# 3rd Edition

# DATA COMMUNICATIONS

## A User's Guide

## Ken Sherman

A RESTON BOOK
Prentice Hall
Englewood Cliffs, New Jersey 07632

Library of Congress Cataloging-in-Publication Data

Sherman, Kenneth.
    Data communications : a user's guide / Ken Sherman. -- 3rd ed.
        p.    cm.
    "A Reston book."
    Bibliography: p.
    Includes index.
    ISBN 0-13-199092-6
    1. Computer networks.  2. Data transmission systems.   I. Title.
TK5105.5.S43  1990
    004.6--dc20                                              89-8433
                                                               CIP

Editorial/production supervision: Joan L. Stone
Interior and cover design: Jayne Conte
Manufacturing buyer: Mary Noonan, Robert Anderson

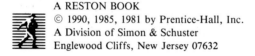A RESTON BOOK
© 1990, 1985, 1981 by Prentice-Hall, Inc.
A Division of Simon & Schuster
Englewood Cliffs, New Jersey 07632

Printed in the United States of America

10  9  8  7  6  5  4  3  2  1

ISBN 0-13-199092-6

Prentice-Hall International (UK) Limited, *London*
Prentice-Hall of Australia Pty. Limited, *Sydney*
Prentice-Hall Canada Inc., *Toronto*
Prentice-Hall Hispanoamericana, S.A., *Mexico*
Prentice-Hall of India Private Limited, *New Delhi*
Prentice-Hall of Japan, Inc., *Tokyo*
Simon & Schuster Asia Pte. Ltd., *Singapore*
Editora Prentice-Hall do Brasil, Ltda., *Rio de Janeiro*

*To Mom and Pop, without whom this book would never be*
*and*
*Barbara G—you will always be with us*

# Contents

# 3

## Carriers, Services, and Regulations  23

# 4

## Communications Media  59

# 5

## Interfaces 83

# 6

## Circuit Types and Their Uses 117

# 7

## Data Codes 123

# 8

## Synchronous and Asynchronous   136

# 9

## Protocols   150

# 10

## Modems and Modulation   189

# 11

# Multiplexers   236

# 12

# Other Network Hardware   252

# 13

# Data Transmission Integrity, Forward Error Correction, Compression, Encryption   262

# 14

## Voice and Data Switching  290

# 15

## Local Area Networks (LANs)  315

# 16

## The Digital World with ISDN   349

# 17

## Packet Switching   384

# 18

## Network Architectures 408

# 19

## Satellites, Video, Radio, Facsimile, and Microwave 445

# 20

## Communication System Transactions, Applications, and Formats 467

## 21

## Transmission Bandwidths and Impairments  486

## 22

## Network Management and Control  502

# About the Author

Dr. Ken Sherman brings to this text over 30 years of direct involvement in all the major areas of communications system design, development, implementation, operations, and management. He has had direct responsibility for large national and international programs and intracompany systems in both the commercial and aerospace/governmental environments, including the SAC Command and Control System, the Federal Reserve Bank Communications Network, airlines message switching systems, and a wide variety of corporate MIS and communications facilities.

Dr. Sherman, an internationally recognized lecturer, has been presenting seminars to the public since 1976. The material generated for those seminars forms the basis for this text. The information was developed specifically to provide an introduction to and overview of the subject of Data Communications from the user's point of view. It is practical, easily understood, and addresses all of the major areas of the subject. Updated with constant feedback from both industry and student sources, this text provides the right mix of depth and clarity.

# Preface

Well, here it is, time to do the preface for the third edition of this text. Since this section is usually one of the last items to be generated, it feels like I have been working on this edition for at least the last four years. With data communications expanding as fast as it is, it seems like every week there is something new that ought to go into the text. Because of the time it takes to put a text into print, the latest information going in is obviously not the latest information when the book finally becomes printed. But people want the absolute latest information regardless. Many students in my class, even when the second edition first came out, commented on the fact that it was not up to date. If that is the kind of information you are looking for, you will only be able to find it in weekly or monthly periodicals.

I have tried to incorporate into this edition the basics of data communications that have been in all of the editions and add in the concepts of the newer services such as local area networks, packet switching, network architectures, and satellites. Putting all the material together has highlighted one very important fact: the rate of change of new products and information is getting faster all the time. Just four years ago, when the second edition was published, it seemed that new products and services were arriving on the scene every month or so (divestiture was just taking place). It now seems that change is occurring on a weekly basis. This has also led to a change in the people who are entering the world of data communications.

Up to just a few years ago, you could assume that people in data communications either started out in data communications (not many) or had at least been in some area related to data processing and were now getting into the communications side of the system. That does not seem to be the case anymore. In my public as well as in-house seminars I am finding more and more people who not only do not have any data communications background, but also don't have any familiarity with fundamental data processing concepts. At the other extreme are people who are getting to be more specialized in specific areas and really need to find out where and how all the pieces fit together. These factors have prompted a few subtle changes in the text where I have added a little more of an introduction as well as a bit more detail to some of the current subjects considered *"hot"* at the moment.

There also seems to be a substantial growth in what I term the *PC-techie* communications area. PC-techies are those people who are heavily involved in PC communications, which, as far as they are concerned, are the only communications worth spending any time in. There is no question that PC communications is one of the bright spots in the world of data communications, but it is still only a spot. Without the standard forms of communications at higher and higher speeds, the volumes of information generated at the PC level could not be moved to centralized sites for processing. It is therefore necessary to understand the entire picture, not just the PC side of it.

In trying to meet the goal of introducing the subject of data communications to a wide variety of potential readers in a user-oriented way, I tried to provide a uniform level of introductory description of how the various products and services interrelate, but in some areas I went into a little bit more detail to help you get the most out of those products and services for your organization. I hope the new material achieves that goal.

The second edition of this text still seems to be selling at a very brisk rate in spite of the heavy competition from a variety of books relating to an introduction to data communications. Being constantly aware of the competitive environment, especially in my public seminars, I have reviewed many of the other texts now available. I still get the very strong feeling that some of them are written in a very academic and tutorial way, so that they are geared for the *college* environment, while others are written extremely simplistically without giving a feeling for how the products and services of data communications can be used to the best advantage. Many of these texts also seem to have significant technical errors in them which have been promulgated throughout the data communications world, so that many believe the statements to be true. A perfect example is the subject of synchronous and asynchronous communications. Many people describe the timing relationship in the synchronous part as being sent from the transmitter to the receiver, which is not true. The timing is actually generated at the receive end in the demodulators, but because most people have been told that the timing information is actually sent on the line from the transmitter to the receiver, some authors say the same thing.

In the preface of the past two editions of the text, I suggested that when somebody describes something to you, have them *draw you a picture*. It is very easy to talk your way through many things when the diagram is not there, but when you have it in black and white, many points become obvious that would not otherwise be so. Don't be afraid to ask questions like *Why?* and *How?* If somebody is describing something to you, they should know how it works or at least be able to find out how it works, and they should not be afraid to draw a picture for you instead of *intimidating* you with words. With more people getting into the data communications business every day, it seems to be becoming easier to throw a few words around to the new entrants to impress them, thereby giving them an erroneous picture of what is happening, which only promotes misunderstanding in the subject.

As I have said before and will continue to say, *the biggest problem in communications is communicating,* because different people use the same terms to mean different things and different terms to mean the same things. I really don't care what you call something as long as I know what it does and how it does it. We then have a common level of understanding. If you don't like my term or I don't like your term for a definition, it really doesn't make any difference as long as we know how it works. With the increasing integration of more and more networks containing diverse applications and equipment, it is even more important to understand how things occur without getting hung up on terminology. Therefore, I have tried to describe many things in this text with diagrams and information flows so that you will get a better understanding of what is happening.

There is one final point that I would like to make sure that you understand. You must be very careful when planning changes or upgrades to your own network. I still feel very strongly that you must solve your problems with hardware, software, products, and services that you are familiar with rather than relying on a vendor's promise (see the end of Chapter 24) so your changes or upgrades will work when you put them in. As I paraphrased the axiom before, ''You can always tell the pioneers by the arrows in their backs.'' This is really not a time to be a pioneer, especially with the heavy cost constraints that are placed on organizations today. I read of a study recently relating to a particular industry that is always at the leading edge of technology. Individual organizations would spend many months or years developing a product or service with all of the attendant costs and time expenditures only to see their competition with an even better version within six to nine months providing the same service. Even if you want to spend the time and money, you must remember that the vendors will learn from your experiences and be able to provide a product or service for less money without development costs for your competitors. Then you will need your original and now possibly outmoded system just to stay competitive yourself. What I am leading to here is that if you let other people do all the pioneering work and get the arrows in their backs, within a relatively short time your own organization should be able to provide the same level of service without the heavy development expenditures. There are enough *pioneers* out there; you don't have to do it yourself. The older I get, the more convinced I am that it is better to be sure that something will work when you turn it on than having the grief that comes with developing a new product or service. Some of you may disagree with this philosophy, but when you are the person responsible for making the decisions and your paycheck depends on having something run, you will end up with a very different perspective on those decisions.

Many of these things were said before, will probably be said again, and the way my seminar business is progressing it is quite probable that I will be talking to you again in the same way another three or four years from now. Since I am also teaching these days at the University of California at Irvine, the next edition has also a much higher probability of occurrence. This text, therefore, was not written just to spew forth facts regarding data communications. It was prepared with the idea of being a very useful adjunct to the teaching of practical data communications—not the academic, theoretical kind, but the practical, everyday-use kind. I hope you feel the effort was worthwhile after you finish this text.

## ACKNOWLEDGMENTS

It is always a pleasure to thank those people who have made an effort such as this text come to life. As in the past, I owe the greatest debt to those students who have continuously provided me with new and updated material for presentation to subsequent classes and eventual incorporation into this text. I cannot list them all individually because there are so many but, for those of you who have helped me, thank you very much. This book could not have been done without you.

The next person I would like to thank I have never met personally, but he has provided invaluable input to the content of the first two texts. His name is Thomas Scott, and he is on the staff of Iowa State University in Ames, Iowa. Tom has used this text for a class that he teaches at Iowa State and contacted me when he found some typos and errors in the text. Not too many people would take the time to write down each of the errors they found and then look me up to let me know what they were. I appreciate that effort, and I think Tom will be surprised when he gets a copy of this book in the mail and sees his name in it. Thanks, Tom.

Next I want to thank a very special person. Since the last edition, my son graduated from Stanford University and went on to medical school. Just prior to moving to San Diego, he married a wonderful girl who is now my third daughter. Her name is Renee. Renee has done most of the typing for this text, for which I am greatly indebted. My son, Mark, did the preliminary diagrams on his Mac, for which he still hasn't reimbursed me but I am really getting my money's worth anyway. The two of them have done a great job. With the extensive hours on rounds at medical school, Mark hardly had the time to complete the diagrams and because Renee works full time in a surgeon's office, she did the typing at night and on weekends while Mark was on call. I know how hard it has been for both of them to do this work (even though it means extra spending money), sometimes under limited time schedules, but the trust has been well rewarded because they have done a fantastic job in putting the materials together for me. Thanks, you two.

Last, but not least, I must thank the rest of my family, who had to put up with more than a year of "I have to work on the book," which meant not doing a lot of the fun things in life like going out for dinner or to a show or whatever. Hopefully, we will now have at least a couple of years before we have to go through this again. Thanks for sticking through it with me.

*Ken Sherman*

# Introduction

Many books have been written about data communications, but their emphasis has been primarily toward the technical types who design communication networks, or, toward the other end of the spectrum, an overview that describes everything but doesn't give you enough information to determine how the functions are performed or what would be the best way to utilize them. This text is oriented toward the data communications user. It provides not only the overview that you need to see how all the pieces fit, but also enough of the application and technical content to answer the questions of how and why the systems work the way they do.

To do this appropriately, you need to have a clear and comprehensive introduction to what makes up a data communications system: the major components, the diagrams of how all of the elements fit together, a good description of terminology, and the differences between the various network carriers and networks.

This text provides information on the assumption that you know little or nothing about the subject, or that you are proficient in one or more areas, but want to see how they integrate with the other areas of communications. You are provided with information on who carries the information and how, through descriptions of the different kinds of carriers and the services they provide, including a basic definition of what a *voice-grade* line really is and many of the current and anticipated services such as packet switching, local area networks, satellite services, ISDN, and others.

To get you to the point where you will begin to understand network and equipment operations, the major interfaces, such as RS232 and all its descendents, are described first. Included are the predominant interfaces described by both the Electronic Industries Association (EIA) for U.S. specifications and the CCITT (Consultive Committee on International Telephone and Telegraph) for international specifications.

The basic differences between asynchronous and synchronous transmission are described, as well as when and where to use each. The subject has caused a considerable amount of confusion because of the overlapping terminology and vendor advertising, which tends to promote the misconceptions that exist in the environment.

All of the major types of protocols are described, such as mainframe to mainframe, terminal to mainframe, PC to mainframe, and PC to PC. This includes the majority of the necessary conversions through protocol converters that allow different types of devices to communicate with each other. Incorporated into this description is an overview of the Open System Interconnect Seven Layer Standard so that you can see where what you have been calling a protocol fits into the International Standard.

Whenever you transmit data it is necessary to validate that the transmission was correct, so many of the ways to find and fix errors are described as well as some of the newer bit manipulative techniques, such as data compression, forward error correction, and encryption, all of which are becoming necessary in more and more applications today.

The major hardware devices are then described, the two primary ones being modems and multiplexers. Modems operating at various speeds in both leased line and dialup environments are covered as well as the mechanism whereby they accomplish their high data rate throughputs. Tables for comparisons between standard U.S. and CCITT defined modems are provided. Uses of the various kinds of multiplexers are described as well as how to get the maximum benefit from statistical techniques. Along with these hardware functions the applicable switches—PBX, Centrex, Matrix Switches, and others—are explained.

How the physical devices are integrated to make up a network is described in detail as well as many of the networks themselves, such as packet networks, local area networks, satellite networks, and digital networks like ISDN, which is the direction toward which most network vendors are moving today.

To complement these descriptions a separate chapter on evolving network architectures from all of the major vendors such as IBM, Unisys, DEC, Data General, and others is provided. You will be able to see what the vendors are planning for their future architectural philosophies and how they anticipate integrating their equipment with others, including SNA from IBM, who seems to be finally admitting that there are other vendors in the world besides themselves. How to test all of these networks is included along with many of the transmission parameters that affect signals in a network.

The text has been updated in this third edition to incorporate the very latest of the vendor announcements regarding products and services so that you will have a complete picture of what is now available for your networks as well as the kinds of products and services that you can anticipate in the near future. Since the world of data communications changes literally on a weekly basis, it is strongly recommended that you always validate what additional products and/ or services are available when you actually need them. The newer products and services will probably not change the basic functional operation of the network, but they may provide additional speed, throughput, reliability, and additional services. How all of this fits into your network from a practical, user-oriented point of view is what the book is all about.

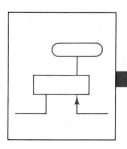

# 1

# Background
# of Data Communications
# and Terminology

The first edition of this text was printed in 1981. At that point in time, most of the people who were involved in data communications had evolved from the data communications world itself or out of the data processing world. Today's environment is radically different. More and more people are getting into data communications without any communications or data processing background. Because some of the terminology has evolved from the data processing world, this edition assumes that the reader would like additional introductory information. It is also assumed, however, that the basic terms of *bit, byte,* and other essential data processing terms are understood by the reader, even though the actual operation of a computer may not be.

## A
## BACKGROUND

The function of communicating has been around ever since prehistoric man developed hand signs and sounds to communicate ideas. The evolution of this process is therefore thousands of years old, but only within the last 150 years or so have we seen the growth of electronic forms of communication.

There is a parallel history in the development of computers, where the last 150 years or so have provided a form of computational capability independent of communications. It wasn't until the mid-1940s, however, that the modern elec-

1

tronic computer evolved. It was still another 20 years before the processes of computing and communications began to merge. Before the early 1960s there were many standalone communications systems based on telegraph or teletype, while the computing systems primarily processed numerical data that was entered into the machine manually, by punched card, or by punched paper tape.

The current worldwide networking environment is therefore little more than 25 years old and, with technology continuing to evolve, it is possible to look forward and see worldwide communications and data processing networks (some of which already exist) tying most of the populated world together within the next 15 to 20 years. It is this environment that most people are entering today. With limited prior experience more and more network users are at least curious to hear how it all came about. The following brief sections will give you a little bit of that history, selecting the key points from both the data processing world and the communications world.

## B
## HISTORY OF COMMUNICATIONS

It is obviously impossible to date some of the historic events in the evolution of communications accurately, so some of them will be described in general while the more recent ones will be given specific dates.

Grunts and other sounds were probably the very first form of communication for prehistoric man, and these eventually evolved into specific spoken languages. Physical signals such as hand and other body movements probably also contributed to this "spoken" communication. While communicating this way, though, information could only be moved as far as the human voice could be heard or a human could be seen to make physical gestures. Communication over greater distances could not be accomplished.

Eventually, the ideas to be conveyed could be represented by symbols. Egyptian hieroglyphics were one of the first forms of symbolic representation of information. Once this symbolism developed, information could be moved over great distances by inscribing it on a medium such as paper (papyrus), wood, or stone. Now messages could be sent over great distances by carrying the medium from place to place.

Still further in this evolutionary cycle, another set of symbols was developed to describe individual *sounds,* and these symbols—the first form of an alphabet— could be put together to form words. The distance over which the information could be moved was still limited, but there was now a way to form a more detailed description of the information to be transmitted, as well as a way to develop more subtle variations which could not easily be shown by simple symbolic idea representation. What was still necessary was to have both the speaker and the listener understand the concepts or meanings of the sounds (the transmitting device and the receiving device had to utilize the same *code set* to be able to communicate with each other).

Besides the alphabets, other methods developed by which information could be transmitted more quickly over greater distances. The Greeks, for example, developed the heliograph, a mechanism for reflecting sunlight off shiny surfaces. Here, too, the transmitter and the receiver must have known the same code set to convey meaningful information. The Romans utilized torches set in groups at varying distances apart (inches or feet) to communicate between mountaintops during wartime. When the heliograph or Roman torch system was used, the *enemy* could also see the information, so the concept of *coding* was developed. Even though there was a common user language, *codes* could be used for specific instances. The transmitter and the receiver had to know what the code was to move information effectively, and the code could be changed at any time as long as both parties knew the new code. This method of moving information could be accomplished over greater distances than the distance the human voice could carry, and although there were plans to develop relay stations to move information over even greater distances, it does not appear that this ever happened. Very long-distance communications were still accomplished by humans who walked, ran, or rode horses to deliver the message to the receiver.

Two other forms of communications used over longer distances were drums, typically in the jungles of Africa and South America, and smoke signals, initially used by the North American Indians. These could only be used as far as the sound could be heard or the smoke could be seen. For the most part, no specific language was developed, but a symbolic representation was again used so that as much information as possible could be produced from as little effort as possible.

As we moved into the modern era, a variety of optical telegraph-type systems evolved in the 1800s. Among these were the *Semaphores,* or flags. We saw the development of the first form of electronic communication, the telegraph system developed by Samuel Morse in 1844. By the end of 1844 a telegraph was in operation between Washington, D.C. and Baltimore, Maryland. By 1849, the first printing telegraph was developed. It recorded messages from an oscillating needle that was sensitive to electronic current flow. Telegraphs will be described in Chapter 2.

In 1861 the first cross-country telegraph was established in the United States, and by the 1860s there was a much higher-speed telegraph unit. During this same time frame, in 1866, a trans-Atlantic telegraph cable was installed.

Electronic communications then grew at a very fast rate, with James C. Maxwell developing the necessary mathematical equations for telecommunications theory in 1873. One year later in 1874, Emile Baudot developed the first *Multiplex Telegraph,* which provided for the movement of information from up to six simultaneous users on a single wire with the individual characters being divided up into a predetermined *code set.*

The next major contribution to the world of communications occurred in 1876, when Alexander Graham Bell developed the telephone in an attempt to communicate with his mother and his wife, who were both deaf. He used existing telegraph circuits, but instead of providing for an electrical current being turned on and off to activate a remote device, Bell's invention was sensitive to sound, and thereby created vibrations in a receiving diaphragm which he hoped could be understood by deaf people and provide communication with them. An ironic fact is that another gentleman, Elisha Grey, applied for the same patent that Bell did four hours later on the same day (February 14, 1876). But for that timing, we might have had the Grey Telephone System instead of the Bell Telephone System.

By 1882 the first manual switchboard, called a *Beehive,* was developed so that a centralized location could be used for connecting people by telephone. Then, in 1888 Heinrich Rudolph Hertz showed that electromagnetic waves existed and that they could be used for moving information over great distances. This would be the forerunner of electromagnetic propagation, or radio transmission.

By the year 1889 a dial-type telephone was invented by Almon B. Strowger, who then perfected it for general use by 1896. In the interim Strowger also developed the first automatic telephone switch, which consisted of five buttons. The first button was called the *release,* which started the switch. The next button was the *100s,* and identified the first digit of a three-digit number to be called. This button was pressed the appropriate number of times to indicate the number being dialed; so was a *10s* button and a *digit* button. For example, if the number 451 was to be dialed, the 100s button would be pressed four times, the 10s button would be pressed five times, and the digit number would be depressed once. The fifth button was the ring button, which would then ring the phone that was being called. Longer telephone lines were being installed during this time, and by 1897 there were both radio and telegraph lines in use all over the United States. In 1892 the New York to Chicago telephone line was installed, and by 1901 there was trans-Atlantic radio communications service. The first transcontinental U.S. telephone line was in use by 1915.

Because the use of telephone lines is sensitive to the time of day (people communicate more by day than by night), it became necessary to develop a methodology for combining two or more voice channels on a single wire. This was known as *multiplexing,* first accomplished in 1918. Telephone lines could then be built to handle different levels of communications requirements over one physical path. This allowed the rapid proliferation of telephone service throughout the United States and the rest of the world. More and more lines were put in to connect suburban and rural areas, and we saw the growth of the modern telephone network, which is described in more detail in Chapter 3.

The next major event in the world of communications occurred in 1948, when Claude Shannon developed his *Mathematical Theory of Communications.* Shannon developed the concept of information theory, which incorporated a measure of what a communications channel could and could not do. It quantifies the message source and channel, and then relates them to each other. If the information rate exceeds the capacity of the channel to support it, then the information is subject to error, all of which would be measurable. Shannon is sometimes described as the father of modern data communications.

By the early 1950s the first microwave communication links were established. They provided high-volume communication over fairly long distances as long as the transmitting and receiving antenna could *see each other* (had an unobstructed line-of-sight path). This was also the decade that saw the development of the transistor, which led to a significant reduction in the size and power requirements of communications equipment. By the mid-1960s the first tone-generating telephones were developed, as well as the first electronic switching systems. Since that time, the proliferation of new products, devices, and services has been occurring at an ever-increasing rate. Not only may information be moved between humans, but data processing and communications can now be integrated into a network form, as in our current environment. It appears that they will be integrated forever.

## C
# HISTORY OF COMPUTERS

When discussing the history of data processing, you are really looking at the history of computing capability utilizing some form of mechanical or electrical capability. As such, the first real computer was the Abacus, or Soroban as it was called, which was developed around 3000 B.C. It consisted of a series of beads mounted on a frame with a wire or rod running through them such that they could be moved up or down individually or in groups. The abacus could be used for quick addition and subtraction of numbers and is still used in many countries today.

From the abacus we have to go all the way to the year 1632 when the next major revolutionary device was developed. It was the slide rule, attributed to William Oughtred, which could provide multiplication and division capability (not addition or subtraction). Slide rules were used primarily by engineers, who added many additional mathematical capabilities such as trigonometric functions and logarithms. Use of the slide rule all but disappeared with the arrival of the electronic calculator in the early 1970s. Ten years after the slide rule was developed, in 1642, Blaise Pascal invented a form of adding machine that could be used to add numbers mechanically.

More than 150 years passed before the next major computational device was developed. It was the punched-card loom, developed by Joseph Marie Jacquard in 1805. This device provided the ability to weave fabrics based on a pattern that was contained in punched cards.

Charles Babbage then developed in 1831 the Difference Engine, which many people consider the forerunner of modern computing devices. It was not until 1885, however, that the first commercial adding machine was developed by W. S. Burroughs, and that was followed five years later, in 1890, by the electronic tabulating machine developed by Herman Hollerith for the 1890 census.

Even though the invention of the electronic digital computer was credited to J. V. Atanasoft at Iowa State University in 1942, the modern world of data processing really started to move quickly in 1944 when the Mark I was developed at Harvard by Howard Aiken. It was called the Analytical Sequence Controlled

Calculator. The following year, 1945, Eniac (Electronic Numerical Integrator and Calculator) was developed by J. Presper Eckert and John W. Mauchly; since then, the development of analog and then digital computers has progressed at an ever-increasing rate. The big spurs to this growth were the invention of the transistor and the utilization of *chip technology,* which substantially increased the actual amount of numeric calculations capable of being processed per unit time.

It was in the 1960s that the worlds of communications and data processing began to come together because of the need to move information from any remote point to centralized points for processing. It is this world that we will be looking at over the next 23 chapters.

Before going on, it is suggested that you go to the back of the book and skim the definitions in the *glossary* to get an idea of some of the terms used in the text. Obviously you should not memorize them, but many of the more common words that you probably have already heard are described there. To get an idea of how they will be used and what they mean when you see them you should scan them now. When people read texts like this one, they tend to continue reading material even if they do not understand all the words. This is a mistake. If you choose not to go through the glossary now, when you come to a word that you do not understand or that is being used in a context with which you are unfamiliar, turn to the glossary and find out exactly what it means. The concepts in this text build on the early information and it is assumed that once a term is used you will know what it means before you proceed. Special care has been taken to avoid using words without defining them, but if you do run across a term that is unclear, find out what it means before going on so that the subsequent information will be understandable to you.

## QUESTIONS

1. What is the functional communications difference between representation of information by hieroglyphics and an alphabet?
2. What was the original reason for the development of codes?
3. Create a time line diagram for the evolution of computing equipment and another one for communications systems.

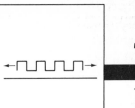

# 2

# Basics
# of Information Flow

## BACKGROUND AND OVERVIEW

There are many different ways to go about introducing the subject of data communications. Depending on your own particular perspective, you may look at data communications as a standalone entity for moving information between two points or as an adjunct to the data processing world. In actuality data communications is one of the functions that must be performed in today's society for the processing of information. It is not a standalone entity any more and must be looked at from the perspective of its integration with data processing, database management, and applications functions. None of these entities is any more or less important than the other, but because of the concentration of effort by individuals in specific areas, more emphasis may sometimes be given to one area. Data communications is only one of the primary functions that make up the integrated process of information movement in today's information-oriented society. Although this text deals almost exclusively with the subject of data communications, systems, database, and applications must also be kept in mind because they are of equal importance.

The minimum components of any communications process are a transmission source, a transmission receiver, and a medium through which the information is to be transmitted. On an elementary level this may be typified by one person talking to another. The person who is talking is the transmitter. The one who is listening is the receiver, and the air is the medium through which the information flows. The information moves because the molecules of air strike each other from the transmitter to the receiver, and when the receiver's ear, which is sensitive to the vibrations of the air molecules, is impacted by those vibrations, the message (information) is received.

Another form of communication is the movement of information via the written word. The author—the transmitter—writes the information. The reader is the receiver, and the medium is the document that is being read. Many such examples can be given, but the important concept to recognize here is that to have communications, not only must the transmitter be able to generate the information and the receiver be able to detect the information, but the medium used must be compatible to both ends and be in a form that does not alter or modify the transmitted information. Only then can the receiver reliably detect what the transmitter is sending as information.

It is also important to comprehend that not only must there be a communications path for the transmitter and the receiver to communicate over, but there must also be multiple levels of recognition of information being sent. For example, one speaker may be talking in English while another is speaking Russian. The basic requirements for a communications system exist (transmitter, medium, receiver), but the two speakers will not be able to communicate with each other because they do not understand each other's language. A second level of understanding deals with the particular *dialect* being spoken. For example, in some parts of the United States there are slang expressions or words that are accented differently, and it is very hard to understand everything being said if you are from a different part of the country. This is also noticeable in the English spoken in different parts of the world, such as in the Caribbean. In those places, even though the two speakers may be speaking the same basic language, the actual meaning of the communications may not be completely understood, or may even be lost, because the dialect is different. Humans may be able to interpret and comprehend ideas without understanding each individual spoken word, but at present machines cannot.

Still another level of communication that must be recognized and understood is the *subject* itself. The level of understanding of words being used must be compatible to both ends of the communication line. If the subject matter is such that one listener has very little comprehension of what the other person is saying, even though the same language and dialect are used, then they are not communicating (like parents trying to discuss the relative merits of heavy metal bands versus rhythm and blues with their teenagers).

Therefore, when relating to a data-communications environment, not only must you have the transmitter, path, and receiver, you must also have exact recognition at each level of the hardware, software, and user at each end of the path. Even though the path exists for moving electrical signals such as bits or bytes of information, if they are in different code sets or use different definitions for the same character sets, or if the actual use and application of the information is different, then effective communication does not take place. Throughout this text, whenever interfaces are discussed, it is assumed that both the transmitter and the receiver are compatible at all levels of understanding so that the information being transmitted can be received and actually *used* by the receiver.

Since most information is transmitted through a network over a medium that may distort the transmission, there must be some means of identifying unrecognizable transmissions and providing a method for the receiver to be aware of a possible error, obtain a retransmission, or correct the transmission at the receiving end. When two people are talking to each other, it is easy for the receiver to ask the transmitter to repeat what was said, but in the case of a written document it is virtually impossible to get back to the author for clarification. What we have in the first case is a real two-way transmission, while in the latter case we have only a one-way transmission.

Data communications can be looked at in exactly the same way. There is transmission equipment, a facility (the medium), and receiving equipment that carries the information from one to the other. In most cases the medium is provided by the telephone company or carrier and, as reliable as it is, errors or distortions in voice or data can occur to the transmission. This text deals primarily with communication of information (data), but because the facilities being used were initially designed for voice transmission and many of the networks in use today still have significant voice facilities, the effects of voice-related characteristics will also be discussed.

## B
## SIMPLE CIRCUIT COMPOSITION

Although there are many components that make up a communications circuit, it is necessary to put them all into perspective before describing all of the features and parameters. Figure 2–1 gives a simplistic diagram of what a circuit may look like in the data communications world today. Each element of the connection is described here, but you must recognize that there are many products and services that impact what is to be done and how it is to be done. This diagram is provided to give an idea of where the major pieces of a circuit fit. Later you will be provided with a more extensive diagram with other products that are also available.

Descriptions of each of the labeled components in Figure 2–1 are as follows:

1. Human who will be transmitting and receiving information to or from the system.
2. The hardware of the terminal to or from which the human enters or receives information.
3. The software for an individual terminal, if it exists, that communicates with a controller-type device.
4. The cable or mechanical interface that connects the user's terminal to a controlling device.

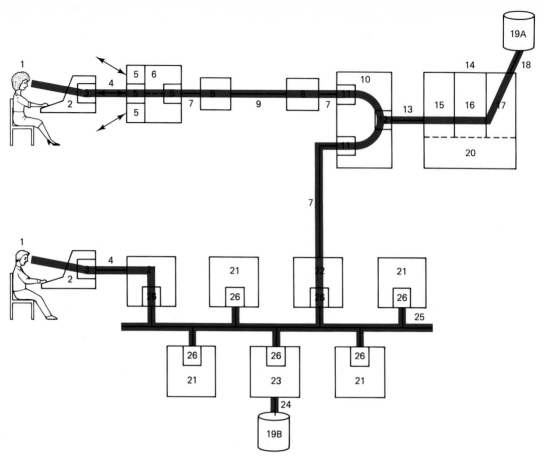

**FIGURE 2-1**
Simple Circuit Composition

5. The software in a controller that communicates to or from user terminals as well as to or from another processing site.

6. The hardware of the controller device, which may incorporate multiple connections to different terminals.

7. Standardized interface for communicating between a user's logical device and a communications device for subsequent transmission of signals over a communications path.

8. A device for interfacing the user's logical world with the carrier circuit. This device is typically a modem when transmitting over analog or voice facilities, described in Chapter 10, or a DSU/CSU for communications in the digital world, described in Chapter 16.

9. The path through the carrier world that connects different locations. These facilities may be your own or provided by some other organization like a telephone company.

10. A controller unit that is used at a large, centralized processing site for interfacing with multiple remote devices.

11. A *port* that is the specific interface connection for terminating a particular communication line that has particular characteristics. Ports can run at different speeds, and they can communicate utilizing different protocols (described in Chapter 9), but they can use only one speed or protocol at any one time. Information here must be transmitted one bit at a time serially or sequentially.

12. An additional port on the communications front end that connects to a host processing device. This port is sometimes called a *channel* and typically runs in parallel with a very high transfer rate. This transfer rate typically takes place a *word* (one or more bytes) at a time.

13. The cable between the channel interface and the host processing unit.

14. The host central site processing unit (CPU).

15. The communications interface that moves information to and from the front-end controller. It is part of the central site host processor.

16. The section of the host processor that is the applications software. These programs physically perform the jobs required by the end users.

17. The database management system (DBMS), which provides the methodology of accessing the data on the storage devices and provides the logical versus physical relationships of the information to be accessed.

18. The channel cable, which connects the DBMS to the peripheral storage devices such as discs or tapes.

19A., 19B. The storage devices, such as tapes or discs, where physical information is stored.

20. The operating system of the processor, which provides the management of the CPU resources and interaction of communications, applications, and database functions. All programs written to perform specific functions in the host processor must be compatible with the operating system of the processor.

21. An interface device for accessing a Local Area Network (LAN); could be a terminal controller or a personal computer (PC).

22. A special interface device that is typically called a *gateway* (described in Chapter 15) and utilized to connect one type of system to another, in this case a LAN to a host processor.

23. Another special interface device, in this case known as a *server,* which connects a database to a LAN such that all users of that network can access the same data.

24. The physical connection from the server to the database if the database is stored on an external device. If you are using a PC, the database may be

integrated directly into that PC and if so a separate external connection is not required.

25. The physical medium through which the various devices on a LAN connect to each other. The physical form shown here is a *bus,* but there are other kinds of connections, which are shown in Chapter 15.

26. The physical interface that converts the logical interaction of the device to the physical medium so that electrical signals can be moved on that medium. It also incorporates the necessary hardware and software controls for the particular mode of access to or from the medium.

Obviously many more devices and interfaces can be described, but here you have both a long-distance connection utilizing various carriers, Item 9, and a network that is utilized internally at the same facility as the CPU, which is a Local Area Network, Item 25. As we go through the text you will find further definition for all of the areas described on this diagram except the CPU functions, which are not normally part of the communications description.

For the remainder of this chapter a little bit of the evolution of the hardware is described as well as what a typical network may incorporate today.

## C
## TELEGRAPH EQUIPMENT

Although we do not use telegraph equipment in the typical modern data communications environment, it was the telegraph that gave us some of the original modes of operation and terminology. For this reason the telegraph is described, so that you may see the origins of some of the terms utilized today. The telegraph system developed in 1844 by Samuel Morse basically included a closed circuit, which had an electrical source, a transmit key that could be opened and closed, and a sensing unit that was either a relay, sounder, or some other kind of indicator. This is shown in Fig. 2–2.

**FIGURE 2–2**
Simplex Telegraph System (information flow only one way)

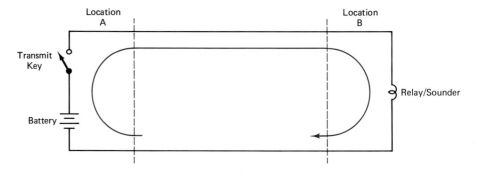

This configuration allows for the transmission of information in one direction only, because the transmit key that controls current flow in the line (and therefore activates the sounder) can be opened and closed at only one location, while the sounder is at the other location.

Since it is usually desirable to be able to transmit information in two directions, alternative telegraph configurations allow either the transmission of information one way at a time or both ways at the same time. These are shown in Figs. 2–3 and 2–4.

Figure 2–3 allows the transmitter at either end to transmit; but since that would provide for the activating of the sounder at both locations, only one end can transmit at a time. This is called a *half-duplex* transmission, because only one transmitter can be active at any one time.

Figure 2–4 shows a configuration by which each end can transmit to the other end at the same time. Note that there are two independent power sources and two independent transmission paths. This mode of transmission is known as *full duplex* because both ends can transmit at the same time, and the receiver at the opposite end will not have any interference or distortion due to its own transmissions.

Since the telegraph mode of communications involved the closing of a circuit and the current from a power source flowing through that circuit, this mode of communication eventually evolved into what is known as the *current loop* interface (defined in more detail in Chapter 5), where a specific current level (20 or 60 milliamperes (mA) was used as a standard for devices, which eventually evolved into such equipment as Teletypes (TTY).

The telegraph required a human interface at each end to recognize the information when it was transmitted because there was no means of storing the information while being transmitted. Teletype equipment, which could store information on paper tapes, was derived from the invention by Emile Baudot in France of what was known as the *Baudot Distributor.* The Baudot Distributor allowed for the segmentation of a predefined character into five unique electrical signals

**FIGURE 2–3**
Half-Duplex Telegraph (information flow one way at a time)

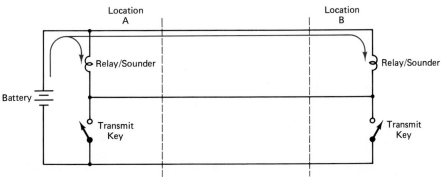

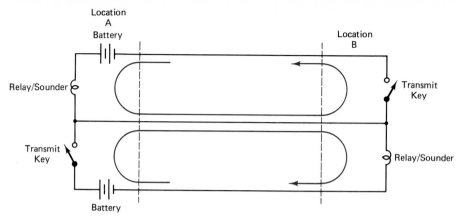

**FIGURE 2–4**
Full-Duplex Telegraph (information flow both ways at the same time)

that could be used to identify the character at the other end of the line and either print the representative character or punch a series of holes in paper tape; thus the receiving location would not have to have a human in attendance. This was significantly different from the telegraph, which required the sequential transmission of dots and dashes that could not be stored on a permanent medium while being transmitted.

Once storage capability existed, sequential transmission of information could be made from either a mechanically or an electrically stored medium at a faster transmission rate than a human operator could physically generate the information at some type of entry device. In actuality, the initial teletypes transmitted information at a rate of 10 characters per second. This rate was determined by the physical limitations of the *distributor,* which was a mechanical ring also called a commutator, and a rotor that rotated ten (10) times per second.

# D
## BAUDOT EQUIPMENT AND TELETYPES

The Baudot Distributor became the forerunner of the modern teletype machine and was the first of the truly sequential data communications terminals. It also provided the first asynchronous form of communications and gave us the term *baud.* It is shown in Fig. 2–5. What the distributor configuration provided was the opening and closing of a circuit at a relatively fast rate, which allowed current to flow or not flow in a transmission line. This current could then be detected by a similar distributor at the other end, and the existence or absence of current on the line could be directly related to a specific element of information, which was known as a *bit.* A bit is a contraction of the term *binary digit,* which identified the existence of two possible states of information (current flow or no current

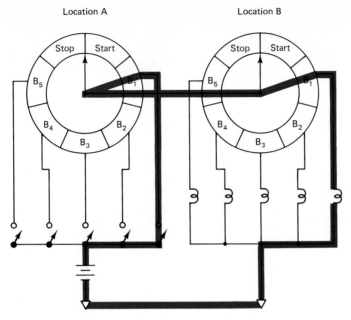

**FIGURE 2-5**
Baudot Distributor

flow). The *zero* or noncurrent flow is known as a *space* or *off* condition, while the current flow state is called either a *mark* or *on* condition. They correspond to a 0 and 1 bit logically.

Baudot developed a code whereby five consecutive bits of information represent a particular alpha or numeric character, and this was known as *Baudot code*. (Codes will be described in Chapter 7.) Operation of the distributor required the receiving device to know when the transmitting device started transmitting, and therefore each set of five information bits was preceded by a special bit called a *start bit* and succeeded by, in the case of Baudot, a *stop bit* which is $1\frac{1}{2}$ bit times long (actually 1.42 bit times long). The segments were actually the same size but the time allowed for the stop bit was an extra half-bit time. These start and stop bits allowed the receiver to recognize when to start its rotational sequence and gave it time to come to a complete stop so that it would then be able to start at the appropriate time for the next character. Start bits are always a zero, while stop bits are always a one. This will also hold true for ASCII and EBCDIC eight (8)-level codes and is called *asynchronous transmission,* which will be described in Chapter 8.

Although it is relatively early in the text, this is a good time to discuss a pair of terms that are probably the two most confused terms in all of data communications. They are the terms *baud* and *BPS*. The term BPS has always represented bits per second, and although it is very common today to use the terms interchangeably, technically they are very different. The differences will be explained here, and then, as long as you know the difference, you can use the terms any way you want. Just make sure the people you are trying to communicate with are using the terms the same way you are.

The term *baud* comes from the Baudot Distributor environment. In order for the engineers who were designing that piece of equipment to determine how far the signal could travel, they had to come up with a method of defining the time duration of the narrowest signal. One of the primary degradations encountered in a communications environment over a pair of wires is that the sharpness of the digital rise and fall time degrades as the signal travels down a pair of wires. This is shown in Fig. 2–6 and is called *rolloff*. The farther a digital, square-wave signal travels on a pair of wires, the more pronounced the rolloff effect becomes, until finally the signal is not recognizable as having two separate and distinct states, which is the method of conveying information. Because the Baudot transmission contained a start bit, five data bits of the same size, and a stop bit which was $1\frac{1}{2}$ bit times long, a method had to be established that would identify the width of the narrower bits which were the most affected by rolloff. The term was called *baud* and was defined as

$$\frac{1}{\text{smallest increment of bit time}}$$

This is the actual technical definition of the term *baud* and provides a mathematical description of the narrowest bit time that may be encountered on the particular line in question.

From a more practical, user-oriented point of view, what this formula really did was to identify the *maximum signal-change rate* on the line. It means the signal could change no faster than the rate identified by the baud value.

For all Baudot-type transmissions, the term baud was used to describe the signal-change rate on the line, while a separate rate, bits per second, was used to describe the actual information flow. Because Teletype distributors rotated for many years at 10 revolutions per second, there were 10 characters generated every second. That means 10 start bits, 50 data bits, and the equivalent of 15 stop bits (actually 10 but each is $1\frac{1}{2}$ bit times long), giving a transmission rate of 75 baud

**FIGURE 2–6**
Signal Degradation from Rolloff

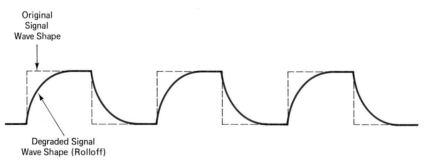

Original
Signal
Wave Shape

Degraded Signal
Wave Shape (Rolloff)

BASICS OF INFORMATION FLOW

but a data rate of 50 BPS. Therefore, there was a very specific difference between baud and bits per second for the Baudot and TTY environments.

As the evolution of data communications equipment progressed, the requirement for moving digital signals on a telephone line arose, but because of the rolloff degradation, the square waves could not be transmitted for any great distance and a loop current-type of transmission method used in Teletype circuits could not be used either. This led to the development of modems that took the digital signals generated by the Teletypes and generated two separate frequencies, one for a logical zero and one for a logical one, which were compatible with the telephone system. At the other end of the line, the same type modem saw the two different frequencies and converted them back to the appropriate ones and zeros.

The terms baud and bits per second then began to be used interchangeably because each signal change on the line (an alternate frequency) represented a bit of information. This bit might be a start, stop, or data bit, but since they were all now the same width, they took the same amount of time and therefore could be discussed as if they were the same width all the time. Since every signal change could represent a bit, whether it was start, stop, or data, baud and bits per second really meant the same thing. This situation remains the same for all modems transmitting at rates of up to 1800 BPS.

It was not until the advent of transmission techniques in the range of 2400 BPS and up (the early 1960s) that modem technology made the interchange of baud and bits per second technically incorrect. This came about because the signal-change rate on the telephone line was no longer equal to the bit-per-second data rate. For example, the actual data rate of 2400 BPS only required 1200 signal changes on the telephone line. (This will be explained in much greater detail in Chapter 10.) Since that time, all modems that have been transmitting at data rates of 2400 BPS and up have a signal-change rate on the telephone line that is typically between 600 and 2400 baud, while the data rate has gone all the way up to 19,200 BPS. In spite of this difference, the term baud is still being used to describe data rates, and even though there is nothing wrong with using them interchangeably, the people who are talking to each other should make sure that they are really referring to the same thing. This is very important for describing digital transmission also, because digital transmission rates are always described in bits per second, and the *baud rate* has no real meaning there.

Getting back to the evolution of asynchronous equipment, for many years separate communication lines were used for telegraph and Teletype transmissions only. This was because of the on/off nature of the current, which in effect was digital-type transmission and, at the time, not compatible with the facilities that existed for voice communications.

As requirements for voice communications grew, it became increasingly impractical to provide separate long-distance circuits for each type of transmission; in addition, it became more desirable for different transmitters and receivers to communicate with each other, and at different points in time. This evolved into the requirement for establishment of a communications common carrier. A communications common carrier is a company whose business it is to supply communications facilities to public users. The different telephone companies are examples of these common carriers.

Because of the proliferation of facilities and carriers, which at one time numbered over 14,000, the U.S. government established the Federal Communications Commission in 1934 to regulate the facilities and services offered by common carriers. This was done so that standards could be established for all users, making it possible for any one user to communicate through any of the common carriers to any other user anywhere within the United States.

With a standardized carrier and facility environment, we now have to take a look at the difference between the Teletype kind of transmission and the voice transmission. Since Teletype transmission consisted of the existence or absence of a current on a line, there was very little need for providing anything other than a conducting path for current flow. On the other hand, voice communications required a totally different kind of capability. The human voice is made up of frequencies with the most energy in approximately the 200- to 4000-hertz (cycles per second) range. Thus whatever medium was used to transmit voice information, at least those frequencies must be supported. Due to the preponderance of voice frequencies in the middle range, it was eventually decided to establish, as a standard, a frequency range from 300 to 3300 hertz (Hz), which would be used for all voice communications on common carrier facilities. Even though the entire bandwidth to be provided was actually 4200 Hz, the usable portion for voice would be between 300 and 3300. The range between 0 and 300 Hz would be used, when applicable, for data transmission at rates of up to 150 BPS; the range from 3300 to 4200 Hz would be available to the carriers for signaling purposes if required.

The multiple-frequency mode of transmission (voice), not being compatible with the loop-current mode of transmission, meant that two separate types of facilities would have to be maintained. Because of the desirability of communicating between Teletype and Teletype-like terminals using the facilities of the voice-grade network, it became necessary to establish an interface that could be used by the Teletype kind of equipment to interface with the voice-grade facilities. The result of this requirement was the establishment of the RS-232 interface, described in Chapter 5, which allowed for the replacement of the current-loop-type interface with a voltage type of interface, which could then be converted through modulation equipment to the frequency range that could be supported on voice-grade facilities. The voltage interface therefore opened up the entire voice-grade network for use by digital-type terminal and computer equipment. Except for the current growth of digital and direct satellite transmission networks, data communications is still almost totally dependent on the voice-grade network for transmission of information.

As the data communications traffic increased, it also became necessary to establish some type of network for movement of information between multiple points that could not be predetermined utilizing the existing voice-grade network capabilities. This involved the specific addressing of traffic between one terminal and another where information had to be routed through one or more central points called nodes. An early manual configuration of this type of connection is shown in Fig. 2–7 and was known as a *torn tape center,* typically utilizing Teletypes. It consisted of the transmission of information manually or from paper tape on one of multiple Teletypes on a particular line to a Teletype machine located at a central site where a paper tape would be punched out. An operator would physically read the tape, tear it off the Teletype it was received on, physically walk over to the line on which the addressed Teletype was resident, and then transmit the message from the central-site Teletype on the outgoing line to the addressed terminal. This mode of communication lasted for many years and in some places is still used. Operators are required to recognize the coded

**FIGURE 2–7**
Torn Tape Center

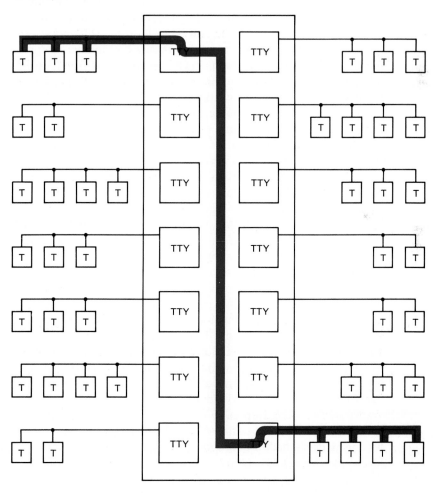

punched paper tape information and then establish the operating process whereby the information is to be transmitted to the final sites addressed. In effect, this consists of what is known as *store-and-forward* communications; it graphically illustrates the problems encountered in almost every single area of data communications routing and handling, the most obvious of which is that all transmitting and receiving equipment must be the same, as well as the code being used by each device.

Some of the other problems that can be seen in a torn tape center are the conditions that arise when an addressed terminal is unavailable, the line is unavailable, or there are messages that were received previously but have not yet been transmitted out on that same line. It is relatively easy for the operator to establish a queuing situation and even a priority transmission situation, but the conversion of those types of functions to an automated mode is an extremely complex and comprehensive process. The entire queue management, buffer management, routing, priority, and validation process must be automated in a software process so that all combinations and permutations of potential conditions that may occur are recognized and handled in the software.

If a single unplanned condition occurs on the line, the program will in all likelihood malfunction or even abort. It is for this reason that the most sensitive interfaces in all networks are those that involve the movement of data between points. This is over and above the problems that are due to the inherent degradations that exist on a communication line itself.

Another area that is important to recognize in the communications environment is that when data processing started to evolve the potential interfaces with communication equipment were not considered. It was not until the late 1940s and early 1950s that the data processing evolution got to the point where it seemed to be desirable to connect remote terminals to computer processing sites using data-communications techniques.

Baudot code, which had no error-checking capability (no parity), and was still used with Teletypes, was not a code that could be utilized to move information from one machine to another because there would be no way for the machines to tell if there were an error in that information. (Note—for the purist, the code being described here is actually known as Murray Code or International Telegraph Alphabet (ITA) #2. It has been called Baudot code for so many years that the terms are used interchangeably even though the original Baudot code was different.) It was not until 1963 that a standardized code was developed that was highly suited for information transmission. This was the ASCII code, which was an eight-level code containing both a parity capability and seven bits for information, which meant that all the possible combinations of alphas, numerics, and controls could be identified with a unique bit configuration. ASCII was upgraded in 1967 with respect to the control characters identified, and this is the predominant code used today as a worldwide standard. At the same time ASCII was being developed, a new Teletype was developed that could utilize the eight-level code (Model 33). Other eight-level code terminals followed shortly thereafter.

What also occurred in the same relative time frame was the integration of communications-type terminals with the data processing machines; but since the data-processing-oriented personnel were more interested in performing numerical functions and applications, they totally ignored the communications interface. For that reason it was left up to the designers of communications equipment, such as front ends, store-and-forward message switches, and concentrators, to design interfaces, mostly in an emulation mode that would take the communication-type inputs and convert them to a form that the data processing machines could interface with. The end result was that, for a long time, the only progress in the area of communications interfaces was made by the manufacturers and vendors of communications equipment. It was not until the mid-1960s that the requirement was so overwhelming that manufacturers and vendors of data processing equipment turned their energy toward developing better communications interfaces.

The situation today, therefore, is one where the vendors of data processing machines are developing software packages that will permit movement of data between different points in a network under individual or centralized control. At the same time the vendors of communications equipment are developing faster and more reliable equipment to operate over the existing and newly emerging communication facilities such as fiber optics and lasers. Added to these areas of progress, we have the new technologies of digital transmission and satellite communications, which are being addressed by both parties. What has continued to develop is an integrated system where data can be processed at multiple points within a network; and if the capability does not exist to process the information at one location, it can be moved quickly and easily to another location where it will be processed. This is the concept of distributed network design.

One other major function that is being developed by the vendors of communication equipment is the capability for performing on-line, real-time monitoring and analysis of communication facilities; thus, when there are problems anywhere in the network, they can be analyzed from a centralized location within a relatively short period of time (like 10 minutes). Better than 90 percent of the line problems that occur can be isolated so that the appropriate maintenance personnel can be called out to fix the problem.

With the development of new products and services coming at such a fast rate, there is still one very significant area that must be addressed by all personnel involved with data communications networks. That is the question of terminology. It has often been said that one of the biggest problems involved with communications is "communicating." Different people may use the same term to mean different things and, at the same time, use different terms to mean the same thing. It is therefore necessary to establish a baseline reference for terminology that can then be used by all parties to discuss, analyze, and then decide on a specific course of action. Everyone involved in the decision-making process will then be fully aware of what the others are talking about and know that all agree to the same course of action, and that course of action will mean the same thing to all the parties.

# MODERN NETWORK CONNECTIONS

Even though it is relatively early in the text, it is an appropriate time to consider the types of connections that exist in a modern communications network. From a conceptual point of view, Fig. 2–1 showed the physical components of a circuit with humans interacting on a network that was connected to a central processing unit. The foldout illustration opposite, with its three segments, gives a more complete picture of the types of equipment that you will run into, all of which are described later in this text. The left side, up to the telco demarc, shows the equipment that may be found at a remote user's site. Every one of these devices will be described in at least one section of the text.

The middle section of the foldout, between the telco demarcs, incorporates the various carrier-oriented facilities that you find outside your facilities. These connections are provided by telephone companies, packet-switching companies, and other specialized carriers.

Finally, the right side, beyond the telco demarcs, shows the host site series of connections, illustrating what might be available at the central processor. What should be especially noted here is the diagnostic equipment; it is one of the fastest growing areas in all of data communications. The foldout provides the complete data communication connection on an end-to-end basis of what exists in state-of-the-art networks.

This diagram was not meant to *scare* you about the detail involved in data communications, but only to show the different devices that you can expect to encounter in the subject. Please do not be intimidated. How each of the devices works and fits into the overall scheme will be described in detail. Let's start with the world of carriers.

# QUESTIONS

1. What are the three basic elements of a communications system?
2. Describe the primary levels of comprehension in a communications system.
3. Draw a diagram of the basic communications circuit and describe the functions of each element.
4. After reading the chapter, draw the diagram and describe the information flow of a half-duplex telegraph system. Do the same for a full-duplex telegraph system. You can use the diagrams in the text, but describe the information flow without going back to the text.
5. Describe the operations of the Baudot distributor.
6. What is the difference between baud and BPS?
7. Define a poll and a call.
8. Draw three different circuits between a remote and a host site with different components at the terminal end, network, and host end.

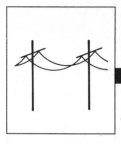

# 3

# Carriers, Services, and Regulations

All forms of electronic communications, in our case voice and data, must travel through some type of medium, which is also called a *facility.* Facilities include hardware, communication lines, switching centers, and all the other support equipment that physically move the electrical signals from the transmitter to the receiver. Many different types of companies provide facilities, as well as specific services to go along with them, and as an industry these companies are experiencing the most significant changes since the beginning of the telephone era. The reason is *deregulation,* under which the giant of the industry, American Telephone and Telegraph Company (AT&T), was ordered by the courts to divest itself into many separate companies, some of which compete with each other. At the same time, independent organizations other than AT&T will compete in specific service and facility areas. The divestiture of AT&T has been described in hundreds, even thousands of articles and documents, but a brief description of the process is warranted here to provide an overview of the carrier world.

Prior to 1984, AT&T consisted of many different organizations providing the full gamut of services to telephone users in the United States. They serviced the local user, connected locations over long distances, supplied equipment, maintained their offerings, and engaged in research and development for new products and services. On January 1, 1984, after a long, involved process as a result of what has come to be known as the Modified Final Judgment (MFJ), AT&T divested itself of all the telephone companies that provided service to the local user. There were 23 of these Bell Operating Companies (BOCs), most of which were owned entirely by AT&T. After divestiture, seven Regional Bell Holding Companies (RBHCs) were created that incorporated the original 23 local carriers. The relationship between the old and new organizations is shown in Fig. 3-1. As can be seen, Pacific Telesis was formed from Pacific Telephone and Nevada Bell. U.S. West developed from Pacific Northwestern Bell, Mountain Bell, and Northwest Bell. Southwestern Bell remained the same, covering the same five states that it covered before (Texas, Oklahoma, Kansas, Missouri, and Arkansas). Ameritech was created from five different local operating companies (Wisconsin Telephone, Michigan Bell, Illinois Bell, Indiana Bell, and Ohio Bell). SouthCentral Bell and Southern Bell became the new Bell South. Bell Atlantic encompassed New Jersey Bell, Diamond State Telephone Company, Bell of Pennsylvania, and the C&P Telephone companies. Finally, Nynex was made up of New York Telephone and New England Telephone. There were a couple of other telephone companies in which AT&T had an interest, but those holdings were also eliminated as part of the divestiture process.

AT&T kept the entire *longlines* organization (now AT&T Communications) as well as Bell Laboratories. Additional organizations were then created for AT&T to provide various kinds of network services which would integrate their own services as well as merge with other vendor services. However, those organizations keep changing over time, so it is not appropriate to include them here. Nevertheless, one of the big areas is the entry of AT&T into the computer field with a wide range of hardware (computers made by Olivetti) and systems.

In 1984 the AT&T organizations could not market their services together, but that ended by 1986 with an ironic twist. AT&T could no longer use the Bell symbol as its trademark, that right passing to the local Bell Operating Companies.

The growth of the non-AT&T companies also will be great for many years to come, although some will have problems because of the enormous amount of capital required. The biggest area open for competition is in equipment, since users are no longer required to utilize telephone company equipment in any part of a network.

Available services will expand at a rapid rate due to the multiplicity of vendors. In addition, in the future the end user will see the growth of services not necessarily related to data or voice communications provided by the local telephone company, the long-distance carriers, and nontelephone company types of vendors.

To put all these factors in perspective, this chapter will describe the different kinds of carriers, their services, and the types of rules and regulations that they must follow.

Before studying the different types of carriers you should be aware that one of the results of divestiture is the process whereby the Regional Bell Holding Companies (RBHCs) can apply every three years to provide additional services. The first of these dates came on January 1, 1987 when the RBHCs applied for an extensive list of new capabilities to provide information-oriented services to end users. Although most of the requests were denied at that time, early in 1988 Judge Harold Greene of the federal circuit court, who was presiding over the

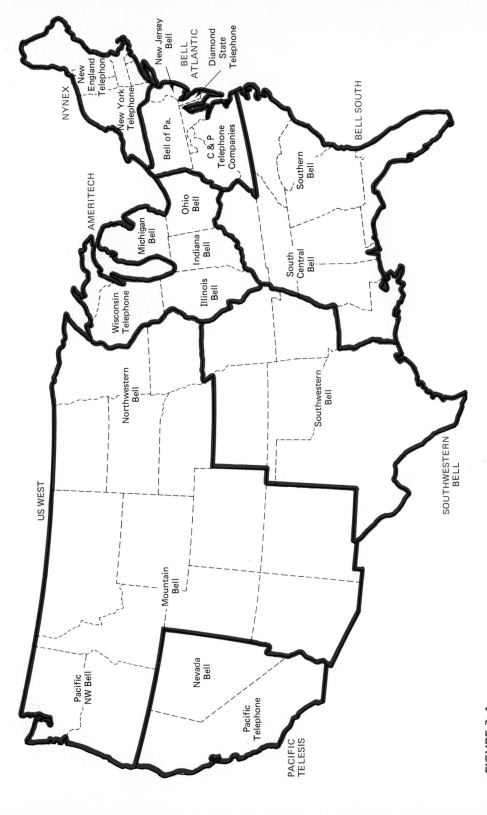

**FIGURE 3-1**
Bell System Configuration

implementation of divestiture, ruled that certain types of services could then be provided by the RBHCs. Some people felt that this decision reflected a significant amount of political pressure, while others felt it was a natural step toward what will eventually be total deregulation in the local environment. Starting in 1988, the RBHCs were able to provide certain information oriented services, such as:

| | |
|---|---|
| Voice Mail | Address Translation |
| Audiotex | Electronic Mail Services |
| Gateways to Information Services | Voice Messaging Services |
| Protocol Conversion | Billing Management |

This ruling means that the RBHCs can provide transmission capabilities to vendors that provide information content based services but cannot provide *content* based services themselves. In other words, they cannot market services like electronic databases but they can provide a *menu* to access those services provided by other vendors. In all likelihood the first users of these systems will be oriented toward Centrex customers (described in Chapter 14), but cannot be provided initially to PBX owners because the carriers own the Centrex but not the PBXs.

There is no doubt that over the next few years the local telephone companies will provide information to end users directly, but only if those services are deemed to be economically sound to the end user will they proliferate.

## A
## TYPES OF CARRIERS

Prior to 1984, there were many telephone companies (as many as 14,000), but they were of two basic types: the local telephone companies (most of which were not owned by AT&T but serving only very limited areas), connecting the user and the telephone network, and the overwhelmingly predominant long-distance carrier, AT&T. Today, however, there are fewer local telephone companies (approximately 1500) and many different types of other carriers. Because some of their services will now overlap, they will be competitive, as evidenced in the long-distance environment. Local competition is at present limited, but there has been talk of deregulating the local environment. The different types of carriers with their capabilities and services are described next.

***LOCAL CARRIER (LOCAL TELEPHONE COMPANY)*** The local telephone companies are usually called *local exchange carriers* (LECs) today. The LEC is the company that almost everyone interfaces with at home or in the office. When interfacing with an LEC it is the carrier that provides the connection from you to the telephone system. This connection has sometimes been described as the *last mile,* because it provides the physical connection from your voice or data instrument to the telephone network. It is also called a local loop, a subscriber loop, a station loop, or an end loop.

The LEC is the only organization at present authorized to install wire under the streets or overhead within a specified geographic area. For this reason the local carrier is also sometimes called a *wire line* carrier. This will be significant later when discussing *cellular radio* service. In almost all cases the LEC is the organization that provides *dial tone* to your telephone.

Of the 1400 plus different (fewer all the time in the post-divestiture environment) local telephone companies, some cover a very wide geographic area, while others serve a relatively small area with a single switch. The local carriers include the divested Bell operating companies, sometimes called Regional Bell Operating Companies (RBOCs) when they exist in one state and Regional Bell Holding Companies (RBHC) when they cross state lines.

Almost all of the former non-Bell carriers were part of an organization called the United States Independent Telephone Association (USITA), but with divestiture the name has been changed to the United States Telephone Association (USTA), and now includes the RBOCs.

Each local telephone company has one or more serving areas within one or more of what is known as a *Local Access and Transport Area* (LATA). Any service within a LATA is considered local, while service between LATAs is considered long distance and must therefore be provided by a long-distance carrier (described next). This is true even for those LATAs that are within a single state's boundaries (previously, only service crossing a state boundary was considered *true* long distance).

Your local telephone company provides service to your home or office and you have the option of obtaining your equipment from many different vendors. When the RBOCs were first divested, they could not provide any hardware, so it was provided initially by AT&T Information Systems. If an RBOC wants to provide hardware it must set up an *arm's length* subsidiary to provide that equipment, but this will change over time so that eventually RBOCs will be able to provide both telephone service and equipment (probably after 1990). In addition, local carriers will eventually be allowed to provide services that are not necessarily directly related to telephone service, such as alarm systems, meter reading, and data processing services. One of the most significant developments for data communications will be the installation of both fiber-optic and microwave digital termination systems as substitutes for metallic wire local loop.

The connections for a local call involving just the local carriers is shown in Fig. 3–2(a). The user has a connection over the local loop to the Class 5 (described later) telephone office from which there may be a connection directly out to a number with the same exchange (first three digits of the telephone number), a connection to another Class 5 over an interoffice trunk for which there are no tolls, or a connection to a Class 4 office through which the call must go when a toll is involved. Once the toll office is accessed the call goes through another interoffice trunk to the destination Class 5 office, and then over the local loop to the person being called. There are variations of these connections, such as

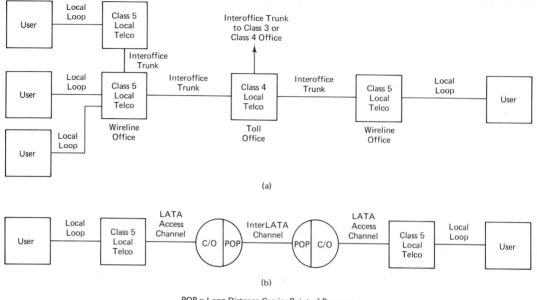

**FIGURE 3–2**
(a) Connection for Local Call. (b) Connection for Long-Distance Call.

having two Class 4 offices within a LATA communicate with each other to get to a remote Class 5 or even a Class 3 office as long as it is in the same LATA. In all cases, however, if the connection crosses a LATA boundary the call must go through a Class 4 office and then to a long-distance carrier, as shown in Fig. 3–2(b).

In this case the connection to the local Class 5 telephone office is over the same local loop, but from there the call will go to a Class 4 central office located at or near a long-distance carrier's *point of presence* (POP). Once the connection is made at a POP, the routing can go through any of that long-distance carrier's facilities until reaching the LATA where the destination local telephone company resides. At that point the signal goes through the POP into the local telco central office (probably a Class 4) and eventually to the local Class 5 office for connection on a local loop to the location being called. Here, too, there are variations in connections, some of which will be described later.

***LONG-DISTANCE CARRIERS*** These organizations provide both intrastate–inter-LATA as well as interstate connections. The largest organization in this arena is AT&T Communications, which was formerly AT&T Long Lines. These vendors provide all connections between local serving areas (LATAs), and although many of them provide both voice and data services on both dial and leased lines, the overwhelming majority of the service provided now is for voice.

Some other long-distance carriers are MCI, Sprint, and ITT. Only AT&T

covers all the geographic areas of the United States while the others, although they are growing, originate service in specific areas only. Most non-AT&T vendors provide call origination from specific metropolitan areas even though calls can be placed to practically anywhere in the country. They typically do this by using WATS or leased lines from AT&T, MCI, or Sprint for interstate service and, in many cases, intrastate WATS for services within a state.

Under equal-access requirements that were established in July 1984, all long-distance carriers have the ability to access local exchange carriers with circuits of equal quality. This *equal access* significantly improved the quality of long-distance connections for users utilizing circuits provided by vendors other than AT&T. The quality issue on local access was no longer significant, and the subjects of service and reliability rather than cost became the dominant issues in the marketing of the non-AT&T carrier services. One of the reasons for deemphasis on pricing is that AT&T is continually reducing charges for their long-distance service, while the other vendors had to pay more for their equal-access lines. This put pressure on the non-AT&T vendors to the point where many of them have significantly scaled back some of their expansion plans. It is probably safe to say that the alternative vendors will always cost something less than AT&T, but that should no longer be the deciding factor as to which vendor to use for your long-distance service.

To give you an idea of the carrier hierarchy, Fig. 3–3 shows the five levels of carrier office as described by AT&T. Most other long-distance carriers have a similar hierarchy. The carrier connection starts at the Class 5 local office, always owned by the local telephone company and which terminates the end-user local loops. There can be connections to other Class 5 offices or to Class 4 offices, called *toll centers.* Any call involving tolls or message units must go through a Class 4 office. These too are almost always owned by the local telephone company.

From a Class 4 office there are connections to Class 3 offices, known as *primary centers,* that service large metropolitan areas. Depending on the size of the local carrier, a Class 3 office can be owned by either the local carrier or a long-distance carrier. If local and long-distance facilities are located in the same office, they are sometimes called *tandem offices.*

From the primary center the circuit goes to a sectional center, which is owned by the long-distance carrier and covers a very large geographic area. Ultimately we connect through a Class 1 office, known as a *Regional Center,* that covers multiple states.

There are over 20,000 Class 5 offices in the United States, where AT&T has 10 regional centers (there are two more in Canada) with the hierarchy in between proportionally increasing toward the lower-level offices. To control this network AT&T has a network control center in Bedminster, New Jersey, which is described in more detail later in this chapter.

Although Fig. 3–3 shows a very structured hierarchy of connections, it is possible for certain levels of office to skip other levels under specific routing conditions. With the new routing software available, an AT&T cross-country call in the United States now goes through a maximum of five carrier offices.

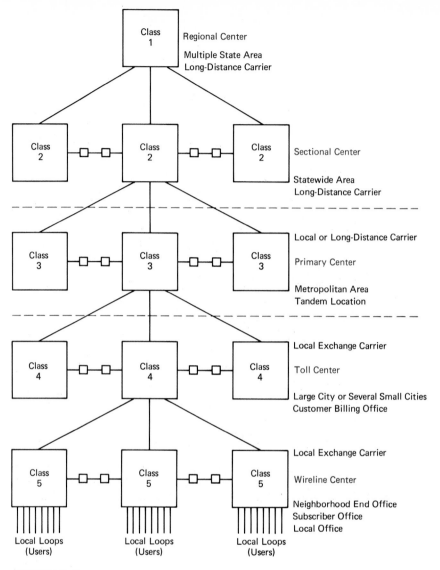

**FIGURE 3-3**
Carrier Hierarchy

*SATELLITE CARRIERS* For the most part, satellite carriers are simply long-distance carriers, but they primarily use satellite circuits for providing communication paths between locations. Typical of these companies are AT&T, GTE, CONTEL ASC, and Hughes. There are other satellite service vendors, but they may not own their own satellites but lease capacity from satellite owners. Satellite owners may not only provide the satellite facility, but they may also provide satellite circuits directly to the end user. Companies that do not own their own satellites lease circuits from other satellite vendors at a bulk or reduced rate and, in turn, sublease the service to the end user with enough margin to make a profit.

**VALUE-ADDED NETWORK OPERATORS** *Value-added network operators* (VANs) provide a network service in which additional value is added to the transmission prior to its reception at the remote location. Instead of just providing a circuit over which the user transmits information end to end (sometimes called a *transport* service), the VAN also provides some form of service, such as message validation, through the network. A typical example of a VAN is a *packet-switching operator* such as GTE Telenet, McDonnell Douglas Tymnet, Compuserve, and ADP Corporation. AT&T and the local telcos have packet-switching services also (described in Chapter 17), but they are limited because of interface differences. In the United States Telenet and Tymnet provide almost 50 percent of available packet services, but there are others who may serve either wide or specific geographic areas. Depending on the relationship to the specific network services provided, a time-share vendor may also be considered a VAN. With the overlapping of services in some of these organizations, it is quite possible for a particular company to fall within the definitions of more than one type of carrier. There are no specific ground rules, and the definitions given here are generalized categories which even the vendors themselves disagree on. The user should not worry about in which category the vendor considers itself, since primary interest is in the particular service provided and whether the required service is available where you need it.

**RESALE CARRIER** A resale carrier is a provider of network services that owns its own switching equipment but generally leases network facilities from other carriers. This type of carrier may also provide services that are leased in their entirety from other carriers. Usually a resale carrier can be found in large market areas, where the costs for providing the same type of service to a smaller market area are not incurred. Typically this service originates in just a few cities, but may terminate in many because of the use of WATS lines, which go to all states other than the originating state. Intrastate WATS may be used to cover cities within the same state. For distances of less than 50 miles, local telephone company (telco) services are probably less expensive to use.

**RADIO CARRIERS** A radio carrier is an organization that provides communication paths through radio links, predominantly in the mobile-radio environment. One service in widespread use today is called *cellular radio,* which will soon be available in almost all major cities. It involves the ability to provide many more channels than were available with the old mobile radio, and therefore the potential area of coverage can be significantly expanded. Cities will be divided into *cells,* each having its own base station, and as a mobile user moves from one cell to another the original base station will hand off communication to the next base station without affecting the transmission in progress. This kind of service can be used for both voice and data, so that many organizations are installing keyboards and hard-copy terminals in their mobile vehicles. It should be noted that if the vehicle is in motion and crosses a cell boundary, a data error will probably occur due to phasing changes, but this will hardly be noticed during voice transmission. Each city that is authorized by the FCC to implement cellular radio will have two providers: first, the local wire-line carrier (local telco), and second, an alternative financially viable carrier. (A more detailed description is provided in Chapter 19.)

**INTERNATIONAL RECORD CARRIERS** *International Record Carriers* (IRCs) are organizations that are authorized to provide international service from the United States. Any communication that extends more than 12 miles beyond the boundary of the contiguous United States (except for Canada and Mexico, which have separate rules) is considered an international call or connection. Therefore there are different rates between calls to the contiguous 48 states and those to Alaska and Hawaii. (This is changing for some services and will eventually be phased out. Puerto Rico is already considered a domestic connection.) The FCC provides coordination with the regulatory bodies of the countries to which connections are desired, and all international tariffs must be in accordance with these agreements. The FCC therefore is the governing body when any international services are to be provided. Typical of some of the larger IRCs are AT&T, Western Union International (a subsidiary of MCI), ITT, GTE Telenet, and TRT Communications.

Some of the services provided by IRCs are

Telex at 50 and 110 BPS

Analog and digital leased lines, alternate voice/data, simultaneous voice/data, data only (up to 56 KBPS)

Store-and-forward message service (a Telex enhancement)

Message switching—from private to public networks up to 1200 BPS ASCII and Baudot code

Packet switching—between the United States and foreign countries

Datel—data to and from a limited set of foreign countries up to 4800 BPS

Due to relatively recent bilateral agreements, connections can now sometimes be made directly between specific organizations in the United States and specific organizations in certain foreign countries without going through an IRC. These connections are dedicated links used almost exclusively for data purposes. As time goes on, more of these specialized connections may be allowed, but for most applications, calls will have to go through an IRC to connect outside U.S. borders.

**DIGITAL TERMINATION SYSTEMS (DTS)** The DTS vendors are relatively new in the communications world. They provide an alternative to having satellite antennas for direct communications to satellites or utilizing local telephone company local loops. They are also called *bypass* vendors because they bypass the local loop. The connections go directly from the user's facility to the long-distance carrier, and therefore are not constricted by the *voice-grade* limitations of the metallic local loop. Since only the local telephone company is allowed to provide cabling in the streets, the majority of the DTS vendors utilize microwave. Generally, the minimum transmission capacity for this type of transmission is 56,000 BPS but, when installed, it is usually utilized at T-1 rates (1.544 MBPS).

Because of the potential competition and because they already have cable rights of way, some local telephone companies are installing their own bypass capabilities by utilizing fiber-optic circuits for DTS. Due to the costs involved, these fiber-optic connections are generally used for concentrated business areas and are not yet available for residential service.

DTS can be used for both data and voice transmission, although the majority of initial installations are for data only. At present, it would appear that unless the user can eliminate six or seven separate local loops, the economics do not justify a DTS. It is expected that more implementations will reduce this rate, so if the user has a substantial amount of local loops DTS could be a viable cost-reduction alternative under current market conditions. As a result of this situation the majority of bypass circuits are being provided by the local carriers bypassing their own copper local loops.

**CARRIER EQUIPMENT**   In discussions of the various carriers, especially the local and long-distance carriers, much reference is made to the classes of office (1–5). There are also many types of switching equipment that have what seem to be the same kinds of numbers. Actually there is a set of numbers for offices and a different set of numbers for equipment. This section describes the differences.

First the offices are listed. This was also done earlier in Fig. 3–3, the carrier hierarchy.

> *Class 5 Office.* An *end office,* neighborhood office, wire line center, and local exchange office, among other names. It is always owned by the local exchange carrier and terminates all local loops from user facilities.
>
> *Class 4 Office.* A *toll center* usually servicing one large city or several small cities. It is the billing office for customers connected to that particular area. The local telephone company typically owns the Class 4 offices (except for the very small telcos who only own Class 5 switches in very small geographic environments).
>
> *Class 3 Office.* A *primary center* servicing a wide metropolitan area. It is sometimes called a *tandem location* because the long-distance connection is typically provided here. In some situations the long-distance carrier owns the office, while in others the local telephone company owns the Class 3 office (when they each own the same level of office switch, it is a tandem office). This is the level that is usually called a point of presence (POP).
>
> *Class 2 Office.* A *sectional center* usually covering a wide geographic area, even an entire state. It is always owned by the long-distance carrier.
>
> *Class 1 Office.* The *regional center* covering a multiple state area; always owned by the long-distance carrier. The Class 2 and Class 1 switches are normally very large automated switches for handling high volumes of calls.

Although there is a wide variety of vendors of telephone switches, the overwhelming majority of switches used in the United States are from AT&T and Northern Telecom, Inc. (NTI). NTI sells primarily to the local telephone companies for service in the Class 5 and 4 offices, although they have made some sales for installation in the Class 3 office. AT&T has historically provided switches to all levels of office, but has a long history of providing switches with numbers that have been confused with class of office. They will be explained in more detail now.

Prior to the use of Electronic Switching Systems (ESS) there was a wide variety of equipment in telephone offices, especially at the Class 5 and Class 4 levels. Some had names like Stepper Switch Office, Cross-Bar Office, and other electromechanical type names. The term Electronic Switching System (ESS) began in the 1960s and to date denotes five types of switches that can be used in different class offices:

*#1 ESS.* A switch designed for metropolitan areas with up to about 60,000 lines. The first one, delivered in May 1965, was designed to replace the #1 and #5 Cross-Bar Switches. The #1 ESS contained some of the features that we are accustomed to in our phone systems today: touchtone®, Centrex capability, call waiting, and three-way calling. A special version of the #1 ESS, delivered in 1966 for special networks like the government AUTO-VON, consisted of a four-wire switch rather than the two-wire switch which was used in commercial applications.

*#2 ESS.* A switch designed for a variety of service size. It came in two versions: the first could handle between 1000 and 15,000 lines and the second one between 4000 and 25,000 lines. The #2 ESS incorporated speed calling, call forwarding, three-way calling, and call waiting as some of its features.

*#3 ESS.* A switch designed for very small communities (less than 6000 lines). Delivered in the early 1970s, it was used in small towns or rural communities. It did not offer Centrex service.

*#4 ESS.* A major upgrade in the AT&T network. Partly analog and partly digital, it was designed to be compatible with all other switches in the network. First developed in 1976, it was designed to be installed in toll switching Class 4 through Class 1 offices (no Class 5 offices). As the equivalent of three or four existing primary centers, it could handle up to 750,000 busy-hour calls. Not only did it replace previous ESS equipment, but it also replaced the #4A crossbar that was used in some higher order telephone switching offices.

*#5 ESS.* The AT&T switch designed on a modular basis so that it would have the potential for virtually unlimited growth. It has two processors, one for small and one for larger applications. It can replace any existing central office switch. The first #5 ESS, delivered in the early 1980s, operated both in a standalone and a remote environment. When used in a remote situation, the modules can be up to 100 miles from the central #5 ESS and serve

up to 4000 lines at that remote location. Thus the #5 ESS can service over 100,000 customers over a 100,000 square-mile area. Almost all of the new features and capabilities being announced, including ISDN with its Signaling System #7, are compatible with the #5 ESS.

As shown, the various types of ESS can function in different class offices. When discussing these devices and offices, you should be clear as to what is being described so that you will know which office levels and what types of switches are being used.

# B
# TYPES OF SERVICE

The carriers provide hardware, physical facilities such as communication lines, and transmission services, which fall into four separate categories. They are voice; data; special services such as alarms, security, and meter reading; and others such as facsimile, television, and radio. The services are provided over either a private line for which the user contracts on a monthly basis or a dial-up line that uses the carrier circuit-switching facilities to establish a circuit every time the user wants to communicate between specific transmitting and receiving locations. The service may be offered with equipment leased from the carrier or a third party, or the user's own equipment, but in all cases either a special interface device called a *data access arrangement* must be installed between the equipment and the telephone line, or the user's device must be registered (certified). Registration/certification involves an FCC ruling, which states that if the user's equipment meets the established interface requirements for connection to a voice-grade line then it can be connected directly to that line. The certification process is described in Section E of this chapter. Both data and voice capabilities can be utilized over either the dedicated or the dial-up facilities. The dial-up facilities are known as *direct distance dial* (DDD) facilities and are by far the most common services offered by the carriers. A leased line may also be called a dedicated line, a private line, a 3002 line, or a data line.

Another widely used service that can be used for voice, data, or both, is *Wide Area Telephone Service* (WATS). WATS is a service for which the user pays a specified rate for any number of calls on a particular line for a predetermined time increment (such as 10 hours, 20 hours, or 40 hours). There is a one-time connection charge and a monthly charge based on the distance over which calls are to be made. The continental United States is divided into *bands,* each of which covers a more extensive area, with band 5 covering all the 48 contiguous states. Each call-initiating location can have a different arrangement of band boundaries. This is known as *outbound WATS.* All calls made on a WATS line are specifically logged as to number of messages and total length of time so that the user can see the usage of that line.

Another form of WATS, known as inbound WATS, is sometimes called dial-in 800 service. When a caller dials an 800 number the call is charged to the receiving party. This service is normally used when the called party is providing some business function, such as hotel, car rental, or airline reservations, in return for which the caller should not have to pay. The above description applies for interstate WATS. There is also intrastate WATS, but it is regulated by the individual state public utilities commissions and may have very different rates from interstate WATS. It is for this reason that most inbound WATS lines may specify one 800 number to be called from outside "state X" and specify a different 800 number "for inside state X" (when the vendor is not lucky enough to get the same 800 number for both interstate and intrastate WATS service). The "state X" number is for callers within the state that the WATS calls are being directed to, that is, the WATS number is *within* the state (intrastate). Because of the potential intrastate rate differences the caller is sometimes requested to make a collect call within a particular state instead of using the intrastate WATS.

Data transmission can take place on any voice-grade facility for those companies who already have WATS lines. If those lines are not utilized for voice to their full availability, they can be used very efficiently for data communications, getting what is, in effect, lower-cost transmission time than dial service. Along with this combined capability is the availability of hardware devices that can monitor and measure specific WATS utilization. These devices will identify the calling extension, location called, and duration of call on any WATS line so that the communications manager can determine whether an effective utilization of facilities is being made. This information can identify if there are times of the day when it would be desirable to set aside specific periods for either voice or data communications so as to use the WATS facility to its maximum benefit. This utilization measurement may also be made as part of an entire network accounting system that also accounts for all other utilization. Carriers such as AT&T, MCI, and Sprint provide varying levels of WATS service with different features, especially call accounting. You should always verify, based on your own usage, which vendor or service is best for you.

It is quite possible that the *banded* 800 service may be coming to an end. Until AT&T introduced their Readyline in 1985, previous banded 800 service required the use of special access lines. Readyline, which was good for the range of WATS usage between 25 and 200 hours per month, involved dialing on any access line. Megacom 800 service also did not require special access lines for those users of over 800 hours per month. This means that you can use WATS services without special access lines, and in all likelihood, in the future you will not be limited by specific *band* limitations because you will be charged by the distance called and time used. The costs will still be discounted from regular, long-distance service.

Another extensively used service is known as *Foreign Exchange Service* (FEX or FX). A foreign exchange service is a leased line that allows a user in one exchange area to make a local call to an exchange area that would normally be a toll call. To implement this service, a leased line is provided from the local exchange to the foreign exchange and is paid for at regular leased-line rates on a monthly basis. Depending on the specific service desired, callers at either end are then able to initiate calls as if they were at the other foreign exchange location. Many companies have extensive foreign exchange networks where they can make calls across the country. They use this service by dialing an access code in their switchboard, which connects them to the specific foreign exchange line to the city they want to talk to. Because regular voice-grade facilities are involved here, too, either voice or data can be transmitted. This is a dial-oriented service.

Another service provided by the carriers is called a *tie line*. A leased line, it connects two specific private branch exchanges (PBXs) so that a call can be made to another geographic location just by dialing the last four digits instead of the entire seven digits. These lines may be connected to multiple switchboards at multiple locations (each connection is a separate tie line).

Finally, there is a whole range of carrier services which are designated CLASS. This stands for Custom Local Area Signalling Services and involves *out-of-band* signalling for its implementation. CLASS services can be provided in a single switch within one telephone office or across multiple switches in either a local or a long-distance environment, but Signalling System #7 (SS#7 described in Chapter 16) is required in order to carry the services across multiple switches.

The features are divided into two basic areas called *inbound* features and *outbound* features. The inbound features are dependent on the calling number ID. They can provide selective screening of inbound calls, rejection of inbound calls, rerouting of inbound calls, automatic callback on busy, distinctive ringing, database lookup on caller, and other services that depend on the specific calling number. On the other hand outbound features can involve user selectable automatic redialing, speed dialing, rejection of specific outbound area codes or numbers, and other limitations you might want to incorporate into your system based on who is making a call.

One of the negatives about CLASS is that there are no common codes defined for activation as yet. Unless a standardized set of codes is developed, CLASS may turn out to be a problem for multiple local telco implementation when connected across a long-distance carrier circuit.

Other specialized services can be provided, mostly at user's facilities, and are determined individually by the capability of the local private branch exchange (PBX) or computerized branch exchange (CBX). Any questions regarding the capability of these services should be referred either to the local telephone company or to the PBX vendor to determine specifically what can be provided and the costs for those services. Other network services will be described in Section H of this chapter.

## C
## REGULATORY AGENCIES

The various carriers are regulated by two different agencies. For services provided between two or more states, the carrier is regulated by the Federal Communications Commission (FCC); for services provided within a single state's boundaries, the carrier is regulated by the Public Utilities Commission (PUC) of that state. The FCC was formed as part of the Communications Act of 1934 to regulate all interstate communications. It also has jurisdiction over the U.S. interface for international communications.

The carrier is accountable to the regulatory agency within specific geographic areas of operation for specified services, for conformance with uniform policies applied to all users, and for establishing a maximum fixed return on investment. (Proposals have been made by the FCC to change this policy to a *rate cap* because under the present rate of return formula there is a disincentive for the carriers to upgrade their equipment. (Extensive discussion will be required before a final determination can be made.) The geographic areas of operation are sometimes called *franchised monopolies* regarding the local telephone company. They prevent duplication of services in high-density areas and absence of service in the other areas. The natural problems of this type of system are the lack of competition and potential lack of choice of services, but both problems are exactly what the regulatory agency has been given the charter to monitor and control in the public interest while allowing the carrier to earn a reasonable profit. (Franchised monopolies, too, are under review with the potential for opening up the local environment to competition. It is the author's opinion that it would be a disaster to overlap these services in the local environment primarily because of the confusion it would cause for the end user.)

# D

## TARIFFS

The document that a carrier submits to the regulatory agency for permission to offer a service is called a *tariff*. The tariff specifies the service to be offered, the rates to be charged, and the requirements to be imposed on both the carrier and the user. The tariff must be provided in sufficient detail for the regulatory agency and the using groups to identify clearly the equipment and/or services being offered, as well as the basis on which the rates will be established. The user's liabilities must be clearly understood, especially concerning such things as penalties to be paid for maintenance or repair eventually found to be the customer's fault. Penalties are also established against the carrier for not maintaining the service to the standards specified in the tariff.

All tariffs that involve interstate service are ruled on by the FCC; tariffs for intrastate service are ruled on by the individual PUCs. For those cases when the dial-up facilities of the telephone company network are used, their terminal and local equipment will be tariffed on an intrastate basis, and only the charge for the specific call itself will be on an interstate or interLATA basis if the call crosses a LATA boundary.

With regard to uniform policies, the carrier cannot show any discrimination toward any user or group of users when offering services to the public. Nor may preferential treatment be given to any user or group of users. Rates must be uniformly applied even though it may actually cost the carrier more to provide service to one particular user than to another, such as for remote compared to local geographic locations.

The money a carrier is allowed to make is regulated according to a specific rate of return on investment (see Section C). The net profit allowed to the stockholders is controlled by the rates allowable for the various tariff services. The regulating agencies have the right to and actually do perform audits of the financial records of the carriers, and all regulatory decisions are supposed to be based on the necessity of or benefit to the using public.

In years past there was an extensive process by which a vendor had to first submit a tariff with written testimony justifying and supporting the new rate or service being offered. Then, after publication of the proposed tariff, a hearing would be held to determine whether the tariff should be approved. The public had an opportunity to comment on those tariffs. Today the process has been significantly shortened and, in most cases, approval is forthcoming by the regulatory agency after their own internal review. Sometimes public comment is elicited, but this is an exception rather than the rule today. The philosophy seems to be that if a vendor provides a service that the public does not want, then the public is free to go to another vendor. There have been cases, however, where a state PUC has determined that actions by a telephone company were detrimental to the using public, and rebates have been ordered in those cases. The tariffs remained in effect, but it was the implementation that was in question; the review showed that the service was not provided under uniform conditions, therefore the rebate. This can still happen, and you should be aware that the various state PUCs may rule differently on the same service.

There still seems to be a lot of confusion regarding the tariffs, especially for the long-distance network. The private line tariff which was primarily used for data was AT&T tariff #260. It established the criteria for what would be carried on a leased line. As a result of divestiture, tariff #260 became obsolete. It was replaced with the interstate private line tariffs #9, #10, and #11. These three tariffs covered different areas of connection.

> *Tariff #9.* This tariff established the rates on interoffice channels between AT&T rate centers (POPs). There were to be three types of Interoffice Channel (IOC): IOC-1 was for basic voice service, IOC-2 was for both voice and data, and IOC-3 was optimized for data only.
>
> *Tariff #10.* This tariff covered the location of the POPs, where the rate centers would be, and what service availability there would be. It covers all the logistical administration for cost calculations.
>
> *Tariff #11.* This tariff established the rate information for AT&T arranged local channel portions of interLATA service and coordinating functions. In other words, when you got an AT&T leased line which originated and terminated in two different LATAs, and AT&T coordinated the entire end-to-end circuit, Tariff #11 applied to the local channel between you and the

local telephone company. In discussing this kind of tariff you should be aware that if a leased line is terminated in a PBX, it is subject to extra charges, because theoretically it can access the local switched network through another line connected within the PBX. Also, conditioning charges (described in Chapter 21) would now be separate for the local loop and interoffice trunks.

Another set of communication line services that were tariffed prior to divestiture but have changed significantly since then are the types of lines. There were four general categories: the 1000 series, 2000 series, 3000 series, and the 8000 series. Because many people still refer to some of these categories of lines they will be listed here along with their capabilities.

| TYPE | SPEED | SERVICE |
| --- | --- | --- |
| 1000 Series | Up to 150 BPS | Teletype or communications |
| 1001 | Up to 30 BPS | Telemetry, signalling, supervisory control |
| 1002 | Up to 55 BPS | TTY, data, telemetry, supervisory control, signalling |
| 1003 | Up to 55 BPS | Radio telegraph |
| 1004 | Up to 45 BPS | |
| 1005 | Up to 75 BPS | Same as 1002—no Morse code |
| 1006 | Up to 150 BPS | Same as 1002—no Morse code |
| 2001 | | Voice |
| 2002 | | Radio telephone |
| 2003 | | Radio telegraph |
| 2004 | | Radio telephone (for civil defense only) |
| 2006 | | Foreign exchange |
| 2007–2010 | | Secure communications for government use only (special conditioning) |
| 3001 | | Control, signalling, telemetry |
| 3002 | | Data |
| 3010 | | Unloaded data line (see Chapter 10) |
| 8800 | Up to 56 KBPS | Data, facsimile, voice |
| 8900 | Up to 56 KBPS | Washington, D.C. area only |

Since AT&T no longer controls a circuit from end to end and provides only the interoffice channels, they have specified the interoffice channels to meet 10 different types or levels of operating capability. When you order lines you will not order the type of line, you will order certain levels of conditioning (see Chapter 21) that will determine the type of IOC you get from AT&T. The local telcos are still using the terminology dealing with conditioning as defined prior to 1984. The 10 types of interoffice channels are as follows:

| TYPE | PRIMARY APPLICATION | SERVICE CHARACTERISTICS |
|------|---------------------|-------------------------|
| 1 | Basic voice | Fixed noise limits and distortion |
| 2 | Trunks to MTS (trunks to local carrier switches) | Less signal loss than type 1 |
| 3 | Radio land lines | Specified signal/noise performance |
| 4 | Low-speed data | Signal/noise at least 21 dB |
| 5 | Basic data | Signal/noise 24 dB minimum and specified envelope delay, phase jitter, and impulse noise |
| 6 | Voice/data trunks (foreign exchange also) | Type 5 plus better envelope delay and harmonic distortion |
| 7 | Voice and data to AT&T | Type 6 plus better phase jitter, envelope delay, and signal/noise |
| 8 | Trunks between AT&T switches | Type 7 plus better envelope delay, harmonic distortion, signal/noise (30 dB minimum) |
| 9 | Telephone facsimile | Type 5 plus better envelope delay |
| 10 | Protective relaying | Type 5 plus better attenuation distortion |

Even though these different types sound very complex with lots of different characteristics available, you can still order lines which were equivalent to the 3002 data line to meet your basic data transmission criteria. With all the changes going on in the carrier environments today, it is quite possible that even more types will be added to this list as well as many other changes. Still, now when these terms get thrown at you, you should have an idea of what they mean.

# E
# INTERCONNECTION AND CERTIFICATION

Interconnection was originally defined as the ability to utilize communications equipment and services that *are not* provided by the local telephone company in conjunction with equipment or facilities that *are* provided by that telephone company. Today interconnection means the attaching of any device to the telephone-company line and includes the devices provided by the carriers themselves such as modems, PBXs, handsets, meter-reading equipment, and alarm equipment.

Prior to 1962 a noncarrier device could not be connected directly to a telephone line. Then in 1962 Thomas Carter in Dallas, Texas, brought suit against the Public Telephone Companies (Southwest Bell and AT&T) to allow direct connection of his Carterphone to the telephone line and, in turn, to the network. This suit eventually resulted in a consent agreement signed by AT&T allowing a noncarrier device to be connected directly to the telephone circuit. This new tariff filed in 1969 provided a connecting arrangement black box called a *data access arrangement* (DAA) that the common carriers were to supply which would enable the interconnection of "foreign" equipment to the public network without any degradation of service or harm to the public network.

About the same time, Microwave Communications, Inc. filed for common carrier status to supply specialized microwave communications services for trucking companies between the St. Louis and Chicago areas. After six years in the courts, MCI was allowed to compete for some of the specialized communications services in parallel with the already existing common carriers (AT&T and Western Union). In 1969 MCI was also granted a construction permit for building a segment of its network between Chicago and St. Louis. The first application was to provide a 2000-Hz bandwidth service, which was different from any of the existing carrier services at that time along that route and was therefore a special service. This in turn made MCI the first of the specialized common carriers.

Also during 1969 the FCC authorized informal technical hearings on the subject of interconnection; they were held under the auspices of the National Academy of Sciences (NAS). The result of the NAS hearing was a report submitted in 1970 that indicated a potential for harm or degradation to the public network by indiscriminate interconnection. The degree of degradation was not stated due to the lack of data, but a program of certification could be implemented that would allow for control of interconnection to the degree that no potential harm would occur to the public network. As a result, in May of 1971 the FCC issued a ruling on the definition of a common carrier. This ruling permitted the formation and operation of specialized common carriers, which were subject to more lenient rules of technical and financial qualification. This ruling fostered the formation of a number of new and competing companies in the communications market, and in the same year additional construction permits were issued to MCI for routes between New York and Washington and New York and Chicago.

In 1973 the State Public Utilities Commission in New York approved a tariff for a direct connection between equipment not owned by the telephone company (Rochester Telephone Company) and the public network. The California PUC also proposed that direct connection of equipment not owned by the telephone company would be permitted if it was certified by a registered professional engineer not to cause harm to the public network. In 1976 most of the states, as well as AT&T, had tariffs that provided for the connection of non-telephone-company-owned equipment directly to the public network as long as the equipment was certified. Certification means that the equipment has been tested by an independently registered professional engineering organization and has been found to meet all the interface requirements established for connection to the public network. In effect, certification allows for the connection of foreign equipment directly to the public network as long as it meets the same requirements as telephone-company-owned equipment. Most terminal and communication equipment vendors now provide certified equipment that can be purchased by the end user and then connected directly into the carrier network. This equipment is registered with the FCC.

A registered device will have a label attached in an inconspicuous spot containing three items of information: the registration number itself, the *ringer equivalent,* and the USOC (Universal Service Ordering Code). The ringer equivalent represents the amount of signal load which the device places on the ringing current. The sum of the ringer equivalents of devices connected to a single line cannot exceed five; if it does, no telephone (not even one) is guaranteed to ring. Individual phones may have ringer equivalents anywhere between 0.2 and 2 (usually not more than 1) or more, so that the total number of phones allowed on one line could be as few as two or as many as 25, depending upon their ringers. The USOC identifies the jack which attaches the device to the telephone line; see Chapter 5 for a discussion of jack types.

In addition to connections to the analog network there will also be connections to the digital network. Since 22 May 1987 all equipment connecting to the digital network must meet a set of criteria established by the FCC for signal power, impedance, and leakage limits. These are contained in part 68.2 and part 68.3 of the FCC rules (existing equipment already connected to the network is *grandfathered*). The coding on the equipment is in three basic forms delineated by the last two characters of the code sequence. The code sequence is in the FCC standard 13-character designation [XXXYYY12345AA(A stands for an alpha character)]. The first of the alpha sequences is DD. The DD signifies that this device complies with all FCC rules for electrical and analog encoded information. Typical equipment that will have the DD designations are the digital telephone and most subrate digital equipment.

The second set of alpha designators is DE. DE signifies that this device complies with all FCC rules except for the analog content protection. This means an affidavit is required for the telephone company indicating that the user equipment does not carry any encoded analog content or billing information that is intended for eventual conversion into voice or analog signals for retransmission within the carrier network. Typical equipment that conforms to this specification are most of the channel service units utilized with dataphone digital service (described in Chapter 16).

The third form of alpha designator is XD, which means the device complies only with the FCC rules for encoded analog content (digitized voice) and it must be connected separately to a registered DE-type device. A typical XD device would be a digital T-1 multiplexer or a channel bank (which would then connect to a channel service unit).

The DD- and DE-type devices connect directly to the communication line (like a modem for analog), while the XD device must connect through the DE device (like an unregistered DTE through a DAA for analog).

Connections to the communication line are through an RJ48 jack. There are many versions of the RJ48 for the various configurations of services. The table on page 44 will give you an idea of the most common ones.

Although it may seem early to get into this depth of description, it is the reference to FCC designations that is important here. Care must be taken when implementing all digital interfaces in the future to make sure they conform to FCC registration criteria.

| SERVICE | DESCRIPTION | JACK NAMES |
|---|---|---|
| Single T-1 | Miniature 8-position jack | RJ48C—same as ISDN<br>RJ48X—same as RJ48C with a shorting bar for loop back, if customer equipment shorting bar is removed |
| Multiple T-1 | Fifty-position | RJ48M—8 four-wire miniature ribbon jack connections with 16 conductors not used |
| Sub rate digital | 8-position keyed jack | RJ48S—pins 1 and 2 are service pair one and pins 7 and 8 are pair two |
| Multiple subrate | 50-position miniature | RJ48T—use digital services ribbon jack, all but 2 pins for transmit and receive |

## F
## CARRIER SYSTEMS

The total bandwidth capacity of different communications media is usually much greater than is actually needed for an individual communications line, and therefore various carrier systems are used to increase media efficiencies. Carrier systems were first introduced in the telegraph industry and later used by the telephone company to divide the available bandwidth into specific channels. Frequency division multiplexing (FDM) was the technique first used to build a carrier system. Teletypewriter or low-speed data channels are multiplexed into voice-frequency (VF) channels (rarely done today), which normally carry telephone conversations. These VF channels are multiplexed into what are known as base groups, super groups, master groups, and finally jumbo groups.

Typical carrier systems for wire media handle from 4 to 10,800 VF channels, while radio systems handle from 600 to 1860 VF channels. Digital carrier systems typically handle data speeds from 1.544 million bits per second (MBPS) to 44.736 MBPS. Figures 3–4 and 3–5 show the AT&T hierarchy for combining voice-grade

**FIGURE 3–4**
Telephone Carrier Systems—Analog

| CARRIER SYSTEM | FACILITIES MEDIA | LINE FREQUENCY BAND | VOICE CHANNELS |
|---|---|---|---|
| Voice-Grade Channel | Wire or Cable (1 pair) | 300–3300 Hz | 1 |
| K | Cable (2 pairs) | 12–60 kHz | 12, Base Group |
| L1 | Coaxial Cable | 60–2788 kHz | 60, Super Group |
| L3 | Coaxial Cable | 312–8284 kHz | 600, Master Group |
| L4 | Coaxial Cable | 0.564–17.548 MHz | 3600, Jumbo Group |
| L5 | Coaxial Cable | 16.6–18.8 MHz | 10,800 |
| TD-2 | MW Radio | 3.7–4.2 GHz | 600, Master Group |
| TH | MW Radio | 5.9–6.4 GHz | 1860, 3 Master 1 Super Group |

MW—Microwave

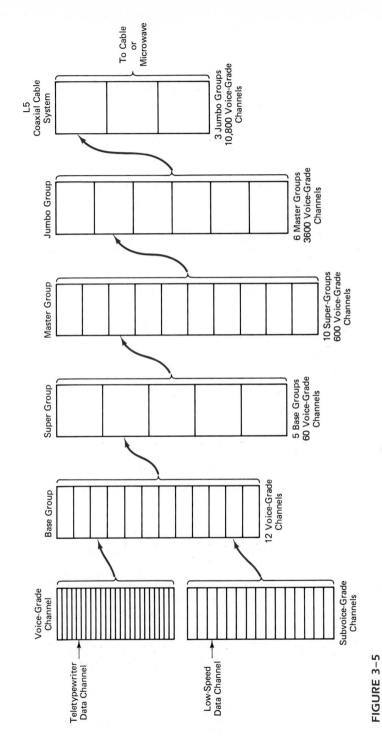

**FIGURE 3-5**
Telephone Voice-Grade Carrier Hierarchy

45

channels at the various levels. An equivalent digital hierarchy which is being implemented today is described in Chapter 16.

# G
## OPEN NETWORK ARCHITECTURE (ONA)

A term being utilized more and more today is *Open Network Architecture* (ONA). ONA is an architecture for the Bell operating companies to offer standardized interfaces to all service providers. It is a mechanism which the local telephone companies will be able to use as a tradeoff in order to provide information services themselves. ONA is more of a philosophy rather than a set of standards, although it is expected that standards will evolve. Still, with both the FCC and Bellcore (Bell Communications Research) not involved, there will in all likelihood be many incompatible plans for ONA interfaces from the Bell operating companies.

The preliminary ONA plans, filed in February 1988, include plans for *unbundled* network services. The services provided by the RBHCs are divided into two segments. First is the Basic Service Element (BSE), which consists of the specific services to and from the local carrier. These are separated from the Basic Service Arrangement (BSA), which is the provision of an end to end line service. By appropriately selecting the BSEs, end users will be able to add those kinds of services to their BSAs. ONA establishes a standardized set of interfaces for both the BSE and BSA environments. Pricing structures are also needed to give to those vendors who want to provide services. This situation is an interesting one because eventually the local carriers will want to provide those services themselves, setting up what appears to be a conflict of interest. As a result carriers seem to be moving very slowly toward ONA and service providers are upset. It is not clear exactly what the outcome will be, but with the FCC mandate, there will be progress toward standardized end-user service interfaces. The question is when?

BSEs are designed to allow Enhanced Service Providers (ESPs) access to the public switched network. Since interface standards have not been established for BSEs, there will probably be different offerings in different states. It will probably be hard to tell the difference between intra- and interstate services in the event of alternate routing. The services defined within a BSE are to be provided on an equal basis to all accessors of the network and will consist of at least the following features: automatic calling number i.d., speed calling, distinctive ringing, abbreviated dialing, screening, three-way calling (conference calls), call distribution, and special billing services.

Functions that are to be provided as part of a BSE will exploit the capabilities of Signaling System #7 (described in Chapter 16), sometimes called IN/2, which stands for Intelligent Network 2. The idea behind this intelligent network is that with it the local telephone company can program its own switches and therefore not be dependent on the switch manufacturer for particular features.

With this kind of capability inherent in each of the local telephone companies there will probably be a substantial amount of incompatibility, especially between different telephone companies, until the end users begin to apply pressure for standard interfaces. IN/2 is anticipated to be operational in the mid-1990s.

There is a tremendous amount of discussion today regarding ONA, which means that there will probably be many changes to its planned implementation before it actually appears. Therefore, when someone mentions ONA or its features, find out exactly what they mean, because it may be different from what you heard before.

# H
## SPECIAL NETWORK SERVICES

### Software Defined Networks

A wide variety of services are offered by the carriers these days: specialized WATS services, special network configurations, special features, and a variety of hybrid network capabilities that involve both dial and leased network connections. It would be impossible to describe all of them here and some would probably be significantly changed by printing time, but a couple seem to have features that will allow them to exist for many years. One of them is known as the *Software Defined Network* (SDN). This is a service from AT&T, which by 1987 was providing service to over 700 locations. Three competing services also performed the same kind of function. MCI offered Vnet, Sprint offered VPN (virtual private network), and Western Union offered its own version of SDN that was available only in limited areas. The idea behind these networks was to have a series of leased circuits between the long-distance carrier offices that could be accessed on demand by dialing from the end-user's facility. It ends up providing the equivalent of a leased line only when required. As a side benefit redundancy is built into the network because when there is a failure you can redial and get the same level of access on another circuit.

The idea behind SDN is for the user to access a local carrier via a dedicated or dial connection. This connection is then routed over predetermined circuits to the long-distance carrier at what is being called an *intelligent* network node. This location is known as an *access point* and all access points of the SDN are connected.

The user will control all connections through addressing, and the addresses can change on user demand. These addresses are stored in the switches at the access points. You make a call just as if you were dialing on the regular switched network. The effect is like a PBX environment where you access locations over a wide geographic area, rather than an in-house environment. A typical connection for an SDN is shown in Fig. 3–6. The user site has a connection to the local telephone company office on a dial or dedicated loop. In this particular case the dedicated loop is a little different from what you might be accustomed to because

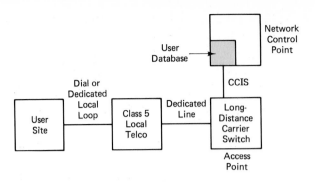

CCIS = Common Control Interoffice Signaling (Out of Band Signaling)

**FIGURE 3-6**
Software Defined Network

it is guaranteed to be of data quality. When you want to make an SDN call you get a dial tone on this special loop. The local telephone company now has a dedicated line to the long-distance carrier switch, known as the access point, from which a separate connection to a network control point is provided. The network control point contains call routing information and authorization codes, provides blocking capabilities, establishes the routing and billing information, contains call screening, and can establish priorities. Not all vendors have the same features.

All of these networks use a standard seven-digit dialing scheme; when you call it seems just like a local call. There are two kinds of calls to be made: *on-net* calls, which originate and terminate within the network, and *off-net* calls where one end of the connection is on the SDN but the other is on the public switching network. You typically need to dial an access code for on-net calls and a different access code for an off-net call (you need to know whether your destination is on or off the net). Also, off-net calls must be the full ten digits, so you need to dial the area code in addition to the regular number.

The cost for SDN-type services is based on distance, time of day, duration, rate bands, access line charges, and any special features. In typical operation the user can make minor network changes but cannot add any new lines or modify existing routes. The initial network is set up based on anticipated traffic patterns and the rates are typically related to *mileage bands*. If users would like to make network changes, they must go to the carrier network control point where changes can be loaded into each of the NCPs via a separate control transmission provided by the long-distance carrier.

As the cost for leased lines increase, and the costs for an SDN-type network come down, it appears that more users will move toward this kind of network. This is another instance where you must keep up to date on the usage and costs of the network, as well as feature changes, so that you will know whether you are getting optimum use out of your network.

One last item: When transmitting data, depending on the vendor, you can transmit up to 9600 BPS between on-net locations because you can get leased, conditioned lines to support that rate (there is no guarantee of the line quality when you go to an off-net location). When going to higher data rates, some locations can support switched 56 KBPS service. In that case you must find out from the vendor whether that service is available from the locations you want to connect.

## Universal Information Systems (UIS)

*Universal Information Systems* (UIS) is not a product or a service but a network concept where software can be incorporated into that network such that all users can be provided with access to any kind of voice, data, or image service, in any place, at any time with the maximum amount of convenience and economy. This sounds like the ultimate network and maybe it is, but it would appear that all of the AT&T services are already evolving toward this concept. It is also an evolutionary step toward Integrated Services Digital Network (ISDN) type services (described in Chapter 16). UIS should not be confused with the Information System Network (ISN), which is really a form of a local area network described in Chapter 15.

## Virtual Telecommunications Network Service

The *Virtual Telecommunications Network Service* (VTNS) was announced in late 1987. It was to be a single source for all customer integrated digital network capabilities. All AT&T digital offerings, including network management, would be part of this service. It was aimed at large customers with many diverse communications requirements and was designed, according to AT&T, in accordance with extensive user input. The initial service was to include data rates of 2400 BPS all the way through 256 KBPS. As time goes on, there will obviously be further definition of what this service will become, so if you are going digital and toward ISDN this is another type of service you should look into. There will probably be equivalent types of announcements from other vendors that should also be evaluated.

Related to all of these services, just as all of the competing long-distance carriers are developing new capabilities and services, in late 1987 AT&T cut over a new network control center in Bedminster, New Jersey to control their nationwide network. This center is designed around a 20-foot-high by 60-foot-wide display of the United States where each AT&T trunk is delineated. This system can detect if even a single call in the entire network fails to reach its destination and typically handles 75 million calls per day in the United States. Also, a new diagnostic network that incorporated 45,000 route miles in 1987 is designed to go to 67,000 miles by 1990, with the entire worldwide network expected to go to 88,000 route miles by 1991.

In addition to the various analog services, AT&T also expects to incorporate digital service to over 400 cities over the same time frame, which will include the United States, Japan, Europe, and the Far East. The route miles described are the *backbone* networks from which other branches emanate to connect to local telephone companies in the various cities where AT&T provides service.

Other long-distance carriers (LDCs) have their own network control centers that perform the same kind of functions, but on a smaller scale because their networks are not as extensive. Even though many of the services and locations reached are the same, the other LDCs utilize AT&T connections in those areas that they do not serve directly.

Finally, the method for dialing long-distance connections today involves dialing a 1 before the area code and then the seven digits of the number—11 digits in all. All area codes at present have either a 0 or a 1 as the second digit. Many of the carriers utilize the 0 or 1 as a second digit as an indication that the number being dialed is a long-distance number, since the area code is recognized with that 0 or 1. There is a problem brewing, however, because the telephone network is running out of area codes. By 1995 it will be necessary to use area codes that can utilize numbers 2 through 9 as the middle digit. This will make 792 possible area codes instead of only 152. As of 1988 only 13 metropolitan areas incorporated the 1-plus dialing as part of their switching structure, which is independent of the middle digit. If your carrier does not utilize the 1-plus dialing, then the equipment in the central offices must be replaced within the next few years, involving a substantial increase in carrier cost, which in turn will probably be passed on to end users.

Many users have PBXs that work on the same basis, so that when area codes contain any three digits, that equipment will have to be replaced also. Because there are still a few years before it will be necessary to make that change, many users are taking the attitude that it is "too far in the future to worry," but planning for that kind of change should begin now. To help end users, both Bellcore and the USTA (United States Telephone Association) plan to initiate a public awareness educational series of announcements to inform both users and carriers. Because network equipment is integrating more facilities as time progresses, you should not incorporate any equipment for the long term that does not have the ability to accommodate area codes with a middle digit that is not a 0 or a 1.

## DOCUMENTATION

This section will describe the source publications that have been issued by AT&T and Bellcore for services in the voice and data environment, especially the new digital and packet interfaces. Table 3–1 contains the most relevant AT&T publications; Table 3–2 contains the most relevant Bellcore publications. Typically, when either of these organizations issues documents like these, other vendors use them as a base for their own documentation so that compatibility problems are reduced

**TABLE 3-1**
Pertinent AT&T Publications

| PUBLICATION NUMBER | PUBLICATION TITLE | SUBJECT AREA | PUBLICATION DATE |
|---|---|---|---|
| Pub 62210 | Access Connections to Baseline Offerings at AT&T Central Office | End user methods of connecting to AT&T Baseline services | May 1985 |
| Pub 54010 | X.25 Interface Specs and Packet Transport Network Capabilities | X.25 specs for user connections | May 1986 |
| Pub 54012 | X.75 Interface Specs and Technical Capabilities | X.75 specs for Internetwork connections | May 1986 |
| Pub 54015 | Customer Controlled Reconfiguration in Accunet T1.5 Service | Describes specs for CCR function | January 1985 |
| Pub 62411 | Accunet T1.5 Service Description and Interface Specs. | Describes T1.5 service in detail | October 1985 |
| Pub 41458 | Special Access Connections to AT&T Switched Network | Interfaces for analog (2-W, 4-W) and digital services such as switched 56K | October 1985 |
| Pub 41449 | AT&T Integrated Services Digital Network Primary Rate Interface Specs. | Describes ISDN Primary (23B + D) Digital interface | March 1986 |
| Pub 41459 | ISDN Primary Rate Interface for AT&T | Describes ISDN features | April 1986 |
| Pub 54020 | AT&T Communications Telecom Canada Spec of CCITT Signaling System No. 7 | Describes SS #7 signaling channel used in ISDN | July 1984 |
| CB 143 | Digital Access and Cross-Connect System Technical References | Describes DACS system and compatibility | January 1983 |

**TABLE 3-2**
Pertinent Bellcore Publications

| PUBLICATION NUMBER | PUBLICATION TITLE | SUBJECT AREA | PUBLICATION DATE |
|---|---|---|---|
| TR-NPL-000334 | Voice-Grade Switched Access Transmission Parameter Limits and Interface Combinations | Describes requirements for connections to switched voice-grade services | June 1986 |
| TR-NPL-000335 | Voice-Grade Special Access Service Transmission Parameter Limits and Interface Combinations | Describes requirements for connections to non-switched voice-grade services | June 1986 |
| TR-EOP-000063 | Network Equipment—Building System Generic Requirements | Describes requirements for building telephone company equipment rooms | August 1985 |
| TR-TSY-000020 | Generic Requirements for Fiber and Optical Fiber Cable | Describes requirements for using fiber-optic facilities | December 1985 |
| TR-NPL-000275 | Notes on the BOC Intra-LATA Networks—1986 | Describes how BOC Intra-LATA networks are organized; who connects to these networks | April 1986 |

or eliminated, though there is no guarantee that that is the case. Other vendors' offerings must be compared on an apples-to-apples basis with either the AT&T or Bellcore specs.

If you need additional information or updated specifications, the latest address at the time of this writing for AT&T publications is:

AT&T Technologies
Customer Information Center
Indianapolis, Indiana 46219
317/352-8557

The Bellcore location for obtaining information is:

Bellcore
Information Operations Center
60 New England Avenue
Piscataway, New Jersey 08854
201/981-5600

Both addresses and telephone numbers change fairly often.

## J
## CANADIAN CARRIERS AND SERVICES

The Canadian data communications industry resembles the United States' and provides an integrated North American network. Part of this similarity stems from the fact that the Bell System technology was dominant in Canada through the early part of the 1900s. Today there are many carriers throughout Canada although Bell Canada constitutes more than half of all telephone operations in the country. The structure of the various organizations within Canada is shown in Fig. 3–7.

In the center we have Telecom Canada, an association of some of the largest Canadian telephone companies. It is a common carrier that provides public telecommunications facilities. Prior to September 1983 it was called the TransCanada Telephone System (TCTS). The diagram shows the major carriers that are part of Telecom Canada, but seven other major carriers as well as many smaller carriers throughout Canada also provide the various services to end users.

The largest member of Telecom Canada is Bell Canada, a privately owned company. Bell Canada services Ontario, Quebec, the Northwest Territories, and various exchanges in the Arctic.

In a related area, Bell created a manufacturing subsidiary in 1882 called Northern Electric and Manufacturing Company to produce telephone equipment for Canadian use. Northern Electric became a separate company in 1895 and in 1976 was renamed Northern Telecom. Northern Telecom was the equivalent of

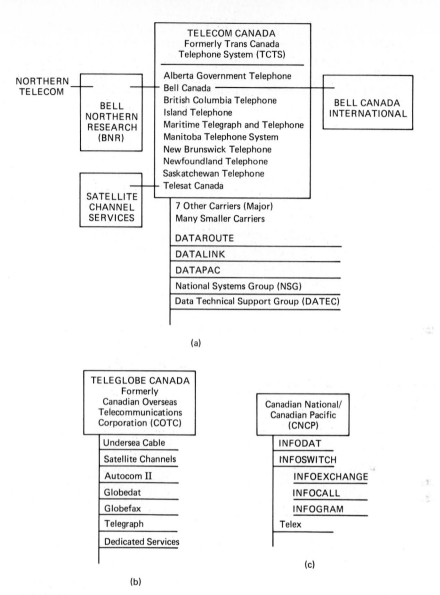

**FIGURE 3-7**
Canadian Carriers

the Western Electric Company in the United States, which today is a part of the AT&T Technologies Group.

To support research and development in the Data Communications area, Bell Canada and Northern Telecom set up a separate organization known as Bell Northern Research (BNR), the equivalent of AT&T Bell Laboratories in the

United States. It is the largest industrial research and development laboratory in Canada. Its U.S. subsidiary is called BNR, Inc.

Another organization formed by Bell Canada is Bell Canada International (BCI). This organization provides consulting services to organizations that require communications capabilities around the world.

Telecom Canada offers various services to the communications users, which will be discussed next.

## Dataroute

Dataroute is a dedicated all digital communications capability serving the entire country. Digital transmission speeds can range from 2400 to 56 KBPS with either half- or full-duplex circuits. Point-to-point and multipoint circuits are available in more than 75 cities in Canada. In areas that are not served directly by Dataroute facilities, users can access the service through dial-up circuits or through existing analog facilities. It should be noted, however, that the advantages of digital transmission's lower error rates are significantly reduced when accessed through analog facilities.

Dataroute's connection to the AT&T Dataphone Digital Service (DDS) is called Dataroute International. It provides all digital circuits between the United States and Canadian cities that have digital access capability.

## Datalink

Datalink is a dial digital service in which transmission is synchronous at speeds of 2400, 4800, and 9600 BPS in a full-duplex mode. Since it is bit-oriented it is transparent to the user's protocol and code set. Datalink is available in all Dataroute locations in which the user has a dedicated local loop connection to the carrier switch supporting the datalink service.

## Datapac

Datapac is a packet-switching service utilizing the X.25 interface. It was first made available in 1977 and uses Dataroute circuits. It provides connections throughout Canada and has gateways to the United States, Europe, and the Far East. A local Datapac node can be dialed using standard analog circuits or accessed via dedicated digital circuits. The Datapac services support the following:

Synchronous devices from 1200 to 9600 BPS
Asynchronous devices from 110 to 1200 BPS
CCITT V.3—ISO poll/select protocol
IBM 2740 terminal at 134.5 BPS

IBM 3270 Bisync

IBM Bisync HASP at 2400 to 9600 BPS

IBM Bisync terminals using contention mode up to 4800 BPS

## National Systems Group (NSG)

The National Systems Group is the organization within Telecom Canada that has the responsibility for providing all data communications services. It was called the Computer Communications Group (CCG) prior to April 1983.

## Data Technical Support Group (DATSG)

The Data Technical Support Group provides personnel for assistance in designing and developing new implementations for users and for providing assistance in solving complex network problems.

## Teleglobe Canada

Teleglobe is an international common carrier that provides both voice and data services between Canada and the rest of the world. It was established as a Crown Corporation in 1950 under the name of Canadian Overseas Telecommunication Corporation (COTC). Teleglobe uses a network of submarine cables, which they own jointly with other countries, that cross the Atlantic and Pacific Oceans. Teleglobe also uses satellite channels that they lease from INTELSAT (International Telecommunications Satellite Organization). Other specific services that are provided by Teleglobe are described in the following sections.

*AUTOCOM II* Autocom II allows storage of messages for both domestic and international forwarding. Users own or lease their terminal equipment from local carriers and connect to Autocom II at speeds from 50 to 300 BPS. Code conversion is provided from Baudot to ASCII, for example, and features a fully redundant backup system. Typical message switching capabilities such as long-term storage, sequence numbering, statistical reports, line polling, and multistation addressing are also provided.

*GLOBEDAT* Globedat is a service at which speeds of 300 to 1200 BPS are common, with higher speeds up to 4800 BPS available to selected countries like the United Kingdom, Japan, and France. Globedat is primarily intended to support the connection of user terminals to host computers over international circuits. The charging mechanism is based on a cost for accessing the network, a charge based on volume of transmission (like a packet), and the duration of the call.

**GLOBEFAX** Globefax is a high-speed facsimile service for document transmission between Montreal and the following countries at present: Australia, Bahrain, Bermuda, Hong Kong, Japan, Singapore, and Switzerland. Documents must be of standard letter or legal size.

**TELEGRAPH** Telegraph is a special leased-line connection for transmission and reception of low-speed teletype transmission in the speed range of 50–200 BPS. Half- and full-duplex circuits can be provided.

**DEDICATED SERVICES** Dedicated services are leased-line services that utilize standard voice-grade channels for international connections. Both satellite and submarine cable facilities can be used. It is possible to use these circuits for alternate voice/data services where voice and data can be transmitted, but only at alternate times. If required, wide-band services can also be provided. Asynchronous data transmissions can be 300, 600, or 1200 BPS, while synchronous transmissions can be up to 9600 BPS. The wide-band circuits can support data at 56,000 BPS.

## CNCP Telecommunications

CNCP (Canadian National/Canadian Pacific) Telecommunications is a joint venture of the two large Canadian railroads, Canadian National and Canadian Pacific. It is a common carrier that provides data-oriented services throughout Canada. CNCP services compete directly with Telecom Canada services and also provide voice service to the Northwest Territories, the Yukon, the northern parts of British Columbia, and parts of Newfoundland. The following services are offered by CNCP:

**INFODAT** In competition with Telecom Canada's Dataroute service, CNCP introduced the all digital transmission service called Infodat in 1973. Transmission speeds of up to 56 KBPS with point-to-point or multipoint capability are provided to the following cities at present: Brampton, Brandon, Calgary, Clarkson, Edmonton, Halifax, Hamilton, Kingston, Kitchener, Lethbridge, London, Moncton, Montreal, Oakville, Oshawa, Ottawa, Quebec City, Regina, St. John, Sarnia, Saskatoon, Sudbury, Thompson, Thunder Bay, Toronto, Vancouver, Victoria, Windsor, and Winnipeg.

**INFOSWITCH** Infoswitch is a nationwide digital packet switching service that was introduced in 1977. Infoswitch provides three separate services:

> *Infoexchange.* Infoexchange allows users to connect standard terminal equipment utilizing RS-232 interfaces and ASCII, BCD, or EBCDIC code sets. This is a circuit-switched type connection where the address of the destination is specified in an originating message, and once connected the user has a dedicated point-to-point connection with the addressed location.

Asynchronous transmission speeds supported are 110, 134.5, 300, 600, and 1200 BPS, while 1200, 2400, 4800, and 9600 BPS can be supported when running synchronously. Typical of the synchronous protocols supported are HDLC (International High Level Data Link Control)–SDLC (the IBM subset of HDLC), and Bisync.

*Infocall.* Infocall provides users with the ability to connect existing terminal equipment which employs various standard protocols such as Bisync, SDLC, and HDLC using the same speed and code sets as are used with Infoexchange. When user data arrives at the network location it is put into a packet format and transmitted through the network as a packet transmission. The packet sizes are established in asynchronous transmission based on either quantity of characters or receipt of a line-feed character, while in synchronous transmission an entire block or predetermined packet size is sent.

*Infogram.* Infogram is very similar to Infocall except that the user's terminal controller must be capable of utilizing the Infogram Network Access Protocol, which is also known as the Infoswitch Protocol.

**TELEX** Telex provides connection to the international telex network, the largest communication system in the world, consisting of over 1,500,000 terminals. In Canada alone there are over 42,000 businesses that use telex while in the United States there are an additional 74,000 telex users. Telex is an international low-speed message delivery service. It utilizes Baudot code and transmits at a rate of 75 baud, which is equivalent to 50 BPS of information. It should be noted that in Baudot transmission baud and BPS cannot be used interchangeably. The CNCP telex service provides a direct connection to the telex services of Western Union in the United States, but it does not provide a connection to the North American TWX network. In the United States there is conversion equipment provided by various carriers to connect the TWX and Telex networks, but that is not available from CNCP. Another unique requirement of the telex service of CNCP is that only vendor-provided terminal equipment can be used. Customer-provided equipment is not permitted.

One last type of service to be described is provided by Telesat Canada. Telesat Canada was incorporated by an act of Parliament in September 1969 as a federally regulated, commercial telecommunications carrier. Even though it is not a Crown Corporation, it is regulated by the government. Telesat Canada is a member of Telecom Canada and is investor-owned by major carriers and the Canadian government. Until recently, Telesat operated as a "wholesaler" of domestic satellite services to other carriers only, but recently Telesat was given the option of marketing the service directly to end users as well.

The satellites used by Telesat are known as the ANIK series, of which there are six presently in orbit with the seventh scheduled to be launched in 1990. ANIK is an Eskimo word for "friend."

As with all providers of communication services, the Canadian vendors are continually upgrading their service features and product availability. Therefore, for those Canadian users or users who must interface with Canadian networks, the latest information should be obtained from the vendor. Make sure that you are aware of all the latest available capabilities and determine whether they are compatible with the networks to which you are connecting, including those to the United States.

## QUESTIONS

1. What is the difference between a local exchange carrier and a long-distance carrier?
2. Draw a diagram of the telephone office connections for a long-distance call. Describe the function of each element.
3. What are the names of the seven Regional Bell Holding Companies? Which local carriers make up each RBHC?
4. List the types of each class of telephone office and what the functions are for each class.
5. What is a VAN and what function does it perform?
6. What are the two primary types of circuits provided by the carriers?
7. Describe four different types of service and typical end-user applications that might make efficient use of those services.
8. Describe two types of communications regulatory agencies and the areas they are responsible for regulating.
9. What are the four categories of telephone lines? What are their primary functions?
10. What is a DAA and what function does it perform?
11. What does the FCC registration process provide?
12. Describe the concept behind ONA.
13. Explain SDN and what it can do for you.

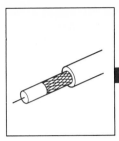

# 4

# Communications Media

## ELEMENTARY COMMUNICATIONS THEORY

The chief reason for communications, whether voice or data, is to move information from one location to another. When the transmitter and receiver are in the same physical location, it is relatively easy to perform that function. When the transmitter and the receiver are removed from one another, or if we want to move extremely high volumes of information in a short period of time, then some form of machine-to-machine communication is necessary.

Of the various available methods, the primary mode of machine-to-machine communication is via an electronically generated signal. The reason for use of electronics is the ease with which a signal can be generated, transmitted, and detected, and the fact that it can be stored transiently or permanently; also, high volumes of information can be transmitted within a short period of time.

The basic concept of communications theory is that a particular electronic signal can be generated so that at least two different states of that signal can be detected. The two states represent a zero or one, mark or space, on or off, etc. As soon as two different states can be detected, the capability for moving information exists. Specific combinations of states, which are known as codes, can then represent any alphabetic, numeric, or control character, so that information can be transmitted either in a pure information form for machines to interact with, or in a representative form (the code) that allows a human to recognize the information. Since most forms of communication are initiated by humans, there must be an interface to convert the information from the human source to machine-readable format. This conversion process then allows the information to be stored, transmitted, and used by the communications devices or data processing devices, and ultimately, if necessary, permits the return of some kind of information, which will be converted back to recognizable information for use by the human.

The primary mode for generating electronic signals for transmission on voice-grade communication lines is what is known as a *sine wave*. The sine wave is a particular frequency (the amount of complete cycles per unit time) during which the signal starts from a zero level, goes positive at a decreasing rate for a period of time, reaches a peak, then moves in a negative direction to the zero level, continues to a level in the negative direction equivalent to its positive direction level, and then returns to the zero level at an increasing rate, at which point the signal begins a new cycle. The more cycles per unit time, the higher the frequency. A sine wave is shown on the left in Fig. 4–1.

For most data processing functions, however, signals occur in an on-and-off configuration, which looks more like a square wave. This is the same general process as for a sine wave, except that it reaches its maximum value almost instantly, stays at that level for the duration of that bit time (0 or 1), then goes to the full negative value almost immediately and then stays at that value (which represents the other bit value 1 or 0). At that point a new bit will either go back to the maximum positive value or stay at the same level if it is the same bit. Figure 4–1 shows both a sine wave and a square wave.

In actuality, however, the square wave is mathematically made up of many individual sine waves, of which there are quite a few high-frequency components. The high-frequency components provide the squareness to the signal. The primary frequency is the frequency at which the square wave completes a single cycle, but in order to square the signal, many high-frequency components have to be added with the resultant figure being the square wave. When representing a single information source this description of a square wave is sometimes referred to as a *baseband* digital signal.

For communication purposes, especially over voice networks that were designed for voice frequencies between 300 and 3300 Hz (discussed in Chapter 21),

**FIGURE 4–1**
Sine Wave and Square Wave

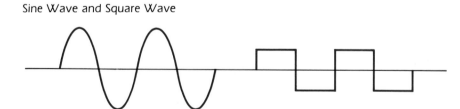

Sine Wave

Square Wave

the majority of the higher frequencies that are required to square the signal cannot be transmitted because of attenuation at those frequencies on the communications line. Therefore, it is mandatory that the frequencies used for communications purposes be totally contained within the 300- to 3300-Hz range. To accomplish this, techniques had to be developed that would permit detectable signal variations of the frequencies within the voice-channel range. There are three ways in which a sine-wave signal can be changed so that information can be correlated with those individual changes: (1) the amplitude or magnitude of the signal; (2) frequency or the number of times the signal crosses the zero level per unit time; and (3) phase, or the relative location where the signal crosses the zero level, referenced to the location at which the signal crossed the zero level on the previous cycle. An example of each of these types of changes is shown in Fig. 4-2.

The actual manipulation of the sine waves that bear a specific relation to the digital information generated by a data processing machine is a process known as *modulation/demodulation,* which is fully described in Chapter 10. Modulation is the inherent capability of taking digital information (square waves) and modifying specific carrier frequencies that can be supported on a communications line in a predetermined relationship such that information can be transmitted from one point to another electronically over those lines. Demodulation is the conversion of the manipulated sine waves back into the original digital form for data processing purposes.

Electronic transmission is not limited to voice-grade lines only. It can also take place at much higher frequencies with the same basic techniques on different types of lines, or *pulses,* that represent the digital signals can also be transmitted over circuits designed specifically for their propagation. Also, for purposes of extremely high transmission rates, an optical system can be used, which is really the modulation of a "light" source. The basic technique still remains the same. Some "carrier" (in this case light) is changed in a very specific manner (usually just on/off but in the future it may be varied in intensity) so that the receiver can

**FIGURE 4-2**
Sine Wave Changes

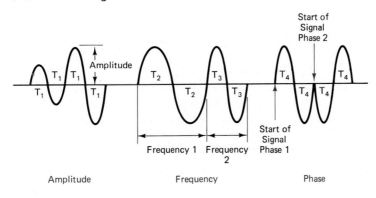

detect those changes and convert them into information that can be used by data processing machines.

No discussion of communications theory would be complete without some words on the biggest problem that arises with communication, *noise,* which distorts the signals being transmitted so that the changes describing the information cannot be recognized. When transmissions are not recognizable or are distorted to the point where they are recognized as something different from what is being sent, information is lost. Since noise exists in all communications-type circuits, it is necessary to recognize the different types and to determine what their impact is on transmission. They are described in detail in Chapter 21.

## B
## COMMUNICATIONS CONDUCTORS

The primary media used for communications lines are, and have been for many years, heavily oriented toward wire conductors. Wire communications paths may be classified into four groups: open wire, twisted pair cable, coaxial cable, and the newest (emerging because of the information carrying capacity available), fiber-optic cable. Actually, fiber optics is not really wire but is classified with wire communications due to the method of implementation. There are also microwave, lasers, and wave guides, each with its own capabilities for specific uses.

### Wire

Open-wire lines are very old but still in use around the world, principally in low-density traffic areas. Wire sizes are measured several ways, the predominant method in the United States being the American Wire Gauge Standard (AWG). The range of open-wire sizes in widespread use is from 10 AWG (0.1019 inch diameter) to 19 AWG (0.0359 inch diameter). The composition of earlier open-wire lines was iron (steel) and was later changed to copper because it was a better conductor of electrical signals and was also able to withstand most of the corrosion problems caused by exposure to moisture. The wires were tied to glass insulators, which were in turn attached to wood crossarms and mounted on utility poles. The resistance to electric current flow of the open-wire line varies greatly with weather conditions, and for this reason the twisted pair cable was adopted.

Twisted pair cable is composed of copper conductors insulated by either paper or plastic and twisted into pairs. These pairs are further twisted into groups called units, and then units are twisted into the finished cable. The cable is covered by lead or plastic and either suspended from aerial crossarms or buried by one of three types of construction. The three types of twisted pair buried-cable laying are direct burial, ducted runs between access vaults, and utility tunnels. The technique used depends on the frequency of required access to the circuits inside the cable; that is, infrequently accessed requires direct burial, and frequently accessed cables and large numbers of cables require cable tunnels. Twisting of the cable pairs and units is done with a different pitch for adjacent pairs or units so that accidental coupling of noise interference, called *crosstalk,* will be minimized. Wire sizes commonly used for twisted pairs range from 19 AWG to 26 AWG.

At transmission frequencies above one megahertz (MHz) for long-distance simultaneous transmission of multiple conversations (carrier type systems), electrical interference in the form of crosstalk between adjacent circuits is the predominant design concern. Attempts to overcome this impairment in twisted pair cables led to the development of coaxial cables. Grounded shields were placed around single copper conductors and, later, pairs of conductors to shield against the noise caused by adjacent pairs. Various kinds of insulation material, including paper and plastics, are used between the conductors and the shield. To carry higher frequencies, representing greater bandwidth or more information-carrying capability, the coaxial cable is constructed with air as the insulator between the current-carrying conductor and the shield. Thin insulating discs support the inner conductor and keep it away from the shield. Up to 20 of these coaxial pairs are twisted into a cable, which is buried in similar fashion to the twisted pair cable. A typical cross section of a coaxial cable is shown in Fig. 4-3.

Because of its use for more than 100 years, twisted pair telephone cable pervades the entire carrier world. Even with all of the newer techniques for moving signals, cable was and will continue to be (because it is already there), the most heavily utilized medium for in-house and short-distance connections to the carriers (new installations are heavily oriented toward fiber in the local loop and coaxial cable inhouse due to data requirements). There are two basic descriptions with respect to the twisted pair cable. The first is defined as outside plant (OSP), which connect users to carriers as well as carriers to carriers; the second is house wiring, which is sometimes called building wiring, physically installed in the user's facilities. OSP cabling is known as *black cable;* house wiring is also known as *grey cable.* Depending on the locale of use and potential distance for transmission, the cables are used in sizes that run from 6 to 3000 pairs and may come in 19, 22, 24, or 26 gauge.

**FIGURE 4-3**
Cross Section of Coaxial Cable

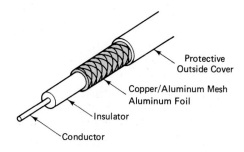

Protective
Outside Cover

Copper/Aluminum Mesh
Aluminum Foil

Insulator

Conductor

For cables greater than 18,000 feet (approximately $3\frac{1}{2}$ miles), the carriers add an *inductive load* (loading coils), which improves the voice response of the circuit. Most modems compensate for these loading coils (except short-haul modems; see Chapter 10), but for digital transmissions they must be removed. When the carriers provide digital circuits, they make sure the loading coils are removed. If the user employs his own cabling, then any loading coils provided for the voice response must be removed before digital transmissions can take place over those cables.

Typical user digital data rates for 24-gauge twisted pair cables range from approximately 6000 feet at 1.544 MBPS to approximately 10 miles at 2.4 KBPS. Smaller diameter wire (higher gauge number) reduces the distance while larger diameter wire (smaller gauge numbers) will increase the distance somewhat.

As recently as 1983, a study was done to determine what the local loops would look like for the future of digital traffic. Results showed that the average length of a local loop was 10,400 feet and that 83 percent of them were not loaded. Of the local loops 40 percent were 26 gauge, 34 percent were 24 gauge, and the rest were 22 gauge.

When digital service is provided by the carrier in your area, the carrier will normally take into account the restrictions on service due to wire capabilities. Even though there is enough capacity and distance available, other effects (due to external noise) may seriously affect the ability to transmit data digitally. Therefore it is expected that many of the digital services, especially ISDN (described in Chapter 16), will first be implemented at a lower data rate (basic rate at 144 KBPS) and will then be moved up to the primary rate of 1.544 MBPS.

When sending data over telephone cables that were originally designed for voice, you must understand some of the evolution of cables from the time when the network was used primarily for voice. The original cables from the telephone company were typically wired in 2700 pair cables which in turn were divided into three separate 900 pair cables. For various voice installations, the cables would be *tapped,* which is known as *bridging.* Over the years, various bridges were added and subtracted so that some bridges exist today that are not terminated properly from an electrical point of view. The technical term for this situation is an *open bridge tap* or an *open tail circuit.* These circuits change the impedance of the overall circuit and will significantly affect the ability of those cables to handle digital transmission.

In order to transmit digital information over these cables you must isolate and remove the bridges. The telephone company can typically do this from their records and from additional testing. If you need digital transmission, you should give the telephone company as much advance warning as possible so they can remove the bridge taps. At the same time it may be possible for the carrier to remove the *loading coils* for circuits which are over 18,000 feet because loading coils cannot be tolerated on digital circuits.

Depending on where you are in relation to the local telephone company, you must also be concerned with the methodology of the cabling to your facility. The various local carriers have a device called an SLC 96 (Subscriber Line Carrier 96) which provides for the derivation of 96 DS1 channels on 10 pairs of wires (T-

1 transmission rates) for a net gain of 86 DS1 circuits. Because of the mechanics in accomplishing this conversion, it is possible that the user's transmission will be affected. You must check with the local telco to see if that is the case in your area. The SLC 96 is typically put into a new serving area to connect a central office to a satellite location with digital fiber (rather than copper) at which point it is connected to end users.

## Fiber

Recent developments in laser technology have led to construction of thin glass fibers that can carry information at frequencies in the visible light spectrum. This technology is already providing very efficient and economical buried cable systems. The optical fibers are either joined by connectors that have a very low light loss or the signal is converted back to electrical form, amplified, and then reinserted onto the next section of fiber cable. Optical fiber is also being used for undersea cable, with present technology allowing over 1.3 gigabit per second information transmission for over 20 miles without amplification. It is anticipated that the transmission rate will increase by a factor of four and the distance by a factor of five in the next few years.

Fiber technology has advanced at a very fast rate. There are presently two basic methods of transmitting through a fiber link but others are being developed. Optical transmissions involve the modulation of a light signal (usually on and off but varying the level of light intensity is being researched now) onto a very narrow strand of glass (called the *core*). Another concentric layer of glass around the core is called *cladding*. After it is inserted into the core the light is reflected by the cladding, which means it follows a zigzag path through the core. Figure 4–4(a) shows single-mode transmission and (b) shows multimode transmission for which three forms of propagation are available.

**FIGURE 4–4**
Single and Multimode Optical Fiber

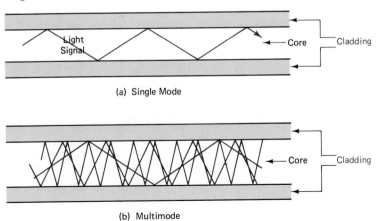

(a) Single Mode

(b) Multimode

*Single Mode* involves the use of fiber with a core diameter of 5 to 8 microns. This fiber has a very low attenuation and is therefore used with just a few repeaters for long distances. It is therefore used primarily for *trunk* type applications and has a bandwidth of approximately 50 GHz per kilometer.

*Multi-Mode/Step Index* is fiber that has a bandwidth of 10 to 20 MHz and consists of a core fiber surrounded by a cladding that has a lower refractive index for the light. Light propagating down the core will continually bounce off the cladding and therefore interfere with transmissions at other frequencies, causing an attenuation of approximately 10 dB/Km. Multi-Mode/Step Index is therefore typically used for distances of less than one kilometer. The cable itself comes in two sizes, 62.5/125 microns or 100/140 micron cable. Because the outside diameter is 1 mm, it is relatively easy to provide connections and splicing.

*Multi-Mode/Graded Index* is a cable where the refractive index changes gradually as you go toward the outer edge of the cable so the light *bends* instead of bouncing off the edge. Attenuation is less than 5 dB/Km and therefore can be used for longer distance communications circuits. The bandwidth is 200 to 1000 MHz, and the cable diameter is 50/125 microns (the core diameter is the first number and the cladding diameter is the second).

Splices also cause loss of signal and are typically in the range of 1 dB. Also, adapters for converting between different types of nonstandard connectors incur an additional 1 dB loss of signal or more. The sources of the light beam can be either a Light Emitting Diode (LED), which is used for transmission up to 150 MBPS, or a laser, which is capable of transmission in the GBPS range.

Single-mode fiber has a much higher bandwidth than multimode because it has much less dispersion due to interference between the multiple light beams in multimode. The single-mode fiber strand is also narrower than the multimode. The wider diameter allows for more propagation paths or *modes* to be used. In multimode the paths vary in length depending on the angles of reflection; the pulses of light can enter at the same time but may come out at slightly different times. The dispersion of individual light beams in multimode transmission is called *intermodal* dispersion, which is in reality an interference between the modes.

Multimode is typically used for connector-intensive applications like LANs because the bigger diameter allows easier splicing and connection to LED sources. It also provides the ability to use lower loss connections. Because of the usual distance parameters involved, LEDs are typically used with multimode fiber while lasers are used with single mode.

The LEDs are typically more reliable than lasers, but since lasers provide more power they can go farther and accommodate connectors with more losses. Because there is less dispersion, lasers are also capable of transmitting at much higher data rates in a single-mode transmission. However, lasers need to be thermally stabilized (extra expense) and must be serviced by more knowledgeable technicians.

One of the most practical uses for fiber is in long-distance transmissions. If the *right of way* is available, the capacity for fiber to handle huge volumes of traffic makes it an appropriate choice for new installations to high-density areas. Voice and data are heavy users of fiber where it exists and there is more fiber being installed all the time. Typical installations are between major cities and in undersea cabling (a new series of cables was installed to support additional traffic starting in 1988). Fiber installation has been steadily replacing satellites for data transmission. The primary reason for retaining satellites seems to be to communicate with remote areas. In 1987, the satellite capacity for handling traffic over North America was more than 30 percent non-utilized, and many of the satellite vendors were either selling out or scrambling for other kinds of business.

Listed here are the installations and anticipated installations for undersea cables through 1995.

| CABLE NAMES | FROM/TO | YEAR OF INSTALLATION |
|---|---|---|
| Transatlantic Cables | | |
| TAT 8 | United States to England/France | 1988 |
| PTAT 1 | United States to Bermuda/England | 1989 |
| TAV 1 | Video Between United States and Canada to England/France/Spain | 1989 |
| TAT 9 | United States to England/France/Spain | 1991 |
| PTAT 2 | United States to England | 1992 |
| Pacific Cables | | |
| PPAC | United States to Alaska/Japan | 1989 |
| HAW 4 | United States to Hawaii | 1989 |
| TPC 3 | Hawaii to Guam/Japan | 1989 |
| JP 2 | Guam to Philippines | 1989 |
| H-J-K | Japan/Korea/China | 1990 |
| Tasman 2 | Australia to New Zealand | 1991 |
| ? | United States to New Zealand | 1993 |
| ? | Australia to Mainland of Asia | 1995 |
| ? | Middle East/Sri Lanka/Singapore/Malaysia | ? |

There is a tremendous amount of activity in fiber, and many of the future cables will probably involve technologies that are under development today.

The TAT 8 cable will consist of two separate fiber circuits, each operating at 280 MBPS. A spare fiber pair acts as a backup in the event of failure of one of the primary pairs. There will be a theoretical maximum of 10,000 voice channels if they are operating at 64 KBPS, but with compression techniques and multiplexing it is quite possible that between 40,000 and 50,000 individual channels will be obtained. It is expected that compression such as ADPCM and a technique called Digital Speech Interpolation (DSI) which fills in the silent periods on existing channels with transmissions of other conversations will be used.

The TAT 8 cable is the first transatlantic cable to require regenerators at distances of only 35 to 40 miles. It is known as a dry multiplexing cable because the regeneration points will be out of the water for power and maintenance purposes. The TAT 9 will use a wet mux, that is, the multiplexing, power, and maintenance capabilities will be incorporated right into the cable itself all along its path.

Fiber-optic transmission stands to improve significantly in the future. By 1987 Nippon Telephone and Telegraph (NTT) had already established a single-mode transmission capability of 1.6 GBPS (23,040 two-way voice channels) for a distance of 75 miles. Various U.S. companies are testing different kinds of materials, such as using fluoride glass rather than silica. Fluoride glass has several orders of magnitude less loss and can potentially go 3000 miles without requiring regeneration. Although these test results have not yet been proven in the field, where connections might have to be made that involve signal losses, thus lowering the practical limit, still, this is a substantial improvement over existing capabilities.

British Telecom has been testing a purely optical light wave regenerator involving true light amplification to replace the current process of requiring the light to be brought back into electrical mode, amplified electrically, and then reintroduced to light mode. Direct light amplification would probably substantially reduce the cost of regeneration, which would lower the overall cost of fiber transmission capability, making it even more economical than at present.

It is also estimated that the compounds with chlorine or fluorine (called halides) may provide one gigabit per second transmission speed for over 2000 miles. Silica glass can transmit up to 180 miles at one gigabit per second while halides can get over 2000 miles at the same data rate. (Relative to the light sources, silica glass has 0.15 to 0.20 dB per kilometer expected loss while halides have 0.001 to 0.01 dB per kilometer loss.) Halide fiber also has potential surgical application. Its biggest disadvantage is that it is substantially more brittle than silica glass, is possibly toxic, and tends to decay over time. These disadvantages will probably be overcome, but potentially at the expense of speed or distance capabilities. Other compounds may be developed which will provide the same or even greater capabilities than silica glass or the halides.

One last technique for fiber transmission is known as *coherent* transmission, which varies the intensity of the light source rather than turning it on and off. Changing in this mode is the same process as a modem that involves varying combinations of amplitude, frequency, or phase. If the light source can be modified in an equivalent form, it is anticipated that transmission capacity could be increased by a factor of 2000 times. Coherent transmission already exists up to the 560 MBPS range and is expected to increase substantially in the near future.

## Microwave

Communications lines are also being constructed using radio signals between a transmitter and receiver. The names of these systems are based on the radio-frequency bands being used or the wavelength (i.e., *very high frequency* (VHF) and *microwave*). Again, as in the case of the coaxial cable and fiber-optics cable, the higher the frequency, the greater the bandwidth. The largest systems today are radio paths operating in the 4- to 14-gigahertz (GHz) bands whose wavelengths are very short (millimeters in length).

Three principal groups of radio systems used for communications lines are broadcast, beam, and satellite. Broadcast radio is limited in that every receiver picks up the signals and therefore each receiver must be tuned to a unique frequency, within the range of the transmitter. Microwave or beam radio has the advantage of being a narrow beam that can be separated in space to form several channels using the same frequency. Beam radio has serious limitations in the distance that signals can travel before they must be repeated due to loss of signal strength, the curvature of the earth, and, most important, the noise introduced because of moisture in the air surrounding the earth's surface. Normal beam radio repeater stations are typically placed about 30 or more miles apart on mountaintops, towers, or the tops of tall buildings. The radio beam is usually on the order of 5° width and operates with up to about 12 watts (W) of power. The power level is kept low to prevent interference with other beams on the same frequency, as is also true of the narrow beams.

Satellite microwave radio is employed to overcome the problem of the curvature of the earth. Earlier systems were orbiting receiver-transmitters; antennas on the earth's surface were directed toward the satellite as it moved across the operating area. Present commercial systems use geosynchronously orbiting satellites that are placed in an orbit over the earth at the appropriate distance from the earth to maintain the orbit and move with zero surface speed relative to the earth's rotation. This distance is approximately 22,300 miles and gives the effect of the satellite being suspended in space over the operating area. Satellites used for domestic communications are positioned at 2° to 4° intervals between 67° and 143° west longitude. This yields an operating area over the entire contiguous United States. By positioning the satellite between 90° and 130° Hawaii and Alaska are included in the operating area, and the power levels are higher than for the terrestrial microwave systems to allow transmission over the greater distances. With satellites, the number of radio signal repeaters is reduced, relative to the terrestrial or beam radio, from several hundred to span the country to one; in addition, the noise interference of the environment near the earth's surface is minimized due to the lesser total distance the signals travel through the earth's atmosphere in going away from and then returning to the surface. Figure 4–5 depicts terrestrial and satellite radio systems.

Present satellite systems use two separate and independent frequency bands for operation. The first is called the C band, which uses the 4- and 6-GHz spectrum; the second, the Ku band, uses the spectrum of 12 and 14 GHz. During 1983 the FCC decided to create more positions in the satellite orbit so that additional satellites could be put up. In the future, therefore, instead of satellites being 4 orbital degrees apart they will all be moved such that they will eventually be 2° to $2\frac{1}{2}$° apart. This will be done over a period of time, moving the C band satellites first to 3° apart and then to 2° or $2\frac{1}{2}$° apart so that vendors will be able to modify their ground stations to accommodate the narrower beam requirements

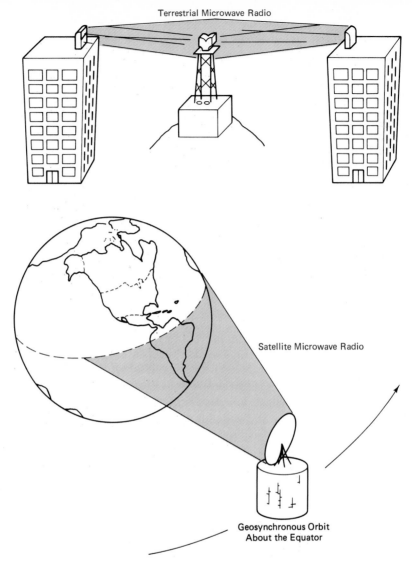

Terrestrial Microwave Radio

Satellite Microwave Radio

Geosynchronous Orbit
About the Equator

**FIGURE 4–5**
Terrestrial and Satellite Radio Systems

necessary for closer spacing. There is also a proposal to use higher-frequency spectrums for future satellites in the range of 27 GHz, which is part of what is known as the Ka band. It is anticipated that satellites to be used in this spectrum will be launched in the early 1990s under present projections.

In the terrestrial world microwave is also utilized for private links between user-owned facilities. As long as those facilities are within *line of sight* of each other and will not interfere with other microwave transmissions (determined by the FCC), a license from the FCC can be obtained. The line-of-sight transmissions do not necessarily have to be between the two end facilities. There can be repeaters along the way as long as there is access to those physical locations. For relatively short distances of 5 to 10 miles the frequency range allocated for this purpose is typically 23 GHz, and for 10 to 15 miles the typical frequency range is 18 GHz. For terrestrial distances greater than 15 miles the allocated ranges are typically between 2 and 10.5 GHz.

Data rates using these various microwave ranges can be as low as 56 KBPS and go up to 44.736 MBPS. For the most part, the decision to implement such a private circuit is usually determined by the economics involved. Another potential disadvantage of microwave compared to the short-distance use of infrared or direct lasers is the fact that an FCC license is required, which may take 6 to 9 months to obtain.

Microwave may also be used from a user's facility directly to a carrier. Direct communication with a long-distance carrier (bypassing the local telephone company loops) cannot be done by cable because of right-of-way problems, so microwave becomes a viable alternative. The physical location of the long-distance carrier connected to is known as the point of presence (POP).

An additional area that will become a very large potential market by the late 1980s will be the direct hand-held device or vehicle device transmitting to and receiving from a satellite. Present technology has tested the use of a 6-inch antenna that will be able to transmit to and receive from a satellite while requiring less than 2 watts of power. Its feasibility has been tested and it is anticipated to be in commercial use by the early 1990s, utilizing the L band.

## Infrared/Laser

This technology has been around for quite a while, but until recently the economics did not justify its direct use. Direct infrared and laser transmissions involve the same techniques as used in fiber-optic transmission, except that the medium is open air. The capabilities are said to be up to 10 miles, although the majority of applications are actually one mile or less. Typically, infrared/laser transmissions are utilized between user facilities when there is no cable available to support the connection and the installation of cables is not feasible. Data rates up to 1.5 megabits per second are typically obtainable at these distances, and a distinct advantage for this technology is that an FCC license is not required. Care must be taken, however, because laser beams may damage human eyesight. Appropriate physical protection must be incorporated within user facilities.

For short distance, short time frame connections (facility locations being moved, for example) infrared/laser transmissions are an excellent choice. They can be up and running within a few days with significantly less expense than for microwave. Networks of these devices have been set up between buildings in industrial parks as organizations temporarily expanded; when applicable for long-term use, cabling was installed.

## Waveguide

One other medium being used for communications is the waveguide, which operates in the millimeter wavelength range. The bandwidth is extremely wide and it is used primarily where low signal loss is required under high power power conditions such as to and from a microwave antenna and a radio frequency transmitter/receiver. Typical applications are in a telephone company office or a user's facility using microwave transmission directly (bypass or satellite).

## C
## OTHER CONSIDERATIONS

When dealing with carrier-provided facilities there really is not very much you can do about the type of connection that is available to you at your local facilities (except to consider one of the bypass alternatives). In-house, however, there are many different considerations that you have control over and therefore you can make your own economic decisions regarding their implementation.

For example, the choice of twisted pair wiring, coaxial cable, or fiber-optic strands depends upon the type of transmission you expect to have, its speed and its distance. Because many vendors require specific cable to work their equipment, you obviously have to use the type of cable recommended or it may not support your system.

IBM recommends RG-62/U coaxial cable for connecting their 3270 CRTs to its controller. This cable provides approximately a 2000-foot distance at the 2.358-MHz analog signal which contains all the information relative to cursor positioning and other screen attributes. On the other hand, Wang uses RG-59/U coaxial cable. These are two very different cables, because the impedance of the RG-62 cable is 93 ohms, while RG-59 is 75 ohms. If you intend to use terminals from both of these vendors, you have to have the right cabling in the appropriate location to support them.

Another consideration is that the required coaxial cable may not already exist in your facility and you may want to utilize twisted pair telephone wiring that does exist. How can you get from a coaxial interface at both the CRT and the controller to and from a twisted pair interface?

The answer is a device called a *balun* (balanced/unbalanced). A balun consists of a coil or impedance matching device that matches the coaxial impedance (whichever one it is) to twisted pair impedance, which is 110 ohms. The balun then provides the capability to go from coaxial to twisted pair at one end and then convert from twisted pair back to coaxial at the other. There are still limitations; for example, instead of having the maximum cable distance between the two devices, utilizing a balun you can connect a CRT with a controller at a distance up to 900 feet while a Wang can be connected only up to about 400 feet. This is only one example of what you might encounter when you have multiple equipment vendors within your facility. You have to consider the unique requirements of each vendor as well as what you are trying to do, especially relative to local area networks where the vendors have even more unique requirements. An example of a balun connection is shown in Fig. 4–6.

There are some other subtle considerations regarding your inside wiring. For example, the carrier provided wiring may have to be accounted for differently. Any wiring that was put into a building before 1982 was typically capitalized and the costs for that installation may not have been recovered yet. Any wiring put in after 1982 had to be expensed, which means the costs are fully recovered. It is not always easy to determine which is which and this may lead to problems with the carrier. In addition, the condition of the wire is not really known, so to determine and fix wiring problems you have a very labor-intensive, time-consuming, hard-to-isolate situation. You might be better off just putting in new wiring and designing it such that it will provide whatever capacity you anticipate needing for many years to come.

Even the internal wiring that may be considered good has some potential problems. For example, when transmitting data over 1 MBPS there could be some *crosstalk* problems from transmissions on adjacent circuits. This crosstalk can also come from strong PBX ringing currents, that is, when your twisted pairs are used for both voice and data, the type of PBX may be significant. If telephone wiring is located near any kind of power wiring it may be impossible to utilize twisted pair for data at all. Voice may be in a noisy environment, which you can live with, but data cannot support any errors.

To summarize the capabilities of the various media some of the trade-off parameters are listed on page 74.

**FIGURE 4–6**
BALUN Implementation

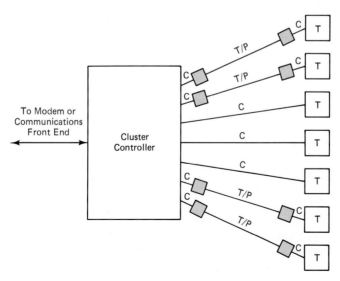

Twisted Pair Telephone Wire
    Least expensive
    Most noise prone
    Most buildings will be wired with it
    Has significant speed-versus-distance limitations

Baseband Coaxial Cable
    Single digital signal
    One-way-at-a-time transmission (half-duplex)
    50 MBPS maximum data rate—usual 10 MBPS max
    Easy access with Taps
    Regenerators can be used

Broadband Coaxial Cable
    Same as CATV
    Multiple signals simultaneously (RF mode of operation)
    Simultaneous two-way transmission (full-duplex)
    Frequency division multiplexing for signal separation (requires modems)
    500 MBPS maximum capacity
    Taps more expensive than baseband
    Splitters must be used for connections

Fiber-Optic Cable
    Four to five times capacity of broadband coaxial maximum
    Longer distances can be traversed than broadband
    Much more expensive to tap into
    Relatively immune from external interference

When considering each of these media, you may also need to prevent unauthorized access to the circuit. If so, fiber provides the best protection, but recently it has been determined that even fiber can be tapped by sharply bending the strand. If some of the cladding is scraped off, some light will escape and can be detected externally. The equipment required to do this is expensive, but if you have sensitive transmissions you need to keep it in mind. You can also determine whether your optical circuit is being *tapped* by measuring the strength of the received signal at the remote end. This, too, takes more expensive equipment. You must perform your own risk analysis to determine whether you will want to spend the money to protect yourself.

## D

## AT&T PREMISES DISTRIBUTION SYSTEM/IBM CABLING SYSTEM

No discussion of transmission media can be complete without a discussion of the AT&T Premises Distribution System (PDS) and the IBM Cabling System. Even though both of these mechanisms were developed primarily for support of LAN-type installations, they are significant in the planning of facilities for future data and voice communications. Both of them will be discussed here, although it should be recognized that other vendors such as Northern Telecom, Inc. and DEC also have methodologies designed for a user to install wiring to support their kinds of networks.

## IBM Cabling System

The IBM Cabling System which was first announced in 1984 was designed to support the IBM token ring mode of operation of their LAN. It has evolved into a wiring mechanism that can support voice and data transmissions of many different forms. A schematic of how the architecture would look is shown in Fig. 4–7. The structure consists of tying all the devices through a distribution panel that terminates up to 64 data connectors and a voice telephone line termination block, typically located in a wiring closet, which is operated in one very large ring. The wiring closets can be *daisy chained* up to 6600 feet apart, depending on the type of cabling used, and there may be different numbers of devices located at different distances from the access unit. The speed of the basic transmission for the token ring is 4 or 16 MBPS and will be described in more detail in Chapter 15.

Many different alternatives for wire use are available with regard to both number of wires and location of use (indoor versus outdoor). They are

Type 1—Data Cable
>Two twisted pair number 22 gauge wires. Each pair has a polyester and aluminum foil shield with an overall shield of braided copper and a PVC jacket.
>>Connects terminal end work stations to wiring closet distribution panels and also connects two distant wiring closets
>>Fire retardant cable not required
>>The user end is terminated in a special data-only wall plate connector
>>Maximum speed: 16 MBPS
>>Maximum cable distance: 330 feet

Type 1—Plenum Data Cable
>Cable is the same as Type 1 Data Cable, but it has a fire retardant TEFLON™ jacket, and it can be used without conduit in air plenums

Type 1—Outdoor Data Cable
>Two twisted pairs of 22-gauge solid copper conductors protected by a corrugated metallic cable shield
>>Used with outdoor aerial installations or dry underground conduit

Type 2—Data and Telephone Cable
>Two twisted pair conductors with a braided shield for data communications and four unshielded twisted pair wires for voice telephone connections

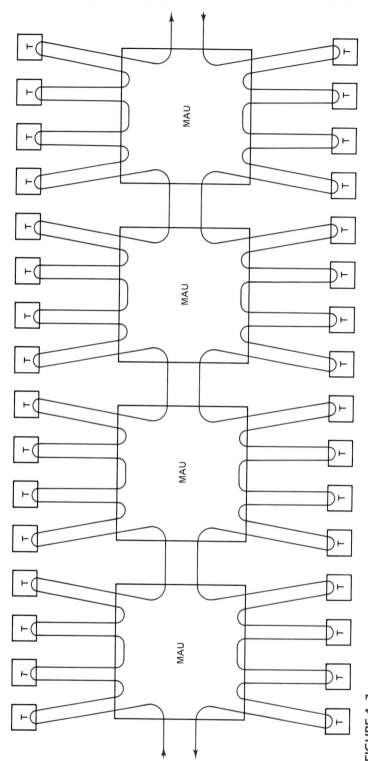

**FIGURE 4-7**
IBM Cabling System

Solid 22-gauge wire with PVC jacket

Allows one terminal and one voice telephone to transmit over the same cable to the wiring closet

Maximum distance: 330 feet

Termination for this cable is a double wall plate where there is a data connector and an 8-pin modular telephone connector

Type 2—Data and Telephone Plenum Cable

This is the same as Type 2 Cable but has a TEFLON™ jacket instead of PVC

Type 3—Telephone Cable

Four pair twisted conductors for voice use

Type 5—Fiber-Optic Cable

Consists of two 100/140 micron optical fibers with a PVC jacket

Used for data only between wiring closets

Can be used in indoor conduit, outdoor aerial lines, or dry underground conduit

Maximum distance: 6600 feet

Transmission used is at 500 MHz at 1300 nanometer wavelength

Type 6—Data Cable

Two twisted pair of 26-gauge wire with a braided shield and a PVC jacket

Stranded wire is used

Only for nonplenum use

Performance characteristics are the same as for Type 1

Sometimes used as a *patch* cable

Type 8—Under Carpet Cable

Two parallel pairs of 26-gauge solid conductor with a PVC jacket in a flat base for installation under carpets

Use is for connecting devices to the wall box where connection to a Type 1 cable is made

Maximum distance for use: 148 feet (to wall box)

From the wall box to the wiring closet the maximum distance can be 33 feet

Type 9—Plenum Data Cable

Two twisted pairs of 26-gauge solid or stranded conductor with a braided cable shield and a TEFLON™ jacket

Used for nonconduit applications in plenums

From the terminal outlet to the distribution panel there can be maximum distance of 220 feet

Using this cable for wiring between closets, the maximum distance is 437 feet

Of the eight wiring types defined to date, type 2, which consists of six pairs of wires (four pairs unshielded for telephone and two pairs shielded for data) is considered the backbone of the cabling system. Each of the others has unique attributes for particular applications and, if connected appropriately, can be used within the distance parameters specified.

The key to this system is the access unit, where all the cables can be *jumpered* or *patched* for distribution to devices that need to access that particular unit. Since some parameters may change, these data should be used as a starting point and updated with whatever current information is available from IBM.

## AT&T Premises Distribution System

The AT&T Premises Distribution System (PDS) is an evolutionary outgrowth of AT&T's Universal Wiring Plan, originally developed for the Dimension and System 85 PBX. It has six separate and independent subsystems, of which subsystems 1 through 3 are shown in Fig. 4–8. Subsystems 4 through 6 are described below. PDS was designed to accommodate all required internal wiring for voice and data, not just for LAN operations.

Subsystem 1 is called the work location subsystem. It consists of four twisted pairs of unshielded telephone cable that connect terminal equipment to a single standard 8-pin modular jack, RJ45. This is the same jack that will be used eventually for connection to ISDN. It can support either voice or data.

Subsystem 2, the horizontal wiring subsystem, also consists of four unshielded twisted pairs of 24-gauge wire. It includes the wiring between the jacks in the offices and the wiring closet on the same or adjacent floor. Full implementation of PDS dictates that two runs of this cable must be pulled to each office with two RJ45s, but in most cases this is not done. The wiring closet is sometimes called the *satellite* wiring closet.

Subsystem 3 is the *backbone* or *riser* subsystem. Sometimes it is called the *feeder* cabling. This large count cable connects the main equipment room to the farthest wiring closet, dropping off pairs as it passes through the interim satellite wiring closets.

Subsystem 4, the equipment wiring subsystem, includes the cable and connectors necessary to connect voice and data switches (PBXs) with subsystems 1, 2, and 3.

Subsystem 5 is known as the *campus* subsystem. For this implementation multipair wiring cables connect buildings within, for example, an industrial complex or campus environment.

Finally, subsystem 6, the *administrative* subsystem, consists of all the patching and interconnect wiring that provide the ability to reconfigure the various office services.

PDS is a *Star* wired topology from wiring closets and AT&T describes their cabling with the use of a term called *Comcode*. It is these cables that will be described along with a comparison to IBM cabling.

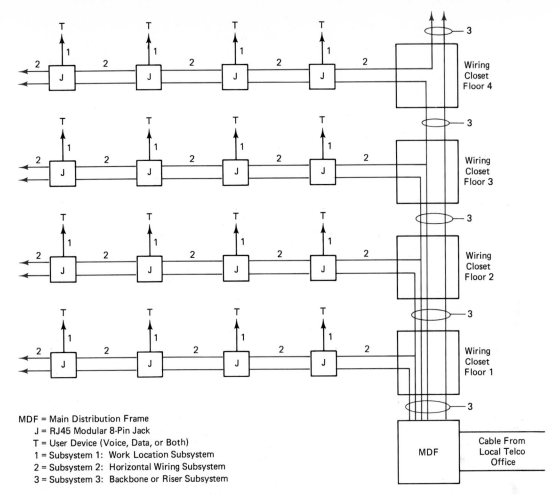

MDF = Main Distribution Frame
 J = RJ45 Modular 8-Pin Jack
 T = User Device (Voice, Data, or Both)
 1 = Subsystem 1:  Work Location Subsystem
 2 = Subsystem 2:  Horizontal Wiring Subsystem
 3 = Subsystem 3:  Backbone or Riser Subsystem

**FIGURE 4–8**
AT&T Premises Distribution System (within a building)

Comcode 105055891

Two twisted pair 24-gauge solid conductors with a polyester aluminum foil shield and a solid *drain* wire

Jacket is PVC

Connects users to satellite wiring closets via conduit or wireway

Terminates in an 8-pin information jack with only the center four pins used for the wiring

Maximum distance: 1200 feet at a data rate of 6.3 MBPS

Equivalent to IBM Type 1 cabling

Comcode 105296412

> Two twisted pair 24-gauge solid copper conductors
>
>> Jacket is fire retardant FEP for individual conductors and overall cable as well
>>
>> Like IBM Type 1 Plenum Cable in performance and application

Comcode 105053680

> Two twisted pair 26-gauge stranded conductors
>
>> Polyester/aluminum foil is used as an overall shield with a stranded 26-gauge drain wire and an overall PVC jacket
>>
>> Can be used with up to 12 pairs of wire
>>
>> Maximum distance: 400 feet at up to 6.3 MBPS
>>
>> Like IBM Type 6 cable

Comcode 105053649 (also called LAN Data/Voice Cable)

> Two twisted pair 22-gauge solid conductors with each pair having an individual PVC jacket and a foil shield for data
>
>> Two unshielded pairs for telephone use
>>
>> Entire cable jacket is PVC
>>
>> One cable can carry voice and data from user to a wire closet
>>
>> The user end termination is a double wall plate with two 8-pin information outlets
>>
>> Can be used at up to 2000 feet at 6.3 MBPS maximum
>>
>> May also come with four voice pairs of conductors
>>
>> Data pair is like IBM Type 2 cable

When configured for voice and data there are typically four pairs of wiring used. Pair 1 is an analog voice pair, while pairs 2 and 3 are for data that is either analog or digital, depending on the terminal. Pair 4 is available to provide power to remote devices. When power is provided, it is usually the standard telephone-company level of 48 volts and is provided from the wiring closet. Typically, subsystem 2 is run with 24 pair cable such that there are six sets of four pairs in the cable. To get an idea of some of the trade-off parameters between the LANs supported under these cabling systems, refer to Table 4–1. You can see the total amount of devices that are supported for IBM's token ring running on either twisted pair or their shielded cabling system; AT&T's StarLAN; and Northern Telecom's Meridian PBX-LAN option. No value judgment is being made here because of the variety of other parameters that must be considered when implementing your own LAN. These parameters will be further discussed in Chapter 15.

Another set of trade-off parameters is shown in Table 4–2, between IBM, AT&T, Northern Telecom, and DEC. These parameters will be changed over time, so always determine whether the current offering meets your specific needs.

Overall, it is not easy to separate descriptions of the media from the various locations where they are used, but by doing it this way there will be a single

**TABLE 4–1**
Distance/Device Criteria: IBM/AT&T/Northern Telecom

| | TOTAL DEVICES CONNECTED | DISTANCE (FEET) | WIRING CLOSETS | SPEED (MBPS) |
|---|---|---|---|---|
| Token Ring | 72 | 300 | 1 | 4 |
| (Twisted Pair) | 72 | 600 | 2 | 4 |
| Token Ring IBM Cabling System | 260 | 1000 | 8 Maximum | 4 (16 announced) |
| AT&T StarLAN | 1200 | 800 | 20 Maximum | 1 |
| NTI Meridian PBX–LAN Option | 1000 | 2000 | 20 Maximum | 2.56 |

**TABLE 4–2**
Cabling System Comparisons

| IBM CABLING SYSTEM | AT&T-PDS | NTI–IBDN | DEC–DEC CONNECT |
|---|---|---|---|
| 6 Pairs of Wire 2 Pairs of Shielded 4 Pairs of Unshielded | 24-Pair Unshielded (6 sets of 4 Pairs) | 4 Pairs Unshielded | 24-Pair Unshielded |
| Fiber Can Be Used | Fiber Can Be Used | Fiber Can Be Used | No Fiber Yet |
| — | RS232 | RS232/423 | RS232/423 |
| 1 Modular Telco Jack 1 IBM Data Jack | 2 Modular Telco Jacks | 1 Modular Telco Jack | 2 Modular Telco Jacks 2 Coaxial Jacks |

PDS—Premises Distribution System
NTI—Northern Telecom, Inc.
IBDN—Integrated Building Distribution Network

**TABLE 4–3**
Location of Media Use

| | IN-HOUSE | LOCAL LOOP | INTRACITY | INTERCITY | LONG-DISTANCE |
|---|---|---|---|---|---|
| Twisted Pair | Yes | Yes | Yes | Some | No |
| Baseband Coax | LAN | Some | Some | Some | Older-Already Installed |
| Broadband Coax | LAN | Campus Type | No | No | No |
| Fiber | LAN | Yes | Yes | Yes | Yes |
| Microwave | No | Bypass | Some | Yes | Yes |
| Laser/Infrared | Building to Building | No | No | No | No |
| Waveguide | To/From Microwave Antenna | Typical Carrier Use Only | | | |

source for comparison of the various media. Each medium will be referenced in the particular chapters where it applies, and the various wiring systems will be discussed in Chapter 15 when describing the LAN systems. As a final comparison, Table 4–3 shows where the various types of media are used in the entire carrier network.

## QUESTIONS

1. Describe five types of communications media and where they would most likely be used. If there are multiple locations for use, describe them also.
2. What is a balun used for? Where would it typically be used?
3. What are the two primary trade-off criteria in the selection of wiring media?
4. Describe the different types of media used in the IBM cabling system and what applications they would be most appropriate for.
5. What is the most significant reason why PDS from AT&T is structured the way it is?
6. What reasons would you use to select among the different wiring systems? Would it make a difference?

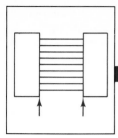

# 5

# Interfaces

## BACKGROUND

In each transmission environment we have many different vendors providing products for their specific services. Unless a predetermined set of interface parameters is specified for operation at that interface, there will be total chaos in trying to connect equipment from different vendors. Part of the problem is accommodated by existing standards, but there are different standards organizations, and therefore different standards. One specific standard, however, is accepted throughout North America and has a comparable standard in the rest of the world. Because it is the most important connection between a user's logic equipment and the device that interfaces to the telephone line, it provides a basis for starting the description between the user and the communications network. This specification is called RS232 and will be described further in this chapter, in addition to other significant interfaces.

## B

## LOOP CURRENT

In the evolutionary development of communications capabilities, one of the first methods for electronic transmissions was the presence or absence of a current in a transmission line. When a current was flowing it represented a signal, which could be used to light a light, close a relay, activate a magnet, or perform any one of the other functions required for what was known as telegraph operation. Also, when used with mechanical teleprinters, the current flowing in the line would indicate a specific "bit" of information that would be considered part of a code and as such be used to generate specific characters or provide controls within the printing device. The most common form of current flow, current loop, is 20 milliamperes (mA). The most common use for 20-mA current has been for the transmission of binary serial asynchronous data. In mechanical teleprinters the current is switched on and off for transmission or recognition of information by a series of carbon brushes rotating over a copper commutator. The commutator has individual segments that relate to the specific bits. As the brushes make contact with each of the segments of the commutator (the brushes rotate around it), a current will flow if a voltage is present at that particular segment. Voltage is present depending on the bit value to be transmitted (voltage-on means a 1 bit and voltage-off means a 0 bit) and is controlled through a switch. At the receive end, an equivalent commutator-brush arrangement exists. It is started by the start bit of the transmitter and rotates at the same rate as the transmitting brushes. Because the receiving brushes will be in the same segment area as the transmitting brushes, if a current is flowing through the line from a particular segment at the transmit end, then the current will also flow through the segment at the receive end. This is the mode whereby individual bits within a character (a character is one complete revolution of the commutator) can be transmitted over the wire (just like Baudot, described in Chapter 2).

The carbon brushes rotating over a commutator have two significant disadvantages. First, significant noise is introduced on the line from the contact imperfections between the brushes and the commutator; second, a specific minimum current, usually 18 mA, must be maintained to keep the surfaces of the commutator relatively clean. The interface with such a device must include circuitry to suppress the noise generated by the brushes–commutator and some kind of filter to reduce the signals generated from *contact bounce,* which occurs when the machines are switched from a local mode of operation to line transmission modes.

As stated previously, a minimum current of 18 mA has to be maintained through the commutator contacts, but due to internal dissipation parameters the upper limit of current is usually 25 mA. Taking this into account, we can look at the available interface with a data processing device. This type of interface may have available voltages of $+5$ and $-15$ volts (V) (others are available and can be used). Because there is approximately 1-V loss at various points in the internal loop, we can assume that of the total 20-V difference (between the $+5$ and $-15$ V) only 19 V are available to generate the necessary line current. If the total interface resistance is approximately 750 ohms we will have slightly over 25 mA of current available for line transmission. If we also assume that 26 AWG copper wire is used for transmission, we can have up to 7300 ft of this wire before its resistance totals 300 ohms. This particular transmission requires a *full loop,* which means the teleprinter could be located half that distance, or 3650 ft away. We also assume that external interference has not affected the operation.

By taking higher initial voltages, additional wire length could be used that could increase the distance at which the printing device can be located. This approach is used by the carriers and other users who have to cover long distances with loop current transmission, which is usually limited to rates up to 150 BPS.

There are other considerations, especially when interfacing with foreign countries, where the specific mode of generation of current loops is important. Some countries require that the carrier provide the loop current, while the hardware merely switches or detects it. In other countries the communications site provides the current and must therefore have the capability for adjusting it. In either case there are two variations, *polar working* and *neutral working*. In polar working, a *mark* is current flow in one direction, and a *space* is current flow in the other direction. In neutral working, a mark is the presence of current, and the space is the absence of current. The currents used in most telegraph systems are typically 20 mA, but another common value is 60 mA.

For most computer-to-teleprinter interfaces that use loop current, the distance between them will not be more than 1500 ft. Therefore, the low-voltage current approach is desirable because it is cheaper and easier to maintain, and the higher voltage interfaces will be used only for the longer distances using a carrier. The high- and low-voltage interfaces are not compatible with each other even though there is the same amount of current in the overall loop.

Although the description here covers the teleprinter environment, the loop current interface is used extensively for in-house connections of terminals to controllers and connections to mainframes since only two wires are required and the interface is very inexpensive. As a matter of fact, almost all PCs have as their standard a loop current interface over which they use primarily a TTY protocol. With the PC environment being so price sensitive and the loop current interface so inexpensive, it is natural that the loop current interface is the primary mode of connection for PCs. Because of the standardization of the RS232 interface, however, each PC vendor has as an option the ability to interface with an RS232-compatible device. This option obviously costs more money because there are more wires involved and a different connector; but since almost all devices that connect to the telephone line are RS232-compatible, this option is mandatory in most cases.

## C

As the evolution of interfaces progressed and AT&T with its associated operating companies was, for all practical purposes, the only provider of communications services, the modems developed at AT&T became industry standards. Even so, both users of modems and independent modem manufacturers who offer equipment for private line use must know what the electrical characteristics of the computer and terminal are to interface with the modem. Therefore, the Electronic Industries Association (EIA), in conjunction with the Bell System, the independent modem manufacturers, and the computer manufacturers, developed a standard for the interface between the data communications equipment (provided by the carrier) and the data terminal equipment (provided by the data processing hardware manufacturers). This specification is known as RS232. The first version was issued in May 1960 and modified in October 1963 to the A revision. The B revision was issued in October 1965 and the C-level revision in October 1969 (reaffirmed in June of 1981). It is the C-level revision that is most commonly used today. But the D-level revision was issued in January 1987 and its use will grow as vendors make their equipment compatible. RS232D is upward compatible with RS232C.

There is another nomenclature point to be aware of, and that is that the EIA is dropping its use of the term RS (recommended standard). All specifications from now on will have an EIA designation; for example, RS232 will be known as EIA232. RS will still be used in this book because of its familiarity, but in the future EIA will grow in popularity of use.

For interface with circuits in foreign countries, the CCITT (Consultive Committee on International Telephone and Telegraph, based in Geneva) has established a standard called V.24 that is very closely aligned with RS232. V.24 is functionally identical to RS232 in almost all areas. V.24 describes the operational parameters of each of the signals and describes what the various logical relationships are. Then, as a subset, another standard called V.28 describes the signal levels themselves. Both V.28 and RS232 only define a binary 1 bit as being a minimum of $-3$ V and a binary 0 bit as being a minimum of $+3$ V. *Typically,* however, a received binary 1 bit is $-5$ to $-15$ V and a binary 0 bit is $+5$ to $+15$ V (the open circuit voltage can be less than 25 V maximum).

The RS232 standard basically defines three specific items:

1. Electrical signal characteristics
2. A functional description of the interchange circuits
3. A list of standard subsets of specific interchange circuits for specific groups of communication system applications

*Note:* A specific connector was not defined through the C level but was defined in the D-level revision. The shape and pin configuration most commonly used is shown in Fig. 5-1. Typically the interface is defined for every specific signal and, in addition, has adequate definition for the combinations and permutations of different types of modems (private line, leased line, dial up) that are

**FIGURE 5-1**
RS232 Connector Configuration

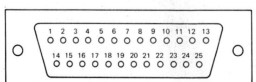

Plug goes on DTE (Male)
Receptacle goes on DCE (Female)
Plug is Connector with Pins (Male)

known at this time. Table 5–1 defines the RS/EIA interface along with the equivalent CCITT designation.

The distance over which the signals will travel is not specifically identified in RS232. However, the maximum amount of *capacitance* allowed on the cable connecting the devices is specified. The value is 2500 picofarads (pF), which is equal to $2500 \times 10^{-12}$ farads (F). For twisted pair connections, this normally comes out to approximately 50 ft, which is why many people think that RS232 has a 50 ft limitation. This is not always true. Different kinds of cable can be used, such as low-capacitance cable, that may significantly extend the distance over which the circuits will operate.

In addition, RS232 specifies a maximum allowable data rate to be transmitted between the DTE and DCE of 20,000 BPS. If you look at the 20,000 BPS at 50 ft, it is logical to assume that a slower data rate can be transmitted over a longer distance because the signals are wider and the rolloff degradation caused by line capacitance has less effect on wider signal widths. None of this higher speed versus shorter distance operation is contained within RS232, so as an end user you might want to try longer distances at lower speeds. In some cases vendors indicate they will support distances greater than 50 ft. One thing to be careful of, however, is that once the vendor's specified distance is exceeded it is quite possible the vendor will not support the connection if problems develop.

The utilization of RS232 connections in a local environment is further discussed in Chapter 10, where modem eliminators are described.

Because of the critical nature and extensive use of RS232, the signal definitions for each circuit and its relationship with the EIA and CCITT circuit equivalents are described here. Listed next are the signals with their functional and operational descriptions.

> *Circuit AA.* Protective Ground. This is a conductor that shall be electrically bonded to the equipment frame and may be further connected to external grounds as required by local codes. (Not used in EIA232D.)
>
> *Circuit AB.* Signal Ground. This is a conductor that establishes the common ground reference potential for all interchange circuits except circuit AA. It may be connected or removed as required at local installations to meet local codes or minimize addition of noise.
>
> *Circuit BA.* Transmit Data. These are the signals generated by the DTE and transferred to the local DCE. The DTE shall hold circuit BA in a mark condition between characters or words and at all times when no data are being transmitted. In all systems the DTE shall not transmit data unless a mark condition is present *on all of the following four circuits* when implemented:
>
> 1. Circuit CA (request to send)
> 2. Circuit CB (clear to send)
> 3. Circuit CC (data set ready)
> 4. Circuit CD (data terminal ready)

## TABLE 5-1
### Electronic Industries Association RS/EIA232 Interface

| | RS 232 C | | | | EIA 232 D | | | | |
|---|---|---|---|---|---|---|---|---|---|
| Pin | CCITT Circuit Name | RS 232C Circuit Name | Direction | Name | Pin # | CCITT Circuit Name | EIA 232D Circuit Name | Direction | Name |
| 1 | 101 | AA | Both | Protective Ground | 1 | | | Both | Shield |
| 7 | 102 | AB | Both | Signal Ground | 7 | 102 | AB | Both | Signal Ground/Common Return |
| 2 | 103 | BA | To-DCE | Transmit Data | 2 | 103 | BA | To-DCE | Transmit Data |
| 3 | 104 | BB | To-DTE | Receive Data | 3 | 104 | BB | To-DTE | Receive Data |
| 4 | 105 | CA | To-DCE | Request to Send | 4 | 105 | CA | To-DCE | Request to Send |
| 5 | 106 | CB | To-DTE | Clear to Send | 5 | 106 | CB | To-DTE | Clear to Send |
| 6 | 107 | CC | To-DTE | Modem Ready | 6 | 107 | CC | To-DTE | DCE Ready |
| 20 | 108.2 | CD | To-DCE | Terminal Ready | 20 | 108.2 | CD | To-DCE | DTE Ready |
| 22 | 125 | CE | To-DTE | Ring Indicator | 22 | 125 | CE | To-DTE | Ring Indicator |
| 8 | 109 | CF | To-DTE | Received Line Signal Detect (Carrier Detect) | 8 | 109 | CF | To-DTE | Received Line Signal Detect Carrier Detect |
| 21 | 110 | CG | To-DTE | Signal Quality Detector | 21 | 140/110 | RL/CG | To-DTE | Remote Loopback/Signal Quality Detector* |
| 23 | 111/112 | CH/CI | Either | Data Signaling Rate Selector/Indicator | 23 | 111/112 | CH/CI | Either | Data Signaling Rate Selector/Indicator** |
| 24 | 113 | DA | To-DCE | Transmit Clock (DTE Source) | 24 | 113 | DA | To-DCE | Transmit Clock (DTE Source) |
| 15 | 114 | DB | To-DTE | Transmit Clock (DCE Source) | 15 | 114 | DB | To-DTE | Transmit Clock (DCE Source) |
| 17 | 115 | DD | To-DTE | Receive Clock (DCE Source) | 17 | 115 | DD | To-DTE | Receive Clock (DCE Source) |
| 14 | 118 | SBA | To-DCE | Secondary Transmit Data | 14 | 118 | SBA | To-DCE | Secondary Transmit Data |
| 16 | 119 | SBB | To-DTE | Secondary Receive Data | 16 | 119 | SBB | To-DTE | Secondary Receive Data |
| 19 | 120 | SCA | To-DCE | Secondary Request to Send | 19 | 120 | SCA | To-DCE | Secondary Request to Send |
| 13 | 121 | SCB | To-DTE | Secondary Clear to Send | 13 | 121 | SCB | To-DTE | Secondary Clear to Send |
| 12 | 122 | SCF | To-DTE | Secondary Carrier Detect | 12 | 122/112 | SCF/CI | To-DTE | Secondary Carrier Detect*** |
| | | | | | 9 | — | — | — | Reserved for Testing |
| | | | | | 10 | — | — | — | Reserved for Testing |
| | | | | | 11 | — | — | — | Unassigned |
| | | | | | 18 | 141 | LL | To-DCE | Local Loopback |
| | | | | | 25 | 142 | TM | To-DTE | Test Mode |

*CG No Longer Used

**See Pin 12

***If SC Not Used Then CI is on Pin 12

88

When implemented, all data signals that are transmitted across the interface on circuit BA during the time a mark condition is maintained on all four preceding circuits will be transmitted to the communications channel.

*Circuit BB.* Receive Data. These are signals that are generated by the local DCE and transferred to the local DTE. Circuit BB shall be held in the mark conditions at all times when circuit CF is in the OFF condition. On a half-duplex circuit, circuit BB shall be maintained in the mark condition when circuit CA is in the mark condition and for a brief interval following the mark to OFF transition of CA to allow for the completion of transmission and decay of line reflections.

*Circuit CA.* Request to Send. This signal is used to prepare the local DCE for data transmission and, on a half-duplex channel, to control the direction of data transmission of the local DCE. On one-way only channels or full-duplex channels, the mark condition maintains the DCE in the transmit mode and the OFF condition maintains the DCE in a nontransmit mode. On a half-duplex circuit the mark condition maintains the DCE in a transmit mode and inhibits the receive mode. The OFF condition maintains the DCE in the receive mode. The DCE initiates the necessary actions and indicates completion of them, returning circuit CG to the mark condition. The mark condition indicates to the DTE that data may be transferred across the interface on circuit BA. A transition from mark to OFF directs the DCE to complete the transmission of all data that were previously transferred on circuit BA and then assume a nontransmit mode or a receive mode as appropriate. DCE then turns circuit CB to the OFF condition when it is ready to respond again to a subsequent mark condition of circuit CA. (*Notes:* A nontransmit mode does not imply that all line signals have been removed from the communications channel. When circuit CA is turned OFF, it shall not be turned to the mark condition again until circuit CB has been turned OFF by the DCE. A mark condition is required on CA as well as CB, CC, and, where implemented, CD whenever the DTE transfers data across the interface on circuit BA. It is allowed to turn CA to the mark condition anytime that circuit CB is in the OFF condition regardless of the condition of any other circuit.)

*Circuit CB.* Clear to Send. The signals on this circuit are generated by the DCE to indicate whether the DCE is ready to transmit data. The mark condition of CG combined with the mark condition on circuits CA, CC, and, where implemented, CD is an indication of the DTE that signals transmitted on circuit BA will be transmitted to the communications channel. The OFF condition indicates to the DTE that data should not be transferred on circuit BA. The mark condition of circuit CB is a response to the occurrence of a simultaneous mark condition on circuits CC and circuit CA, delayed as may be appropriate to the DCE for establishing a communications channel (including the removal of the MARK HOLD clamp from the Receive Data Interchange Circuit of the remote data set) to a remote DTE. Where circuit CA is not implemented in the DCE with transmitting capability, circuit CA shall be assumed to be in the mark condition at all times, and circuit CB shall respond accordingly.

*Circuit CC.* DCE Ready. The signals on this circuit are used to indicate the status of the local DCE. A mark condition on this circuit indicates the following:

1. The local DCE is connected to a communications channel ("OFF HOOK" in switched service).
2. The local DCE is not in test, talk, or dial mode.
3. The local DCE has completed, where applicable, any timing functions required by the switching system to complete call establishment and the transmission of any discrete answer tone.

Where local DCE is not transmitting an answer tone, or where the duration of the answer tone is controlled by some action of the remote data set, the mark condition is presented as soon as all three conditions or conditions one, two and the first part of three are satisfied. The circuit shall be used only to indicate the status of the local DCE. The mark condition shall not be interpreted as either an indication that the communication channel has been established to a remote location or the status of any remote equipment.

The OFF condition shall appear at all other times and shall be an indication that the DTE is to disregard any signals appearing on any other circuit with the exception of circuit CE. The OFF condition shall not impair the operation of circuit CE or CD. When the OFF condition occurs during the progress of a call before circuit CD is turned OFF, the DTE shall interpret this as a lost or aborted connection and take the necessary action to terminate the call. Any subsequent mark condition on circuit CC is to be considered a new call.

*Circuit CD.* DTE Ready. Signals on this circuit are used to control switching of the DCE to the communications channel. The mark condition prepares the DCE to be connected to the communications channel and maintains the connection established by external means (e.g., manual call origination, manual answering, automatic call origination). When the station is equipped for automatic answering of received calls and is in the automatic answering mode, connection to the line occurs only in response to a combination of a ringing signal and the mark condition of circuit CD. However, the DTE is normally allowed to present the mark condition of circuit CD whenever it is ready to transmit or receive data except as indicated here.

The OFF condition causes the DCE to be removed from the communications channel following the completion of any "in process" transmission from circuit BA. The OFF condition shall not disable the operation of circuit CE. In switched network applications, when circuit CD is turned OFF, it shall not be turned to a mark condition again until circuit CC is turned OFF by the DCE.

*Circuit CE.* Ring Indicator. A mark condition of this circuit indicates that a ringing signal is being received on the communications channel. The mark condition shall appear approximately coincident with the mark segment of the ringing cycle (during rings) on the communications channel. The OFF condition shall be maintained during the OFF segment of the ringing cycle (between rings) and at all other times when ringing is not being received. The operation of this circuit shall not be disabled by the OFF condition on circuit CD.

*Circuit CF.* Receive Line Signal Detector. The mark condition on this circuit is presented when the DCE is receiving a signal that meets its "suitability" criteria. These criteria are established by the DCE manufacturer. The OFF condition indicates that no signal is being received or that the received signal is unsuitable for demodulation. The OFF condition shall cause circuit BB to be clamped in the mark condition. On half-duplex circuits, this circuit is held in the OFF condition whenever circuit CA is in the mark condition and for a brief interval of time following the mark to OFF transition of circuit CA.

*Circuit CG.* Signal Quality Detector. Signals on this circuit are used to indicate whether there is a high probability of an error on the received data. A mark condition is maintained whenever there is no reason to believe that an error has occurred. An OFF condition indicates that there is a high probability of an error. (Not used in EIA232D.)

*Circuit CH.* Data Signal Rate Selector (Using DTE Source). Signals on this circuit are used to select between the two data signaling rates in the case of a dual-rate synchronous modem or the two ranges of data signaling rates in the case of a dual-range nonsynchronous modem. A mark condition shall select the higher data signaling rate or range of rates.

*Circuit CI.* Data Signal Rate Selector (DCE Source). Signals on this circuit are used to select between the two data signaling rates in the case of dual-rate synchronous modems or the two ranges of data signaling rates in the case of dual-range nonsynchronous modems. A mark condition shall select the higher data signaling rate or range of rates.

*Circuit DA.* Transmitter Signal Element Timing (DTE Source). Signals on this circuit are used to provide the timing information relative to the transmitted signals. The mark to OFF transition shall nominally indicate the center of each signal element on circuit BA. When circuit DA is implemented in the DTE, the DTE shall normally provide timing information on circuit DA whenever the DTE is in the "power on" condition. It is allowable for the DTE to inhibit timing information on circuit DA for short periods provided circuit CA is in the OFF condition. (This may be done for maintenance purposes.)

*Circuit DB.* Transmitter Signal Element Timing (DCE Source). Signals on this circuit are used to provide the DTE with timing information. The DTE shall provide a data signal on circuit BA in which the transitions between signal elements normally occur at the time of the transitions from OFF to mark conditions of the signal on circuit DB. When circuit DB is implemented in the DCE, the DCE shall normally provide the timing information on this circuit whenever the DCE is in a "power on" condition. It is allowable for the DCE to inhibit timing information on this circuit for short periods provided circuit CC is in the OFF condition. (This may be done for maintenance purposes.)

**Circuit DD.** Receiver Signal Element Timing (DCE Source). Signals on this circuit are used to provide the DTE with receive signal timing information. The transition from mark to OFF condition shall nominally indicate the center of each signal element on circuit BB. Timing information on circuit DD shall be provided at times when circuit CF is in the mark condition. It may, but not necessarily, be present following the mark to OFF transition of circuit CF.

**Circuit SBA.** Secondary Transmitted Data. This circuit is equivalent to circuit BA except that it is used to transmit data via the secondary channel in reverse channel modems. The DTE shall hold circuit SBA in the mark condition during intervals when characters or words and at all times when no data are being transmitted. In all systems the DTE shall not transmit on the secondary channel unless a mark condition is present on all the following circuits where implemented: SCA, SCB, CC, CD. All data signals that are transmitted across the interface on circuit SBA during the time the above conditions are satisfied shall be transmitted to the communications channel. When the secondary channel is used only for circuit assurance or to interrupt the flow of data in the primary channel (less than 10 baud capability), circuit SBA is normally not provided, and the channel carrier is turned to a mark condition or OFF by means of circuit SCA. Carrier OFF is interpreted as an "interrupt condition."

**Circuit SBB.** Secondary Received Data. This circuit is equivalent to circuit BB except that it is used to receive data on the secondary channel. When the secondary channel is used only for circuit assurance or to interrupt the flow of data on the primary channel, interchange circuit SCF is usually provided instead of circuit SBB. In that case, the mark condition shall indicate circuit assurance or noninterrupt condition. The OFF condition shall indicate failure or interrupt.

**Circuit SCA.** Secondary Request to Send. This circuit performs the same function as circuit CA, except that it performs that function for the secondary channel.

**Circuit SCB.** Secondary Clear to Send. This circuit performs the same function as circuit CB, except that it performs that function for the secondary channel.

**Circuit SCF.** Secondary Received Line Signal Detector. This circuit is the same as Circuit CF (receive line signal detect) and indicates the reception of the carrier signal on the secondary channel.

**Circuit LL.** Local Loopback. The signals on this circuit are used for control of the LL test condition in the local DCE. The ON condition of circuit

LL causes the DCE to transfer the normal output of the modulator to the normal input of the demodulator through the appropriate circuitry that would allow for proper operation of the demodulator. After going into the LL test condition, the DCE turns on Circuit TM (test mode), after which all of the interface circuits may be tested. The OFF condition of Circuit LL restores the DCE to standard operation. (Newly specified for EIA232D.)

*Circuit RL.* Remote Loopback. Signals on this circuit are used to control the RL test mode in the remote DCE. The ON condition of circuit RL causes the local DCE to signal the remote DCE to go into the RL test condition. After circuit RL is put in the ON condition and an ON condition is also detected on Circuit TM, the local DTE can test the circuitry of the local and remote DCEs. The OFF condition of Circuit RL reestablishes standard operational configuration. (Newly specified for EIA232D.)

*Circuit TM.* Test Mode. The signal on this circuit indicates whether the local DCE is in a test condition. The ON condition of circuit TM indicates that the DCE is in a test mode and shall be in response to an ON condition of Circuit LL or Circuit RL. The OFF condition of circuit TM indicates that the DCE is in normal operational mode. (Newly specified for EIA232D.)

Other changes have been incorporated into EIA232D, such as the formalization of pins 9 and 10 being reserved for testing. Pin 11 is still unassigned. Also, as was indicated in the functional signal descriptions, signal quality detector (Signal CG) is no longer used. If secondary carrier detect (SCF) is not used, then Signal CI data signaling rate selector/indicator is utilized on pin 12.

The establishment of EIA232D was in response to the requirement for standardized test capabilities in the modem world. It is upwardly compatible from RS232C in that all the pin connections are the same, and only the addition of new signals and formalization of existing procedures have been quantified. The methodology of implementation will probably be that as new equipment is produced, it will be EIA232D compatible even though only one side of the DTE/DCE circuit may be upgraded at any one time. Eventually, at both sides of the interface, equipment will be compatible.

The definitions provided here are standards that are used worldwide, but that does not mean that these are the only signals that can be provided on the individual pin assignments. For those modem equipments that do not use all the defined parameters for their operation, vendors sometimes use the same pins for other functions (not defined within the RS232 interface). These devices are then not compatible with devices that use the standard interface with the functions that had been predefined on those leads. The user should always verify with the vendor whether their devices are, first, RS232 compatible and, second, whether they use any of the leads for defining some other signal that is unique to their own operation.

RS232C is equivalent to MIL-STD-188C in the U.S. military environment except that MIL-STD-188C specifies a lower-level current at the interface than RS232C so that less electromagnetic radiation is generated. The same is true for the D-level revision.

## RS449, RS422, RS423, AND EIA530

Over the years, RS232 has been more than adequate for the speeds and distances encountered in the data environment. However, as users wanted to transmit higher data rates at longer distances in house, the requirement evolved for a specification that would perform that function. Finally, in 1975 the EIA issued a specification identified as RS449, which was supposed to supersede RS232. RS449 is both a mechanical and functional specification that also contains two subspecifications which identify the specific electrical interface standards. The first electrical interface standard is RS422, which is known as the *balanced* electrical interface. It is less noise sensitive and can transmit over a greater distance at a faster data rate than the other electrical standard, RS423, called the *unbalanced* electrical interface. The basic difference between the two is that the balanced interface uses a differential amplifier that allows half the signal to be transmitted on each wire of the pair that is used. Because of the method of signal generation and detection, this is much less noise sensitive (a detailed description of differential amplifiers is included in Chapter 10 under Line Drivers). The unbalanced electrical circuit provides for the transmission of the signal only on one of the wires, very much the same way as it is done presently in RS232.

The connectors used are in the same basic shape but not the same size as RS232 and there are two of them. First, there is a 37-pin connector that contains all the primary functions and is designed to be the only connector to be used in the final configuration. A separate 9-pin connector is used for those interfaces where the device at one end of the DTE/DCE connection is RS232 compatible, while the device at the other end is RS449 compatible, and the interface requires a split channel or reverse channel operation (also described in Chapter 10 under Split Channel Modems). The 9-pin connector is optional.

Figure 5-2 shows the difference in capability between RS232 and RS449. As can be seen, the RS232 distance is nominally 50 ft up to 20,000 BPS, whereas RS449 allows operation up to 4000 ft. When using the RS423 unbalanced electrical circuit the 4000-ft distance can support up to 1200 BPS, and then the distance decreases while the data rate increases until at 40 ft the transmission rate supported is 100,000 BPS.

If the RS422 balanced circuit is used, a data rate of up to 100,000 BPS can be supported for up to 4000 ft, and then the distance decreases while the data rate increases until at 40 ft the capability still exists for transmission at 10 million BPS.

For additional comparison, Table 5-2 shows the pin connections for RS449 as they relate to the RS232C circuits and it also describes the mnemonic identified by the EIA, the category of circuit (category 1 requires two wires and pins while category 2 requires only one wire and 1 pin), the pin numbers, the circuit classification (G = ground, C = control, D = data, T = timing), the equivalent RS232C circuit, the direction that the signal travels, the equivalent EIA RS232 mnemonic, and, finally, the equivalent CCITT code. The same information is

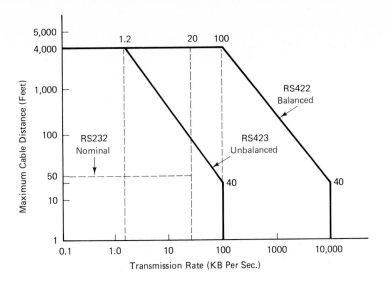

**FIGURE 5-2**
Performance Characteristics of RS449 versus RS232

shown in Table 5-3 for the 9-pin optional connector for those situations where it is used.

One would expect with this extension of distance and speed capability that RS449 would have been accepted universally almost immediately. This was not the case, however, because at about the same time Xerox Corporation came out with a method of connecting devices in a local environment called Ethernet. Ethernet was one of the first of the *local area networks* (LANs), which will be described further in Chapter 15, and although it is not an interface but a *system,* it provided an alternative connection. The Ethernet specification allowed for the transmission of data at up to 10 million BPS for up to 2.5 kilometers. Ethernet permitted the user to retain all existing RS232 interfaces because it provided an interface module to connect directly within a few feet to your device, and then provided the conversion for the Ethernet connection on the network side of the interface module.

Many people looked at a LAN as being an upgrade to RS232 instead of to RS449, with the result that very few RS449 interfaces were built (AT&T Dataphone II modems are one of the few). In addition, many vendors are building alternative interfaces besides Ethernet, and these will also be described in Chapter 15.

Some areas in which RS449 was being used were for connections between CPUs and satellite antennas, which typically operate at 1.544 MBPS (T-1 carrier) over distances of a few hundred feet. Also, RS449 can be used for those interfaces over which video signals must be sent, because typically in-house video is in the range of 3.6 MBPS and must be transmitted on in-house cables that at times run

hundreds of feet. It does not appear, however, that RS449 will be used much longer, because in March 1987 the EIA issued specification EIA530 to replace RS449.

As described previously, RS449 required two connectors, one of which was a 37-pin connector, to totally replace RS232. Because the connector was so much bigger, extensive physical changes would be required if the user were to try to upgrade to RS449. As only one end of the interface typically gets changed at a time due to cost considerations, the eventual upgrade would involve significant amounts of money and time. To make the transition easier and still provide the ability to transmit at higher data rates over longer distances, the Electronic Industries Association issued EIA530, which would accomplish the same electrical functions as RS449, but with a 25-pin connector that was the same as RS232. RS422A and RS422B (now called EIA422A and EIA423A) are still the electrical subspecifications that are used within EIA530. By utilizing these electrical interfaces the transmitted data signals can be driven over much greater distances at higher speeds, still in accordance with Fig. 5–2. A direct comparison between RS449 and EIA530 is shown in Table 5–4.

The circuits fall into two categories with respect to their electrical characteristics. Category I circuits are the following:

Circuit BA—Transmit data

Circuit BB—Receive data

Circuit DA—Transmit clock (DTE source)

Circuit DB—Transmit clock (DCE source)

Circuit DD—Receive clock (DCE source)

Circuit CA—Request to send

Circuit CB—Clear to send

Circuit CF—Received line signal detect

Circuit CC—DCE ready

Circuit CD—DTE ready

(clock equals signal element timing)

Category I circuits use EIA422A as the specification for the electrical characteristics.

Category II circuits use the specification EIA423A to identify their electrical characteristics. They are the following:

Circuit LL—Local loopback

Circuit RL—Remote loopback

Circuit TM—Test mode

Signal ground (Circuit AB) is the return line for Category II circuits.

The functional operation of each circuit conforms closely to the operation of the comparable circuit in RS232. They will, therefore, not be described in

**TABLE 5-4**
A Comparison Between EIA449 and EIA530

| EIA-449 SIGNAL NAME | EIA NAME | CCITT NAME | PIN NUMBER | PIN NUMBER | CCITT NAME | EIA NAME | EIA-530 SIGNAL NAME |
|---|---|---|---|---|---|---|---|
| Shield | — | — | 1 | 1 | — | — | Shield |
| Send Data | SD(A) | 103 | 4 | 2 | 103 | BA(A) | Transmitted Data |
|  | SD(B) |  | 22 | 14 |  | BA(B) |  |
| Receive Data | RD(A) | 104 | 6 | 3 | 104 | BB(A) | Received Data |
|  | RD(B) |  | 24 | 16 |  | BB(B) |  |
| Request to Send | RS(A) | 105 | 7 | 4 | 105 | CA(A) | Request to Send |
|  | RS(B) |  | 25 | 19 |  | CA(B) |  |
| Clear to Send | CS(A) | 106 | 9 | 5 | 106 | CB(A) | Clear to Send |
|  | CS(B) |  | 27 | 13 |  | CB(B) |  |
| Data Mode | DM(A) | 107 | 11 | 6 | 107 | CC(A) | DCE Ready |
|  | DM(B) |  | 29 | 22 |  | CC(B) |  |
| Terminal Ready | TR(A) | 108 | 12 | 20 | 108 | CD(A) | DTE Ready |
|  | TR(B) |  | 30 | 23 |  | CD(B) |  |
| Signal Ground | SG | 102 | 19 | 7 | 102 | AB | Signal Ground |
| Receiver Ready | RR(A) | 109 | 13 | 8 | 109 | CF(A) | Received Line Signal |
|  | RR(B) |  | 31 | 10 |  | CF(B) | Detect (Carrier Detect) |
| Send Timing | ST(A) | 114 | 5 | 15 | 114 | DB(A) | Transmit Signal Element |
|  | ST(B) |  | 23 | 12 |  | DB(B) | Timing (DCE Source) |
| Receive Timing | RT(A) | 115 | 8 | 17 | 115 | DD(A) | Receiver Signal Element |
|  | RT(B) |  | 26 | 9 |  | DD(B) | Timing (DCE Source) |
| Local Loopback | LL | 141 | 10 | 18 | 141 | LL | Local Loopback |
| Remote Loopback | RL | 140 | 14 | 21 | 140 | RL | Remote Loopback |
| Terminal Timing | TT(A) | 113 | 17 | 24 | 113 | DA(A) | Transmit Signal Element |
|  | TT(B) |  | 35 | 11 |  | DA(B) | Timing (DTE Source) |
| Test Mode | TM | 142 | 18 | 25 | 142 | TM | Test Mode |
| Send Common | SC | 102A | 37 |  |  |  | Not used |
| Receive Common | RC | 102B | 20 |  |  |  | Not used |
| Terminal Inservice | IS | 135 | 28 |  |  |  | Not used |
| Incoming Call | IC | 125 | 15 |  |  |  | Not used |
| Signal Quality | SQ | 110 | 33 |  |  |  | Not used |
| New Signal | NS | 136 | 34 |  |  |  | Not used |
| Signalling Rate Indicator | SI | 112 | 2 |  |  |  | Not used |
| Select Frequency/Signal | SF/SR | 126/111 | 16 |  |  |  | Not used |
| Rate Selector |  |  | 32 |  |  |  |  |
| Select Standby | SS | 116 | 36 |  |  |  | Not used |
| Standby Indicator | SB | 117 | 3,21 |  |  |  | Not used |
| Spares |  |  |  |  |  |  | Not used |

detail here since descriptions under RS232 are adequate for the level of detail within this text. If more detailed or additional information is required regarding the EIA530, the specification can be obtained from the Electronic Industries Association.

## E

## CCITT INTERNATIONAL INTERFACES

Many different types of interfaces are recognized by groups around the world. For purposes of this text, three types will be described. The first will be the Electronic Industries Association (EIA) specifications, which are always preceded by the letters RS (Recommended Standard) or EIA. The second set will be the CCITT standard interface specifications, which are always preceded by the letter V, and the third series of specifications, also established by the CCITT, are always preceded by the letter X. A V specification deals primarily with telephone circuits, while the X specifications deal primarily with data interfaces and public data networks. The most common specifications in use today are identified below.

*EIA-232-D.* Interface between data terminal equipment and data communication equipment employing serial binary data interchange (January 1987).

*EIA-269-B.* Synchronous signaling rates for data transmission (January 1976; identical to ANSI X3.1-1976).

*EIA-334-A.* Signal quality at interface between data processing terminal equipment and synchronous data communication equipment for serial data transmission (August 1981) (also adopted as ANSI X3.24-1967).

*EIA-334-A-1.* Addendum No. 1 to EIA-334-A and EIA-404. Application of signal quality requirements to EIA-449.

*EIA-357.* Interface between facsimile terminal equipment and voice-frequency data communication terminal equipment (June 1968).

*EIA-363.* Standard for specifying signal quality for transmitting and receiving data processing terminal equipment using serial data transmission at the interface with nonsynchronous data communication equipment (May 1969).

*EIA-366-A.* Interface between data terminal equipment and automatic calling equipment for data communication (March 1979).

*EIA-404-A.* Standard for start/stop signal quality between data terminal equipment and nonsynchronous data communication equipment ANSI approved (January 1986).

*EIA-404-1.* Addendum No. 1 to EIA-404 and EIA-334-A. Application of signal requirements to EIA-449.

*EIA-410.* Standard for electrical characteristics of class A closure interchange circuits (April 1974).

**EIA-422-A.** Electrical characteristics of balanced voltage digital interface circuits (December 1978).

**EIA-423-A.** Electrical characteristics of unbalanced voltage digital interface circuits (December 1978).

**EIA-449-1.** General-purpose 37-position interface for Data Terminal Equipment and Data Circuit terminating Equipment employing serial-binary data interchange. (The electrical signal characteristics for EIA-449 are defined by either EIA-422 or EIA-423, since EIA-449 is only a mechanical and functional definition standard) (February 1980).

**EIA-470-A.** Telephone instruments with loop signaling. Performance and technical criteria for connecting and interfacing various elements of the public telephone network.

**EIA-491.** Interface between a numerical control unit and peripheral equipment employing asynchronous binary data interchange over circuits having EIA-423-A electrical characteristics (October 1982).

**EIA-496.** Interface between data communication equipment (DCE) and the public switched telephone network (PSTN). ANSI approved (May 1984).

**EIA-530.** High-speed 25-position interface for Data Terminal Equipment and Data Circuit Terminating Equipment. ANSI approved (March 1987).

**V.** CCITT code designation: CCITT is the Consultive Committee on International Telephone and Telegraph (the name is really French—this is the English translation). Based in Geneva, Switzerland, it is the organization responsible for establishing a wide variety of specifications. The V. series deals with telecommunications and analog facilities, the X. specifications deal with the public data network (packet switching), and the I. series deals with ISDN recommendations. The CCITT is involved with other areas, but these are the most pertinent to the subject of data communications. Many people are curious as to how the CCITT operates, so it will briefly be described here.

Any country that is a member of the United Nations can be a member of the CCITT. Its 15 study groups are each responsible for a different area of communications. Each group, composed of any number of experts, develops standards for its own specific area, and the recommendations must be unanimous from the study groups. (You can understand why some of these specifications take so long in coming to fruition.) Every four years the CCITT meets in plenary session, where the previous four years of activity can be reviewed. Recommendations are reviewed, approved, or sent back to committee, and objectives are established for the next four years of study. Many times, however, interim recommendations are issued for guideline purposes only so that work may continue in the vendor or end-user environment in anticipation of the issuance of a final specification. Although it is not a final document, many organizations act on the interim recommendation. The CCITT is one of the most influential bodies in the world in establishing standards in the world of data and telecommunications.

***V.1.*** Equivalence between binary notation symbols and the significant conditions of a two-condition code.

***V.2.*** Power levels for data transmission over telephone lines.

***V.3.*** International Telegraph Alphabet No. 5.

***V.4.*** General structure of signals of International Telegraph Alphabet No. 5 code for data transmission over public telephone network.

***V.5.*** Standardization of data-signaling rates for synchronous data transmission in the general switched telephone network.

***V.6.*** Standardization of data-signaling rates for synchronous data transmission on leased telephone-type circuits.

***V.7.*** Definition of terms concerning data communication over the telephone network.

***V.10(X.26).*** Electrical characteristics for unbalanced double-current interchange circuits for general use with integrated circuit equipment in the field of data communications (and provisional amendments, May 1977).

***V.11(X.27).*** Electrical characteristics for balanced double-current interchange circuits for general use with integrated circuit equipment in the field of data communications (and provisional amendments, May 1977).

***V.15.*** Use of acoustic coupling for data transmission.

***V.19.*** Modems for parallel data transmission using telephone signaling frequencies.

***V.20.*** Parallel data transmission modems standardized for universal use in the general switched telephone network.

***V.21.*** 300-bit/s full-duplex modem standardized for use in the general switched telephone network.

***V.22.*** 1200 BPS full-duplex modem standardized for use in the general switched telephone network and on point-to-point two-wire leased telephone-type circuits.

***V.22bis.*** 2400 BPS full-duplex modem using the frequency division technique standardized for use on the general switched telephone network and on point-to-point two-wire leased telephone-type circuits.

***V.23.*** 600/1.2K BPS modem standardized for use in the general switched telephone network.

***V.24.*** List of definitions for interchange circuits between data terminal equipment and data circuit terminating equipment (and provisional amendments, May 1977).

***V.25.*** Automatic calling and/or answering equipment on the general switched telephone network, including disabling of echo suppressors on manually established calls.

***V.25bis.*** Automatic calling and/or answering equipment on the general switched telephone network using the 100 series interchange circuits.

***V.26.*** 2.4/1.2 KBPS modem standardized for use on four-wire leased telephone-type circuits.

*V.26bis.* 2.4/1.2 KBPS modem standardized for use in the general switched telephone network.

*V.26ter.* 2.4 KBPS full-duplex modem using the echo cancellation technique standardized for use on the general switched telephone network and on point-to-point two-wire leased telephone-type circuits.

*V.27.* 4.8 KBPS modem with manual equalizer standardized for use on leased telephone-type circuits.

*V.27bis.* 4.8 KBPS modem with automatic equalizer standardized for use on leased telephone-type circuits.

*V.27ter.* 4.8/2.4 KBPS modem standardized for use in the general switched telephone network.

*V.28.* Electrical characteristics for unbalanced double-current interchange circuits.

*V.29.* 9.6 KBPS modem standardized for use on point-to-point four-wire leased telephone-type circuits.

*V.31.* Electrical characteristics for single-current interchange circuits controlled by contact closure.

*V.32.* A family of two-wire, full-duplex modems operating at data signaling rates of up to 9600 BPS for use on the general switched telephone network and on leased telephone-type circuits.

*V.35.* Data transmission at 48 KBPS using 60- to 108-kHz group band circuits.

*V.36.* Modems for synchronous data transmission using 60- to 108-kHz group band circuits.

*V.37.* Synchronous data transmission at a data signaling rate higher than 72 KBPS using 60–108 kHz group band circuits.

*V.40.* Error indication with electromechanical equipment.

*V.41.* Code independent error control system.

*V.50.* Standard limits for transmission quality of data transmission.

*V.51.* Organization of the maintenance of international telephone-type circuits used for data transmission.

*V.52.* Characteristics of distortion and error-rate measuring apparatus for data transmission.

*V.53.* Limits for the maintenance of telephone-type circuits used for data transmission.

*V.54.* Loop test devices for modems.

*V.55.* Specification for an impulsive noise measuring instrument for telephone-type circuits.

*V.56.* Comparative tests of modems for use over telephone-type circuits.

*V.57.* Comprehensive data test set for high data signaling rates.

*V.100.* Interconnection between public data networks (PDNs) and the public switched telephone network (PSTN).

*V.110.* Support of data terminal equipment (DTEs) with V-series type interfaces by an integrated services digital network (ISDN).

*X.* CCITT recommendation designation.

*X.1.* International user classes of service in public data networks.

*X.2.* International user facilities in public data networks.

*X.3.* Packet assembly/disassembly facility (PAD) in a public data network.

*X.4.* General structure of signals of international alphabet no. 5 code for data transmission over public data networks.

*X.20.* Interface between data terminal equipment and data circuit-terminating equipment for start/stop transmission services on public data networks.

*X.20bis(V.21).* Compatible interface between data terminal equipment and data circuit-terminating equipment for start/stop transmission services on public data networks.

*X.21.* General-purpose interface between data terminal equipment and data circuit-terminating equipment for synchronous operation on public data networks.

*X.21bis.* Use on public data networks of data terminal equipment that is designed for interfacing to synchronous V-series modems.

*X.24.* List of definitions of interchange circuits between data terminal equipment and data circuit-terminating equipment on public data networks.

*X.25.* Interface between data terminal equipment and data circuit-terminating equipment for terminals operating in the packet mode on public data networks (and provisional amendment, April 1977).

*X.26.* Electrical characteristics for unbalanced double-current interchange circuits for general use with integrated circuit equipment in the field of data communications (identical to V.10).

*X.27.* Electrical characteristics for balanced double-current interchange circuits for general use with integrated circuit equipment in the field of data communications (identical to V.11).

*X.28.* DTE/DCE interface for start/stop mode data terminal equipment accessing the packet assembly/disassembly facility (PAD) on a public network situated in the same country.

*X.29.* Procedures for exchange of control information and user data between a packet-mode DTE and a packet assembly/disassembly facility (PAD).

*X.30.* Standardization of basic model page-printing machine in accordance with International Telegraph Alphabet No. 5.

*X.31.* Characteristics, from the transmission point of view, at the interchange point between data terminal equipment and data circuit-terminating equipment in a 200 BPS start/stop data terminal.

*X.32.* Answer-back units for 200 BPS start/stop machines in accordance with International Telegraph Alphabet No. 5.

*X.33.* Standardization of an international text for the measurement of the margin of start/stop machines in accordance with International Telegraph Alphabet No. 5.

*X.92.* Hypothetical reference connections for public synchronous data networks.

*X.95.* Network parameters in public data networks.

*X.96.* Call progress signals in public data networks.

*X.500.* A specification defining the universal interconnectivity of public electronic mail networks. X.500 implies a global directory for *all* of the different services, not just electronic mail; services include telephone, Telex, and other networks. X.500 is in its early stages of development. To create a database incorporating the addresses of all of these different networks would appear to be unattainable at this time, so what is expected initially would be a standard to link several autonomous databases within an existing electronic mail network. In other words, one directory leads to another in a hierarchical form in the order of country/network/organization/person.

Some of the attributes yet to be defined are response time, which may be in the range of hours because electronic mail is not real time, and how changes will be incorporated into these directories. Changes must be inserted quickly to maintain the viability of the directory. What also needs to be determined before this specification becomes standard is whether you will be able to browse through the directory, if you will be able to send *junk mail* using the directory, and what you must do if you want an *unlisted* number. Though X.500 will probably not be required in a network until the early 1990s, work is being performed on its development now.

*X3.1-1976.* Synchronous signaling rates for data transmission.

*X3.4-1976.* Code of information interchange.

*X3.15-1976.* Bit sequencing of the American National Standard Code for Information Interchange in serial-by-bit transmission.

*X3.16-1976.* Character structure and character parity sense for serial-by-bit data communication in the American National Standard Code for Information Interchange.

*X3.24-1976.* Signal quality at interface between data processing technical equipment for synchronous data transmission.

*X3.25-1976.* Character structure and character parity sense for parallel-by-bit communication in the American National Standard Code for Information Interchange.

*X3.28-1976.* Procedures for the use of communication control characters of American National Standard Code for Information Interchange in specified data communications links.

*X3.36-1977.* Synchronous high-speed data signaling rates between data terminal equipment and data communication equipment.

*X3.41-1977.* Code extension techniques for use with seven-bit coded character set of American National Standard Code for Information Interchange.

*X3.44-1977.* Determination of the performance of data communication systems.

*X3.57-1977.* Message heading formats for information interchange using ASCII for data communication system control.

There is a tremendous amount of confusion regarding the different kinds of interfaces that are available today for the different types of networks. Even with many of the standard organizations coming up with methods to tie the different networks together, the proliferation of terms is making everything very confusing. In an attempt to put some of them into limited perspective, Fig. 5–3 shows where some of the public data network standards from the CCITT are applicable, what they mean in simple terms, and a block diagram of the interface specified by that standard. The basis for these standards are

1. Connections are not limited to certain vendors.
2. Interfaces will be provided for both the circuit-switched and packet-switched networks.
3. The definitions will meet the appropriate national and international standards.

*X.3.* A packet assembler/disassembler (PAD) device that resides in the network and looks like a DCE to an Asynchronous DTE. Within X.3 there is a list of operating parameters for each Asynchronous Interactive DTE.

*X.25.* This is a specification for a packet-mode DTE interfacing with a packet-switched network DCE.

**FIGURE 5–3**
Packet Interfaces

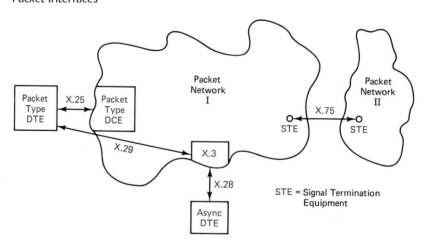

**X.28.** This specifies specific terminal functions of an asynchronous device that is connected to an X.3 PAD when connected in an X.25 packet network.

**X.29.** These are specific X.3 PAD options selected for virtual circuit management and provided by an X.25 packet-mode DTE; in other words, a special interface for the packet-mode DTE to interface with an X.3 PAD.

**X.75.** This is an expanded X.25 for internetwork communications between different packet-switching networks and includes the international call establishment procedures.

**X.121.** This is nothing more than an international numbering scheme for identifying the various networks in a multinetwork communication environment.

The CCITT has also established a series of specification numbers to describe those areas where specifications are being established for ISDN. They are

**I.100.** General ISDN concept that includes the structure of records, terminology, and general methods

**I.200.** Service features

**I.300.** Network features

    **I.310.** Architectural considerations

        Lower-layer capabilities at 64 KBPS and higher for both circuit-switched and nonswitched circuits, packet-switching capabilities, and common channel signaling capabilities

        Higher-layer capabilities

**I.400.** Network/user interface features

**I.500.** Internetwork interfaces

**I.600.** Maintenance requirements

There is a basic set of equivalent specifications for communications interfaces between the EIA and CCITT specifications. The most common ones are as follows:

| EIA | CCITT |
| --- | --- |
| RS232 | V.24/V.28 |
| RS449 | V.24/V.10/V.11 |
| RS422 | V.11/X.27 |
| RS423 | V.10/X.26 |

Another equivalent set of standards is RS449 and MilSTD 188C/114. In all likelihood this set will be upgraded to incorporate the new EIA530 specification that is making RS449 obsolete.

Finally, picked out of context, there is ANSI X.12, an American National

Standards Institute specification for Electronic Data Interchange (EDI), used for business documents such as purchase orders, invoices, bills, insurance claims, and tax returns. It will be used in networks that incorporate EDI services. ANSI X.12 was developed to fill the need of almost every organization today for a proprietary format for the internal forms they have. In order to move the information electronically, a standard set of interfaces is required. EDI will no doubt be one of the hot data communications topics in the 1990s.

Although there is a multitude of additional definitions included in each one of the standards described, the definitions given should at least give you a way to begin to relate the terms to each other.

## F
## DATA ACCESS ARRANGEMENTS

An older interface still used with non-FCC registered DTEs, the data access arrangement, DAA, connects all devices that are not certified for direct connection to the DDD network. The DAA was required to prevent any harm that might result from nonstandard interfaces connecting to the telephone network. There are three types of DAAs—a manual type, a voltage type, and a contact type. An example is shown in Fig. 5–4 along with definitions of the individual signals. The CDT is a manual coupler, which must have a telephone set provided. All telephone calls are manually made and answered, and then the data key is actuated for data transmission. In the meantime, the CBS and CBT are both automatic couplers, which make the telephone set optional. The interface leads are voltage type in the CBS unit and contact closure type in the CBT unit, and the power supply may be supplied by the user or the telephone company in the case of the CBT. Since these devices are no longer necessary with certified units and will be phased out over time, a further detailed analysis of their operation is not provided. Telcos no longer provide DAAs, so if you still have a nonregistered device and want to connect it to the telephone line, you must obtain a registered DAA from another vendor to interface between your device and the telephone line. This is shown in Fig. 5–5.

## G
## PBX INTERFACES

Other interface standards are being talked about, with some preliminary announcements being made by the organizations promoting them. One of these is the Computer to PBX Interface (CPI). This is a standardized type of interface developed by Northern Telecom (NTI) and DEC and was initially supported by Rolm, Mitel, and Intecom. It is an interface that is really on the user's side of the PBX for connection with the CPU and was intended to provide the necessary descriptions for what was identified as the T1 channel (1.544 MBPS, a method of

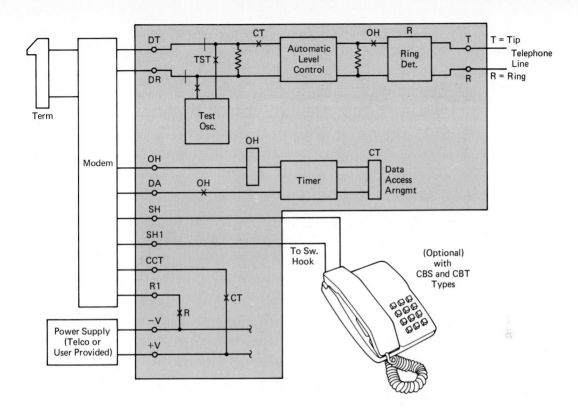

| Manual CDT | Type Voltage CBS | Contact CBT | Direction | Function |
|---|---|---|---|---|
| DT | DT | DT | Both | 600-Ohm Transmission Leads. |
| DR | DR | DR | Both | 600-Ohm Transmission Leads. |
| * | OH | OH | To DAA | Control of "Off Hook" Relay. |
| * | DA | DA | To DAA | To Request Data Cut Through. |
| * | RI | RI | To Modem | Ringing Signal Present. |
| * | SG | * | Both | Signal Ground (CBS only). |
| * | CCT | CCT | To Modem | DAA Data Path Cut Through. |
| * | SH | SH | To Modem | Status of Hook Switch. |
| * | * | SH1 | To Modem | SH Return (CBT only). |
| * | * | +V | To DAA | Positive DC Power (CBT only). |
| * | * | −V | Both | Return for DC Power and common for all contacts except SH, SH1 in CBT. |

**FIGURE 5-4**
Data Access Arrangement Configurations

multiplexing digitized voice-grade channels). CPI identified 24 64-KBPS channels with signaling for definition of those channels contained within the individual data band itself. That signaling uses the least significant bit in each byte to carry the signal information, which in turn reduces the usable byte size in that band to 7 bits and limits the channel speed to 56 KBPS effectively. This limits the data

G. PBX INTERFACES

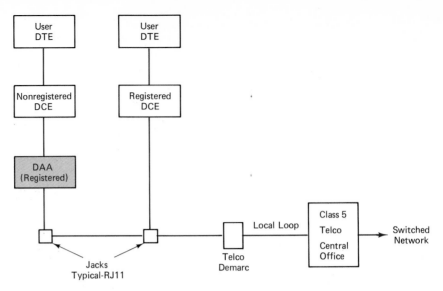

**FIGURE 5–5**
Data Access Arrangement (DAA) Connection

capacity of the channel, so in 1987 NTI announced that CPI would be upgraded to full 64-KBPS capacity in 23 channels and signal in the twenty-fourth channel. This would also be ISDN compatible.

On the other hand, there is the AT&T definition for this same interface, which is Digital Multiplexed Interface (DMI). This was developed in conjunction with Hewlett-Packard and Wang Laboratories. DMI consists of the same 1.544 MBPS and already divides that bandwidth into 23 separate channels of 64 KBPS and provides a single full band for signaling purposes which is ISDN compatible. This interface allows a full eight bits in a byte and provides for full 64-KBPS digitized voice, which was the initial standard (described in Chapter 16 in more detail). This type of separate channel signaling is compatible with existing common control interface signaling (CCIS), which AT&T has been using for years for circuit establishment in the long-distance network; it is also being considered by the CCITT as an interface standard for one of the channels of the Integrated Services Digital Network (ISDN), which will also be described in Chapter 16.

Both CPI and DMI describe the necessary protocol definitions to support data transport at all the standard transmission rates between the PBX and the user's front-end equipment.

In connection with the DMI interface, AT&T announced in 1984 a method of effectively doubling the T1 circuit capacity for voice digitization by defining a 32-KBPS compressed digitization methodology. It provides for 44 digitized voice channels along with 4 separate signaling channels, all operating at 32 KBPS. Although the technical details may sound very complex, the operational interface is of interest to all users who are thinking of digitizing their voice transmissions.

The interface and service were announced as part of Accunet T1.5, which requires the use of special customer premises equipment (CPE), as well as a matching device at the AT&T *serving* office. This means that the transmission would be transparent to the local class 5 telephone office. In other words, this new capability *rides on top of* existing facilities, so if you have standard AT&T T1 service now, the new service is directly compatible.

Conversely, if you are not using AT&T digital service, and are not using AT&T switches, you may not be compatible with the digital switches of other vendors, since they use a different method of establishing circuits for digital transmission. AT&T has released the algorithm to accomplish the compression so that potential customers or other hardware vendors can build this equipment. The technique uses adaptive differential pulse code modulation (ADPCM), which has also been endorsed by the CCITT. There is no apparent degradation in voice quality but there is an impact to data transmission. Modulated data transmissions above 4800 BPS at present cannot be split. In other words, at 7200 BPS, 9600 BPS, and higher, an entire T1 subchannel of 64 KBPS must be used. It is possible however that in the future additional speeds may be an added feature to the compressed service. Additional descriptions of CPI and DMI are provided in Chapter 14.

## H
## AUTOMATIC CALL UNIT (ACU)

The next major interface in many networks is the automatic call unit (ACU), which is represented by the 801 series of AT&T devices. The interface specification for this unit is EIA (RS)366. The definition of the interface is shown in Table 5–5 and the sequential operation of an ACU with a modem and DTE is shown in Fig. 5-6. The DTE and its interface with the ACU are responsible for four separate functions:

1. Ensure that the DCE is available for operation.
2. Provide the telephone number to be dialed.
3. Decide to abandon the call if unsuccessful.
4. Supervise the call to determine when to abandon the connection. This is usually done by the modem after the call has been established.

To perform the first task, the PWI signal is referenced to determine whether the ACU has power on. The DLO signal is then referenced to determine whether the communications line is currently in use. To initiate control of the communications line, the CRQ (call request) lead must be activated. To do this and to obtain dial tone, the DTE interface checks to determine that the ACU has power on and that there is no one else using the line. If these conditions are met, the DTE turns on the CRQ. At the same time the data terminal ready signal may also be presented at the interface to the modem. The communications line is

**TABLE 5-5**
Automatic Call Unit Interface Bell Series 801

| PIN NO. | CIRCUIT | DIRECTION | DESCRIPTION |
|---|---|---|---|
| 1 | FGD | Both | Frame ground |
| 2 | DPR | To ACU | Digit present |
| 3 | ACR | To Terminal | Abandon call and retry |
| 4 | CRQ | To ACU | Call request |
| 5 | PND | To Terminal | Present next digit |
| 6 | PWI | To Terminal | Power indication |
| 7 | SGD | Both | Signal ground |
| 8 | | | Unassigned |
| 9 | | | Unassigned |
| 10 | | | Unassigned |
| 11 | | | Unassigned |
| 12 | | | Unassigned |
| 13 | DSS | To Terminal | Data set status |
| 14 | NB1 | To ACU | Digit lead |
| 15 | NB2 | To ACU | Digit lead |
| 16 | NB4 | To ACU | Digit lead |
| 17 | NB8 | To ACU | Digit lead |
| 18 | | | Unassigned |
| 19 | | | Unassigned |
| 20 | | | Unassigned |
| 21 | | | Unassigned |
| 22 | DLO | To Terminal | Data line occupied |
| 23 | | | Unassigned |
| 24 | | | Unassigned |
| 25 | | | Unassigned |

now placed in the *off hook* condition by the ACU, and the telephone switching equipment returns a dial tone to the ACU.

Once the dial tone has been recognized, it is time to undertake the second task, which is providing the telephone number to be dialed. The lead called PND is activated from the ACU to the DTE, which, when ON, indicates that the ACU is ready to be told which digits are to be dialed. The digits-to-be-dialed information is presented from the DTE to the ACU over the four leads referred to as NB1, NB2, NB4, and NB8. The transfer of information on the digit leads is provided in parallel. At the same time the strobe signal is provided by the DPR lead. With most ACUs it is permissible for the interface to present the digit information and the DPR simultaneously, but in all cases the DPR must not be provided unless the appropriate information is presented on the digit leads. The ACU next indicates that it has accepted the digit for dialing by negating the PND lead. The digit lead information and the DPR signal must not be changed until this negation occurs.

The ACU then reasserts PND when it has completed dialing the digit. The DTE may then present new information on the digit leads and then reassert DPR to indicate that the new digit should be dialed. The process of presenting digit information proceeds until the last digit has been dialed, at which time the DTE places the EON (End of Number) code on the digit leads. Having dialed the

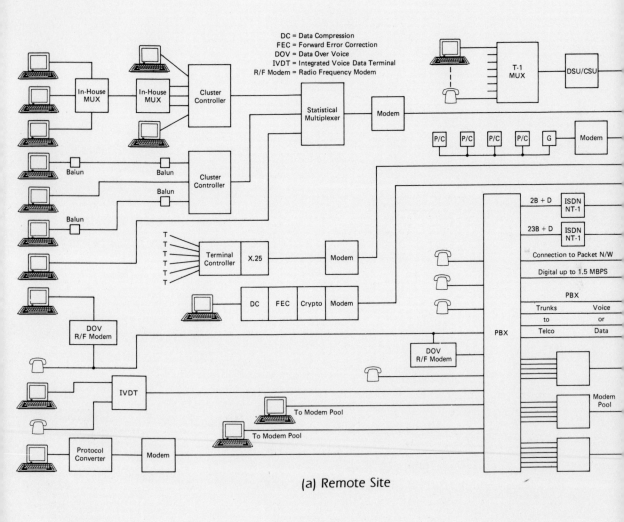

DC = Data Compression
FEC = Forward Error Correction
DOV = Data Over Voice
IVDT = Integrated Voice Data Terminal
R/F Modem = Radio Frequency Modem

(a) Remote Site

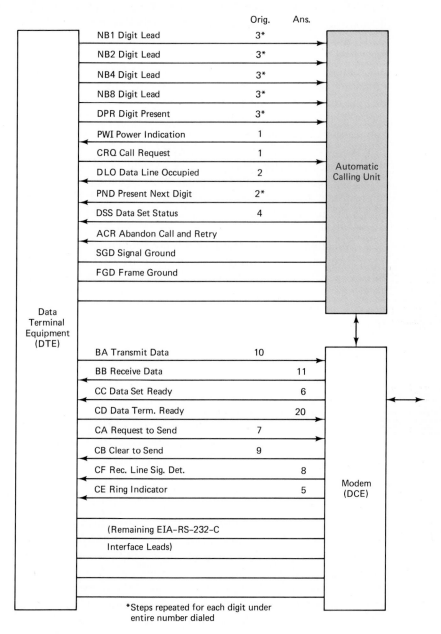

**FIGURE 5-6**
Operation of ACU

number, the ACU and modem are now ready for the third function, which is abandoning the call if unsuccessful.

When the EON code is presented on the digit leads, an *abandon call timer* is initiated. If the call is answered by a data terminal, a tone is received by the ACU, and the abandon call timer is turned off. If the call is not answered or is answered by something or someone other than a data terminal, the timer continues running, and after 10 to 40 seconds (selectable) the ACU initiates signal ACR (abandon call), which directs the DTE to disconnect. The call is disconnected by turning off signal CRQ. If the call is successfully answered by a data terminal, the ACU transfers control of the line to the modem, which continues to hold the connection under the control of the data terminal ready lead, which must be provided by the DTE at the time. The call request lead may then be dropped without disconnecting the call, and the modem interface, in conjunction with the DTE, then controls the data terminal ready signal and disconnects the call when appropriate. Most of these functions are now available in modems used with PCs and the overall cost of automatic calling and answering has been reduced substantially.

A related interface, although it is not standard, must be reviewed in relation to the transmission of information. It is the acoustic coupler, which converts the bits of specific characters to multiple tones that can be transmitted on a communications line. In conjunction with either rotary or tone calling systems, the acoustic coupler can be utilized as an interface to transmit information from a terminal to a central site. The most prevalent use of this type of interface is with portable terminals, which can then be used at any location where such a calling system exists.

## OTHER INTERFACES

Many other interfaces can be examined in detail, but for most that level of examination is not applicable to this text. One, however, is getting a lot of publicity because of its ability to provide access to dial circuits. It is X.21, originally released in 1976. X.21 is an interface for public circuit switching data networks. It provides the automatic calling capability directly between the DTE and a DCE with significantly fewer interchange circuits than other interfaces. For example, Fig. 5–7 shows the standard interface in the top half of the diagram and X.21 in the bottom half of the diagram. An RS366 interface requires a separate 25-pin connection (in addition to the connection to the modem), and itself has a cable to the modem. Once the circuit is established through the automatic calling unit, control for the circuit is handed over to the modem for data transmission. When the call is terminated, control goes back to the automatic calling unit, which can then initiate another call. X.21 provides this interface directly between the DTE and the modem.

The natural question is, Why do I need this complex mechanism when so

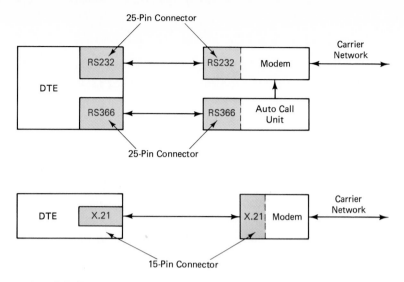

**FIGURE 5-7**
X.21 Interface

many dial-up modems are available in the market today? Almost all of the dial-up modems are designed for establishment of circuits for asynchronous transmission. The Hayes AT command set, the most common in use, allows automatic dialing, *but only for asynchronous transmissions* (described in detail in Chapter 10).

The bottom diagram of Fig. 5–7 shows a 15-pin connection between a DTE and a modem through which both calling and data transfer can occur for full-duplex synchronous transmissions. All of the interchange circuits in X.21 are balanced, that is, they meet the electrical requirements of X.27 and RS422A. The signals can be transferred up to 1000 meters at a rate of 100 KBPS. X.21 describes the actual limit on data transmission as 48 KBPS. Data can be transferred in a full-duplex (simultaneous two-way transmission) mode, so it can also be used for a circuit that is four-wire or leased, but for the most part it is intended to be used on dial circuits.

When a call is made from a terminal, the typical sequence of operations is for the terminal (DTE) to enter the *dial mode*. The number to be called is then entered or accessed by software if it is already stored. When the circuit is established through the modem, at which time the information can be transmitted, the call will be terminated with a disconnect.

Even though this particular interface has been around for quite a while and is standardized, it does use a 15-pin connector. Based on previous experience with the low-speed modems, another standard may very well be established for use with all other modems based on the 25-pin connector utilized for RS232, V.24/V.28, and EIA530. More information on synchronous dial-up is provided in Chapter 10.

1. What is the functional difference between a loop-current interface and RS232?

2. Name the four functional types of circuits in RS232. Into which categories do each of the 24 signals defined in RS232 fit?

3. What are the purposes of the request-to-send and clear-to-send signal sequences?

4. What was the primary purpose for the evolution of RS449? Why is it not used today?

5. What are the three primary areas of interface specifications defined by the CCITT? How do you know which areas the specifications refer to?

6. What does a DAA provide for you?

7. What is the primary difference between DMI and CPI?

8. Describe a typical application in which you would use an ACU.

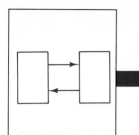

# 6

# Circuit Types
# and Their Uses

## BACKGROUND

When discussing a network and the circuits that comprise it, many definitions come to mind. Because of the different definitions used by the telephone company, vendors, and users, a very limited definition of a network will be used for this text: A network is *the configuration of carrier facilities that is incorporated to connect the different geographic locations of the user's system.* The other definitions that relate to the mode under which information is transmitted, such as packet, multiplex, and satellite, will be described separately under those particular headings. For purposes of this chapter, the method of functionally connecting the geographically separated points will be described.

Prior to describing the types of connections, two definitions must be made as they apply to all the different network configurations. They are *half-duplex* (HDX) and *full-duplex* (FDX). These definitions refer to the physical facilities provided to the user for connecting to a voice-grade line. (Further definitions of HDX and FDX relative to the movement of information will be made in Chapter 9.) The term *half-duplex* referring to a circuit provided by the telephone company consists of a two-wire connection between two or more points. This is shown in Fig. 6–1(a) and 6–1(b). The two-wire connection consists of a signal lead over which the information is transmitted in either direction; the other wire is a refer-

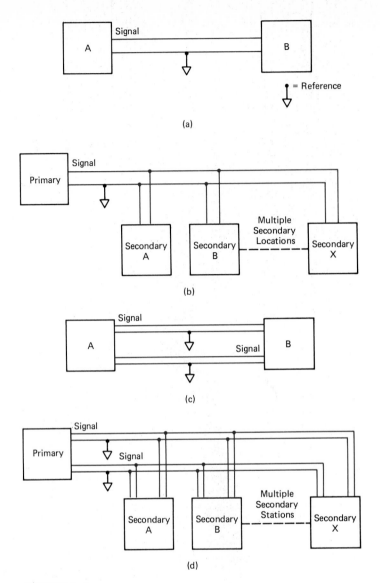

**FIGURE 6–1**
Half-Duplex and Full-Duplex Circuits

ence connection (ground) over which no signals are transmitted. When drawing a network configuration the reference connection ground wire is usually not shown.

A full-duplex connection is a four-wire connection between two or more physical locations. The four wires actually consist of two two-wire pairs and are usually used for transmitting information in one direction on one pair while transmitting information in the other direction on the second pair of wires.

A full-duplex four-wire connection is provided by the carrier on a leased basis only (you could dial two two-wire connections in a backup mode to set up a four-wire circuit). When talking about a half-duplex circuit or a full-duplex circuit, nothing more is implied than a two-wire or a four-wire connection. There is a circuit known as a *simplex* (SPX) circuit, which in reality is a two-wire circuit, but data moves only in one direction. Unless such a circuit is specifically requested and unidirectional amplifiers are installed, an SPX circuit is the same as a half-duplex circuit (two wires). Full-duplex circuits are shown in Fig. 6–1(c) and (d). A simplex circuit would look the same as Fig. 6–1(a).

It should be noted that data flow is not described here because it is not relevant. Data flow can be half-duplex or full-duplex on either a half-duplex or full-duplex circuit (full-duplex data on a half-duplex circuit is like interrupting someone while they are talking to you).

## B
## POINT TO POINT

A point-to-point circuit is the connection of a two- or four-wire circuit between two points and only those two points. A point-to-point connection can be either a dial-up type of connection or a dedicated connection that belongs to the user on a monthly basis. A point-to-point connection is shown in Fig. 6–1(a) and 6–1(c). All dial-up connections are point to point and are also two wire.

## C
## MULTIPOINT/MULTIDROP OR MULTISTATION

A multipoint/multidrop circuit connects three or more points on a common circuit. There are usually a single master site and two or more slave sites connected on such a circuit. An example is shown in Fig. 6–1(b) and 6–1(d). In the past this type of circuit was sometimes called a multistation circuit, but no longer, as multistation referred primarily to Teletype configurations where any Teletype could talk to other Teletypes on that line directly. This is different in a multipoint/multidrop configuration where there is a definite master/slave relationship in that the master is the only site that can talk to the individual slave sites. If a slave site wants to transmit a message to another slave site, it must first go through the master site, where the message will be routed back onto the same circuit to go back to the second slave site. Multipoint circuits must be leased because only under very limited conditions with special equipment can a multipoint circuit be dialed (these cases usually involve dialing multiple locations and patching the individual dialed lines together at a central site for a temporary connection). Additional connections are shown in Fig. 6–2.

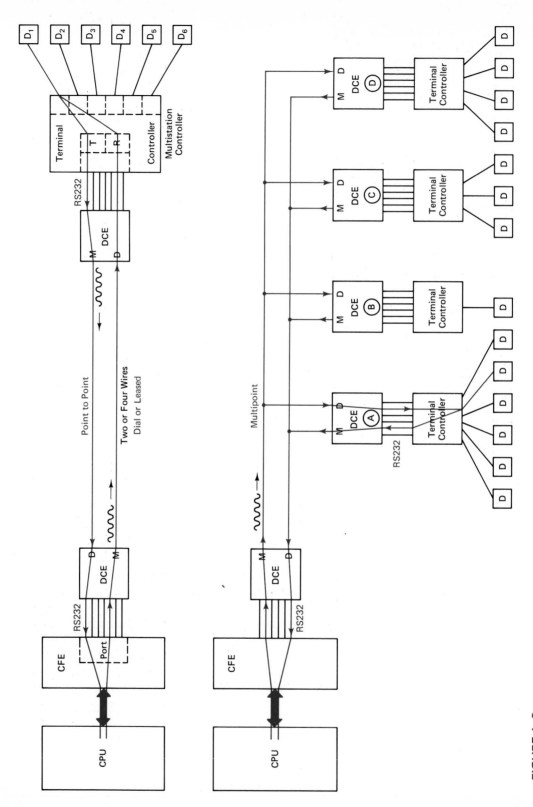

**FIGURE 6–2**
Multistation Controller and Multipoint/Multidrop Configuration

# D

## DIAL NETWORK

The dial network (DDD) consists of all the different carrier facilities over which the standard telephone type of dial connection is made. Either a rotary dial or tone dialing can be implemented to make a direct connection between the end user locations. At both ends there is a circuit known as a *local loop* which connects the user site to the closest telephone company serving office. All the dial connections are routed through the local telephone company serving office regardless of the length or distance of the call. There are five levels of telephone company serving office where the carrier equipment will automatically route the call via the most efficient means for equipment utilization. Thus it is possible for a call from San Francisco to Denver to actually be routed through midwestern or eastern cities if equipment used by the carrier determines that it is the best route to take at that particular time. The user still only pays for the airline mile distance between the two cities but has no control over the route that the switching centers may take to get the call from one location to the other. If problems are encountered on a particular line on the dial network, the call should be terminated and then redialed, as the probability of getting the same physical connection is almost zero. All dial-up calls are point-to-point half-duplex circuits. Also, under very limited conditions with special equipment, two separate half-duplex circuits can be dialed which are then configured in a point-to-point arrangement as if they were a full-duplex circuit. What must be considered here is that if the terminal is going to operate in a half-duplex mode (transmitting only one way at a time) then connecting them with a full-duplex circuit established by two separate calls may be unnecessary.

# E

## DEDICATED

Dedicated lines are also called private lines, leased lines, data lines, or 3002 lines, but all mean the same thing. A dedicated line is obtained from the carrier on a monthly basis for unlimited usage between the individual points to be connected. It can either be point to point or multipoint and cannot be dialed because they are two different types of service (there are some new services such as Software Defined Network from AT&T that allow local dial access to long-distance leased circuits, which are described in Chapter 3). A dedicated line is also the only kind of line that can have conditioning applied to it. Conditioning is described in Chapter 21. As a general rule, if the traffic volume or cost of dial connections is such that a dedicated line is warranted, it pays to get a full-duplex line instead of a half-duplex line. The difference in rates is usually at most about 10 percent, and the capability for utilization of a full-duplex protocol and the elimination of modem turn-around time is then possible (modem turn-around time is described in Chapter 10).

## QUESTIONS

1. How do a half-duplex and a full-duplex circuit differ?
2. Describe the data flow on a typical multidrop line.
3. How does a multistation controller move information from a group of terminals to a host site?
4. What is the primary limitation of a multidrop circuit?
5. What is the difference between a dial line and a leased line?

| |
|---|
| A = 11000001 |
| B = 11000010 |
| 1 = 00110001 |
| 2 = 00110010 |

# 7

# Data Codes

## A
## BACKGROUND

There are many different code sets available today that are used for both data processing and data communications functions. For this particular section of text, we will concentrate on codes that are used for data communications. In effect, this means that we will discuss the various code sets that enable one automated machine to talk to another. Although a message may be destined to go from one human to another human who has to read the final text, the physical function of moving the information from one machine to another will most likely be accomplished by using one of the code sets defined in this chapter.

One definition of information is *any signal or set of signal elements that conveys a particular message or communication, especially one assembled and processed by automatic machines.* A totally predictable message sequence will contain no information since the receiver already knows what is to be transmitted. Therefore, information is a quantitative term that is measured by the degree to which it clarifies an unknown quantity.

In data communications the smallest element of information is the *bit,* a term derived from the contraction of "binary digit." The machines being discussed here are used to store and carry this information in a binary manner. A binary manner means on or off, mark or space, or yes or no.

Some very confusing terms that have evolved in the data communications environment are *bits per second* and *baud*. Although there is a very specific difference between these two terms, the newer modes of communication have blurred the meanings. Originally, baud was defined as the maximum quantity of signal changes that can appear on the line in one second. It can be specified by dividing the time span of the narrowest width signal into one second. These signal changes do not necessarily pertain to information regarding specific characters. They may contain signals that establish the start and stop positions of the characters and therefore do not convey any user information, but the signals are required because they do contain very important machine control information. Thus the amount of user information bits transmitted may be less than the quantity of signal changes that occur on the line per unit time. At the other end of the spectrum, today's modems carry multiple-user information bits with each signal change on the telephone line giving the exactly opposite effect (more bits per signal change).

The baud (rate of signal changes) can also describe each of the bits for information purposes when each signal change identifies one information bit; but for those codes or transmission sequences that require additional overhead bits (start and stop sequences) to define the beginning and the end of characters, the total amount of signals transmitted may not accurately describe the actual amount of user information bits transmitted.

For example, we can use the Baudot code, which is used on all Teletypes up to and including the Model 28. Baudot code (Baudot will be specifically described later in this chapter) has five information bits, one start bit, and a stop bit that is one and one-half bit times as long as either the start or information bits. It is transmitted by teletypewriters at a rate of 10 characters per second. If 10 characters are transmitted every second, there will be a total of 75 bit times transmitted on the communication line. Of these, there will be 50 information bits (5 bits of information for each of the 10 characters), 10 start bits, and an equivalent total of 15 stop bits ($1\frac{1}{2}$ for each character). Therefore, the baud (total amount of signal changes on the line) is 75 (75 baud). On the other hand, the BPS rate, which describes the actual user information, is only 50 BPS. Therefore, a 75-baud transmission using Baudot code is the same as a 50 bit per second transmission.

This particular type of definition was important during the time when low-speed Teletype equipment was being used on loop current type telegraph circuits where the transmission rate of information (BPS) was always less than the baud. When modems began to be used for interface to telephone lines, each signal change represented one bit and the BPS rate included the start and stop bits, so BPS equalled baud. Today, however, with the synchronous multibit modulation schemes described in Chapter 10, you have individual changes of amplitude or frequency or phase (signal changes) identifying more than one information bit. For example, in a multibit (dibit) modulation scheme, there are two bits of information contained in four different phases; each phase change (signal change) that contains two bits of information is really the equivalent of the baud, but the information transfer is actually twice the signal-change rate and therefore twice the baud. The end result of all this is that in today's higher-speed modems (2400 BPS and above), the true BPS information transfer rate is greater than the baud (exactly the opposite of what it was on low-speed Teletype lines).

For these reasons, the BPS rate and baud are being confused even more extensively today and, in turn, the terms are used almost entirely interchangeably. A communication line described as a 2400-baud line is actually a facility that is accommodating 2400 BPS. For the ASCII code, where we have eight information bits (7 information and 1 parity), a 2400 baud/BPS communication transmission rate will support 300 characters per second (8 bits per character) synchronously or 240 characters per second (10 bits per character) asynchronously.

The final result of all these definitions is that, even though there is a semantic and technical difference between the terms *baud* and *bits per second,* they are still used interchangeably today. It is therefore up to the user to determine what the mode of transmission (synchronous or asynchronous) will be, and from that, to determine what the useful amount of information to be transmitted will be. Interchangeability of terms should definitely not be promoted, but in this case, where such interchange already exists, the use may be tolerated as long as the users of the terms are aware of the difference and know exactly what the other is saying.

## B
## CODE SETS AND PURPOSE: BAUDOT, BCD, EBCDIC, ASCII, AND OTHERS

The first true code that was used in electronic data communications was *Morse code.* Samuel Morse developed the code that bears his name when he invented the telegraph system. This code is based on what are known as *dots* and *dashes.* A dot is a single short bit, while a dash is a single long bit. For those instances where short and long cannot be identified, a dot is a single entity while the dash is two quick dots. So a dot followed by some time frame is still a dot, while two quick dots indicate a dash.

Even during the time when Morse was developing his code, he was interested in the efficiency of information transmission. He reasoned that the most often used characters in the English alphabet, if represented by the least amount of dots and dashes, would decrease the total amount of time it took to transmit a particular message. He therefore went to a friend who owned a printing shop (at that time all printing was set a character at a time) and borrowed the type box where all the individual characters were stored. He counted the characters in each of the type box slots, and those where the most characters of a particular letter were stored were chosen to use the least amount of dots and dashes. As we all know, E is the most commonly used letter in the English alphabet and it is therefore represented by a dot, T a dash, and so on. The entire code is represented in Fig. 7–1.

Morse code lasted as the primary communication code for many years, until

Morse Code

| | | | | | |
|---|---|---|---|---|---|
| A | • – | N | – • | 1 | • – – – – |
| B | – • • • | O | – – – | 2 | • • – – – |
| C | – • – • | P | • – – • | 3 | • • • – – |
| D | – • • | Q | – – • – | 4 | • • • • – |
| E | • | R | • – • | 5 | • • • • • |
| F | • • – • | S | • • • | 6 | – • • • • |
| G | – – • | T | – | 7 | – – • • • |
| H | • • • • | U | • • – | 8 | – – – • • |
| I | • • | V | • • • – | 9 | – – – – • |
| J | • – – – | W | • – – | 0 | – – – – – |
| K | – • – | X | – • • – | . | • – • – • – |
| L | • – • • | Y | – • – – | , | – – • • – – |
| M | – – | Z | – – • • | ? | • • – – • • |

Baudot Code

| Character Case Lower | Character Case Upper | Bit Pattern 5 4 3 2 1 | Character Case Lower | Character Case Upper | Bit Pattern 5 4 3 2 1 |
|---|---|---|---|---|---|
| A | – | 0 0 0 1 1 | Q | 1 | 1 0 1 1 1 |
| B | ? | 1 1 0 0 1 | R | 4 | 0 1 0 1 0 |
| C | : | 0 1 1 1 0 | S | ' | 0 0 1 0 1 |
| D | $ | 0 1 0 0 1 | T | 5 | 1 0 0 0 0 |
| E | 3 | 0 0 0 0 1 | U | 7 | 0 0 1 1 1 |
| F | ! | 0 1 1 0 1 | V | ; | 1 1 1 1 0 |
| G | & | 1 1 0 1 0 | W | 2 | 1 0 0 1 1 |
| H | # | 1 0 1 0 0 | X | / | 1 1 1 0 1 |
| I | 8 | 0 0 1 1 0 | Y | 6 | 1 0 1 0 1 |
| J | Bell | 0 1 0 1 1 | Z | " | 1 0 0 0 1 |
| K | ( | 0 1 1 1 1 | Letters (Shift)↓ | | 1 1 1 1 1 |
| L | ) | 1 0 0 1 0 | Figures (Shift)↑ | | 1 1 0 1 1 |
| M | . | 1 1 1 0 0 | Space (SP) = | | 0 0 1 0 0 |
| N | , | 0 1 1 0 0 | Carriage Return < | | 0 1 0 0 0 |
| O | 9 | 1 1 0 0 0 | Line Feed ≡ | | 0 0 0 1 0 |
| P | 0 | 1 0 1 1 0 | Blank | | 0 0 0 0 0 |

1 = Mark = Punch Hole
0 = Space = No Punch Hole

**FIGURE 7–1**
Code Sets: Morse and Baudot (International Telegraph Alphabet—ITA #2)

Emile Baudot developed the Baudot distributor. This unit provides for the transmission of five consecutive units of information (bits) representing a character of information to be transmitted on a line between two electromechanical devices. A receiving station identifies the five bits of information, which were generated electrically at the transmitting station, because the receiving device has an identical distributor with a rotor rotating at the same speed (see Chapter 2). Because the rotors at both ends start rotating at the same time and speed, they are in the same relative position in each device. If the distributors are segmented and the segments electrically isolated from each other, signals can be sent from segments on the transmit end to correlating segments on the receive end. If a signal exists on the line, the bit is a 1 while if there is no signal on the line, the bit is a 0. This particular distributor is capable of transmitting asynchronous characters 10 times a second and is what the basic Teletype transmission rates evolved from. Baudot code, which is really International Telegraph Alphabet (ITA) #2, is also shown in Fig. 7–1 and is still in heavy use throughout the world. As an inherent part of its design, Baudot code uses five information bits per character (32 combinations). There is no method of error detection, so the reader of the information must determine if a possible transmission error exists. If there is an error, the human at the receive end can request the human at the transmit end to retransmit the message. For that reason, Baudot code has a major drawback to its use in a totally automated environment, where machines must use the information without human intervention.

There is another inherent problem in that the code is *sequential*. Sequential means that a particular control character defines the subsequent series of characters for a period of time until a new special control character is recognized. The two control characters that identify the bit configurations in Baudot code are *letters* (LTRS), which is represented by an arrow pointing down, and *figures* (FIGS), which is represented by an arrow pointing up. These two characters do the same thing that the shift lock on a typewriter does. The lowercase or LTRS shift means that all characters after it are alpha characters, as shown by the lowercase under the Baudot description, and when a FIGS character is recognized it means that all succeeding characters are in the uppercase mode, which are all the numerics and the special characters as shown in the code description. For Teletypes, where the means of storage is paper tape with holes punched in it, if a particular FIGS or LTRS character were missing, an entire portion of a paper tape message would have to be physically cut out, repunched correctly and then reinserted, or repunched entirely. This obviously requires great time and effort, so in actuality all the characters in error are usually repunched so that they are eliminated (all LTRS characters). The result of all this is that the entire sequence of transmitting Baudot code via punched paper tape is a slow and tedious process.

As technology evolved and machines had to start communicating with other machines without humans involved, better and more efficient codes had to be developed for transmitting information so that the machines themselves could recognize the information and automatically request a retransmission when necessary in the event of an error. This led to the development of many other codes, which were usually designed with specific hardware devices in mind. They are described in the remainder of this chapter.

In parallel with the development of data communication codes, when data processing first evolved data processing machines used their own codes. One of the first codes used was the *binary coded decimal,* which is shown in Fig. 7–2. Binary coded decimal (BCD) was used to perform calculations internally within a data processing device. As can be seen, there are no alpha characters, so this code is not usable as a communications code and cannot be used for anything but storing of numeric information.

As soon as data processing required communication with humans, and therefore printed characters from some type of printing device, the *binary coded*

Binary Coded Decimal

| Numeric (Decimal) | Binary Equivalent | BCD Code | | |
|---|---|---|---|---|
| 0 | 0 | | | 1010 |
| 1 | 1 | | | 0001 |
| 2 | 10 | | | 0010 |
| 3 | 11 | | | 0011 |
| 4 | 100 | | | 0100 |
| 5 | 101 | | | 0101 |
| 6 | 110 | | | 0110 |
| 7 | 111 | | | 0111 |
| 8 | 1000 | | | 1000 |
| 9 | 1001 | | | 1001 |
| 10 | 1010 | | 0001 | 1010 |
| 11 | 1011 | | 0001 | 0001 |
| 12 | 1100 | | 0001 | 0010 |
| 13 | 1101 | | 0001 | 0011 |
| 14 | 1110 | | 0001 | 0100 |
| 15 | 1111 | | 0001 | 0101 |
| 16 | 10000 | | 0001 | 0110 |
| 20 | 10100 | | 0010 | 1010 |
| 63 | 111111 | | 0110 | 0011 |
| 64 | 1000000 | | 0110 | 0100 |
| 255 | 11111111 | 0010 | 0101 | 0101 |
| 256 | 100000000 | 0010 | 0101 | 0110 |

Binary Coded Decimal Interchange Code

| | | | 3 | 0 | 0 | 0 | 0 | 1 | 1 | 1 | 1 |
|---|---|---|---|---|---|---|---|---|---|---|---|
| Bits | | | 2 | 0 | 0 | 1 | 1 | 0 | 0 | 1 | 1 |
| | | | 1 | 0 | 1 | 0 | 1 | 0 | 1 | 0 | 1 |
| 6 | 5 | 4 | | | | | | | | | |
| 0 | 0 | 0 | | SP | 1 | 2 | 3 | 4 | 5 | 6 | 7 |
| 0 | 0 | 1 | | 8 | 9 | 0 | #/= | @/, | : | > | √ |
| 0 | 1 | 0 | | SP | / | S | T | U | V | W | X |
| 0 | 1 | 1 | | Y | Z | = | , | %/( | γ | \ | ⧺ |
| 1 | 0 | 0 | | – | J | K | L | M | N | O | P |
| 1 | 0 | 1 | | Q | R | ! | $ | * | ] | ; | |
| 1 | 1 | 0 | | & + | A | B | C | D | E | F | G |
| 1 | 1 | 1 | | H | I | ? | ¤/) | [ | < | ‡ | |

Commercial Usage ——
Scientific Usage ——

Example:
Bits:  6 5 4 3 2 1
1 1 0 0 0 1 = letter "A"
0 0 0 0 1 0 = number "2"

FIGURE 7-2
Code Sets: BCD and BCDIC

*decimal interchange code* (BCDIC) was developed, also shown in Fig. 7–2. This code can be used for complete communication between a human and a machine, but it is not good for machine-to-machine communications purposes because there is no error detection capability. Therefore, it suffers from one of the same drawbacks that Baudot did, in that a machine could not recognize an error that had occurred during transmission.

The parity problem was corrected by using the *extended binary coded decimal* (Extended BCD) code, which was also called the *paper tape transmission code* (PTTC). This code was first developed for the IBM Selectric typewriter, which could be used to create information in a hard copy and, at the same time, generate a code for transmission over a communication line. This code had six bits for information and a parity bit, which enables a transmission device to determine whether an error has occurred within a particular character. As can be seen, however, PTTC is a sequential code because a shift character is required to differentiate between upper- and lowercase characters. Therefore, even though the communications error detection part of the code was now acceptable, the fact that upper- and lowercase were required made efficient utilization of this code less than optimum. Extended BCD is shown in Fig. 7–3.

The next code that was used extensively was *extended binary coded decimal interchange code* (EBCDIC). EBCDIC has the capability of accommodating 256 combinations because it is an 8-bit code. The standard definition for EBCDIC is shown in Fig. 7–4. A seeming step backward was taken from a communications viewpoint, because even though more bits are available to be used for character representation, there are no bits set aside for parity detection. To overcome this absence of parity, IBM, its primary user, established a method of error detection called block check character or checksum (described in Chapter 13). The user should be aware, however, that with all the bit configurations not defined, two different users can select different definitions, which means incompatible devices.

The next level of code to be developed was the *American National Standard Code for Information Interchange,* which is also called ANSCII or ASCII. This code was first developed in 1963 without lowercase. It was changed in 1967 to include 52 letters (upper- and lowercase), 10 numerics, 33 control codes, and 33 symbols. It conforms to the American National Standards Institute (ANSI) X3.4 standard, which was issued in 1977.

ASCII code, which is a 7-bit code plus 1 bit for parity, giving 8 bits, is shown in Fig. 7–5, where the 7 bits for information are described completely. The eighth bit, which is a parity bit, could be either odd or even depending on what the user desires, and could even be ignored entirely. ASCII is now the most extensively used communications code in the United States and has become a government standard. Even the military establishment, which for years generated codes of its own that were more efficient for its particular applications, has now adopted ASCII as its standard.

Something of the same problem exists for ASCII utilization, however, as does for EBCDIC, where codes were redefined for control purposes. Not all the control codes or special characters defined in ASCII are used by all users who, for their own applications, needed other functions to be redefined (technically

(Paper Tape Transmission Code)

|       | 6 | 0 | 0 | 0 | 0 | 1 | 1 | 1 | 1 |
|-------|---|---|---|---|---|---|---|---|---|
| Bits  | 5 | 0 | 0 | 1 | 1 | 0 | 0 | 1 | 1 |
|       | 4 | 0 | 1 | 0 | 1 | 0 | 1 | 0 | 1 |

| 3 2 1 | 000 | 001 | 010 | 011 | 100 | 101 | 110 | 111 |
|-------|-----|-----|-----|-----|-----|-----|-----|-----|
| 0 0 0 | SP / SP | : / 4 | / 2 | ' / 6 | = / 1 | % / 5 | ; / 3 | / 7 |
| 0 0 1 | − / − | M / m | K / k | O / o | J / j | N / n | L / l | P / p |
| 0 1 0 | ¢ / @ | U / u | S / s | W / w | ? / / | V / v | T / t | X / x |
| 0 1 1 | + / & | D / d | B / b | F / f | A / a | E / e | C / c | G / g |
| 1 0 0 | * / 8 | PN / PN | ) / 0 | UC / UC | ( / 9 | RS / RS | '' / # | EOT / EOT |
| 1 0 1 | Q / q | RES / RES | | BS / BS | R / r | NL / NL | ! / $ | IL / IL |
| 1 1 0 | Y / y | BY / BY | EOB / EOB | | Z / z | LF / LF | | / , | PRE / PRE |
| 1 1 1 | H / h | PF / PF | | LC / LC | I / i | HT / HT | ⌐ / . | DLE / DLE |

Upper Case ——→  
Lower Case ——→

Example:

| Bits: | P | 6 | 5 | 4 | 3 | 2 | 1 |            |
|-------|---|---|---|---|---|---|---|------------|
|       | 0 | 1 | 0 | 0 | 0 | 1 | 1 | = letter "A" |
|       | 1 | 1 | 0 | 0 | 1 | 0 | 0 | = number "9" |

(Odd parity)

Nonprinting Characters

| | |
|---|---|
| SP  = Space | LF  = Line Feed |
| PN  = Punch On | HT  = Horizontal Tab |
| RES = Restore | EOT = End of Transmission |
| BY  = Bypass | EOB = End of Block |
| PF  = Punch Off | UC  = Upper Case |
| BS  = Backspace | LC  = Lower Case |
| P   = Parity Bit | IL  = Idle |
| RS  = Reader Stop | PRE = Prefix |
| NL  = New Line | DLE = Delete |

**FIGURE 7–3**
Code Sets: Extended BCD

then, this is no longer ASCII but the user community still refers to it as ASCII). In those cases they redefined the standard ASCII definitions for their own purposes. This in turn means that two or more users who developed a modified ASCII code independently and try to talk to each other may have characters that are undefined or defined differently. Of all the problems encountered with the utilization of ASCII code, this is by far the most prevalent. When implementing a particular communication system (unless there are special requirements), the use of ASCII code is recommended in the format that exists in Fig. 7–5. If changes are necessary, they must be uniform throughout the environment where

| Bits | | | 4 | 0 | 0 | 0 | 0 | 0 | 0 | 0 | 0 | 1 | 1 | 1 | 1 | 1 | 1 | 1 | 1 |
|---|---|---|---|---|---|---|---|---|---|---|---|---|---|---|---|---|---|---|---|
| | | | 3 | 0 | 0 | 0 | 0 | 1 | 1 | 1 | 1 | 0 | 0 | 0 | 0 | 1 | 1 | 1 | 1 |
| | | | 2 | 0 | 0 | 1 | 1 | 0 | 0 | 1 | 1 | 0 | 0 | 1 | 1 | 0 | 0 | 1 | 1 |
| | | | 1 | 0 | 1 | 0 | 1 | 0 | 1 | 0 | 1 | 0 | 1 | 0 | 1 | 0 | 1 | 0 | 1 |
| 8 | 7 | 6 | 5 | | | | | | | | | | | | | | | | |
| 0 | 0 | 0 | 0 | NUL | SOH | STX | ETX | PF | HT | LC | DEL | | | SMM | VT | FF | CR | SO | SI |
| 0 | 0 | 0 | 1 | DLE | DC1 | DC2 | DC3 | RES | NL | BS | IL | CAN | EM | CC | | IFS | IGS | IRS | IUS |
| 0 | 0 | 1 | 0 | DS | SOS | FS | | BYP | LF | EOB | PRE | | | SM | | | ENQ | ACK | BEL |
| 0 | 0 | 1 | 1 | | | SYN | | PN | RS | UC | EOT | | | | | DC4 | NAK | | SUB |
| 0 | 1 | 0 | 0 | SP | | | | | | | | | | ¢ | . | < | ( | + | \| |
| 0 | 1 | 0 | 1 | & | | | | | | | | | | ! | $ | * | ) | ; | ¬ |
| 0 | 1 | 1 | 0 | − | / | | | | | | | | | | , | % | − | > | ? |
| 0 | 1 | 1 | 1 | | | | | | | | | | | : | # | @ | ' | = | '' |
| 1 | 0 | 0 | 0 | | a | b | c | d | e | f | g | h | i | | | | | | |
| 1 | 0 | 0 | 1 | | j | k | l | m | n | o | p | q | r | | | | | | |
| 1 | 0 | 1 | 0 | | | s | t | u | v | w | x | y | z | | | | | | |
| 1 | 0 | 1 | 1 | | | | | | | | | | | | | | | | |
| 1 | 1 | 0 | 0 | | A | B | C | D | E | F | G | H | I | | | | | | |
| 1 | 1 | 0 | 1 | | J | K | L | M | N | O | P | Q | R | | | | | | |
| 1 | 1 | 1 | 0 | | | S | T | U | V | W | X | Y | Z | | | | | | |
| 1 | 1 | 1 | 1 | 0 | 1 | 2 | 3 | 4 | 5 | 6 | 7 | 8 | 9 | | | | | | ¤ |

PF  – Punch Off  
HT  – Horizontal Tab  
LC  – Lower Case  
DEL – Delete  
SP  – Space  
UC  – Upper Case  

RES – Restore  
NL  – New Line  
BS  – Backspace  
IL  – Idle  
PN  – Punch On  
EOT – End of Transmission  

BYP  – Bypass  
LF   – Line Feed  
EOB  – End of Block  
PRE  – Prefix (ESC)  
RS   – Reader Stop  
SM   – Start Message  
Others – Same as ASCII  

**FIGURE 7–4**
Code Sets: EBCDIC

the code will be utilized. One final point to mention is that many terminal vendors today are using ASCII code for the creation of individual characters from the keyboard; but instead of using the eighth bit for a parity bit, they are using it to define another 128 combinations of bits (characters) to be used in the local environment, such as in generating special format controls, peripheral accesses, and local data processing. If one of these terminals is used, the user should be aware of the potential ramifications if the same terminal is to be used in a communications environment also. 8-bit use is sometimes called *extended ASCII*.

# C
# CONTROL CODES

To use a code set efficiently in a data communications environment, the user must be able to transmit not only the alphanumeric type of information, but also the necessary controls to identify to the receiver what is to be printed, how it is to be printed, and what to do in the event special actions are to be taken. To control the transmission of information, a series of characters must identify the

American
National Standard Code
for
Information Interchange

| Bits | | | | 7 | 0 | 0 | 0 | 0 | 1 | 1 | 1 | 1 |
|---|---|---|---|---|---|---|---|---|---|---|---|---|
| | | | | 6 | 0 | 0 | 1 | 1 | 0 | 0 | 1 | 1 |
| 4 | 3 | 2 | 1 | 5 | 0 | 1 | 0 | 1 | 0 | 1 | 0 | 1 |
| 0 | 0 | 0 | 0 | | NUL | DLE | SP | 0 | @ | P | \ | p |
| 0 | 0 | 0 | 1 | | SOH | DC1 | ! | 1 | A | Q | a | q |
| 0 | 0 | 1 | 0 | | STX | DC2 | " | 2 | B | R | b | r |
| 0 | 0 | 1 | 1 | | ETX | DC3 | # | 3 | C | S | c | s |
| 0 | 1 | 0 | 0 | | EOT | DC4 | $ | 4 | D | T | d | t |
| 0 | 1 | 0 | 1 | | ENQ | NAK | % | 5 | E | U | e | u |
| 0 | 1 | 1 | 0 | | ACK | SYN | & | 6 | F | V | f | v |
| 0 | 1 | 1 | 1 | | BEL | ETB | ' | 7 | G | W | g | w |
| 1 | 0 | 0 | 0 | | BS | CAN | ( | 8 | H | X | h | x |
| 1 | 0 | 0 | 1 | | HT | EM | ) | 9 | I | Y | i | y |
| 1 | 0 | 1 | 0 | | LF | SUB | * | : | J | Z | j | z |
| 1 | 0 | 1 | 1 | | VT | ESC | + | ; | K | [ | k | { |
| 1 | 1 | 0 | 0 | | FF | FS | , | < | L | \ | l | ¦ |
| 1 | 1 | 0 | 1 | | CR | GS | – | = | M | ] | m | } |
| 1 | 1 | 1 | 0 | | SO | RS | . | > | N | ∧ | n | ~ |
| 1 | 1 | 1 | 1 | | SI | US | / | ? | O | – | o | DEL |

Example:

Bits:  P*7 6 5 4 3 2 1

1 1 0 0 0 0 0 1 = letter "A" (Odd Parity)
0 0 1 1 1 0 0 0 = number "8" (Odd Parity)

P* = Parity Bit

**FIGURE 7–5**
Code Sets: ASCII

different portions of the message and what to do with the text from a recognition point of view. The characters that perform this function are called *control characters* or *control codes* and are shown in Fig. 7–6 for ASCII. As can be seen, there are 27 different controls, with a specific function defined for each. Within these controls there are different functions to which the controls relate. There are first the controls used in transmission of individual characters, and these are identified by the letter A. These characters are usually sent on an individual basis and have to do with bits being transmitted on the line that do not affect the information content.

The second type of control character (labeled B) defines the various parts of a message being transmitted. The individual segments of a message, as well as

## ANSCII CODE SET ABBREVIATIONS

| | |
|---|---|
| A — NUL (Null) | The all zeros character, used for time or media fill. |
| A — SYN (Synchronous Idle) | Used for character synchronization in synchronous transmissions. |
| A — DEL (Delete) | Used to erase in paper tape punching. |
| B — SOH (Start of Header) | Used at the beginning of routing information. |
| B — STX (Start of Text) | Used at the end of header or start of text. |
| B — ETX (End of Text) | Used at end of text or start of trailer. |
| B — EOT (End of Transmission) | Used at end of transmission, i.e., end of call. |
| B — SO (Shift Out) | Code characters that follow are not in the code set of the standard code in use. (Predefined as to which code you shift to.) Typically used to define graphics character extensions. |
| B — SI (Shift In) | Code characters that follow are in the code set of the standard code in use. (94 characters in ASCII.) |
| B — DLE (Data Link Escape) | Used to change the meaning of a limited number of contiguously following characters. Use of DLE for additional controls is described in ANSI specification X3.28. |
| B — ETB (End of Transmission Block) | Used to indicate end of a block of data. |
| B — CAN (Cancel) | Disregard the data sent with. |
| B — EM (End of Medium) | End of wanted information recorded on a medium. |
| B — SS (Start of Special Sequence) | As named. |
| B — ESC (Escape) | Provides for an alternate set of control characters or a different code set. This is described in ANSI specification X3.64. |
| B — FS, GS, RS, US | (File, Group, Record, Unit Separators) |
| C — ENQ (Enquire) | Used as a request for response; "who are you." |
| C — ACK (Acknowledge) | Used as an affirmative response to a sender. |
| C — BEL (Bell) | Used to call for human attention. |
| C — DC1, DC2, DC3, DC4 | (Device Controls) Characters for the control of auxiliary devices; i.e., start, pause, stop. DC1 = Xon and DC3 = Xoff. |
| C — NAK (Negative Acknowledge) | Used as a negative response to a sender. |

**FIGURE 7–6**
*Control Codes*

the controls for going to different codes in the middle of a message transmission and the blocking of information within the message, are all defined within this particular segment of control characters. The third set (labeled C) involves the controls on the line that identify whether a particular terminal is to transmit and whether a message was received correctly. Many terminal vendors today use these particular single character codes for controls in a different mode from that just described here as a standard, and when these codes are used they should be analyzed in detail to determine their specific function and how it relates to the user's

C. CONTROL CODES

133

operation of the machine. It should also be recognized that many of the control characters, such as those listed as "separators," are redefined by users when not required and, in turn, may mean something totally different. This is one of the primary areas where users of ASCII code may be incompatible with each other, because codes defined for special purposes may be defined differently at the different locations.

When discussing the control codes in ASCII, one must also consider the codes that are used for *flow control*. Flow control characters are used within the data stream (in band) itself to tell different devices whether they should turn on or off, start transmitting or stop transmitting. These codes are normally used for serial on-line printing when the print speed is lower than the transmission speed. Using flow control, the transmitter can be turned off temporarily until the printer gets caught up. With parallel printers, a separate control line can be set *busy*, so they are controlled in a different way. Parallel printers do have a limitation of cable distance because of the *race conditions* (receipt of simultaneously generated signals at different times) of the signals at the parallel interface.

The primary flow control modes are Xon/Xoff. For most vendors they correspond in ASCII to DC1/DC3. When Xon is provided to a device, it is allowed to transmit, and when Xoff is sent to that device, it is supposed to stop transmitting. Some vendor products are designed such that an Xon will turn them on, but an Xoff will not turn them off until they have finished sending the block that they are in the process of transmitting. If you are using Xon/Xoff, make sure that Xoff will be treated in all cases as a true turnoff signal. (See Chapter 9 for additional flow control protocols.)

There also seems to be some confusion in the method of generating the various ASCII control characters. In general, the operator depresses the *control key* simultaneously with another key to generate the particular control character. If you look at Fig. 7-5 under the column headed by the @ sign and at alphas below it, you will see that they correspond to the first column of control characters if depressed with the control key. For example, Control A = SOH, Control B = STX, Control C = ETX, and so on. In turn, the next column of alphas corresponds to the control characters in the second control character column. For example, Control P = DLE, Control Q = DC1, Control R = DC2, Control S = DC3, and so on. Again, since all vendors do not follow the same ground rules, be sure that your vendor does; if the vendor does not, generate the control characters the way the vendor specifies for its terminal.

**D**

## FORMAT EFFECTORS

Along with the control codes shown in Fig. 7-6, there is another set of codes called *format effectors*. These are contained within a particular message and pertain to the control of the printing device that will be printing out the message. The format effectors consist of those characters defined in Fig. 7-7. As shown,

| | | |
|---|---|---|
| BS | (Backspace) | Moves a printing device back one space on the same line. |
| HT | (Horizontal Tab) | Moves a printing device to the next predetermined position along a line. |
| LF | (Line Feed) | Moves a printing device to the next printing line. |
| VT | (Vertical Tab) | Moves a printing device to the next predetermined printing line. |
| FF | (Form Feed) | Moves the paper to the next page. |
| CR | (Carriage Return) | Moves the printing device to the left margin. |
| SP | (Space) | A format effector, used to separate words. |

**FIGURE 7–7**
Format Effectors

these particular control codes permit control of a printing device for the printout of forms using tabs or form feeds, so that the total transmission does not require extra characters transmitted as blanks, or no characters, when particular formats such as columnar printing are required.

It should be noted here, however, that for the Baudot Teletype mode of operation there are times when particular sequences of control characters have different functions. For example, a message may be started by using the sequence carriage return/carriage return/line feed, CR/CR/LF. Some users who still have Baudot Teletypes will use ZCZC for end-of-message, while others may use NNNN. The receiving hardware will recognize the special sequence as being the end of the message and will then start looking for a new start-of-message sequence.

Users in the ASCII environment may also have to consider the use of alternate characters as meaningful controls for interface purposes but if another unused control character cannot be redefined to specify the newly required function an incompatibility may exist between communicating devices.

## QUESTIONS

1. Why is a data code required?
2. What are the two major drawbacks to the use of Baudot as a communications code?
3. What problem does a user face when establishing a connection between two locations for the first time even when those locations use the same basic code?
4. Why are control codes necessary in a code set?
5. What are the two most common codes used in data communications today?

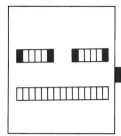

# 8

## Synchronous
## and Asynchronous

## BACKGROUND

Next to the terms half-duplex and full-duplex, the two most confusing terms in data communications are probably *synchronous* and *asynchronous,* because both terms are used to describe different types of circuits, modems, protocols, and other transmission attributes. In actuality, the terms refer to a methodology of moving information in different formats on a transmission line.

As was seen in Chapter 1, part of the history of data communications involved the development of a Baudot distributor, which provided the capability of sending information one character at a time whether those characters were generated independently or contiguously (characters coming one after the other without a time interval in between). This was the standard mode of data transmission until the early 1960s when the first modems using a new form of modulation that could move information at speeds of 2400 BPS were developed. Because of the bandwidth limitations of the telephone line, the previous method of modulation, FSK, could not be used. There was not a sufficient amount of carrier cycles available for the demodulator at the receive end to detect the required amount of changes of carrier frequency each second. A method had to be developed for transmitting information such that individual signal changes on the telephone line would convey more than one information bit each time the signal on the line changed. (The method of modulation that accomplished this function is described in detail in Chapter 10.)

The technique was described as *synchronous* in its movement of data. The term synchronous implied a specific relationship to a separate signal, which was called a *clock*. The remainder of this chapter will describe in more detail the characteristics of both asynchronous and synchronous transmission and their uses.

# B
## ASYNCHRONOUS TRANSMISSION

Asynchronous transmission involves the generating and transmitting of characters that have a specific start and stop sequence associated with each character. The definition used in this text for this mode of transmission is *character-framed data*. Character-framed data are normally generated at terminals that have human operator interfaces. It is relatively inexpensive to implement an asynchronous interface because each character can be handled separately, and since transmission started at low speeds, the methodology is well-suited for terminal to CPU transmission.

Prior to cost reductions in the buffer environment, it was much easier and less expensive to generate characters one at a time and send them directly on the line to the host end from a terminal. In this mode of transmission it was necessary for the receiving devices to be able to accept characters that came in at random intervals. This was accomplished by having a specific start-of-character identification, which turned out to be a single bit called a *start bit*. In addition, the receiving hardware had to be able to determine when the end of the character was received so it could reset itself to look for the next start-of-character bit. This was accomplished by putting in a stop bit sequence, which, depending on the type of device, would be either one or two bits. Since the operation is conceptually the same, and since it is also much more prevalent, only the one-bit stop sequence will be described. Once the sequence of bits is identified, it is easy for the hardware to accept contiguous characters or characters arriving with varying time intervals between them. An example of both sequences is shown in Fig. 8–1.

Asynchronous characters may be transmitted as generated, or they may be buffered and transmitted contiguously. If the connection is directly between the two communicating devices in a local environment, asynchronous transmission can take place at any speed up into the MBPS range. Once the analog telephone line is involved and modems are used, the highest practical speed for true transmission of asynchronous characters is 1800 BPS. Although you may already transmit asynchronously at higher data rates on the telephone line, you should be aware of the fact that even though the transmission appears to be asynchronous, in reality the modems must transmit synchronously. For applications where asynchronous transmission is required at rates higher than 1800 BPS using the

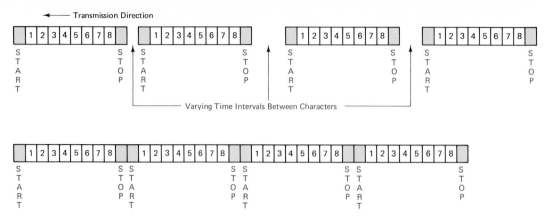

**FIGURE 8–1**
Asynchronous Transmission

telephone network, the modems have built-in circuits that convert the transmitted asynchronous characters to a synchronous transmission stream. At the receive end, the modems put the characters back in an asynchronous form. Therefore, you have asynchronous-to-synchronous conversion at the transmit end and synchronous-to-asynchronous conversion at the receive end. The primary reason why the entire sequence is not synchronous is that the circuitry in the DTEs becomes much more complex and substantial cost increases are involved. It is much easier for modem vendors to provide you with the appropriate conversions and allow you to operate with your existing equipment, but at a higher speed.

Figure 8–1 shows 8 information bits along with a single start and single stop bit. The 8 information bits may be 7 bits plus 1 parity for ASCII or 8 total bits for EBCDIC. ASCII is usually the code used in those machines where 1 start and 2 stop bits are involved (Model 33 Teletypes), but other devices that are not TTYs also use the 1 start and 2 stop bit sequence.

To tie the Baudot equipment back into this environment, Baudot has 1 start and 1 stop bit, although the stop bit for Baudot is longer in time than all the other bits (1.42 bit times long). This was described in Chapter 2. Despite the differences in character length and the size or quantity of start and stop bits, all asynchronous cases involve transmission in the same mode, one character at a time.

## C

# SYNCHRONOUS TRANSMISSION

Synchronous transmission involves the moving of both character-oriented information and bit-oriented information, or *binary stream*. There is no character differentiation in synchronous transmission, and the data are always buffered because an entire message must be transmitted at one time, not just one or a few characters at a time. For this reason, the definition used in this text for synchronous transmission is *message-framed data*. Message-framed data means the information is transmitted in an envelope that includes a *start sequence* and an *end sequence*. The start sequence involves a specific character or bit sequence telling the receiving hardware that the beginning of a message is arriving. The end sequence is usually an end-of-message type character that tells the receiving hardware that the end of the message has arrived, so the receiving hardware can now look for a new start of message. In synchronous transmissions there can be varying time intervals between messages but definitely not between bits or characters.

A typical sequence for a synchronous transmission is shown in Fig. 8–2. As can be seen, a typical synchronous transmission sequence begins with two *sync* characters, which are in whatever code set is being used for the transmission. The synchronization sequence will be described later in this chapter. The next character is a start-of-message (SOM) character, which indicates the beginning of the actual data transmission. In many cases there are more than two sync characters prior to receipt of an SOM character.

Following the SOM, there may be one or more control characters that specify to the receiving hardware what is to follow. These may include message controls such as sequence numbers, addresses, and priority; they may also indicate that within this particular message there are changes in the code set or that information, instead of being in a code, is in binary stream, such as graphics, facsimile, or compressed data. You then reach a variable-length data segment, which, again, can be bit and/or byte oriented (the characters for doing this bit to byte and back to bit sequence are shown in Chapter 7).

Eventually you receive a sequence that is used for error control, which most commonly today is the cyclic redundancy check (CRC), described in Chapter 13. Following the error control sequence you have an end-of-message character, which tells the receiving hardware that here is the true end of the transmission. In some environments the sync characters are sent continuously between messages so that the receiver is always looking for a start of message character, which identifies a new message. The synchronous transmission mechanism is used for all telephone line transmissions at 2400 BPS and up. This is due to the method in which the modem must operate and is required because of the multibit modulation technique used (described in Chapter 10).

Figure 8–3 illustrates the basics of synchronous circuit operations. The pri-

**FIGURE 8–2**
Synchronous Transmission Block

SYNC = Synchronization Character
SOM = Start of Message
EOM = End of Message

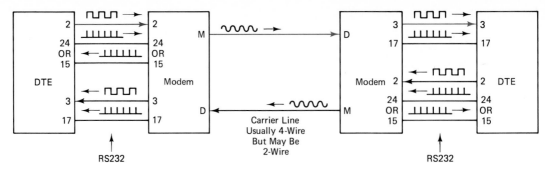

**FIGURE 8-3**
Synchronous Transmission Circuit Operation

mary pieces of equipment, the signal interface between them, and the pin numbers associated with RS232 are identified. The carrier line will probably be four wires for a leased line, but with the newer modems this operation may take place on a two-wire dial-up line with the full-duplex modems that are described in Chapter 10.

Since the operation will be the same in both directions only one way will be described, left to right. At the top is pin 2, the connection for transmit data. It is the same pin 2 whether synchronous or asynchronous transmission is utilized, but in the synchronous case, a special method is used to get the data from the DTE into the modem. There are two alternatives for this. In the most common case the modem will determine when the information is to be brought in from the data buffer in the DTE. The modem has an *oscillator,* used for creating a *clock* signal internally. This clock is most often used to bring the data in, and the signal is sent from the modem to the DTE over the connection on pin 15. The actual methodology is fairly complex, but the end result is that the clock pulses bring each data bit into the modem from the DTE. There are conditions, however, when the DTE might be required to provide the clocking signal for the data. For those situations an equivalent clock signal is provided on pin 24 from the DTE to the modem. It makes no difference whether the clock signal is on pin 15 or pin 24 for transmission purposes, but only one of them can be used. The transmission side of synchronous transmission is strictly an orderly way to bring data bits into the modem at the appropriate rate and at the appropriate time for providing the modulation to the carrier signal. As will be described in Chapter 10, two or more of these data bits are utilized to create a change in the carrier signal, and that is what really makes up the basic mechanism of synchronous transmission.

Once the modem carrier signal has been modulated, it is transmitted throughout the carrier network. As far as the end user is concerned the network should be transparent to the transmission, but this is no longer the case, especially since the digital world of ISDN is moving in. One of the techniques, T1 transmission, involves the utilization of 64 KBPS transmission channels (to be described in Chapter 16). Normally the digitization technique converts the modem output to binary bits, then converts those binary bits back into the modem carrier signal at the receive end. When full pulse-code modulation (PCM) is utilized at 64 KBPS, the modem carrier is regenerated accurately enough to portray data at any rate. However, some of the newer techniques utilized for voice, which convert the analog signal at the rate of 32 KBPS or less, do not regenerate a modem signal accurately enough to give reliable data transmission at rates over 4800 BPS. As a matter of fact, if 16 KBPS digitization is used, the reliability of transmission over 1200 BPS is questionable.

Assuming the optimum situation of no *digitization*-caused errors, the demodulator will receive the modem carrier signal on the local loop at the receive end. Given the predetermined signal-change rate of the carrier (baud) and the amount of bits contained within each baud, only the demodulator can determine exactly where each bit is supposed to be, and in turn generate a clock signal that will allow the DTE to determine accurately whether a particular data bit is a 0 bit or a 1 bit. That signal is the received clock signal, which is generated only by the modem internally. It is derived from the same internal oscillator as was used for the transmit clock, but which is now used separately and independently. It is adjusted forward or backward relative to the data signal on pin 3. The mechanization of this process and the time it takes to accomplish the process is known as *modem training time* (MTT), *line training time* (LTT), or *modem synchronization time.*

Elapsed time for MTT varies with the data transmission rate. At the low end, MTT for 2400 BPS is usually in the 3–5 millisecond (ms) range up to 19.2 KBPS, where it can take many seconds to occur. For point-to-point transmissions the MTT is not critical, but in the case of multidrop circuits the MTT can be extremely critical at the higher speeds because of the requirement for each remote modulator to resynchronize with the host demodulator on the initiation of each transmission. The operation of this *switched carrier* is shown in Fig. 8–4. When the circuit is turned on, the modulator at the host site turns on and puts its carrier out onto the circuit. Each one of the remote demodulators goes through the normal synchronization time to become synchronized to the host. (By the same process everybody in a room hears a speaker simultaneously.)

The modems at the remote locations on this multidrop line are not allowed to turn on simultaneously because there would then be multiple carriers on the line. The host-site demodulator can only accept input from one specific modulator at a time. Therefore, all remote site modulators are in the OFF condition. If two or more remote modems transmit simultaneously and one will not turn off, the condition is known as modem *streaming*. When a modem streams on a multidrop line, the entire circuit is inoperable because no other remote modem transmission can be recognized.

If a poll is sent to one of the remotes, such as Location A, all of the remote sites will see that poll. Only the addressed location should answer if the system is working correctly. In order for Location A to respond, the modulator at Location A is turned ON, and the carrier is now transmitted on the line back to the demodulator at the host site. The demodulator must then go through the appropriate synchronization time before it can adjust the internal clock signal to detect

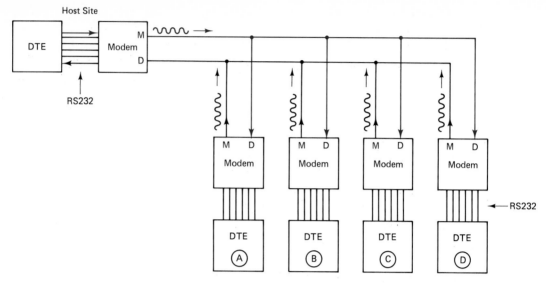

**FIGURE 8–4**
Synchronous Multidrop Operation

the incoming bits accurately. During the synchronization time, no data bits can be sent.

The control for this process resides at the RS232 interface where the DTE will typically turn on the Request-to-Send signal. The modulator will go through the appropriate turn on of the carrier and initiate the synchronization process at the demodulator. Only when an appropriate time has elapsed that would guarantee synchronization will the transmitting modem return a Clear-to-Send signal to the DTE. At the point in time when the CTS signal is received, the DTE can transmit data to the host in a normal manner. Upon conclusion of the transmission, however, the modem must turn off its carrier to leave the incoming line at the master site open again for one of the other remote sites to transmit. The host will now go out and poll another location where the same process must be repeated. If remote site A has not turned off its carrier, then the carrier from host site B will overlap that carrier and the demodulator at the host site will not be able to recognize either one. This synchronization process is repeated every time a remote site must transmit back to the central site.

You might ask what difference this turning on and off of remote carriers makes, especially when you have to move large amounts of data at high speeds and want to utilize the higher transmission speeds. The problem is in the synchronization time, as shown by Table 8–1. For a typical message length of 150 characters (1200 bits), the shortest time to transmit from a remote is at 4800 BPS due to the extended synchronization time. With a 600-character (4800 bit) message the 9600 BPS is the fastest, and in both cases the 14.4 KBPS is the slowest. This *switched network* operation has forced many organizations who operate multidrop lines to limit their rate to 4800 BPS.

**TABLE 8-1**
*Multidrop Synchronous Operation*

ASSUME MESSAGE LENGTH = 150 CHARACTERS (1200 BITS)

| AT(BPS) | MTT | Msg Transmit Time | Total Transmit Time |
|---------|------|-------------------|---------------------|
| 2400 | 5 ms | 500 ms | 505 ms |
| 4800 | 50 ms | 250 ms | 300 ms |
| 9600 | 250 ms | 125 ms | 375 ms |
| 14.4K | 5 secs | 83.3 ms | 5083.3 ms |

ASSUME MESSAGE LENGTH = 600 CHARACTERS (4800 BITS)

| AT(BPS) | MTT | Msg Transmit Time | Total Transmit Time |
|---------|------|-------------------|---------------------|
| 2400 | 5 ms | 2 secs | 2005 ms |
| 4800 | 50 ms | 1 sec | 1050 ms |
| 9600 | 250 ms | 500 ms | 750 ms |
| 14.4K | 5 secs | 333 ms | 5333 ms |

The vendors, realizing the multidrop limitation, have come out with products that increase the capability to operate multidrop at higher data rates. For example, some newer modems will synchronize at 9600 BPS within 53 ms. In those cases they would obviously be the preferred modem. It is mandatory, however, that you know what the average message length will be on your circuit, because for very short transmissions it may still be to your advantage to utilize a lower transmission rate for throughput optimization.

Another method implemented by some vendors is a *split-stream* modem. This device can operate at one speed on the transmit side and a different speed on the receiving side. Unless the DTE is compatible with this mode of operation, though, split-stream modems will not work.

Considering all of the preceding factors, the user must have an accurate picture of what to expect when transmitting in a multidrop environment from the remotes with respect to the volumes of data and the specific message lengths. In other words, a higher transmission speed does not necessarily mean higher throughput. It is up to the user to determine which mix is the best.

The operations in Fig. 8-3 are performed in the same way in both directions. It is possible for the modem at one end to use pin 15 to bring data in while the modem at the other end receives an external clock for transmission on pin 24. The transmission mechanism ends up being the same.

It is extremely critical to recognize that there is no real relationship between either of the transmit clocks and the receive clock and *SYNCHRONIZATION DOES NOT TAKE PLACE BETWEEN THE TRANSMIT MODULATOR AND THE RECEIVE DEMODULATOR.* Synchronization is an internally generated process within the modem where the clock pulse is adjusted relative to the data. In other words you don't synchronize the receiver to the transmitter. You actually synchronize the receive clock to the receive data signal on pins 17 and 3 at each end independently. Even though the internal oscillator in the modem is the source for both the transmit clock on pin 15 and the receive clock on pin 17, they are generated and utilized in a totally independent manner internally. The clocking process will be described in more detail now.

The inherent operation just described of synchronous modems is prone to higher error rates due to transmission line characteristics which make the bits being received by the demodulator sometimes seem to change their width as well as their timing relationships to each other. The only device that knows what all the relationships are, and where the data bits actually are, is the demodulator; therefore, it is only the demodulator that can create a timing signal to be used by the DTE to sample the information bits at their most stable point.

The forms of degradation that affect the modems when they operate synchronously are shown in Fig. 8–5. The top line shows the ideal received bit stream on pin 17, which is both symmetric and exactly *square*. The second line shows what happens when *rolloff* is encountered, in which the sharpness of the signal rise and fall time is degraded due to the length of the connecting cable between the modem and the DTE. *Jitter* implies that the start and end times of the bit are not always exactly where they should be. The signal actually jitters back and forth with respect to the rise and fall time of the square-wave signal. This degradation is also called *phase jitter*.

The fourth line shows the degradation known as *positive bias,* which means the positive-going output bits are wider than the negative-going output bits, while the fifth line shows a *negative bias,* which is just the opposite. A modem can have either positive or negative bias but not both at the same time. This degradation is also called *marking* and *spacing* distortion and occurs due to internal modem circuitry anomalies.

At the bottom is a series of arrows that show the optimum sample times for the DTE to determine what the actual received data bit is, even with all the

**FIGURE 8–5**
Synchronous Signal Degradation and Timing

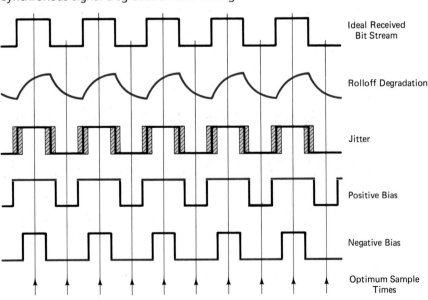

Ideal Received
Bit Stream

Rolloff Degradation

Jitter

Positive Bias

Negative Bias

Optimum Sample
Times

degradations. Unless the sample times are very close to the middle of the receive bit time, the probability of one or more of the combination of degradations giving you an erroneous bit gets higher and continues to increase as you get closer to the rise and fall time of where the bit is supposed to be. Since only the demodulator knows where the exact middle of the data bit is, it is the demodulator that sets up the clock sample times to be in the correct position as already described. This is known as modem synchronization or *modem training time* (MTT).

When a modem is said to lose synchronization, the circuits inside the demodulator *think* that the sample times are in the wrong place and begin to move them closer to the rise and fall times. As soon as it is recognized that this is incorrect, the clock signal is moved back to the middle of the bit. Whatever the specified MTT is for the modem is now the time required to bring the sample point back to the middle of the bit.

What has just been described has nothing to do with the two sync characters at the beginning of the message. MTT must take place prior to receipt of the first sync character, as will be described shortly. All synchronous transmissions using analog telephone lines and modems require a bit synchronization time to be completed prior to sending data. If not, the entire message may be lost because the sync and/or the SOM characters may not be recognized if the bits representing those characters are not detected as such.

Once the MTT has taken place, the next sequence required for the receiving DTE is to determine where the sync characters are. This will provide what is known as a *character* or *frame* sync, which in turn allows the receiving hardware to recognize a true start-of-message character. This sync/sync/SOM sequence is mandatory, because prior to receiving the sync characters, random bits are being recognized on pin 17 of the receiving modem, especially during the MTT time, and it is quite possible for these random bits to accidentally represent an SOM. An erroneous SOM will initiate the receiving hardware because it thinks a real message is actually coming in. Probabilities of this occurring during random bit reception are very high, and therefore a scheme is necessary to prevent the erroneous start-of-message reception. The methodology selected was the sync/sync/ SOM sequence, which provides a 24-bit predetermined start sequence that has an extremely low probability of random generation instead of an 8-bit sequence. The reason two sync characters are required at the beginning of the sequence is that the first may be modified by transmission errors so there will still be another sync character left before the real SOM.

An example is shown in Fig. 8–6, which gives the typical sequence of what can occur in a synchronous transmission. The sequence at the top shows random bits preceding two sync characters and SOM in ASCII code using odd parity. The second sequence shows some of those random bits for which each 8 bits in the DTE is looked at to see if it is a sync character. The first three samples are performed in what is referred to as a *bit shifting* mode (looks at a defined quantity of bits, which in this case is 8, then looks at the same quantity but shifted by 1 bit—bits 2 through 9—then looks at the same quantity but shifted by another bit—bits 3 through 10—and so on); each looks at a total of 8 bits and does not find what appears to be the sync sequence, but the fourth one does. As it turns

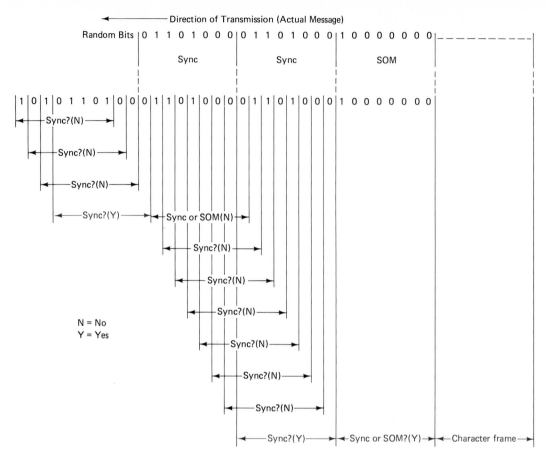

**FIGURE 8-6**
Synchronous Transmission Character Framing

out, the sequence that finds a sync character happens to include the first 0 bit of the real sync character. The DTE *frames* on what appears to be a valid 8-bit sync character and in effect shifts gears; so instead of bit shifting again, it looks at the next 8 bits as a full character to see if it is a sync or an SOM character. Since the first bit of the real sync has already been included in the previous sync character frame, this character is neither a sync nor an SOM. The DTE goes back to looking for a sync character in a *bit shifting mode* again.

Notice that for the next six samples the sync character is not found, but on the seventh one it is found. The DTE then again looks for either sync or an SOM for the succeeding 8 bits and finds an SOM. The DTE now "shifts gears" again such that it is again in character frame mode and assumes that a valid message has been initiated. If (still referring to Fig. 8-6), there were only one sync character at the front, then a valid SOM character might have its first bit included in the frame after recognizing sync and the real SOM would no longer be recognizable as a start of message. If, after seeing a sync, either a sync or an SOM were recognized in a bit shifting mode, the probability of finding an SOM sequence would still be very high. For that reason a minimum of two consecutive sync characters are required prior to receipt of an SOM so that erroneous starting of the DTE on receipt of a random SOM is practically nonexistent.

After the true SOM is recognized, the DTE is in a character frame mode, and will then look at the control characters to determine address, sequence number, and priority, and will also look for the controls that determine whether the remainder of the message stays in the character frame mode, goes into binary stream mode or even into another code set. The method for doing this was shown in Chapter 7.

## D
## OTHER RELATED FACTORS

Numerous other factors relate to both synchronous and asynchronous operation, although many of them are confusing because they do not necessarily relate to the transmission environment. Listed next are some of the descriptions that relate to the use of synchronous and asynchronous operation.

1. *Bisync.* Bisync is the name of a protocol developed by IBM (it is described further in Chapter 9). It stands for binary synchronous communications and is sometimes abbreviated BSC. Bisync uses synchronous transmission and is therefore used at speeds of 2400 BPS and up. The fact that bisync is a half-duplex protocol (transmits in one direction at a time only) has nothing to do with the fact that it transmits synchronously.

2. *Bit Sync.* Bit sync refers to the modem synchronization process of moving the clock signal to the middle of the data bit. It means that the DTE is in a position to recognize the received bits reliably when received during a synchronous transmission.

3. *Byte Sync.* Byte sync may refer to either character or frame synchronization in a synchronous transmission. There are many other related definitions but they all boil down to the receipt of character-oriented information. Although it is sometimes used with reference to asynchronous transmission, the more common use is with synchronous transmission.

4. *Isochronous.* There are many different definitions and uses of the term isochronous, but again they all boil down to a method of transmitting asynchronous characters synchronously. The unique trait about isochronous is that when the characters are not contiguous they are separated by timing differentials that are an integral number of character times. In other words, the characters are not transmitted randomly; they are transmitted as required, with the hardware making sure that there is an integral number of character times between them. In some environments this may mean inserting *fill* characters between the actual data characters.

5. *Protocols.* There are various synchronous and asynchronous protocols, with most of the low-speed TTY protocols and simpler terminal protocols being asynchronous. The synchronous protocols are typically Bisync, SDLC, 2780, 3780, 3270, ICL, Honeywell VIP, CDC-UT200, Univac U-100, and others. The vendor determines whether a protocol is synchronous or asynchronous. Except for the SDLC-type protocols (described in Chapter 9), the others are almost all half-duplex protocols.

6. *Personal Computer Interfaces.* In the PC world now the majority of the protocols are asynchronous because they were designed to run at 300 or 1200 BPS. Starting in 1987 newer modems came on the market that allowed asynchronous dial-up operation at 2400 BPS. Still other modems now provide a capability to operate at 4800 BPS and 9600 BPS asynchronously with the DTE because they do the async/sync/async conversion internally.

7. *Digital Environments.* Since the digital transmission world is designed to operate at 2400 BPS and up, all digital transmissions are synchronous, but no modem clocking is available. Instead, the DSU provides clocking information to the DTE so that the DTE can use the clock as if it were getting data and clock signals from a modem in the form of a synchronous reception. No MTT (modem turnaround time) is involved with digital transmission because digital circuits remain in synchronization all the time. This results from a single network clock that must be used not only to keep the DSUs in sync but also the intermediate switching equipment.

8. *Advantages and Disadvantages.* The primary advantage of asynchronous transmission is cost and ease of implementation. There is much less circuitry involved, and with the timing not as critical, asynchronous is used extensively, especially when there are humans generating information, which is at a very low speed compared to the line transmission rate. On the other hand, even though synchronous is much more expensive, there is an immediate reduction of two bits out of each character, providing a 20 percent improvement in transmission efficiency. As will be seen in Chapter 13, the use of parity is also no longer required, and therefore the parity bit can be eliminated in ASCII also. Eliminating the start, stop, and parity bits from an asynchronous transmission means a potential 30 percent reduction in total bit transmission. Combined with other types of data compression, the total efficiency of transmission can be improved even more. Also, new error-detection schemes such as CRC are designed for synchronous transmission. All in all, when there is a requirement for high-speed transmission, synchronous transmission is mandatory and can be utilized in both analog and digital environments.

## QUESTIONS

1. Give a simple definition for asynchronous transmission. Synchronous transmission.

2. What transmission speeds are typical for asynchronous transmissions? Synchronous transmissions?

3. Draw the character envelope for asynchronous data. What are the functions of each main component?

4. Draw the message envelope for synchronous data. What functions does each element perform?

5. Describe the operation of a multidrop line transmitting synchronous data.

6. What are the four primary forms of signal degradation for synchronous transmission?

7. What are the differences among bit sync/byte sync/bisync/frame sync?

8. What is the primary trade-off between synchronous and asynchronous transmission?

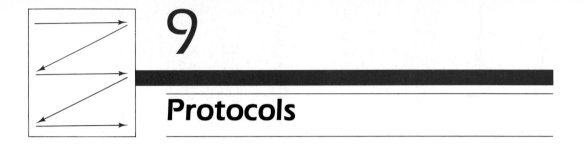

# 9

# Protocols

## A
## BACKGROUND

When talking to users and vendors, and reading textbooks available on the subject, one comes up with many different definitions of a protocol. There are also many ways in which the classifications of the different portions of the protocol can be defined. Because this particular text is user oriented and will probably be used in conjunction with the understanding of and design and operation of an entire network, the approach taken here is to define the functions of a simple protocol, describe the methods in which a simple protocol can be implemented, and then provide an example to give the reader a practical idea as to how the simple protocol functions in the real world.

A network protocol, as opposed to a simple protocol, describes multiple levels of functions that include the interaction among many levels of logical and physical functions. Network protocols are usually described in the context of the International Standards Organization (ISO) Open System Interconnect (OSI). The OSI has seven separate layers of protocol, each performing a specific function. A simple protocol corresponds to the second, or to the first and second layer of the OSI model. Because it is such an extensive subject, an entire chapter has been dedicated to network protocols and their relationship to network architectures. The network protocols, including OSI, will be fully described in Chapter

18. This chapter will deal with the simple protocol that moves information between two points and corresponds to the second layer of the OSI model.

For purposes of definition in this text, a simple protocol will be defined to have two major functions, handshaking and line discipline.

*HANDSHAKING*   This is the sequence that occurs on the communications facilities between the communication equipment (modems) and establishes the fact that a circuit for transmission of information is available and operational. The signals that describe the electrical interface between the modem and the user equipment (RS232) were described in Chapter 5. This chapter will describe the functions of a protocol that move the information and the techniques for doing so, as opposed to the interface-only digital signaling control that was described in Chapter 5.

*LINE DISCIPLINE*   The line discipline is the sequence of operations that actually transmits and receives the data, handles the error-control procedures, handles the sequencing of message blocks, and provides validation for information received correctly. This is the portion of the simple protocol that most vendors call a protocol.

The line discipline portion of the protocol can be further segmented to describe the sequence for movement of the data and may be called half-duplex (HDX), which means transmission in one direction at a time regardless of the available facilities, full-duplex (FDX), which means transmission in both directions at the same time between the same two points, and full/full-duplex (F/FDX) (which the author has defined to describe a unique capability), meaning the transmission of information in both directions at the same time on a *multidrop line*—specifically where a master site can be transmitting to one point on the multidrop line, while simultaneously receiving from a different point on the multidrop line.

The F/FDX protocols are defined as full-duplex protocols by the vendors, typically SDLC from IBM. They are capable of transmitting in both directions at the same time between the same two points. A separate definition is given for the full/full-duplex type of capability because it is this mode of operation on a multidrop line that gives these particular protocols a significant advantage in a distributed network, where some terminals on multidrop lines can have high volumes of traffic destined for the central site, while others on the same line can have high volumes of traffic destined to them from the central site. Without the capability of transmitting and receiving from different terminals on the same line, the effective line utilization decreases significantly. This decrease is due to the fact that, if only one terminal location can communicate with the central site on a multidrop line and there is a long message in one direction from that terminal, all other terminal locations on that line must wait their turn before they will be able to communicate with the central site. So, for the special limited case of multidrop lines with data link control-type protocols, the new definition of full/full-duplex protocol will be used.

Examples of the functional flow of information between the various types of protocols are shown in Table 9–1. Half-duplex protocols move information one way at a time between the same two points. Whether polling/calling, flow control, or any other mode of control, the information only moves one way at a time. Examples of these are shown in the last column.

A full-duplex protocol moves information in both directions simultaneously between the same two points and is typified by HDLC, SDLC, DDCMP, and ADCCP. When a full-duplex protocol is used on a multidrop line, the DLC-type protocols have the ability to allow the master site to transmit to one slave location while simultaneously receiving from a different slave location, that is, the master would poll the individual slave sites on a multidrop line one at a time when it has nothing to transmit itself (transmission will always take precedence). When one of the slave sites begins to transmit to the master as a result of a poll, and if at that point in time a message at the host site comes from the CPU to the communications front end, the CFE can *call* whatever site the message is destined for and then transmit the message. In this case, the *called* location is not required to respond to the call. In fact, its response would interfere with the other site that is already transmitting to the master (modem signals will overlap). At some time later the master will go back to the slave site which it called previously and transmitted information to see if the previously transmitted blocks of data were received. Both ends of the path keep track of all messages that are transmitted and received so that even if the acknowledgments come back later, the blocks are always in synchronization with those that were transmitted and received correctly.

Because many protocols prior to the DLC type did not have this ability, the author decided to give this feature a unique name and then describe its capability. The examples for the full/full-duplex protocols are the same as the full-duplex (because only this unique multidrop operation differs) and they are HDLC, SDLC, DDCMP, and ADCCP.

**TABLE 9–1**

Protocol Comparison

| TYPE OF PROTOCOL | FUNCTION | DIRECTION | SEQUENCE | LOCATIONS | EXAMPLES |
|---|---|---|---|---|---|
| SPX Protocol | Moves Information | One direction | Only | Between same two points | Typically proprietary |
| HDX Protocol | " | Two directions | One way at a time | " | TTY Flow Control Bisync |
| FDX Protocol | " | " | Simultaneously | " | HDLC SDLC DDCMP ADCCP |
| F/FDX Protocol | " | " | " | Multidrop M → Sx M ← Sy | " |

The full or full/full-duplex protocols can operate in a half-duplex mode, but the half-duplex protocols cannot operate in either a full- or full/full-duplex mode. Also, the full/full-duplex protocols can operate in either the full-duplex or half-duplex modes, also depending on the traffic requirements.

## B
# HALF DUPLEX

The line discipline portion of a half-duplex protocol allows data transmission to occur in one direction at a time between the same two points. For all practical purposes, the relationship during a specific transmission sequence will always be a master-slave type of arrangement where one end will determine who transmits and when. Half-duplex protocols are almost always used at the lower speeds (up to 2400 BPS), but sometimes up to 9600 BPS, and almost always on dial-up circuits. For applications that are *interactive,* a half-duplex protocol is more applicable, because each transmission, regardless of which way it goes, is dependent on the previous transmission. As such, the functions that occur can only be in sequence, giving a one-way-at-a-time operation, which fits perfectly within the definition of a half-duplex protocol.

A very important advantage of a half-duplex protocol is that in most cases a single block of information is transmitted and then a positive acknowledgment must be received prior to the transmission of the next block. Thus only one buffer has to be allocated at the remote site and one buffer at the central site for transmission of information. In full-duplex protocols the additional buffers required and the management of them adds a significant level of complexity.

Bisync will be described here in a little more detail because it is one of the most commonly used forms of a half-duplex protocol. TTY or Teletype-type protocols are also half duplex and used extensively for low-speed applications, especially with personal and small business computers, but because they vary over such a wide range in individual operation, bisync was chosen to illustrate the concept of half-duplex information flow. It is very important to remember that while this chapter discusses the types of protocols, at no time will the type of circuit over which these protocols are transmitted be mentioned. A matrix will be provided to tie the protocols together with the circuits to show how the definitions are used, and will help to eliminate the confusion with respect to half duplex and full duplex, which is probably the most misunderstood area of definition in all of data communications.

Bisync, an IBM-developed protocol, has been in use since 1966 for communication primarily between computers and terminals, but it is also used from computer to computer, especially in a dial-up mode. It is a half-duplex protocol that uses special characters to delineate the different fields of a message and to control the required protocol functions.

Figure 9–1 shows the format of a typical bisync message. The header portion is optional, but if it is used it begins with a start-of-header character and

| SYN | SYN | SOH | Header | STX | Text | ETX or ETB | BCC or CRC |

Bisync Message Format

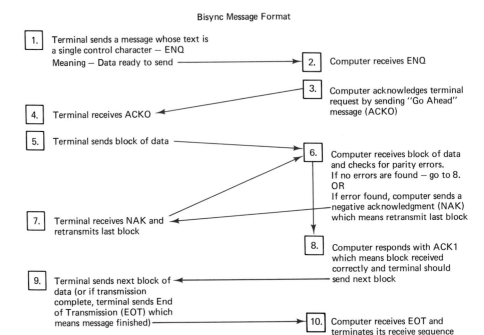

1. Terminal sends a message whose text is a single control character — ENQ
Meaning — Data ready to send

2. Computer receives ENQ

3. Computer acknowledges terminal request by sending "Go Ahead" message (ACKO)

4. Terminal receives ACKO

5. Terminal sends block of data

6. Computer receives block of data and checks for parity errors. If no errors are found — go to 8. OR If error found, computer sends a negative acknowledgment (NAK) which means retransmit last block

7. Terminal receives NAK and retransmits last block

8. Computer responds with ACK1 which means block received correctly and terminal should send next block

9. Terminal sends next block of data (or if transmission complete, terminal sends End of Transmission (EOT) which means message finished)

10. Computer receives EOT and terminates its receive sequence

**FIGURE 9–1**
Bisync Contention Mode Format and Sequence

ends with a start-of-text character. The sync (SYN) characters are required to establish a mechanism whereby the individual message control and information characters can be identified. This will be described in detail later in this section. The SOH and STX characters are special format control characters, and the specific bits required to form them are found solely in ASCII and EBCDIC, the two most common codes used with bisync. The contents of the header are specified by the user, except for status and test request messages. The text portion is variable in length and may contain bits that are not character oriented. The character recognition logic of the receiver has to be turned off so that a data pattern resembling either ETX or one of the other special characters will not confuse it. To turn off the character recognition at the receiver, the bit-oriented data are delimited by a DLE (data link escape character) STX, and DLE ETX or DLE ETB; these special characters indicate the end of the text field and the beginning of the trailer section, which contains only the block check character or characters. The line-discipline portion of bisync employs a rigorous set of rules for moving the data between transmitter and receiver. A typical sequence between a terminal station and a computer on a point-to-point line is shown in Fig. 9–1. Note that the individual functions that occur on the transmission line occur one way at a time. This is a true half-duplex protocol.

To detect and correct for errors occurring during transmission, bisync uses either a combination vertical–longitudinal redundancy check sequence (VRC/LRC) or a cyclic redundancy check (CRC), depending on the information code being used (parity checking will be described in Chapter 13). For ASCII, a VRC check is performed on each character, and an LRC check is performed on the entire message. In the case of ASCII, the LRC in the trailer field of the message is a single 8-bit character. If the code is EBCDIC, no VRC check is made; instead a 16-bit CRC is calculated for the entire message. When errors are detected, a negative acknowledgment sequence (NAK) is transmitted back to the originator (shown in Fig. 9–1). To correct the error, bisync requires that the block be retransmitted in its entirety (one block storage at a time). It is up to the user to determine how many retransmissions will be tried before it is assumed that the line is nonoperational or that the originally transmitted message contained an inherent error.

When a transmitted block check matches the block check calculated at the receiver, the receiver sends a positive acknowledgment, ACK 0 for an even-numbered block or ACK 1 for an odd-numbered block. This alternating between ACK 0 and ACK 1 checks for sequence errors and can detect duplicated or missing blocks. The acknowledgment messages are sent as separate control messages rather than being incorporated within a specific data message.

Because they are used so extensively throughout the world, some additional information will be provided on the IBM 3270 and 3780 type interfaces. They both use bisync as a protocol and can both use ASCII or EBCDIC code, although some of the IBM product families that interface with these products do not allow the use of ASCII. ASCII, when used in this environment, utilizes the LRC mode of error check, while EBCDIC utilizes the CRC16 for error checking (described in Chapter 13).

Synchronous modems must be used because bisync utilizes a synchronous transmission. Either half-duplex or full-duplex lines can be used, and circuits can be either point to point or multipoint. It is also advantageous to use bisync because it can use many different codes, not just ASCII or EBCDIC.

There are two separate modes of operation:

1. *Contention Mode.* This mode uses point-to-point lines and is almost always on a dial-up connection (two points). No addressing is required, and when there are no data to send, the line is idle. The station that wants to transmit must get permission to do so by sending to the master site the sequence of sync/sync/enq. Permission is given with an ACK 0 response. If there is a simultaneous requirement for the host to transmit to the station, the host has priority.

2. *Polled Mode.* This mode takes place on either a point-to-point or a multipoint line and is therefore almost always used in a leased-line environment. There must be an addressing scheme for individual controllers (single terminal location) and multiple terminals on a cluster controller. It is a two-level

scheme in which the first address is the cluster controller address (the device physically connected to the line), and the second-level address is the terminal address, which is the device connected to the cluster controller. There can be a maximum of 32 controllers (single or cluster) on a line and 32 devices on each cluster controller.

In bisync, a poll is defined as a *Poll* and a call is described as a *Select*.

## C
## FULL DUPLEX

A full-duplex protocol moves data in both directions at the same time between the same two locations. This method of data movement is functionally the same whether the circuit is point to point or multidrop. In a point-to-point circuit, either end can be the master site, although in most instances the user has predetermined that one of the ends will be the master and the other the slave. For a multidrop circuit, there can be only one master site, and all the rest of the locations on the line must be slave sites. The term *terminal* is used to identify remote sites, which for the most part use some form of lower-level capability data processing; but a multidrop network configuration could also have a series of different computers connected to a single line for which a single predefined location could serve as the master site.

Since there is a multitude of full-duplex protocols that permit transmission in both directions at the same time between the same two points, with no single type being a *de facto* standard as bisync is for half-duplex synchronous protocols, a specific sequence of data movement descriptions will not be provided. For a better understanding of full-duplex operation however, the SDLC example given in the next section can be used as a full-duplex description when transmitting between two points at the same time in both directions. This can be done because the full/full-duplex definition for SDLC described earlier is a more complex sequence, and point-to-point operation can be considered a subset of it.

## D
## FULL/FULL DUPLEX (SDLC)

As stated previously, a full/full-duplex protocol is a special case for a standard full-duplex protocol. Only the newer DLC (data link control) protocols have the capability of transmitting to one remote location while receiving from a different remote location over a multidrop line (protocols doing this have been written by individual users, but none are available as a product offering). The method most widely used to implement this technique is IBM's SDLC, which stands for Synchronous Data Link Control.

Other protocols do very much the same things as SDLC and are produced by the other major mainframe vendors. Burroughs has BDLC, Honeywell has their own version of HDLC, and CDC has CDC DLC; but these, if available, are part of a complete system offering. Digital Equipment Corporation (DEC) has a protocol named Digital Data Communications Message Protocol (DD-CMP), which functionally performs the same operations as SDLC but in a different mode. It is used only with DEC equipment. Whereas SDLC is defined as a bit-oriented protocol, DDCMP is defined as a character-count protocol. Although there is a difference of opinion, especially between vendors, the fact that one protocol is bit oriented while the other is character oriented really makes very little difference to the user, because the protocols almost always come with hardware, firmware, software, and ancillary support. The user therefore, when selecting a vendor, has no real choice, but gets what the vendor has, and the capabilities are comparable anyway. Since SDLC and DDCMP are different in operation and incompatible with each other and SDLC is being implemented by many different vendors while DDCMP is unique to DEC or vendors communicating with DEC, SDLC will be described in detail here along with an example.

Figure 9-2 depicts the format of SDLC and the functional characteristics that make up the pieces of the format. SDLC is described by IBM as a bit-oriented, full-duplex, serial by bit transmission, centralized control, synchronous, data communications message protocol. In reality, SDLC is not only a full-duplex protocol, but, as described previously, it can function as a full/full-duplex protocol when in a multidrop environment. Also, the centralized control concept can be carried further to a *bus* arrangement, whereby any CPU on an interconnected common bus at the same physical location can be a master. With respect to this bus operation, IBM does not support any configuration other than a predefined master–slave relationship.

By referring to Fig. 9-2, the line-discipline functions of SDLC will be apparent. The first set of bits to be generated in the format is called a *flag*. The configuration of this flag byte is always 01111110, and this sequence will never be repeated throughout the entire message transmission until the end flag with the same configuration is transmitted. To ensure this operation everytime, when a sequence of five 1 bits in a row is recognized by the transmit hardware after a start flag is generated (except when the end flag has to be generated), an extra 0 bit will be added to the bit stream between the fifth 1 bit and the next bit, regardless of whether that next bit is 0 or 1. This technique is called *zero stuffing*. The hardware at the receive end will always remove a 0 that is detected after five consecutive 1 bits, before it is passed on to the recognition logic and therefore the bit stuffing will end up being transparent to the user.

SDLC itself is totally transparent to the user, in that all the bits that are added to the front and back of the message at the transmit end will be removed at the receive end, so the user will get back the original bit stream starting with the first user character to be generated and ending with the last user character to be generated. In this manner SDLC can be looked on as a functional black box into which a user at the transmit end inserts information in a serial bit form and gets out at the receive end the same serial bit stream exactly the way it was put in.

SDLC is a bit-oriented, full/full-duplex, serial by bit transmission, centralized control, synchronous, data communications message protocol.

| Flag | Address | Control | Info | CRC Frame Check Sequence | Flag |
|------|---------|---------|------|--------------------------|------|

Flag is always 01111110 (If a sequence of 5 "1" bits occurs in the middle of a transmission, the transmitter "stuffs" in a "0" bit and the receiver removes it.)

Address is the Station Address on a particular line.

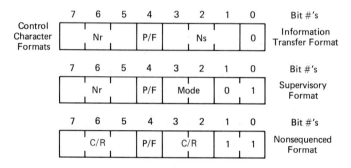

Ns is Sending Sequence Number = 000 through 111 and then repeats

P/F is Primary Station Poll when = 1 from Primary Station
    Secondary Station Final when = 1 from Station on the line

Nr is Receiving Sequence Number = 000 through 111 and then repeats

Mode is Receive Ready (RR) when 00
    Receive Not Ready (RNR) when 10
    Reject (REJ) when 01

C/R is Command from Primary Station or Response from Secondary Station

Commands:
- Nonsequenced Information (NSI) = 000–00
- Set Normal Response Mode (SNRM) = 100–00
- Disconnect (DISC) = 010–00
- Optional Response Poll (ORP) = 001–00
- Set Initialization Mode (SIM) = 000–01
- Request Station ID (XID) = 101–11
- Request Task Response (TEST) = 111–00
- Configure for Test (CFGR) = 110–01

Responses:
- Nonsequenced Information (UI) = 000–00
- Nonsequence Acknowledgment (UA) = 011–00
- Request for Initialization (RIM) = 000–01
- Command Reject (FRMR) = 001–01
- Request Online (DM) = 000–11
- Test Response/Beacon (BCN) = 111–11
- Disconnect Request (RD) = 010–00

Info is Information = Variable Length for Information Transfer
    Prohibited for Supervisory Format
    Variable Length for Nonsequenced Format with NSI
    Fixed Format with CMDR

CRC = Cyclic Redundancy Check Remainder

**FIGURE 9–2**
SDLC Format

158

Since the flag sequence will only occur at the beginning and the end of the message, it is relatively easy to view it as both a start-of-message and an end-of-message delimiter. The only other time 01111110 can occur in sequence is due to a transmission error somewhere between the two flags. If this is the case, the receive hardware assumes that the second flag was preceded by a 16-bit CRC check sequence. When the calculated CRC at the receive end is compared with the assumed CRC that resulted from the transmission error, they will be found to be different, and therefore the message is determined to be in error and will have to be retransmitted. A further description of this will be given later.

The next byte after the start flag is the *address byte,* which consists of 8 bits giving 256 combinations. This particular address refers to the address on a particular communication line. It has nothing to do with the address that the user may define for the system. The address byte therefore allows 256 unique addresses to be accommodated on every single individual communication line in the network, but because the probability of using that many on one line is extremely remote (16 being a practical limit), many of the other vendors who have SDLC-type protocols have taken bits from the address byte to use for other functions. These other functions could be used for more control or for transmission of more blocks of information before an acknowledgment must be received. (This will be described under the control byte definition.) Since the address byte on a link is unique to that link, there must be a table somewhere that will convert the user's defined mnemonic and/or logical addresses to the specific link address on that particular line. This information must be provided to the SDLC interface so that the link address can be inserted correctly.

The third byte of the format is the heart of the protocol. It is called the *control byte.* The control byte can have any one of three different formats depending on what is to be transmitted. As can be seen from Fig. 9–2, if bit "0" is a 0, it is called an *information transfer format.* If bits "0" and "1" are a 1 and a 0, it is a *supervisory format,* and if bits "0" and "1" are a 1 and a 1, it is called a *nonsequenced format.* When bit "0" is a 0, the next three bits identify the sequence number of the block being transmitted (by either the master or the slave). Since there are eight combinations available with 3 bits, no more than eight blocks of information can be sent before this segment will start repeating itself. Therefore, it would appear that the maximum limitation of blocks that can be sent prior to the repeating of message identification would be eight. In reality, however, only seven blocks can be transmitted before an acknowledgment for at least one of the blocks must be received. The eighth block identification is reserved for positive acknowledgment of the preceding seven, because, as will be seen in the example later, the mechanism whereby SDLC informs a transmitter that a block has been received in error is to use that sequence number to request a retransmission. Therefore, if eight blocks are transmitted, there would be no unique way to tell whether all eight blocks were received correctly or if only the first block was actually received in error. (The example provided later will show this clearly.) IBM has added the *extension* capability to SDLC so that the amount of blocks in transit can now be up to 127. Operation is the same as with the seven-block limit except for the greater amount allowed now (at user option).

The next bit location in the control character is the same for all three formats; it is called *P/F bit.* When being transmitted from the master location it is called a *P bit* and, if set to one, identifies a *poll message.* If set to 0, it is not a poll message, and the slave that is being addressed should not answer. If coming from a slave location it is called an *F bit* (final message of a sequence), and if it is a 0, then at least one more block of information will be following the block in which this control character is contained. If the F bit is a 1, this block will be the last block in the present sequence to be transmitted by that slave site. Since the F bit occurs at the very beginning of a block being transmitted by a slave site, the firmware at the master site can use this information to interrupt its transmission of a multiblock sequence of information to another location on the same multidrop line at the end of the block in progress, wait for the end of the incoming transmission from the slave site that is in the process of transmitting, and, at that time, poll a different location on that line for information to be brought in from that new location. As soon as the newly polled site begins to transmit to the master, the master can go back and finish the interrupted multiblock transmission to the original slave site to which it was transmitting. This is the mechanism whereby the full/full-duplex capability is implemented in a multidrop environment.

The last three bits of the control byte contained in the information transfer format are the next block number that the transmitting end (master or slave) expects to get from the other end the next time a transmission takes place. As we will see, this is the mechanism whereby acknowledgments are accomplished.

For the supervisory format, where bits "0" and "1" are a 1 and a 0, the next two bits are defined as the *mode,* shown in Fig. 9–2 as being either receive-ready, receive-not-ready, or reject. These controls are used to identify whether a particular terminal can receive or not. The P/F and Nr bit segments are the same as for the information transfer format.

**NONSEQUENCED FORMAT (NOW CALLED UNNUMBERED)**   The nonsequenced format is defined by bits "0" and "1" of the control byte being 1 and 1. When the nonsequenced format is identified, then bit numbers 2, 3, 5, 6, and 7 must be looked at together as being a command or a response. These commands/responses are shown in the bottom half of Fig. 9–2 in the brackets assigned for each. Nonsequenced formats are used primarily for establishing the initial synchronization, for ultimate disconnecting of a terminal site, and for testing.

The next segment in the SDLC format is what is known as the *information portion.* This segment is the total user transmission and starts with the user's first character and ends with the user's last character. If the user has his own capability for error detection in addition to the SDLC capability, it will also be included in this segment before the user EOT and the SDLC CRC. This CRC (cyclic redundancy check) is described in Chapter 13, in which all the transmission integrity functions are included. It is also called the frame check sequence and guarantees that the transmission is correct to an extremely high reliability.

After the SDLC CRC is the final flag byte. This final flag identifies the end of the present block, and a new flag sequence must be transmitted to initiate the next message or block.

Further points on the information portion of the format are the following:

1. It is of a variable length (DDCMP requires multiples of 8 bits).
2. It is prohibited for the supervisory format.
3. It is of variable length for the nonsequenced format when used with UI (nonsequenced information).
4. It is of a fixed format with the use of the command reject (FRMR) response by a slave to the master.

Probably the best way to understand the concepts of SDLC is to go through a specific example describing the functions being performed. Two examples are provided and are shown in Figs. 9–3 and 9–4. The example that will be described in detail is Fig. 9–3. This is the easier one to understand for the first-time user because the functions will happen sequentially in what is really a half-duplex mode of operation. The desirability of SDLC operating in a half-duplex mode is very low from a transmission efficiency point of view, and it is therefore shown here only for explanatory purposes. It should be noted, however, that those applications upgraded from HDX protocols may retain the same hardware and therefore operate SDLC in an HDX mode. After going through the sequence of operations in Fig. 9–3, the reader should be able to go through the example shown in Fig. 9–4, where the true full/full-duplex operation is depicted.

Four major functions are described in Fig. 9–3: an initial synchronization sequence, a two-way transmission without an error, a two-way transmission with an error and a retransmission, and finally a disconnect command. The functions are described by identifying the individual format segments, expanding out the control byte, and then describing the operation that has occurred. The left column shows the transmission from the master site to the slave site, and the arrow shows the direction in which the transmission occurs. To the right of the arrow is a column that shows what the slave is transmitting back to the master, and to the right of the vertical line is a description of what has occurred. Where applicable, the initial synchronization sequence required for handshaking must take place prior to transmission of the initial flag character. This may not be required on point-to-point transmissions between the master and slave sites as long as there is a high percentage of traffic (to keep synchronized), but it is a mandatory transmission each time a slave site initiates a transmission on a multidrop line.

We start off with a transmission from the master to the slave with the flag byte, the address (B), and then the control byte, which starts off with a 01 (a supervisory format looking at the bits from right to left). With the P/F bit coming from the master set as a 1, this is a poll. The CRC and end flag follow, and as can be seen under Remarks, the master has polled site B. Coming back from B now we have the flag, and notice here the slave identifies itself. If the slave were to put in the master's address, it would be redundant information, because

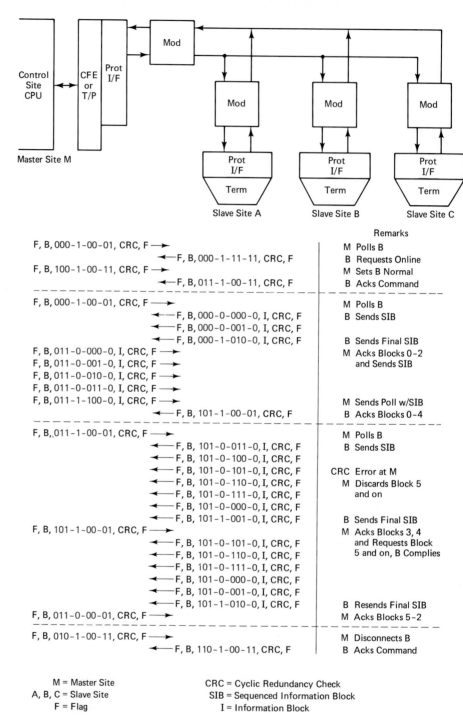

FIGURE 9-3
SDLC-HDX Operation Sequence

162

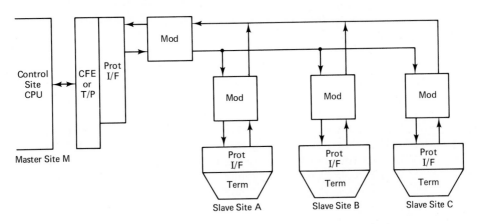

Master Site M

Slave Site A   Slave Site B   Slave Site C

| | Remarks |
|---|---|
| F, B, 000-1-00-01, CRC, F → | M Polls B |
| ←F, B, 000-1-00-01, CRC, F | B Has No Send Data |
| F, C, 000-1-00-01, CRC, F → | M Polls C |
| ←F, C, 000-0-000-0, I, CRC, F | C Sends SIB to M |
| F, B, 000-0-000-0, I, CRC, F → | M Sends SIB to B |
| ←F, C, 000-0-001-0, I, CRC, F | |
| F, B, 000-0-001-0, I, CRC, F → | |
| ←F, C, 000-1-010-0, I, CRC, F | C Sends Final SIB to M |
| F, C, 110-0-00-01, CRC, F → | M Acks Blocks 0-2 to C |
| F, B, 000-1-010-0, I, CRC, F → | M Sends Final SIB to B |
| ←F, B, 110-1-00-01, CRC, F | B Acks Blocks 0-2 to M |
| F, A, 000-1-00-01, CRC, F → | M Polls A |
| ←F, A, 000-1-00-01, CRC, F | A Has No Data to Send |
| F, B, 000-1-00-01, CRC, F → | M Polls B |
| ←F, B, 011-0-000-0, I, CRC, F | B Sends SIB to M |
| ←F, B, 011-0-001-0, I, CRC, F | |
| F, B, 000-0-011-0, I, CRC, F → | M Sends SIB to B |
| ←F, B, 011-1-010-0, I, CRC, F | B Sends Final SIB to M |
| F, B, 011-1-100-0, I, CRC, F → | M Sends Final SIB to B and Acks Blocks 0-2 |
| ←F, B, 101-1-01-01, CRC, F | B Acks Blocks 3, 4 and Advises Is Busy |
| F, C, 110-1-00-01, CRC, F → | M Polls C |
| ←F, C, 000-1-00-01, CRC, F | C Has No Data to Send |
| F, A, 000-1-00-01, CRC, F → | M Polls A |
| ←F, A, 000-1-00-01, CRC, F | A Has No Data to Send |
| F, B, 110-1-00-01, CRC, F → | M Polls B (Still Busy?) |
| ←F, B, 101-1-00-01, CRC, F | B Has No Data to Send and Is Normal |

M = Master Site
A, B, C = Slave Sites
F = Flag

I = Information Block
CRC = Cyclic Redundancy Check
SIB = Sequenced Information Block

**FIGURE 9-4**
SDLC-F/FDX Operation Sequence

163

the slave can only talk to the master. Therefore, in each case when a slave transmits to the master in the address byte, the slave site puts its own address. The control byte starts off with an 11, which identifies the transmission as a nonsequenced format, which, looking at Fig. 9–2, is seen as a "request for on line." With the P/F bit set as a 1 from the slave, the master knows that this is the final block being transmitted from the slave, and there will be no blocks after it. This is followed by the CRC and the end flag. B has requested on line.

The master now transmits flag, the address of B, the control byte starting with 11 (which means a nonsequenced format), and a set normal command. With the P/F bit being a 1, this is also a poll. This is followed by the CRC and flag. B then comes back and sends a flag, its own address, a nonsequenced control byte format acknowledging the command, and the P/F bit a 1, which says this is the final block of this sequence, followed by the CRC and end flag. These four steps now complete the sequence that establishes initial synchronization between the master and the slave, and this sequence must now occur between the master and every other slave site on the line to establish a basic synchronization of buffers. With this logic synchronization complete, the master and the slaves now know which messages are being transmitted and which ones are to be acknowledged. If desired at this time, the reader should draw a line across the page under the fourth line, and these four steps can be referred to as a typical synchronization sequence.

Next let us take a look at a transmission sequence where information must be passed in both directions. Remember we are showing this in a half-duplex arrangement for simplicity. Actually, the transmissions would be occurring in both directions at the same time. Figure 9–4 shows this mode, and the arrows in opposite directions could be taking place at the same time in Fig. 9–4 but cannot take place at the same time in Fig. 9–3.

The master starts off by sending a flag byte, B address, and then a supervisory format with a poll included. In other words, the master polls B. The assumption is made that B has three blocks of information to send, so it returns flag, its own address, and then an information format that has as the sending sequence number (Ns) 000. Note here that the P/F bit is a 0, which means that at least one more block is coming after this block is completed. The Nr is 000, which means the slave will expect to receive block 000 from the master when the master transmits information. I stands for an information block regardless of the length. This is followed by CRC and a flag. B then sends block 001 and block 010. Along with block 010 the P/F is set to a 1, which tells the master that this is the last block to be transmitted. The master waits for the end of the transmission, and in the meantime has put together a five-block message that must be sent to B.

We now have a flag byte and an address for B. In the control byte we have a 0, which specifies an information format, and then 000 for the first block to be transmitted. The P/F bit is next and is a 0, which means this is not a poll, and then Nr, which is set to 001. The fact that the master expects to get block number 011 from the slave the next time the slave transmits tells the slave that all blocks up to 010 have been received correctly. In this mode, SDLC has acknowledged three blocks of information being received from the slave site with a single transmission, and up to seven blocks can be acknowledged this way. Either individual or multiple block sequences can be acknowledged in this manner. The master then sends its information block, followed by a CRC and a flag.

Following this transmission block are blocks 001, 010, 011, and 100. Along with block 100 is a poll in the P/F bit position so that B is being polled. B does not have a message to send back to the master at this time, so it acknowledges by transmitting a flag, its own address, and a supervisory format acknowledging blocks 000 through 100 by putting a 101 into the control byte in positions 6, 7, and 8 (Nr). This is followed by the CRC and a flag. Between the line drawn above and this description line is a two-way transmission without an error. The reader may draw a line here under "B Acks Blocks 0–4" across the page, which will indicate a successful two-way transmission. Again, remember that in a true SDLC operation these transmissions would be occurring at the same time in a full-duplex mode.

Next let us take a look at a transmission where an error is recognized. The master sends out to site B a flag, B address, a supervisory format with a poll, a CRC, and a flag. B now has an eight-block message to send. B starts transmitting by sending a flag, its own address, and an information format starting with block 011 (note the block identification continues on). Block 100 is then sent, 101, 110, 111, 000 (wrap around now), and 001. Along with 001, the P/F bit is sent as a 1, because up to this point no acknowledgment has been received; and because this means seven blocks have been transmitted, the slave must stop transmitting until it gets an acknowledgment. An assumption is made that an error has been detected in block 101 at the master site.

To initiate the retransmission sequence, the master therefore sends back a flag, B address, and a supervisory format that indicates in the Nr segment that the next block expected is block 101. Included within this message is a poll. Since B has transmitted not only 101, but all succeeding blocks through 001, by definition of the SDLC protocol operations B recognizes that 101 was received in error. Also by definition of the protocol, not only must block 101 be transmitted, but all blocks after 101 that had been transmitted must also be retransmitted. This is known as the *Go back N Technique* and is significant in that only a maximum of seven buffers must be available to store the seven blocks of information at both ends of an SDLC communication link. For other vendor protocols like SDLC, where many more blocks can be in transit before an acknowledgment is received, many more buffers will be needed at either end to store information for the case where acknowledgments have yet to be received.

B, recognizing that block 101 was received in error, now transmits blocks 101, 110, 111, 000, 001, *and* block 010. B can send block 010 now because the first two blocks of the original sequence were acknowledged as part of the previous transmission, and there were only six blocks in this sequence to be transmitted. The master answers back now with an acknowledgment indicating that the next block to be received is 011. This tells B that all blocks through 010 have been received correctly now, and therefore no additional retransmissions are required. The reader can now draw a line under "M Acks Blocks 5–2," and this sequence can be considered a two-way transmission where one of the sequences contains an error.

The last two lines show a disconnect command, which is used when a terminal site is to be taken out of service in an orderly manner. The master sends a flag, B address, a nonsequenced format, which is interpreted as a disconnect command, followed by the CRC and a flag. Included within this transmission is a poll. B then answers back with a flag, its own address, and a nonsequenced format that acknowledges the command, and at the same time indicates this is a final transmission. At this time B disconnects, and now a brand new synchronization sequence must be initiated before the master can talk to B again.

A true full/full-duplex operation is depicted in Fig. 9–4, although no error transmissions are shown. When going through the sequence, keep in mind that when arrows are in two different directions those transmissions may be occurring at the same time. This is the way true SDLC can operate on a multidrop line.

# E
# HALF-DUPLEX/FULL-DUPLEX COMPARISONS

At no time during the description of circuits in Chapter 6 was the flow of information described, and at no time in the description of simple protocols in this chapter was the circuit described. Yet, both circuits and protocols have been described as being half duplex and/or full duplex. Not only has this been a very confusing situation but it is not complete, because modems are also described as being half duplex or full duplex, and there is yet a fourth entity, called Echoplex, which is also described as half duplex or full duplex. This section will put all of them into perspective so you can describe any one of the situations functionally rather than having to rely on the definition of a term that very few people agree on anyway.

By referring to Table 9–2, you can see a matrix of all of the half-duplex and full-duplex definitions for a circuit, protocol, and a modem. You can have a half-duplex protocol on a half-duplex circuit, but the modem you use, depend-

TABLE 9–2
HDX/FDX Comparison

| CIRCUIT | PROTOCOL | MODEM | EXAMPLE |
| --- | --- | --- | --- |
| HDX | HDX | 2-wire—HDX or FDX | Bisync on a dial line |
| | | 2-wire—FDX | PC on a dial line |
| FDX | HDX | 4-wire—HDX or FDX | Bisync on a leased line |
| FDX | FDX | 4-wire—FDX | SDLC on a leased line |
| HDX | FDX | 2-wire—FDX | SDLC on a dial line |
| FDX | F/FDX | 4-wire—FDX | SDLC on a leased, multidrop line |

ing on your particular DTE, must be specifically an HDX or an FDX modem, as seen under the example column. All PCs have a very simplistic TTY-type protocol that does not allow the modem being used to instantaneously reverse direction of transmission (*Line Turnaround* or *Modem Turnaround* [LTA or MTA]). Therefore a modem that is capable of transmitting both ways at the same time must be used for a PC. Even though the modem is only used here for transmission one way at a time, it must be capable of transmitting both ways simultaneously so that the logic of the protocol, which provides no delay between reception and transmission of a new message, can be accommodated.

On the other hand, bisync has all the necessary controls to accommodate modem turnaround, and so does any other protocol that uses *Request to Send* and *Clear to Send* (described in Chapter 5). Therefore, bisync and these other protocols can utilize a half-duplex modem. A full-duplex modem can also be used by bisync, in which case there is no time delay between reception of a message and a transmission back to the other end (because the RTS/CTS delay will be eliminated).

The second example shows a full-duplex circuit with a half-duplex protocol, where a four-wire modem is necessary. It can be an HDX or FDX modem if bisync is used, and bisync will probably be the protocol of choice on a leased line. If a PC is used on a leased line it is probably emulating a terminal, and if the terminal has something like RTS/CTS, then the PC does not look like a PC on the line, but looks like the terminal it is emulating.

The third example shows a full-duplex protocol on a full-duplex circuit, which needs a four-wire full-duplex modem because SDLC, or something like it, is typically how this circuit is implemented.

On the fourth line we have a full-duplex protocol like SDLC on a half-duplex circuit, which would occur when there is a dial situation. The modem here must be a two-wire modem, and must also be FDX to support the simultaneous two-way information flow.

The final example is the FDX circuit with an F/FDX protocol, which is the way SDLC would operate on a leased, multidrop line. A four-wire FDX modem is necessary here because information flow must be supported in two directions on the leased line, which is four wires.

As can be seen, the circuit, protocol, and modem can all be described as half- or full-duplex. If there is apparent confusion regarding the definition of the terms, the user must remember that there are no definitions for these terms agreed upon by everyone. It will be much better to describe *functionally* what is occurring and not use the terms *half duplex* or *full duplex* at all. If the people understand the process that is going on, no one will have to rely on different definitions of the same term.

Another term described as being half duplex or full duplex is the term *Echoplex*. Echoplex came from the world of Teletype many years ago when the only storage medium was paper tape. This gave rise to two separate modes of operation. In the first mode, a user at a TTY location would depress a character on the keyboard. Two choices were then available. The character could be transmitted on the line to the other end, stored there, and then sent back for display on the local printer. The alternative was to key the character in locally, display it (on the printer), and then transmit the character without any return. Because the Teletype world was one in which only one device could be transmitting at any one time, there was never a problem of interleaved information between multiple devices on the same line. Today's world, however, is much different. Terminals rarely transmit *on line*. They are buffered and transmit entire messages (or at least blocks of data) upon operator completion.

When the operator must wait for an **echo** before display, it is described as full-duplex echoplex. When the display is immediate and the transmission takes place without an **echo,** it is known as half-duplex echoplex.

The two terms seemed to have disappeared from the vocabulary for a while, but with the advent of PCs, the term *echoplex* is back. Because PCs have the TTY protocols that contained echoplex in the first place, echos are now available when PCs are used as communicating terminals with the TTY protocol.

Interesting situations arise when a PC is configured as a terminal because of options regarding the use of the echo in either or both the modem and the operating system of the computer. The result may be that the character is not displayed when it is keyed in, or that the same character is displayed up to three times. If the PC is put in FDX mode and both the modem and operating system are put in the HDX mode, the character will not be displayed on the screen because the user is transmitting with the expectation of receiving an echo, while the modem and operating system do not echo. On the other hand, if the PC is set in HDX mode and the modem and operating system are set in the FDX mode, there will be three separate displays, one when the character is keyed in, and one each time the modem and the operating system echo that character back. Obviously, depending on the configuration set up, there can be one, two, or three displays of the character. Although there is always a recommended way for a particular application to set up the switches in the echoplex configuration, the documentation is not always clear as to what switch settings will actually do.

Figure 9–5 shows the circuit that provides for the different echos. *A* comes from the local PC, *B* comes from the modem, and *C* comes from the host site. Any one of them can be enabled or disabled, which is why the displays can range from none to three.

Because of the many uses of the terms *half duplex* and *full duplex* that may be used in your organization, the terms must be defined each time carefully. It is always recommended that a diagram be drawn describing the functional operation to supplement the definitions and to show what is actually occurring instead of relying on ambiguous terminology.

## F

## ARQ HALF-DUPLEX PROTOCOLS

Since the first edition of this text, many students have requested further information on the type of half-duplex protocols called *automatic repeat request* (ARQ). Each of these types of protocols has a different mechanism for its transmission

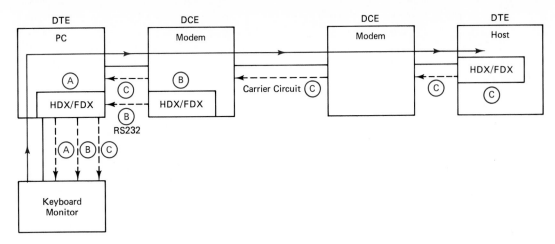

**FIGURE 9–5**
Echoplex

and acknowledgment sequence. This section will deal with the different types of ARQ protocols.

Discussed first is the *Stop and Wait* ARQ, typified by a protocol where one block is sent at a time, with another block not being sent until an acknowledgment has been received for the first, just like bisync, which was described earlier. If a negative acknowledgment (NAK) is received after a particular block is transmitted, that same block will be retransmitted before any new block is transmitted. If either the ACK or NAK is no good, the protocol will *time out* and then retransmit the same block. A diagram of a Stop and Wait ARQ protocol is shown in Fig. 9–6 where you can see block 1 being acknowledged, block 2 being NAK'd, block 2 NAK'd again, then block 2 ACK'd, and then finally block 3 ACK'd.

The next type of ARQ protocol is *Continuous* ARQ, shown in Fig. 9–7. In the top part of the diagram, you have five consecutive blocks transmitted, then an acknowledgment for six. ACK 6 indicates that the next block requested by the receiver is block 6, which in turn tells the transmitter that the first five blocks were received correctly. Blocks 6 and 7 are then transmitted and followed by ACK 8, which means the next block that the receiver wants is block 8. That message tells the transmitter that blocks 6 and 7 were received correctly.

In the bottom half of Fig. 9–7 is the transmission of the same five blocks with an ACK for block 4 returned instead of an ACK for 6, which tells the trans-

**FIGURE 9–6**
Stop and Wait ARQ Protocol

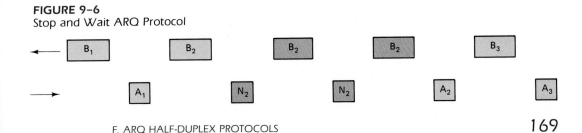

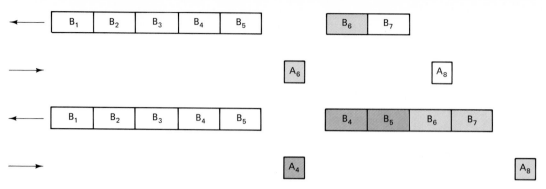

**FIGURE 9–7**
Continuous ARQ Protocol (also called Go Back-N)

mitter that block 4 was received in error and must be retransmitted. The second block stream shows blocks 4 through 7 all being sent together with an acknowledgment for 8 being returned, which tells the transmitter that blocks 4 through 7 were received correctly. This technique is also known as the *Go Back N* technique, which was also described under SDLC and is unique in that the ACK identifies the *next* block the receiver wants to see, and not the last block received correctly.

Finally, we have Fig. 9–8 which describes the *Selective Reject* ARQ protocol. In this sequence you see five blocks being transmitted, and if we make the assumption that an error was received in blocks 2 and 4, the following sequence is what occurs. A NAK for message 2 is returned, which causes block 2 to be retransmitted. Then a NAK for 4 is returned, which causes block 4 to be retransmitted. Now an ACK for 6 is returned, which means that block 5 was received correctly and the next block to be transmitted is block 6. If either block 2 or 4 were retransmitted and still received in error, a NAK for that block would be returned, and this process would be repeated until all blocks were received correctly or the quantity of retransmissions exceeded the amount set by the user in the software at which time the error handling mode of operation would be initiated.

One last question seems to come up when discussing any one of these protocols: "What does transparent mode mean?" It means a capability to transmit all the information bits of a message without worrying about what those bits repre-

**FIGURE 9–8**
Selective Reject ARQ Protocol

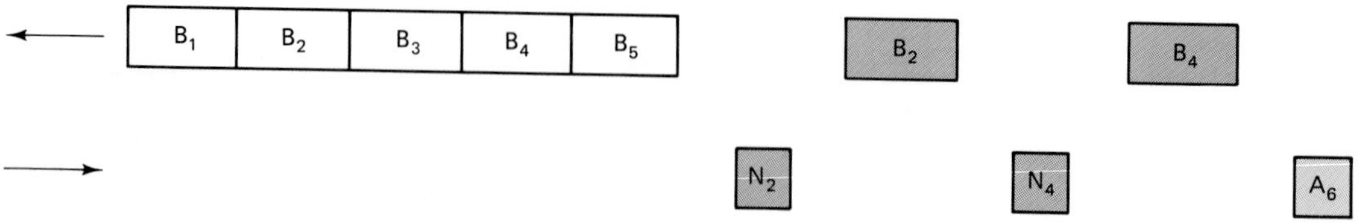

| SYNC | SYNC | SOM | CNTRL | Count | Variable Length | Error Detect | EOM |
|------|------|-----|-------|-------|-----------------|--------------|-----|

**FIGURE 9-9**
Transparent Mode Format

sent. It is used when transmitting in either binary stream mode or some code set other than that being used by the DTE. It is a transmission (must be synchronous) with a header portion that identifies the beginning of the message, a value that tells the receiver how long the variable portion is, and then some form of error detection at the end. The contents of the variable portion will not be decoded until it reaches the point in the DTE or application program in the CPU where information is to be interpreted (not necessarily in the transmitted code set). A diagram of this type of message format is shown in Fig. 9-9.

# G
# FLOW-CONTROL PROTOCOLS

Another type of protocol that was common many years ago and is getting renewed attention in the PC world is the *Flow-Control* protocol. Flow-control protocols consist primarily of low-speed asynchronous-type communications between PCs and peripherals, but are also applicable when terminals are talking to computers. Flow control allows transmission on a continuous basis until there is a specific instruction not to transmit anymore. One of the most common of these is the so-called Xon/Xoff protocol. It is also known as an *inband* protocol because an ASCII character is used to define the Xon/Xoff functions. An Xon character is sent by a device to let another know that it can accept data at any time. The Xoff is sent when data can no longer be accepted. Typically this is the sequence of events in a terminal to a printer communication with the printer sending an Xon when it can receive data in its buffer and an Xoff when its buffer is filled. The cycle continues until the entire message is sent.

A second form of flow-control protocol is called the DTRon or DTRoff protocol. DTR is the Data Terminal Ready signal in the RS232 interface. When a DTR signal is on it means that the device can accept information, and when the DTR signal is off, it means that the device can no longer accept information. This operation is the same as Xon and Xoff in that as a buffer is filling in a printer the DTR can be high, and as soon as the buffer gets full the DTR signal can be turned off.

A third form of flow control is called ETX/ACK, which is an acronym for End of text/Acknowledge. The ETX/ACK is also similar to Xon/Xoff in that it is a software-type flow control. In this case the data must be sent in a block of a predetermined length, which is defined based on the size of the buffers in the devices between which the information is being sent (the smallest buffer determines the block size). A block is sent in the predefined length and terminated with an ETX character. An ACK must be returned by that device before another block of the same length can be sent. The block being transmitted is sent with an ETX character at the end regardless of its length, and the transmitting device will then not send any additional data until the recipient returns an ACK character. Notice that the ACK in this case does not signify receipt of error-free transmission like standard data communications protocols. It only means *send another block*.

# H
## PC PROTOCOLS

PCs have radically changed the communications world. There are all kinds of products and services oriented toward the PC as a standalone device and the PC as a terminal. Products change literally on a daily basis, so even though there is an enormous amount of information available, a lot of it becomes obsolete by continuously updated announcements. There is no doubt that by the time this text gets into print there will be much more that is obsolete. Therefore, this section will deal with the PC protocols for data communications purposes over standard communication links. Because the methodology of PC communications is changing so fast, only the generics will be described here. For current information, the user must get it from the vendors *on the fly*. The special applications that deal with PCs operating in a local area network environment will be covered in Chapter 15 on LANs.

The majority of PC interfaces connected to communication networks have been low-speed asynchronous TTY-compatible-like protocols connected directly to a device at the other end of the circuit that communicates utilizing the same protocol. TTY protocols have serious limitations in that they cannot tolerate modem line turnarounds (described earlier in this chapter). Therefore PCs must be used with full-duplex modems unless they have some form of protocol conversion interface, which will be described in Section J. In addition, PCs have no inherent method of error detection and correction because TTY protocols did not incorporate that. As such, the majority of PC communications have to be validated by applications software if it exists. This is obviously a very dangerous way to transmit information if files are being moved from one PC to another without operator intervention. Recently error-detection schemes have been incorporated into some of the modems that operate in the PC environment. They will be described separately in Section I, Modem Protocols.

PC-to-PC communications cannot be viewed the same way other terminals are. Other terminals typically communicate with hosts using predetermined protocols that are already incorporated into both ends of the circuit. When it comes to PCs, almost everything has to be done from the ground up. Therefore, before we get into the different kinds of PC protocols we will take a look at the physical PC interface.

A PC will typically have communication ports that are labeled COM 1/2/ 3 and so on. Then they have a whole series of parameters for the selection of a particular operation. Seven bit characters are used to transmit ASCII files; 8-bit characters are used to transmit binary files such as word processing documents. To transmit binary the switch must be set for 8 bits, which will incorporate both the ASCII and the binary transmission. However, to use *parity* when transmitting with ASCII, the 7-bit transmission must be used.

The next setting on the PC is parity, which can only be used for text files (ASCII). The options are:

*Mark/Space.* Parity is not used for error detection here but as a position filler (mark is always 1 and space is always 0). Parity is not generated by the transmitter or checked by the receiver.

*None.* No parity is generated or expected.

*Odd.* The number of 1 bits in the character is odd.

*Even.* The number of 1 bits in the character is even.

The next parameter to set is the amount of *start* and *stop* bits. These come in two forms, predominantly one start and one stop. One start with two stops is common in certain older machines. A setting might be 8N1, which would stand for 8-bit characters/no parity/one stop bit, or 7E2, which would stand for seven data bits/even parity/two stop bits.

Finally there is the setting for the echoplex, which is half duplex (HDX) or full duplex (FDX). HDX means you transmit one way at a time (transmit a character and display it at the same time) and FDX means simultaneous two-way transmission (key character in and transmit, then display the return).

The settings will depend on the particular application and the kind of information to be moved. When the information is moved, there are two kinds of transfer, both called *file transfers*. The same protocol must exist in both the PC and the device it is communicating with (another PC or a host). The first type is a *blind* transfer in which the information sent is captured by the other end without any verification that it got there correctly. The second kind of transfer is a *protocol* file transfer, in which a predetermined sequence of actions takes place to move the file, which may include a form of acknowledgment that the information was received correctly. In most of these cases, to receive text on a PC from a host you must instruct the host to list a file and then capture that file to your memory. Everything received then becomes part of the captured data including the necessary controls, which means the file can be printed the way it was intended to appear. Secondly, to send data to the host, put the host editor in *input* mode. Then, while the editor is expecting specific keystrokes, tell the communications program to send an entire file. A warning: If the editor is not fast enough, *flow control* (described in Section G) may be needed.

The typical flow control used is Xon/Xoff. If Xon/Xoff is not utilized in the host, a specific transfer character like carriage return (CR) may be needed. Be very careful when using CR for file transfers because some editors may turn off when they receive two consecutive CR characters and that will shut off the new transmission. Instead of a CR a predetermined time delay can be used before sending the next character or line, but that may cause a severe reduction in transfer efficiency.

The file-transfer protocols operate with a copy of the protocol in both machines. Many protocols are both proprietary and in the public domain. By 1987 there were over 50 different file-transfer protocols, each with its own advantages and disadvantages. Without getting into the trade-offs between the various protocols, for which 50 different users may have 50 different opinions, what will be described here are some of the more common protocols being used for file transfer.

One of the most common protocols is XModem, sometimes called XModem/Checksum. Data is put into 128-byte packets (data is 8-bit characters). A checksum byte is calculated for error detection, and the receiver compares it to the checksum it calculates independently on receipt of the transmission. If they are the same, an acknowledgment is sent for that packet. Packets are continually sent until the message has been completed. It is possible for the checksum byte to allow some errors to get through, so XModem CRC may be used because it incorporates a much better error detecting scheme based on a 16-bit CRC (described in Chapter 13). XModem moves data one way at a time (HDX).

Two variations to XModem add to the features just described: (1) YModem transmits information in 1024-byte packets instead of 128-byte packets, and (2) ZModem does not wait for individual packet acknowledgment before sending out the next packet. In other words, the entire file becomes a *window*.

Another fairly common file-transfer protocol is *Kermit*. Kermit can be utilized in almost all machines and handles batch files very well. It requires only a 7-bit data byte, but an 8-bit byte version is also available. The packet size is less than 128 characters, so it is somewhat slower than XModem, but as an added feature it can handle file name conventions and wild card file specs. KERMIT is also called Sliding Window KERMIT. It is referred to by this name because KERMIT is capable of transmitting any number of blocks up to 32 before an ACK must be received. When a NAK is received, KERMIT utilizes the Go Back N technique, which means the block in error must be retransmitted as well as all subsequent blocks because they have been ignored by the receiver (part of the protocol definition). In contrast ZMODEM uses *only* NAKs, at which time it uses the Go Back N technique. For both protocols to be efficient the packet size should be 3 to 12 Kbytes and should be used with MNP Class 6 (described in Section I) for optimizing information throughput.

Another PC protocol with fairly wide implementation is BLAST II. This is a very efficient protocol that is able to handle variable propagation delays. If there is any kind of problem BLAST II will retransmit from the point of interruption rather than start at the beginning. BLAST II can handle both synchronous and asynchronous transmissions.

As mentioned before, there are many different protocols for use with PCs and the descriptions here should not be taken as recommendations, only as a description of what functions are available. There are others, some of which may be better for a particular use, so before implementing any PC-oriented file-transfer protocol, the user should find out what the latest software is and if it is better suited to that particular application.

Another level of PC protocol is not truly a PC protocol but an information-transfer capability that includes one of the file-transfer protocols (or multiples) within its domain. Protocols having this capability provide modem management, terminal emulation, communications port management, user interface (including application log ons), file management, and run the file-transfer protocol. One popular package is *Smartcom* from Hayes, which comes in many different versions for different machines (and different levels as new features become available). Another popular package is *Crosstalk* from Microstuf. To operate these programs the user needs to know how the PC is configured, whether the screen is monochrome or color, how many communication ports there are, what kind of printers and ports are connected, what kind of modem is connected, and where the modem connected. Also needed are the details of each of the systems that the programs will communicate with and how that communication will take place. This includes whether the connection is direct or if a dial function needs to be performed, whether telephone numbers are required, and the speed, parity, bit length and other parameters for operation. If these are not defined, a set of *default* conditions will be incorporated automatically.

In the sequence of events that takes place when dialing to a host location, the user first identifies the host. The program then loads the appropriate parameters for that particular host and sets up the communications port with the appropriate speed and parity for that connection. Next it sends the necessary commands to the modem to dial the host. Once the modem responds that the connection has been established, the program initiates the appropriate *log on* macro. If accepted by the host, the program then prompts the user with a "ready," indicating that the session is ready to begin.

Programs like Smartcom and Crosstalk automate many of the functions that the user would otherwise have to perform manually, from the set-up of the appropriate parameters to the dialing sequence, to the actual log on for a particular application. Many people who use these programs don't realize how much is being done for them in this automated mode. Several of the file-transfer protocols can be incorporated into these programs, creating a wide variety of uses and applications, multiplied by the many versions of Smartcom and Crosstalk and the additional features that are continually being incorporated. In addition, there are differences between the two programs. For example, Crosstalk is a command-driven program with multiple commands available for the user to initiate, while Smartcom is menu driven and has no commands. Depending on personal tastes the user may like one or the other based on particular features that are available on one and not the other. Once again, the user should verify the latest versions of the programs and check to see if other programs might be currently available that would do even more.

Many other types of programs used with PCs are sometimes called protocols, but they are more like applications software, and so they are not discussed here. Additional software is available for accessing local area networks, some of which will be covered in Chapter 15.

## MODEM PROTOCOLS

There really are no true modem protocols. What have been described as modem protocols are really error-detection and correction functions incorporated into modems to make up for the lack of error-detection capability on dial-up asynchronous links, common when accessing a packet-switching network at 300 BPS and 1200 BPS. Any errors generated in this path will not be recognized. Therefore, for data going from the terminal to the host, if errors are generated on this type of connection (terminal to packet node) they will not be recognized until they are detected in the host processor. Once the bits arrive at the node from the PC, the bit integrity is guaranteed throughout the packet network until it reaches the host as long as the host is X.25 (described in Chapter 17) compatible. If the user is communicating to another PC at the other end of the packet network, the connection between the final packet-switching node and the other PC will also suffer from the lack of transmission integrity.

The process also works the other way, in that the user can transmit without errors into the network, get all the way to the host and have the host return a message to the packet-switching node, but an error is generated when the local node transmits to the originating PC. You don't know where the error came from, but there is an error that can show up in a variety of forms at your PC.

The so-called modem protocols provide a mechanism on the link between the user and the packet node (or from the user directly to another PC) for detecting errors on that link. They put the information in block form in an internal buffer. The block is transmitted to the modem at the other end of the link (packet node or other PC), at which time the block is checked for errors. If an error is detected, the software in the modem goes back to the transmitting modem and requests a retransmission of that block. The retransmission is repeated until the block is received correctly. The methodology used for detecting the errors is CRC (see Chapter 13).

There are many other applications for error detecting algorithms. The two major *protocols* that provide error detection today are MNP and X.PC. X.PC was originally promoted by TYMNET and is based on X.25 characteristics, which make it very much like a dial-up X.25-type connection. In competition with X.PC, TELENET recommended MNP (Microcom Networking Protocol), which functionally operates the same way. There was controversy concerning the two, and for a while they were used in modems on an essentially equal basis. In 1987, however, the use of MNP began to grow in relation to X.PC. Although there are other proprietary products that perform the same kind of function, it seems that MNP will be the one that will primarily be used for PC-to-PC or PC-to-packet network communications.

As was described, MNP is not a true protocol because information is not moved between DTE type devices. As an error detecting algorithm, however, it has one very important application. Figure 9–10 shows the configuration of an asynchronous terminal such as a PC communicating through a packet network to a host site X.25 interface. In a packet node under normal operations, all communications in the packet network have error detection capability as part of the HDLC protocol. In communicating to an X.25 port, the user also has error detection on the link between the packet network and the host site. The problem occurs with the connection between the originating PC and the local node. Asynchronous transmissions do not have error detection capability built in because parity is no longer a valid method for detecting errors (described in Chapter 13). Some of the modem vendors have incorporated the MNP protocol into their modems so that asynchronous transmissions can be put into *block form* in either modem and sent out over the connection between the user and the asynchronous pad with a CRC, which in turn can be used to detect errors in that transmission. This

**FIGURE 9–10**
Use of MNP for Packet Interface

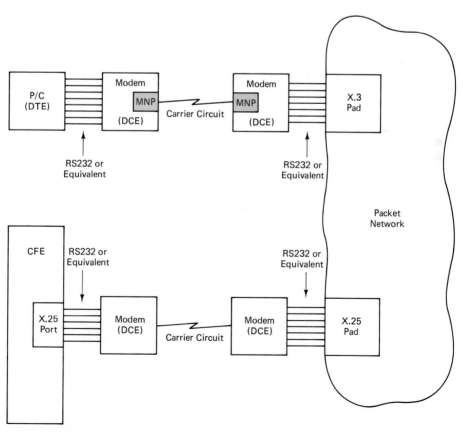

methodology is transparent to the end user but provides a complete end-to-end error detection capability.

By providing this process the user can be reassured that transmissions on an *end-to-end* basis will not contain any errors. This is very important for those dial-up connections, where the quality of the circuit cannot be guaranteed and where most errors are introduced into the transmissions. Of course MNP is not limited to modem-to-modem transmission. It can be used within a PC file-transfer protocol also but to date has only limited use in that area.

MNP provides the ability for modems to communicate with each other and incorporate both error detection and, in later versions, data compression capabilities. There are multiple levels (sometimes called classes) of MNP protocols. They are

*Class 1.* Used for asynchronous, byte-oriented, half-duplex, block transmission of data. It is approximately 70 percent efficient and is rarely used today.

*Class 2.* Adds full-duplex capability to Class 1. It is 84 percent efficient but is becoming less popular as the higher levels become available.

*Class 3.* Used for asynchronous, bit-oriented, full-duplex transmissions where data packets are used to eliminate the start and stop bits for asynchronous characters. Because of this, it is approximately 108 percent efficient.

*Class 4.* This level of MNP incorporates an adaptive packet-size assembly capability that provides longer packets as error rates decrease. As such when there are less errors, the packets are longer, which in turn provides a higher level of transmission efficiency because the overhead and framing bits do not change. Class 4 MNP will provide up to 120 percent transmission efficiency.

*Class 5.* Adds data compression to Class 4, utilizing a proprietary mechanism with a real-time, adaptive algorithm. The compression will typically vary between 1.3:1 and 2:1 so that typical efficiency can run up to 200 percent.

*Class 6.* At this level there is the addition of a Universal Link Negotiation (ULN) capability and what Microcom calls Statistical Duplexing Capability to Class 5. ULN allows a single modem to operate at speeds between 50 and 9600 BPS by starting at the lowest speed and negotiating upward with the modem at the other end. Naturally, the modems at each end of the line must both have this level of capability in order to provide the negotiation. With statistical duplexing there is a very fast line turnaround for half-duplex modems like the V.27 and the V.29 modems. Class 6 software will monitor the data waiting and change the transmit direction when applicable to simulate full-duplex operation as close as possible.

*Class 7.* This level adds an adaptive encoding technique to the process that provides up to 300 percent data throughput efficiency.

*Class 8.* The additional feature here is the provision of a V.29 *fast train*

capability and emulation of full-duplex data transmission. Class 8 still incorporates enhanced data compression.

*Class 9.* Incorporates V.32 technology and provides a full-duplex throughput data capability of up to 300 percent more than standard V.32 modems.

Classes 1 through 4 were already in the public domain by 1988, while the rest were still proprietary. Future classes are expected to have encryption capability incorporated.

With all the talk about error correction being performed between modems, a spec identified as V.42 has been issued by the CCITT for standardizing modem error correcting protocols. It involves the ability to negotiate which protocol to use without any user intervention. Because of political considerations, there are two protocols that are incorporated into V.42. The first one is LAPM, a subset of the X.25 LAP protocol, that was originally desired by the CCITT. V.42 also incorporates the Microcom MNP Classes 2–4 protocols because there were almost one-half million modems in use by the time V.42 came out. To keep those modems from becoming obsolete overnight, MNP was incorporated.

The implementation will be on the modems which meet the V.22bis and V.32 protocols. If the user would like to add data compression which is already available with higher-level MNP protocols, then a proprietary protocol must be used.

## J

# PROTOCOL CONVERSION

When PCs first emerged in the early 1980s, incorporated into them were the simplest of all communications protocols, TTY. As mentioned before, TTY does not have the ability to accommodate modem/line turnarounds, nor does it have a lot of the controls that would be inherent in protocols for terminals with more communications capability. The PCs did quite a bit of standalone processing early on and then, in a minimal form, communicated with other PCs. It was soon recognized that the PC was a very powerful processing tool that could function like a terminal in a network environment. The problem was that it did not look like any other terminal and the PC had completely alien interfaces. The best the host could hope to do was to communicate utilizing the archaic TTY protocol. For many years TTY was the dominant protocol for PCs to communicate with host site mainframes. This connection is shown in Fig. 9–11(a). The PC functions as a standard DTE and communicates utilizing the TTY protocol through a modem such as the 212 or V.22 that is capable of transmitting at 300 BPS or 1200 BPS (the V.22 actually transmits at either 600 BPS or 1200 BPS). At the host site the modem is connected via an RS232 interface to a port on the communications front end (CFE). The port is configured to be TTY-compatible.

The typical speeds for this connection were 300 BPS or 1200 BPS. In the mid-1980s the V.22bis modem came out, which allowed this connection to operate at up to 2400 BPS. All transmissions were asynchronous.

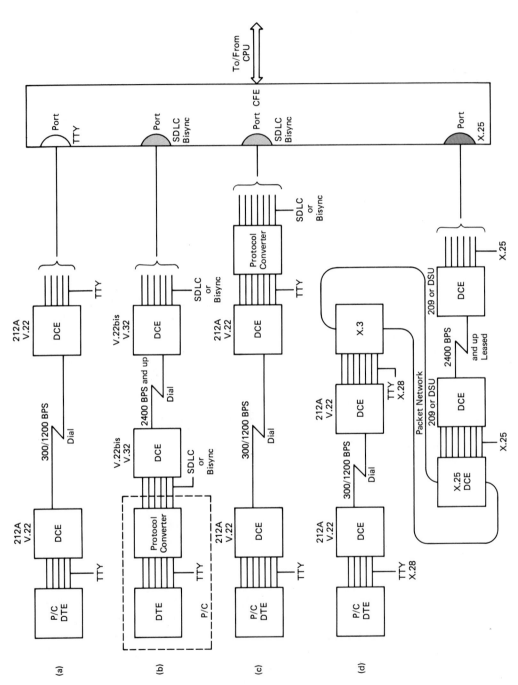

**FIGURE 9–11**
Protocol Conversion

180

Parallel to this mode of operation, IBM announced that they would not support low-speed asynchronous interfaces in future SNA implementations. Thus no devices communicating in an SNA environment could use the TTY protocol, and they all had to be compatible with either Bisync or SDLC. As a result the development of *Protocol Converters* began in earnest. A protocol converter makes a device look like a different one when connected on a communication line. One method for doing this is shown in Fig. 9–11(b). The PC is still the same and it communicates via its TTY protocol, but in this instance the output goes to the protocol converter, which can be in a standalone box or on a card that is installed in an expansion slot of the PC. The box shown in the diagram around the DTE and the protocol converter is the configuration, with the protocol converter in one of the slots. Coming out of the PC now is either the SDLC or Bisync protocol. Notice that the PC has not changed at all, but it looks like it has because it is communicating via a different protocol. The interface here is to a modem that must communicate synchronously at 2400 BPS and up, such as a V.22bis or V.32 modem. At the host site the modem is now connected to a different port that is configured to communicate with either SDLC or Bisync (one or the other, and it must be set up as part of the original configuration). Bisync cannot be transmitted one time and then SDLC another time into the same port unless the port is reconfigured to communicate using the other protocol.

An alternative method for performing this kind of protocol conversion is shown in Fig. 9–11(c) where this time the conversion is performed at the host site. The port still thinks it is communicating with either SDLC or Bisync, but the conversion is done locally rather than at the remote site.

The arguments for using one configuration or the other in Fig. 9–11(b) and (c) are many and are usually determined by the particular application and who owns which pieces of equipment. For example, if the user owns the host site and other people own the remote terminals from which they dial in, the user would probably say that the others ought to do the conversion and pay for the converters. If the user owns both ends of the link, he or she may feel that a higher throughput can be achieved by putting the converters at each site, keeping in mind that transmitting at a higher speed does not mean a higher throughput. Many people discover when they go to 2400 BPS or higher that their throughput is not as great as they had thought it would be, in some cases even less than at 1200 BPS. The reason for this is that the communication line between the terminal and the host may not be capable of supporting the higher-speed transmission and the amount of errors keeps the overall throughput down.

Another important consideration: If many terminals are in the remote environment, not all of them will be busy at the same time and there is a limited number of ports in the CFE for communicating with them. Let us say there are 200 remote locations and 50 ports. Only 50 remotes can be busy at any one time, so if a converter is put at each of the remote locations, the user is paying for 200 protocol converters as well as 200 pairs of higher-speed modems, which are more expensive. On the other hand, if a higher throughput can truly be achieved on the dial lines at 2400 BPS, for example, the amount of time spent on the communication line is less and will therefore cost less money. The problem is that you cannot foresee how good the lines are going to be until the higher-speed equipment is actually installed at the remote sites. Each one of these situations must be determined on an application-by-application basis, and it is strongly suggested that tests be performed from the remotes if you anticipate dialing in at a transmission speed greater than 1200 BPS.

Another common form of protocol conversion is performed in the packet-switching network, shown in Fig. 9–11(d). Communication is still via the teletype protocol to a local packet-switching node where the line is terminated in an X.3 PAD (described in Chapter 17). The transmission is made at the 300 BPS or 1200 BPS rate (or 2400 BPS in some nodes). In the packet network the transmission is converted to an X.25 form so that when it gets to the host node location, the transmission to the host may also utilize the X.25 protocol. A big advantage to this type of connection is that the port in the CFE can support up to 1024 terminals simultaneously (it is rarely done, but the port can support hundreds of independent terminals simultaneously because they are operating at a low speed while the port is operating at high speed and interleaving the communications of the various remote locations). This kind of configuration is very good for a diverse geographic distribution of remotes with random call-in patterns. The big negative is that the X.25 port is very expensive (when first announced for the IBM 3725 it was $12,000). Still, if many remote locations will be calling in at random times, the user can communicate with most or all of them through a single port rather than many low-speed ports. Even though the low-speed ports are much less expensive on a per-port basis, the total may approach or exceed the cost of the single X.25 port. Utilizing this last mechanism, the throughput will still be somewhat less than any of the others and the response time a little longer because the packet network provides a store-and-forward function in addition to the communication with the node at 300 BPS or 1200 BPS.

Many of the companies that build protocol converters today are providing additional conversion for a wide variety of devices—Bisync to X.25, SDLC to X.25, and others that came on the market when the volume of conversion made it economically feasible to develop such devices. More will no doubt become available as the interconnection of networks proliferates.

Protocol converters are also called *terminal emulators,* although some vendors build terminal emulators as complete standalone terminals in which the emulation is done directly in the terminal. Regardless of what the device is called, the end result is the same, making one device look like a different device on a communication line.

K
## DIAL-UP AND DEDICATED HANDSHAKING

Up to this point we have been discussing the line-discipline portion of a protocol. Even more critical, before the data transmission can start, a valid circuit must be established that can support the information transmission. The technique for validating the availability and operability of a circuit is called *handshaking*. Different modes of handshake are applicable to the different kinds of circuits involved (see Chapter 6). This section will cover the details of the handshaking procedure as they apply to both types of circuits and all descriptions will be made using the RS232 nomenclature as a reference.

Four of the most common handshaking procedures are shown in Figs. 9–12 through 9–15. Figure 9–12 shows the procedure that takes place at an RS232C interface for a private-line full-duplex circuit operation. Figure 9–13 shows the RS232C interface for a half-duplex private-line interface. (Note that in most cases a user, when leasing a line, will get a full-duplex line and not a half-duplex line because of the minimal difference in cost.) Figure 9–14 describes the RS232C interface for a dial-up half-duplex mode of operation, and Fig. 9–15 describes the handshaking sequence that occurs on a full-duplex leased line with reverse channel. These are some of the handshake sequences on typical point-to-point type connections, but very much the same sequence takes place in a multidrop private line between the master and each remote site. Once the handshaking is complete and the circuit is confirmed, information can be passed back and forth until one end decides to terminate the sequence.

Because the descriptions are presented in the same format and at the same level of detail, all the sequences will not be described. Only the full-duplex private line (Fig. 9–12) will be described.

The handshaking sequences are described with respect to their relationship at the RS232C interface, which was described in detail in Chapter 5. Referring then to Fig. 9–12, we find on the left side of the page the definition of the signal and its designation, the direction of the signal transmission between the controller and the modem (designated by the arrows), the functions that occur on the modem (or line), the arrows depicting the direction of signal at the central site end, and finally the definition of the signals at the central site.

Starting off at the top line, we have the frame ground (not used in RS232D), which ties the modem and the controller together at each end of the line. Then we have the signal grounds that provide common return paths for all signals. At the remote end the "terminal ready" signal is sent to the modem from the terminal while the "modem ready" signal is sent back to the terminal from the modem. This indicates that both units are capable of operation. At the other end of the line at the same time, we have "modem ready" being transmitted to the central site controller port (like the terminal) and the control port indicating to the modem that it is ready.

From a DTE data viewpoint, therefore, both ends are ready to transmit. If we assume that both ends would like to transmit at the same time, the protocol on the digital side of the interface will initiate the "request to send" signal. At the modem, only because this is full duplex, the signal is "strapped" back to the "clear to send" signal interface so that the digital side is now ready to transmit. Since synchronous transmission requires modem training time (described in Chapter 8), the first transmission of a sequence must allow for that time delay so the first message will not be lost. Subsequent messages in a sequence do not have to be resynchronized because the modem will stay in sync as long as data

184

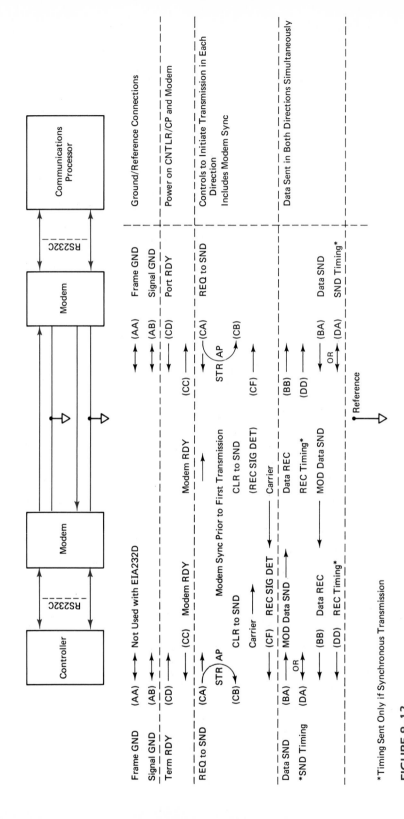

**FIGURE 9-12**
FDX Private-Line Handshaking

*Timing Sent Only if Synchronous Transmission

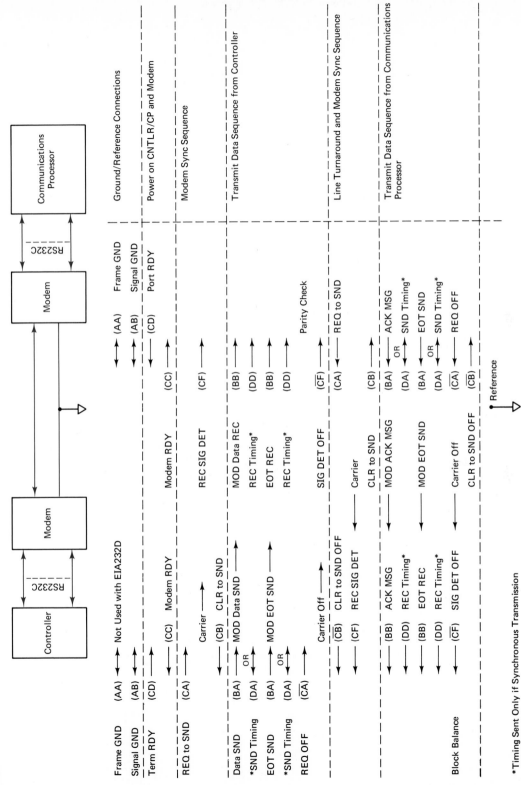

**FIGURE 9–13**
HDX Private-Line Handshaking

*Timing Sent Only if Synchronous Transmission

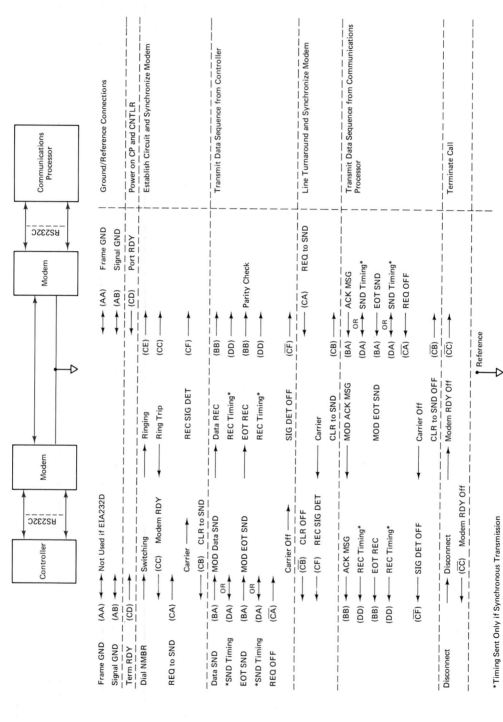

**FIGURE 9-14**
HDX Dial-Up Handshaking

186

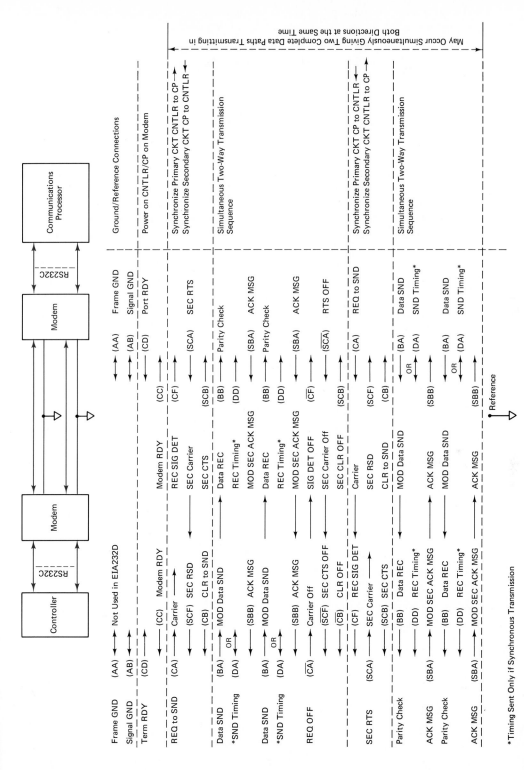

**FIGURE 9–15**
FDX Reverse-Channel Handshaking

*Timing Sent Only if Synchronous Transmission

187

are being transmitted. The carrier now comes up in one direction on one pair of wires and in the other direction on the other pair of wires, indicating that the transmission line will now be transmitting data.

From the remote end you have data being sent via pin BA over the line and being output on pin BB at the central site, while at the same time pin BA at the central site will be sending data out on the line, which will be output from pin BB at the remote site. At exactly the same time that the data is being sent, both ends are also sending timing information through pin DB. The timing information is combined with the data in the modulator so that the modulated carrier will contain sufficient information for the demodulator to determine both. This will come out as phase-corrected receive timing at the receive end so it can be used by the DTE equipment to recognize the data reliably.

When each end comes to the end of this transmission (possibly at different times), the "request to send" will be removed, which in turn takes the carrier off the line, and the link now waits for the next "request to send" to come up. If during or between transmissions the modem-ready signal is no longer being detected, it is assumed by the DTE that the line is no longer available and the transmission is terminated. Also, when the carrier comes up there is a signal called *receive line signal detect* that indicates a carrier is on the line. The same functions, unique for their particular handshaking sequence, are shown in Figs. 9-13 through 9-15.

## QUESTIONS

1. What is the difference between a simple and a network protocol?
2. Explain the difference between a half-duplex protocol and a full-duplex protocol.
3. Give an example of a protocol functioning on a type of circuit for all combinations of half duplex and full duplex.
4. What is echoplex? How does it work?
5. What is a typical application for the use of transparent mode format?
6. Describe the error mode of operation for a continuous-mode ARQ protocol.
7. What are typical uses of a flow-control protocol?
8. What characteristics of different protocols used with PCs involve information flow?
9. What do so-called modem protocols really provide?
10. Draw a diagram of three configurations for providing protocol conversion.

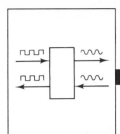

# 10

# Modems
# and Modulation

## A
## BACKGROUND

In the computer environment today, moving signals from one part of a device to another is usually accomplished by sending digital pulses in the form of either square waves (defined in Chapter 2) or actual pulses. The digital mechanism works extremely well for short distances and over wires of a relatively small gauge (diameter). Once the signals have to be transmitted over longer distances, a whole series of options opens up to the user. These options result from the fact that the square waves or pulses cannot travel down a metallic wire without in some way degrading. This degradation rounds off the rise and fall time of the signal and decreases the total energy level of the signal itself. The losses are caused by the resistance of the metallic wire, which in effect consumes some of the energy initially injected into the line, which therefore cannot be available at the end of the line. The reason why the round-off occurs is that mathematically an electrical square-wave signal is made up of many different frequencies, of which the very high frequencies give the squareness to the signal. The characteristics of metallic wire are such that the very high frequencies are degraded the most as the wire gets longer. With the loss of the higher frequencies, the square wave or pulse loses its sharp rise and/or fall times and therefore gets rounded. The electrical characteristic that causes this degradation is called *capacitance*. In summary, resistance causes loss of signal amplitude while capacitance causes a change of signal shape.

## B
## DISTANCE VERSUS TRANSMISSION RATE CONSIDERATIONS

It is the rounded off signal, in conjunction with the loss of energy, that is interpreted at the receive end with much less reliability than the original signal would be. Degraded electrical signals cannot trigger the detection circuitry at the same points as the original signal, which results in all kinds of distortions and loss of information. Thus some other technique must be used for transmitting the digital signals over longer distances.

The distance over which a signal must travel is probably the key criterion in determining the method that must be used for that transmission. Close behind is the transmission rate of the required information. The five most common methods of transmitting data, each more expensive than the previous, are listed here.

1. Direct connection by wire
2. Line drivers that reshape distorted pulses (some versions may utilize digital signaling techniques)
3. Limited-distance modems (short-haul modems), which are in effect simplified versions of conventional modems
4. Medium-distance modems
5. Standard telephone line modems

As discussed in Chapter 5, the RS232C specification is the most prevalent interface specification used in communications. Its inherent limitations concern the transmission rate of information versus the distance over which the electrical signals can travel without being degraded to the point that they cannot be recognized. When that distance is exceeded, a method must be used that maintains the signal integrity over the greater distance. The primary form of this mode of signal transmission is called *modulation.* The process is performed by a device called a *modem,* which is a contraction of the two words *modulator/demodulator.*

A *modulator* is a device that converts the computer-generated digital signal to a form that can be transmitted on a telephone line (which was designed to handle only voice frequencies between 300 and 3300 Hz), while a *demodulator* converts the signal back to a digital form for the computer at the receive end to act on. For digital transmissions the connections are basically the same, but the modem is replaced by a device called a *digital service unit* (DSU), sometimes called a *data service unit.* Instead of converting the computer-generated digital signal to an analog form for transmission over the voice network, the DSU converts the computer-generated signal into a special pulse transmission, which will be described in Chapter 16. Functionally, however, as you will see, the diagram will look the same.

The first connection is shown in Fig. 10-1(a). This is a direct connection. Due to the limitation of cable capacitance, which was described in Chapter 5, the limit of this connection is normally approximately 50 ft, although at lower transmission rates it is possible to go a greater distance. The typical trade-off values here, as defined in RS232, are a signal at a transmission rate of up to 20,000 BPS and a cable that has less than 2500-pF capacitance regardless of its length. Since typical connections have 2500 pF at about 50 ft, the nominal RS232 limitation is 50 ft. By using low-capacitance cable or lower transmission rates, it

**FIGURE 10-1**
Device versus Distance Connections

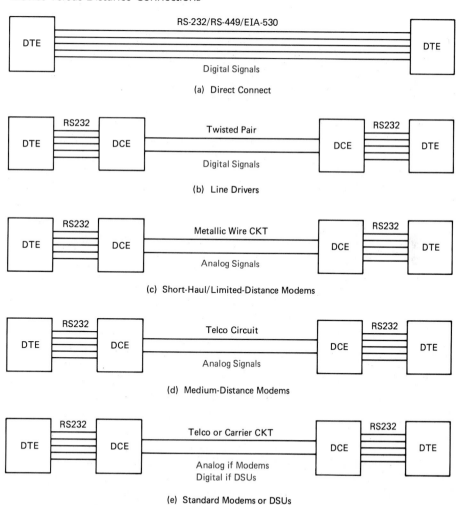

(a) Direct Connect

(b) Line Drivers

(c) Short-Haul/Limited-Distance Modems

(d) Medium-Distance Modems

(e) Standard Modems or DSUs

is possible to increase the distance between the two DTEs, and many vendors allow this; but if you exceed the distance limitation specified by the vendor most will not provide support without extra charge when there are problems.

Again, as described in Chapter 5, using RS449 or EIA530 it is possible to transmit at higher data rates over longer distances, but there are not many vendors who make these kinds of interfaces. Another factor that can be considered here is that there are now LANs (described in Chapter 15) that will also have an impact on connecting devices within approximately a 5-mile cable radius.

Once the DTE distance exceeds the capability of the direct connect interface used, the next type of device that can be utilized is a *line driver*. A line driver provides the capability to transmit data over distances usually of up to 2000 ft with data rates up to 19,200 BPS. A twisted pair wire is normally used for the connection between the line drivers, although coaxial cable may also be used. The technique implemented by the line driver is known as *differential signaling,* which transmits half of the signal on one wire and half on the other wire of the pair in the opposite *polarity.* At the receive end, one signal is polarity reversed and then the two signals are added to each other to recreate the original signal. What is unique about this method is that any noise encountered would cause the same polarity transient on both signals, so when one of the two signals is reversed and combined at the receive end the noise pulses cancel themselves. This makes a line driver much less noise sensitive and allows transmission over greater distances. These devices are very inexpensive and in many cases can be inserted right into the cable itself; or, as some vendors have done, the line driver can be put into the RS232 connector housing shell. The line driver configuration is shown in Fig. 10–1(b).

Once the distance over which a line driver can be used is exceeded, the next device that can be used is called a *short-haul, limited-distance modem* (SHM/ LDM). LDMs can transmit information up to approximately 10 miles and up to 19,200 BPS, but not at the same time. These devices are true modems in that they convert the DTE digital signal to an analog signal for transmission over the circuit, but they do not have the sophisticated equalization and filtering circuitry that allow very long-distance connections. Without these circuits, the cost is substantially less than for longer-distance modems.

As an additional limitation LDMs must communicate over a *metallic wire* circuit, which means that a metal cable must be run between the two LDMs (no microwave, fiber-optic, or carrier system). It must either be done via a user's own direct connection or through the telephone company circuits, which are limited to going in and out of the same exchange (first three digits of the telephone number), and the local loops must be less than approximately 18,000 ft. If the connection goes between telephone exchanges or the local loop is more than 18,000 ft, the carrier normally puts *loading coils* on the circuit to improve voice response. But the coils degrade the ability of a modem to send data, and that is one of the reasons why standard modems have more extensive compensation circuitry. It is possible to order a circuit without loading coils from the telephone company for short-distance direct connections or local loops; they are known as 43401 circuits (AT&T Specification 43401). At rates of 9600 BPS, LDMs are roughly one-fifth the cost of standard long-distance modems. An SHM/LDM configuration is shown in Fig. 10–1(c).

A relatively recent product line announced by several vendors is called a *medium-distance modem* (MDM), shown in Fig. 10–1(d). An MDM is capable of transmitting up to 19,200 BPS at distances up to 50 miles, but not necessarily simultaneously. An MDM has some of the compensation and equalization circuitry to allow it to transmit through the telephone trunk circuits even with loading coils on them, and since it has been estimated that up to 70 percent of an organization's communications needs are within a radius of 50 miles (50 percent within 1 mile), this type of modem is aimed at a particular market area because of its capability at reduced cost.

Once the user wants to go through the standard telephone network at longer distances, the device to be used is a standard modem [shown in Fig. 10–1(e)] if analog transmission is to be used, or a DSU if digital transmission is to be used, which is described in Chapter 16. Since Chapter 16 will deal with digital transmission specifically, the discussion here will stay with analog parameters.

Standard modems are capable of transmitting data up to 19,200 BPS without compression at almost any distance. Some of the higher data rates, such as 16,800 BPS and 19,200 BPS, require that specific *line conditioning* be applied to the circuit, and this will be described in Chapter 21. Typically, the distances can be variable through either the switched network (dial up) or on leased lines, and transmission rates of 14,400 BPS are becoming more common. However, despite vendor promises to the contrary, even 9600 BPS, which is very common today, may not be attainable without special line conditioning.

In each of the diagrams of Fig. 10–1, there is an RS232 connection between the user's device and the circuit terminating device (DCE). This connection must never exceed the distance specified for RS232 (unless you use the RS449 or EIA530 interface). In most instances, this means that the DTE and the DCE must be within the approximate 50-ft limit imposed by RS232. If experience shows that your particular circuit will work at more than 50 ft with negligible degradation, there is no problem in using that circuit. The 50-ft limitation is sometimes a shield behind which vendors will hide when they do not want to service specific user configurations. If it works, let it be.

## C

## SIGNAL SHAPES

As described earlier in this chapter, a modem provides a conversion for a digital or square-wave signal into a form that can be transmitted onto an analog telephone line. Many users do not realize that the internal digital data signal shape can vary over a wide range of alternatives. Some of these alternatives are used for direct communication between two devices not using an RS232 interface; others are used just to move signals between internal components of a processing unit or between a processing unit and its various peripherals.

For informational purposes, Fig. 10–2 shows some of the wave shapes that may be encountered in different environments. The top signal [Fig. 10–2(a)] shows a *make/break* or *mark/space* type of signal. This is typical of a loop current type of signal where the current flows only in one direction. This is not an RS232 compatible signal as the interface circuits themselves are different. Typically, this signal form is used in all TTY interfaces and is compatible with PC interfaces that are described as TTY compatible.

Figure 10–2(b) describes a *polar voltage signal* or a *bipolar current loop* interface where current flows in alternating directions. It also describes the voltage signal where positive and negative voltage levels are used to describe the signal shape. When used as a voltage reference signal, this is the shape of an RS232 signal. Notice that the 0 bit is a positive level, whereas the 1 bit is always a negative level for the entire length of the signal period. If there are two consecutive bits of 1s or 0s, the voltage level stays the same for two bit periods.

Figure 10–2(c) is known as a *return to zero* signal (RZ) and is self clocking. The bit, regardless of its value, has a transition during the signal period. Zero bits start at the 0 reference level, go negative for half a signal period, and come back to the 0 voltage reference level for the remaining signal period. One bits go positive for half of the signal period and then come back to the 0 voltage reference level for the remainder of the signal period. Some conventions have return to zero signals where the 0 goes positive and the 1 goes negative just like the RS232 (sometimes called return to zero inverted). Therefore, all return to zero interfaces should be validated such that the RZ method is the same for the devices communicating with each other.

Figure 10–2(d) is called *nonreturn to zero* or differential encoding and the unique property of this signal waveform is that there are transitions only when a 1 bit is present. The first 1 bit causes the signal to go positive; the next 1 bit causes it to go negative. The signal stays at that level until the next 1 bit, when it goes positive again, and so on. Since the 1 bit may cause either a positive or a negative transition, there is always a match between the two ends of a communication path because it is the transition that signifies the bit, not its specific level.

The next signal pattern is called *Biphase-M,* shown in Fig. 10–2(e). Biphase-M is used when transitions are necessary for synchronization purposes. It is a unique type of pattern in which each timing period has at least one level transition. Also, the 0-bit time periods alternate between high and low levels with the signal staying the same for the entire period. One bits go high immediately after a low-level 0 bit and go low immediately following a high-level 0 bit. This is shown in the sequence of bits in Fig. 10–2(e).

Figure 10–2(f) is called *Biphase Manchester,* which is signified by a transition in the middle of every timing period. Zero bits always go from high to low, while 1 bits always go from low to high. Because there is a transition in the middle of every signal bit, this pattern is used when critical synchronization requirements are involved. A typical example is that Biphase Manchester coding is used in Ethernet LAN transmissions.

The last pattern is shown in Fig. 10–2(g). This waveform describes *bipolar* voltage pulses that are used for digital transmissions. What is unique about this

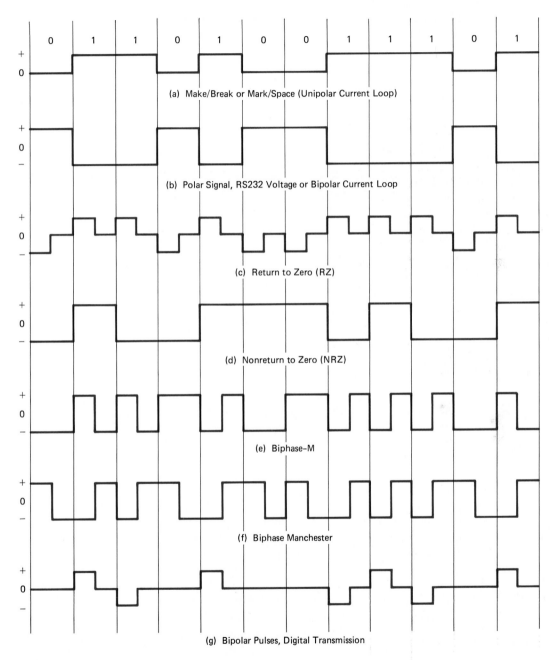

**FIGURE 10-2**
Digital Signal Waveforms and Patterns

sequence is that there are transitions only when a 1 bit is involved and the pulses alternate polarity. Polarity alternation provides a very easy method for hardware to detect errors generated by noise. Noise will generate one or more adjacent pulses going in the same direction that can be detected in the receiving hardware as an erroneous condition since the code requires that alternating pulses be received. The specific pulse in error cannot be determined, but the fact that an error exists can be identified before any of the user's software does error checking. This mechanism was recently incorporated into the ESF (described in Chapter 16) form of digital transmission by AT&T to isolate specific segments of a data link causing errors.

## D
## ANALOG MODES OF MODULATION: AM, FM, PM

When discussing the various modes of modulation, the reader must have some understanding of a sine wave. A sine wave is a mathematical description of a varying waveform that has specific mathematical properties. It is not necessary to know what those specific properties are other than that the signal starts at some predefined reference level, increases toward a positive peak, at which time it comes back down to the reference level, goes through the reference level to a negative peak, and then comes back to the reference level, at which time a new cycle can start. The number of cycles that occur during a 1-second time interval is known as the *frequency.* This frequency, in cycles per second, is known as hertz (Hz). The frequencies used in the voice-grade telephone environment are those between 300 and 3300 Hz.

Because the original telephone system was developed for moving human voice signals, which are *analog* in form, the electrical characteristics of the telephone circuits do not allow square-wave, computer-generated digital signals to pass for any great distance. Therefore, the modem is used to provide a method of moving the digital information through an analog medium. The method, stated very simply, is to create a signal that looks like a human voice signal, and then to modify that signal in direct relation to the digital bits being generated by the computer or terminal, transmit that modified signal through the telephone environment, and then convert the modified signal back into the original digital bit stream at the receive end. There are many ways to accomplish the function, and those most commonly used will be described.

Figure 10–3 shows the three simplest forms of modulation. These conversions are performed by the modulator at the transmit end onto the telephone line and by the demodulator at the receive end from the telephone line.

The first form of modulation is shown in Fig. 10–3(a) and is called *frequency modulation* (FM). It is sometimes called *frequency shift keying* (FSK). In frequency modulation there are two signals, known as *carriers.* Each of the two carriers represents a different bit. For example, a 0 bit could be represented by a low-frequency carrier while a 1 bit could be designated by a higher-frequency carrier. Figure 10–3(a) shows a 0 represented by the low frequency and a 1 repre-

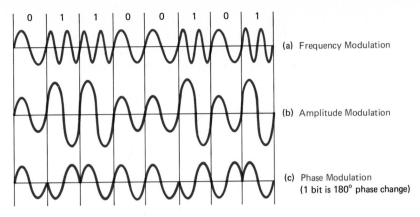

| 0 | 1 | 1 | 0 | 0 | 1 | 0 | 1 |

(a) Frequency Modulation

(b) Amplitude Modulation

(c) Phase Modulation
(1 bit is 180° phase change)

**FIGURE 10-3**
Simple Modulation, 1 Bit per Baud

sented by a high frequency, with a single cycle shown for the 0 bit and two cycles for a 1 bit. This signal form was specifically chosen, because one frequency modulation modem will use a frequency of approximately 1200 Hz to represent a 0 bit and a frequency of approximately 2400 Hz to represent a 1 bit. Typical modem carrier frequencies and their relation to specific modems will be shown later in this chapter.

Frequency-modulation modems are used almost exclusively for asynchronous transmission up to approximately 1800 BPS but in today's world are rarely used over 600 BPS. They are the least expensive modems to build, many can fit on the same circuit card, and they are not very noise sensitive. Therefore, they are excellent for all low-speed transmissions, especially for terminals or PC oriented applications, where the software has been designed for generating and transmitting asynchronous characters. The specific differences between synchronous and asynchronous were described in Chapter 8.

The second form of modulation is shown in Fig. 10-3(b) and is called *amplitude modulation* (AM). Amplitude modulation is depicted with only a single carrier frequency. For simplicity, the diagram shows a single cycle for each bit period, with the 0 bit being represented by a low-level signal and the 1 bit represented by a higher-level signal. If the carrier were 1200 Hz, then the data transmission rate would be 1200 BPS because there is a single bit represented by each cycle. To carry this one step further, if the carrier were 1800 Hz and the signal changed every $1\frac{1}{2}$ cycles, the data rate would still be 1200 BPS because there is still one bit for every signal change. This is a significant point, because as the more complex modems are described we will get into the true difference between bits per second and baud, which was briefly described in Chapter 2. AM modems are rarely used alone because they require more power and are more noise sensitive. AM is used in conjunction with PM or phase modulation only.

The third phase of simple modulation is *phase modulation* (PM), sometimes called *phase shift keying* (PSK). PM is depicted by a change of phase that is the same as changing the point at which the cycle starts. One way that phase modulation is implemented is that a 0 bit always stays the same phase as the bit before it, while the 1 bit always changes phase by 180° (or one-half of a cycle). Figure 10-3(c) shows phase modulation, and if you follow along the carrier you can see that everytime there is a 1 bit there is a half-cycle phase change, while 0 bits just continue on in the same phase.

PSK modems are used at data transmission rates of 1200 BPS and above and can be used in either a synchronous or an asynchronous environment. They are the most expensive and complex of the modulation only modem methods (other features such as error detection, error correction, and encryption, will add costs to any modem in which they are implemented), but they are very reliable. This methodology is used either by itself or with AM by all major high-speed modem vendors.

A point to recognize here is that most modems typically work asynchronously to 1800 BPS and synchronously at 2400 BPS and up (asynchronous transmission methods at higher rates are described later in this chapter). This does not necessarily mean your DTE has to be synchronous. When specified for use with asynchronous DTEs, the modem takes care of the conversion and reconversion process. Synchronous transmission is necessary at the higher data rates because the modulation technique, combined with the degradation of the signal on the line, requires a *clocking* signal to be transmitted along with the information. The actual method is to *derive* the clock from the modulated signal so that the receiving modem can tell the DTE where to sample the data. This was described in detail in Chapter 8. FSK can only be used for transmission rates up to approximately 1800 BPS, while amplitude and phase modulation are technically feasible for use at 2400 BPS and up. This means all transmissions below 2400 will typically be FSK, except for modems that transmit two ways simultaneously on the same wire (to be described later in this chapter) at rates of 1200 BPS or more each way. Vendors usually use a form of PSK in these modems, and although the transmission appears to be asynchronous to the user, the actual method of modulation is synchronous with PSK. This will be discussed later in the chapter.

## E
## MULTIBIT MODULATION

Once it became necessary to transmit information at higher data rates than 1200 to 1800 BPS, because of the inherent line characteristics that degrade the carrier signal, a method other than 1 bit per signal change (described previously) was required. In its simplest form it is called *multibit modulation* and normally involves the use of either PSK or AM; but it can involve both at higher-speed transmission rates. Simple multibit modulation is shown in Fig. 10-4 for both the AM and PM case. Figure 10-4(a) shows amplitude modulation with four different amplitudes. If there are four different states for the level to be described, each level can contain two information bits. The data stream coming into the modulator would be at whatever the user's transmission rate is, and the signal change rate on the line would be half that rate. Therefore, a carrier rate

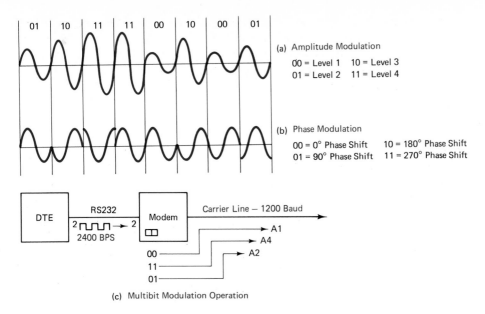

| 01 | 10 | 11 | 11 | 00 | 10 | 00 | 01 |

(a) Amplitude Modulation

00 = Level 1    10 = Level 3
01 = Level 2    11 = Level 4

(b) Phase Modulation

00 = 0° Phase Shift    10 = 180° Phase Shift
01 = 90° Phase Shift   11 = 270° Phase Shift

(c) Multibit Modulation Operation

**FIGURE 10–4**
Simple Multibit Modulation, 2 Bits per Baud (AM and PM only)

of 1800 Hz changing every $1\frac{1}{2}$ cycles gives a 1200-baud rate (signal change rate); and with each signal change providing two data bits, the effective transmission rate for the user is 2400 BPS. The operation is transparent to the user's equipment but has a significant effect on the communication line, because as far as the communication line is concerned the signal is still only changing 1200 times a second. The example of an 1800-Hz carrier is being used because most vendors use carriers in that range. In actuality, the carriers range somewhere between 1650 and 1800 Hz, with the signal changes not occurring at specific full- or half-cycle increments. Most vendors try to get their signal change rate to be not much less than a full cycle, but, as we will see later, some of the new higher-speed modems (14,400 and 19,200 BPS) must have a baud rate of 2400, which means that a carrier of approximately 1800 Hz would be changing approximately every three-quarters of a cycle. The ultimate limit is a half-cycle according to Shannon's law, which states that in order to define amplitude or frequency or phase, an absolute minimum of a half-cycle must be available. The practical limit for trying to reach a half-cycle is such that the expense incurred as you get closer to the half-cycle makes the modem economically unfeasible.

The same methodology as is used with four levels of amplitude modulation can be implemented with four different phases using phase modulation or PSK. Figure 10–4(b) shows four different phases each giving 2 bits per phase change. Like multibit amplitude modulation, each 2-bit (dibit) phase combination causes a specified change in which the cycle will start. Using the 1800-Hz carrier again, changing every $1\frac{1}{2}$ cycles, you have four different phase changes each representing two data bits, providing a 2400-BPS data transmission rate.

E. MULTIBIT MODULATION

199

In the example, for ease of explanation, only a single cycle is shown, where a 0° phase shift means the two bits represented will be zero/zero; a 90° phase shift from the previous phase will mean a zero/one combination; a 180° phase shift from the previous phase will be a one/zero bit combination; and finally a 270° shift from the previous phase means a one/one bit combination. Most 2400-BPS modulation schemes use phase modulation alone, while the higher data rates use a combination of phase and amplitude modulation.

An operational example of this multibit modulation is shown in Fig. 10-4(c). The DTE is putting out information at 2400 BPS. That information enters the modem via pin 2 of the RS232 interface. In the modem there is a 2-bit buffer. When the first bit, which is a 0 bit, comes in from the DTE, it is stored in the first position of the 2-bit buffer. Nothing happens at this time on the outgoing carrier line. When the second bit comes in, it is also a 0 bit, and at that time amplitude one (A1) of the multibit amplitude modulation scheme is put out on the carrier line.

When the third bit comes in (let us assume it is a 1 bit), it is stored in the 2-bit buffer but nothing changes on the carrier line. Then, when the fourth bit comes in, if it too is a 1, at that point in time A1 is taken off and amplitude four (A4) is put out on the carrier line.

If the fifth bit coming in is a 1, it is stored in the 2-bit buffer of the modem and there is no change on the outgoing carrier line. If the sixth bit is a 0 bit, that combination is amplitude two (A2), which is now put on the carrier line instead of A4.

In other words, every two data bits coming into the modem on pin 2 cause a decision to be made as to which carrier amplitude level is to be put on the line. If the two new bits are the same as the two bits that were in the buffer before, the amplitude stays the same. If the two new bits in the buffer are different from the two bits that were there before, a new amplitude is put on the carrier line. All of this means that the signal on the carrier line is changing at one-half the rate that the data bits are coming in to the modem. Therefore, if the data is coming in at a 2400 BPS rate, the modem carrier signal is changing on line at a rate of 1200 times a second or 1200 baud.

The same mode of operation is applicable if phase modulation is used, except there will be four different phases representing dibit combinations. The exact same concept can be used when there are combinations of amplitude and phase modulation where the different values of combined *states* each represent a unique sequence of bits. The modulator must be very accurate in creating the specific value of the amplitude and the phase combinations, while the demodulator must be sensitive enough to detect those combinations and to put out the appropriate data bits on pin 3 of RS232 at the receive end. Recognition of amplitude and phase combination states must be made with a signal that has been degraded by transmission line characteristics. More will be described about this later.

QAM, *quadrature amplitude modulation,* is a unique form of modulation. In quadrature amplitude modulation two carriers of the same frequency are modulated and then added together. One carrier is a sine wave and the other a cosine wave that are 90° apart, that is, in quadrature. In order to get the appropriate signal point in this form of modulation, the *X*-axis is modulated by the cosine wave while the *Y*-axis is modulated by the sine wave. The two signals are then combined and transmitted on the carrier line. The demodulator will see the combined signal, separate the two components, and then demodulate each of them. The result is called a *signal point,* a combination of a pair of amplitudes that can be represented in a two dimensional diagram known as a *signal constellation.* The demodulator is designed such that it anticipates receipt of a particular signal within a constellation of multiple signals, where each point represents two or more data bits. When the specific signal point generated by the received signal is calculated in the demodulator, it is compared with the points in the anticipated or expected map. The data bits are those that the demodulator has determined the signal point to be, and they are output on pin 3 of the demodulator.

Examples of the most common signal constellations are shown in Fig. 10-5. The constellations shown here are for the most common AT&T modems as well as the CCITT modems. Some of these constellations are applicable to modems transmitting in a half-duplex mode, while others are transmitting in a full-duplex mode on a half-duplex circuit. Each will be defined in more detail later.

Starting with the 212 or the V.22 modem, we have four signal points, which means there are 2 bits per point. Whatever the baud rate will be, the bit rate will be double that (for these modems specifically, 600 baud and 1200 BPS). The V.22bis modem has 16 different points so that each point represents four data bits, in this case 600 baud and 2400 BPS. The 201 constellation is just like the 212

**FIGURE 10–5**
Signal Constellations

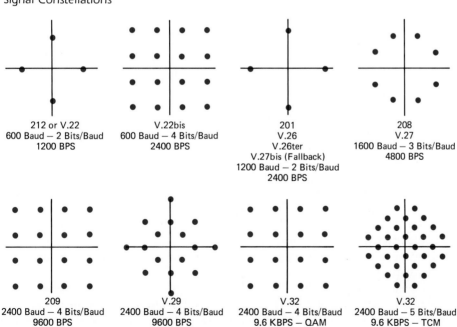

| 212 or V.22 | V.22bis | 201 | 208 |
|---|---|---|---|
| 600 Baud – 2 Bits/Baud | 600 Baud – 4 Bits/Baud | V.26 | V.27 |
| 1200 BPS | 2400 BPS | V.26ter | 1600 Baud – 3 Bits/Baud |
| | | V.27bis (Fallback) | 4800 BPS |
| | | 1200 Baud – 2 Bits/Baud | |
| | | 2400 BPS | |

| 209 | V.29 | V.32 | V.32 |
|---|---|---|---|
| 2400 Baud – 4 Bits/Baud | 2400 Baud – 4 Bits/Baud | 2400 Baud – 4 Bits/Baud | 2400 Baud – 5 Bits/Baud |
| 9600 BPS | 9600 BPS | 9.6 KBPS – QAM | 9.6 KBPS – TCM |

except that in these modems the baud rate will typically be higher (1200 baud), so the data rate will be higher (2400 BPS). The 208 modem has eight points with 3 bits per point, and this unit transmits 4800 BPS at 1600 baud.

The 209 and the V.32 have equivalent-looking signal constellations to the V.22bis, but because of the different baud rates they operate at totally different data rates. The V.29 modem has 16 points, giving 4 bits per signal point, while the V.32 modem has 32 points, which provides 5 bits per signal point. The V.32, however, does not utilize all the bits for just data. It utilizes another mechanism for improving the throughput of the modem, called *trellis coding* (Trellis Coded Modulation—TCM), which is a form of *forward error correction*. Many modems use trellis coding at the higher data rates because TCM provides 3dB less noise sensitivity for the carrier in a modem transmission.

Without getting into the detailed mathematics of trellis coding, the mechanism provides for the addition of an extra (redundant) bit to be added to each symbol interval (baud). For example, the V.32 modem has a transmission rate of 9600 BPS and a baud rate of 2400. This would normally involve only 16 signal points, but as can be seen from Fig. 10–5 there are actually 32. The redundant bit is mapped into the 32 signal-point constellation. Only the last 2 bits of the symbol set are encoded. The three encoded bits (two data plus one trellis bit) belong with one of eight subsets, each consisting of 4 points. The two remaining bits then identify which of the 4 points from the subset is to be selected.

The redundancy ensures that only certain sequences of bits are valid by eliminating other subsets that the mathematics say cannot be valid. A good trellis code ensures that any two valid sequences are far enough apart so they can be more easily differentiated.

At the demodulator, the trellis decoder compares the sequence of bits with all possible signal points and selects the best fit. Because there are dependencies between consecutively transmitted signals, only certain sequences will be valid. The decoder will pick the most likely sequence. A modem using this technique is typically described as a TCM-type modem.

The primary value in having a TCM-type modulation scheme is that it provides a much lower error rate (but at a higher cost). At the higher data rates a modulator transmits many more possible amplitude/phase signal points and they will be much closer to each other due to the carrier-imposed limits on the magnitudes of signals that can be transmitted on a telephone line. In other words, there is a maximum envelope into which all the points can fit. TCM mathematically reduces the amount of valid points to be selected from.

Each time the amplitude states are doubled, existing noise that did not cause a problem before will now be more likely to make one amplitude look like another. In addition, other line degradations will make phase changes become distorted so they will also be closer to each other, which means the likelihood of one or more bit errors being generated is substantially increased. The degradations that are added to or subtracted from a modulated carrier may cause the demodulator to think it sees a valid signal point, but at a different location, which in turn will cause erroneous bits to be output to the user and leave the recognition of those errors up to the user protocol software. As an additional note, the errors do not increase linearly; they go up exponentially. By doubling the data rate you may actually end up with less throughput. Operation might have been marginal at the lower rate, and now at the higher rate there will be a substantial increase in errors, thus reducing the overall data throughput. An example of a signal constellation incorporated into a modem by a vendor, Fig. 10–6, shows the signal constellation of a Paradyne 14.4 KBPS modem utilizing 64 states, a proprietary scheme that has worked very well on both leased and dial lines with transmission in only one direction at a time.

Two other examples of proprietary schemes are shown in Figs. 10–7 and 10–8. Figure 10–7 shows a Codex modem operating at 16.8 KBPS utilizing trellis coded modulation. With a baud rate of 2400 there would normally be 7 bits per baud, requiring 128 states. With TCM, however, an eighth state is needed, which brings the total to 256 states. This modem must be used on a conditioned, leased line. A related Codex modem that is pushing the state of the art is the Codex model 2680, which operates at 19.2 KBPS. Here again there is a proprietary scheme for transmission in that user data is combined into a 28 bit sequence represented by a combination of four symbols (signal points). The baud rate is 2743 and three of the 28 bits are put through a 64-state convolutional encoder, which adds an extra bit. The resulting 29 bits are mapped into the four signal points, each selected from a 160 point constellation. Codex calls this a 64 state–8 dimensional trellis coded modem. This mechanism is provided through proprietary chips and operates at what is considered the upper limit today in practical analog modem operation.

One of the outgrowths of the use of signal constellations is the ability to provide test equipment that will display these constellations. You don't have to be very knowledgeable in the operation of modems to look at a display and compare it with an ideal representation. If there are missing or distorted points you will get a very good idea of whether there is a problem, and if you are looking at the transmit carrier, you will know it is a transmitting modem problem. On the other hand, you can tell a lot about the quality of the received signal from looking at the receive line and then make further tests to determine whether the transmitting modem or the lines are causing those degradations.

**FIGURE 10–6**
Signal Constellation of Paradyne 14,400 BPS Modem (64 states—2400 baud/6 bits per baud)

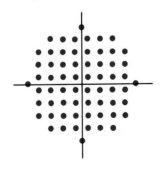

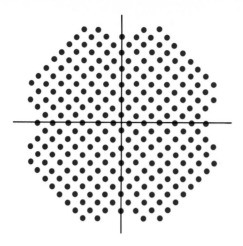

**FIGURE 10-7**
Codex Modem at 16.8 KBPS with TCM (256 states—2400 baud/8 bits per baud)

Figure 10-9 shows what the typical effects of impairments would be for a four signal state modem. On the left there is no impairment with small signal points. Harmonic distortion makes those points radiate out from the axis while noise and/or attenuation make the dots much bigger than normal. Phase jitter will cause the different signal points to oscillate in an arc-type arrangement. When the points get close enough to overlap, data errors are probably encountered. Many modem vendors today are not only providing standalone test equip-

**FIGURE 10-8**
Codex Modem at 19.2 KBPS with 160-Point Signal Constellation

2743 Baud.
Four Symbols @ 7 Bits Each.
Three of 28 Bits Through a
64-Bit Convolutional
Encoder for 29th Bit.
Four Points Selected from
160-Point Constellation

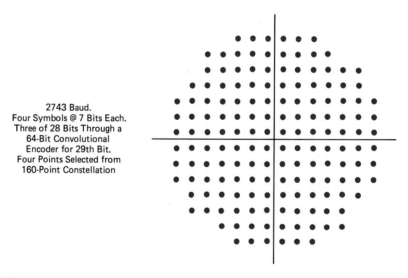

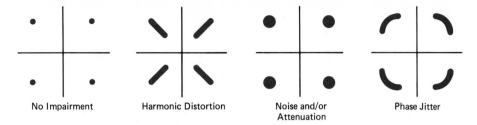

| No Impairment | Harmonic Distortion | Noise and/or Attenuation | Phase Jitter |

**FIGURE 10–9**
Effects of Impairments

ment but are also integrating signal constellation displays into the front panels of their modems. Although it is technically incorrect to call them so, these displays are sometimes called *eye* patterns. It is the received eye patterns that enable the signal points to be displayed as individual dots. From a test equipment point of view, if you are considering the implementation of your own network test center, it is mandatory that you have equipment that will give you signal constellation displays. A single unit can be utilized for all lines by patching capabilities, but you might also want to consider having two pattern generators in the event that one becomes inoperative.

Up to this point the descriptions have been for modems that transmit utilizing one pair of telephone lines in one direction or two pairs of telephone lines (one pair for each direction). These modems are typically referred to as four-wire leased line modems or two-wire half-duplex modems (transmit only one way at a time). These modems, however, do not address the *dial-up* situation. Because of the two-wire limitation, both the transmitting and receiving ends must share the same line. They must divide the 300–3300 Hz bandwidth so that both can transmit simultaneously. These modems are known as two-wire full-duplex modems.

The primary mode of operation of these modems is to utilize half of the bandwidth for transmitting in one direction and the other half for transmitting in the opposite direction. A diagram of this is shown in Fig. 10–10. This full-duplex mechanism is sometimes described as *split-channel operation* and, in some limited cases, reverse-channel or backward-channel.

Because the AT&T 212A modem is one of the most widely used modems in North America, its mode of operation will be described here. The 212A can transmit at either 300 BPS or 1200 BPS, but each mode operates in a radically different manner. At 300 BPS the modem splits the telephone line into two segments and uses FSK in each channel for transmission. To identify which channel will be used, the modems at either end are defined as either *originate* or *answer.* Your modem must be in originate mode when initiating a call, and in answer mode when receiving a call. That way there is never any question about who will be transmitting in which channel. The FSK operation takes place utilizing 1070 Hz as transmit zero bit and 1270 Hz as transmit one bit for the originate end. For the answer end, 2025 Hz is transmit zero and 2225 Hz is transmit one. This is 1

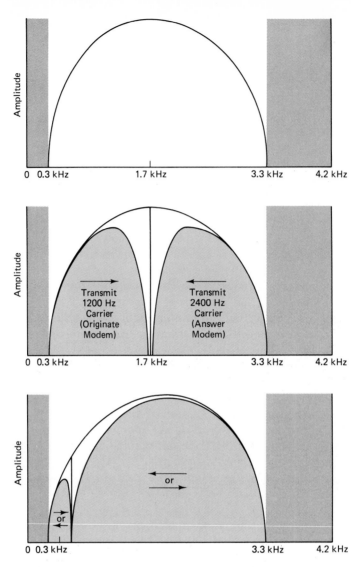

**FIGURE 10-10**
Split-Channel and Reverse-Channel Modems

bit per baud asynchronous-type transmission because the modem carrier signal will change from one frequency to another for each bit.

At 1200 BPS, however, the 212A modem actually transmits in a synchronous form because it uses PSK at 600 baud with four phases so that each phase represents two data bits. A diagram of the 212A modem operating at 1200 BPS, which is indicative of almost all full-duplex modems, is shown in Fig. 10–11. The originate end carrier is 1200 Hz and the answer end carrier is 2400 Hz. Both signals exist simultaneously on the telephone line between the modems. To demod-

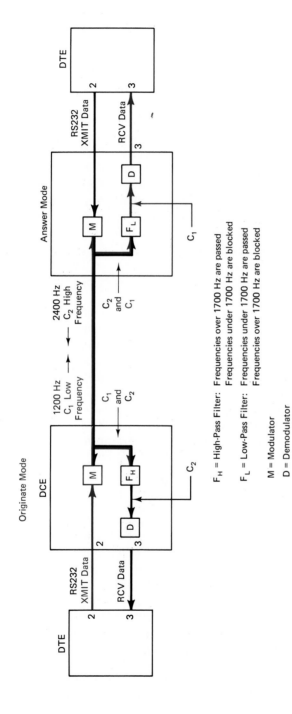

$F_H$ = High-Pass Filter: Frequencies over 1700 Hz are passed
Frequencies under 1700 Hz are blocked

$F_L$ = Low-Pass Filter: Frequencies under 1700 Hz are passed
Frequencies over 1700 Hz are blocked

M = Modulator

D = Demodulator

$C_1$ = Low-Frequency Carrier or Carriers

$C_2$ = High-Frequency Carrier or Carriers

**FIGURE 10–11**
Split-Channel Operation

207

ulate the received signal, the originate modem will utilize a filter that eliminates the locally generated carrier (low frequency), leaving the high-frequency modulated carrier to be demodulated so the received information can be output on pin 3. At the answer mode modem location, the exact opposite occurs—a low pass filter is used to prevent the locally generated high-frequency carrier from passing through. The low-frequency carrier is then demodulated so that data can be output on pin 3. What is important to remember is that both modems are actually transmitting in a synchronous mode because they are using multibit modulation, but they operate almost exclusively with asynchronous DTEs. Any conversions back and forth are transparent to the user, so even though the modems are described as being asynchronous or synchronous compatible, in almost every single case they will be used with asynchronous DTEs only.

The 212A modem operates primarily in the 1200 BPS mode, but when degraded conditions warrant it can *fall back* to 300 BPS and operate at that rate. It is interesting to note that the CCITT equivalent, the V.22 modem, also operates at 1200 BPS, but its fallback mode is 600 BPS. If you intend to operate on an international level where modems are typically provided by the host country Postal Telephone and Telegraph companies (PT&Ts), you will probably have to utilize a V.22 equivalent in North America because the fallback mode of the two modems is not compatible, the 212A being 300 BPS/FSK while the V.22 modem is 600 BPS/PSK.

A chart of the various AT&T and international modems is shown in Table 10–1. This table gives the most common modem types, their data rates (multiples when applicable), the actual baud rate at each data rate, the typical modulation method, half- or full-duplex mode operation, and finally the carrier frequencies that they use. Each of the terms is self-explanatory, but to eliminate confusion under the modulation method, PSK means two phases. DPSK means four phases with 2 bits per phase. PM means phase modulation with 2 or more bits per phase. QAM is quadrature amplitude modulation, and TCM is trellis coded modulation.

It should be noted that full-duplex modems are mandatory for operation with PCs, because the standard protocol utilized in PCs is based on Teletype operation where there is no provision for time delays between transmitting and receiving. As soon as a TTY-type protocol receives the end of a transmission from a remote location, it is immediately in a position to transmit back. If standard modems are used on a telephone line, a process called *line turnaround,* or *modem turnaround,* must be accommodated. If you refer to Fig. 10–11 and assume that you are transmitting in only one direction at a time (typically the way a PC operates), the modulator at the originate modem will transmit to the demodulator at the answer modem. When the transmission is completed the modulator at the originate modem must turn off, which turns off the carrier. The demodulator at the answer modem then turns off, indicating to the DTE that no more data is being received. The DTE at the answer mode location then turns on its data immediately, which will go to the modulator and causes a carrier to be put on the line. The originating modem then connects its demodulator to the line to begin decoding the received signal. This process must be repeated each time the modems change direction of transmission. The time involved in this turn-

**TABLE 10-1**
Modem Comparison Chart

| MODEM TYPE | DATA RATE (BPS) | BAUD RATE | MODULATION METHOD | HDX/FDX | CARRIER FREQUENCY |
|---|---|---|---|---|---|
| 103 | 300 | 300 | FSK | FDX —2 Wire | 1070/1270—Originate<br>2025/2225—Answer |
| V.21 | 300 | 300 | FSK | FDX —2 Wire | 980/1180—Originate<br>1650/1850—Answer |
| 202 | 1200 | 1200 | FSK | HDX—2 Wire<br>FDX —2 Wire | 1200/2200<br>387 Backchannel |
| V.22 | 1200<br>600 | 600<br>600 | DPSK<br>PSK | FDX —2 Wire<br>FDX —2 Wire | 1200/2400<br>1200/2400 |
| 212 | 1200<br>300 | 600<br>300 | DPSK<br>FSK | FDX —2 Wire<br>FDX —2 Wire | 1200/2400<br>1070/1270—Orig.\2025/2225—Ans. |
| V.23 | 1200<br>600 | 1200<br>600 | FSK<br>FSK | HDX—2 Wire<br>HDX—2 Wire | 1300/2100\390/450 Backchannel<br>1300/1700\390/450 Backchannel |
| 201 | 2400 | 1200 | DPSK | HDX—2 Wire<br>FDX —4 Wire | 1800 |
| V.22bis | 2400<br>1200 | 600<br>600 | QAM<br>DPSK | FDX —2 Wire<br>FDX —2 Wire | 1200/2400<br>1200/2400 |
| V.26 | 2400 | 1200 | DPSK | FDX —4 Wire | 1800 |
| V.26bis | 2400<br>1200 | 1200<br>1200 | DPSK<br>PSK | HDX—2 Wire<br>HDX—2 Wire | 1800<br>1800 |
| V.26ter | 2400<br>1200 | 1200<br>1200 | DPSK<br>DPSK | FDX —2 Wire<br>FDX —2 Wire | 1800<br>1800 |
| 208 | 4800 | 1600 | PM | HDX—2 Wire<br>FDX —4 Wire | 1800 |
| V.27 | 4800 | 1600 | PM | FDX —4 Wire | 1800 |
| V.27bis | 4800<br>2400 | 1600<br>1200 | PM<br>PM | FDX —4 Wire<br>FDX —4 Wire | 1800<br>1800 |
| V.27ter | 4800<br>2400 | 1600<br>1200 | PM<br>PM | HDX—2 Wire<br>HDX—2 Wire | 1800<br>1800 |
| 209 | 9600 | 2400 | QAM | HDX—2 Wire<br>FDX —4 Wire | 1650 |
| V.29 | 9600<br>4800 | 2400<br>2400 | QAM<br>DPSK | FDX —4 Wire<br>FDX —4 Wire | 1700<br>1700 |
| V.32 | 9600<br>4800 | 2400<br>2400 | QAM or TCM<br>QAM | FDX —2 Wire<br>FDX —2 Wire | 1800<br>1800 |
| V.33 | 14,400 | 2400 | QAM | FDX —4 Wire | 1800 |

around is called line turnaround (LTA) or modem turnaround (MTA). Depending on the modem, this time can be up to a few hundred milliseconds.

If the protocol in the DTE is one that begins to transmit as soon as it receives the last bit of information from the opposite site, any information transmitted during the LTA will be *clipped,* or lost. A full-duplex modem provides the ability to accommodate an LTA of zero time, because both paths are available simultaneously. Even though the information is transmitted half duplex (one way at a time) and the circuit is half duplex (two wire), the modem must be a full-duplex device (capable of transmitting both ways simultaneously) so that data transmissions without time-delay capability built in can be accommodated. This was described in more detail with all the combinations in Chapter 9.

Full-duplex modem operation is also available at higher speeds. The V.22bis modem operates at 2400 BPS (600 baud/4 bits per baud) and is being pitched very heavily to users who have to move higher volumes of information on a dial-up line. The V.32 modem provides both 4800 BPS and 9600 BPS in a full-duplex two-wire mode of operation and many vendors have V.32-equivalent modems in their product line today. There are also other proprietary schemes for rates above 2400 BPS/FDX but line quality is extremely critical in determining whether these modems can operate at their stated data rates. In many cases to date, testing has shown very low throughputs for these modems on many lines. It is therefore incumbent on the user who needs high-volume dial-up capability to test the modem being considered in the environment in which it is to be used. This way the user will know ahead of time whether to spend the extra money for the anticipated higher-speed capability. It should be noted that with data compression, throughput of these modems can be increased by up to a factor of 4 (38,400 BPS).

A typical application these modems include is for high-volume transmissions in one direction and low volume or acknowledgments in the opposite direction. To accommodate this, the CCITT is working on an *asymmetric standard,* which is anticipated to provide for operation at 9600 BPS or greater in one direction with the reverse channel providing for acknowledgments and error control at a lower rate such as 150 BPS. It is also anticipated that these modems will be capable of operating in a half-duplex mode, and if they have to, fall back in transmission speed when line conditions warrant.

The methods of operation described here for modems do not depict operations for all vendors' products. For example, Telebit Corporation offers a modem that contains up to 512 carriers within the 300–3300 Hz band with each about 7.8 Hz apart. It operates at a baud rate of 7.5 with the different carriers containing different quantities of bits. In a typical mode of operation, the amount of bits per carrier in each range is as follows:

| | |
|---|---|
| 0–300 Hz | 0 bits per carrier |
| 300–700 Hz | 2 bits per carrier |
| 700–1300 Hz | 4 bits per carrier |
| 1300–2800 Hz | 6 bits per carrier |
| 2800–3300 Hz | 4 bits per carrier |
| 3300–3400 Hz | 2 bits per carrier |
| 3400–4200 Hz | 0 bits per carrier |

The modem automatically measures the signal-to-noise ratio at all carrier speeds and sends either 2, 4, or 6 bits at each usable frequency. There are typically 400 usable carriers. By sending approximately 2400 bits at a 7.5 baud rate, the approximate throughput is 18,000 BPS. Data is typically sent in packets with dynamic adjustment of transmission speed based on line quality parameters. The overhead being sent along with the individual bits means that the actual user throughput will be less than the transmission rate. By utilizing an ARQ protocol with CRC 16 error detection, the throughput is very reliable, but the actual amount of user bits being throughput per second must be determined by measurement and could be 12,000 BPS or less.

As the industry continues to evolve other proprietary schemes for modem transmissions at the higher rates will emerge. Regardless of the claims, however, a modem really needs to be tested in the intended environment to determine whether it will work as expected.

## F

# MODEM CONSIDERATIONS

The following discussions examine various other options that can enhance the modem's ability to move data reliably.

## Scrambler

The term *scrambler* describes certain modem operations. A scrambler modifies the output of a modulator such that the bit patterns being transmitted appear random even for a constant input. If there is a long string of zeros or a long string of ones when no data is being transmitted, it is quite possible that the modem will lose synchronization. The scrambler provides a continually varying pattern that can be used by the demodulator to maintain synchronization. A modem with a scrambler is less likely to lose synchronization and so a scrambler is typically utilized in those modems transmitting at high data rates.

## Echo Suppressor Disable

In all dial-up circuits an echo suppressor or echo canceler may be incorporated into the circuit (operation to be described later). In North America the tone that disables an echo suppressor is one between 2010 and 2240 Hz lasting for at least 400 milliseconds. In the international environment the V.25 option says the answer tone will be 2100 Hz but there are still many circuits that are 2225 Hz or 2250 Hz. Thus when North American-type modems are used in the international environment, the North American modems recognize the CCITT echo suppressor disable tone, but the reverse may not be true. Therefore, care must be taken with an international connection to verify that the modems at both ends are generating the appropriate disable tones to eliminate echo suppressors from the circuit. The suppressors must be disabled because they take time to drop out of the circuit. This will cause *clipping* if the data starts back in the opposite direction before the suppressor has been disabled or turned around (make the line full duplex). This is very much like the half-duplex versus full-duplex, line turnaround mode of operation, where the protocol starts to transmit before the circuit is ready to support it.

Because some carriers now use echo cancelers instead of echo suppressors, if you utilize the V.32 modem standard for dialing up at 9.6 KBPS, there is an additional potential problem involving the echo cancellation techniques between the modems themselves and the public telephone networks where both use echo cancelers. The problem arises when there are four cancelers on the circuit. The cancelers compete with each other, which is called *dueling*. The result is that the modem will not work.

The CCITT has a solution: the installation of a specific tone for turning off the network's echo cancelers (Recommendation G.165 specifies a 2100 Hz tone with slow phase alternations for at least one second). Many modem manufacturers have incorporated the tone into their equipment. If you are going to use V.32 modems you must first determine whether your intended carriers (AT&T, Sprint, MCI, etc.) have the ability to recognize the canceler turn-off tone. If they cannot recognize this tone, then they have no method of turning off their cancelers and your dial-up modems will not work.

## Call Waiting

The call waiting feature, now available from many carriers in North America, is provided by a temporary disconnect condition that lasts somewhere between 50 ms and 200 ms. V.22bis modem specifications provide for a disconnect after 40 ms to 65 ms while the 212A modem can accommodate between 600 ms and 700 ms before it drops its carrier detect signal. As a result, a V.22bis modem may not be usable in those areas where call waiting is available. Since almost all the two-wire 2400 BPS/FDX modems are V.22bis compatible, you must find out whether call waiting exists on your circuits and, if it does, you may have to have it removed or disabled.

## Carrier Line Connection

Telephone companies require that signals coming in from users on local loops have a signal level no greater than $-12$dBm (dBm will be described in Chapter 21). If the level is too great (more positive value than $-12$dBm), then clipping circuits that limit the magnitude of the signal may be utilized so that no harm will come to the telco equipment. In addition, the carrier may cut off service and/or impose penalty charges on the user. In order to alleviate this situation, there are three common ways for the user to connect to the local loop.

The first method is known as a *permissive* jack that uses an RJ11C 4-pin voice jack, shown in Fig. 10–12(a). Normally it is up to the user to measure the actual loss in the local loop and then add whatever additional loss is required to get the level to $-12$dBm. Since most users in the data world do not have this equipment and would not know how to use it if they did, modem manufacturers typically set the output level of their dial-up modems to $-9$dBm and assume that the local loop will make up the rest of the loss. Although most of the time there

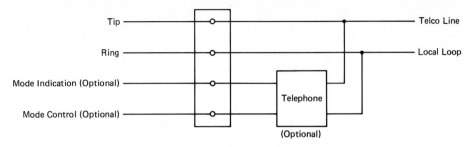

**(a)** RJ11C Jack Arrangement

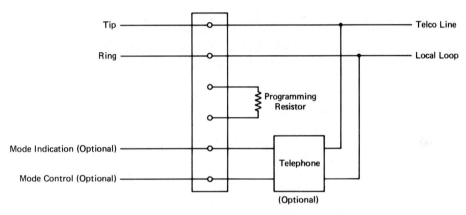

**(b)** RJ45S Jack Arrangement

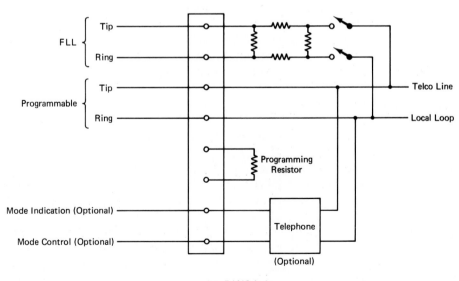

**(c)** RJ41S Jack

**FIGURE 10–12**
Jack Configurations

213

should be no problem, if you are too close to the telephone office your signal may be too strong; if you are too far from the office your signal will be too weak, which will probably lead to transmission errors.

The second method of connection utilizes a 6-pin, RJ45S *programmable* jack which is usually used on a leased line where the local loop is considered to be of data quality. A diagram of an RJ45S is shown in Fig. 10–12(b). In this connection a resistor set by the installer is used to set the output level of the signal to the required value. A variation of this jack called RJ27X can connect up to eight modems to eight different lines. The RJ27X, which is also called a multiline jack, utilizes a 50-pin connector where each of the eight lines will look like a separate RJ45S connection.

The third method, called *fixed loss loop* (FLL), utilizes an 8-pin RJ41S jack. This is shown in Fig. 10–12(c). In this case a resistor (called a pad) sets a fixed loss of 9dBm on the circuit; since modems connecting to an RJ41S are normally set to transmit at a level of −3dBm, the level at the carrier office will be −12dBm.

## Training

As described in Chapter 8, all modems that transmit in a synchronous mode must go through a *training,* or synchronization, sequence. This sequence can vary from just a few milliseconds at lower speeds up to a few hundred milliseconds at 9600 BPS and many seconds at higher data rates. For point-to-point connections this is not a very significant problem, but in multidrop circuits it is a major consideration. Figure 10–13 shows that the modem at the master site can be transmitting a carrier all the time. Each demodulator at a remote location will synchronize to that master modulator. The transmission back from the remotes is not that simple. When a logical poll goes out to Location A, it is recognized by the DTE at that location. To respond to the poll, the modulator at A must turn its carrier

**FIGURE 10–13**
Multidrop/Switched Carrier Operation

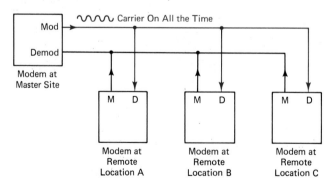

on, at which time the demodulator at the master site must go through the synchronization process to receive the data response. If there is no data to send, there is still a transmission (usually just an ACK) indicating that such is the case. Upon completion of the transmission from remote site A, the modulator at A must be turned off. The master site can now poll remote site B. At that point the modulator at B will turn on its carrier and the host site must synchronize to it. Remote site A had to turn off its carrier upon completion of its transmission because two or more carriers cannot be received by the master demodulator at any one time. If that occurred, the master site could not synchronize and, in turn, determine who was transmitting. You may have heard the term *streaming* modem. A streaming modem is one that has turned on its carrier signal and does not turn it back off. If streaming occurs on a multidrop circuit where one of the remotes does not turn off its carrier, the entire line will be inoperable.

If the training times for modems are in the range of a few hundred milliseconds, transmitting at a higher data rate may mean a lower throughput. Examples are shown in Table 10-2.

Assuming a message length of 150 characters or 1200 bits (a reasonable message length) and typical training times of 5 ms at 2400 BPS, 50 ms at 4800 BPS, and 250 ms at 9600 BPS, you can see that the training time added to the data transmission time gives an optimum data throughput at 4800 BPS. Even though the transmission time at 9600 BPS is half the time it takes at 4800 BPS, the data actually gets through in less time at 4800 BPS because of the training time. As you make the messages longer it becomes more feasible to utilize the higher transmission rate, but many applications, especially those that are inquiry or response oriented, have even shorter transmissions, which means the 4800 BPS transmission is probably optimum for most applications.

Vendors have realized for a long time that this is the case, and so they have developed modems that can synchronize faster at the higher data rates. *Fast-train* modems are now becoming available in the 20–60 ms range. If you require multidrop operation and you have messages of different lengths at different times, it would benefit you to consider the modems with shorter training times so you can operate at higher data throughput rates.

Another alternative is a *split-stream* modem, which provides the option of transmitting at one rate while receiving at a different rate. To support this opera-

**TABLE 10-2**
Multidrop Training Time Comparison. Assume Message at 150 Characters (1200 bits)

| AT | MODEM TRAINING TIME | DATA TRANSMIT TIME | TOTAL TIME |
|---|---|---|---|
| 2400 BPS | 5 ms | 500 ms | 505 ms |
| 4800 BPS | 50 ms | 250 ms | 300 ms |
| 9600 BPS | 250 ms | 125 ms | 375 ms |

tion the DTE must be compatible with a split-stream modem, which means the DTE must be capable of transmitting and receiving at different rates also.

Finally in late 1987 there was still another announcement of a new modem capability. Both Codex and Racal/Milgo announced a *multidrop* modem, which provides for two or three separate applications running simultaneously on a single multidrop line. In the Codex modem there are two separate applications that are frequency division multiplexed (FDM) on the incoming line at 4800 and 2400 BPS. The outgoing path transmits at 9600 BPS using TDM (FDM and TDM are described in Chapter 11). The Racal/Milgo was advertised to operate at 14.4 KBPS in a multidrop with three applications running simultaneously in both directions, apparently through some form of frequency division multiplexing because of the amount of synchronization time required in going from the remote locations back to the host. There is no doubt that additional devices will be doing the same thing in the future. This may be an economical way to reduce the amount of multiplexers used in a network because the net effect of this operation is that two or three separate channels communicate simultaneously, which is the same as multiplexer operation.

Along with the potential for different training times, some modems *train on data,* that is, instead of utilizing particular synchronization sequences when starting up, the modems themselves can train on bits that are received on start up. When a modem carrier signal is on the line, bits are output even if you don't send data. They appear to be random data bits. The modems can now stay in synchronization as long as data is being transmitted. You must still wait the minimum amount of training time on start up to be capable of recognizing the data at the receive end.

## Dual Tone Multifrequency

There appears to be some confusion between the carrier signals put out by a modem and the tones generated by tone dialing telephones. They are totally unrelated to each other. The *dual tone multifrequency* (DTMF) tones generated by a telephone are used by the carriers to establish circuits through their switching systems, and although they take place within the voice range they have absolutely nothing to do with data. Some older systems, however, use DTMF tones to transmit both alpha and numeric data. Numbers were sent by depressing the key one time for a numeric value, two times for the first alpha, three times for the second alpha, and four times for the third alpha, all in rapid succession so the receiving devices can understand what the transmitter is trying to say. Because of the human interface here, there is quite a bit of room for error and misinterpretation, so this method is obsolete today. For numeric interaction only, or for automatic answering systems (depress digits in response to a query) the key pad can still be used. Fig. 10–14 is provided to give you an idea of what the DTMF tones are.

The DTMF is activated when one of the keys on a handset is depressed. Then a single frequency from the low group and a single frequency from the high

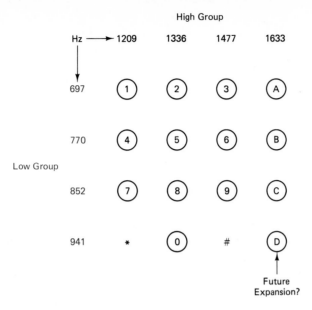

**FIGURE 10-14**
DTMF Tones

group are generated simultaneously. Both frequencies must exist for the carrier equipment to utilize the signal. These frequency pairs are used throughout the world where tone signaling is utilized (the term Touch-Tone℠ is a trademark of AT&T and therefore can only be used by them).

## Code Division Multiplexing

In 1987 AT&T announced a method of incorporating diagnostic information into modem transmissions in a way that would not detract from bandwidth allocations, as is the case with reverse or backward channel modems. By utilizing the entire bandwidth, not only could data be transmitted at high rates, but also diagnostic information could be included with it. It was called *code division multiplexing*. Diagnostic information would be carried in the same stream by adding to the signal constellation points. Figure 10-15 shows how it would work. Given a normal signal constellation of 16 points (4 bits per signal point), 1 point in each quadrant would be designated as a potentially dual signal point. As shown, 2 points in each quadrant convey the same information bits, but depending on which of the signal points are used they could also represent a 0 or a 1 bit from a separate data stream such as diagnostic information. This data can transmit information as well as control signals for initiating other operations. It remains to be seen whether AT&T will incorporate this mechanism into their modems.

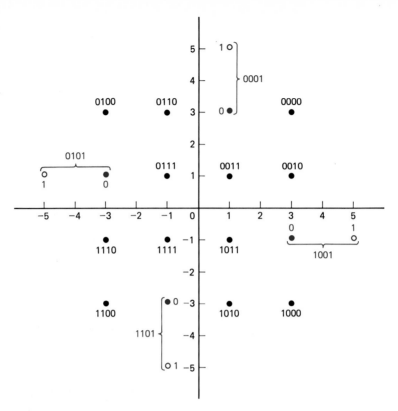

**FIGURE 10–15**
Code Division Multiplexing

## Compression

The various techniques for compressing data will be described in Chapter 13, but there are many modem vendors today already using those techniques (described in Chapter 9) to increase the throughput of their modems. Both standard and nonstandard techniques are being used to reduce characters into fewer bits so that higher effective throughputs can be realized. Because data compression is a technique that can be utilized by end users independently, if a modem vendor already incorporates a form of data compression into a modem, any other reduction in bits to be sent with their corresponding higher data throughput may not be feasible. It is therefore necessary for the user to identify the technique used by the modem vendor to obtain high data rates. If compression is incorporated, then the user may not be able to perform external compression with any additional gain in throughput.

# OTHER MODEM-RELATED EQUIPMENT

There are many different types of equipment that relate directly to modem implementation and operation. They will be described in this section.

## Acoustic Coupler

The acoustic coupler converts ordinary binary digital bits to audio tones in a low speed asynchronous environment. Typically the transmission speed is up to 1200 BPS in each direction. Depending on the protocol used, the coupler may transmit simultaneously in both directions or one way at a time. An acoustic coupler does not have to be registered with an FCC number because it does not connect directly to the telephone line. It is used in conjunction with a telephone handset, which is plugged into the telephone line. Many portable devices (keyboards, printers, etc.) have built-in acoustic couplers so that they can be carried to any location where there is a telephone. The transmit end converts binary bits to tones for transmission on the telephone line, while the receive end converts the tone back to binary bits for use there. It is not anticipated that acoustic couplers will be used for transmission above 1200 BPS. Acoustic couplers are usually compatible with AT&T 103/113 modems at 300 BPS and AT&T 212 modems at 1200 BPS. If possible, acoustic couplers should be avoided because of the added signal distortion and/or noise they introduce to the transmitted signal.

## Autobaud Modem

An autobaud modem is used predominantly in dial-up situations where a central site may have to communicate with multiple remote sites potentially operating at different speeds. Typically the two speeds are either 300 or 1200 BPS, and the common mode of communication is for the remote to dial into the autobaud modem at the central site and transmit a character such as a carriage return, which the autobaud modem will recognize. The modem sets its internal speed for the speed of that particular remote device. The same speed is maintained for the duration of the connection. As soon as the connection is terminated, the host site modem (autobaud modem) goes back to a mode where it will look for either 300 or 1200 BPS from the next caller.

With the advent of V.22bis modems transmitting full duplex at 2400 BPS, the autobaud operation at the fallback speeds can now be reduced to either 1200 BPS or 600 BPS if true V.22bis compatibility is incorporated. If 212A compatibility is incorporated, it also needs to be backed up at the lowest data rate of 300 BPS. For those applications in North America where a V.22bis modem is utilized, the user would probably be better off getting a modem with 212A compatibility also and, if reduced transmission is required because of line degradations, then go from 2400 BPS to 1200 BPS and ultimately to 300 BPS. The 600 BPS fallback mode should only be used on international circuits when operating with V.22bis modems.

Another type of autobaud modem monitors line conditions and/or error rates. When error rates exceed a certain level set by the user, these modems may automatically switch speeds to a lower rate. From 14.4 KBPS, speed may be switched down to 9600, 7200, 4800, or 2400 BPS. Both ends of the line must obviously be the same type of modem, and it is very important in this particular mode of operation that both user devices (DTE) be capable of dynamically changing the speed at which they will transmit or accept data. Many DTE vendors prohibit this dynamic changing, so the autobaud modem in such a case would not be applicable.

This type of autobaud modem is only used at the higher synchronous data rates, and in order not to interrupt data transmissions, the speed changes will only occur when no data are being transmitted on the line. The advantage of these modems is that they can operate over lines where degradation changes with time. The disadvantage is the lack of user interfaces for dynamically changing speeds and the possibility of continuous changing up and down as the line parameters change, which slows down the effective throughput rate of data transmission.

## Equalizers in Modems

Almost all modems today, especially those used for transmission rates of 2400 BPS and up, contain some form of equalization. The terms *equalization* and *conditioning* (conditioning will be discussed in further detail in Chapter 21) are used interchangeably and refer to the process of correcting line impairments in attenuation and delay making them closer to the same value (equalized) at all frequencies. Equalization is mandatory for all high speed modems to reduce error rates.

The first type of equalization is *fixed equalization,* which assumes a standard voice-grade circuit from end to end and provides a predetermined amount of compensation or filtering for its equalization. Because fixed equalizers correct for impairments anticipated on typical long-distance circuits, a fixed amount of equalization may actually make the line worse than if it had no fixed equalization at all (overcompensation). We can compare this to wearing a pair of sunglasses when driving. For the most part the sunglasses will prevent sunlight from bothering you, but if you happen to go through a tunnel, the amount of light blocked will make it very hard for you to see. At the other end of the spectrum, if you are facing the sun, even with sunglasses it may still be too bright for you to see. A voice-grade line is in many ways like a road with bright sun and tunnels, and the best way to compensate for these variations is to have some form of adaptive equalization.

*Adaptive equalization* allows modems to communicate with each other prior to or while transmitting data, and to adapt their filtering and equalization circuitry to compensate for the dynamic line changes as they are encountered during a particular connection or a particular sequence of segments on a leased line. In addition, adaptive equalization, which today uses many digital filtering elements, can even compensate for degradations on the line that vary during transmission. Almost every single modem operating at 2400 BPS and up uses some form of digital filtering technique to reduce the possibility of errors received at that transmission rate. Even though many vendors say you do not need to have telephone company line conditioning installed for the equipment to operate at higher data rates, some lines are so poor that the internal modem equalization is not adequate and therefore some form of external equalization is still required.

Some modems today operate at higher transmission rates than 9600 BPS, such as at 14,400 BPS or greater, and vendors usually say that external equalization is required for these applications. Again, conditioning and equalization will be described in Chapter 21.


## Modem Eliminator/Emulator/Simulator, or Null Modem

When two DTEs are within the 50-ft RS232 operating limitation, there is another potential problem that must be resolved: What do you do with the signals that normally connect to modems for transmission and reception of signals when the two DTEs connect directly together? For example, pin 2 is Transmit Data and pin 3 is Receive Data. If two DTEs were connected directly together, the two transmitting signals would be on the same line (the output to the modulators if they were there), while the two receive signal pins would be connected (the input from the demodulators if they were there). If this connection were made there would be no transmission of information. The two transmitting DTEs would be sending their data signal on the same physical line and nothing would be coming into the receive circuits.

Also, many of the control signals for the protocol such as Data Terminal Ready, Data Set Ready, and Carrier Detect may be required for normal operation, but there are no modems to provide the appropriate signal generation and termination. As a final point, for synchronous transmission between the two DTEs there would be no modem clock, which is mandatory for reception of synchronous inputs.

This entire situation is resolved by the use of a device (if you can call it that) that goes by many names, including modem eliminator, modem emulator, modem simulator, and null modem. This device performs the necessary functions for tying two DTEs together in the local environment when they are both RS232 standard compatible. In Fig. 10–16 you can see the different connections that are provided for various types of operation in the local environment. Pin 7 is the required ground signal and therefore the two are tied directly together. Pins 2 and 3 in the cable connecting the two connectors are reversed such that pin 2 at one end connects to pin 3 at the other end, and vice versa so that Transmit Data at each end can get to the Receive Data pin at the other end.

Pins 20, 6, and 8, which are Data Terminal Ready, Data Set Ready, and Carrier Detect, are tied together so that if any one of the signals is turned on at one end all three signals at that end will be activated. This simulates the terminal being turned on, the modem being turned on, and a carrier signal being received from the modem, which says the DTE should be ready to receive data.

For protocols that require Request to Send and return of Clear to Send prior to transmitting data, pins 4 and 5 are strapped together. If necessary, they go through a separate timing circuit that will insert the appropriate RTS/CTS delay when required.

The preceding connections constitute the necessary interfaces for a full asynchronous modem eliminator. Not all the connections may be required for all protocols, but if required, the asynchronous modem eliminator can be obtained with all the necessary connections to accommodate all situations.

Below the asynchronous modem eliminator connections are two more connections, which are terminated in a clock generator. The clock generator is required for a synchronous modem eliminator because it generates the appropriate

**FIGURE 10–16**
Modem Eliminator/Emulator/Simulator or Null Modem

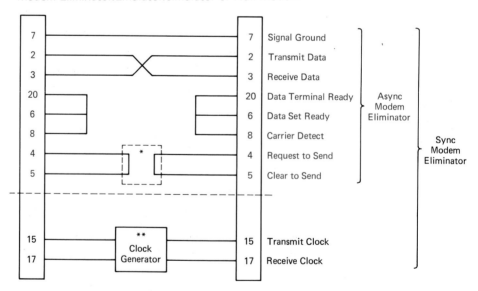

*Inserts RTS/CTS delay if required
**Set for specific standard transmission rates

clock signals as if a modem was in the circuit. The clock generator must be set to the appropriate transmission speed and usually requires all the asynchronous connections to be there also.

Many vendors provide DTE equipment that has a separate product number for local or remote operation. The primary difference in these devices is that the local device is configured for a direct connection to the CPU without the requirement for a modem eliminator. Personal computers that have an RS232 interface may require a modem eliminator (usually asynchronous) for direct connection to another PC or mainframe. If this is the case, be aware that there are some PCs that will not turn on their Data Terminal Ready signal until they get a Data Set Ready signal from the modem. Because the modem is not there, both the Data Set Ready and the Carrier Detect signal will never be turned on, and you will be in what is known as a *deadly embrace*, with the PC never turning on. It may therefore be necessary to connect an external battery and jumper pins 20, 6, and 8 to get the PC to operate.

There is much confusion regarding the null modem because it goes by many names and performs many different kinds of functions. If, after connecting two DTEs together, they do not work, you should go back to the manuals and try to identify the specific signals that are required at the interface and which ones must be active for each DTE to operate. You should then be able to identify the specific modem eliminator pins that must be *jumpered* (connected together) to initiate operation.

There are other variations to null modems, one of the primary ones being the connection of DTR at one end to DCD and DSR (strapped together) at the other end. In the particular instance shown in Fig. 10–17, when a device at one end is ready to transmit (turns on its DTR signal), the DCD and DSR signals are activated at the remote end so that the remote can receive. In other words, instead of your own terminal turning on your DCD and DSR, you allow the device at

**FIGURE 10–17**
Alternative Null Modem (shown for async only)

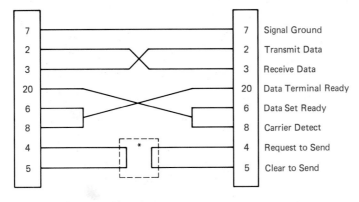

| 7 | | 7 | Signal Ground |
| 2 | | 2 | Transmit Data |
| 3 | | 3 | Receive Data |
| 20 | | 20 | Data Terminal Ready |
| 6 | | 6 | Data Set Ready |
| 8 | | 8 | Carrier Detect |
| 4 | | 4 | Request to Send |
| 5 | | 5 | Clear to Send |

*Inserts RTS/CTS delay if required

the other end to do it. This configuration seems to have as many proponents as tying a DTR signal back to its own device DCD and DSR. Depending on your application one might be better than the other, so you need to know what sequence of signals is best for your particular DTE.

Another area related to null modems is the need to determine if a device such as a computer or PC is really a DTE or DCE. A way to do that is to look at the signal on pin 2 relative to pin 7. Since a DTE puts out a constant logical 1 (negative voltage) when it is not sending out any data, if you see a negative voltage on pin 2 the device is a DTE. This is especially important for those interfaces where PCs are communicating with peripherals through an interface that is *described* as RS232. The voltage is one of the functions to verify first if the PC/ peripheral interface doesn't work when first connected.

## H
## CIRCUIT DEVICES AND OPERATION

Since the existing telephone circuit environment was developed for voice transmission, many functions required to make the circuits operate better for voice may cause problems for data transmission. Some of the more significant problems will be described next.

### Echo Suppression

All transmission lines suffer from *impedance mismatches,* which result in the reflection of some of the energy being transmitted for both voice and data back to the originator. When distances are not too great it is hard to recognize these reflected signals, but as the line gets longer the signal appears to be an *echo.* To eliminate echoes, especially on long-distance circuits, AT&T started inserting echo suppressors in circuits that exceeded the distance where voice echoes could be recognized by humans. Figure 10–18 shows how these initial echo suppressors worked. When connecting between locations A and B through a long-distance carrier circuit, an echo suppressor would be associated with that line. If the individual at location A began to speak, the echo suppressor would pull into the circuit, making it *unidirectional* from A to B. When location A stopped speaking, the echo suppressor would drop off the line and come into the line in the opposite direction once location B began to speak. In this mode of operation, only one person could speak at a time and there was no way to interrupt that person once they were talking.

In the data transmission environment this is a significant potential problem because some communications, especially those involving PCs, require the capability for immediate initiation of transmission in the opposite direction (immediate line turnaround). In addition, even if there was a capability for accommodating some line turnaround time, if the echo suppressor does not drop out fast enough, the transmission coming from the opposite direction may have the initial

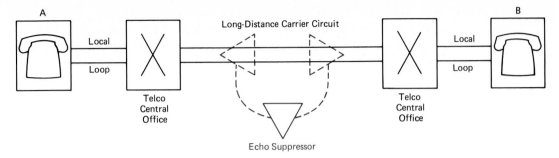

**FIGURE 10–18**
Echo Suppression

bits *clipped* off, which means the response will be incomplete and therefore erroneous.

AT&T recognized the potential echo suppressor problem many years ago and began to upgrade the network by putting in echo suppressors that could be *turned around* by a higher-volume input from the opposite direction. This was good for voice communications when the listening party wanted to interrupt the transmitting party, but in the case of data, with the modems putting out the same level of signal, the line could not be turned around.

Therefore, AT&T began installing *hybrid circuits,* which converted the two-wire local loop circuit to a four-wire circuit for long-distance connections, and then at the far end converted the four-wire circuit back to a two-wire local loop. By appropriate wiring configuration of the hybrid (which was nothing more than a transformer), each pair of wires in the long-distance circuit could be made unidirectional, yet the people or devices communicating at each end would have what appeared to be true two-way, simultaneous communication. This circuit is depicted in Fig. 10–19.

All two-wire *leased* circuits are in this configuration, which is the primary reason that two-wire and four-wire leased circuits cost approximately the same. The only additional things you get in a four-wire leased circuit are four-wire local loops (2 two-wire pairs) at both ends. If you are going to lease a circuit then, it

**FIGURE 10–19**
Hybrid Circuit

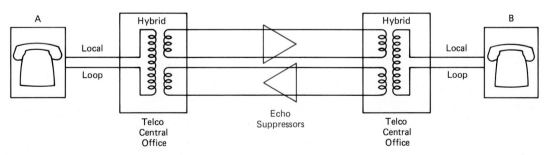

is much better to get the four-wire circuit from end to end so that you will not have to worry about the turnaround times involved in two-wire modem communications (you could also use a split-channel modem). If you have enough volume to lease a line, lease it four-wire all the way.

As a separate function involved in this area, there is a signal known as a *disable* tone (between 2010 and 2240 Hz in the United States, 2225 or 2240 Hz in Europe) that causes the echo suppressor to operate during a particular call connection. This is the approximate frequency of the connect tone that you get from a computer when you complete the dial connection. It does not help modem turnaround time but allows you to use split-channel modems.

Still another device has been incorporated into the telephone circuits in today's satellite environment. It is known as an *echo canceler,* shown in Fig. 10–20. The local loop is still two wire for both voice and data dial up, but in this case the telephone offices connect to a satellite ground station for a major portion of the circuit distance, and that is where the echo cancelers are incorporated.

An echo canceler is an *active* device. It does not make the line unidirectional, but instead measures the energy at each frequency coming from the local and remote end. Built into it is a mathematical model of the satellite circuit, which identifies the distance and, in turn, the total propagation time. This mathematical model is used to predict when all echoes will be returned and at what level the returned signal will be; in other words, the magnitude of the echo. The echo canceler is designed to eliminate only the amount of energy at each frequency that is due to the echo. If the transmitter at the other end uses the same frequencies, they will propagate all the way through, because only the amount of energy due to an echo will be eliminated by the echo canceler.

Echo cancelers are obviously very sophisticated devices, but they work very well in today's satellite environment. You can always tell when one of them is not working, because the echo is very pronounced and occurs somewhere between 600 and 750 ms after you speak. The circuit is so good that you appear to hear

**FIGURE 10–20**
Echo Cancelers

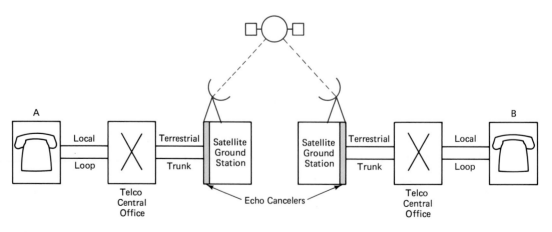

your own echo at the same level that you are speaking. Echo cancelers permit simultaneous two-way communication and therefore will not affect data transmission. Remember, however, that because satellite circuits have such a long propagation delay the protocol time-outs must be considered.

## Bridge

Two types of devices are known as *bridges*. The first is used like a hybrid, but instead of converting a two-wire circuit to a four-wire circuit, it takes the circuit coming in from a master site and splits it into two circuits, one for a local drop on a multidrop line, and the second for transmission onto the next site on that multidrop line. There will be a bridge at every Class 5 office on the circuit where there is a multidrop termination. This is shown in Fig. 10–21.

The other type of bridge is a connection used in a monitoring and control environment where signals can be monitored without affecting the operation of the line. There are both analog and digital bridges that allow monitoring of the signals on both sides of the modem. Normally the bridge circuit is connected through a *patch panel,* which provides convenient bridging (connections) to all circuits into and out of a site.

## I
## AUTODIAL MODEMS

Two very different areas deal with the subject of autodialing. First is the low-speed asynchronous autodial, typified by the Hayes-type commands; the second area, synchronous autodialing, is much newer and only recently became available to end users. Both will be discussed.

Years ago when connections had to be established between remote modems and central sites, it was necessary to establish the circuit with a telephone handset. The circuit would physically be established by dialing with the handset and then a switchover to the modem connection would be made, obviously a cumbersome way to establish the circuit since it always required human intervention.

With the growth of the PC in the early 1980s, there was an obvious need for automatic circuit establishment so that the time delays involved with human intervention could be eliminated. Many more calls could be made within the same time frame, and more efficient use of the equipment could be incorporated. Although there were quite a few different mechanisms to set up an automatic dialing scheme, the system set up by the Hayes Corporation has become a de facto standard for dialing at 300 BPS and 1200 BPS. There are other command sets for asynchronous autodialing established by Concord and AT&T Information Systems (ATTIS). The Hayes mechanism is known as the *AT* command set because the ASCII character *A* or *T* is required before any command is sent. It defines a simple modem control language (the command set) that a terminal or

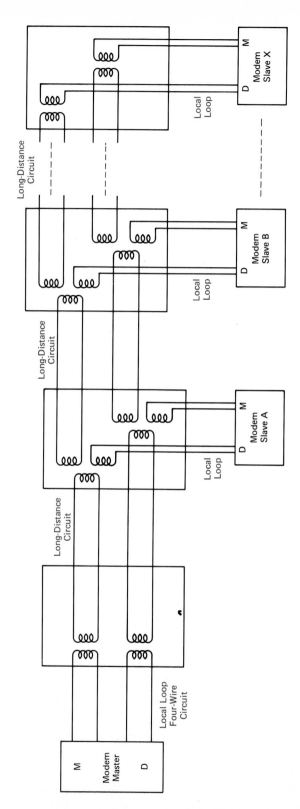

**FIGURE 10-21**
Bridge for Multidrop Circuit

computer can send to a modem to set up a call automatically by autodialing and autoanswering.

The command set only sets up the connection. It does not involve the movement of data. It is the set of commands between the terminals or computer and the modems to initiate circuit establishment and verification.

Because of the command set's extensive use, the commands are listed here but the user must remember that they are continually being upgraded so modems with different levels of commands may not necessarily be compatible with each other. The full name of the Hayes AT command set is *Smartmodem 1200 Minimum Command Set*.

AT Characters          Commands

A—Initiate answer mode data call.

C0—Turn carrier off.

C1—Turn carrier on, pause for secondary dial tone—approximately two seconds; modem reenter command state after dialing.

Ds—Dial the number string "s."

E0—Do not echo characters keyed when in command mode.

E1—Echo characters keyed when in command mode.

F0—Half-duplex. Echo characters keyed during a data call.

F1—Full-duplex. Do not echo characters keyed during a data call.

H0—Hang up.

H1—Go off hook.

I0—Request product index code.

I1—Request product revision code.

O—Return to data mode.

P—Dial using pulses.

Q0—Enable status message.

Q1—Disable status message.

R—Reverse current connection mode.

Sr?—Read command register "r." "r" may be 0–12 or 16. Result will be in the range of 0–255.

Sr=n—Set command register "r" to "n."

T—Dial using tones.

V0—Status messages will be abbreviated to one digit.

V1—Status messages will be in English.

X0—Enable only the basic status message set.

X1—Enable the 1200 BPS connect status message set.

Z—Reset.

The AT characters must be in upper case and provide the attention sequence which initiates the process. The command characters are then sent and they may be in upper or lower case. Finally, the carriage return is sent. The modem uses the AT characters to adapt to the speed because the speed of the commands is the same as the speed of data. The AT characters are also used to adapt to parity, which is either odd, even, mark, or space. Because the A character has an even number of one bits and the T has an odd number of one bits, by checking both characters the modem can determine what method of parity is used.

As an example of how the AT command sequence works, if you wanted to automatically dial the number 1-800-555-1212, the command sequence would be ATDT9,18005551212 ⟨carriage return⟩. This assumes that you are dialing through a PBX onto an outside line, which requires a pause for a secondary tone. The number 9 secures the outside line, at which time you must pause and wait for the connection to the outgoing telephone line.

Some communications protocols like Smartcomm and Crosstalk automate these commands so the user does not have to perform them. If additional features are to be incorporated they will probably be added by expanding the X commands, such as Xx, Xy, Xz, and so on.

The asynchronous autodialing takes place these days up to 2400 BPS with the V.22bis modem. There are, however, needs for dialing automatically at higher data rates. Right now the CCITT V.25bis specification is the best description that can be used, although at the moment there are quite a few gaps in its definitions. When design specifications are unclear, vendors make decisions on their own for manufacturing, which results in almost certain incompatibility among modems from different vendors.

When deciding how to use modems in asynchronous dial-up transmissions, there are three primary methods that must be considered because it is the combination of modem hardware and software that determines the actual operation. What you are really trying to do is get as close as possible to a *pseudo full-duplex* transmission, which means approximating a high-speed asymmetric transmission.

The first method is sometimes called *ping-pong half-duplex*. In this mode of operation the transmission direction is changed based on the required volume of transmission for a particular direction. If the volume from one direction is higher than the other, then the direction of transmission is set up to accommodate that high volume. Periodically, the direction of the transmission is changed to allow ACKs and/or NAKs to be sent. The line turnaround when this occurs will cause a slowdown in throughput, so you would be well advised to utilize some form of compression capability if possible. This type of transmission is used extensively when you have heavy one-way file transfer.

The second method is to have two separate channels with a high-speed channel in the direction of the higher volume of data flow, and a low-speed channel set up for transmission of ACKs and NAKs. The low-speed channel can also handle error control transmissions and *echos* and can be at either the high or low end of the voice-grade band. This particular mechanism is also good for one-way file transfer.

The third method is to operate like the first method (one-way high-speed transmission) when the application is one-way file transfer, but if the application is interactive, then the modem would operate like a 212 full-duplex modem at 1200 BPS in each direction.

Synchronous autodialing requires a separate process because the characters that represent the numbers to be dialed are in an *envelope* encased between flag, sync, or control characters instead of being standalone asynchronous characters (characters with a start and stop bit on each). There has to be an entirely different sequence of determining what the parameters are when the circuit is being established. Until recently, you needed to have an RS366 computer port at an approximate price of $10,000, plus a separate AT&T 801 automatic calling unit, which costs approximately $500. Because of this cost, there are only a few applications that could support utilization of synchronous autodialing (typically from the mainframe going to the remote world).

From the growth of high-speed data requirements in a dial-up mode, there will be a great movement toward synchronous autodialing. It has already started with modems like the UDS *Syncup* modems that came out in 1986. More than 20 software houses support this mode of operation, which is designed for 2400 BPS half-duplex modems. The limitation of these was that they were BSC protocol compatible only.

The RACAL-VADIC series of modems incorporates a public domain autodialing protocol for synchronous transmissions. It is called *SADL,* which stands for Synchronous AutoDialing Language. SADL incorporates procedures for Bisync, SDLC, and HDLC. It eliminates the need for a Bell 801 type Automatic Calling Unit (ACU) and the requirement for an RS366 port.

SADL sends and receives in the applicable protocol and uses a block format for dialing functions such as commands, polls, acks, call progress signals, recovery from errors, and recovery from failed calls. It is used at 2400, 4800, and 9600 BPS and also has the ability to differentiate between the various call progress signals such as dialing, ringing, answer tone, busy, failed call, no dial tone, invalid, and others.

Somewhat like SADL is the CCITT V.25bis spec. V.25bis cannot be used for IBM transmissions, however, because it specifies 7-bit ASCII code with odd parity, whereas IBM uses EBCDIC code with no parity. Another specification in use today for autodialing is V.25, but it is limited because it does not define the various modem option setting commands nor the specific call progress functions.

# J
## OTHER TRANSMISSION MECHANISMS

Excluding local area networks, which will be described in Chapter 15, there are many other ways to move data. Most of them do not use modems. Some of those methods will be described here.

## FM Radio Transmission

In the world of television, sound is transmitted utilizing the FM radio band. In that environment a substantial amount of excess bandwidth called *sidebands* are not used. In FM this is called *subcarrier;* in TV it is called the *vertical blanking interval* (VBI). These schemes involve a one-way transmission only, unless you have a separate mechanism for transmitting information back to the originator, such as Videotex. Transmission using sidebands is user- and distance-insensitive as long as you are within the broadcast range of the station transmitter.

In March of 1983 the FCC allowed FM stations to broadcast virtually any type of programming on the unused portion of their station bandwidth. In the FM world stations are assigned 200 KHz in the 88.1–107.9-MHz range. If the FM station transmits monaural, it uses approximately ± 20 KHz around the carrier frequency, and if it uses stereo, ± 53 KHz around the carrier frequency is used.

Since the total bandwidth assigned to a station is 200 KHz, even with stereo transmission there is 46 KHz at each end of the assigned frequency spectrum for what is called *subcarrier* use.

Before 1983, use of the FM subcarrier world consisted primarily of foreign language broadcasts, background music, reading services for the blind, and other smaller services. In order to receive these transmissions, however, the user would need a special subcarrier receiver tuned to the specific sideband that the transmission is on. In the United States those bands consisted of 57 KHz, 67 KHz, and 92 KHz.

Once the sidebands were deregulated in 1983, their use was primarily for transmission of financial information with secondary services being news transmission, weather, E Mail, and private network transmissions. This is an area that has been growing in metropolitan environments for users who need to have information broadcast within a localized geography.

The advantages in using FM subcarrier is that existing transmission facilities can be used and the receivers must be just within the range of the transmitter. Typically, the receiver will cost under $1000 and could be even less than $500. For the typical station, the radius of reception is between 10 and 50 miles depending on the transmitter power. Another advantage is the fact that whether there are one or 20,000 listeners, the cost for the transmitting equipment is the same.

To put the transmission radius into perspective, you can utilize the distance at which a stereo signal can be recognized as the distance at which subcarrier transmissions can also be recognized (due to transmitter power differences). The maximum data rate for FM subcarrier transmissions at this point in time is 38.4 KBPS with error rates approximately the same as an analog telephone line. The path degradations which affect the signal integrity are things like obstructions and signal bounce (which causes duplicate signals to be received at the remote site). You can always utilize land lines or VSATs for backup.

As the utilization begins to increase, more and more applications will find themselves appropriate for FM subcarrier use. One of the more recent ones is the electronic advertising signs that provide not only news, weather, and other general information, but can also provide specific advertising. Many banks are beginning to use these in their branches so that customers waiting in line will get general information as well as advertising. This kind of application will no doubt grow quickly in the future.

## Spread Spectrum

A form of transmission called *spread spectrum* can be used on local telephone loops that are unloaded. It can be used simultaneously with voice transmissions.

Spread spectrum is a technique that provides at least two forms of data transmission that are used when security is required. The first generates a very low-power signal on an existing voice channel so that it appears to be background noise and will therefore not interfere with a voice conversation. Each of the data bits is encoded in a predetermined sequence called a *chip* and is transmitted sequentially. The 0 bit is encoded as the complement of the 1 bit. For example, if the 0 bit (data) is encoded as 01110001, then the 1 bit (data) will be encoded 10001110. Because of the sequence required to represent each individual bit, the actual data rate typically is slow. This method is called *direct sequence* spread spectrum. The chip sequences must be known to both ends of the path for proper decoding, but it would be relatively easy for an unauthorized listener to figure the encoding out. If a more secure method of transmission is required, this may not be good enough.

As an alternative to direct sequence, there is a method called *frequency hopping*. In this form, multiple frequencies are used to represent the data bits. The carrier frequency changes with each transmitted bit in a predetermined sequence, and direct sequence encoding can be used on top of frequency hopping. Frequency hopping is therefore applicable to secure environments because the receiver must know not only the frequencies used, but also the specific sequence for representing each of the data bits.

Both methods can be used for data transmission, but will probably only be used in those environments where the application can take advantage of the unique properties of these techniques. Spread spectrum transmission is used primarily for communicating between facilities that are either within an industrial park or within a couple of miles of one another. It is very expensive right now, but in the future it is anticipated that the cost will be down in the $500 per end range. The technique is well proven, since it has been used by the military for many years and is now becoming available commercially. Extensive use of this technique can be incorporated for radio transmissions in which digitized voice can be transmitted in addition to data.

## Infrared

To communicate between buildings that are within a five-mile radius without running a cable, you may want to use infrared transmissions. Sometimes known as laser transmissions, they use the infrared frequency spectrum. Infrared can take the place of local microwave and is substantially easier to incorporate because there are no FCC filings for frequency allocations, with their inherent delays. The signal is a baseband digital (most common) or analog signal that is modulated onto a high-frequency carrier. The preferred form of modulation is FM. The modulated carrier goes first to an infrared LED and is then sent to a solid-state laser where the output infrared beam is modulated. It is typically good for up to one mile, especially in the 23-GHz range. The speed of transmission is comparable to T carrier rates up to T3 (45 MBPS).

Multiple transceivers can be near each other because of the narrow spread of the beam. Besides use in those areas where cable cannot be made available, infrared can be used to bypass local copper circuits to the local telephone company, or as a *final hop* in a connection to the long-distance carrier for a bypass operation. Laser transmitters have to be protected so it is not possible for humans to look directly into the beam because of the potential harmful effects on the eye. Each transmitter is labeled with a rating established by the federal government that indicates the level of potential hazard. With the proper precautions, potential danger should not be a significant factor in the decision as to whether to use it. Costs for infrared transmission are becoming very competitive at T1 rates and are expected to be reduced even further as more units are built.

Another form of infrared transmission, a system developed in late 1987 provided in-house transmissions to and from transceivers located in individual rooms. Any device with an infrared transmitter could communicate with the transceiver located in the ceiling of the room. The initial use was intended to be something like a PBX without wiring to individual units, or a form of LAN, but it can also be used to communicate between terminals regardless of where those terminals reside. The system is capable of routing any transmission from any device to any other device anywhere in the network as long as the appropriate access codes are used. In this mode of transmission there can be no break in the line of sight between the device and the transceiver in the ceiling or the transmission will be interrupted. More information on this will be described in Chapter 15 on LANs.

## QUESTIONS

1. What are the speed versus distance limitations for direct connection? Line driver? Short-haul modem? Medium-distance modem? Standard modem?
2. How can you tell the difference between a 0 bit and a 1 bit for a polar signal? Nonreturn to zero signal? Biphase Manchester signal? Return to zero signal? Bipolar signal?
3. What are the three basic forms of simple modulation?
4. Describe the concept of multibit modulation operation.
5. What is QAM?
6. What is trellis coded modulation?

7. What does a modem eye pattern represent?
8. What factors limit the data throughput on an analog telephone line?
9. Draw a diagram of a full-duplex modem. Describe the sequence of data flow on the telephone line.
10. What is the difference between an echo canceler and an echo suppressor?
11. Describe three jack-type interfaces that provide a connection for a modem to a telephone line.
12. Draw a diagram and describe the switched network operation for a multidrop circuit.
13. What is the difference between an autobaud modem and an automatic equalization modem?
14. Which signals are used in a null modem? What does each one of them do?
15. What functions does a bridge perform?
16. What are the primary considerations between autodialing for synchronous and asynchronous data transmissions?
17. What is a typical application for spread spectrum transmission?

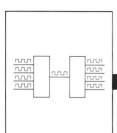

# 11

# Multiplexers

## A
## BACKGROUND

The term *multiplexer* (MUX) is derived from the Latin words *multi* meaning "many" and *plex* meaning "mix." A multiplexer combines the individual data transmission volume requirements of multiple low-speed lines in such a way that a specific grouping of them can be transmitted on a single higher-speed line. The overall effect is that instead of having a significant quantity of low-speed lines connected from a single transmitting location to the same receiving location, the low-speed lines can be combined at the remote location, and only a single line (at a higher speed) will be required to transmit all the information to the receiving site, and vice versa. This allows for a significant decrease in overall cost because the quantity of lines will be significantly reduced. At the same time, each remote location will still appear to have a direct line access to the central site because the multiplexer is, in fact, transparent to their operation (except during failure modes). For those situations where the user has a multidrop line with response times continually increasing due to heavier and heavier data transmission requirements, the use of multiplexers is a primary alternative to consider. (Implementation will depend greatly on the geographic locations of terminal sites.) A typical multiplexer configuration is shown in Fig. 11–1.

The configuration includes both local and remote connections to a remote

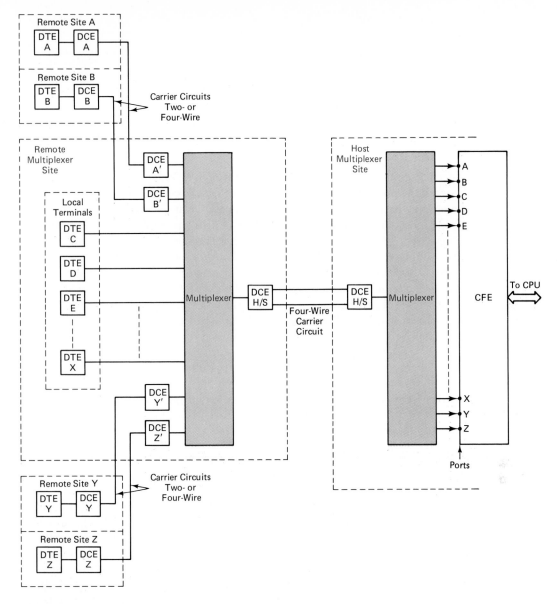

**FIGURE 11-1**
Multiplexer Configuration

multiplexer without identifying the specific multiplexer type, which will be identified later in this chapter. Remote site A and remote site B contain terminal devices
connected through an RS232 interface to a modem and then over either two- or
four-wire carrier circuits (almost always four-wire leased circuits) to the remote
multiplexer site, at which time the data are converted back to digital form, and

then through another RS232 connection to the multiplexer. Terminals C, D, and E through X (any number allowed by the multiplexer vendor) are connected directly to the multiplexer. In addition, remote sites Y and Z are also connected through carrier circuits into the remote multiplexer site.

As an example, remote site A may be Seattle, Washington; remote site B may be Portland, Oregon; the remote multiplexer site may be San Francisco; remote site Y may be Los Angeles; and remote site Z may be San Diego. San Francisco would be chosen as the remote multiplexer site because it is approximately equidistant between the cities involved, and it also has the most devices to be tied into the multiplexer.

The multiplexer would typically go through a DCE with an RS232 interface between them and then out over the carrier network to the host multiplexer site, which may be in a city like New York. The DCE in New York connects via an RS232 interface to the multiplexer, which in turn has an individual connection to separate ports on the communications front end for each remote terminal. This gives all the remote users the impression that they have a direct connection to the host-site computer. In reality they do, but instead of having separate circuits from each of the remote cities to New York, which would be very expensive, the multiplexer provides the mechanism whereby the excess line costs can be reduced with only one long-distance line required. The cost of the multiplexer configuration must include the modems and circuits between the remote cities and San Francisco.

There are many different ways to configure circuits, and different types of multiplexers can be used. Therefore, the remainder of this chapter deals with the various types of multiplexers and their particular applications.

## B
## BASIC THEORY

There are two basic kinds of multiplexing techniques, *frequency-division multiplexing* (FDM) and *time-division multiplexing* (TDM). Most FDM units are used to combine very low-speed circuits onto single voice-grade lines for transmission to a central site, while the TDMs are used for both low- and high-speed lines for the same purpose. An FDM is an analog device in which the inputs are combined to share the same voice-grade line, and therefore an external modem is not required (each subchannel has its own built-in modem). A TDM is a digital device, so a modem is required between the transmit multiplexer and the receive multiplexer (the receive portion of a multiplexer is called a *demultiplexer*). This will be described in more detail later.

Frequency-division multiplexing is also implemented at the voice-channel level by the telephone company for long-haul transmission on both coaxial cable systems and microwave radio. These are known as *carrier* systems. This capability allows the telephone company to combine many voice-grade lines for long-haul transmission between specific cities using what are known as *wideband* lines.

Time-division multiplexing is also being used by the common carriers for transmitting data at different speeds, as well as to transmit voice using the pulse code modulation techniques described in Chapter 14.

A TDM is basically a digital device. Its theory of operation is that the digital bits and bytes will share the time available on a high-speed line, so each of the low-speed incoming channels will have a dedicated portion of the high-speed outgoing line assigned to it. This will be explained in more detail later in this chapter.

## C
## PHANTOM CIRCUIT

One of the earliest attempts to transmit more than one channel of information on a particular circuit was the use of the phantom circuit shown in Fig. 11–2. The phantom circuit allows three channels of information to be carried on two circuit facilities. Subsequent developments allowed a more efficient means of *stacking* different frequencies onto the voice-grade line for transmission so phantom circuits are now obsolete.

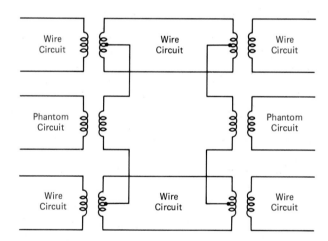

**FIGURE 11–2**
Phantom Circuit Configuration

## D
## FREQUENCY-DIVISION MULTIPLEXING

The telephone company multiplexes voice channels to utilize the capabilities of wideband long-haul facilities more efficiently, but multiplexing at these levels is both transparent and unavailable to typical voice-grade line users. What is avail-

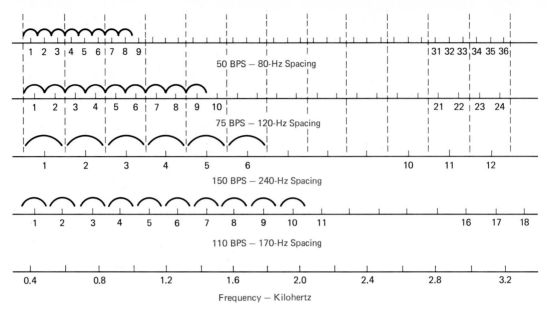

**FIGURE 11-3**
Frequency-Division Multiplexing Voice-Channel Spacing

able to voice-grade line users, however, is the capability to multiplex very narrow (low-speed) circuits into the standard voice-grade channels using FDM. Figure 11-3 shows a typical subvoice band FDM channel and frequency assignment chart. This specific segmentation follows the standard CCITT recommendations in that a nominal guard frequency band separates each channel from the adjacent one. The filters used for channel isolation normally have a 30- to 35-dB attenuation in the middle of the guard frequency band.

Frequency-division multiplexing is shown diagrammatically in the upper half of Fig. 11-4, which compares it with time-division multiplexing, shown in the lower half of the diagram. FDMs are usually used for low-speed applications (50 to 300 BPS) and are connected on a full-duplex voice-grade line, which may have conditioning applied to it but for all practical applications today is obsolete like the phantom circuit.

**E**

## TIME-DIVISION MULTIPLEXING

Time-division multiplexing has been in use for many years, but only recently with the advent of less expensive solid-state components and increased use of computers has TDM become more applicable as a means of conserving line efficiency. A TDM is a digital device and can therefore select incoming bits digitally and apportion them over a particular higher-speed bit stream in the same time inter-

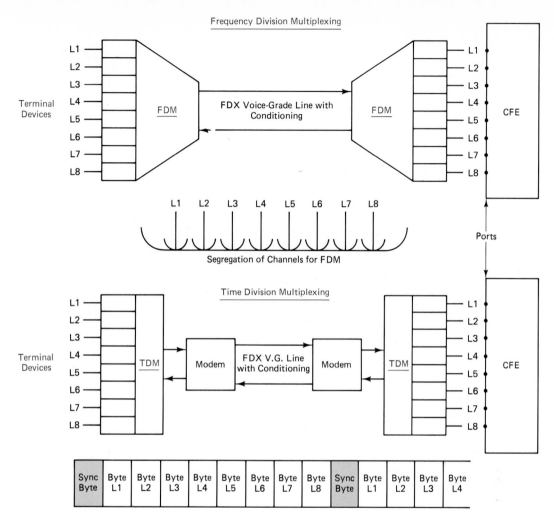

**FIGURE 11-4**
Multiplexing Techniques

val. The transmitting multiplexer will put a bit or a byte from each of the incoming lines in a specifically allocated time slot, and the demultiplexer at the other end, knowing where the bit or byte from each of the incoming lines is located, can output those bits or bytes on appropriate output lines at appropriate speeds. This is also shown in the lower part of Fig. 11-4.

TDMs have three basic modes of operation: bit multiplexing, byte multiplexing, and block multiplexing. For purposes of this text, only the byte multiplexing technique will be described, although the others are functionally implemented in exactly the same way.

In a byte multiplexing TDM the digital information that comes from the low-speed lines is combined in the form shown at the bottom of Fig. 11-4 so that the sequence starts off with a predetermined sync byte that defines the start of the sequence. This is followed by a byte from line 1, a byte from line 2, a byte from line 3, and so on, until a byte from each line has been transmitted. At that time another sync byte is sent and the sequence is repeated. This goes on continuously from end to end, from the multiplexer through the modulator over the voice-grade line to the demodulator, then to the demultiplexer, and then to the specific output line to which the character belongs. To both the remote site and the central site, it appears that there is a direct connection between them. If any errors are detected, the messages are sent back and forth as if there were a direct connection at the low-speed transmission rate. The TDM will therefore appear to be transparent to the low-speed line and the central site. If a particular line does not have any data to be transmitted, it is advisable from a user's point of view to transmit some kind of identifiable character such as an ASCII sync character to verify that the line is operational. If all zeros or blanks are sent, it is possible for one end of the line to think that the other end is nonoperational. TDMs in general utilize synchronous transmission modes on full-duplex conditioned leased lines between them.

Some TDMs are single ended, which means they will multiplex at the remote end, but at the central site or computer end the computer itself will do the demultiplexing. Demultiplexing by the computer may be required because of the non-availability of communications ports, although it does create a much heavier load on the CPU in that many more CPU cycles are required to do the demultiplexing function. Single-ended FDMs are not available because they are analog devices.

Multiplexers can also accommodate incoming lines with different speeds, as long as the total bit-carrying capacity of the incoming lines does not exceed the bit-carrying capacity of the single outgoing line. If a mixed group of incoming lines is being accepted, a *complex scan* technique is used by which the higher-speed lines (of the low-speed inputs) are sampled and transmitted more often within a particular sequence between sync bytes than the lower of the low-speed inputs. For example, if one low-speed line is twice as fast as another, it will have two bytes transmitted in any sequence for each one of the half-speed lines. All the descriptions here assume that both ends of the multiplexer pair are specified so that each incoming low-speed line at the remote end will be specifically related to an identified line coming out at the demultiplexer end. It is much easier to diagnose specific TDM than FDM logic problems, because the information is digital and can be measured more accurately with standard test equipment.

FDMs, being analog, have much more complex requirements for performing diagnostics and monitoring. Various levels are measured, the frequencies and distortions of which, because they are analog, leave much of the interpretation of what the problem really is up to the maintenance personnel. On the other hand, FDMs are in general less expensive on a per-line basis and are very reliable for low-speed circuits, such as those for Teletypes or Teletype-compatible terminals, which may include PCs using TTY protocols. Finally, because of the ever decreasing costs of chips, FDMs are being replaced by TDMs and are rarely used in North America today.

# INTELLIGENT/STATISTICAL MULTIPLEXERS

Along with the newer technological capabilities that are available due to VLSI and ULSI (very large scale integration and ultra large scale integration) components, it has been recognized by network designers that, in general, most buffered terminals require actual communication line time less than 1 percent of the time they are in use. Thus for 99 percent of actual clock time a buffered terminal will not require line time for transmission or reception of information. (These types of terminals are single-device controllers. If multiple devices on a cluster controller are used, required line utilization may increase.) If it were possible to identify the terminals that require transmission time and to only allocate time when required, it would definitely be feasible to have many more low-speed lines connected to a multiplexer than it would be possible to support if they were all busy at one time.

The device that can take advantage of that capability is called an *intelligent* or *statistical multiplexer* (statmux). This device, shown in Fig. 11-5, is a microprocessor-based unit that contains the necessary software to control both the reception of the low-speed data coming in and the high-speed data segments going out. Only those inputs that are active will be provided capacity on the output line. Therefore, the output transmissions may vary in length. There are many different methods of implementing the statmux functions, so only the most common will be described here.

Statmuxes are buffered devices; the buffer is used to absorb those time intervals when more bits are coming in on the low-speed side than the high-speed line has available to transmit. A diagram is shown in Fig. 11-6. In addition, for control purposes the statmux also puts together packets of information with bits and/or bytes from the various lines coming in. The overhead involved in creating and transmitting these packets also has an effect on the throughput capability. A typical frame used to move the high-speed data is shown in Fig. 11-7. This is a format that is typical of those vendors who use a packet scheme for transmission. Other vendors may use message blocks that are not specifically packet oriented, but the philosophy is the same.

The overhead techniques can vary, which will obviously affect efficiency. It would be possible, as some vendors do, to use Huffman coding techniques (described in Chapter 13) to increase the high-speed line efficiency by up to 50 percent. In addition, asynchronous characters will have their start and stop bits stripped off, while bisync will have the sync characters and padding characters stripped off. With the various methods of improving line efficiency, there may be up to a 50-percent difference in high-volume performance between vendor devices.

In typical statmux operations, a unit that performs bit multiplexing has a delay of 2 to 3 *bit times,* and a character-oriented multiplexer has a delay of 2 to 3 *character times,* while block- or message-oriented statmuxes can have a delay of

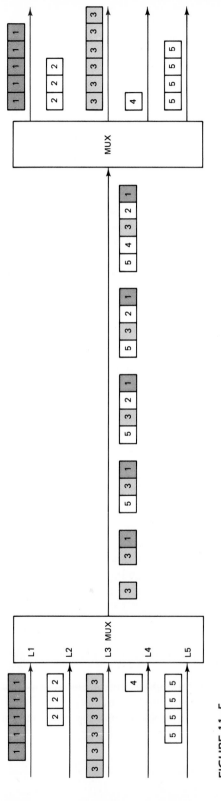

244

**FIGURE 11–5**
Statistical Multiplexing Transmission Sequence

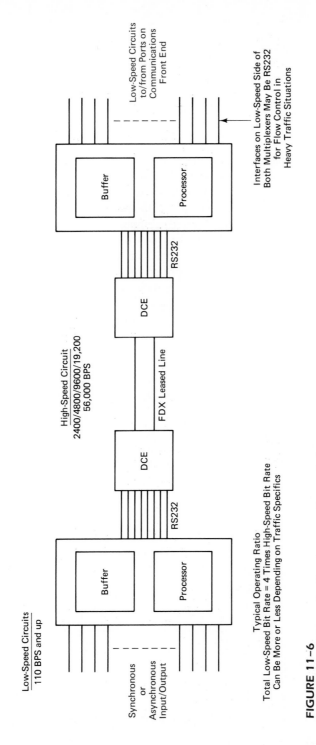

Low-Speed Circuits
to/from Ports on
Communications
Front End

Buffer

Processor

Interfaces on Low-Speed Side of
Both Multiplexers May Be RS232
for Flow Control in
Heavy Traffic Situations

RS232

DCE

High-Speed Circuit
2400/4800/9600/19,200
56,000 BPS

FDX Leased Line

DCE

Typical Operating Ratio
Total Low-Speed Bit Rate = 4 Times High-Speed Bit Rate
Can Be More or Less Depending on Traffic Specifics

RS232

Buffer

Processor

Low-Speed Circuits
110 BPS and up

Synchronous
or
Asynchronous
Input/Output

**FIGURE 11-6**
Statistical Multiplexer for Synchronous Transmission

| Flag (Start) | Destination MUX Address and Frame Number | Control | Additional Addresses if Necessary | Data | Error Detection CRC | Flag (End) |
|---|---|---|---|---|---|---|
| 8 Bits | 8 Bits | 8 Bits | 8–16 Bits | | 16 Bits | 8 Bits |

**FIGURE 11–7**
Format for Statmux Transmission

20 to 100 ms because of the frame formation, buffering, and checking involved. Statmuxes can intermix synchronous and asynchronous low-speed lines with the synchronous lines getting priority because they are delay sensitive (bits must be contiguous). Sometimes, depending on the protocol, the statmux will introduce *sync-fill* characters to the DTE to compensate for those cases where there are delays. This is done to keep the synchronous transmissions as a single block. Some protocols like DECs DDCMP cannot tolerate sync-fill characters, so in those cases the entire block is formed in the multiplexer at the remote end and the block is sent and delivered in its entirety at the host end. This will cause greater delays than those transmissions where the bits are intermixed.

As a general rule, vendors have established a criterion for the low-speed lines coming in on a statistical multiplexer. They may have a maximum of four times the bit-carrying capacity of the single high-speed or trunk line going to the host site. It is possible, however, again depending on conditions, to have bursts of eight to ten times the trunk capacity; but if this continues, the buffer in the multiplexer will fill up and there will either be greater delays or, in the worst case, erroneous messages for those synchronous inputs that must remain contiguous but had intramessage delays forced on them.

Some of the features to consider when looking at the overall operation of a statistical multiplexer are items such as the following:

Transmission efficiency
Delay
Protocol handling
Throughput
Routing
Buffer management
Diagnostics and monitoring
Synchronous and asynchronous capability
Programmability
Switching capability
Port contention
Automatic speed changing
Multiple trunk routing capability for backup or sharing

Ease of operation
Maintenance support available
Upgrade capability
Flexibility for new functions and interfaces
Pricing

Additional features to consider when evaluating the buffer management capability depend very much on the intended use, but the following items will affect efficiency:

Size of total buffer pool: should be six to eight times the trunk capacity for dynamic allocation and up to ten times the trunk capacity for nonallocated lines
Buffer allocation by channel or groups of channels
Buffer capability to absorb peak transmission bursts

Along with buffer management capabilities, a feature critical to all network operations is the capability of diagnosing and isolating errors. Software, therefore, must be available as well as hardware for at least the following:

Local and remote loopbacks
Generation of test messages
Memory and component checks
Self-testing on power up
Isolation of faults down to printed circuit board level
Understandable indicators to operators
Information to be made available for user analysis:
    Messages (totals)
    Configuration parameters
    Operational reports
    Statistics
    Processor utilization
    Buffer utilization
    Retransmission rates
    Terminal utilization
    Compression efficiency if used

The user must then also evaluate how easy it is to operate the multiplexer and to reconfigure the incoming and outgoing lines in the event of problems. When trying to evaluate a statmultiplexer's utilization, four formulas are used to compare them. This is for gross comparison only and does not necessarily mean that one device is better than another, because the previously mentioned factors must also be considered. The efficiency factors are as follows:

1. Gross efficiency $= \dfrac{\text{total bit-carrying capacity of incoming lines}}{\text{bit-carrying capacity of trunk line}} \times 100\%$

2. User protocol efficiency $= \dfrac{\text{total single-channel bit-carrying capacity including all bits}}{\text{bit-carrying capacity of trunk line}} \times 100\%$

3. High-speed link efficiency $= \dfrac{\text{data actually being sent over the trunk line}}{\text{bit-carrying capacity of trunk line}} \times 100\%$

4. True efficiency $= \dfrac{\text{total bit-carrying capacity actually being input on low-speed side}}{\text{actual bit-carrying capacity output in bits}} \times 100\%$

Along with all the operational considerations of the multiplexer, the user should evaluate the capability for handling required data flow control signals such as Xon and Xoff, which are *in-band* signals that must be recognized as part of the data stream. Also, controls for the *out-of-band* type of signaling, such as the Request to Send (RTS)/Clear to Send (CTS) or Data Set Ready (DSR)/Data Terminal Ready (DTR) controls, must be available if needed. Finally, the ability to handle additional user-programmable *in-band* controls such as ENQ/ACK (Enquiry/Acknowledge) must also be considered.

There is one last item to mention with respect to multiplexers in general: In the remote multiplexer location, where there are external lines connecting to further remote locations, those circuits are sometimes called *tail* circuits. Tail circuits can almost always be identified as having a connection through either modems or DSUs to the farther remote site.

Throughout this description of multiplexers, it should be recognized that the modem can be very easily replaced by a DSU for transmission through the digital network instead of the analog network.

## G

## T-1 MULTIPLEXER

In 1982 AT&T filed tariff #270, which covered the High Capacity Terrestrial Digital Service (HCTDS). This tariff described a data transmission capability at 1.544 MBPS.

The service begun by AT&T in 1984 that incorporated that capability was part of what is known as Accunet T1.5. This service was a significant upgrade to the previously available digital transmission services, which were limited in most cases to 56 KBPS for data and 64 KBPS for digitized voice. With T1.5, the capability existed for transmitting most combinations of digitized voice and/or data at rates of up to 1.544 MBPS. When first announced this service provided the T-1 connections in various configurations, ranging from the connection between two user end sites to connecting two carrier serving offices, with the user itself providing the connections to the end site, or combinations of the two. The different combinations were required because of the divestiture parameters that established standalone local telephone companies. The result is an arm's-length type of relationship between the long-distance carriers and the end users.

As soon as the 1.544-MBPS standard was established, many vendors developed specific multiplexer devices to interface with that T-1 circuit. A functional description of what the T-1 multiplexer might look like is shown in Fig. 11–8. On the left you can see various combinations of data and/or digitized voice, some of which are coming through submultiplexers that combine lower-speed channels into higher-speed outputs or bring in further distanced remote sites into a concentration point, very much like Figure 11–1, which is a standard multiplexer configuration. At the host end there may also be submultiplexers if the quantity of ports available on the T-1 multiplexer is inadequate to handle all the lines that must be accommodated.

The T-1 multiplexer does not differentiate between the data and the digitized voice circuits, and it is up to the user to terminate those lines in the appropriate devices for end-to-end communications.

The T-1 multiplexers must connect through a channel service unit (CSU) or equivalent. If the multiplexer does not have the correct output data format parameters to interface directly with a CSU, an AT&T 306 modem or equivalent is required between the multiplexer and the CSU. A disadvantage to putting in this type of modem is that the total bandwidth capability on the T-1 trunk is reduced to 1.35 MBPS. This is equivalent to losing three 64-KBPS channels and is therefore very important when considering the type of T-1 multiplexer you would be interested in.

The T-1 multiplexer is a true time-division multiplexer in that it can handle synchronous, asynchronous, data, or digitized voice inputs. Typically, asynchronous lines from 50 BPS to 19.2 KBPS can be supported, as well as synchronous inputs of 2400 BPS and up (to 1.544 MBPS including digitized voice at 64 KBPS).

The T-1 multiplexer may be divided into 24 separate digitized voice channels of 64 KBPS, for which the user may have to use external submultiplexers to combine lower-speed inputs to get up to that speed for nonvoice applications, while other vendors have inputs as low as 50 BPS. For vendors who do have the lower-speed inputs, be aware that, depending on the vendor, they may sometimes take an entire 64-KBPS channel, which is a substantial waste of bandwidth. These trade-offs must be evaluated when comparing different vendors.

Almost all the T-1 multiplexers are either bit or character multiplexers that

250

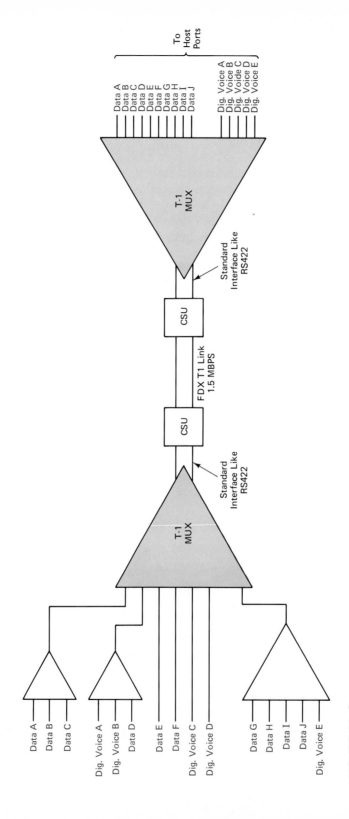

**FIGURE 11-8**
Multiplexer Configuration

operate on a full-duplex point-to-point circuit. Because of the difference in transmission speed between the United States and foreign vendors, many T-1 multiplexers have output speeds that can be either 1.544 MBPS or 2.048 MBPS.

Typical interfaces provided by the T-1 multiplexer to the end user are RS232C, RS449, RS422, RS423, CCITT V.24/V.28, V.10, V.35, Military Standard 188-114, and AT&T 303 (EIA530 available since 1988).

Besides the technical parameters and the availability of sufficient transmission requirements to warrant a T-1 circuit, the user should also look at features provided by the vendors such as diagnostics, maintenance support, power backup capability in the event of power failure, ability to reconfigure network parameters by manual switches or software, and the ability to allocate output bandwidth based on priority, such as having a fixed bandwidth available for high-priority inputs and a variable bandwidth availability for low-priority inputs (where the T-1 multiplexer acts like a statistical multiplexer for the low-priority inputs).

As the higher-speed digital circuit market matures there will be more vendors providing more products with more services. Just because a service is available does not mean it has to be used. The only time a newer device should be implemented is when there is a demonstrated business and economic need for the additional service. Another point to consider is that the more you try to put through the same *pipe,* the more you should take into account what would happen if the pipe degrades or breaks, which will affect every single input and output in that pipe.

Finally, some statistical TDMs are called *concentrators* by vendors, but for this text, and in almost all cases, a concentrator is a store-and-forward device that handles entire messages and will be described in more detail in Chapter 12.

## QUESTIONS

1. What is the primary function of a multiplexer?
2. What are the two most commonly used forms of multiplexing? Where are they typically used?
3. Draw a diagram of a multiplexer from the DTEs at one end to a host DTE at the other end.
4. What is the relationship describing the information transmission rate between multiplexers and the capacity from the user to and from the multiplexer for a standard multiplexer? For a typical statistical multiplexer?
5. What is the primary difference between a standard multiplexer and a T-1 multiplexer?

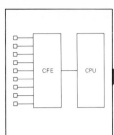

# 12

## Other Network Hardware

## BACKGROUND

In the data communications environment many items of hardware are required for the physical movement of information from one site to another, for the logical processing of the information to get it ready for transmission, and to validate its correct reception at the receive end. Even though this equipment is not identified specifically as performing a communication line function, it is mandatory to complete the process of moving information between two locations.

At the remote sites, there are the various terminal controllers and since this remote environment has historically been considered unique, with only very specific functions to be performed, it is fairly easy for most users to relate to the capabilities provided in that equipment.

At the other end (the central CPU or processing site), the function delineation is not so sharp. Many kinds of equipment were developed as special-purpose devices, while others were designed to handle all the necessary logical functions that are performed at that site. To make matters a little worse, some designers took the special-purpose devices and gave them some, but not all, of the additional attributes of the multipurpose machines. So even though there was at one time a fairly sharp differentiation between the functions of the devices with different names, that is no longer the case.

252

Therefore, for what is described in this chapter we use the names of equipment that are most common, with the classical definition of the functions that used to be performed uniquely by these machines. The reader should be aware, however, that many vendors describe their offerings with names that are not necessarily descriptive of the functions they perform. As such, the user should review the functions that the device performs to see how they meet the user's requirements and not rely on only the name for a description of the functions to be performed. For example, statistical multiplexers, described in Chapter 11, are sometimes called *concentrators* by certain vendors.

## B
# CONCENTRATORS

Chapter 11 described the various types and uses of multiplexers. Standard multiplexers are usually bit- or byte-oriented devices with very limited storage capability (one or two characters at a time), and except for statistical multiplexers, very little logic is involved in the combination of multiple low-speed lines onto individual high-speed lines. If it is desired to perform some kind of processing function on the information, for purposes such as routing, editing, or error detection, the information being transmitted can no longer be handled on an individual character-oriented basis. The information must be handled on a message basis, and even more so in a store-and-forward mode. Store and forward means the reception of a complete message at a particular location, the validation that the transmission was correct, and then the acknowledgment back to the transmitter that the message was received correctly. On an evolutionary increase-in-capability basis, the next level of equipment over and above a multiplexer is called a *concentrator*. The concentrator is basically a store-and-forward device that takes information on a message basis from multiple incoming lines, high speed or low speed, and retransmits those messages to a central site on a *single line* for processing. Retransmission to the central site may occur in either a local or a remote environment (today, most are local) and can occur on more than one line at a time. In effect, the concentrator acts as a master to all the remote site terminal locations and, in turn, acts as a terminal site itself to the central site master. If the central site master is in the same location (local environment), the concentrator may transmit to that central site in either a serial mode over a communications line or in a parallel mode over a local emulation-type interface such as a disk or tape (sometimes described as *channel attached*). It is also possible for the serial path in a local mode to be a direct wire connection at extremely high data rates (megabits per second).

A typical concentrator-type configuration is shown at the bottom of Fig. 12–1. Concentrators are usually implemented to relieve the network-control overhead from the central site hardware. In that regard, the concentrator will poll and call all the remote sites, bring the information in on a message-oriented basis, and in turn pass that information on to the central site as a slave in a master–

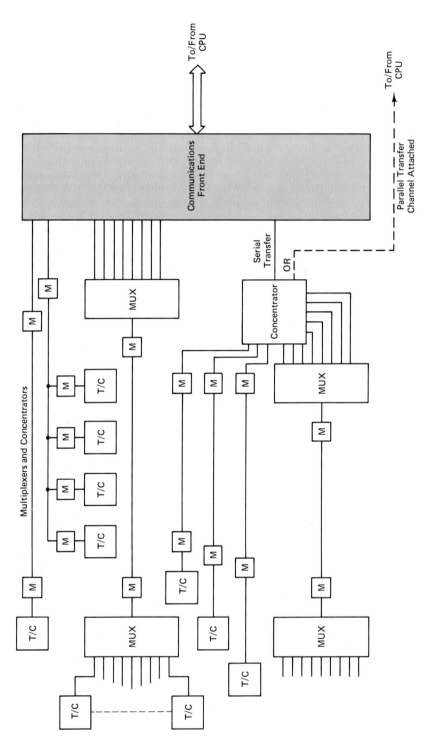

**FIGURE 12–1**
Concentrator/Front-End Configuration

slave relationship at a higher speed. In a local environment, the probability for transmission errors at the high speeds becomes extremely remote. Concentrators can be looked on as message buffering locations, which can also reduce loads on the central site hardware by storing messages on their own peripherals during failure or degraded modes of operation and send the messages on to the central site only when the capability exists to process those messages.

Concentrators can also perform data compression functions, forward error correction, and other network-related functions, which also takes additional overhead off the central site hardware. For the most part, concentrators will not perform any unique routing functions. They take information from a central site and distribute it to remote sites and take the remote site transmissions and transmit them only to the central site. Terminal-to-terminal communications that require routing are performed in either message-switching equipment or front-end processors, which will be described in Sections C and D. Concentrators are considered data processing devices and in most cases today are built around minicomputers.

## C

# MESSAGE SWITCHES

A message switch is a store-and-forward device just like a concentrator except it also performs the full range of routing functions with their inherent software considerations. Message switches were originally developed for the movement of traffic between terminals located in different parts of a network, and they performed no data processing function other than to route information coming in on one line and going out on another. The software required for operation of a store-and-forward message switch was extremely complex, however, in that all the possible combinations and permutations of network problems had to be incorporated to accommodate the many various types of network malfunction. For example, the standard polling and calling arrangement to bring information in from remote terminals and send it back out has several possible abnormal possibilities. The following list includes some of those situations:

1. Terminal down
2. Line down
3. Terminal does not answer
4. Wrong terminal answers
5. Terminal sends garbled information
6. More than one terminal transmits at a time
7. Terminal never stops transmitting

Each case has to be handled completely and correctly so as not to affect any other part of the system. In addition, if a particular line or terminal is down for a period of time, the store-and-forward message switch has to have the buffering and queue management capability to stack the traffic destined for that site and send it out in accordance with a predetermined set of guidelines when the terminal or line becomes operational again. These situations cause a significant amount of overhead software to be incorporated in message switches, because when there are very large queues destined for a particular line or terminal, it is quite possible for a newly received message to be sent out immediately because of some kind of priority situation. A store-and-forward message switch has to have not only a queuing capability, but a priority handling capability by terminal and by line.

In the event there are multiple terminals and multiple priorities, the queue management software has to be able to go in accurately and open up a particular queue, insert a message, and then close the queue again. Problems will obviously arise if the queue chain gets broken for one reason or another (hardware or software). The tail end of the queue will never come out of the system unless there is software available to go in and find the broken queue chains and determine where the messages must be sent. The queue management mending software may have to be done in an off-line mode because of memory or cycle time limitations; but if it is not done, more and more of the peripheral storage will be taken up with what are in reality *headless queues* that can never be sent (also called *broken chains*). Eventually, if they are not removed, the peripheral will be filled with these broken chains, there will be no room for new traffic, and the system will probably come to a halt.

Along with the queue management software that must be incorporated, the proper criteria must be established for transmission of the queues when a period of time passes before the message can be transmitted. This requirement stems from the fact that many messages are time dependent and therefore have no use or applicability if they are not transmitted within a particular time frame. If one looks at an airline system for a moment, it can be seen that a particular flight manifest must be transmitted to the boarding gate prior to the flight departure, because after the flight departure the manifest will have no meaning at the boarding gate. The necessary software must be incorporated to make this timing determination, usually in the header of each message, if a queue management system is to operate correctly in the store-and-forward switching mode.

Many minicomputer networking systems use store-and-forward techniques, but without any of the large peripheral storage devices. In this mode they use some form of core or semiconductor buffering for the individual messages and are therefore subject to degraded or shutdown modes of operation if a particular line is down and a queue builds up for that line that cannot be transmitted. This in turn uses up all the available buffer area, which does not leave enough buffers for other lines and their applicable queues. Devices that operate in this mode are sometimes called *transaction processors*. They have rules governing the handling of such transactions, including their elimination from the system once a certain time frame has passed.

There are two basic differences between a concentrator and a message switch. First, a concentrator passes all its traffic on to a central site, while a message switch takes in all the traffic and routes that traffic either to a central site or to other remote sites. Second, a message switch may or may not be connected to a central site for processing purposes. If it is connected to a central site, that site will have its own unique address and will be treated as a separate line or lines connected to the message switch. A diagram of this configuration is shown in Fig. 12-2.

The *real-time* message switching world has changed significantly in the last few years with more organizations going toward *non-real-time* delivery of messages. The rationale behind this change is the extensive overhead software required to validate message delivery in real time. The software for real-time store-and-forward message transmission involves all of the abnormal and error conditions that must be incorporated, such that when they occur they will not cause the program to hang up or abort (these include line busy, terminal busy, queue for delivery, and no acknowledgment). It is not so much the actual programming that is a problem, but defining all of the possible combinations of those events that demands all of the time, effort, and most importantly, previous expertise. As many of the people who used to be involved in real-time message switching have moved upward in an organization or left, much of the expertise has not been passed on to newer personnel in the field. Therefore real-time message switching is designed from the ground up almost every time it is needed. A small percentage of the actual program coding involves the data movement, while an overwhelming majority of the code involves all of the *what happens if* conditions.

Both vendors and users have tried to get away from this situation for many years and it looks like they may succeed. The obvious answer to eliminating the requirement for real-time delivery of messages is to make them non-real time. Applications are not as time dependent as they used to be, and even if they are, putting the responsibility of delivery on the system has become an inordinate burden. What is the obvious answer? Electronic Mail (EM). EM takes the responsibility for delivery of messages away from the system and gives it to the receiver. In other words, if someone needs to send you a message by a particular time, and they put the message into your electronic mailbox before the appropriate time, you now have the responsibility to get the information on time. All the information that needs to be sent between individuals, typically for administra-

**FIGURE 12-2**
Store-and-Forward Message Switch

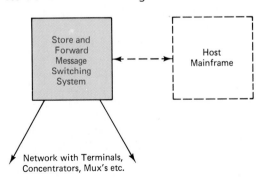

tive purposes, can be put into the system and taken out at the receiver's convenience. There is no longer a requirement to store the information until the terminal is available. It's now up to the recipient, who may be performing other tasks, to look for mail at convenient times. This almost totally eliminates the overhead required in the software for real-time message handling when the message cannot be delivered. Also, the transmitter does not have to wait for an acknowledgment in real time. If an acknowledgment is required, it will come in the form of a message generated and returned by the recipient.

There are still some applications that require real-time delivery of message traffic, but they are primarily in the governmental, military, and emergency services environments. Even airlines, one of the biggest users of message switches in the past, have been moving away from message switching toward multiple copies of a database for use in the local airport environment, with a primary copy for system use if necessary. This way information can be down line loaded as required to a local location and accessed by all personnel there, rather than everyone having to go to the system-wide database, which incurs substantially more network traffic, and, in turn, resources. This is very much dependent on application, because for some databases there can only be one copy. This mode of operation, however, is an excellent alternative for applications that are time sensitive and where decision making must take place at the remote sites in real time.

Overall the use of real-time store-and-forward message switching is definitely on the wane. Even though it may not disappear entirely because certain applications still require it, it will never reach the extensive implementation it once had. For those instances when it is still required, you must go to a vendor who still offers a product that performs the function. Two of the mainframe vendors who still have products that can perform store-and-forward message switching in the large environments are IBM and UNISYS (Univac provides this capability for international airlines). For large or small environments, Tandem can also perform store-and-forward message switching functions.

## D
## COMMUNICATIONS FRONT ENDS

The Communications Front End (CFE) goes by a wide variety of names such as Front End Processors, CPUs for Communications, Transaction Processors, Communication Controllers, Line Controllers, and probably many more. Their primary function, as shown in Fig. 12–3, is to interface the host processor to the network where all of the user devices reside. The CFE provides the DTE interface at the host site and performs all of the polling, calling, error detection, retransmission, and other protocol functions. The reason behind having this device is to remove those functions from the mainframe so that they will not take up so many CPU memory cycles for what is actually a special purpose function.

Since computers work on a byte or word at a time and data transmission

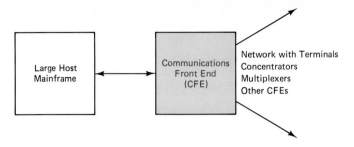

**FIGURE 12-3**
Communications Front End

occurs serially, there must be a serial/parallel and parallel/serial conversion performed at the host site for all communications lines to the remotes. This process used to be performed entirely in the CPU, then by software in the CFE, and now it is performed almost exclusively by chips that perform those specific functions at the DTE interface. For asynchronous interfaces, the device is called a *Universal Asynchronous Receiver Transmitter* (UART). For synchronous interfaces the device is called a *Universal Synchronous/Asynchronous Receiver Transmitter* (USART). The required serial/parallel and parallel/serial conversions are done here, while the actual information flow with error detection, retransmission, and validation is done at a higher level of processing within the protocol. CFEs have many *ports* that are designed to have specific physical interfaces such as RS 232, EIA 530, and V.35. After the physical interface is specified most vendors require a software definition for the protocol that the port must support such as SDLC, Bisync, VT-100, and X.25. A CFE usually does not provide any intelligent processing of the information content other than moving the message to and from the host site and then validating message integrity if defined within the protocol. It does not perform any concentration or switching functions.

Almost every CPU vendor has a device identified as their CFE (or one of the other names) to perform all of the necessary functions to interface with that particular vendor's host processor. This is not done in the PC world because the PC has ports built directly into it (typically RS232), and it still takes the necessary CPU cycles to make the data transmission compatible internally. For example, because of their heavy use in the world today, there are CFEs such as the IBM 3705 (no longer supported by IBM, but many are in use), 3725, 2720, 2725, and new 3745. It is probably only a matter of time before the 3725 is phased out also because it is limited to 400 ports and cannot support some of the new functions to which IBM will be interfacing. The 2725 is a high-volume switch that not only supports RS232, but that will also support Token Ring, X.25, V.35, and T-1. A smaller version, the 2720, only has 64 ports but will support RS232, V.35, and Token Ring. It is the Token Ring support in these devices that make them a very important product for IBM because many of the network capabilities being performed today are in Token Ring networks. By coming through one of these CFEs, any user on a Token Ring can also access a mainframe for support.

A recent change in the CFE environment is the capability to access a host processor from a very high-speed device without going through the CFE itself. This is sometimes called a channel-to-channel device or channel-access device, which at a minimum can handle T–1 transmission rates. An example of this device is the IBM 3737 remote channel-to-channel interface, which can handle interface signals that have 32 wires in parallel (for interface to 370s and others). The output to a T–1 will be serial, and the reason you might want something like this is that at present the typical channel-access interface transfer is 3.4 MBytes/second (27.2 MBPS) while the standard front-end processor slows this rate down to 256 KBPS. By going through a channel-to-channel interface the T–1 rate can be fully supported. In addition, T–3 connections run at a rate of 44.736 MBPS. Interfaces like this are used for high-volume applications where there is a consistent requirement for large volumes of data transmission, such as laser printing or volume file movements.

Finally there are other devices that are sometime confused with a CFE, such as a PBX, Data PBX, and a Matrix switch. These devices perform different functions and are all described in Chapter 14.

Typically you do not have a choice in most environments to select a CFE from a third party, since the host mainframe vendor usually will not support your network unless you use their CFE (IBM is an exception, where third-party CFEs are available), therefore you need to have a good idea of the size of your network and the types of traffic it must support. You can then identify for the vendor what those parameters are so the appropriate CFE can be chosen for your network. At one point IBM's versions had many clones, such as ComTen, Amdahl, Memorex, Codex, and others. Even though many of those devices performed the same functions as the 3705 and 3725 more efficiently, and for less money, their use began to diminish in the mid-1980s because of the data communications environment. IBM would make changes continuously in their existing equipment, but the other vendors might have to reprogram major portions of their CFE to incorporate the same change or upgrade. Users did not like having to incorporate a new software package, or in the worst case get a new CFE, so they tended to remain with IBM, especially when integrated networks started to blossom. You really do not want to be in a position where you cannot incorporate changes and upgrades into your network without major expenditures of time and effort. For that reason more and more networks are incorporating the CFE from the mainframe vendor instead of clones from alternate CFE vendors. Network and diagnostic support are mandatory, and the CFE is a critical device in that process. It must be totally compatible with all the other hardware and software elements, so even though you may not like the idea of being forced to stay with a single vendor you are probably better off doing so. If you would still rather do it on your own, you will need substantial support from knowledgeable people who must remain up to date on all the new features and services that must be incorporated into your network as you upgrade it. This makes you very dependent on your own people, who may not always be there when you need them (a lot of knowledge and history go out the door if one of your key network people leaves). Vendors at least have a much bigger base for support.

# QUESTIONS

1. What is the difference between a concentrator and a statistical multiplexer?
2. What is the primary function that a message switch performs that a concentrator does not?
3. What system is replacing message switches? Why?
4. What is the primary function of a communications front end? By what other names is a CFE known?

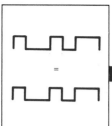

# 13

# Data Transmission Integrity, Forward Error Correction, Compression, Encryption

## BACKGROUND

One of the most significant problems facing the user of data communications today is that much of the information to be transmitted between two points must still go over facilities that were not originally intended to carry digital information. As described in Chapter 10 relative to modems and the techniques for moving information, and as will be seen in Chapter 22 describing the different kinds of problems encountered on a communications line, the least reliable portion of a communications system is the communication line itself. As data transmission rates in the voice-grade environment get higher, the need for more reliable communication capability exists, but in actuality the error rate goes up (not linearly but exponentially). The mechanisms that we use to treat those errors will be discussed in this section.

There are three basic modes of operation for detecting or correcting errors. The first is recognition of an error and flagging the transmission when an error has occurred. This means the receiving unit identifies that an error has been received and provides an output indicating that an error is contained in this particular transmission. This mode of operation is prevalent in process-control types of applications where there are uncontrolled terminals with no memories. With no memory, information cannot be retransmitted, and therefore the best a user can do is to flag the fact that an error has occurred. There are also instances when analog information is digitally coded and digitally transmitted where an error cannot be corrected because the original analog information is no longer available. This situation is typical where voice communications are digitally encoded and transmitted to a different location where the voice is reconstituted.

If there is a particular segment of digitized voice that contains an error, it is not possible to go back and tell the originator to repeat a portion of a word that was being said. If the segment in error is large enough that the human at the receive end cannot understand the word being spoken, then the listener will request the originator to repeat the original statement. The fact that the digital information had an error that could not be corrected in this case is overridden by the fact that the human can request retransmission. In general, however, the mode of only flagging errors is used when the transmitter cannot regenerate the information for retransmission. If a retransmission cannot be made, it may be possible to establish specific operational procedures or software on an application basis to handle the invalid transmission.

The second mode of error handling is when the information has been transmitted from a buffered location and is therefore available for retransmission in the event an error occurs in the initial transmission. When the receiving hardware recognizes an error, it will automatically request the transmitter to retransmit the same information. The message will be retransmitted and verified until the information has been received correctly. The user must be aware, however, that in some cases the error is being generated by the transmitter every single time, so a reasonable limit must be placed on the amount of times a message can be retransmitted before a different course of action must be taken. This may be done in the software of the user's equipment, or it may be done as part of a limit that can be set within the protocol (discussed in Chapter 9). The use of retransmission techniques is the most common alternative for correcting errors in a communication system and is typically called *automatic repeat request* (ARQ). There are many variations to using the ARQ technique in the protocols available today. The key, however, to the identification and retransmission of erroneous information is the error detection method itself. Some of the many methods available to do that will be described in this chapter.

As the last mode of providing data transmission integrity, we have the situation in which we add enough additional information in the original transmission so that when an error is detected at the receive end, the original transmission can be recreated. This is a forward error correcting mode of data transmission and is implemented in various ways. The basic idea is first to detect the error and then to go through some form of mathematical algorithm to recreate the original bit stream. Various methods of doing this will be described in this chapter. To summarize the three methods of error correction:

1. Flag the error at the receive end.
2. Detect and request a retransmission.
3. Forward error correction.

# ECHO CHECKS

One of the earliest modes of automatically detecting and correcting an error was the use of what is called an *echo check*. This particular technique consists of the receiver sending the character received back to the originating terminal. In this manner the originating terminal can determine whether the character it sent was the character that was received by the receiver. Even though two different communications paths must now be accommodated (originator to receiver and receiver back to originator), which will double the probability of an error, the closed-loop mechanism of this technique ensures that the receiver has detected and stored the correct character. The probability of an error going in one direction and being compensated by an error coming back in the other direction is remote and therefore not considered a significant problem.

The growing use of personal computers has created an interesting situation relative to echo checking. Depending on the setting of the various switches on the network components, there can appear to be more than one return of a character in the echoplex mode. This switch setting deals with the HDX/FDX switches on the PCs, local modems, the operating system of the PC host at the receiving end, or the protocol being used when communicating between a PC and a mainframe. The definitions on the use of these switches are *definitely* ambiguous. In general, the HDX and FDX switches should be the same on the terminal as they are on the modem, but this is not necessarily true; so what you may have is the possibility of a single character being generated at a terminal and an echo coming back from the terminal itself, the modem at the terminal end, and the operating system at the host end. One way to get rid of these multiple echoes (multiple displays of the same character on the CRT) is to set the HDX/FDX switches selectively in the other position so as to eliminate the extra echoes. It would appear that only *playing* with the circuit will determine the switch positions that will provide only a single echo; then you must decide where you want the echo from so that you will know how far up into the circuit the echo is coming from. Trial and error seems the only sure way at this time to get a single display on the screen when echo check is being used, but you will have to use some investigative techniques to figure out where it is coming from.

There are significant limitations in using the echo check mode of transmission, because, first, the operator must be on line transmitting a character at a time. With the human being as the slowest user of a system, it means that the available line capacity will be grossly underutilized. The second major limitation is the speed of transfer, which is limited to a character at a time. During the time that one operator is on a multidrop line, no other terminal can be operational on that same line. Therefore, other terminals on the same line will have to wait until that operator is through before they can use the line. In general, this is the reason why on-line terminals requiring echo checks are rarely used in today's multidrop line environment. Buffered terminals are used instead. Echo checking is also called echoplexing and is used extensively in in-house environments where direct connection to the port of a communications processor is possible. Also, it should be recognized that echoplexing terminals could be used in a remote location as long as they connect through a buffered controller at that site, because it would be the buffered controller that communicates over the telephone line, not the terminal directly (the terminal device echoplexes with the cluster controller).

# C
## PARITY CHECKS: VRC, LRC, BCC, CHECKSUM

Even though parity was covered briefly in Chapter 7, it will be repeated here in detail as it is an integral part of the topic of transmission integrity. Of all the possible techniques to determine whether an error has occurred during the transmission of a message, the technique most widely recognized is known as *parity*. Parity consists of the addition of some noninformation-carrying or redundant bits to another specified group of bits so that a particular mathematical calculation can be made at the receive end to determine whether the group of bits including the parity bit or bits are the same. If so, it will indicate that the original information was received correctly.

The first type of parity used was called character parity or VRC (vertical redundancy checking). VRC is used on a character level to determine that the bits of a particular character were received correctly. When information was transmitted one character at a time at relatively low speeds, this was the best and most reliable means of detecting individual character errors. Due to the multibit modulation schemes in use today, the same noise that used to cause an error in a single bit of a character will now cause errors in multiple bits of a character, thereby making this particular scheme not as reliable as it once was because of compensating errors (described later). VRC consists of adding a single bit at the end of a character to create either an *odd* parity or an *even* paraity. Thus if you use ASCII code with 7 bits per character, the parity bit is added to make the total of "1" bits odd if odd parity is used, and if even parity is used the sum of "1" bits is even. Vertical parity probably got its name from the days when characters were punched out on paper tape, because on the paper tape the individual characters are in a vertical position. Parity was not used with Baudot code but was used with most 7-bit codes such as ASCII.

Using VRC in the PC environment is causing some diagnostic problems because some programs describe a *mark* parity, while others allow a *space* parity (1 or 0). To make it even worse, some programs do not even care about parity, so the eighth bit in an ASCII transmission can be either a 1 or a 0. When diagnosing line problems you must know the parity configuration to know if there is a problem with the generation or recognition of parity bits.

Any code can be created so that it has an odd or even parity as long as the hardware at the transmit end is generating the same kind of parity that the hardware at the receive end is looking for.

Before going on to describe the parity mode of operation, you should be aware that the handling of parity errors is different in different programs when there is no retransmission. Sometimes the error is denoted by a special symbol; at other times, if the terminal is capable of doing so, the character received in error will blink. Other programs will substitute a question mark or some other conventional symbol; still others will display a blank so that when the information is read the reader will know that there is an error. Sometimes this blank is not good enough, because the printout may have many other blanks already in it, and an additional blank may not register with the reader as an error. What may be even worse is when information is stored in a memory directly. The error indication will also be stored and, in turn, there will be missing data in the storage medium for eventual use when the original information is no longer available to be retransmitted.

As the speed of data transmission increased in the early 1960s to 2400 BPS and above, the incidence of errors that could not be detected began to increase, because VRC can only detect an odd number of bit errors in a transmission. If 2 bits within a particular character were reversed, the sum of the 1 bits would still be the same, and the parity bit would still be the same, even though the character is now incorrect. With the advent of 2400 BPS transmission and the utilization of multibit modulation schemes of 2 or more bits at a time, the errors that used to cause only single-bit errors were now causing a much higher incidence of compensating multibit errors.

To overcome this limitation an additional level of parity detection was implemented that was called LRC (longitudinal redundancy checking) or BCC (block check character). Using LRC for a specific block or message, an additional 7 bits were added at the end so that an odd or an even parity was created for each longitudinal row of bits. The LRC parity sequence provided for the first bit of each character of the message (looking horizontally) to have a parity bit associated with it, all of the second bits, all of the third bits, and so on, until each row of bits in all characters had a bit at the end, giving either odd or even parity appended to the end of the message. The LRC character itself must contain the same type of parity as is used for individual characters of the block.

By using an LRC, if there were compensating errors in a particular character, the character would check out okay, but the block check character would show errors in the message. This mechanism provided a significant amount of additional capability to detect what would have otherwise been an undetected error in a transmission. As an additional capability with the use of LRC characters, some vendors set up a situation in which all the even characters in a block would have their own block check character, and all the odd numbered characters in a message would have their own block check character. By segregating the odd and even block check characters, the probability of an undetected error was further reduced, because transmission errors usually occur in bursts and if errors were to occur, they would probably be in adjacent characters as opposed to nonadjacent ones. LRC was in use for many years until the more common use of higher-speed communications (4800 BPS and up) required an additional level of parity checking due to the higher probability of compensating errors occurring in contiguous and noncontiguous characters at those speeds.

IBM used a variation of the LRC for their communications with EBCDIC. Because EBCDIC is an 8-bit code, there is no VRC and only an 8-bit parity character at the end, which was called a *block check character* (BCC).

An example of VRC and a combined VRC/LRC are shown in Fig. 13–1.

As shown in the diagram, odd parity was used for the example. For even parity, the state of each of the parity bits is reversed. This applies to both the vertical and longitudinal modes.

An example is also shown of what happens when errors occur in the transmission. For the VRC diagram, a single bit is changed in the first column from a 0 to a 1. When the VRC is calculated at the receive end, the parity comes out to be a 0 instead of the 1 that was transmitted, which indicates that an error has occurred in the transmission. You do not know what the error is, but you do

**FIGURE 13–1**
VRC and LRC Parity

Vertical Redundancy Checking

| Bit Position # | Information Characters #1 | #2 | #3 | #4 | #5 |
|---|---|---|---|---|---|
| 1 | 0 | 1 | 0 | 1 | 1 |
| 2 | 1 | 0 | 0 | 1 | 0 |
| 3 | 0 → 1 | 0 | 1 | 1 | 0 |
| 4 | 0 | 1 → 0 | 1 | 1 | 1 |
| 5 | 0 | 0 → 1 | 0 | 1 | 1 |
| 6 | 0 | 0 | 0 | 1 | 0 |
| 7 | 1 | 1 | 1 | 1 | 1 |
| Parity* | 1 → (0) | 0 → (0) | 0 | 0 | 1 |

*Odd

(For Even Parity Reverse the State of Each Odd Parity Bit)

Longitudinal Redundancy Checking

| Bit Position # | Information Characters #1 | #2 | #3 | #4 | #5 | Block Parity Char. |
|---|---|---|---|---|---|---|
| 1 | 0 | 1 | 0 | 1 | 1 | 0 |
| 2 | 1 | 0 | 0 | 1 | 0 | 1 |
| 3 | 0 | 0 → 1 | 1 | 1 → 0 | 0 | 1 → (1) |
| 4 | 0 | 1 → 0 | 1 | 1 → 0 | 1 | 1 → (1) |
| 5 | 0 | 0 | 0 | 1 | 1 | 1 |
| 6 | 0 | 0 | 0 | 1 | 0 | 0 |
| 7 | 1 | 1 | 1 | 1 | 1 | 0 |
| Parity* | 1 | 0 → (0) | 0 | 0 → (0) | 1 | 1 |

*Odd

know that there is an error in the character. Character 2 on the other hand shows 2 bits being changed, a 1 to a 0 and a 0 to a 1. The parity for the VRC for this particular character is calculated to be a 0, which is the same as the parity bit transmitted. To the hardware this looks as if the character was received correctly, when in reality it is incorrect. The term used to describe the receipt of information that contains an unrecognized error is *undetected error.*

Another compensating error situation is also shown for the LRC, where in character 2 two bits are changed, and in character 4 two bits are changed. In the vertical mode, both characters 2 and 4 indicate no error because the errors compensate for each other; rows 3 and 4 contain compensating errors also. The end result is that there are two characters in error but neither one is found as a character error nor are they found as longitudinal errors. Obviously, a better technique for determining errors in transmission is needed.

As a method of improving the capability to detect errors, a scheme known as CHECKSUM was developed (sometimes called BCC). CHECKSUM adds together the numerical values of all the characters in the block and defines the least significant 16 bits of the total as the CHECKSUM. Because EBCDIC is an 8-bit code, CHECKSUM is the prevalent method for detecting errors with EBCDIC.

## D
## CYCLIC REDUNDANCY CHECK (CRC)

As transmission speeds increased, undetected errors continued to increase, so a new means of reliably detecting errors had to be implemented. Any new techniques had to be based on all of the bits transmitted as part of a message or a block, and not just the individual characters in a character orientation. This was even more critical because many of the newer transmission techniques were not character oriented but bit oriented, synchronous, or both.

Two earlier techniques that were used to check an entire block of bits, *spiral redundancy checking* (SRC) and *interleaving,* were better than VRC and LRC but required more complex mathematics. SRC is the same technique as LRC except that the individual bit positions of the characters are calculated on a diagonal instead of on a straight horizontal. Even if the bits making up the message are not character oriented, they can be set up in sequences of 8, and the spiral checking can take place. At the top of Fig. 13–2 we can see that the bit position 1 of character 1 is combined with bit position 2 of character 2, 3 of 3, and 4 of 4 until we get to the eighth bit of character 8, when we go back to the first bit of character 9 and start the sequence over until we get to the very end. When we get to the very last character in this mode we can add a single SRC character at the end, which provides an odd or an even parity for all the bits contained in the message. If the message is bit oriented and there are not enough bits to fill out the last character, the hardware will "pad out" the last 8-bit sequence so that there is an integral number of 8-bit segments. Due to the fact that only a single character is used as the SRC character, it turns out that mathematically there is

Spiral Redundancy Checking

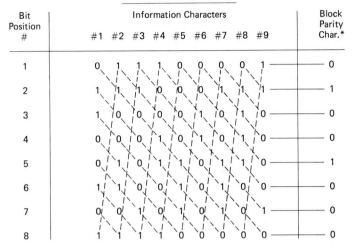

| Bit Position # | Information Characters | | | | | | | | | Block Parity Char.* |
|---|---|---|---|---|---|---|---|---|---|---|
| | #1 | #2 | #3 | #4 | #5 | #6 | #7 | #8 | #9 | |
| 1 | 0 | 1 | 1 | 1 | 0 | 0 | 0 | 0 | 1 | 0 |
| 2 | 1 | 1 | 1 | 0 | 0 | 0 | 1 | 1 | 1 | 1 |
| 3 | 1 | 0 | 0 | 0 | 0 | 1 | 0 | 1 | 0 | 0 |
| 4 | 0 | 0 | 0 | 1 | 0 | 1 | 0 | 1 | 0 | 0 |
| 5 | 0 | 1 | 0 | 1 | 1 | 0 | 1 | 1 | 0 | 1 |
| 6 | 1 | 1 | 0 | 0 | 1 | 0 | 1 | 0 | 0 | 0 |
| 7 | 0 | 0 | 1 | 0 | 1 | 0 | 1 | 0 | 1 | 0 |
| 8 | 1 | 1 | 1 | 1 | 0 | 0 | 0 | 0 | 0 | 0 |

Interleaving

Original Characters

| A 12345678 | B 12345678 | C 12345678 | D 12345678 | E 12345678 | F 12345678 | G 12345678 | H 12345678 |
|---|---|---|---|---|---|---|---|

Interleaved Characters

| ABCDEFGH 11111111 | ABCDEFGH 22222222 | ABCDEFGH 33333333 | ABCDEFGH 44444444 | ABCDEFGH 55555555 | ABCDEFGH 66666666 | ABCDEFGH 77777777 | ABCDEFGH 88888888 |
|---|---|---|---|---|---|---|---|

**FIGURE 13-2**
SRC and Interleaving

very little improvement over a straight LRC detection. The advantage is in the probability of errors occurring in bits that are further removed from each other. Because of the extensive mathematical calculation required and limited improvement, SRC is not used today.

A second method of attempting to detect compensating burst errors is known as *interleaving*. Interleaving is shown at the bottom of Fig. 13-2. There are 8 characters of 8 bits each (ASCII type) where all the 1 bits from each character are put together, all the 2 bits, and all the 3 bits until all 8 bits are put together in an eighth segment to be transmitted. At that point the ninth character starts off as if it were the first character again, and the sequence continues for 9 through 16, then 17 through 24, and so on. If there are not enough characters to complete a full sequence of 8 characters at the end, the additional characters can be padded out by the hardware or a short interleave can be generated. For this configuration an unusual set of error conditions causes compensating errors, and therefore interleaving is better at detecting compensating errors than the straight VRC and LRC characters; but, again, due to the extensive manipulation of information and the fact that interleaving is still not that much better than straight VRC and LRC detection, it also is not used.

The technique used most extensively today for bit-oriented checking of errors on a block or message basis is called *cyclic redundancy checking* (CRC). CRC has been designed to validate transmission of a bit- or character-oriented transmission sequence and is done by the use of a mathematical polynomial that is known to both the sender and the receiver. The specific polynomial interacts through a predetermined mathematical algorithm on the data being transmitted and then on the data being received at the receive end to create a remainder, which is transmitted in addition to the data (the remainder comes from dividing the polynomial into the transmitted bit stream). If the calculated remainders at both the transmit and receive ends are the same, the data are known to have been transmitted correctly.

The two polynomials most widely used for error detection are called CRC-16 and CCITT V.41. They are

CRC-16: $\qquad X^{16} + X^{15} + X^2 + 1$

CCITT V.41: $\qquad X^{16} + X^{12} + X^5 + 1$

Their use is based on a unique property of *prime numbers* (numbers that can only be divided by one or themselves without leaving a remainder). If an integer containing a specific number of digits is divided by a prime number (within certain limits to be described later) then the remainder is unique for all integers with the same number of digits.

For the case of data transmission, a serial bit stream (of a maximum predetermined length) is divided by one of the above described polynomials. The remainder is then appended to the transmission and the same division is performed at the receive end on the entire transmission including the transmitted remainder (the same divisor polynomial must be used as in the transmitter). If there is no remainder after the calculation, then the transmission had no errors. If there is a remainder after the calculation, then one or more of the bits was changed during the transmission, which indicates an error is contained in the received data. At that point in time it is up to the protocol being used to determine what to do next (flag the error, repeat the transmission, or forward error correct).

Since the polynomial divisor has 17 bits, the remainder can have only 16 bits, and the maximum length of message that can be transmitted is related to this remainder length. The limit on the length of the data message is $2^n - 1$, where $n$ is the number of bits in the remainder. If $n$ is 16, then $2^n - 1 = 65,535$, which is the maximum message length (good enough for almost all present applications). If you need longer block lengths for transmission, there are chips available that have 24-bit remainders. A schematic representation of CRC error detection is shown in Fig. 13–3.

To get an idea of the estimated probability of an undetected error occurring, CRC redundancy checking utilizing the 17-bit polynomial has been calculated to allow only 1 bit error for every $10^{14}$ bits transmitted. If transmitting at 9600 bits per second, 24 hours a day, 365 days a year, it would take approximately 330

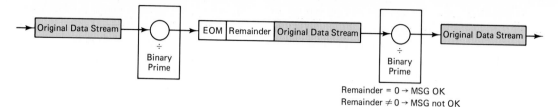

Remainder = 0 → MSG OK
Remainder ≠ 0 → MSG not OK

**FIGURE 13–3**
CRC Error Detection and BCH Forward Error Correction

years for a single bit of undetected error to occur. At a 1 MBPS transmission rate, it would still take over 3 years before a single undetected bit error would occur based on statistical probability. CRC/16 is therefore, by far, the most powerful practical tool today for detecting what would otherwise have been undetectable errors.

CRC is so widely used today that some chip manufacturers have implemented the algorithm in chips that can be purchased and implemented by the user independently of any other technique now being used. Many vendors have even incorporated the CRC method of error detection into their communication protocols, and typical of these are all the new SDLC-type-protocol vendors, as well as DEC with their DDCMP. CRC is even used in some of the error-detection mechanisms that are called either PC or modem protocols, the Microcom Networking Protocol (MNP) and X.PC, which are utilized to check errors on asynchronous links where otherwise there would be no error detection. They are included as part of the modem process and are, for all practical purposes, transparent to the user's equipment. A more detailed description of X.PC and MNP is included in Chapter 9. For any application that requires a high reliance on the integrity of the data, and where the data transmission rates will be 2400 BPS or greater, the CRC method of error detection is by far the best to implement.

# E

## FORWARD ERROR CORRECTION: HAMMING, BCH, CONVOLUTIONAL, BLOCK

So far in this chapter we have been discussing the means of detecting errors in the transmissions. Without some means of correcting the erroneous messages, the detection methods are academic. Since the flagging technique does not correct any errors but only identifies them, we will not consider them further in this chapter. Also, the error detection schemes described in Sections C and D can be implemented within specific protocols to provide appropriate retransmission sequences. The various methods whereby information that has been received in error can be corrected without retransmission will be considered now. In discussing the means of correcting errors in data transmissions, we have to pay careful attention to the mode in which the information is being controlled. This is dealt with extensively in Chapter 8, where the sequence of retransmitting blocks or messages in error is identified.

The relationship between the protocol and the method of error correction is shown in Fig. 13–4. We have first, at the top, a block-by-block transmission and at the bottom, a series of blocks transmitted from one end with acknowledgments coming back at some later time while the transmitter is in the process of sending subsequent blocks. The block-by-block transmission method is really a half-duplex mode of transmission. Each block is sent, but only after the preceding block has been acknowledged as received without error. Block 1 will be followed by ACK 1, block 2 by ACK 2, and so on, until there is a block with an error. The error block will be retransmitted as many times as the protocol allows before some other action must be taken if there is a continuous error in that particular block. In the bottom portion of Fig. 13–4, where we have the continuous mode of transmission that represents a full-duplex protocol, we have a sequence of blocks transmitted with acknowledgments coming back in the opposite direction. When a particular block is received in error, a NAK is transmitted back to the originator, and upon completion of the block in progress, the block that was received in error will be retransmitted.

As can be seen, the line utilization in the block-by-block (HDX) transmission is relatively poor, while the utilization in an FDX sequence is much better. This is not the overriding consideration, however, in that other factors must be considered when deciding on whether to use block-by-block transmission or a continuous mode of transmission.

A primary consideration is the buffer requirements that exist for each of the two cases. In a block-by-block transmission, only one block of information must be stored at a time at either end. Since a particular block must first be received correctly by the other end, there is no need to store a second block until

**FIGURE 13–4**
*HDX/FDX Transmissions*

Block by Block Transmission (HDX)

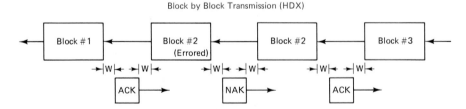

W = Wait Period Due to Propagation and Turnaround

FDX Mode Transmission

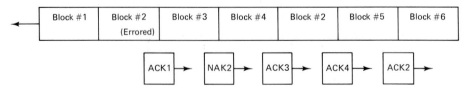

DATA TRANSMISSION INTEGRITY

the first block has been acknowledged. If there are many different locations or many different central sites, the user can come to a predetermined definition of the amount of buffering required to handle this entire system. This is not the case in a continuous mode of transmission where both the remote sites and the central sites must maintain multiple blocks of information, because each block has to be acknowledged in sequence. In all the standard vendor protocols, if one block is not received correctly all the subsequent blocks must be stored until that block is received correctly. If we make the assumption that the same block can be in error more than once, then depending on the transmission rate and the propagation delay (especially considering satellites), many blocks may be stacked up waiting for the arrival of a block that has to be retransmitted. If we consider the case of a 56-KBPS transmission, which is standard in satellites, with block sizes of 500 characters (4000 bits) and a satellite propagation delay of approximately 1 second, we have a situation where a single block in error will require storage of 12 total blocks of information before the error block can be retransmitted. Since it takes another 1-second time frame to acknowledge the error block that was retransmitted, we have a situation where 24 blocks have been stored at both the transmit and the receive end with only one block in error. One can imagine the situation if a protocol allows multiple retransmissions of the same message or if the transmissions take place at higher data rates, such as T–1 (1.544 MBPS) or even T–3 (44.736 MBPS).

Suppose a standard number of three retransmissions is required before a different error sequence must be followed. With one error requiring 24 blocks, two errors would require 36 blocks, and the third error would require a total of 48 blocks of information to be stored at both ends. Multiply that by the total amount of lines and/or terminals available, and it is easy to see how the user, at a central site especially, can run out of buffer space very quickly. This is extremely critical for those systems that have transaction processors utilizing solid-state memory for buffers (no disk or tape peripherals). These machines use a buffer pool arrangement and do not have very many spare buffers to begin with. Therefore, it is quite possible for a single line having multiple errors to use up a majority of the buffer pool available, which in turn will slow down or cut off the entire remainder of the system communicating with that one CPU. Some compensation is available with satellite delay compensation units (SDCU), which are described in Chapter 19.

The preceding methods of retransmission have to do with the recognition of an error and retransmitting the information block that was received in error. There are many instances, especially where long propagation delays are involved (such as satellites), where it may not be feasible to go back to the originator to retransmit information. For these situations, the user has available a capability for adding additional overhead information on top of each message so that if, under specific conditions, an error is recognized, the original bit stream can be recreated without going back to the originator for retransmission. These particular techniques are known as *forward error correcting codes*. Two of the initial methods used were Hamming and BCH (Bose, Chaudhouri, and Hocquengham).

When developed, the Hamming code was used extensively as an error-detecting scheme (and still is) but it is not utilized for forward error correction very much because it can only forward error correct for a single-bit error.

Another method of forward error correction that was being considered was the BCH forward error correcting algorithm, which is based on the same type of Euclidean algorithm as was described for CRC error detection. In the case of the BCH code, the remainder is transmitted along with the data and then used by the receiver to recalculate the original data stream.

The BCH algorithm is performed by calculating the remainder for all combinations of bits of a specific message length to determine which one fits the unique remainder. The problem with this form of message regeneration is that as the message gets longer (each additional bit doubles the time it takes to recalculate the original bit stream), the computer power at the receiving end may not be able to determine the original bit stream for what could be seconds, minutes, hours, days, or even longer. Therefore, even though BCH may have its place for short messages, it is not really practical for longer transmissions.

The two previously described forward error correcting codes, Hamming and BCH, have been around for quite a while. There are many others, estimated to be 50 or more, that are available, some of them utilized in military and deep space transmissions. More recently some of those techniques have been implemented in the communications and data processing environment. As a matter of fact, FEC techniques have been used for years when writing information to mass storage media to provide additional reliability in reading the same information out as was originally written into the storage device.

There are basically two different types of FEC: convolutional and block coding. In convolutional coding, each bit of a user's data stream is compared with one or more of the bits sent immediately before it. The value of each bit may be changed by the FEC algorithm and is therefore directly related to the value of other bits. There are additional redundant bits added for every specified group of bits (to be described later).

In the block method of FEC there are whole blocks of bits that are loaded into a specific sized buffer and then processed by the algorithm as a block. Redundant bits are still added but the process is obviously different from convolutional. This is the methodology that is used primarily on storage media.

In both types of FEC the overhead is fixed for each size block and therefore the total amount of bits per block can always be projected. The overhead can range up to 50 percent of the entire transmission block, where there is a redundant bit added for every user bit. The more redundant bits added, the greater the error correcting capability. The *code rate* is defined as the ratio of user bits/total bits sent. If one overhead bit is sent for every four user bits the code rate is 4/5. The 4/5 code was included in the CCITT V.32 specification for modems operating at 9600 BPS simultaneously in both directions on the same channel. This method is called the Trellis code although it is not really a code but a diagram which may represent any convolutional FEC. Many vendors now use this technique to improve throughput capabilities at modem rates of 9.6 KBPS and higher.

Some of the comparisons between block and convolutional codes are

| TYPE | MAXIMUM DATA RATE | TYPICAL CODE RATES | | TYPICAL THROUGHPUT DELAY | BIT ERROR BURSTS CORRECTED |
|---|---|---|---|---|---|
| Block | Over 100 MBPS | 7/8 | 15/16 | 2000 + bit times | up to 100 |
| Convolutional | Generally less than 50 MBPS | 1/2 4/5 | 3/4 7/8 | <1000 bit times | usually < 20 |

In general the convolutional code is used when error bursts of 5 to 6 bits long are expected, which is typical of what occurs in data transmissions. It should also be recognized that with the very short time delay involved, even with 2000 bit times delay, FEC of digitized voice transmissions can be realized with relatively little effect.

Although there may be other FEC codes that are developed in the future, their use in data communications will not grow very fast until the economics improve. Instead of being in the $1000 to $1500 range, if the cost gets down below $500 per end, it will be much more feasible to incorporate. However, it would appear that for the majority of existing applications, retransmission of errored blocks is still the way to go. The practical use of FEC is limited today to transmissions where the information is not stored at the transmit end, such as process control and deep space probes. For the commercial world it would appear that practical use involves those transmissions where there are high transmission speeds (T–1 or greater) in conjunction with long propagation delays, such as satellite hops. Most end users today are utilizing terrestrial links for high-speed communications over fiber-optic facilities rather than having to make allowances for the delay inherent in satellite transmissions. Until there is a stronger requirement for FEC, it will be limited to special purpose applications.

# F
# DATA COMPRESSION TECHNIQUES

As data transmission rates and the distances over which they must be transmitted increase, the time frame for correcting these errors requires extensive buffering at the transmit and receive end of the communications path. This delay is significant on those links where satellite transmissions and multiple satellite links in a single path are involved.

With the use of forward error-correcting codes, we have a mechanism whereby requirements for retransmissions are substantially reduced. However, another technique called *data compression* can also be used to further improve the probability of a successful transmission when long block lengths are involved. Data compression means the elimination of specific bits of information without changing the total information content. The various techniques for implementing data compression will be described in this section.

One of the simplest modes of compression applies to the technique using punched cards (believe it or not, still being used today in many systems). If only 60 columns in an 80-column punched card have information, then only 60 characters' worth of information should be transmitted. This also applies to output devices, such as a typical computer printer where there are 132 columns. If only 75 valid characters are to be printed, only those characters should be transmitted. These techniques do not require any particular kind of coding technique other than to identify that the end of a particular line or block has been transmitted via control characters.

Another relatively simple form of data compression is to delete fixed information from a form, that is, to identify a format at both the receive and transmit end and then transmit only the variable information along with a definition of the format that was used. The receiver can then apply the information it detects to the appropriate fields of the previously identified form.

Redundant characters can be coded so that after identifying the coding technique a long alpha sequence can be compressed with an alphanumeric transmission. For example, if there are five of the same ASCII characters to be sent, then the transmission would be changed to have a control character specifying that a compressed stream is coming, then a numeric ASCII 5 (since there are 8 bits in this character, up to 255 identical consecutive characters can be specified) and then the character itself transmitted. Three characters (control, quantity, alpha) will represent the original five characters. This method only has very specific applications such as suppressing *nulls* and therefore is used only in a limited number of cases.

One of the most often used methods of data compression is the binary representation of ASCII numeric characters. If there are transmissions that involve many numbers of large orders of magnitude, it is much more efficient to transmit them in binary form. Since each ASCII character is represented by 8 bits, up to a numeric 256 can be described within that 8-bit sequence. For a 16-bit sequence, a numeric value up to 65,535 is represented; so instead of sending 8 bits for each numeric character (40 bits total—5 × 8), there can be a significant reduction in the total amount of bits being transmitted if the numbers up to 65,535 are coded in binary (16 bits versus 40 bits). This technique is especially applicable where there are many numerics to be sent, although, depending on the application, alpha characters can also be included as long as the overhead of going back and forth between the alpha representation and the binary representation does not exceed the quantity of data compression realized by implementing the binary.

For those applications where program development is being undertaken and many computer dumps must be transmitted over a communication line for debug purposes, hexadecimal code can be used, where 4 bits will represent all the numerics to be transmitted as well as the alpha characters A through F. This of course is a very specific application, although in a distributed-type system where development is going on at different locations it can be a highly effective means of allowing multiple users to interact and debug the same problem at different locations.

The preceding techniques are known as *brute-force* types of data compression. There is another area of data compression techniques based on mathematical algorithms, which are designed to work on the probability of specific sequences occurring and coding those specific sequences with a shorter sequence of bits. In other words, those sequences of fixed length that are used most often would be represented by a sequence of bits that is much shorter. The less often a particular sequence occurs, the more bits it may take to define that particular sequence, but overall the quantity of bits being transmitted is significantly reduced.

One technique that assigns shorter bit sequences to frequently occurring symbols and longer bit sequences to less common symbols is called *Huffman coding*. The technique is very much like the one that Samuel Morse used for Morse code; that is, the most often used characters in the English language were represented by the least amount of dots and dashes. The probability distribution of the source information must be known in the Huffman code, and from this a code sequence can be defined using a method known as the *tree method*. An example of the tree method is shown in Fig. 13–5. For a given set of symbols (8),

**FIGURE 13–5**
Huffman Code Compression

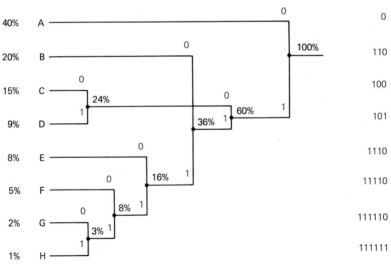

| | 20-Character Bit Stream | | |
|---|---|---|---|
| A → 8 TIMES | 8 | 24 | |
| B → 4 TIMES | 12 | 12 | |
| C → 3 TIMES | 9 | 9 | |
| D → 2 TIMES | 6 | 6 | |
| E → 2 TIMES | 8 | 6 | 12 Bits Reduced = 20% |
| F → 1 TIME | 5 | 3 | |
| G → 0 | 0 | 0 | |
| H → 0 | 0 | 0 | |
| | 48 Bits Sent | 60 Bits Required | |

a probability factor is worked out based on some quantity of actual data being sent. A tree is then developed that will give a unique set of variable length codes that are inversely proportional to the specific probability of the characters being transmitted.

Figure 13–5 provides a brief description of how the technique works. The first column shows the predetermined utilization of the character (these quantities were defined arbitrarily for this simplistic diagram to show the capability of the Huffman tree). The second column shows the particular symbol that is being represented (characters A through H for this example). Then we have the tree itself.

The idea is to keep combining the two lowest probabilities of occurrence in the tree, and when that is done, to assign a 0 and a 1 bit to the two legs of the branches being tied together. For example, G and H being tied together as the two lowest probabilities gives the G leg a 0 and the H leg a 1 for a combined total of 3 percent utilization. Combining the 3 percent with the 5 percent for F, we give the F branch a 0, and the combined GH branch a 1. This continues, combining only the two lowest probabilities at each junction until we end up with 100 percent utilization in the upper-right corner.

The right column then shows the specific character representation. This was obtained by starting at the 100 percent junction and tracing back the branches of the tree until the symbol was reached. For example, to get the character A, all you pass through is a single 0 bit, so A is represented by a single 0 bit. This means that all other symbols must start with a 1 bit and be unique in their representation such that there is no ambiguity as to what character is being represented. To show what character F is we start at the 100 percent and go down through a 1 bit, then another 1 bit, then a third 1 bit, then a fourth 1 bit, and then a 0 bit, at which time we arrive at the symbol F. Notice that none of the previous characters have been defined by the sequence of bits until we arrive at F (none of them begin with four 1 bits and none of them are defined by any of the bits that make up the F character). This applies for all characters A through H.

To show the amount of reduction that can be accomplished utilizing the probabilities of occurrence shown in column 1, a sequence of characters and their quantities of times in the character stream are shown at the bottom of Fig. 13–5. If A occurs eight times, B occurs four times, C occurs three times, and so on, the corresponding amount of bits transmitted appear in the second column under the 20-character bit stream heading. Since there are 8 symbols to be transmitted, 8 symbols can normally be represented by a total of 3 bits each, and this is shown in the required bit stream column. By comparing the two we see that only 48 bits would have to be sent using the compressed sequences to represent what 60 bits would represent if 3 bits per character were actually sent. This occurs even though characters E, F, G, and H require more than 3 bits for their representation. Because they occur so rarely (in this instance G and H do not occur at all), the end result is a significant reduction in actual bits to be sent. For the simplistic example here, there was a 20-percent reduction.

The Huffman tree method can be used for any code set, with the ultimate result being somewhere between a 30- and 50-percent reduction in actual bits required. The reason for the significant reduction is that many of the control characters are sent either once per message or not at all, while some of the typographical characters may never be sent because they are not used. In addition, if you look at the EBCDIC code set definition given in Chapter 7 you will see many blanks for configurations that are not defined. These never have to be sent and therefore do not even have to be defined. If they were defined, it would make no difference if they contained 20 or 30 bits each because they would never be used.

Because of the noncharacter orientation of Huffman code compression, the transmission must always be synchronous, which means that the header of the message must identify the fact that compressed bits follow. This in turn will tell the DTE to go through the appropriate expansion module to give you back your original character orientation. A block diagram of how Huffman coding ties into the other capabilities is provided later in Fig. 13–7.

Huffman character compression is already being used in some modems and multiplexers to reduce the amount of bits sent on line. A 9600-BPS transmission capability can actually provide 19.2-KBPS transmission throughput utilizing 50-percent compression. In addition, mathematical techniques have been proposed for further compressing the Huffman code by compressing the Huffman sequences, such that an additional 2-to-1 reduction ratio can be realized (giving a total 4-to-1 compression). With other compression algorithms there have been mathematical predictions of up to 76 KBPS on a dial circuit and 100 KBPS on a dedicated line using existing analog transmission facilities, but these are not commercially available yet. If at some time in the future they do become practical, it would cause a serious reevaluation of the requirement to go to higher-speed transmission equipment and lines, because with existing modem equipment you may be able to get enough bit throughput on a line to accommodate your growing requirements (digital facsimile is an excellent example).

Costs for these units are running $2000 each, but with the growth of the market combined with mass production the price should come down significantly, because it is estimated that the chips themselves will cost a hundred dollars or less shortly. Some of the newer units even advertise that they can dynamically respond to transmission characteristics. If you are running in a heavily alpha-oriented mode, the compression table will be established based on that mode. If you then go into a heavily numeric-oriented mode, it will be sensed by the compression units, and after a period of time a new table will be created and loaded at each end of the line so that the new numeric information can be transmitted more efficiently. With elimination of the start bit, stop bit, and the parity bit in ASCII transmissions, the end result of alpha-numeric compression utilizing Huffman codes can be up to 80 percent. For all practical purposes, however, you can be fairly sure of obtaining at least a 50-percent reduction in bits to be transmitted whether you use asynchronous or synchronous transmissions. The location in the transmission sequence will be shown later in Fig. 13–7.

In addition to character compression, with a hybrid form of compression that involves *string coding* (which is the technique for combining multiple identical characters) and Huffman-type coding together it is possible to get other types of bit streams reduced substantially. For example, a method is under development to reduce video transmission (normally requiring 3.6 MBPS) down to the range of 56 KBPS. The methodology used is to first utilize only 20 of the 30 frames that are transmitted in a normal TV transmission every second. Next the pixel value is established for each picture element (color dot) on the screen. Each of the pixel values is stored in memory, and if the changes occurring on a frame-to-frame basis do not exceed a certain minimum defined value, no additional information is required to be transmitted. A further description will be provided in Chapter 19. A Huffman technique is used on the pixel value differences so that the amount of bits required for the differences is reduced. The end result is a very good full-color, full-motion video *when there is relatively little movement*. More than 20-percent movement could cause *blurring,* but this methodology would be very good for teleconferencing; and since the bandwidth is so narrow, existing facilities can be used to transmit this video. Many other compression applications like these can be used for reducing the bandwidth requirements for moving a user's data. The trade-off will always be cost versus capability; but when you consider that the cost of network facilities is going up at a very fast rate, and that the cost for data compression will be coming down, it would appear that the market for compression capability will grow exponentially.

Currently the dial-up modem vendors are simultaneously incorporating new techniques for error correction and compression into their devices. Some of the most common of these are the Microcom Networking Protocol devices that started off with error-correction capability (utilizing the MNP protocol with CRC in each modem at both ends of the circuit). The first four classes of MNP are in the *public domain* and incorporate error-correction capabilities only. Classes 5 through 7 incorporate data compression along with error correction. As of the early part of 1988, Class 5 MNP was being licensed to other vendors; Class 6 is a half-duplex protocol; and Class 7 was not yet being licensed. The Class 4 MNP seems to be a de facto standard for asynchronous dial-up error correction.

The MNP Class 5 is the most common compression algorithm used in modems, although there are others by different vendors. In potential competition with MNP Class 5 is the method developed by Adaptive Computer Technologies (ACT) which is claimed to be as good as MNP 7 and is endorsed by many modem vendors, such as Racal/Vadic, Concord, and Universal Data Systems. The ACT algorithm was designed for use with dial-up modems such as V.22bis to obtain a throughput of up to 7200 BPS. Of course the modem at each end of the line must be the same.

One very important feature for modems using both error correction and data compression is that in the future, if they contain different levels of error correction and/or data compression, they must go through a *negotiation* for a common base. MNP and ACT can do that, so both modems will end up operating at the capability of the device with the highest level of compatibility. If a modem has a particular level of capability but no *negotiating* software, then it can only be used with another modem that has exactly the same capability. For public-oriented networks, this can be a serious drawback for the vendor and must be taken into account by users who will be calling many different locations.

To help overcome some of this incompatibility, the CCITT is working on a negotiating method between the Link Access Protocol M (LAPM) and MNP 4. LAPM is a hybrid of LAPB and LAPD, which are defined and utilized in other networks such as Packet Networks and ISDN. No doubt there will be other techniques developed to provide interoperability in the future, but in the meantime it is the user's responsibility to ensure that different levels of compatibility can be accommodated in any given environment.

Finally, there is a form of compression that is used extensively in the digitization of voice. Instead of 64 KBPS, which is the standard PCM form of conversion, there are techniques that will reduce the required bits to be transmitted down to 32 KBPS, 16 KBPS, and even 2400 BPS. These techniques are described in more detail in Chapter 14.

# G

## ENCRYPTION

With more and more data being sent over facilities like satellites from which anybody with an antenna can pick up the transmission, the requirement for *masking* information is increasing. Data dealing with personnel, banks, marketing information, accounting information, proprietary information, and the like must be kept from unauthorized listeners such as competitors. In the government and military environment the classification of information has existed for many years, and special equipment is used to modify the information such that an unauthorized listener will not be able to tell what the transmission represents. This technique is called *encryption*. It involves the substitution or transposition, or both, of the bits that represent a known data transmission sequence. The method of performing the modification is sometimes called *ciphering*. The cipher can be in any level of complexity and is usually judged by a *work factor,* with the higher work factor being a cipher that is harder to break.

Early ciphers included direct substitution codes, as well as mechanical devices that were used by the Greeks over 2000 years ago. Sparta developed a mechanism whereby a long, thin sheet of paper could be wrapped around a cylinder with a unique shape such that the characters were written across all the tape segments. Unless you had a cylinder of the same size and shape to wrap the paper the same amount of times, you could not read the message. The tape was worn as a belt by the messenger, and because there were different shapes of cylinders (direct cylinder sizes or cones of varying angles), it was not very easy to decode the messages even if the messenger was captured.

Electromechanical devices were developed during early World War II based on specific characteristics. If you had the same type of device as the enemy, you could decode what the *enemy* was transmitting. Obviously, this was not adequate enough, so with the development of the computer came the mathematical capability to modify bits so that they appear to be random but in reality represent the original data stream in a specific predetermined but modified order.

Devices that utilize this technique are called *cryptos.* The typical operation of a crypto is represented in Fig. 13–6. The known data stream, called *cleartext,* enters the crypto device serially. An encryption algorithm performs the mathematical modification of the data stream so that an encrypted data stream called *ciphertext* is then transmitted on the carrier circuit. At the receive end the same algorithm is removed from the encrypted data stream, giving you the original data stream (cleartext) back out. Two things must be known. The first is the algorithm, and the second is where the sequence of known data starts. To provide a substantial amount of flexibility, a *key,* which may be changed, can be applied to the encryption algorithm. Thus even if two locations had the same encryption algorithm, unless they had the same key they would not be able to communicate with each other.

Keys come in various levels of capability. Because of its extensive use in the industry today, the Data Encryption Standard (DES) will be described here. It has been endorsed by the National Bureau of Standards (NBS). The DES was originally developed by IBM but is manufactured and used by a wide variety of vendors today. Because the key can be changed as often as you desire, whatever process it takes to break your code will have to be performed over and over again each time you use a different key. Although there are some detractors who feel that the DES may be relatively easy to *break* because of what is known as mathematical *trapdoor techniques,* it will still keep unauthorized listeners off your system today.

The DES involves modifying specific blocks of bits by the algorithm. There is a 64-bit data segment (cleartext) that involves 56 data bits of the user and 8 additional bits for parity, which are not used by the encryption algorithm. These are mixed with a 64-bit key of which only 56 bits are active. The result is 64 bits of *ciphertext,* which is then transmitted on the carrier circuit. When fed back into the same DES chip with the same key, out will come cleartext again. When establishing the circuit, however, the cryptos must be synchronized, and this may take 1 to 2 seconds which must be added to the synchronization sequence for the modems at the higher data rates. If used in a dial-up environment, the continual *turning around* of the line will cause a very slow overall transmission unless full-duplex modems are used.

**FIGURE 13–6**
Encryption Process

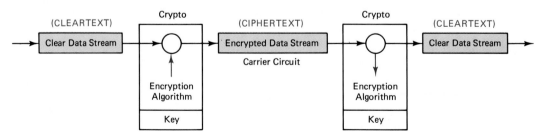

The way a user implements a crypto system is to obtain as many of the DES chips as needed, set the keys physically into the chips, and then install them in the appropriate devices at the transmit and receive end (a block diagram for the location of the installation is shown in Fig. 13-7). By using all the devices described in this chapter you will have information going from a DTE through a data compression chip, to a forward error-correction chip, to an encryption chip, to a DCE, then out through the carrier environment, and back through the reverse process at the remote site.

No one knows how strong a cipher really is. Theoretically a cipher is unbreakable if the key is randomly selected, the key is as long as the plain text, and it is used only once. Obviously this cannot be done in the end-user environment, and therefore some methodology is needed to control the utilization of the keys. One of the most significant problems in the utilization of cryptos is the handling and control of what the keys are, where they are located, where they are used, and when they are used. There has to be a substantial amount of human control over the establishment and delivery of keys.

The establishment and control of procedures necessary to implement cryptos at multiple sites is called *crypto key management.* There are various ways to accomplish this in the commercial environment (government and military security environments are handled differently due to special requirements and will therefore not be discussed here). General requirements for handling crypto key management are described in Federal Standard (Fed Std) 1027-Telecommunications: General Security Requirements for Equipments Using DES and ANSI X9.17—Financial Institution Key Management. If manual key management is to be used, there must be dual locks on the container holding the keys with two

**FIGURE 13-7**
Transmission Manipulation Sequence

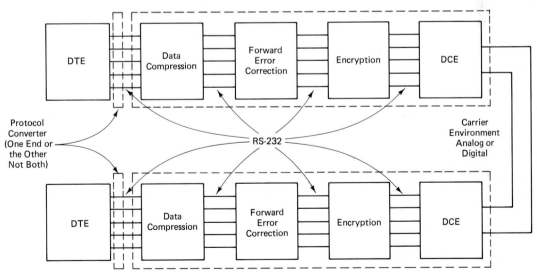

separate individuals holding separate keys. Another document applicable to this environment is the Federal Information Processing Standard (FIPS) #46, which defines the DES.

There are three levels of automated crypto key management to be considered, as follows.

*Single Key.* Keys are manually loaded into individual cryptos at each end of the circuit.

*Double Key.* The encrypting key is loaded into the transmit end manually, and then a new key is downline loaded to the receiving device at the remote location when required. This method provides for reduced access to manually loaded keys in environments where the physical security may not be as strong.

*Triple Key.* This method utilizes a public key to distribute the initial key encrypting key electronically. The public key, also called a master key, is utilized to send encrypting keys to a remote location. The keys are different, but mathematically related. There is one key for encryption and another key for decryption. The user preloads a large number of keys in the remote device and provides an index to access each one. To use a particular key the index of that key is sent to the remote device. The appropriate key will then be used for decrypting data following the index. You can have a different key for every single transmission by utilizing a different index each time. The process by which this takes place is known as *authentication* and is described as follows.

Host site dials remote location. (Process can be initiated from remote to host also.)

Remote location acknowledges.

Remote location sends a known block of data that is to be encrypted.

Host site encrypts the received block of data and transmits it back to the remote.

Remote validates the encrypted transmission using the appropriate indexed key.

If the validation is acceptable, then the communication is allowed to proceed with index changing for each transmission.

There is one encryption algorithm for transmission in one direction and one or more encryption algorithms for the return retransmission. Knowing the encryption key for one direction is not enough to determine the two-way information content. Even if one of the return keys is broken at some point in time, it is much harder for a potential intruder to obtain both transmissions because the return transmission will utilize a different key each time. The same scheme can also be used for downline loading of additional keys when required.

For many years, until the end of 1984, there was another code that was also known as a public encryption code. Also called the *Knapsack* code, it involved the establishment of a key that contained 100 numbers, each 60 digits long. Added all together, they would yield a specific 62-digit sum. To break the algorithm, each one of the individual numbers had to be known as well as the specific sum. The knapsack code was considered fairly secure to use in the public domain until a mathematician utilizing one of the *trapdoor* techniques figured out a relatively simple way to break it. Because it was done on a PC in real time, for all practical purposes the knapsack algorithm was no longer usable. Here the basic algorithm was broken, not just the key. It must be recognized that if you break a transmission utilizing a particular key you will be able to determine all transmissions utilizing that key, but you cannot decipher any transmissions using another key. If, however, you break the algorithm itself, any key utilized in the transmission can be broken.

Some terminology regarding encryption operations and functions are

*Eavesdrop.* To monitor what is being transmitted.

*Spoof.* The process whereby a remote device is simulated with a device that is inserted in the line to emulate the valid remote. Spoofers are counteracted by encryption keys sent along with a verification code to be returned by the remote (there can be multiple verification codes) so the Spoofer cannot break into the circuit in real time. Unless the particular keys are known to the Spoofer, the classified remote locations cannot be emulated.

*Hacker.* An idiomatic expression describing an individual who attempts to access protected locations by a variety of means. Most hackers can be negated by a system of callback procedures in which the device at the called location allows an initial log on with a verification sequence, then terminates the circuit. The callback device then calls the originator at a prestored number. If the original calling device does not answer the call, or answers the call with a different validation procedure, then the connection is terminated. This process is good for internal systems where everyone is at a fixed location, but not for those systems with access from hundreds or thousands of locations in real time. This is especially applicable to communications through the packet network.

The subject of crypto use and management always leads to the discussion of network security in general. Network security is a subject that requires a separate text for adequate coverage, but there are a couple of items that you should be aware of. The best way to protect a system is to take whatever steps are necessary at the very beginning to prevent unauthorized access. Security is typically considered to be good enough if it costs the intruder more than the potential gain from the information that would be obtained. Of course you should not pay too much for security to protect information that may not be of great value. This is a very subjective evaluation and the cause of much controversy not only between organizations but within organizations.

Some simple steps that can be taken to protect a system when there is dial access are

*Unauthorized Entry Tries.* If there is more than a predetermined number of entry tries on a particular line utilizing the same invalid access code, or if there are some user determined minimum number of other invalid access tries within a predetermined amount of time, they must be flagged. At that time either automated or manual action should be initiated to try to track down the unauthorized intruder.

*Training.* Personnel should be trained in the operation and use of all access processes and equipment. Actual cases have shown that the majority of unauthorized accesses come from authorized users who are accessing parts of the system that they were not authorized to get to. Procedures must be established to identify and track those unauthorized accesses, which can be done by logging all accesses and checking who is doing the access either constantly or at unannounced, random intervals.

*Billing.* Even when there are authorized accesses to the system, if use is a chargeable process review should be made of changes in volumes of activity.

*Who Uses the System and When.* Check access to the system by authorized users to see if there are changes in patterns. Statistics can be used to determine typical access times and access lengths. If there are variations in these statistics, it would be a good idea to find out why those changes are occurring.

*Automated Verifier.* This method allows the called location to establish a user code that is scrambled and retransmitted back to the caller, where it must be decoded and returned correctly to determine if the caller is authorized to access the system.

*Encoded Cards.* These are actually electronic keys that must be inserted into the hardware to provide access to the alternative site. This process requires additional hardware at the remote end and may not be economically desirable.

Many of the preceding items can be incorporated into a system that includes extensive *audit trails* that can collect the necessary information needed to determine who is accessing the system. But remember, audit trails do no good unless you actually look at them to try to determine what is happening.

Other procedures that may be used for guarding against intrusion have been used for many years without encryption or special planning. Some of these are the sequential numbering of messages both in and out to determine if there are breaks in the sequence; utilizing passwords for both hardware and the human user, and then comparing the two to make sure that the combination is an allowable one; and automatic logoff in the case where a terminal is inactive for a period of time. Automatic logoff is an excellent way to keep unauthorized users off the system when a terminal has been logged on, validated, and authenticated, then left unattended or not turned off. Of course, there is always physical security, where authorized terminals are kept under human or automated surveillance to make sure that only authorized users are allowed to use those terminals.

All of the preceding processes involve the use of a system by humans. There are other security considerations dealing with just the hardware. All electronic devices that generate characters, such as keyboards, radiate different forms of signals, including possible electrostatic, electromagnetic, and/or acoustic radiations. If an unauthorized intruder can pick up those emanations, it is possible to determine what information is being transmitted by picking up the signals before they ever get put on the transmission link. For almost any practical commercial application this is not a serious consideration, but in military and government environments it may be extremely critical. Protection against this type of unauthorized access is covered under what the Department of Defense calls *TEMPEST* testing. TEMPEST stands for *Transient Electromagnetic Pulse Emanations STandard*. TEMPEST specifications and use are classified for most devices, but if you are in a commercial environment where heavy security is needed, there are unclassified processes that can be used to protect your equipment from those radiations.

Another item of interest regarding cryptos is that they can operate either asynchronously or synchronously, depending on need. They can also operate in either a dial-up mode or a leased-line mode. When used in the dial-up mode, a full-duplex modem must be used to eliminate the modem turnaround time and resynchronization of the cryptos each time the transmission changes direction. Some of the companies that make the crypto chips are Motorola, Fairchild, Western Digital, American Microdevices, and AT&T Technologies. In this fast growing market, by 1988 more than 80,000 of the DES chips alone were being made annually.

Recently a long sought after methodology was developed to provide encryption in packet networks. It is an *end-to-end* process (rather than link-to-link) in which a message can be encrypted at the transmit end to look like binary stream data. The block is then packetized, with each packet getting the overhead information of addressing in the clear. The packets are transmitted through the network and the encrypted block is reassembled at the final packet node, from which it is sent to the final destination as an ecrypted block of bits. The end-user receiving location then decrypts the transmission. This process may take place in any direction and between any two points set up to accommodate the process.

Extensive work is still going on in the mathematical world on how either to break the existing codes or develop better methods for encryption. Until a better method comes out, however, the public key methodology can be used when there are multiple users in the same network who do not want to have the other users access their data (obviously, the trade-offs of security versus cost versus control versus operational considerations, etc., must be considered).

For an in-house environment where you are in control of both ends of the link, including the keys, the public key system is probably not necessary. However, if you have dial connections an intruder may be able to access your system, and if they also have access to a valid key, you do not know that an unauthorized user is on your system.

As a final note to encryption, it is the author's feeling that as the time and expense of breaking keys get to be too much for the individual intruder or organization, the intruder will try to get the information from an individual in your organization: in simple words, to buy, steal, or coerce the information. Since many people have a *price* (if the offer has not been made yet, how do you know you would not accept it?) it may be just a question of whether the intruder organization feels the information is worth that price.

## H
## INTEGRATION OF FUNCTIONS

By referring back to Fig. 13–7 you will see the functional representation of how the various bit manipulation processes are tied together. The network product manufacturers will probably develop these capabilities, not the CPU or terminal vendors. For one thing, the interface will be standardized around RS232 so that any pair of chips at either end can just *plug in* to the appropriate location to provide that function. Some vendors already provide data compression within their DCEs, while others are offering encryption either as part of the DCE or as a separate device. It is only a matter of time before forward error correction is also incorporated. In all likelihood the DCE will have either card slots available for plugging in the particular function as an option, or cards already installed in the DCE with chip sockets mounted on them such that you can mount the chips into those sockets when you want to activate that function.

Ultimately there will probably be a microprocessor built solely to perform one or more of these capabilities, which will then be a strappable option provided by the DCE vendor. Cost will obviously be a significant factor, but as the functions are combined and mass producing of the products evolves, the total cost for these functions will come down significantly.

Finally, it makes no difference whether the carrier environment is analog or digital because all the functions taking place for bit manipulation are on the digital side of the DCE. Therefore, whether the DCE is a modem for transmission in the analog environment or a DSU for transmission in the digital environment, the manipulation is transparent to the network.

## QUESTIONS

1. What are the three primary processes for handling errors on a communication line?
2. Describe the process of parity checking. What is the limitation in the use of parity?
3. How does CRC error detection work?
4. What is the concept of Huffman-type data compression? Develop a code tree with 16 symbols.

5. Describe the crypto process. What does the key do?
6. Describe the sequence of implementation for protocol conversion, data compression, forward error correction, and encryption. Why must the sequence always be in a specific order?
7. What situation would require a protocol converter at *both* ends of a circuit?

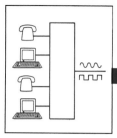

# 14

# Voice and Data Switching

Since divestiture in 1984, the world of the telephone switch has undergone a major revolution. Because the original tenets of the divestiture process dictated that local telephone companies could not provide *enhanced* services, Centrex type services (a switchboard in the telephone company environment) could not be enhanced. This meant that one of the primary services provided by the local telephone companies for end users, a switchboard capability, could no longer be improved upon. The private switch, called a *Private Branch Exchange* (PBX), then grew at an enormous rate. This was a major blow to the local telephone companies, who stood to lose a substantial part of their revenue base, and they continued to petition for relief. Eventually, in 1986, that relief was given in the form of the capability to provide enhanced features on Centrex systems.

What had been a booming PBX market then became flat, and the Centrex world took off again. After a relatively short two-year period, Centrex seems to be coming back as a major player in the telephone switching arena. This chapter will deal with the various types of voice and data switches that are coming together in today's world.

# TERMINOLOGY

Before getting into more detailed descriptions of the functions and operations of switching equipment, certain definitions must be made so that all the pieces can be kept in perspective. Although there is general agreement on many of these terms, there are also quite a few variations. For this text, the following definitions will be used:

*PBX (Private Branch Exchange).* A PBX is a manual device in which an operator must plug patch cords into specific jacks on a switchboard to establish physical connections.

*PABX (Private Automatic Branch Exchange).* In the PABX the jacks and patch cords are replaced with stepper switches and crossbars.

*EPABX (Electronic Private Automatic Branch Exchange).* In the EPABX the mechanical switching matrices are replaced with electronic switching matrices. These devices may use either analog or digital switching techniques. This device is sometimes called a *solid-state* PBX.

*CBX (Computerized Branch Exchange).* The term *computerized* refers to the use of a microprocessor to control the operation of the switch. The term was first applied to the ROLM PBX in 1975 but has come to relate to most digital switchboards available today. Many people utilize the terms PBX and CBX interchangeably today.

*Digitized.* *Digitized* refers to the conversion of an analog signal to a digital signal. The digital signal in this case is not binary bits but a variable height digital pulse, which will be described in Section D of this chapter.

*Digital Switching.* Digital switching refers to the switching matrix being used as digital (either variable height pulses or binary bits). Again, this was first provided by ROLM in 1975 with the announcement of their original CBX. It describes devices that utilize microprocessors for switching purposes.

*TDM (Time Division Multiplexing).* TDM, described in Chapter 11, is applicable to a PBX because all current PBXs convert the analog voice signal to a digital signal of variable height pulses, known as pulse amplitude modulation, then convert the digital signal to binary bits (pulse code modulation). The PBXs then switch the binary bits through a TDM mechanism. Prior to connecting to the analog network the signals are converted back to analog form. This entire process will be described later in this chapter.

*Blocking.* *Blocking* refers directly to the fact that there are many more in-house connections to the PBX than there are circuits *within* the PBX to connect them. Thus all internal users cannot be active at the same time. The reason to use this mode of operation is primarily cost because not all the lines are normally required to be busy at the same time. This is particularly true in voice communications where blocking statistics normally involve less than 200 connections for every 1000 lines connected to the PBX. Data connections, however, are usually active for a much longer period of time. Therefore one of the big pitches used by some of the PBX vendors is the nonblocking internal capability—where everyone can have access to the PBX when they want it. Many people don't recognize, however, that nonblocking only means they will get a *dial tone* when they pick up the receiver. It does not mean that they will be capable of communicating with anyone *outside* of their own switch. They will definitely be able to communicate with another line connected to their PBX internally, but if there are connections required to other PBXs or connections to outside telephones, they may still be blocked because those lines (called *trunk lines*) may be in use. A totally nonblocking switch would have as many outgoing lines as there are internal connections, and that is simply not economically feasible.

***Tip and Ring.*** *Tip and ring* are terms used to describe the twisted pair wires that connect a voice instrument or a modem to the Class 5 telephone-company serving office. They make up the two-wire pair for the *local loop*. The names describe the physical parts of the plug that the telephone operator used to use. Depending on which type of (digital) switch you have in your Class 5 telephone office, the polarity of tip and ring connections may or may not be important (it is important for analog switches).

***Ringer.*** *Ringer* describes the circuit that provides the necessary signaling for ringing a telephone. The circuit itself is always between the tip and ring pair when the phone is *on hook* (hung up). It is a *high impedance* circuit that never interferes with conversation or data transmission, which takes place in an *off-hook* condition on a low-impedance circuit (described shortly). Ring voltages are normally in the range of 50 to 90 V and are in the range of 20 to 30 Hz.

***Off Hook.*** *Off hook* is used by the telephone company to describe the situation that exists when a telephone handset is off its cradle. When the handset is lifted a contact is made that provides a path between the tip and ring wires looping the circuit back to the telco Class 5 office (hence the name *local loop*). For those who are interested in the technical description, the connection is *low impedance*. This type of connection is called a *loop start* because the battery in the telephone office causes a current to flow through the loop (through the tip and ring pair). The current is detected by the central office switch, which gives you a *dial tone*. There are, however, other methods of connection to get a dial tone. One is known as *ground start,* in which the off-hook switch provides a connection between the tip lead and a separate electrical ground, typically used in older pay-telephone circuits.

***Dial Tone.*** *Dial tone* describes the condition of the circuit when a device known as a *line finder* in the Class 5 telephone office recognizes that you would like to establish a connection (by going off hook). Appropriate switch contacts are established to allow you to set up a circuit through the switch to *trunk lines,* which are connections to other switches. In a rotary-dial environment, an *interrupter* switch will open and close at a predetermined rate—up to ten times for each number—so that the switch can detect the specific number you are dialing. In tone dialing, the tones are detected by the line termination equipment of the Class 5 office on the local loop for establishment of the circuit.

*Touch-Tone*℠ (a registered trademark of AT&T). *DTMF (Dual Tone Multifrequency)* is a method of generating tones in which one tone is generated for the row that the digit is in, while the second tone is generated to indicate the column. There are four rows and three columns on the keypad of the telephone handset, and the combination of the two tones establishes the specific digit being depressed. If only one of the tones is generated, the switch will not react.

*Trunk.* *Trunk* describes the connection between telephone office switches at all different levels and typically does not have meaning in the end-user environment. The PBX manufacturers, however, also use the term *trunk,* but in their case trunk means the connection between a PBX and a Class 5 office (really the local loop for the local telephone company). Even though it may sound a little confusing, it is reasonable to make this definition in the PBX world because as far as the PBX is concerned, the connections to the instruments are its own local loops, while the connections to the telephone office are its trunks. If the PBX is considered an *on-premises customer switch* (which it is), then its definition of trunk makes sense. Still, the term should be utilized in the correct context when relating to other individuals.

The various types of switching equipment will now be described.

## B
## KEY SYSTEMS

When telephones came into general use many years ago, the connections were typically made to and from the telephone offices with no in-house distribution of connections. When it became necessary to provide internal distribution, operator-controlled switchboards provided physical connections to circuits in house so that an individual could communicate through the switchboard into the public telephone world. Obviously, a human operator was necessary to perform this function.

One of the first systems designed to provide a form of automated or multiple connections was called a *Key System,* which AT&T dubbed the 1A in the 1930s. The 1A key system contained the mechanical connections that were used to close an electrical circuit to the local telephone central office.

The 1A key system was used until the 1950s, when the 1A1 key system was produced, and, shortly thereafter, the 1A2, where for the first time there were modular, standardized components for connection to the telephone lines. The 1A2 was a common electromechanical system consisting of two basic components. First was the Key Service Unit (KSU), the equipment cabinet that contained all the necessary switching capabilities to provide the desired connections. The second component was the Key Telephone Unit (KTU), which held the circuit cards used to access the individual station lines, the central office trunks, intercom connections, and any other special features.

Also provided was a power supply to provide local power to the equipment and station equipment, which consisted of 6- and 10-button telephones. These systems could support from 2 to 40 stations and up to 15 trunks to the telephone company central office. At least 25 pairs of wires were needed to run to each telephone set, which meant that connections were both bulky and expensive to install and rewire.

Today's electronic key systems still have KSU and KTU terminology and form, but a microprocessor is used for all the controls. The microprocessor is provided with the necessary software to incorporate all of the features that were previously available in the 1A2 key system. Typically, an electronic key system today runs between 4 to 70 stations with up to 30 trunks to the telephone office. Two- or four-pair wiring goes to each telephone handset. Each handset used with a key system must be specially adapted for that key system and therefore will be more expensive than the *plain vanilla* telephone that used to be provided by the telephone company. A handset for one of these key systems may be in the $150–400 range instead of the $50–80 range for the older handsets.

Key systems have their primary application in smaller businesses that utilize up to the 30-trunk capacity. Some have operator-attended stations to intercept all incoming calls and distribute them, while others allow direct incoming calls that can be answered by any one of the handsets. Typically, when an organization outgrows the particular key system they are in (original maximum amount of lines, trunks, or both), they must get a whole new system: either another key system or a PBX.

Still within the classification of a key system there is a series of devices known as *hybrids*. A hybrid is similar to a PBX internally in that it may have some blocking and looks like a PBX to the outside world. Other PBX features included in a hybrid are the methodology of handling calls, system management capability, and various system features. Some of these features include conferencing, paging, music on hold, and push button signaling.

There are also *softkey* controls in a hybrid that provide programmable-type access to specific features like call forwarding, call waiting, call back, speed dialing, speakerphones, and even communication ports. Hybrids may also provide automated route selection, Station Message Detail Recording (SMDR), and Direct Inward Dialing (DID). Hybrids are still classified as a key system because they are designed primarily for internal communications, not external communications. The capacity range for a hybrid goes up to approximately 130 stations and approximately 40 trunk lines.

Although the pricing structures obviously change with features, capabilities, lines, and other factors, a plain key system will cost approximately twice as much as a 1A2, while a hybrid will cost three to three-and-a-half times as much as 1A2 and a PBX will cost at least four times as much as a 1A2.

Some of the terms used in this section need to be defined:

*Call Forwarding.* When a particular number is dialed, it rings at a different location specified by the intended receiver.

*Call Waiting.* Call waiting is an indication to talking parties on a line that another call is coming in. It can be a *clicking* sound or a *tone*. Only the party being called can temporarily put the existing conversation on hold and communicate with the new caller. If there are two calls ongoing (one party on hold), a third caller will get a busy signal.

*Camp On.* If the line is busy a new incoming call will be held until the call in progress is terminated. If the waiting caller is still on the line, the called extension will be rung immediately. If the waiting caller is not on the line, the waiting caller extension will be rung first, and when picked up, the receiving station will be rung.

*Pick Up.* After a predetermined amount of rings the call is routed to another extension or back to a central operator for messages.

*Auto Call Back.* If the line is busy or no one answers the call is reinitiated at predetermined intervals. In the public telephone environment, there are regulations regarding the amount of times a device is allowed to recall the original number to prevent overloading of telephone networks. A human must come back on the line to reinitiate a call once the prescribed amount of automated calls have been made (15 was the maximum in 1987).

*Rotary.* This term designates a mechanism whereby a caller dialing a single number is connected to any one of a series of lines starting at the top end of the rotary. As lines are busy the call will be routed to the next available line in the rotary. Typical use for this kind of operation is in a reservation-type system.

*Direct Inward Dialing (DID).* DID is used to describe a process by which an outside caller has to dial only seven specific digits to ring directly at an internal extension, thus going directly through the PBX without operator assistance to reach a single, specific station. It is relatively complex for PBX vendors to handle because of the way signals are generated at the telephone company office. With DID the PBX cannot determine when the connection has been completed or when the call has been terminated at the far end. The signals that indicate these functions are all contained within the local carrier's Class 5 telephone office equipment and are not available to the PBX. The only signal the PBX actually sees from the central office is the incoming ringing signal. For this reason, DID is normally provided by Centrex (to be described later) equipment and not in the PBX. Some PBX manufacturers, however, have recently indicated that they can handle DID. If DID is an important feature then consider it as part of the vendor's capability when evaluating equipment (remember, this means no operator to screen incoming calls).

*Restrictors.* Restrictors are calling or switch-access restrictions based on predetermined authority levels.

*Speed Dialing.* By depressing a combination of two, three, or four digits the user can automatically dial frequently called seven- or ten-digit numbers, thereby reducing the time required for human dialing.

*Least Cost Routing.* Least cost routing is usually provided in a PBX. The PBX determines the route that will cost the least amount of money, such as the use first of dedicated lines, then foreign exchange lines, tie lines, WATs lines, third-party carriers, and, ultimately, direct dial. Access to these types of connections may also be subject to limitations by level of authorized user.

*Station Message Detail Recording (SMDR).* SMDR includes all of the administrative information regarding the use of the system. It typically includes information such as who made a call, the call destination, time of day, length of call, route and type of service, and cost (this requires continual updating of tariff tables, which contain the cost information based on service vendor and route).

Not only are many other features available, but new ones are being offered all the time. Always evaluate what is available versus what is needed for internal utilization before deciding on a particular system.

## C
## PBX EQUIPMENT GENERATIONS

Before describing the mechanics of PBX operation and their alternatives, it would be useful to categorize the capabilities of the different equipment that has evolved since the mid-1970s. Although many vendors have their own designations for levels of equipment generation, there are really just four generations of PBX that can be described generically.

**FIRST GENERATION** First-generation PBXs were PBXs that were in service prior to 1975. They are voice-only in that they can handle only analog signals (modem signals, being analog, can be moved through these devices because they appear to be the same as voice signals). Typically, the first generation PBXs were electromechanical and used analog circuit switching. All of these devices (unless specially designed) were *blocking* due to cost.

**SECOND GENERATION** Second-generation PBXs were the devices developed between 1975 and 1980 primarily by ROLM and Northern Telecom. Voice signals were digitized and transferred through the switch (the signal was still not binary bits because it was a pulse amplitude modulated digital signal). These switches were typically voice only but could be modified to carry data. Second-generation switches were under the control of a computer for implementing their switching functions and required separate voice and data ports. They were relatively slow for data switching and were also *blocking* due to cost. Typical second-generation devices were the ROLM CBX and the AT&T Dimension PBX System.

**THIRD GENERATION**  PBXs developed starting in 1980 were third-generation devices. They are characterized by the use of a *CODEC* (coder/decoder), which converts analog signals to a series of binary bits. The technique used is known as Pulse Code Modulation (PCM), which differs from the second generation in that the switching is done utilizing binary bits, while in the second generation a varying height digital signal (PAM) was used. The third-generation switches operate like standard time division multiplexors where each of the incoming lines is assigned a particular *slot* in the internal bit stream. These switches can be either blocking or nonblocking depending on the configuration. Third-generation switches are the most common in use today because of their flexibility and capability for providing almost all of a user's needs for voice and data switching (to be described later).

**FOURTH GENERATION**  The fourth-generation PBXs were developed around 1984. The primary difference from previous generations was that they combined all of the voice and data switching capabilities into a LAN method of distribution. The capabilities of these devices were extensive and included additional features such as electronic mail, voice mail, and voice messaging, but their cost has proven to be much too high for general use. With typical costs for fourth-generation PBXs in the range of up to $2000 per line, compared to third-generation PBXs' $800 to $1200 per line, the market for fourth-generation PBXs was very small. By 1987 one of the two companies making a fourth-generation switch had already gone out of business and the second one was going through major reorganization. The fourth-generation PBX illustrates a case of the available technology going beyond the ability of the end user to afford those capabilities and has already faded from the scene. It is therefore anticipated that third-generation PBXs will continue to flourish along with the use of Centrex capability.

## D
## ANALOG TO DIGITAL CONVERSION (CODECS)

Since this text will deal primarily with the current third-generation PBXs, a description of the methodology for converting voice to binary bits is in order. The device that performs this function is called a *CODEC,* which stands for coder/ decoder. The coder converts the analog signal into binary bits, while the decoder converts the binary bits back to analog signals. The reason behind the popularity of these devices is that it is much easier now to operate and maintain a digital switch with the advent of VLSI and ULSI chip technology. With digital transmission technology itself over 25 years old, it is well seasoned, reliable, and commonly available.

The whole process started in 1962 when AT&T decided to eventually convert their entire network to digital operation. They needed a method for converting analog voice signals to binary form. The methodology used is shown in Fig. 14–1. Start off at the top with an analog signal depicted by a *sine* wave, which is *sampled* 8000 times per second with a pulse carrier, shown below the sine wave. To get a good representation of the analog signal when binary signals are reconverted back to that form, sampling must be performed at a minimum of twice the highest frequency being sampled. Since the highest frequency sampled is approximately 3300 Hz, double that would be 6600 samples per second, the theoretical minimum amount of sample times. Since theoretical limits cannot be achieved, AT&T arbitrarily selected 8000 times per second as the sampling rate that would give *toll quality* voice at the receive end.

There are three ways to convert the analog signal to a pulse-oriented signal. The first one is by utilizing *Pulse Amplitude Modulation* (PAM), which gives a variable height digital representation of the analog signal. The second form is called *Pulse Duration Modulation* (PDM) where the digital sampling pulses have a wider width as the analog signal has more amplitude and a narrower width as the analog signal has a smaller amplitude. The third form of conversion is *Pulse Position Modulation* (PPM), which gives more sample pulses when the analog signal is higher and fewer pulses when the signal is lower.

After all of the factors necessary to provide reliable and accurate conversion processes were taken into consideration, Pulse Amplitude Modulation was selected as the only method for converting an analog signal to pulse form. The PAM signal alone is used in second-generation PBXs. Because of the extensive amount of circuitry involved in processing PAM signals, and even though it was more expensive, it was ultimately decided to convert each PAM signal into binary bits (called PCM). The number selected, again to give toll quality representation at the receive end, was 8 bits per sample. The method selected for converting the PAM signal to binary bits, known as $\mu$-LAW North American Standard, was incorporated into the DS-1 signaling algorithm which is now used in all T-1 environments (see Chapter 16).

The first bit determines whether the signal is above or below *zero*. Bits 2, 3, and 4 provide eight levels of approximation for the height of the signal. These eight major bands give a gross approximation of where the analog signal is. When the signal comes out between levels, the lower level is the one that is used. Bits 5 through 8 then give 16 levels of precision within each of the previous eight gross levels of definition. By utilizing this mechanism an extremely accurate approximation of the exact signal height at the time of the sample can be determined. Eight thousand samples each second are converted to binary bits, which are then utilized for switching and even transmission if digital transmission is used.

At the receive end, the binary bit stream is assembled such that each of the eight-bit segments identifying the particular height of pulse is identified. The pulses are reconstructed back into their original heights, and then a circuit called an *integrater* is used to *smooth* the transition between levels of adjacent pulses.

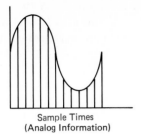

Sample Times
(Analog Information)

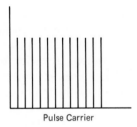

Pulse Carrier

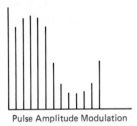

Pulse Amplitude Modulation

Pulse Duration Modulation

Pulse Position Modulation

**FIGURE 14-1**
*Pulse Modulation Techniques*

Since this smoothing does not provide an exact duplicate of the original signal there is some distortion. If the human ear is not sensitive to that distortion, so that no audible difference can be determined, then the regenerated sound is considered to be *toll quality.*

The minimum transmission speed for this mode of operation, called pulse code modulation, is 64 KBPS. It is the standard for voice conversions today. There are many other forms of converting analog signals to binary form, with many different characteristics that may not provide the same level of received signal quality. Because many of these methods are being utilized today in different areas of the network and in PBXs, they will be described here. It should be kept in mind that even though the standard of toll quality is used by AT&T as a subjective reference for determining the quality of a voice signal that has been digitized and then converted back to voice, there are many applications in the end-user world where that level of quality is not required. A variety of techniques that convert voice to binary bits utilize substantially fewer bits and therefore take up less line capacity. Current descriptions of most of the major techniques are listed here.

*PCM (Pulse Code Modulation).* As described, PCM is the worldwide standard of 8000 samples per second with 8 bits per sample. This form of pulse modulation provides high quality voice. Modem signals that are converted utilizing this technique are recreated in a form with such a minimal level of degradation that it appears to the receiving modem that no conversion has taken place. There is also a standard 16-bit sample for analog-to-digital conversion that is used by professional audio recording equipment and for compact discs. With 16 bits there are 65535 possible signal amplitudes (instead of only 255 with 8 bits).

*ADPCM (Adaptive Differential [Delta] Pulse Code Modulation).* ADPCM is another standard used extensively throughout the world. It provides for a 32-KBPS analog-to-digital conversion. ADPCM predicts the shape of voice signals by transmitting the difference between the measured amplitude of the actual pulse and the expected amplitude of the next pulse. It is very good for voice and gives toll quality capability, but if a modem transmission is converted using ADPCM the highest data rate that can be transmitted reliably is 4800 BPS. The difference in data rate capability is accounted for by transmitting only 4 bits of information rather than 8 for each sample. The current version of ADPCM that is acceptable in the carrier world is the 1984 CCITT standard G.721.

*APC (Adaptive Predictive Coding).* APC is the Bell Labs approach to compressing analog signals to 32 KBPS or less. It predicts more factors than plain ADPCM with respect to the next sample. The three submethods of APC that have unique properties are

APC/AB—with adaptive bit allocation

APC/HQ—with hybrid quantization

APC/MLQ—with maximum likelihood of quantization

These three have special uses that are not necessarily applicable to this text, but you may run into them if you get involved with compression techniques. Companies doing work with APC say that the technique can provide toll quality at 16 KBPS, regular quality at 9600 BPS, and comprehensible voice quality at 2400 BPS. Until the techniques can be accepted and mass produced, many of them will continue to be used only in laboratories or very special application environments.

***VQL (Variable Quantum Level Coding).*** VQL is like PCM, except that the absolute amplitude of the pulse is recoded into a relative value. VQL is very sensitive to telephone-company switching processes but is excellent for data. It cannot be used for compression below 32 KBPS.

***LPC (Linear Predictive Coding).*** LPC provides voice compression down to 300 BPS, but is typically used in the 2400 to 9600 BPS range. It is very complicated, involving the establishment of a model of the voice tract. LPC is used primarily to look for intelligible sound, not necessarily recognizable voice. This technique has been used in *vocoding,* which is the oldest of the conversion techniques, originally developed in 1928. It is not good for data.

***DM (Delta Modulation).*** DM is a technique in which the difference between two consecutive samples is transmitted. The typical rate is 32 KBPS with 32,000 samples per second. If a new level is higher than the previous level, a binary 1 is transmitted. If the new level is less than the previous level, a binary 0 is transmitted.

***CVSDM (Continuously Variable Slope Delta Modulation).*** CVSDM monitors the status of the difference between individual samples and changes the step size as the difference changes. It provides for voice transmission at 16000 BPS.

***SBC (Sub-Band Coding).*** With SBC voice is split into two or more frequency bands and each one is treated separately. SBC is usually utilized with another technique such as ADPCM or APC.

***ACET (Adaptive Sub-Band Excited Transform).*** ACET is a GTE-developed technology, for which they have applied for a patent. ACET is designed to provide toll quality voice at 16 KBPS and to handle data reliably at 9600 BPS. It is a hybrid of sub-band coding and transform coding, which breaks the signal into blocks and encodes the factors that describe the amplitude of the signal. ACET can accept either an analog signal or a PCM at 64 KBPS. The methodology involves sending only the actual voice energy in each *sub-band* of a 22.5 millisecond segment or window. Only information, not the entire spectrum of sound, is sent by this mechanism. The amount of bits in each sub-band varies; only the amount of bits necessary to describe the information is allowed to be sent. The result is the removal of redundant or unneeded information from a digitized transmission.

***RELP (Residual Excited Linear Prediction).*** RELP transmits information similarly to ADPCM but in a much more complex form. It is better than ADPCM for voice, but data at or above 9600 BPS cannot be transmitted.

***TDHS (Time Domain Harmonic Scaling).*** TDHS edits human voice patterns and deletes repetitive signals in the *harmonics.* It can be used directly (with transform coding) or with APC. With the TDHS form of compression it is possible to get data up to 9600 BPS; however, the method is very complex and may not be economically feasible.

***DSI (Digital Speech Interpolation).*** DSI is a very different technique from all the others. It recognizes the periods of silence on digital circuits and does not transmit any bits during those times. DSI is the successor to TASI (Time Assigned Speech Interpolation), which is used for analog circuits. Although DSI may save some time and line capacity for transmission of digitized speech, it is totally unacceptable for data transmission where there is continuous information being transmitted. DSI may be used in the future as a technique for combining voice transmissions with data during the silent periods, but that requires a form of multiplexing that is only under development today.

Although it may seem like overkill to go into the details of the preceding mechanisms for compressing voice, any mechanism that can reduce the total amount of bits to be transmitted in a network is a potentially usable technique for adding capacity to the network. With voice still a large percentage of network utilization, any mechanism that can enlarge the capacity to handle voice must be considered. You should know the differences between the techniques, if and when a vendor tries to sell you one of them.

## E

## PBX

Because of the preponderance of third-generation-type PBXs and the fact that they will be around for a long time, all descriptions of PBXs in this section will be relative to the third-generation, or digital, PBX. Typical examples are the ROLM CBX II (being replaced by IBM 9751 which has the same conceptual operation but a different sampling rate), AT&T System 75 and 85, and Northern Telecom's Meridian.

There are four basic components of a PBX, as shown in Fig. 14–2. First, the necessary system controls, contained in memory, describe which devices are to do what, when, and how. This information is table-oriented and therefore capable of being modified by the user. Part of the system control includes the management reporting and facility selection, such as automatic least-cost routing. Any reconfigurations become part of the system control.

The second basic component is the actual switching matrix. Three forms have been used. Originally there were the *space division* matrices that provided physical circuit connections like the older electromechanical switches. They are not used anymore. The *frequency division* matrix involved setting up a communication path with certain electrical frequencies for extensions performing the call-

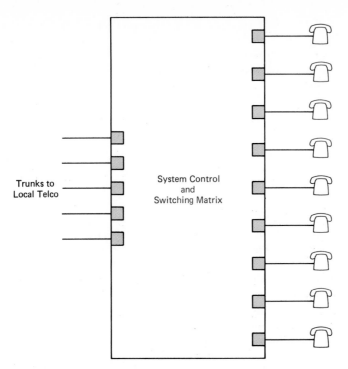

**FIGURE 14-2**
Basic Structure of PBX

ing function and others for those being called. This is not used anymore either. Finally, the *time division* switch provides every individual line with a dedicated *time slot* for the bits (data or digitized voice) being transmitted to or from that particular device. As was described previously for blocking, there are just so many slots available within the PBX, and only if a slot is available will a user be able to transmit and receive from another in-house extension.

The system control and matrix is contained in the center of the diagram in Fig. 14-2. The connections that go to the in-house users, the third major component, are on the right side; they are circuits terminated by telephones, terminals, or combined voice and data devices. All of those devices must be compatible with the particular switch being used. There is also a possibility of having an attendant console that can function as an operator intercept station for incoming calls if desired. Each in-house line needs a separate *line card* for termination in the switch, and if there is a separate terminal and voice device on a single line, each of them must have a separate line card.

Finally, on the left side of Fig. 14-2 is the trunk interface to the local telephone company central office. The trunks are connections that normally make up the local loops, but they may also be connections to other PBXs. In any event, when internal users want to communicate to a location outside the local environment they must utilize one of the trunk lines. Even though the switch may be described as nonblocking, if there are not enough trunk lines you may not be able to communicate to those other locations. This is a very common misconception about the use of PBXs and should always be kept in mind when a vendor tells you how good a nonblocking PBX is. To reiterate, nonblocking means only that you will get a dial tone and you can communicate with anyone else internally, but you may not be able to communicate outside your site because of a lack of trunk lines.

Typically, each line into a third-generation PBX is terminated by a codec to convert any of the analog signals into binary bits. The codec is the little box drawn at the connection of each line into the PBX. All the internal switching is done in binary bit form and then, when communication must go back out of the switch, the signal goes through another codec to give you back your analog signal. It should be noted, especially on the trunk side, that many of the newer PBXs have a digital interface that can communicate at a T-1 rate. If that kind of interface is available, then a codec is not necessary, but another device to put the signals into a T-1 framing format is required (a channel bank, described in Chapter 16).

Very simply described, outgoing calls can be made by dialing from a handset (it must be compatible with the PBX in use), the routing will be performed within the switching matrix, and a logical connection will be provided to either another in-house line or one of the trunk lines going to the local telco. Providing a connection was the original reason for having a PBX, but in today's world the PBX is also being presented as a device for providing data switching.

There are two primary methods for providing data switching with a PBX as the switching device. The first is *Data Over Voice* (DOV). DOV is shown in the top portion of Fig. 14-3. With DOV a terminal is connected through a device called an RF modem, where RF stands for radio frequency. These modems actually have a carrier frequency somewhere in the range of 40–50 KHz. When utilizing a modem with this carrier frequency the person talking on the phone cannot hear the signal because it is out of the human hearing range and at the same time the voice codec in the PBX will not be sensitive to those signals and will not transmit them on the voice line.

At the PBX end of the circuit another RF modem will interpret the information and put it into a separate data line card, which provides a separate path in the PBX for independent routing. The added modem allows you to utilize your in-house telephone wiring for both voice and data purposes—a big selling point for this kind of PBX. There is added expense for the RF modems, but they are not very costly these days and do create an economical way to provide both voice and data transmission on existing in-house wiring. The jack that is used to connect the RF modem into the telephone line is a standard RJ11C. This DOV mechanism is also usable in Centrex environments where the switching matrix is in the telephone company office (to be described in the Centrex section later).

The second mechanism for transmitting voice and data simultaneously on in-house wiring is called *integrated voice and data*. The devices that are used to connect telephones and terminals into the house wiring are known as *Integrated Voice Data Terminals* (IVDTs), depicted in the bottom part of Fig. 14-3. The IVDT box provides a multiplexing capability, so that after the voice is digitized

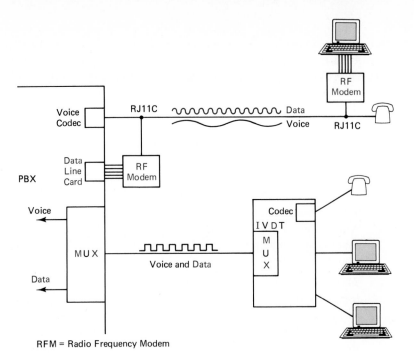

**FIGURE 14-3**
Voice and Data PBX

it can be multiplexed with one or more data streams into the PBX, where a demultiplexer takes out all of the individual data streams and provides a separate switching path for each of them. The limitation here is the distance over which the transmission can be recognized. A typical distance versus speed trade-off for the ROLM CBX 2 (a widely used device) is 4500 feet with 24-gauge wire and the data stream at 256 KBPS, consisting of 96 KBPS voice in each direction and 64 KBPS for data. As the CBX 2 is replaced by the IBM 9751, the digitized voice will be generated at 64 KBPS, which is then compatible with all other third-generation equipment. The AT&T System 75 and 85 provide voice at up to 12,000 feet on 24-gauge wire and up to 5000 feet with 24-gauge wire for voice and data combined at 136 KBPS full duplex (64 KBPS for data in each direction and 8 KBPS for control signaling). The Northern Telecom SL1 provides the capability for transmitting 4000 feet on 24-gauge wire with 64 KBPS full duplex and signaling at 8 KBPS on a separate wire pair.

What you need to be aware of, which is one of the points made by the LAN vendors, is that you never really know where your telephone wiring goes. If it is in the walls and ceiling and runs near other wires that can cause external interference, you can have very high error rates. Fluorescent lights, motors, and other extraneous signals can cause errors in any data transmission, and even though they may have some effect (like static) on voice that may be tolerable, they cannot be tolerated for data.

Going into further detail on specific PBX features and options other than those described in the section on key systems would not be appropriate in this text because of the continuous change and addition of new parameters, but there is one more area that you must pay special attention to, and that is the availability of management software.

The five areas that must be considered for PBX management software are

*System Parameters.* System parameters make up the system profile, which is an inventory of equipment and the location of that equipment. The information is utilized to create an on-line directory so that you know where all of your devices are and what their capabilities are, feature by feature.

*Work Order Generator.* The work order generator is a current listing of what changes are on order, in process, and completed. It is a method of making sure that you are always up to date with all of the changes that you may have in process.

*Financial Management.* Financial management software develops the necessary financial information on the fixed and variable assets of your system. Fixed components are the stations, inside plant facilities, and switches. The variable assets are the message units and toll charges. Service and maintenance charges should also be included here. Part of overall financial management, and mandatory to all systems, is the *Station Message Detail Recording* (SMDR), which tells you about the operational costs of your system (also included in the variable assets).

*Rate Comparison.* Rate comparison is a mechanism for incorporating the rates for the various vendors you use in your network utilizing tables that are updated on a continuous basis so that, if available, your PBX can select least cost routing alternatives. As new and updated information goes in, you will also be able to evaluate new rates and services.

*File Conversion.* File conversion can be used when your management software is not contained directly in the PBX. The information from all the different devices you use must be converted into a standardized format. To give you an idea of the sizing involved, an external device to handle up to 5000 lines would be equivalent to an IBM PC/AT with 512 kilobytes of RAM and a 4-megabyte hard disk. Smaller systems will obviously require a smaller machine. If you want to optimize the use of your network, you must have a continuously updated picture of the use and cost of that network.

One last item before comparing PBXs with LANs: the topic of *modem pooling*. Modem pooling involves the use of a pool of modems on the trunk side of a PBX so that multiple internal users can share those modems. If you have data coming into the PBX on the in-house side, whether from direct connection, DOV, or IVDT, you may want to communicate externally over standard analog lines using modems. By dialing specific numbers or identifying the transmission as data, the PBX can select one of the modems in a modem pool. If all of the modems are in use, then you will get a busy signal when you try to dial out. This pooling reduces the need for each terminal to have a separate modem because they can share the pool. Depending on your application, and the priorities under which your terminals must be used, modem pooling can be a significant potential source of cost savings.

## F

## PBXs VERSUS LANs

One of the major struggles going on in the PBX world is the competition from Local Area Networks (LANs). The trade-off frequently comes down to whether you want to install new wiring for LAN use or utilize existing wire for moving data through the PBX. It is not the cost of the wiring that is significant, but the cost of installing it. As such, when many organizations are building new facilities today, they put in all of the cabling ahead of time for both narrow-band LANs, wide-band LANs, telephone twisted pair, and even fiber. That way the flexibility exists for the future if and when they want to use it. On the other hand, if you must decide whether to install new wiring in an existing building, the economics change radically. For some there may be no choice because of the external interference created by signals that are near the telephone wiring, but in other cases when the telephone wiring can be used, a whole variety of operational and cost considerations must be considered.

The basic trade-offs between LANs and PBXs are that LANs can handle high peak data rates in the megabit range while the PBX is limited typically to 64 KBPS max; LANs can handle multiple destinations simultaneously with broadcast-type transmissions, while PBXs typically have point-to-point connections; and the PBX takes a longer period of time than LANs to set up a circuit (which may not be acceptable in some applications). However, the PBX can set up a permanent circuit with no subsequent switching time, but only between two specific devices. If multiple devices have to communicate simultaneously at high speed, then you probably are limited to using a LAN. Since most applications are still terminal-to-host-oriented, the use of a PBX as a mechanism for routing is still a viable service. Also, since most of the data rates from terminals are 19.2 KBPS maximum, the PBX again is still adequate, but as time goes on, with the growing use of higher speed devices like video and graphics, the need for a higher capacity medium will become more prevalent. That decision is typically a dynamic one where the conclusion may change over time, but there seems to be no question that a LAN can handle all the data needs you will ever want. Although LANs do not handle voice yet, this may change in the future with products like Datakit (described in Chapter 15).

When you evaluate the trade-offs you should also look at the ratio of utilization between voice and data. Even in organizations that are very heavily data oriented, the voice versus data utilization usually runs in a ratio of more than 10 to 1. If this is the case and you use a PBX, you are utilizing a switch designed for voice to move your data, with the data requiring less than 10 percent of the switch use. In this situation, maybe you ought to consider a separate data PBX (DPBX) or other device that will switch your data traffic independently. Even the DPBXs that handle low-speed traffic (typically up to 19.2 KBPS, although some run at higher speeds) may be a better alternative for you. If you figure out the cost of your PBX for both voice and data use, you will typically have a line cost of $1000–1200 per line, whereas a plain voice PBX may run in the range of $500–600 a line and a DPBX, at the low end, between $100–200 per line. These economics show that you will probably be better off running your data through a separate switch. The DPBX will use the same twisted pair wiring as your standard PBX, so you also have the same limitations due to external noise. If you also have high-speed lines required for your terminals there are other DPBXs that can handle speeds up to T–1, and provide the same types of features that PBXs provide, such as directories, on-line help, camp on, information for billing purposes and even limits on access for security. Some even have gateways to LANs available. From an operational point of view you can also get *port contention,* which allows a large number of terminals to contend for a limited amount of ports on the CFE at the host site, and *port selection,* which provides a connection for several host-site CFEs to a single DPBX so that switching between host CFEs will be available.

There is probably a lot more flexibility in having separate voice and data PBXs, but many users prefer for convenience purposes to have both features in the same device, which is not always an economical decision. Additional alternatives will be described later, in section G on data switches.

## Centrex versus PBX

No section on the use of a PBX would be complete without describing the Centrex alternative, which is like a PBX that physically resides in the telephone company Class 5 central office. As was described at the beginning of this chapter, Centrex appeared to be doomed in 1984 when, as a byproduct of divestiture, enhanced services could not be provided by the local telephone company and additional Centrex features could not be added. When that restriction was removed in 1986, the Centrex world boomed once again.

The concept behind Centrex is that users on the customer's premises are served by separate lines from the telephone company central office (CO). Switching takes place in the CO and there is a user predetermined amount of lines between the customer's premises and the CO. If all those lines are in use, the user will not get a dial tone and cannot initiate a call. The capabilities that the user can take advantage of depend on the capabilities that physically exist in the switch. Centrex lines are partitioned into groups, with each group having a set of basic features with other optional enhanced features. Those features vary widely from switch to switch and from state to state. Centrex is typically available in local COs with electronic switching equipment such as the AT&T 1ESS, and 1AESS.

Centrex is typically an analog service, although there is a new digital Centrex when there is a digital switch in the CO. The AT&T 5ESS and NTI DMS 100 can provide digital Centrex. The service usually appears the same as analog Centrex, and, although it may not have as many features as analog Centrex yet, the future holds tremendous potential. Digital Centrex, although more expensive, can also provide digital switching on an end to end basis and an evolutionary path for transition to ISDN. It is also compatible with switched 56 kilobit service (dial digital).

Some of the trade-offs between Centrex and PBXs are as follows:

| CENTREX SERVICES | PBX |
|---|---|
| Regulated environment | Unregulated |
| Functions in telco CO | Functions on user premises |
| Leased only | Lease or Buy |
| Reliability because of redundancy | Reliability when user pays for redundancy |
| Full maintenance always available | Maintenance not always on site (may require user personnel for service) |
| Growth practically unlimited | Finite growth limitations |
| No capital outlay necessary (installation may be amortized) | May require purchase or significant up-front cash outlay |
| Multiple buildings may be connected to same Centrex through CO | Separate PBXs usually required |
| Upgrade features can be continuous | Significant upgrade may require new PBX |
| Simultaneous voice/data available | Simultaneous voice/data available |
| Relatively limited SMDR information | Full SMDR information available |
| All wiring twisted pair | Wiring may be twisted pair or coaxial cable |
| May have high monthly cost per line | Line cost amortized over time in service |
| No space or power required | User space and power required |
| Telco personnel provide maintenance | User may need dedicated maintenance personnel |
| Rate stability plans available | Rate stability not available |

You should be aware that not all COs support Centrex, and if more than one CO supports a particular location, they all may not provide the same Centrex capability. Centrex is regulated by the PUC and the FCC.

Summarizing the trade-offs, it would appear that the advantages for Centrex are the lower initial costs and flexibility in adding new features as they become available in the switch, while on the PBX side, there is much better reporting information and lower ongoing cost if you utilize the PBX over a period of time. Another potential advantage for utilizing a PBX in a network rather than Centrex is that the billing cycles may not be synchronized across the different Centrex areas so that you don't get the same level of detail in your billing. The PBX can move or change locations of equipment from an in-house console much quicker than a Centrex, and although Centrex is getting better in allowing changes to be made on user premises, it is still not as good as PBX.

As can be seen there is a wide variety of parameters that must be considered when evaluating PBX versus Centrex, and there is no simple way to determine that one is better than the other for a particular end-user environment.

Utilizing a PBX from the same vendor at different locations will give you a network with the same features and capabilities at all locations. That cannot be guaranteed when you use Centrex. Also, you can get centralized and uniform SMDR from a single type of PBX, which you cannot always get from Centrex.

As time goes on it is becoming apparent that more and more features are being added to Centrex to make it competitive with PBX, while the PBX vendors are providing additional features and capabilities to stay competitive. In other words, the two are getting closer from an operational as well as from a cost viewpoint. Ultimately you may end up making decisions based on a subjective evaluation of whether you want to operate and maintain your own switch versus having the local telco do it for you.

It is the author's opinion that if one factor will influence the decision process, it will be that a Centrex can be continually upgraded with new features, such as T-1, and ISDN, as they become available from the carrier, whereas a PBX may not be capable of incorporating the new service as an upgrade and may have to be entirely replaced. Still, it may be years before this kind of decision has to be made, so in the interim you need to consider the capabilities that are available today and the life span that you expect from the service. Centrex would definitely have an advantage if your company may be changing size and facility locations very quickly. Centrex can accommodate changes over a much wider range than a key system or a smaller PBX, but if you are in a more stable environment you might be better served to consider PBX as an alternative.

A couple of other interfaces dealing strictly with the PBX should also be looked at. First is the potential future interface with ISDN, and there are two basic structures being used here. The first one is the *Digital Multiplexed Interface* (DMI), from AT&T. DMI is designed to provide an ISDN primary rate type interface between the PBX and terminals connecting to it. The idea is to allow 23 separate terminal environments to access a host computer through a PBX without having individual port cards for each connection in the CFE. Each of the 23 terminal bit streams will be 64 KBPS, while the twenty-fourth channel is used for signaling between the PBX and the computer. If the DMI is utilized appropriately, there can be T-1 type connections for computers to terminals in an in-house environment. Because of the changing environment from the old D4-type data formats, AT&T provides three modes of operation for DMI. Mode 0 is a full 64 KBPS synchronous full-duplex transmission on each of the 23 information channels. Mode 1 is a 56 KBPS full-duplex synchronous transmission, which is compatible with Dataphone Digital Service (DDS) and Mode 2 is an asynchronous input that is capable of operating up to 19.2 KBPS.

On a competitive basis, Northern Telecom (NTI) has an equivalent interface they call the *Computer to PBX Interface* (CPI). This comes in two versions. CPI-1 meets a very high percentage of the existing installed PBX base by using all 24 channels at 56 KBPS synchronous or 19.2 KBPS asynchronous, which means the framing is DID (described in Chapter 16) with *robbed bit* signaling. That signaling is not compatible with ISDN so NTI has come out with CPI-2, which is a path for migration to clear channel 64 K on each of the 23 information channels and the single channel for signaling like DMI does today. If you expect to go the digital or T–1 route and to have an interface directly in your PBX, you need to look at CPI-2.

A separate but related capability that is provided in conjunction with PBXs is a *Voice Messaging System* (VMS). This system allows you to call someone and leave a message in your own voice. This is not just an answering machine, but more like a voice mailbox. VM also allows a whole series of functions to be performed and is used to reduce labor costs for operator intensive services. For example, when you call an organization like a bank with many possible kinds of questions, the voice messaging system will have you depress a particular key for the particular type of service you want. An operator does not have to answer each call and route it separately to the appropriate department for answering. The *fall-through* condition provides the ability to talk to a human when none of the predetermined routes is applicable. There are VM systems that *interface* to a PBX, and there are VM systems that are *integrated* with a PBX. The trade-offs between the two may not seem significant, but depending on your application they could be. For example, on an integrated VM system you can have a personalized greeting from the individual being called, but with a VM system that interfaces to a PBX you only get a generic greeting. You then key in the user's specific extension to get the appropriate mailbox for storage of your message. VM systems are proliferating at a very fast rate today. Because of the dynamics of the situation, you must take a look at the specific features available with the VM system as well as how it can best be interfaced to your existing or planned PBX.

# G

## DATA SWITCHES

When talking about data switches, you must consider not only data PBXs, but a wide variety of other devices that sometimes go by the same name. There are matrix switches, port selectors, port contention devices, and a variety of others. Functionally, a matrix switch provides the ability to have $X$ lines on one side and $X$ lines on the other side. One basic mode of operation is where all inputs are connected to all outputs, but the outputs can be switched from one device to another. Figure 14–4 shows two matrix switches (A and B), each terminating 32 lines (the numbers are arbitrary, and any number of lines can be connected to either switch). Under normal operation, lines 1–32 go to CFE A while lines 33–64 go to CFE B. In the event one of the CFEs fails, the matrix switch can provide a connection so that all of the lines can be connected to the other operational CFE. As an alternative, some organizations have two CFEs with one operating all the time and the second in *hot standby.* Full system operations take place on one CFE all the time, and if it fails or has to be taken out of service for maintenance purposes (once a week or once a month, for example) the matrix switch

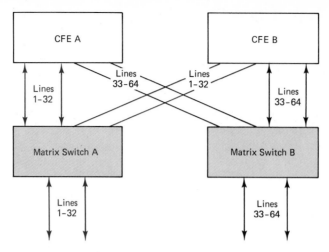

**FIGURE 14-4**
Matrix Switching

can provide switchover to the alternate CFE. The user does not have any control over the individual paths. All of the lines coming in are switched at the same time to a predetermined set of outputs. Typically, the matrix switch can have source-only ports, destination-only ports, and paths to other switches. It may also have RS232-type interfaces that utilize either 16 or 20 wires and are usually used between the modem and the CFE. There are other matrix switches that provide the same kind of transfer capability for the analog side of the modem.

Controls for a matrix switch can be provided through an independent console. You can also connect matrix switches to provide additional paths. A matrix switch usually comes in a 16 × 16 configuration, but can be obtained in larger sizes. As the switch gets larger, however, there are many more connections, which can be a physical problem. Matrix switches are used in large network environments where the user cannot afford to have any downtime due to failures of front-end equipment.

A related device (actually works the same way) is called the *Port Selector* or *Port Contention* device (the terms can be used interchangeably). Operationally, the device works the same as a matrix switch except you specifically have more lines coming in than you have going out. This is normally known as an *X/Y* relationship with *X* lines coming in and *Y* lines going out, where *Y* is a smaller number than *X*. A diagram for a port selector is shown in Fig. 14-5. There are 64 lines coming in to the port selector but only 8 lines going out to the CFE. Of the 64 lines that come in, only 8 can be active at any one time. Port selectors are used in environments where there are requirements for many devices to communicate, but not all at the same time. It is up to the user to determine how many ports are to be available at any one time. In this particular case, only eight devices can be active at any one time. If it is desired to have more lines active, during peak times, for example, connections to additional ports must be provided. Because of the cost of ports on a CFE, a port selector can save a lot of money with a minimal amount of delay to the external users. Of course, a good analysis must

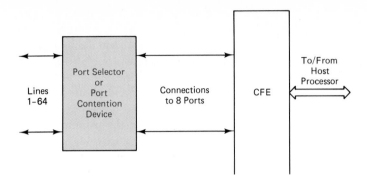

**FIGURE 14–5**
*Port Selection/Contention*

be made of the traffic volumes, especially during peak times, to make sure that delays to get in to the host are not too long.

A port selector would take the place of a telephone rotary, with the added potential of providing priorities on the network side. Depending on the number given to the end users, separate groups of ports can be accessed. Features such as synchronous and asynchronous connections, broadcast capabilities, automatic call back when busy, and others are available in some port selectors. A port selector is sometimes also called a Data PBX, although by the terms used by this text they are different devices because the Data PBX will have many more capabilities. It should be noted that the internal connections in port selectors do not physically connect the incoming lines to a particular output port but, rather, a method of time division multiplexing is used in which the outputs of the port selector sample the data on a bus that integrates the bits from the input lines. It is a rather complex mechanism, but very reliable in operation.

Most port selectors can handle both synchronous and asynchronous inputs up to approximately 19.2 KBPS. Although some of the devices are rated by their manufacturers as having a throughput of 20 MBPS, you really must consider the various device speeds and quantity of ports at their specific operating speeds to determine actual throughput.

In general, the port selector works with a terminal just like a telephone works with a PBX. The user would key in a *call request* from the terminal which might be a single carriage return character (or two of them) along with the RS232 signal *DTR-ON*. The port selector will provide a *prompt* at which time the terminal will send information to the destination. Disconnects can be provided through time-outs, DTR-OFF, disconnect command, break, and others. During the connection, data will be transferred through the data PBX by either a sampling technique or transmission of entire characters. At the higher speeds it is typically done in a character mode.

Finally, from a statistical point of view, Data PBXs typically provide the same kind of information as a PBX relative to Station Message Detail Recording (SMDR). This is the information regarding the usage of the Data PBX. It should also be noted that this device is called by many different names although port selector and Data PBX are the most common  Here again you must describe the functional requirements that you require rather than just a generic name.

Only a few vendors actually make matrix switches and port contention devices, but they are usually good enough so that some of the major vendors such as IBM and AT&T will OEM the devices from those manufacturers and put their own name on it. OEM (Original Equipment Manufacturer) is a process whereby vendor A will build a product for vendor B and put vendor B's name on it. This is very common for special-purpose devices in the communications industry, so when a vendor does not want to manufacture particular equipment itself, it can actually get that equipment built to its own specifications from a third party, and then sell it as its own. As the communication industry continues to grow and the market expands for particular products, the larger vendors who have been OEM-ing some equipment will be more willing to manufacture equipment themselves in the future rather than pay to have it done by an OEM manufacturer. There is nothing wrong with OEM equipment because it is backed up by the selling vendor who has its own name on it. As more and more special-purpose devices become available, they may then become the new OEM devices.

## QUESTIONS

1. Describe the concept of blocking versus nonblocking.
2. What kind of environment is a key system most applicable to?
3. What are the four generations of PBX? Which one is primarily used today? Why?
4. Develop the sequence of steps for obtaining a Pulse Code Modulation representation of voice.
5. What is the primary consideration when selecting a method for converting analog signals to binary bits?
6. Describe the two methodologies for moving data and voice over the same circuit.
7. What is a typical application for modem pooling?
8. What are the primary trade-off criteria to use when evaluating a PBX versus Centrex? Which are the ones that most affect future use?
9. What is the difference between a matrix switch and a port contention switch? Describe their operation.

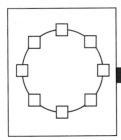

# 15

# Local Area Networks (LANs)

## BACKGROUND AND OVERVIEW

Local area networks (LANs) can be described in many ways. Depending on your perspective, you tend to look at what you are interested in, and how all of the LAN characteristics relate to that. The orientation in this text is based on the primary interface characteristics of how the user actually accesses the LAN. That means if a separate interface device provides a connection to a physical medium with the signals transmitted on the medium representing bits only, it is different from a LAN where the interface is integrated right into the accessing device. Through this differentiation the first major functional type of LAN is called a *public* LAN, and the second is called a *PC* LAN.

In the public LANs such as Ethernet and Wangnet, an interfacing device converts the user information to a predetermined electrical signaling sequence on a communications medium. Many types of user devices can connect to these public LANs through standardized interfaces such as RS232. On the other hand, the PC LANs have hardware incorporated right into the user devices (PCs) so that they all form an integrated network with a higher level of communicating capability. As will be seen later, this integrated network is required because PC operating systems are so slow when accessing their peripherals. Their integrated hardware emulates the operating system so that peripheral access is much faster and the

315

PCs can live up to their potential of multimegabit per second transmissions. Only devices with the same hardware interfaces can communicate with each other.

Another form of differentiation is the topology. *Topology* refers to the configuration of the devices on the communications medium. Many people describe LANs with respect to topology only, while others describe LANs with a third form of differentiation: *narrowband* or *wideband.*

All of the definitions are interrelated and will be described here in this chapter.

# B
## TOPOLOGIES

The LAN is a privately owned network and therefore not subject to regulation by either the FCC or the state PUC. Because most businesses move more than 80 percent of their data within their own facilities, it would seem that a method for moving that data at a high speed, reliably, on end-to-end facilities owned by the user would potentially have a large market. A LAN was designed to be just such a system.

The original idea was to establish a separate wiring system within a facility such that all devices that must communicate with each other could be tied together through some form of common interface. Ethernet, developed by Xerox and announced in 1977, was one of the first of these systems (ARCnet from Datapoint was an earlier version of a LAN but designed only to connect Datapoint equipment). Ethernet provided a method of moving information at up to 10 MBPS over a common cable to any device connected to that cable. Only one device could be transmitting at any one time (all users share the same line), so when other vendors began to design networks that would operate in very much the same way, there also evolved another set of LAN networks in which multiple users could be communicating simultaneously. Ethernet came to be known as a *narrowband* LAN, while the others with multiple users came to be known as *wideband.* Both of these terms will be described in more detail later.

Regardless of the narrowband versus wideband designation, LANs function the same conceptually. They are made up of the same four basic components: (1) the *user workstation,* which is the user device that performs a particular application; (2) a *protocol control,* which logically takes the user information and converts it to a form that can be moved through the transmission medium of the LAN network to reach the desired location; (3) the *medium interface,* which is required for creating the electrical signals to be physically moved on the medium; and (4) the actual *physical path.* The physical path can be almost any form of communications media today such as twisted pair, coaxial cable, or fiber.

For purposes of discussion at this point, all PC-type LANs, such as Novell, 3 Com, and IBM's PC LAN, are considered narrowband. They do have different operating characteristics that will also be described later.

To put all of the characteristics into context, the topologies will be described first. They are shown in Fig. 15–1.

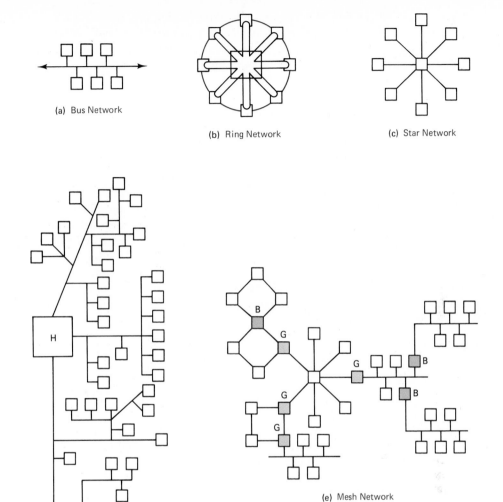

(a) Bus Network

(b) Ring Network

(c) Star Network

(d) Tree Network

(e) Mesh Network

**FIGURE 15–1**
Topologies (Network Configurations)

**BUS NETWORK**  The bus shown in Fig. 15–1(a) shows the typical Ethernet configuration, where each device is connected directly to a cable. Each of the squares represents an interface device, the medium interface to which the user's device connects. A detailed operational description of this type of connection will be provided in Section E of this chapter. In baseband bus networks there can be only one transmitter at a time. Most PC LANs are connected in a bus configuration.

**RING NETWORK**  Fig. 15–1(b) shows a ring configuration that is typical of the IBM token ring. Each of the devices is connected sequentially in a ring configuration which is shown as the solid line between all of the devices. In this particular instance, the squares represent both the user device and the medium access device. Because the failure of a single device would break the ring, the actual wiring configuration is a series of loop-type connections from a centralized location called a *Multistation Access Unit* (MAU). The MAU provides for the *short circuiting* of any device that fails so that the integrity of the physical ring can be maintained. Additional descriptions of the ring operation will be provided later under the IBM token-ring section.

**STAR NETWORK**  In a star network, all devices on the network are connected to a centralized device from which control may emanate, shown in Fig. 15–1(c). The star network is also used where a centralized location, such as a PBX, controls the user devices and where the available medium is twisted pair wiring. Star networks are also configured without controls to take advantage of existing house wiring where terminals are connected to centralized locations like telephone company wiring closets and the wiring closets are then connected in a bus arrangement. StarLAN from AT&T is an example of this configuration.

**TREE NETWORK**  Although the tree network is conceptually very much like a star network, the tree network shown in Fig. 15–1(d) is utilized primarily for wideband networks. The square labelled H is called the *headend*. Each of the remote devices communicates to and from the headend via a separate preassigned transmit-and-receive frequency so that multiple devices can communicate at the same time. The incoming frequencies make up a predetermined set that correlates specifically with an outgoing set of frequencies. The headend is the device that provides the conversion. A more detailed description of a tree network will be provided later in Section D, Bandwidths.

**MESH NETWORKS**  Many terms are used to describe mesh networks, but they all refer to the connection of different types of LANs. One possible configuration of a mesh network is shown in Fig. 15–1(e), where there are rings, buses, and a star. Without getting too complicated at this point in the description, the various individual LANs can be either narrowband or wideband within certain limitations (described in more detail in Section E), but two specific types of devices should be described here.

The squares labeled *B* are known as *bridges*. The primary function of a bridge is to connect two LANs of the same type. The squares labelled *G* are called *gateways*, which are designed to connect two different types of LANs. There are other descriptions for these specialized interfaces, such as *routers* and *protocol converters*, which will be described later. Their configuration also involves the connection of the same or different-type networks into one large-scale network. These mesh networks are all *in-house* networks, even though other gateways may connect them to wide area networks. Those connections will also be described later.

# C

## STANDARDS

Before getting involved in the descriptions of how the different types of LANs work, it should be recognized that many LANs have been designed with interfaces that are being incorporated into the OSI (Open Systems Interconnect) environment, a standardized set of parameters described in more detail in Chapter 18. The first three layers of OSI are the most applicable to the LAN world.

The standards relating to LANs are well enough along in their establishment so that chips for interfaces can be developed. The Institute for Electrical and Electronic Engineers (IEEE) 802 Standards Committee is specifically developing this set of interface specifications. To date, they have established nine areas of standards:

***802.1*** 802.1, known as the higher-level interface standard, deals with internetworking, addressing, and network management. This specification is the least defined because it involves a lot of interfacing with other networks that are still under consideration.

***802.2*** 802.2 is known as the *Logical Link Control Standard* and is roughly equivalent to the second layer of OSI. It provides the point-to-point link control between devices at what is typically the protocol level. Many of the specific applications designed to date using LANs incorporate the 802.2 standard so that they can interface with the higher layers of OSI. A comparison between the OSI standard and the IEEE 802 is shown in Fig. 15–2. The physical layer for OSI is incorporated into the 802.3/.4/.5 set of specifications, but in the IEEE version there is an additional level, called the *Medium Access Control* (MAC). MAC provides the logical connection for the electrical signals onto the physical medium. Above the MAC layer is 802.2, which is the *Logical Link Control* (LLC). 802.2 provides an interface from the physical functions to the logical functions of routing and

**FIGURE 15–2**
ISO versus IEEE 802

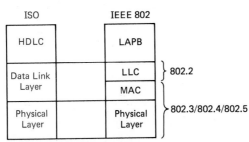

LAPB = Link Access Protocol B
LLC = Logical Link Control (802.2)
MAC = Medium Access Control

also a relatively simple interface to the third level of OSI, which is the routing layer. In the 802 version, the *Link Access Protocol-B* (LAPB) is the protocol version that is used and LLC provides this interface in a simple form. Functionally, therefore, there is not an exact relationship between the layers of the two standards, but the combined result of 802.3/.4/.5 with 802.2 is the equivalent of the first two layers of the OSI model. Because of this similar structure, IEEE 802 becomes directly compatible for those vendors who would like to incorporate LAN communications into their products for the first two layers. Each of the three types of network, 802.3, 802.4, and 802.5, can talk directly with another LAN of the same type, but a gateway is needed for communication between different type LANs.

**802.3**  802.3, 802.4, and 802.5 are detailed descriptions of the actual operation of the LAN with respect to signal flow between user devices. 802.3 is known as *Carrier Sense Multiple Access/Collision Detection* (CSMA/CD). It describes an Ethernet type operation and will be described in more detail in the next section. An overview of this operation involves the capability of any device on a bus to transmit when the medium interface determines that no other device is already transmitting. If two medium-interface devices simultaneously decide that no one else is transmitting, their transmissions will overlap, causing a *collision*. The mode of operation with and without collision is what is identified in 802.3.

**802.4**  802.4 describes the token bus method of operation whereby each device transmits only when it receives a *token*. The token is passed in a user-predetermined sequence and guarantees that each transmitting device will have access to the medium within a maximum amount of time. 802.4 is known as a *deterministic* transmission mechanism, while 802.3 is known as a *probabilistic* method of transmission. The trade-offs between the two will be described in the next section.

**802.5 Token Ring**  802.5 is the mechanism utilized in the IBM token-ring LAN. *Token ring* is a proprietary mechanism for operation on a LAN, with the rights owned by a Swedish designer, Olaf Soderblum, from whom IBM has contracted for unlimited worldwide rights to its use. All other vendors who develop a token-ring approach must obtain rights from Soderblum, who is very active in prosecuting those cases where licenses have not been granted.

As time goes on you will see more incorporation of 802.3, 802.4, and 802.5 specifications into more and more applications. Since many vendors are developing architectures for their equipment that are in accordance with OSI, they will probably incorporate these 802 standards into the lower levels of their own architectures.

**802.6**  Metropolitan Area Network (MAN). The committee that set up this specification was originally brought together in 1981 for the task of coming up with the specifications for networks that were more than five kilometers in distance between two or more points. The original MAN networks were the Cable T.V. Systems (CATV). CATV started out as unidirectional five-channel cables, but were eventually increased to 70 channels on a single cable or a dual cable with 54 channels each (108 total). In anticipation of future applications, the FCC directed that all CATV be two-way cable after 1972. The MAN was designed to support voice, data, and video, while the original LAN specification was for data only. The applications that will be incorporated into a MAN environment will be very much like the wideband LANs which already overlap into the MAN area except they will operate over a much greater distance.

**802.7**  802.7 is a committee established as the working group for establishing broadband LAN operating specifications.

**802.8**  This is the working group that is responsible for the establishment of fiber-optic LAN operating standards.

**802.9**  Another working group, 802.9 is involved with establishing the standards for integrated voice and data operation on a LAN.

# D
## BANDWIDTH

One of the primary differences in describing the technical operation of a LAN is the use of the terms *narrowband* and *wideband*. They are not only different in utilization but also in the applications that they can support. Listed here are the major differences between the two.

| NARROWBAND | WIDEBAND |
|---|---|
| Also called baseband | Also called broadband |
| Typical is Ethernet | Typical is Wangnet |
| Operation up to 10 MBPS | Up to 480 MBPS total |
| StarLAN at 1 MBPS | |
| 500 meters without regenerators | 5–10 miles with amplifiers |
| One transmitter at a time | Multiple users in different channels |
| Good for short, bursty traffic (data) | Good for data/video/graphics/facsimile/etc. |
| Utilizes twisted pair or coaxial cabling | Utilizes coaxial or fiber-optic cable |
| Direct connection to cable | Requires modems for different channels |

As shown, there is a wide diversity in capability. Even though baseband systems far outnumber broadband systems at present, it is anticipated that the future will hold more broadband-type utilization because of the integration of multiple locations in a *campus* environment. A broadband network may incorporate multiple baseband-type operations in different channels so many users on a broadband network have access to different applications on that network (by changing the modem transmit and receive frequencies). At the same time, the broadband can also support applications such as graphics, facsimile, video conferencing, and others. You must also recognize that the stated LAN transmission speed is not necessarily the throughput from an applications point of view. Many other factors affect user throughput; the preceding table only relates to general characteristics of the LANs.

# E
## OPERATIONAL CHARACTERISTICS

### Background

Different vendor products usually exhibit a relationship to a specific topology, and in order to correlate the products with the topologies some of the major vendor offerings will be described. Even though the specific parameters for one vendor may not be the same as for another vendor, the overall concept of operation will be the same. As we go through the various offerings those relationships will become more evident.

### Ethernet

Ethernet was developed in the mid-1970s by Xerox Corporation and operates within the category of the Carrier Sense Multiple Access/Collision Detection (CSMA/CD) mode of operation. Figure 15–3 shows the CSMA/CD configuration. There is a cable to which all devices are connected through an interface device labeled I/F. Conceptually the operation is as follows: If any device (D) requires access to the cable, it informs the interface device of that fact. The I/F then looks at the cable to see if anyone else is transmitting. If no one else is transmitting, then the I/F generates a Biphase Manchester (described in Chapter 10) signal to be transmitted on the line. All devices on the cable can see this signal and the addressed device takes it in. Upon completion of the transmission any other device on the cable can access it through the same process.

However, two interface devices may make the transmit decision at the same time. When this happens it is called a *collision*. A collision is recognized when there are two simultaneous sets of signals on the cable (seen by all of the devices). At that point the two transmitting interface devices back off the line and go through an internal algorithm that says they will not try to transmit on the line again at the same time. Since they are the only two devices that are going through this back-off algorithm, either one can collide with a third device when they try to transmit, at which time the new colliders will go through the back-off algorithm again.

When traffic is relatively light and occurs in a short, bursty form, such as data, collisions are relatively minimal. Many studies have been made to identify when the amount of traffic becomes a problem for a collision detection type of operation. Those who favor Ethernet seem to feel that the collision problem be-

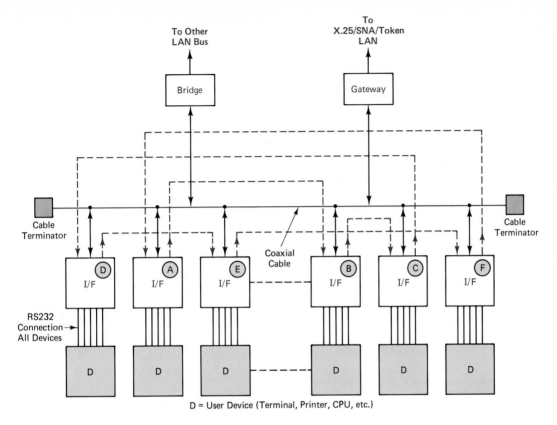

**FIGURE 15-3**
Ethernet (contention bus) and Logical Ring (token passing on a bus)

comes serious when cable utilization approaches 70 percent, while the Ethernet detractors seem to feel that collision detection is a problem in the range of 20-percent utilization. The actual number is probably somewhere between those two values. Suffice it to say at this time that Ethernet and its clones are used extensively for those applications that require short, bursty traffic, like word processing, document processing, and other office automation-type applications.

The number of stations that can be connected to an Ethernet cable is up to 1024, and the transmissions are *code independent,* which means that any code set can be used. Maximum station separation is 2.5 kilometers, or 8202 feet. Because of the collision detection operation there can be no guaranteed response time in an Ethernet mode of operation (probabilistic).

The physical interface for Ethernet is the IEEE Spec 802.3. Fifty-ohm coaxial cable is used and transmission rates can be up to 10 MBPS. Cable segments can be as long as 500 meters (1640 feet) and five segments can be connected through repeaters. Each of the cable segments can accept up to 100 *taps,* each at a point designated by colored rings on the cable. Tap rings are 2.5 meters (8.2

feet) apart and are points at which a transceiver (interface device) or a repeater can be connected to the cable. The transceiver interface consists of four sets of twisted pair wires, as shown in Fig. 15–4. There is one pair each for power, transmit data, receive data, and collision detection. The user's device can be up to 50 meters (164 feet) from the tap.

There can be no more than two repeaters and 1500 meters (4921 feet) in a path between any two stations. The connection to the cable is made through what is called a *vampire tap* which means that the cable does not have to be cut open and *spliced*. It connects simply and directly into the cable at the appropriate location.

The actual Ethernet transmission takes place in a packet format as shown in Fig. 15–5. The format for transmission is broken up into eight segments, of which seven are actual bit sequences. The first segment, called the *preamble,* consists of 8 bytes. The preamble is called a *wake-up* or synchronization sequence and typically consists of a string of 1,0,1,0, and so on, with the last two bits being a 1,1 sequence. The next three segments, the *header,* consist of a 48-bit destination address, a 48-bit source address, and a 16-bit type field utilized to identify the higher level protocol with which this transmission will interface. The type field is an identifier on how to interpret the data. The user data field must then have a minimum of 46 bytes (368 bits), and if there is not enough data to equal 46 bytes, then it must be *padded* out. The data is followed by a 32-bit CRC error-detection segment (described in Chapter 13) and a guard time, which is not actual data, but insures a 9.6 microsecond time delay to avoid packet overrun.

Ethernet transmission provides only the physical movement of bits between one transceiver and another. The logical relationships between message transmissions and acknowledgments are up to the user terminal device. Ethernet is strictly

**FIGURE 15–4**
Ethernet Transceiver

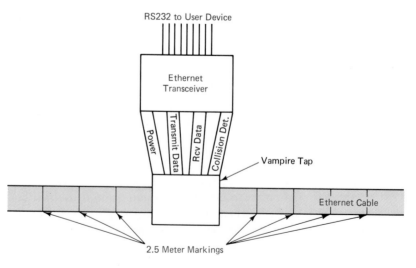

| Preamble (8 Bytes) | Destination Address (6 Bytes) | Source Address (6 Bytes) | Type Field (2 Bytes) | User (46 Bytes Minimum (1500 Bytes | Data — Pad if Required) Maximum) | CRC (4 Bytes) | Guard (12 Bytes) |
|---|---|---|---|---|---|---|---|

**FIGURE 15–5**
Ethernet Transmission Format

a *bit-moving* function to get bits from one point to another. Message acknowledgments must be done at the logical level between user devices.

Recently, because of the expense of installing coaxial cable, significant advancements have been made in the utilization of Ethernet over different media. For example, there is Ethernet transmission over a *thinner* coaxial cable, which limits transmission distances. Even more significant is the mechanization of Ethernet over twisted pair wires. In late 1987 both DEC and 3COM announced an Ethernet interface that provides for transmission over standard twisted pair telephone wiring, which allows a transmission distance of 250 feet at 10 MBPS. A *passive* line impedance matcher/conditioner is used at each end of the twisted pair to provide the appropriate impedance match between the coaxial cable and the twisted pair. Since most studies have shown that more than 98 percent of the user devices to be connected to the cable are within 250 feet of a telephone company wiring closet (junction or amplifier location), this seems to be a convenient way to tie those devices together utilizing existing in-house twisted pair wiring. However, external interference that occurs near the twisted pair could have a significant impact on the utilization of house wiring for a LAN.

When using Ethernet over twisted pair there is also a method for integrating user devices from twisted pair into the standard Ethernet coaxial cable for transmission over a greater distance. Individual terminal devices can be connected to the standard Ethernet cable over these twisted pair connections and can also utilize the thinner coaxial cable. In other words, the entire Ethernet is not on twisted pair. Only those segments that are used to connect devices to the Ethernet cable are on twisted pair, while the backbone is coaxial cable.

When discussing Ethernet and 802.3, you must be aware of the differences between the two. Data-framing formats may be different and there are other potential variations so that even though Ethernet meets the basic 802.3 criteria, it may not be compatible with another LAN that is also 802.3 compatible. Because the various data-framing formats can be different in the 802.3 LANs, there may be a misunderstanding of the control messages that provide for the routing of messages. For the two 802.3 networks to communicate, a separate adapter board is needed, which is actually a bridge but also called a *router* (described later in this chapter).

Ethernet can also operate on a single channel of a high-speed broadband LAN that is called IEEE 802.3 10Broad36, which means it operates at 10 Mbits/second on the broadband cable up to 3600 meters. Some of the networks that have used this kind of transmission are the IBM PCnet, Ungerman-Bass NetOne, Bridge, and Applitek.

Other versions of Ethernet that people may be familiar with, along with a summarization of their capabilities, is as follows. They are sometimes referred to as Ethernet Version 2, which was developed by DEC, Intel, and Xerox, and consists of four components. They are

*IEEE 802.3 10Base5.* This capability involves transmission of Ethernet information at 10 Mbits/sec over a maximum distance of 500 meters. There are some minor differences with the standard Ethernet with regard to signal characteristics, connector pin assignments, and cable grounding.

*IEEE 802.3 10Base2.* This is sometimes called *Cheapernet* or *Thin Ethernet* and involves transmission at 10 MBPS for a maximum distance of 200 meters.

*IEEE 802.3 1Base5.* This is indicative of the AT&T *StarLAN* and provides a 1 MBPS transmission capability for a maximum distance of 500 meters.

*IEEE 802.3 10Broad36.* This is the capability described above for transmission on a broadband cable where the transmission rate is 10 MBPS over a maximum distance of 3600 meters.

Because of the propagation delay of repeaters used in an Ethernet transmission (used when connecting 500 meter segments together), the practical limitation for narrowband Ethernet is five segments with four repeaters.

As a separate but related mode of transmission, AT&T has provided a LAN on twisted pair that they call *StarLAN*. StarLAN provides for the transmission of data at 1 MBPS utilizing the CSMA/CD of 802.3 and is designed to run on unshielded twisted pair wiring. StarLAN provides a distance of 500 meters at 1 megabit per second on 22-gauge wire. Because of their higher resistance, use of 24- or 26-gauge wire limits use to shorter runs.

StarLAN operates like an 802.3 LAN and is normally connected in a star configuration in the telephone company wiring closet, through a Network Extension Unit (NEU), which provides the necessary physical connections for all devices connected to it. Each NEU can support up to 10 devices in a cluster and up to 11 clusters can be linked together. StarLAN was designed to integrate single or groups of PCs and then connect to larger processors or PBXs through the NEU. StarLAN supports the UNIX and MSDOS 3.1 operating systems and a wide variety of IBM and AT&T processors. Because StarLAN operates at a 1 MBPS transmission rate, it is a separate subset of the IEEE 802.3 standard called the 1 Base 5 standard. As technology improves, greater distances and/or more devices will be connected to this LAN.

As part of their effort to continue upgrading their StarLAN product line, AT&T announced a new 10 MBPS StarLAN in May of 1988 that would be capable of transmitting on coaxial cable as well as fiber, so StarLAN will no longer be limited to twisted pair. The StarLAN interfaces announced with the new media and speeds would be capable of supporting over 1200 users on a single network. In addition, AT&T announced that they anticipate having a 4 MBPS token-ring operation some time in 1989. Of course, by that time not only will IBM have their 16 MBPS token ring but they will be very close to their FDDI fiber-optic token ring running at 100 MBPS (all described later in this section).

There is some competition for StarLAN from Northern Telecom, who has a 2.56 MBPS LAN capable of transmission up to 2000 feet that they use to and from their PBX equipment. IBM is also a competitor because they have a 4 MBPS transmission over a 45-meter distance utilizing unshielded twisted pair cabling (although the logical operation is different).

One more item should be mentioned in this section: the utilization of *Collision Avoidance* (CA). CA involves the same mode of operation as Ethernet when there is no transmission on the line (detection of someone else transmitting), but a different method is implemented to get onto the line. A handshake takes place prior to transmission of data, which is a shorter-type transmission requesting use of the cable. If there is no collision, then there is a guaranteed data transmission without a collision. If there is a collision in the handshake process, then a predetermined mechanism is utilized to determine who will transmit. The throughput on a CA system is typically less than on a standard Ethernet because of the negotiation time and it is therefore not utilized as much.

## Wangnet

Wangnet is one of a variety of LANs known as *wideband* LANs. A wideband LAN involves the utilization of coaxial or fiber-optic cabling to provide multiple users with access to the cable simultaneously. Individual devices that need to communicate with each other for like applications utilize the same frequency channels on the coaxial cable through modems, while different applications use different frequency bands for their transmission. In a single cable system the transmit and receive sets of frequencies typically utilize the low and the high band of the frequency spectrum, respectively. The *headend* provides the conversion from the low *transmit* frequency to the high *receive* frequency, which all devices then receive. If a dual cable system is used, one of the cables carries all of the frequencies for transmit purposes while the second cable carries all of the frequencies for receive purposes. The frequency bands for the single cable system are described as follows: The *forward band* is for transmission to the remotes; the *return band* is used for transmitting from the remotes; and a *guardband* is utilized to separate the forward and return bands. At the headend a *translator* converts the low-frequency incoming transmissions to the high-frequency outgoing transmissions. It should be recognized that the frequency splits do not have to be equally divided between the forward and reverse bands.

The topology of a wideband LAN such as Wangnet is known as a tree, shown in Fig. 15–6. Many applications can utilize the network simultaneously because a radio frequency carrier from a modem is utilized on a coaxial cable in a frequency division multiplexing mode. Devices can be connected to the cable anywhere in the network, and no single device can cause a *system* failure. A single device can potentially cause a channel failure if it turns on and does not turn off (streaming).

Because CATV technology is used in wideband LAN operation, it is possible to have many users communicating simultaneously in both directions on the same cable. To do this, however, you need to have a method for accessing the circuit such that you can communicate with other users of your applications and at the same time not interfere with users of alternate applications in other frequency bands.

Figure 15-7 shows how that is done. Every device has a modem that connects it to the wideband LAN cable. The modem is known as a *frequency agile modem* which has a particular transmit and receive frequency pair. When transmitting the modem utilizes one of the predetermined carrier frequencies in the low portion of the LAN, which is received by the *headend,* which functions as a *frequency translator* only (there is no intelligence here). Every incoming frequency has a specific outgoing frequency associated with it, and the headend provides that translation. In this mode of operation multiple modems can be transmitting simultaneously because they use different and therefore noninterfering frequency bands. Under the wideband LAN mode of operation you can have any number of techniques for moving information, including CSMA/CD, polling and calling, token passing, master/slave, or any other mode of control except token-ring—even video applications. As one example, if a mechanism such as CSMA/CD is used and two modems try to transmit at the same time, it will constitute a collision because the output translation will be garbled. The various applications required by the user can be supported in the different available bands, and the end user can change applications by switching the carrier frequencies (transmit and receive) of the modem being used to connect to the cable. Wideband LAN technology has been around for a long time already and is very reliable.

**FIGURE 15-6**
Wideband LAN Configuration (tree)

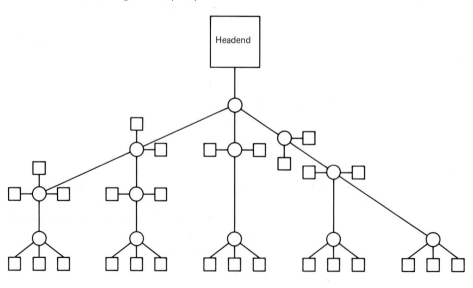

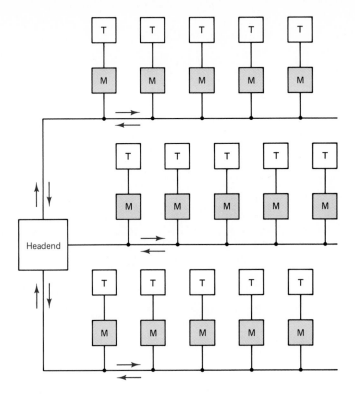

**FIGURE 15–7**
Wideband LAN Operation

As an example of a wideband LAN in a tree topology, Fig. 15–8 describes the makeup of the Wangnet user spectrum, which provides for the integration of many different types of applications. The Wangband is utilized for a CSMA/CD type of operation at 10 MBPS for Wang-type devices. The P band is utilized for a polling and calling type of operation at 4.27 MBPS, also for Wang devices. PCs can be connected on the PC service band, which runs at a 2.5-MBPS rate and utilizes a CSMA/CD mode of operation. An interconnect band is available for non-Wang devices at a wide variety of transmission speeds for both synchronous and asynchronous data transmissions. These transmissions can be multipoint or point-to-point type connections at 9600 BPS or up to 64 KBPS. The SIM band, which may be used for graphics applications, runs in a token passing mode (described later) at 5 MBPS. A utility band is set aside for the use of TV channels 7–13 and may be used for videoconferencing. The Wangnet/PCnet band is a 2-MBPS CSMA/CD band, and finally, there is an IEEE 802.3 band for CSMA/CD type operation at 10 MBPS for non-Wang devices. By utilizing all of these bands separately, a wide variety of applications can be supported simultaneously. The Wangnet type of network is typical of those wideband LANs that allow multiple simultaneous users to access the same *backbone* cable.

As additional explanation of the SIM band operation, it utilizes a mode of

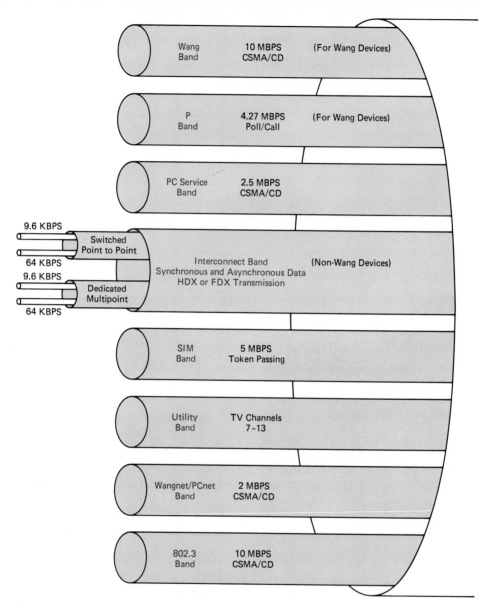

**FIGURE 15-8**
Wangnet User Spectrum

control called *token passing* (different from token ring, which is described in the next section). In the Wang case the SIM band is designed for the connection of desktop computers, performing a wide variety of applications. Token passing provides each device with a predetermined maximum length of time within which it will be able to access the cable. When network architectures are discussed in

330    LOCAL AREA NETWORKS (LANS)

Chapter 18, a more detailed description of other applications such as the Manufacturing Automation Protocol (MAP), which uses token passing, will be discussed. Token passing involves the use of a *token,* which is transmitted from device to device in a user-predetermined sequence to access the cable. The token functions as a *permission slip* so that a device can only transmit when it has the token. If a device does not have anything to transmit when it gets the token, the token is passed to the next device in the sequence. The token gets passed from location to location so that all devices have an equal opportunity to transmit. If the user desires a particular device to transmit more often, like a server or central computer, the token can be passed to that device or location after each one of the remotes has an opportunity to get the token in sequence. In other words, the token can be passed from the master to remote A, back to the master, then to remote B, back to the master, then to remote C, back to the master, and so on. For applications that have mandatory cable access times, token passing is an excellent method for providing that control.

## Token Ring

The token ring described in Fig. 15–1 consists of tying together multiple user devices in a sequential *ring* configuration. The devices, however, are actually wired physically in a *star* form so that malfunctioning devices can be easily eliminated from the ring. To examine the operation of the token ring, look at Fig. 15–9, which describes the mode utilized by IBM, which is by far the most prevalent form of token-ring implementation.

The IBM token ring is a narrowband operation on a *star wired ring.* The transmission rate is 4 MBPS (16 MBPS announced in November 1988), and there can be up to 260 devices in a ring if coaxial cable is used at distances up to about 300 meters (1000 feet) between devices. The ring can contain a maximum of only 72 devices at distances up to 100 meters (330 feet) if unshielded twisted pair telephone wiring is used. It is anticipated that IBM will soon announce a mode of operation that utilizes fiber-optic cabling, and it is also expected that the transmission rate on that cable will be much higher (100 MBPS). Physical movement of information in the ring is in accordance with IEEE 802.5, for which IBM provided the major input.

In the token ring a user's device tells the interface that it wants to transmit. When a token arrives at the interface device, the token is modified to put the source and destination address in the token, along with a message, and the token then becomes a *frame.* Each interface device on the ring monitors the ring and regenerates the frame upon receipt. As the bits arrive they are examined, regenerated, and sent on to the next device. The entire message is not stored before retransmission. (An analogy is a freight train rolling through a station without stopping. A flag on the front describes whether the train is empty—a token—or contains data. Another flag identifies the addressee. The information is read out while the bits move past the station.) The addressed interface device copies the message and sets an acknowledge or *copy* bit in the trailer of the frame. The

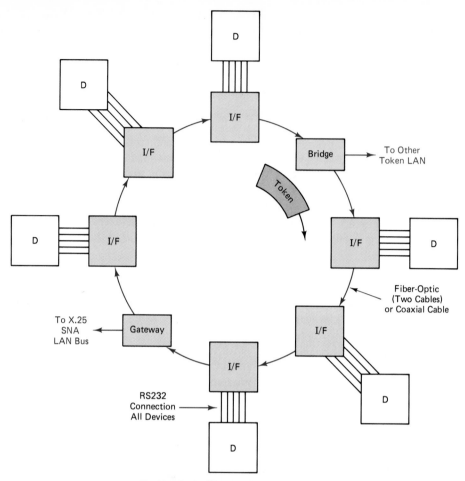

D = User Device (Terminal, Printer, CPU, etc.)

**FIGURE 15-9**
Token Ring

message continues around the ring so that the sender can validate that the message coming back is the same as the message that went out to determine if there was any corruption during the transmission.

An interface device is not allowed to transmit two frames in a row. It must wait its turn until everyone else in the ring has had an opportunity to transmit before it can transmit again, although a method of prioritization is available that will be described later.

The actual wiring mechanism for the IBM token ring is for all access devices to be connected to a central wiring location called a Multistation Access Unit (MAU). The MAU provides for the sequential connection between each one of the terminal devices (up to eight maximum) and a method for short circuiting malfunctioning or failed devices out of the ring. The cables can support full-duplex transmission because they consist of two twisted pairs per cable, two coaxial cables, or two fiber strands. This provides a parallel ring in case of failure of the primary ring. The ring is unidirectional and provides for repeaters in one direction only. Because narrowband signals are used, relatively simple repeaters can be used.

Since each one of the devices is wired to the MAU independently, there can be an intermix of media between them and the MAU. At the MAU end of the cable the connectors have a bypass capability built into them in the event a terminal is disconnected or fails. To provide operational control of the ring, one of the interface devices is designated as the *control unit* (CU). The CU monitors the ring on a continuous basis to make sure that there is always data or a token moving on the ring. Failures are detected by a complete loss of signal or absence of a token or data for a predetermined amount of time. Data errors are recognized in a logical form by each of the access units, which look to see if the bits they sent out are the same bits they receive back after the message goes around the ring.

Detailed operation of the token ring is better understood by looking at the formats for transmission. The token format consisting of a total of 3 bytes is shown in Fig. 15–10. The first and third bytes are the starting and ending delimiters that identify an empty token. The middle byte is the access control byte that contains 8 bits of control information with four discrete functions. They are

> ***Priority Bits.*** The three *priority bits* (P) identify the level of priority (or higher) that a device must have in order to *grab* the token for transmission of a data frame. After completion of a data frame a device sends out a token with its own level of priority unless the reservation bits (described below) require a different level. The first device that sees the token and has the same or higher level of priority can grab the token and send data. If the token goes all the way around the ring without being grabbed, then the device that generated the token will reduce the priority by one level and send the token out again. This process continues until the lowest level of priority is contained in the priority bits. During this process, however, if a token comes by with a level of priority *below* a device defined level, that device can grab the token and transmit a data frame. Upon completion of the data frame, a new token with the level of priority of the last device is set in the P bits and the process continues. The user can define up to eight levels of priority for a device, but care must be exercised, especially when there are *servers* involved, that everyone does get a chance to transmit.

**FIGURE 15–10**
Token-Ring Token Format

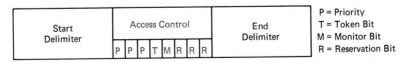

**Token Bit.** The *token bit* (T) is the bit that defines whether the token is empty or contains data. If a device wants to transmit data, it looks at the priority bits to make sure the level of access is acceptable and then looks at the token bit. If it is a 0, the token is empty. The device then changes the token bit to a 1 and proceeds to send out a data frame. After the data frame goes around the ring, the transmitting device changes the token bit back to a 0 (a device is not allowed to transmit two data frames in a row).

**Monitor Bit.** The *monitor bit* (M) provides a capability for a particular type of malfunction detection and correction. Based on the address of each device in a ring, one of them becomes a *monitor* device (every device in a token ring has a different address burned into the ROM of its address card at the factory; the address is determined by the IEEE 802.5 committee). When a data frame comes by the monitor device it changes the monitor bit to a 1. If the same frame comes by a second time (source address is the same), it is obviously an error, so the monitor device grabs the frame and generates a new token allowing the ring to continue in operation.

**Reservation Bit.** The three *reservation bits* provide a mechanism for a lower-priority device to transmit sooner than it might otherwise be capable of doing. If an empty token comes by a device with a higher level of priority than the device has, the device can set the reservation bits to its own level. Upon reaching the source device, instead of decrementing the priority down by just one level, it is adjusted down to the level requested in the reservation bits. That still may not guarantee access to the ring because a higher priority level device can put in a higher level reservation before getting back to the source device, or a higher level priority device can grab the token before it gets back to the initial requestor. Again, care must be used to make sure adequate access is available to all devices on the ring.

One area of potential problems when using token rings is the orientation of most significant to least significant bit. Normally that is on a left-to-right basis, but IBM uses it right-to-left. The IEEE 802.5 committee has opted to utilize the IBM form, so any time there is a bridge or a gateway to another LAN this must be taken into account.

When a device needs to transmit data and it receives a token with a 0 T bit and appropriate priority level, it changes the T bit to a 1 and thereby creates an information frame format, shown in Fig. 15–11. When transmitting information

**FIGURE 15–11**
Token-Ring Information Frame Format

| Start Delimiter (1 Byte) | Access Control (1 Byte) | Frame Control (1 Byte) | Destination Address (6 Bytes) | Source Address (6 Bytes) | Routing Information (Variable Length) | Information Field (4048 Bytes Max.) | Frame Check Sequence (4 Bytes) | End Delimiter (1 Byte) | Frame Status (1 Byte) |
|---|---|---|---|---|---|---|---|---|---|

|←———————————Header 15 Bytes———————————→|←———————Information Field———————→|←——————Trailer 6 Bytes——————→|

there is a single byte start delimiter and the access control byte with the same bits as in the token format. Following that is a frame control byte, which tells the receiver the type of frame it is going to be and how to buffer it. Then there is a 6-byte destination address field and a 6-byte source address field telling all receivers who is to get the information and who sent it. Together these 15 bytes make up what is known as the *start header*.

The next field, of variable length, is called the *datalink control* or *routing information field*. It contains the necessary routing information that is typically utilized by bridges or gateways to go to other rings. Following the routing information field is the actual data or information field, which can be 4048 bytes maximum. The information is followed by a four-byte frame check sequence utilized for error detection and then a single-byte ending delimiter (just like the end delimiter of the token). The end delimiter is followed by a frame status byte used for acknowledgment purposes by the addressed device. The frame check sequence, end delimiter, and frame status byte together are known as the *trailer*.

Although the IBM token ring is compatible with IEEE 802.5, IBM puts in many more control-type messages and network management functions than are defined in the 802.5 specification. Also, token rings can be tied together in a series of small rings that are joined into a single, larger ring, shown in Fig. 15–12. Any one of the individual devices connected to an MAU can be a bridge to another ring, or a gateway to a different network.

## AT&T Datakit and ISN

Two unique forms of LAN connections are the Datakit and ISN systems from AT&T. Conceptually they are very much the same but in operation there is a

**FIGURE 15–12**
Multiple Token Rings

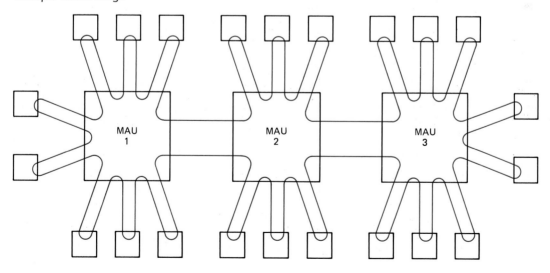

slight difference. Their original purpose was to provide a LAN capability for end users in the carrier environment. Because of divestiture, AT&T could provide a system directly to an end user only if AT&T could be accessed directly. Where direct access was not available, another scheme was needed to enable the local telephone companies to provide the same service. For that reason, Datakit, which is provided to the local telcos by AT&T, is sometimes called a Central Office (CO) based LAN. By utilizing existing local loops, or by using a Centrex system, the switching equipment for providing the LAN could be located on the carrier's site.

Two big advantages of a CO-based LAN are the ease of providing the capability initially and the ability to provide rearrangements right in the central office. Also, no new cable is required and there are no hardware installation problems because the local carrier is responsible for the installation maintenance. In addition, there can be access to other networks or the long-distance carrier environment, which, in the final analysis, would eventually allow integration of all user facilities regardless of their geographic location.

The Datakit version of the CO based LAN is the system provided to the local telephone companies or the end user. A diagram of its configuration is shown in Fig. 15–13. A key to the operation of Datakit is the availability of a wide variety of interface modules (I/Fs). I/Fs connect to the end-user device with whatever protocol is required by the user, such as low-speed TTY, other asynchronous protocols, Bisync, SDLC, or HDLC, and others. The interface device is then connected to a switching module via a coaxial cable.

The operation of Datakit is as follows: Whenever a user wants to transmit information to another location (one user per interface) the I/F goes *off hook,* which indicates that it wants to transmit information to another I/F. Since two or more devices may want to transmit at the same time, each of the I/Fs must contend for access on the contention bus, accomplished by putting a priority code and module address on the bus bit by bit. The I/F device reads the bus at the same time the priority code (which is the originating module address) is put on the contention bus. If the value on the bus differs from what is being transmitted by that device, then another I/F with a higher priority wants the bus also. The lower-priority I/F will drop out of contention. After the priority/address transmission there will only be one I/F left in contention, which then transmits the address of the destination device and information. The transmission is received at the switch module, which replaces the originating address with the destination address or broadcast address. The information follows and is retransmitted to all modules on the receive bus. Only the addressed I/F module accepts the information.

There cannot be a random-type of access on the contention bus as in CSMA/CD. In order for Datakit to operate in a controlled manner, AT&T has provided a clock module that provides synchronization on the transmit bus at a rate of 8.36 MBPS of information per second. The clock module provides the necessary timing pulses to allow each of the I/F devices to transmit on the contention bus simultaneously. The switching module is told which destination address to put on the message at the call set-up time by the transmitting I/F (described above), and the address of the destination station is then stored in the switch

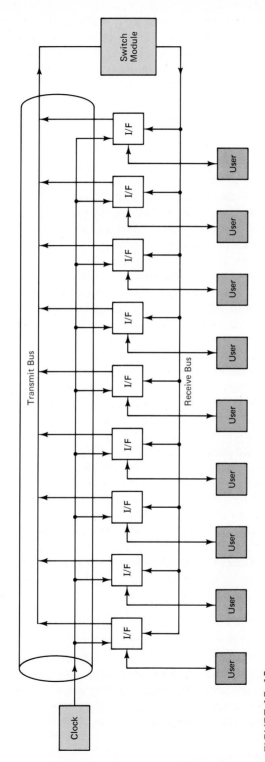

**FIGURE 15–13**
Datakit Virtual Circuit Switch

337

module memory. From that time, all transmission from the transmitting I/F will be addressed to the same receiving I/F until the connection is terminated (just like hanging up the telephone). This mode of operation provides a path between the transmit I/F and the receive I/F only for the time it is physically needed. As such, Datakit is known as a *Virtual Circuit Switch* (VCS). Hundreds of simultaneous paths can exist in a Datakit arrangement, but information is transmitted only when it is actually required.

By 1988, the data rates from the *user* devices to the switch were 75 BPS through 56 KBPS. It is anticipated that this will eventually go up to T-1 rates. Datakits can talk to each other at a rate of 56 KBPS on standard telephone circuits using Dataphone Digital Service, or at 8.36 MBPS over a fiber link when connected within a 3000 meter distance.

There are many variations of implementations of Datakit, some of which are provided by other vendors. The present specification for Datakit provides a total capacity of 44,000 packets of information per second with 16 characters per packet. There can be 3500 connections per node because the bus is used only when transmission is required. Everyone, therefore, shares the same bus. *Star-keeper* is used for Datakit diagnostics and maintenance and can handle up to 40 different nodes. Datakit is compatible with expected ISDN technology.

The Northern Telecom offering that provides both voice and data access to a digital Centrex is called DIALAN, which stands for DMS Integrated Access Local Area Network. DIALAN integrates a DMS 100 switch with a Meridian digital Centrex and commercially available integrated voice/data modules (IVDMs). In actuality, therefore, this is NTI's version of a central-office-based LAN.

A practical example of the preceding type of operation with a Centrex LAN is Intellipath II from New York Telephone Company, which offers simultaneous voice and data connections and incorporates various levels of security for determining authorized access.

ISN, provided by AT&T, implements the same form of operation, except instead of a single bus for both transmission and contention there are two separate buses, as shown in Fig. 15-14. With this mode of operation, while transmission is taking place on the transmit bus, contention is simultaneously taking place on the contention bus for the device that will transmit the next. To reiterate, ISN is provided by AT&T for connection by the user into the AT&T environment directly, while Datakit is provided to either the local telephone company or the end user.

## PC LANs

The final operational methodology to be discussed in this chapter is that of the PC LANs. Although it is obvious that many books could be written about the PC LANs, it is also obvious that by the time they get into print, they will probably be out of date. Not a week goes by without some new announcement of a product or enhancement that becomes available for tying PCs together. Therefore, this

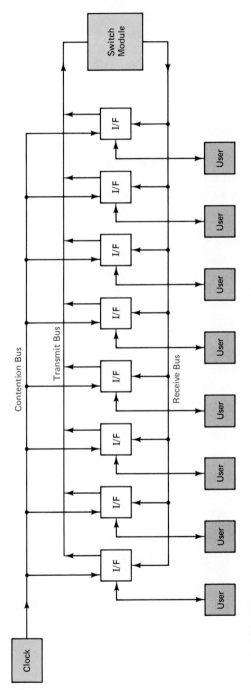

**FIGURE 15-14**
ISN from AT&T

339

section will concentrate on the philosophy behind PC LANs and some of their primary characteristics.

PC LANs are typically narrowband LANs that operate on a bus using one of the token mechanisms. The idea behind a PC LAN is for PCs to share information for files, printing, applications, and the like. Previously, terminals would operate with hosts where the host had all the intelligence and the terminal did nothing more than transmit and receive information that was held and processed at the host. With the advent of PCs came the ability to provide remote computational capability, so PCs could be used both as terminals and as host devices.

Because of their relatively limited capabilities compared to larger host processors, PCs were generally given a specific task when they were connected in a network configuration. Some of the PCs would operate as terminals that processed information and provided applications required by the user while other PCs would provide services like file storage and printing. Multiple terminal emulating PCs could then share the resources of files and I/O requirements from a single source rather than from duplicated facilities dedicated for each PC.

In the early 1980s, the primary limitation of networking PCs together was the operating systems that were very slow in providing access to peripheral devices such as disks. This meant that even though there were transmission capabilities in the 4–8-MBPS range, actual data throughput was in the range of 30–50 KBPS. To overcome this deficiency many vendors provided hardware and software to be installed within a PC that would emulate the existing operating system but provide operation and access to the peripherals at a much faster rate. The larger vendors in the late 1980s were Novell and 3Com, with others sharing market segments oriented toward specific characteristics.

A typical configuration of a PC LAN is shown in Fig. 15–15. There can be a number of PCs all connected to the same cable through the LAN board provided by the same vendor. Some number of the PCs will operate as terminals, while others will operate as servers. Pictured are a single printer server and a

FIGURE 15–15
Generic PC LAN Configuration

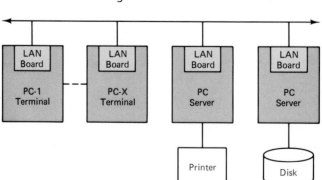

single disk server. There can be many of all types as long as appropriate controls are incorporated to make sure there is no overlapping of definitions.

Many of the PC networks today offer connections to another of the same type network through a bridge and to different networks through gateways. Interfacing is a very fast changing and growing environment because of all the individual applications needed within a large organization, but it should be kept in mind that there is always a need to eventually communicate with other networks and/or computers. Therefore, when you choose a PC LAN vendor, you should make sure that the appropriate interconnections will be available for you to tie the individual applications together as well as into the larger network environment. As this requirement grows you will probably see the vendors offer devices that will allow any type of LAN to talk to any other type of LAN through a single interface. Banyan offered such a device as early as the mid-1980s through their *Virtual Networking System* (VINES), which incorporated a whole series of conversions into a single device. As more and more applications are required to communicate with other applications, the economics for providing an *all-in-one* type of interconnection device will grow.

# F
## INTERCONNECTION

Before going on to describe other forms of networking utilizing different media, it is necessary to describe some of the devices that are used for interconnecting different LANs. Although there is a wide diversity of devices and names given to those devices with corresponding overlaps in definitions, four devices will cover almost all of these connections.

### Bridge

A bridge is typically a device that links LANs that have identical protocols so that two or more physical networks can be combined to form a single logical network. This mode of operation is similar to the second layer of the OSI protocol (the datalink layer). A bridge allows you to move information between LANs as if they comprised one big LAN and a typical bridge is shown in Fig. 15–16. There are three different LANs, possibly performing three different applications. They could also be performing different portions of the same application. Because this is a bus arrangement, there would be a high probability of collisions due to the multiplicity of using devices if everybody was tied together on the same cable. By configuring three different LANs only common application users will have to compete for the cable access. If a device on one LAN needs to talk to a device on another LAN, the bridge can be used to get to the other LAN. You

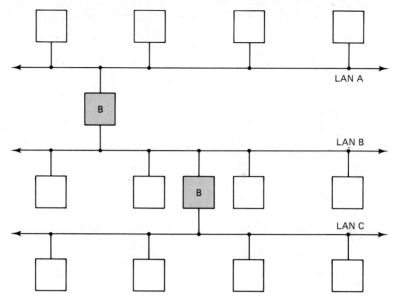

**FIGURE 15–16**
LAN Bridges

end up with three separate LANs, with three access capabilities operating simultaneously. Only for those instances where traffic is destined for another LAN will the transmission go through one or more bridges to get to that LAN.

You must be careful when utilizing a bridge that the addresses on the different LANs are all unique and that the frame size of the transmission is compatible (different fixed lengths or variable lengths). A typical application is in a graphics environment where designers work on different portions of the same product and need to communicate with each other to get the entire product put together. The same thing holds true for working on different portions of the same document.

## Gateway

A *gateway* is a device that may be described as providing either six or seven layer support for the OSI protocol structure. It is designed to link networks that have entirely different protocols. What is important about this device is that information transfers can be initiated in either direction, unlike terminal emulation which is only one way (host to terminal). Gateways involve the incorporation of the various characteristics of different networks into one device to provide storage plus full protocol conversions. Gateways are used to connect one kind of LAN to another, like an Ethernet to a token ring, and also to connect a LAN to a different network such as an SNA or X.25 network. The term *gateway* is also used to describe a device that will connect two non-LAN networks together, such as an X.25 to SNA gateway.

### Router

A *router* falls somewhere between a bridge and a gateway in that it typically operates at the third layer of OSI. Its use is to route packets between the same type of LAN networks (such as Ethernet to Ethernet) that may have different packet sizes. The difference between the router and a bridge is that the router provides the necessary buffering for packet size differences and may also include addressing capabilities for connection to ultimate networks that may not be adjacent. Depending on the source, you may find a router described as either a bridge or a gateway, but in any case it performs the unique function of moving information between LANs with different packet sizes.

### Protocol Converter

*Protocol converters* are sometimes referred to as gateways because protocol conversion is the primary function of a gateway, but if the function of the remote device or terminal is only to provide a file transfer in a terminal emulation mode, the device may be called a protocol converter. Because of this mode of operation, protocol converters fall between bridges and gateways in that they provide more capability than a bridge and router but less than a gateway. The biggest difference between a protocol converter and a gateway is that the protocol converter does not allow initiation of transfers in both directions like a gateway. This is evident in the IBM environment, where a 3274-type controller cannot initiate a transmission to a host. A protocol converter will operate just like the 3274, whereas the gateway would allow the device that is performing the 3274-type functions to initiate a transmission to the host or a host emulator.

A separate topic relating to all LANs is the need to provide a single network monitor for all the networks that are connected (many vendors are in the process of developing this). Most individual networks have individual network managers, but in the future they must be able not only to talk to each other but also to provide a single centralized source for integrated network management.

## G
## OTHER TYPES OF LANS

Besides all the LANs just described, there are other ways to move information within a facility. Some are commercially available and are listed as follows:

## LANs on Power Lines

Moving information on residential power lines has been done for many years at 300 BPS. Today most energy management and building control environments use a broadcast radio frequency in the 50–450 KHz range on those lines. Two such companies are Gridcomm and Secom General. They utilize FSK to split the bandwidth into different channels. Secom, for example, utilizes four discrete channels with each one transmitting information using FSK. They call the network *Powernet*. The four channels are utilized as two separate half-duplex networks or a single full-duplex network that can handle up to 500 devices, although initial implementations were limited to 50. Powernet is designed to allow data transmission at 9600 BPS, but with inherent error-control capabilities the actual data transmission is up to 4800 BPS. *Gridnet,* the system offered by Gridcomm, provides for up to 32 users with eight separate devices that can transmit simultaneously at rates up to 19.2 KBPS.

Applications for power line transmissions are typically electronic mail, file transfer, and peripheral device sharing. Standard transmission with polling and calling in a master/slave relationship can be set up or a token passing operation may be used.

## Microwave

Another method for setting up a LAN is with in-house microwave transmission utilizing the frequencies between 600 MHz and 39 GHz. A company that provides a network like this is Broadcom, with a system they call *Synap Z*. Synap Z uses a *phased array retrodirective* antenna, which provides for transmission of radio beams in the exact reverse direction in which a transmission came in. The same frequency can thus be used for multiple paths without interference because there is no overlap. The approximate distance over which one of these systems can operate is a little over one mile when there is no electrical interference. Because telephone and data terminals can move, this might be a very good way for maintaining communications with devices that must be moved all the time, as there is no wiring required.

Multiple locations can be tied together with microwave. Each building can have a node for all the devices within that building, and the nodes can communicate between themselves by the same microwave method or by wire. Inside the building intermediate frequencies link to specific terminals through ceiling antennas set up like a sprinkler system. The calling device has no selection logic in it. It generates an address by its own transmitting frequency, the time slot it transmits in, and its location (all devices are given a particular time slot for transmitting). The microwave system is good for data and video, with possible future application in the voice world. However, until it can be demonstrated as an economically feasible product without excessive microwave transmitter power levels, this system is not likely to gain wide acceptance.

There have also been proposals for infrared LANs, which are related to the microwave type of operation, although they are not in the same frequency range.

## RS232 Networks

The RS232 or EIA530 form of connection is not really a LAN, but could provide a LAN support function. The idea is to have a LAN arrangement set up in any one of the previous forms which is then interfaced to the user device through the standard RS232 interface. The LAN in this case operates strictly as a bit-moving medium with the user devices responsible for all logical levels of communication. The RS232 interface compensates for different data rates, frame formats, flow controls, and other parameters that must be standardized when going through RS232. A significant advantage of this type of interface is that the device can be connected to the LAN over a much greater distance than other typical LAN interfaces (especially if EIA530 is used). Uses for an RS232 type network could be for port contention or port switching to access different CPUs, device sharing, and reducing overall RS232 wiring since communication between multiple devices can be routed over the LAN.

There are many other types of vendor products, but as was said at the beginning of this chapter, even though the details may be different, they are conceptually similar to the LANs that have been described here. The best way to compare LAN capabilities is to determine what your requirements are with respect to throughput, error detection, distances between locations, and speed of individual devices. You may find that you need a combination of LANs to take care of all of your applications. In those cases, you may want to utilize multiple different types of LANs with gateways or protocol converters between them. The future of LANs seems to be leaning toward the integration of various networks into one big logical network, so that any user can talk to any other user regardless of where they are connected and what application they are performing. If users need to utilize the same application in the future, the goal is to allow them to physically communicate over one or more of the existing, in-house networks.

One additional point to consider here which is very important for the future of all LANs is the issue of security. *Security* in this instance refers to the fact that anybody on a LAN can *see* whatever is being transmitted on that LAN. No one even knows that an intruding device is on the line, because there is no way to identify all the valid *listeners*. Without ever being an active device, an intruder can tap into a LAN and monitor all transmissions on the line, acting as a *passive listener* able to record all transmissions. If you are in a situation where security is important, some new products becoming available will allow for encryption of individual information portions of selected transmissions. There is a fair amount of overhead involved with this, but as the use of fully integrated networks grows, security will become an even more significant problem, especially if you want to transmit out of your local environment and tie into a long-distance network to a remote location. All of your data could potentially be accessed in a passive mode by an external, unauthorized listener. By the same token it probably is possible for one of the unauthorized intruders to emulate one of your valid devices and access your system the way many telephone hackers are doing today. If security is a potential problem for you, you must either develop your own external precautionary steps, or remain vulnerable until applicable products are available.

## H

## FIBER DISTRIBUTED DATA INTERFACE

Finally, one of the communications media that LANs are moving toward for the future is a fiber-optic based cabling system. To make all of the potential users of fiber compatible, the American National Standards Institute (ANSI) X3T9.5 committee is in the process of developing a standard that will be called the *Fiber Distributed Data Interface* (FDDI). The idea behind this protocol is to make use of the high-speed potential of fiber. The FDDI will provide for 100-MBPS transmission in a token-passing scheme. The standard calls for a redundant dual ring for fault tolerance purposes.

Both asynchronous and synchronous transmissions can be accommodated in FDDI. The asynchronous transmissions will be used for short, bursty traffic, like data, while the synchronous transmission will be used for transmitting voice, video, robotic control, and any other application that needs a guaranteed bandwidth and/or access time.

The criteria for network configuration will provide for up to 500 separate stations connected in the ring with a total path length of 100 KM. The stations that connect to the ring will have two classes. A Class A station provides for two physical links to the ring and looks like a *serial* device in the ring. If a Class A station goes out of service, a bypass capability is provided so that it will not break the ring.

A Class B station has only a single physical link to the ring, but can act like a concentrator-type node with other devices connected to it. In other words, multiple devices can be connected to a single Class B station so that they are part of the overall ring, but only the Class B station is an integral part of the ring. If a Class B station goes out of service, all of the other stations connected to it will go out of service as well.

Operation of the ring takes place in two separate modes. The first mode is called the *setup* and provides for the establishment of the ring in a predetermined methodology. At first, each station provides a connection to its neighbor station on a link-by-link basis. When those individual links are established, each of the stations negotiates a link to its neighbor on the other side. Linking continues until all the devices in the entire ring are linked together in a single, continuous ring. There are two separate paths for each of the rings, which provides for redundancy. Bad links are found during negotiation, causing the ring to double back on itself by providing a path connecting the forward and backward rings. The redundancy is then eliminated, but the integrity of the ring is maintained because the loopback process occurs on each side of the break. Two separate breaks in the ring will cause some portion of the stations to be inaccessible, because the loopback will go up to one break on one side of the ring and up to the second break on the other side of the ring. The devices between the two breaks cannot be accessed.

The second portion of the setup process involves the separate negotiation for a maximum delay through the ring, performed by a complex *bidding* process. The node or station that requires the shortest time delay before it receives the token again ends up with the priority for establishing the maximum delay time allowable. Once the ring and the maximum delay time are established, operation can start.

The transmission mechanism for FDDI is very much like the IEEE 802.5 token-ring specification, but there are some significant differences. First of all, 802.5 uses a *differential Manchester code,* which involves a transition in the middle of each bit, plus, *if a bit is a 0, a transition is also required at the beginning of the bit time.* An example of this is shown in Fig. 15–17. FDDI does not use differential Manchester, but instead uses a special coded sequence in which each 4 bits of data are encoded into a 5-bit sequence, so that on the network there is a guarantee of a maximum of 3 bit times between level transitions, which in turn provides adequate *clocking* information. The reason for doing this is a reduction in total bandwidth. With differential Manchester, utilizing 100 MBPS would require 200 MBPS bandwidth, while 4 bits encoded into 5 will require only 125 MBPS of bandwidth.

The individual stations, or *nodes,* of FDDI operate at the IEEE 802.2 level (the Medium Access Control—MAC) and work on half byte increments (called a *nibble*), which makes them very efficient and quite different from 802.5, where individual bits must be processed.

Another major difference between FDDI and 802.5 is that a new token can be initiated immediately after the transmission of the last packet of a transmission. The station does not have to wait until receiving its own transmission around the ring before issuing a new token, thus making much more efficient use of the total bandwidth of the ring.

Another significant feature of FDDI is the incorporation of a priority scheme (somewhat like 802.5). Also, connections that *break* after the ring is in operation are *self-healing* through another internal operation called *beaconing,* which is like the ring initialization previously described. Beaconing finds a break

**FIGURE 15–17**
Differential Manchester Code

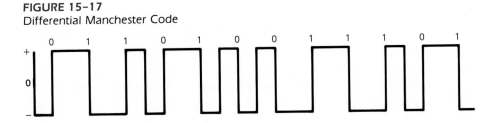

and provides the looping back between the rings to give a complete path again up to both sides of the break. Before allowing data to be transmitted again, however, a new negotiation process for the maximum delay time of the token transmission must be established for the new ring. The renegotiation maintains the specific maximum delay integrity of the reestablished rings.

A 32 bit CRC is used to detect link errors, so marginal links or devices can be identified. Each identified error, not corrected, increments a counter and is then passed on unchanged. When an erroneous transmission is passed on, a bit is set that tells the next station on the ring that an error is contained in this particular transmission. That bit tells the second workstation not to increment its error counter, so that only the device that first receives the error will increment the error counter. By taking a look at the various error counters, the user can determine which links are causing a problem.

Given the additional speed of fiber, FDDI should definitely be considered where applications require large volumes of data or quick response time. IBM has already stated that they will go to FDDI (probably because they already operate in a token-ring mode), but probably in stages. IBM announced a 16-MBPS ring in 1988 and it would probably incorporate then a form of FDDI by the end of 1990. Other vendors may follow, but if their modes of operation are different (CSMA/CD or Token Passing), there will probably be other considerations before they decide to change or come up with a different mode of operation.

## QUESTIONS

1. Describe the major differences between a narrowband LAN and a wideband LAN.
2. What are the five most common topologies used in a LAN network?
3. What does the IEEE 802 series of specifications describe?
4. Describe the operation of data flow for a CSMA/CD LAN with and without collisions.
5. Describe the token-passing operation on a bus.
6. Why do you need a cable terminator at the ends of your LAN cable?
7. What is the difference between Ethernet and StarLAN?
8. Why does the Ethernet message have a minimum required length?
9. Describe the operation of a typical wideband LAN for information flow between multiple users in different applications.
10. Describe the operation of a token-ring LAN.
11. What is the operational difference between Datakit and ISN?
12. What is the primary difference between a PC LAN on a bus and a public LAN on a bus?
13. Describe the functions of a bridge, gateway, router, and protocol converter.
14. What is meant by the term deterministic? Probabilistic?

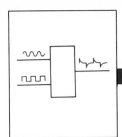

# 16

# The Digital World
# with ISDN

## BACKGROUND

Since the advent of modems in the 1950s, the majority of data transmissions have been in analog form to utilize the voice-oriented telephone network. Starting in 1962, with the growth of satellite transmission and the conversion of higher-level telephone switching offices to digital switches, digital transmission has been one of the fastest growing areas in data communications. Not only is the amount of voice traffic being digitized growing, but the total amount of data to be transmitted is also growing at a substantial rate. If we add to the voice and data volume the expanding requirements for video, facsimile, graphics, and other forms of information, the desirability of maintaining an end-to-end digital capability is obviously becoming a major criterion for network decisions in today's communication environment.

Until recently, the biggest problem facing the implementation of a digital communication path was the *last mile*, which is the connection from the Class 5 telephone office to the user's site—the local loop. Because local loops are predominantly twisted pair copper wire they cannot support a digital signal for a long enough distance (due to resistance and capacitance of the wire, described in Chapter 4) for the signal to be recognized in the local telephone office and regenerated for transmission into the remainder of the telephone network. Not only

349

was the local loop a bottleneck, but a significant proportion of the Class 5 offices could not handle digital transmissions.

Excluding user-owned networks, which could transmit via satellite transponders directly, AT&T was the first to come out with generally available service that would support end-to-end digital transmission in the late 1970s. The service identified the appropriate Class 5 switching offices in specific cities and provided them with digital switches and enough capability in the local loop to support end-to-end digital transmission. Originally, *regenerative repeaters* were put in the local loops approximately every 3000 ft (1 km) to regenerate the signal between the user and the telephone office. In today's environment, extensive amounts of fiber-optic cables are being installed that can support digital transmissions for longer distances than twisted pair copper. This chapter will deal with digital transmission and many of the applications for which it is well suited.

## B

## THE DIGITAL CIRCUIT

Functionally, a digital transmission circuit looks identical to an analog transmission circuit except that some of the devices create and work with pulses instead of analog carriers. A typical circuit for digital transmission is shown in Fig. 16–1. The connection starts with a standard user DTE and an interface that is RS232, EIA530, or V.35-compatible, depending on the distance and the transmission speed between the DTE and the digital interface device. The device that connects to the DTE is still a DCE, but instead of an analog signal output, the standard RS232 data signals are converted to a specific bipolar digital signal. The bipolar signal (described in more detail later in this chapter) generates pulses only when there are 1 bits, and the pulses alternate direction, positive and negative, sometimes called *alternate mark inversion*.

The *data service unit*, or *digital service unit*, as it is sometimes called (DSU), which functions as the interface to the user DTE, cannot be implemented as a standalone unit. When digital services first evolved, the local telephone company provided a device on the user's premises called NCTE (Network Channel Terminating Equipment). AT&T provided the DSU and the local telephone company provided the NCTE to terminate the local loop. The NCTE provided the necessary impedance matching, loopback capability, and diagnostic capabilities for the local telephone companies to service the local digital loop. As part of the divestiture process, however, the local Bell telephone companies were no longer allowed to provide NCTE, so it became known as a *channel service unit* (CSU). Even though it performed exactly the same function, it had to be provided by a vendor who was not part of the local Bell telephone company.

The result is that the DSU and CSU could be provided by different vendors and connected by a cable with 15 wires. An alternative is a DSU/CSU combination device, which is more commonly used.

The CSU is connected to a four-wire local loop that can accommodate bipo-

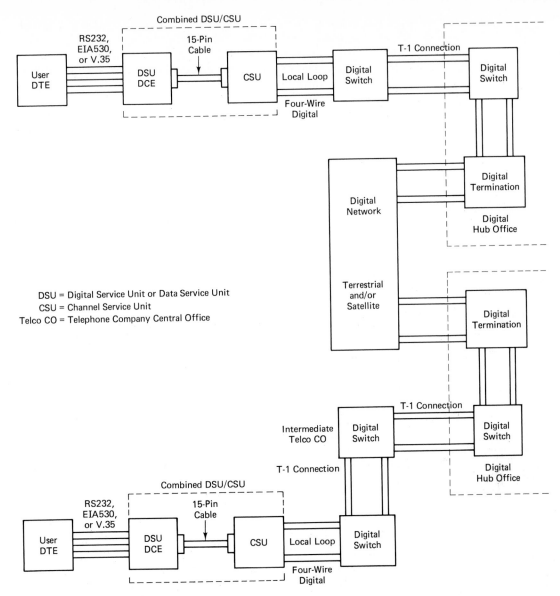

**FIGURE 16–1**
Digital Circuit Configuration

lar digital signals. The CSU connection can only be made to those local telco Class 5 switches capable of terminating the digital circuits and then accessing T-1 circuits (described later in this chapter) that connect to other digital switches for propagation through the network. The final connection is made to the same type of Class 5 digital switch at the remote location. The final digital switch connects a four-wire local loop to another CSU, which can be either an independent device or a combined CSU/DSU. Therefore as far as the user is concerned, the modems are replaced by DSUs, and from an operational point of view, that is the only visible effect on the connection.

Some history might be appropriate here to get an idea of how the digital network evolved. It all started in 1962 when AT&T saw that it would be less expensive to design and develop digital circuits and equipment than to continue with the existing analog technology. Chips made it much less expensive to provide comparable circuit capability with pulses in place of analog signals. In addition, it would provide a much easier method to diagnose and find circuit problems in the digital circuits than in analog circuits, where degradations could be intermittent and varied.

Some very basic decisions were made, the primary one being the implementation of DS-1 signaling, which involves the establishment of 24 separate and independent channels that convert voice to binary bits. By utilizing Pulse Code Modulation (PCM), the voice signal is sampled 8000 times per second, and each of these samples generates 1 byte of information (8 bits). To incorporate all 24 channels into one transmission sequence, the term *frame* was established. It consists of 1 byte from each channel, or 192 bits. An extra bit, called a *framing bit*, is added to each of the frames for synchronization purposes, which actually makes the frames 193 bits long.

Expanding on the mathematics, 8000 frames per second at 193 bits each gives a required transmission rate of 1.544 MBPS, called the T-1 transmission rate utilizing DS-1 signaling (a detailed description of T-1 operation will be provided later in this chapter). This method has been used in the long-distance network ever since and ultimately became available on an end-to-end basis for end users in 1983.

The T-1 transmission rate has been incorporated into a hierarchy for multiplexing purposes. The hierarchy, shown in Fig. 16–2, allows the user of common network facilities to handle extremely high data rates incorporating hundreds or thousands of simultaneous voice conversations.

The channel bank is a very important piece of equipment in the digital environment. A *channel bank* converts the analog voice signals to binary bits, and vice versa. The D-1 channel bank was the first of these devices that was compatible with the original DS-1 signaling working with one frame at a time. The D-2 channel bank came next. It introduced the *superframe* format, which consists of a 12-frame sequence. The 193rd bit forms a unique sequence for frame synchronization so the equipment knows where each frame starts and ends and which eight bits belong to which channels. The superframe framing bits are repeated every 12 frames. The D-2 frame also utilized *stolen bit signaling*, which consists of the least significant bit in frames 6 and 12 carrying line signaling and status information.

The D-1D channel bank made the D-2 frame compatible with the original D-1 channel banks. This evolution continued into today's environment, where the D-4 channel bank is the most prevalent device being used. D-4 significantly improved the hardware capability for the digital network.

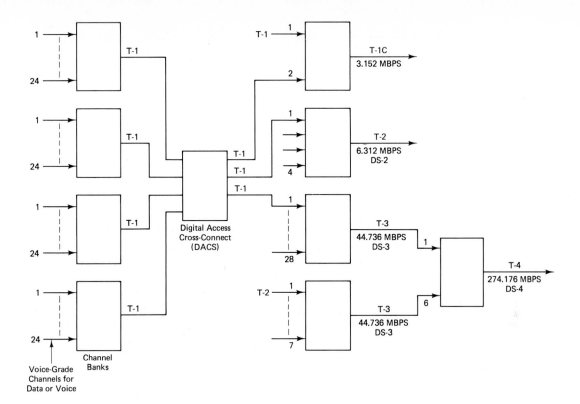

**FIGURE 16-2**
Digital Hierarchy

There is another upgrade that AT&T is beginning to incorporate into the network today, called the *extended superframe* (ESF), which is also based on DS-1 requirements, but the 193rd bit is used differently. ESF was originally proposed in 1979 to find line problems while the circuit was still in service. A detailed description of this operation will be incorporated into Section E of this chapter.

It is anticipated that continuing upgrades will be made in the network, especially as the need for ISDN services grows. It is also quite possible that these upgrades may mean substantial replacements of existing equipment. The changes may not be readily incorporated due to the investment involved in existing equipment. Therefore, the potential network user must constantly be aware of the status of circuits being interfaced because different levels or capabilities of service may be available at different locations, and they may not be compatible with each other in terms of their capabilities. What this means is that all of the features available at one end may not be available at the other end of the circuit, and therefore you may not be able to take full advantage of the capabilities being offered.

To understand the operation of the digital network it is first necessary to get an idea of the various equipment that makes up the network. Since most equipment available today comes from AT&T, their devices will be described as the typical examples. However, other vendors do provide equivalent offerings of both hardware and network services.

## DSU/CSU

The DSU/CSU is the device that interfaces the user's DTE to the digital line. The AT&T designation for the DSU/CSU when used by itself is WE500A, which can transmit at rates of 2400, 4800, 9600, and 56,000 BPS (newly developed equipment is anticipated to have 19.2 KBPS capability also). In addition to converting the RS232 signal to a bipolar baseband signal (a single transmitter at any one time), the WE500A also performs clock recovery, signal regeneration, and automatic equalization of the circuit. It also provides analog and digital channel loop back for trouble isolation and can be tested end-to-end with the same type of DSU/CSU at the other end.

Another type of DSU from AT&T, designated the WE500B, is utilized when the user has his or her own external clock recovery, regeneration, control code recognition, and zero suppression capability, otherwise provided by the WE500A. When the WE500B is used, however, a separate CSU must be used. The CSU is a line driver and receiver that provides a transmit pair of wires, a receive pair of wires, a ground, and status leads. It acts as a circuit interface to the four-wire local-loop circuit and can perform channel loop-back functions.

## Channel Bank

The channel bank provides carrier conversion between the voice channel and a T-1 circuit. The D-4 channel bank is the most common today and can accept up to 50 different inputs. The outputs can be

2—DS-1 outputs at 1.544 MBPS each

1—DS-1C output at 3.152 MBPS each

$\frac{1}{2}$—DS-2 output at 3.152 MBPS when multiplexing two D-4s into a single DS-2

The D-4 channel bank can also have data inputs at 2.4, 4.8, 9.6, or 56 KBPS. A diagram of a simple D-4 channel bank as it is most often used is shown in Fig. 16–3. There are 24 voice channels integrated into a single T-1 channel at the DS-1 signaling rate.

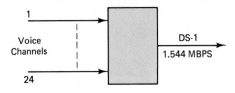

**FIGURE 16–3**
Channel Bank

## Digital Cross-Connect (DCS)

The digital cross-connect provides a connection between various T-1 circuits. It allows the splitting up of T-1 channels into their individual voice channels and then recombining the individual channels in a different grouping onto another T-1 channel. A typical example is shown in Fig. 16–4. Within AT&T the DCS is known as a DACS (Digital Access Cross-Connect System) and comes in a variety of forms and capacities that allow multiple channels of incoming T-1 circuits to be integrated into any desired combination of other T-1 circuits for routing purposes.

The DCS can be thought of as a nonblocking, time division digital switch that interconnects multiple synchronous bit streams. The DCS has been compared with a solid-state version of a wiring patch panel. One of the larger units used by AT&T provides for the integration of 128 DS-1 channels, of which AT&T uses one for test purposes, leaving 127 DS-1 channels or 3048 DS-0 channels (voice channels) that can be cross connected and put into any combination of composite T-1 circuits. An entire DS-1 channel can be switched, or the individual DS-0 channels can be switched, to any other DS-1 channel on the switch. For the future, AT&T has already stated that they anticipate that their DACS equipment will at least incorporate capabilities like protocol conversion, message handling, store and forward applications, and diagnostic network features. This channel manipulation function is sometimes referred to as the separation and concentration of individual DS-0 channels.

As digital cross-connect equipment evolves, different terms are being used to describe the various input and output capabilities. A 1/1 DACS allows T-1 channels on the input to be rerouted to other T-1 channels on the output. A 3/1 DACS integrates T-1 channels with T-3, and a 3/3 DACS allows T-3 channels

**FIGURE 16–4**
Digital Cross Connect (AT&T—DACS)

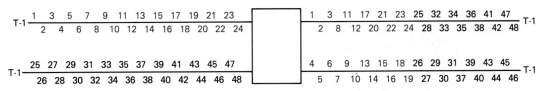

to be intermixed with other T-3 channels. Another use for a DACS will be for routing around circuit breaks.

## Multiplexers

The multiplexers actually do just that. If you refer back to Fig. 16–2 you will see the digital hierarchy in which the various multiplexers are described with each of their capacities. For convenience they are listed here in tabular form.

| CIRCUIT DESIGNATION | DIGITAL SIGNAL DESIGNATION | DATA RATE | EQUIVALENT VOICE CHANNELS |
|---|---|---|---|
| T-0 | | 64 KBPS | 1 |
| T-1 | DS-1 | 1.544 MBPS | 24—PCM/48 ADPCM* |
| T-1C | DS-1C | 3.152 MBPS | 48 |
| T-2 | DS-2 | 6.312 MBPS | 96 |
| T-3 | DS-3 | 44.736 MBPS | 672 |
| T-4 | DS-4 | 274.176 MBPS | 4032 |

*PCM: Pulse Code Modulation; requires 64 KBPS for digitized voice
ADPCM: Adaptive Differential Pulse Code Modulation; requires 32 KBPS for digitized voice

There is another set of multiplexers for digital transmission that can be utilized by the end user. The first one is a standard point-to-point multiplexer that supports a single active T-1 link supplying access to each of the individual 24 channels at the user's own facilities. This type of multiplexer is called a *T-1 multiplexer* and is described in Chapter 11.

The second type of multiplexer is known as a *drop-and-insert* multiplexer, shown in Fig. 16–5. The drop-and-insert multiplexer is utilized where the user needs to remove some DS-0 channels, add others, and at the same time maintain T-1 capacity between the individual locations along a circuit path. The drop-and-insert locations are normally geographically dispersed, so a substantial amount of network capacity can be incorporated into the system by utilizing the available DS-0 channels that exist in each point-to-point connection. The result is that there may be a single T-1 capacity connection on an end-to-end basis, but the individual point-to-point connections may have different users in the individual DS-0 channels.

A third type of multiplexer sometimes used is called a *networking multiplexer*, with which several T-1 circuits can be configured with a DCS such that entire DS-1 channels or individual DS-0 channels may be switched at individual user locations.

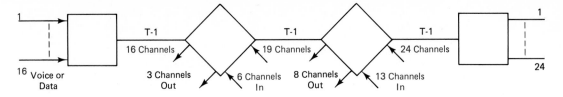

**FIGURE 16-5**
Drop-and-Insert Multiplexers

# D

## DIGITAL SERVICES

### DDS and DDS-2

There are two primary services that are being provided by AT&T initially, Dataphone Digital Service and dial digital. Dataphone Digital Service (DDS) involves providing a four-wire leased circuit to the customer premises with connection to the digital network on an end-to-end basis. Figure 16–1 is representative of what such a circuit would look like. Digital circuits are available anywhere the local telephone companies have the ability to provide both a digital local loop and connection to a long-distance digital carrier, but keep in mind that many areas of the country will not be capable of accommodating digital service until their Class 5 central offices are replaced. If you can't get to the local telephone office digitally, and the AT&T Point of Presence (POP) is not close enough, you may not be able to obtain digital service at all (unless you go via direct satellite). Many people are surprised to find out that the local telephone company cannot provide the level of service they need when they build new facilities in suburban or rural areas. It wasn't until 1987 that Chicago became the first major city in the United States to be capable of providing digital service to all locations in that area, so even though there may be digital service around you, you need to find out from either the local or the long-distance carrier whether digital service will be available for your specific facilities.

DDS involves specific rates of data transmission: 2400, 4800, 9600, and 56000 BPS. In 1987 it was announced that 19.2 KBPS would soon be available, and 64 KBPS clear channel will eventually be available also. Each one of these subrates requires a full 64 KBPS DS-0 channel within which the specific subrate being used is identified. Information is routed through the digital network using only digital transmission, resulting in a very low error rate. Under certain conditions it is possible that there may be an analog link somewhere in the circuit; if so, it is strongly recommended that you not go digital at all because the analog distortion will cause additional errors in the data being transmitted.

One of the new features available with DDS is the ability to provide multiplexing for you in the carrier's office. This means you can then have circuits in a multidrop configuration without putting multiplexers on your own site. The multidrop configuration allows incorporation of multiple users into higher speed circuits that can eventually be integrated into T-1 or T-3 circuits.

In setting up a DDS circuit the DSU is configured for the particular rate to be utilized, as is the interface at the Class 5 telephone office. It would seem that changing rates later should be a relatively easy process because the capability is all in the same device, but nothing could be further from the truth. The mechanics of implementing new data rates on digital circuits involve the administrative over-heads of ordering an entirely new line, so you cannot just *flip switches*. You may even get an entirely different local loop and leased line. If this is the situation in your area, and you anticipate increasing the transmission rate within a relatively short period of time due to volume growth, it is suggested that you go with the higher data rate to begin with. Since all local and long-distance telephone companies vary in their mechanization schemes, it always pays to check on what the implementation time for a new line or a changed line would be if you anticipate changing rates.

At the time of this writing it appears that AT&T is developing a global strategy for network management and control to tie together and upgrade their existing services, including ISDN. Based on what they have done in the past AT&T will probably come up with their own draft specifications for this strategy, but it is likely that they will conform somewhat to the global network standards being considered by organizations such as the American National Standards Institute (ANSI) and the International Standards Organization (ISO).

Part of the global strategy involves the integration of various local telephone company services where, for one, it is no longer necessary to go through AT&T hubs for DDS timing purposes. As a result the local operating companies can now provide appropriate hubbing and timing for DDS circuits within a LATA.

A potential area of concern for users that became effective in 1988 was approval of the request made to the FCC by the local operating companies that they no longer be required to provide DC power to customers on T-1 local loops. In all standard metallic telephone circuits the local telephone company provides the necessary power to drive the terminal interface equipment. This is not a prob-lem for metallic circuits but could be a significant problem for fiber circuits, because power cannot be provided over fiber strands. Extensive amounts of fiber are being installed in local loops these days and the process is anticipated to con-tinue for a long time. If local loops do not provide power to the CSU/DSU (a *dry* circuit) then the end users will have to provide that power on their own, which must be done very carefully because of the power level and grounding requirements needed to provide safe and reliable service. In addition, dry circuits would make obsolete a substantial amount of equipment already in use, so the transition to all dry circuits will probably take place over an extended length of time.

As a separate but related service for leased DDS there is DDS-2. The pri-mary capability of the DDS-2 offering is the provision of a *secondary channel* to be used for diagnostic purposes. Without DDS-2, if you have a problem with

DDS service, troubleshooting takes place from any one of five tests centers located in different areas of the United States. During testing and troubleshooting the line is inoperative. With the provision of a secondary channel for diagnostic purposes, just as in the analog telephone environment, the user has a much greater capability for diagnosing and identifying the DDS network problems independently.

For utilizing DDS-2, the existing transmission facilities, such as circuits, will remain the same, but there will definitely be equipment differences, especially on the customer site. Any existing DDS equipment will have to be replaced by new DDS-2 equipment. There must also be some changes in the local telephone company hubs because the transmitted bit streams must be handled differently. Pricing is more expensive than standard DDS, but if you don't want to perform the diagnostics yourself, then DDS-2 may be what you want. However, standard DDS may be more than adequate for your purposes if the carriers can isolate and correct problems, with the trade-off being the cost of the service versus the anticipated diagnostic benefits of shorter outages.

Listed here is a comparison of operating rates for DDS and DDS-2.

| CURRENT DDS DATA RATE IN BPS | DDS-2 DIAGNOSTIC RATE IN BPS | ACTUAL OPERATIONAL RATE IN BPS |
| --- | --- | --- |
| 2400 | 133 | 3200 |
| 4800 | 266 | 6400 |
| 9600 | 533 | 12,800 |
| 19,200 | To be determined | To be determined |
| 56,000 | 2666 | 64,000 |
| 64,000 | To be determined | To be determined |

As shown, the numbers differ from typical operational data rates, which is why equipment needs to be changed to accommodate DDS-2. Of significant interest to the end user is that if non-AT&T vendors want to be compatible with DDS-2 they not only have to provide compatible user equipment, but they also have to make sure that the switch at the telephone company office is capable of handling their diagnostic channel. With the technology and costs changing fast, and with the advent of ISDN, before you commit you should always make sure that the most current information is available, especially with regard to the existing and future compatibility of services offered by equipment vendors and carriers.

## Dial Digital

The other major digital service currently available is the *dial digital* or switched 56 KBPS capability. AT&T calls their service *Circuit Switched Digital Capability* (CSDC), while Northern Telecom (NTI) calls theirs *Datapath*. When first announced in 1983 these services were radically different in implementation. The differences meant that the user had to know what kind of vendor switches were in the Class 5 central office and had to have specific site located channel terminating equipment that could interface with those specific local carrier switches. For AT&T the user needed to have a No. 1AESS with digital interface capability or a higher level switch, and for Northern Telecom a DMS-100 was needed. The call establishment procedures were also different. AT&T used a four-state calling setup sequence, which made it necessary first to establish an analog circuit and then to switch to digital transmission; NTI required a proprietary handshake procedure and reversed the information bit sequence being transmitted to the carrier office.

Also, the actual methods of transmission were different, with AT&T using a *ping-pong* approach (one-way-at-a-time transmission) at 144 KBPS, while NTI used 160 KBPS ping-pong. With these incompatibilities, and the proliferation of NTI switches in the local carrier environment, it is no wonder that dial digital was tariffed in only two areas with very limited service until 1987. Then, AT&T and NTI made a historic agreement to compromise on dial digital service. AT&T agreed to eliminate their four-state call setup and NTI agreed to accept a circuit establishment procedure that did not require their proprietary handshake. In addition NTI agreed to reverse the bit sequence for transmission to make it network compatible. As a change for both of them, they agreed to change their transmission methodology from ping-pong to *echo cancellation*. Echo cancellation refers to determining what the signal echo would be at each end of the local loop and then electronically generating a signal that eliminates the echo when it returns, providing a received signal that consists of information only. Both vendors incorporated this procedure because by 1987 technology had advanced enough to make echo cancellation economically feasible.

Dial digital services are expected to be available at the same data rates as standard DDS and will be used for establishing short-term reliable circuits for data flow and as backup circuits for existing leased circuits in case of outage.

The Federal Reserve system already utilizes dial digital for their leased-line backup. They have many four-wire leased lines connecting locations all over the country. If those lines become degraded in any way the users can dial a special number at the local Class 5 office that connects to a special dial access arrangement at an AT&T office. The user enters a security code and the dial access equipment automatically places a call on another line preprogrammed into the unit. The destination receiving unit then calls back using a predetermined number and enters a different security code, which results in a four-wire circuit being established. The backup circuit can then handle the required traffic utilizing the new four-wire connection. This particular case is an example of a dial backup to a leased line providing full four-wire service. Under other conditions, when you dial you only have a two-wire local loop (unless you dial two separate circuits yourself). Only the Federal Reserve system may use this operation today because of regulatory limitations, but it could very well be available to other users in the future. AT&T announced in April 1987 that they were preparing a switched digital capability of 384 KBPS for video services, which, as will be seen later in this chapter, is definitely in line with ISDN-type services.

Dial digital is also referred to as switched 56 KBPS service, but with the advent of clear channel 64 KBPS capability in ISDN, dial digital may eventually also be called switched 64 KBPS service.

The impact that ISDN will have on dial digital transmission when fully implemented is not yet clear. All the capabilities of leased and dial digital could be incorporated into ISDN-type services, so it remains to be seen exactly how AT&T and the other carriers will provide for them in the global ISDN world (described later in this chapter).

One last item: There is a whole series of AT&T high-speed digital services grouped under the name *Accunet*. Accunet services typically start at 1.544 MBPS and are provided on either terrestrial or satellite circuits. In 1987, AT&T announced Accunet 45, which provides digital service at T-3 transmission rates of 44.736 MBPS.

# E

## T-1

Although T-1 and ISDN are usually discussed in the same context and are very much related, they really deal with two different entities. T-1 deals with the signal-level parameters and transmission rate capability, while ISDN deals with the types of services that will be provided to the end user. To appreciate the capabilities of ISDN services you must first understand what is involved in the various transmission parameters within T-1. This section will deal with the T-1 parameters; while Section F deals with specific ISDN services.

A digital line is nothing more than a circuit over which digital signals are transmitted. The equipment at either end of the circuit determines the rate of transmission, although the circuit itself has an impact on the maximum rate due to impedance considerations.

T-1 first came into being in 1962 when AT&T began the conversion of their analog telephone network into a digital network. T-1 is described as a digital transmission capability and is not limited in any way to a particular medium for transmission. The mechanism for control of information to be transmitted through a T-1 link is described as a DS-1 signaling. The parameters of a DS-1 signal are

1.544 million clock intervals per second containing either a 0 or a 1 bit

Each clock interval is nominally 650 nanoseconds (ns)

Signal levels are nominally 3.3 volts (including overshoot) in amplitude for 50 percent of the interval

A 1 bit is either a plus level or a minus level

A 0 bit indicates no pulse during the interval

24 channels (separate data streams) are transmitted as a frame

Each channel contains 8 bits (for a total 192 bits per frame)

There is an additional bit in each frame for synchronization purposes, which means a frame is actually comprised of 193 bits

There will be 8000 frames per second

The signals identifying 1 bits will alternate between plus and minus levels (called a bipolar pulse or alternate mark inversion and is shown in Fig. 16–6)

The format for a DS-1 frame with its 24 channels and 193rd bit for synchronization is shown in Fig. 16–7.

In the original derivation of DS-1 signaling it was necessary to provide some form of call progress information within each channel. In a process known as *bit robbing*, the least significant bit from the sixth frame of the twelve-frame super-frame sequence in each DS-0 channel was replaced with a call progress signaling bit for that channel, called the *A bit*. The least significant bit was also stolen from the twelfth frame of the superframe format and replaced by a signaling bit called a *B bit*. This allowed four different signaling states for call control such as idle/busy, ringing/no ring, and loop open/loop closed. By utilizing the least significant bit from two frames out of 12, there was negligible impact on the voice transmission.

The framing pattern for the *F bit* (193rd bit) of the superframe was established as the sequence 100011011100, which identifies the particular 12 frames of a superframe and could in turn be used by the receiving equipment to identify where the 8 bits of each of the 24 channels were. The D-2 channel banks were the first hardware devices to use the superframe. The D1D channel bank provided a superframe compatible with the original D-1 channel banks. In today's telephone network the D-4 is the most common channel bank in use; its operation

**FIGURE 16–6**
Digital Signal for DS-1

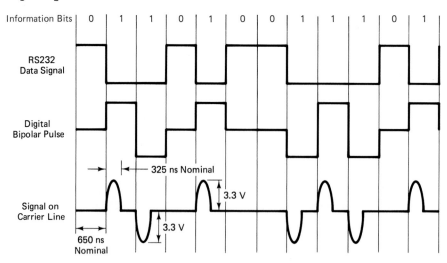

| Channel No. 1 | Channel No. 2 | . . . | Channel No. 12 | . . . | Channel No. 23 | Channel No. 24 | F |
|---|---|---|---|---|---|---|---|

```
1 FRAME:   24 Channels
           8 Bits/Channel
           1 Extra Framing Bit
           193 Bits Total in Frame
```

**FIGURE 16-7**
DS-1 Frame

was described in Section C on digital equipment. There are D-4 channel banks that can handle either two T-1 channels at 3.152 MBPS or four T-1 channels at 6.312 MBPS, allowing either 48 or 96 separate 64-KBPS channels to be handled within a single D-4 channel bank. AT&T has indicated they may be considering a new D-5 channel bank that might be available by the time this book is in print, but the capacity and other specifications had not been published as yet.

The D-4 framing format was developed to further multiplex the individual DS1 frames and was called a *superframe*. The superframe was first used in 1977 and became a network carrier requirement in 1985. It involves the use of 12 consecutive frames where the F bit would repeat itself in each series of 12 frames. This repetition allows the transmission equipment to keep the bit stream in synchronization. The pattern used in the F bit starting with the first frame is 100011011100. The superframe format is shown in Fig. 16–8 with the bits in the appropriate framing pattern sequence.

As stated previously, every sixth and twelfth frame is used to carry channel signaling information. In those frames the eighth bit of each voice channel (DS-0) is used for signaling. If all 24 channels are used there will be 24 signaling bits every sixth and twelfth frame and from every superframe there will be a single AB pair for each DS-0 channel.

The superframe format became standard for all T-1 type transmissions, but contained a serious flaw. In the event that there were errors or line degradations, the entire circuit had to be taken out of service to find the problem because a regenerative process is used in the T-1 network. If noise creates new signals or eliminates existing signals between regenerators, the regenerators *clean up* the

**FIGURE 16-8**
DS-1 Superframe

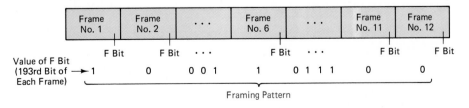

signals. Therefore, the signals going on to the next regenerator look like valid signals occurring at appropriate times. Clean up includes the regeneration of existing signals, so the data stream starts out at each regenerator as a brand new signal string. This is not a problem for voice communications but is intolerable for data.

Because the DS-1 signal is bipolar it contains *no DC component* and could therefore be used with transformers and coils that might exist on the carrier circuit. This was necessary because the analog telephone networks are filled with transformers and coils. If a signal travels through the coils in one direction only, a bias signal level builds up in the coil until no more signal can pass through.

Initially, logic errors can be detected in the D-1 through D-4 framing *only if the line is out of service.* A specific test signal sequence must be generated to insert bits at the transmit end, and the receive end must watch for the known test sequence. Under normal conditions the service provider only performs this test after a customer complains about high error rates. Because of the nature of network conditions, it is quite possible that the trouble may no longer exist by the time the carrier runs the test. If the problem is intermittent, extended outages or periods of degradation could occur from repeated testing.

To eliminate the testing problem, AT&T developed the *Extended Superframe* (ESF) format, which utilizes the F bits of two consecutive superframes in a new predetermined sequence that helps to isolate problems.

Figure 16–9 shows the relationship of the channels to the frame and superframe. Each of 24 channels with their F bits in a single DS-1 frame becomes one of 12 frames in a superframe format (there are 12 bits in this sequence), and 24 DS-1 frames are included in an extended superframe (24 F bits in this sequence).

**FIGURE 16–9**
Channel and Frame Relationships

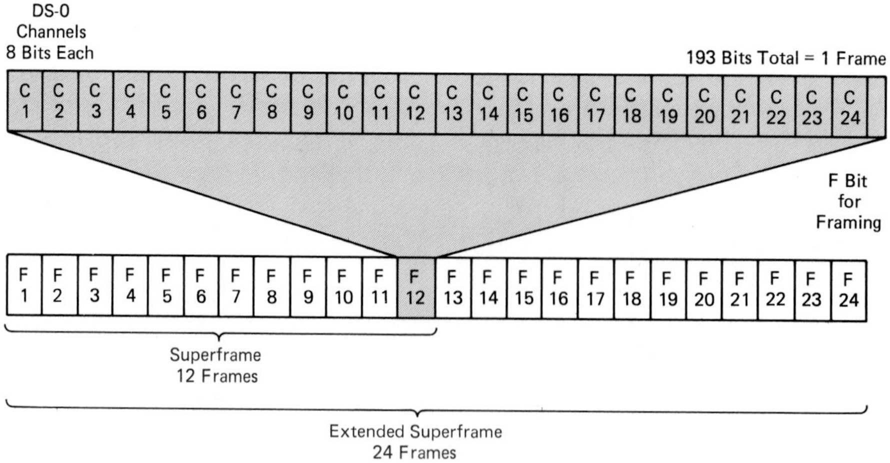

THE DIGITAL WORLD WITH ISDN

The utilization of the F bits provides the necessary functions of synchronization and control.

Figure 16–10 shows the relationships of the F bits. The superframe format has 12 F bits, which occur in the predetermined sequence described previously, 100011011100. The F bits repeat themselves every 12 frames so that the transmission equipment can determine where each of the channels in the frame are.

With the extended superframe format 24 bits are available, also shown in Fig. 16–10. The utilization is as follows. There are 18 bits used for information purposes. Of those 18 bits 12 can be used for data providing a separate data channel at 4 KBPS (sometimes referred to as M bits). The remaining 6 information bits are utilized in a Cyclic Redundancy Check mode (CRC-6). The CRC-6 operation utilizes a modulo 2 arithmetic (no carries or borrows) and performs the operation on 4632 bits. With this level of CRC check there is a 1 in 64 probability that errors could be generated in a compensating way where an appropriate remainder matches the changes caused by bit errors. The result is a 98.4-percent

**FIGURE 16–10**
Superframe and Extended Superframe F Bit Designations

| Frame Number | Superframe Format Value of F Bit | Use | Extended Superframe Format (ESF) Value of F Bit | Use |
|---|---|---|---|---|
| 1 | 1 | $F_T$ | I | D |
| 2 | 0 | $F_S$ | I | CRC |
| 3 | 0 | $F_T$ | I | D |
| 4 | 0 | $F_S$ | 0 | $F_S$ |
| 5 | 1 | $F_T$ | I | D |
| 6 | 1 | $F_S$ | I | CRC |
| 7 | 0 | $F_T$ | I | D |
| 8 | 1 | $F_S$ | 0 | $F_S$ |
| 9 | 1 | $F_T$ | I | D |
| 10 | 1 | $F_S$ | I | CRC |
| 11 | 0 | $F_T$ | I | D |
| 12 | 0 | $F_S$ | 1 | $F_S$ |
| 13 | | | I | D |
| 14 | | | I | CRC |
| 15 | | | I | D |
| 16 | Repeat | | 0 | $F_S$ |
| 17 | of | | I | D |
| 18 | First | | I | CRC |
| 19 | 12 | | I | D |
| 20 | Frames | | 1 | $F_S$ |
| 21 | | | I | D |
| 22 | | | I | CRC |
| 23 | | | I | D |
| 24 | | | 1 | $F_S$ |

$F_T$ = Terminal Framing Bit  
$F_S$ = Multiframe Alignment Bit  } F Bits  
I = Information Bit  
D = Data @ 4 KBPS (M Bit)  
CRC = Cyclic Redundancy Check Bit (C Bit) — 2 KBPS

probability in detecting errors—not perfect, but still an excellent way to measure *in-service* errors in real time.

The information bits can also be used for other purposes such as additional diagnostic information (user oriented) or for actual data itself.

The remaining 6 bits, designated as F bits, are the framing bits used to frame or align the bit stream. Only 6 frames out of the 24 are required for framing because of the evolution of equipment over the years. The sequence of bits required to maintain framing is a 0 bit in frame 4, a 0 bit in frame 8, a 1 bit in frame 12, a 0 bit in frame 16, a 1 bit in frame 20, and a 1 bit in frame 24 (001011). ESF can be used in any DS-1 transmission and is compatible with clear channel 64 KBPS because the information that was formerly contained in the *stolen* bits of the sixth and twelfth frame of the DS-1 sequence can now be included in the data portion of the F bit sequence in the ESF signal sequence.

To take full advantage of the ESF frame more customer premises equipment (CPE) is required. The CPE needs to collect and store a wide variety of information. In turn, it can only be utilized with the appropriate software, and at the moment that software is proprietary to AT&T. Analyzing received bits to find errors could provide end-to-end network management and diagnostics, a service that could easily carry a separate charge. External equipment vendors and users, as well as local telephone companies, have limited access to the 4-KBPS channel, and to make matters worse, AT&T can preempt that information for purposes they alone deem necessary. As a final limitation, any addressing on the 4-KBPS data channel other than those specified by AT&T may encounter a problem in being recognized and routed through the system. Utilization of ESF may be coming, but probably in an extended time frame.

The CPE must be able to accommodate at least the following functions if it is to be compatible with the existing ESF format:

1. Detect errors using CRC-6 of the T-1 bit stream
2. Calculate and store
   a. The current line status, which consists of 8 bits (255 states)
   b. All error events, which consist of 16 bits (65,535 total)
3. Errored seconds and failed seconds for
   a. The current 15-minute period
   b. The previous 95 periods of 15 minutes
   c. The previous 24-hour period
4. Respond to network commands that
   a. Retrieve any of the error values
   b. Reset any counters
   c. Activate/deactivate any local loopback test capabilities
5. Decipher and generate messages based on the AT&T proprietary protocol
6. Be capable of responding to commands within 50 ms preempting all other datalink usage

## Zero Bit Suppression

There is one more critical requirement for all T-1 transmissions. In accordance with AT&T interface specification PUB 62411, the occurrence of 15 consecutive zeros is prohibited in the DS-1 bit stream, and there must be a minimum of three 1 bits within each 24 bits, which means there must be an overall ratio of more than $12\frac{1}{2}$ percent of 1 bits to 0s in any transmission sequence. If the sequence fails this criterion it is called a *format error*. A second type of format error is the simultaneous occurrence of two or more pulses in the same direction regardless of the time frame between them, called *bipolar violations*. Bipolar violations, which may occur due to line degradations, are typically corrected in the network equipment at the regeneration points. Because of this they cannot be detected until they show up as logic errors in the user DTE, but if ESF is used they can be detected at each of the regeneration points and at the customer's end site. As a result the link where errors are occurring can be isolated.

To guarantee that the ratio of one bits to zero bits meets AT&T's specification (required for bit synchronization/clocking purposes) there are two potential methods. The first method, which is compatible with existing equipment, is called *Zero Byte Time Slot Interchange* (ZBTSI). With the ZBTSI, any byte that contains all zeros is replaced with the next byte in the frame. Then, within that same frame, information is transmitted to the next location, identifying which of the frames are all zeros so that they can be reinstated at the appropriate locations in the sequence. The most important feature of this method is that it is compatible with all existing T-1 facilities.

The ZBTSI function is entirely performed in software, so that no hardware changes are involved (the other method, B8ZS, requires hardware changes). Because it is all software, the ZBTSI can be put into both the transmit and receive equipment and the signal propagation will not be affected. The transmitter puts 96 total bytes (equivalent to four frames of 193 bits each) in a buffer. If one or more bytes are zeros, those bytes are removed (if no bytes are all zeros then the data will go out as is). Any nonzero bytes are moved toward the back end of the frame to fill in the gaps, leaving one big gap at the beginning of the buffer. The first byte of the gap is then used to identify where any of the all-zero bytes were located. It is done with a seven-bit binary number giving positions 1–96. The eighth bit of each byte indicates whether there are more all-zero bytes to be identified. There is a flag at the beginning of the overhead framing that identifies whether there are any all-zero bytes in a particular frame. If there are, a 0 bit appears; if not, a 1 bit appears.

AT&T has also come up with another method of eliminating all-zero bytes that they call *Binary 8 Zero Substitution* (B8ZS). This method replaces a byte of eight zeros with a particular bipolar violation sequence in positions four and seven. An example of this is shown in Fig. 16–11. Two bytes are shown in two separate sequences. In the first sequence there are four 1 bits in the first byte and then all zeros in the second byte. Notice that the B8ZS signal inserts a bipolar violation signal in the fourth bit position of the all-zero byte, and an opposite polarity signal in the fifth bit position. In the seventh position of the all-zero byte

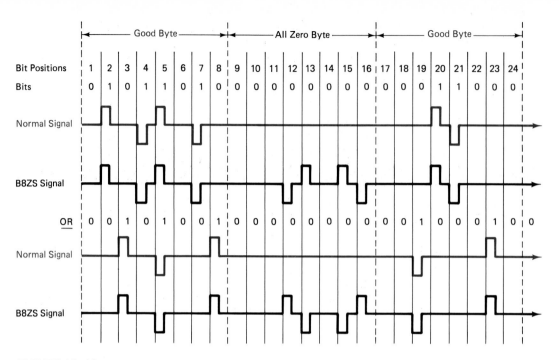

**FIGURE 16–11**
B8ZS—Zero Bit Suppression

there is another bipolar violation signal, and in the eighth position, a signal of the opposite polarity.

As shown in the two examples, regardless of whether the final bit in the good byte is a positive or negative pulse, the bipolar violation in the B8ZS byte is in the fourth bit position occurring in the same direction. By having two pairs of these bipolar violations, a known, predetermined sequence can be established so that all equipment processing this bit stream will recognize the substitution and be able to handle it. Another characteristic is that if you observe the first good byte together with the next good byte, eliminating the all-zeros byte, you will see that the integrity of the normal bipolar transmission is maintained, as if the B8ZS byte did not exist.

Utilizing B8ZS, the entire DS-0 channel can be used for data, resulting in the clear channel 64 KBPS that will be coming with ISDN. The problem is that very few T-1 facilities can support the B8ZS mode of operation. B8ZS is not compatible with existing T-1 circuits because the equipment doing the multiplexing (the DACS) converts the bipolar signal into unipolar signals internally before regeneration. They are then multiplexed before being put back into a bipolar form when going out. Any bipolar violations that exist on input then look like good 1 bits on output, which means corrupted data. Therefore, in order to use B8ZS there must be a significant upgrade in existing network switches and equipment, and in some cases total replacement. Many of the local telephone companies have large investments in existing T-1 superframe capabilities and would therefore be reluctant to go to new equipment in the near future.

## T-1 Standards: North America versus Europe

There are additional points of information that may or may not be important in the decision to utilize digital transmission. For example, the United States' T-1 rate is 1.544 MBPS, while in Europe the T-1 interface is 2.048 MBPS, which consists of a 256-bit frame size. Europeans utilize 32 frames for their equivalent DS-1 signaling, where frames number 1 and 16 carry overhead information. In Japan a variation of the 1.544 MBPS U.S. T-1 rate is utilized.

When the various countries want to communicate with each other using T-1 rates, the translation is done in a device known as *Network Node Interface* on an asynchronous interface basis. Asynchronous means that a large amount of overhead framing information must be sent within the individual data streams so that multiplexed channels can be appropriately identified and sorted out at the receive end. The asynchronous mode is a very inefficient way to interface, but at the moment it is the only way.

The CCITT is working on a new synchronous interface to try to eliminate most, if not all, of the required overhead framing bits. The rate at which this common basis will be established was fixed at 135.168 MBPS in mid-1987 for ISDN. This number was favored by the Europeans. The United States favored 138.240 MBPS, which would still be compatible with the asynchronous transmissions and therefore allow for more gradual upgrading of equipment.

Still to be established are the network node rates, with the United States suggesting 149.7 MBPS (three 44.736-MBPS channels plus overhead) while Europe and Japan are backing the 139.264-MBPS rate with no overhead. Optical rate interfaces are also to be decided upon, although one already exists in the United States, called *SONET*, which will be described in the next section. Another question that still has to be answered is whether the network node interface is to be just between carrier equipment or between carrier and user equipment also. If a carrier-to-user interface must be accommodated there must be a new channel structure for the users.

## Syntran and SONET

The media used for T-1 transmission can be almost any of the existing forms. Twisted pair can be used for up to 100 miles total as long as the signal is regenerated approximately every 6000 feet. The transmit and receive lines must be isolated from each other to prevent crosstalk, and the circuit cannot have any bridge taps (unterminated connections) or loading coils. Coaxial cable and fiber can be used, and digital microwave will be used extensively. The actual selection of the media to be used will typically be a carrier decision and depend on cost, distance, and environmental factors.

Other factors to consider are the higher transmission rates above T-1. Currently, as the carrier signals are routed through the network the multiplexing technique takes the data rate from T-1, to T-1C, to T-2, and then to T-3 at 44.736 MBPS (referred to as 45-MBPS service). When going up and down in this hierarchy, there must be multiplexing from level to level and *dummy* bits inserted so that signals of different rates can be sent at the higher rate with all appropriate framing information maintained. At the receiving end the bit stream must be broken down (demultiplexed) to be put back into the original form of the lower data rates. In other words, DS-1 must go to DS-2 and DS-3 on the transmit end and then do the reverse on the receive end.

A potential solution to this waste of bits for multiplexing is a mechanism called *Syntran*, which stands for Synchronous Transmission, designed for operation up to 45 MBPS. Bellcore (the research organization of the local Bell operating companies) first described this methodology in a 1984 Technical Reference that has been updated many times since. Syntran allows efficient access to individual DS-0 channels at 64 KBPS, as well as to DS-1 data streams, which in turn eliminates the need to go through the intermediate level of DS-2 multiplexing. All signals entering the Syntran device are multiplexed with a single master clock so their specific locations are known, and they can be individually added or dropped from the DS-3 data stream wherever and whenever needed. Up to 1.2 MBPS of overhead dummy bits are eliminated and made available for information transfer. DS-3 is the equivalent of 7 DS-2 circuits, 28 DS-1 circuits, or 672 voice channels. The use of Syntran is expected to grow very quickly, as Bellcore estimates that there will be over 1 billion DS-3 circuit miles by 1990.

Because Syntran will only be used up to the DS-3 transmission rate and media such as fiber can support data rates much higher than that, another method has been proposed for transmission at rates above DS-3, called *SONET* (Synchronous Optical Network). The basic starting transmission rate is 49.920 MBPS, but the development is anticipated to utilize SONET up into the gigabit per second range over the next couple of years. At present there is no guarantee that national standards will be developed in accordance with the same parameters, but if SONET's incorporation into the U.S. network is extensive enough it may become a de facto standard, and users within the North American network will have access to it.

Even though AT&T has been mentioned throughout this section, it should be emphasized that there are many other vendors of T-1 service, such as MCI Telecommunications, Sprint, U.S. Transmission Systems (ITT), Contel ASC, and, in Canada, Telecom Canada.

# F

## ISDN–INTEGRATED SERVICES DIGITAL NETWORK

ISDN is probably the most talked about subject in communications today. Vast amounts of literature are being published and new tests are being announced all over the world on a continuous basis. It is the implementation of the ISDN capabilities in the individual locations that is drawing the most publicity, but before describing them, one must look at the overall concept to get an idea of how the service will provide some form of advantage, technical or economic, over existing network capabilities. A simple overview diagram of ISDN is shown in Fig. 16-12. As you can see there is a wide variety of applications, including voice, data, video, alarms, and telemetry. The signals may or may not be multiplexed through a single DS-1 multiplexer, but in any case there will be a network interface that will carry the signals to the local telephone company office Digital Access Cross-connect System (DACS). The DACS will provide the necessary channelization of all the inputs so that they can be routed separately and/or in groups. The connection between the ISDN network interface on the user site and the DACS at the telephone office is being called the *digital pipe*. It is the digital pipe, actually a local loop, that is providing all of the excitement. Digital service was initiated in the long-distance world by AT&T in 1962, but availability to end users has always been limited by the last mile, or local loop, which prevented end users from accessing the capabilities of high-speed digital service. With the recent implementation of digital capability in the local loop, access to the long-distance digital network is now at hand.

**FIGURE 16–12**
ISDN Concept

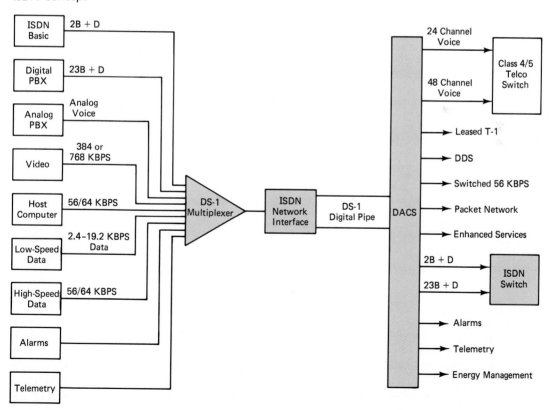

None of this would be of interest if there were not some benefit to the end user. This benefit seems primarily to be reducing the cost for accessing services in the carrier network. Previously, every circuit had to be separate and independent from the user to the carrier and only supported a single voice conversation or a single data channel. With the advent of T-1 service in the local loop there are 24 channels available that can all be provided on the same pair of wires. There is extra equipment at each end, but by 1987 the typical cost of providing those local loops at a T-1 rate was equivalent to the cost of six or seven regular analog local loops. Therefore the local loops between 7 and 24 (17 local loops) are literally *for free*. The cost for typical ISDN services had not been established as of this writing, but in the meantime the circuits can be used to reduce the cost of accessing the carrier. Even though this is not yet truly ISDN, it is definitely an evolutionary step toward that end.

Various services generated on the user's site can be incorporated into channels on a higher speed transmission facility, and then separated by application by the carrier and routed to the appropriate facilities or networks. If an entire network is available, the same kinds of facilities exist throughout the network and at both ends of the circuit, so like applications can be tied directly together. This section covers the various methods and applications that will eventually be incorporated into the ISDN network.

## Services

Some of the potential ISDN services that will be evolving over the next few years are listed here:

| DATA | IMAGE | VOICE |
|---|---|---|
| Alarm services | Cable television | Audio conferencing |
| Circuit switching | Facsimile | Dedicated lines |
| Database access | Graphics | Digitized voice |
| Dedicated lines | Imaging | Music |
| Electronic mail | Picture retrieval | Voice response services |
| Packet switching | Surveillance | |
| Telemetry | Teleconferencing | |
| Teletext | | |
| Telex | | |
| TWX | | |
| Utility meter reading | | |
| Videotex | | |

Some of the services are being provided as part of various tests going on in different parts of the world, but these tests are relatively simplistic in that they deal with data and very limited imaging capabilities. It has been estimated that general ISDN capabilities will not be available for general use until the early 1990s. Even then the capabilities will not necessarily exist in all locations, nor will all the necessary facilities be available for the user to have end-to-end connections. It is therefore necessary to look at the entire ISDN services picture to see which services, when available, can provide the capabilities you need at a reasonable cost.

There is a serious problem for all potential ISDN users concerning the different interface and operating parameters under which services are being set up by the various carriers. For example, AT&T has their defined ISDN interface and the local carriers have their own. Unless the local and long distance carriers can come up with a common form of interfacing, ISDN services will be limited to intralata services. Of course no one expects that to happen, but during the process of developing compatibility it is possible that equipment you may have already bought or will buy soon will be made obsolete by the upgrades required to interface with other carriers. There is no doubt that ISDN is coming, but the real question for the potential user is: What specific equipment should I buy, and when?

Before going any further you should be aware of the definitions of terms used extensively throughout the ISDN world. They are included here so that the rest of this section can be read with understanding.

*Basic Rate Access.* An ISDN-defined service rate equivalent to 144 KBPS. It is made up of two B channels at 64 KBPS each for information and one D channel at 16 KBPS for signaling.

*B Channel.* A signal channel at 64 KBPS that can be used for either digitized voice or data.

*D Channel.* A signaling channel that can operate at the basic or primary rate. For basic rate access the D channel operates at 16 KBPS; at the primary rate the D channel operates at 64 KBPS.

*Primary Rate Access.* A transmission capability at 1.544 MBPS that consists of 24 channels of 64 KBPS. Of the 24 channels, 23 are B channels for information at 64 KBPS and one is a D channel for signaling at 64 KBPS.

*Signaling System #7 (SS#7).* A newly developed (1987) carrier network signaling system used in the 24th channel of primary rate access to provide the necessary signaling and control information to describe what is to be done with each of the other 23 channels.

## Interface Definitions

Many different elements make up the ISDN network. Equipment, interfaces, protocols, and channelization techniques must all be standardized for different types of user equipment to communicate on the same network. Figure 16–13 (a) and (b) show the primary interface definitions along with the equipment designations.

Figure 16–13(a) is a detailed description of the specific user and carrier interfaces. Starting on the left side there is a TE-2, which is defined as a non-ISDN terminal such as a printer, terminal or a PC. The TE-2s are the devices that exist

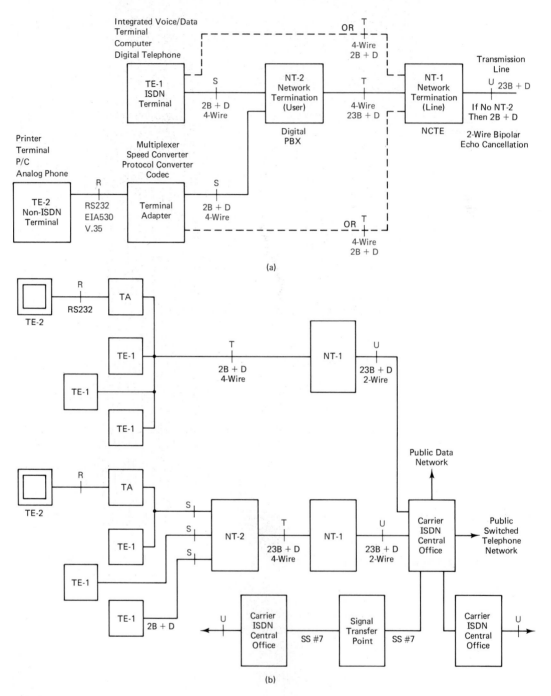

**FIGURE 16-13**

(a) ISDN Terminal Interfaces; (b) ISDN Network Interfaces.

374

today that are not ISDN compatible and typically have interfaces like RS232, EIA530, and V.35.

A TE-2 device connects to a Terminal Adapter (TA) through the R interface, which is defined within ISDN as a non-ISDN interface. The terminal adapter is typically a device that performs at least one of the following: protocol conversion, codec, speed conversion, or multiplexing. The output of a terminal adapter is a 2B + D channel, which is an S or T interface depending on which device it connects to. The S interface is a 144-KBPS transmission that connects to the user side of an NT-2 network termination device. The S interface is the CCITT-defined boundary between the user and the network. However, in the United States the user to carrier boundary is the U interface.

If the terminal adapter is not connected to an NT-2 device it connects via the T interface (still 2B +D) to the NT-1 network termination device. The NT-1 is defined as a device that interfaces the user environment to the carrier network. NT-1 is typically Network Channel Terminating Equipment (NCTE), while the NT-2 equipment is typically a digital PBX.

Still referring to Fig. 16–13(a), there is also a TE-1 device that is already ISDN-compatible, such as an integrated voice/data terminal, a computer, or a digital telephone. The output of this device is again either an S or a T interface depending on the device it connects to, and is in a form that is 2B + D. It is anticipated that a majority of installations will have an NT-2 type device that will provide a four-wire 23B + D connection to the NT-1 network terminating device.

On the carrier side of the NT-1 device is the U interface, which is actually the local loop. The connection is at the 23B + D primary rate and is a two-wire connection on which there is bipolar digital transmission with echo cancellation capability for full-duplex transmission.

In late 1987 the American National Standards Institute (ANSI) T1D1.3 committee rejected a proposal to allow users as well as service providers the ability to initiate diagnostics over the proposed ISDN U interface. The U interface is the demarcation between the customer's premises and the network itself. The committee proposed that only the service providers (carriers) would be allowed to initiate diagnostics through an operating channel that crosses the U interface. However, there is still a possibility that the D channel may have the ability to run high-level diagnostics using its out-of-band channel.

The T interface is defined by the CCITT to be on the customer side of the NT-1 device. It is the same as the S interface when dealing with basic rate access, but may be a 23B + D rate when connecting to an NT-2 device.

The TA provides compatibility for non-ISDN devices with ISDN standardized interfaces. Its output is the S or T interface to an NT-1 or NT-2. The R interface is typically RS232, and the TA can be either a standalone device or plug-in board.

The TE-2 terminal is sometimes called Terminal Equipment Type 2, which is a non-ISDN terminal and needs a TA to access the ISDN interface. The TE-1 terminal is sometimes known as Terminal Equipment Type 1, which is a user device that already supports the ISDN basic rate of 2B + D. It, too, can attach to either the S or T interface of an NT-1 or an NT-2.

The NT-1 device is always a customer premises device that performs switching and multiplexing like a PBX. It will terminate the primary rate access from the local ISDN central office switch. The NT-2 device is also a customer premises device, but its primary function is to convert the two-wire transmission line (local loop), which is the U interface, to four-wire internal customer distribution wiring, the T interface. An NT-2 also supports network maintenance functions like loop testing. Up to eight terminal devices may be connected to a single NT-2.

Figure 16–13(b) shows a typical series of connections for all the different types of terminals with their interfaces, as well as the connections that are made from the local carrier's ISDN central office. Any time there is switching for connection to other ISDN central offices, the switching must be controlled by signaling system #7, which is the ISDN-defined method for control of how individual channels are switched between central offices. If there is a node between two central offices, it is known as a signal transfer point (STP), and it too must be compatible with SS #7 to route the channels appropriately. SS #7 is a protocol for routing of ISDN traffic over the network and will be described later in this section.

## Channels

Information transmission in ISDN takes place in what is known as a *channel*. There are many different definitions of channels and some different uses. The basic structure of the network, however, is based on a T-1 transmission rate of 1.544 MBPS divided into 24 channels. Of these channels, 23 are used for information and one is used for signaling. A definition of each of the channel types is described here.

| CIRCUIT TYPE | BIT RATE (KBPS) | NETWORK ACCESSED | USES |
|---|---|---|---|
| B | 64 | Circuit switched | Digitized voice<br>Data<br>Digitized facsimile |
| D | 16 | Packet | Signal information for ISDN circuit switching (user to carrier)<br>Low-speed user data<br>Telemetry |
| D | 64 | Packet | Signal information for ISDN circuit switching; may be used with PBX interface |
| E | 64 | Packet | Signal information for ISDN circuit switching; used with SS #7 |
| H0 | 384 | Circuit switched | Fast facsimile<br>Video<br>High-speed data |
|  |  | Packet | Packet switched information |
| H11 | 1536 | Circuit switched | Same as H0 |
| H12 | 1920 | Circuit switched | Same as H0 |

Wideband ISDN, known as WISDN, sometimes called Broadband ISDN (BISDN), is being developed. In mid-1987 the channel rate for BISDN was established at 135.168 MBPS, which will be used for full motion color video, multiple channels with voice and data, CAD/CAM, teleconferencing, and other applications that need a very wide bandwidth capability.

Signaling for wideband ISDN will be done at 1.544 MBPS, while full motion color video, video telephones, and video messaging will utilize a data rate in the range of 45–90 MBPS. Bulk data, facsimile, and enhanced video will need a data rate in the range of 150 MBPS. Finally, broadcast-quality TV (cable), or high-resolution TV as it is also called, will require a data rate of up to 750 MBPS.

The initial implementations of ISDN will be the 2B + D (144 KBPS) and the 23B + D (1.544 MBPS) rates. They will be used for the transmission and routing of digitized voice and data in and out of individual or standalone Class 4 or Class 5 telephone company central offices. When SS #7 becomes available those services will be expanded to incorporate multiple carrier switching offices. The channels for voice and data may be divided up such that some or all can be used for either voice or data simultaneously. At different times of the day a channel may be used for voice, later on for data, and still later, for voice again. Ultimately, ISDN will allow the combination of multiple channels and the independent routing of each channel through the network with the information contained in the D channel.

The signaling information contained in the D channel is controlled by a protocol that is defined in two parts. CCITT Q.921 describes the link control procedure while Q.931 describes the information. Q.921 is very much like HDLC (the second level of the OSI protocol), except that only the extended addressing mode is used and the address field specifies the desired service. Q.921 is the link layer protocol that will support the peer-to-peer communications for *feature* networking. At present there are three services, with more to be added later. The current services are circuit switching, packet switching, and management control between the customer premises equipment and the carrier access switch.

Q.931 is the third level of the protocol, but is very different from X.25. Q.931 covers the call control, but not the hold, three-way calling, authorization codes, ring again, or key systems.

The D-channel controls on the local loop will be used for interfacing with the D channel of SS #7. If SS #7 is not locally available, users will only be able to talk to each other through the same switch. SS #7 became generally available during 1987. As an *out-of-band* signaling system, it will replace the existing signaling system, #6, which had been used by AT&T since the late 1960s. SS #6 was known as *Common Channel Interface Switching* (CCIS) and was capable of sending information at 2400 or 4800 BPS. These are 180-bit messages that could support 2.1 million call attempts per hour and control somewhere between 2000 and 4000 total circuits. SS #7 sends information at a 56-KBPS rate and has the ability to control up to 30,000 different circuits. The messages are 256 bytes that can support 12 million call attempts per hour. SS #6 and SS #7 are different with respect to format, message length, routing methods, protocol architecture, and other factors that make the upgrade possible only by replacement.

With the D channel, not only can you have signaling, but you can also have an information content for such things as telemetry, security and alarm signaling, meter reading, and any other data that will be transmitted in a packet switched mode. The D channel is typically used for monitoring services and videotex applications.

A potential problem with the D channel is identifying the address where you want to establish a connection. The ISDN numbering plan is based on the standard telephone numbering plan, but has 15 numbers instead of 12. The extra three numbers are the network destination code, which will be used for international connections. The ten-digit North American numbering plan will continue to be used in the United States.

It is fairly obvious that to determine whether ISDN is a service for you, you must know the costs for it. Most of the tests that were initiated and in process by 1988 did not have those costs delineated. In May of 1988, however, AT&T announced their primary rate ISDN interface, the *Primary Rate Interface* (PRI), with specific services that were to be provided. The PRI is to be installed in 18 cities to start, but only with AT&T's largest customers. The PRI will enable customers to utilize and control all of the channels within a specific T-1 communication link.

Included in PRI is a service called *Information Forwarding-2* (INFO-2). INFO-2 uses an automatic number ID that identifies the caller at an end location. Many applications may be developed that can utilize the caller ID for database lookups, such as credit card validation and other customer service applications where files can be associated with specific originating telephone numbers.

INFO-2 also includes a call service selection that allows each channel to access any one of several switched services, such as MegaCom 800 (*WATS*) and call groups. Depending on the time of day, the customer can change the allocation of different channels within a T-1 link to the services obtained from AT&T. An important fact about PRI is that it establishes a pricing structure for specific services so that an end user can determine on an application by application basis whether it is worth using.

Initial indications are that expansion will be based on customer demand, and to help move that along the System 85 PBX already supports PRI and System 75 will do so in 1989. As a final point, PRI will also be capable of supporting 64 KBPS clear channel data operation, which is one of the significant upgrades in ISDN capability.

As ISDN testing evolves, it appears that France is moving faster and further than other countries in implementing ISDN capabilities. France Telecom implemented ISDN service in early 1987 when circuit switched 64 KBPS service was provided, and they are now in the process of setting up a pilot for transborder ISDN with West Germany by late 1989. France Telecom anticipates connecting their ISDN services to Great Britain and Italy shortly thereafter.

With the various ISDN tests in progress it is worth pointing out that there are potential differences for the users. For example, France will incorporate the Telephone User Part+ (TUP+), which is an interface defined by the European Conference on Postal and Telecommunications Administration (CEPT). On the other hand, West Germany is using at the same interface ISDN Services User Part (ISUP). The Japanese have stated that they will utilize both TUP+ and ISUP in their networks so that they can communicate with anyone, while the United States has been promoting ISUP. There is no doubt that a common methodology will be established for these international ISDN communications, but it may take the form of a gateway process rather than a standardization on a specific interface to which all parties will conform. Japan initiated ISDN services in three cities in 1988 and has indicated that communications will be a *strategic asset* for future development. In other words the Japanese feel that communications is critical to their country's economic development and will move strongly toward implementing and integrating ISDN services in all future implementations.

## Tests

To support ISDN transmissions in the network world, there are different types of central office switches that can interface with the user's site. They are

> AT&T: No. 5ESS with 5E4 generic software
> Northern Telecom: DMS100
> GTE: GTE-5EAX
> Siemans: EWSD
> NEC: NEAX-61
> Ericsson: AXE10

The switches listed here have the ability to terminate the local loop and be upgraded with software to incorporate SS #7 for full network operation. At the toll level (long distance) the AT&T No. 4ESS with 4E11 generic software is another device that can be used for switching.

It is interesting to note that the majority of ISDN interfaces being discussed are fiber and coaxial cable, but at the end of 1986 there were over 100 million copper local loops with an estimated value of $40 billion, and it will be a long time before they are phased out. The distance limitation of the copper local loops depends on the gauge. For local loops that are 26-gauge wire, the maximum distance digital transmissions can travel will be $3\frac{1}{2}$ miles. For 24-gauge wire the distance is four miles, and for 22-gauge the distance is five miles. It is mandatory for these loops to be nonloaded (have loading coils removed). Access to business users with higher volumes will be supplied first, so services to the residential user might be many years in coming.

There are currently more than 50 different tests of ISDN services being performed around the world that were developed by various local carriers in the United States and the PT&Ts in Europe. A complete description of all of the tests is not practical because of the wide variation in services and applications. There are two tests, however, which have received significant attention, and they will be described here. First is the McDonald's test in Illinois, the object of which is to tie together the various McDonald's facilities to reduce network costs. Some of the applications are

PC/PC file transfer

Asynchronous terminal to asynchronous host data access

Asynchronous terminal or PC to IBM host access

Elimination of 3270 coaxial cables

Provision of an X.25 interface to host computers

Modem pooling

Group IV facsimile

Enhanced database access capabilities

Some of the benefits that McDonald's expects to have is a uniform wiring plan throughout all of their facilities and the ability to have a single *information outlet* on each desktop for all transmissions of voice, data, and video. The long-term goal is the integration of many different networks into one network so that all users can access all facilities through a single communications network. The service is being provided by Illinois Bell.

A second test that received a heavy dose of publicity was Pacific Bell's Project Victoria. Project Victoria was originally tested in 1986 in Danville, California, with 200 users having access to many different databases through Apple computers that were provided to them for the test. Pacific Bell said the test was a success and announced an implementation date for Project Victoria on a commercial basis in the Los Angeles area in late 1987.

Although Project Victoria was being billed as an ISDN test, it is really different from all others in that it conforms to a standard known as 1B + D, which is a total of 80 KBPS (64 KBPS + 16 KBPS). A simplified diagram is shown in Fig. 16–14. As shown, the B channel is split into two 32-KBPS voice channels, while the D channel of 16-KBPS total is split into a single data channel at 9600 BPS and four separate data channels at 1200 BPS each. An optional signaling channel is available for information like telemetry (alarms and meter reading).

Pacific Bell indicated that ISDN would typically not be used for long-dis-

**FIGURE 16–14**
Project Victoria from Pacific Bell

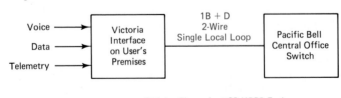

2 Voice Channels at 32 KBPS Each
1 Data Channel at 9600 BPS
4 Data Channels at 1200 BPS Each
Optional Signaling Channel

tance end-to-end communications for a long time to come. Therefore, they would provide a localized service that can support such things as point-of-sale, home banking, electronic mail, fire/burglar alarms, meter reading, support for debit card terminals, and pay-per-view TV program ordering. All of this can be done in and out of a single switch, and if they could get a foothold it is quite possible that many customers would be locked into Pacific Bell because of the system's proprietary operation.

Project Victoria needs a multiplexer on the user's site to perform the process of combining user signals into the 1B + D signal stream. Until Pacific Bell can sell equipment, the multiplexer must be provided by a third party (due to restrictions of the Modified Final Judgment). Because of local loop limitations, Project Victoria users must be within 18,000 cable feet away from the switch (nonloaded circuit). If the transmission rate goes up to the basic rate access speed of 2B + D (144 KBPS), the distance will probably be limited to 12,500 cable feet.

Project Victoria was chosen for description not only because of its direct relevance to user applications, but also to point out the overall situation in the ISDN test environment. Different vendors will be providing different systems, and therefore they may not be able to connect to each other. Furthermore, for Pacific Bell to provide this service on an *interlata* basis would require one of the long-distance carriers to have a compatible interface that does not yet exist. A diagram of that required interlata connection is shown in Fig. 16–15.

As shown, the end user can transmit voice and data through a PBX or Centrex into a local telco ISDN central office switch. If the destination is connected to the same switch, there is no problem because it is controlled by the local telephone company. The same situation would exist for other central office switches located in the same LATA, again because the local telephone company has control over the entire circuit as well as the switches at each end. The problem obviously arises when it becomes necessary to communicate across a LATA boundary. If the long-distance carrier does not have the kind of interface to support the particular application or service provided by the local telephone company, there is no way at present that the local telephone company can communicate across the LATA boundary. For Project Victoria this may all be academic, because in early 1988 (due to an unfavorable regulatory ruling) Pacific Bell announced they would no longer provide Project Victoria service themselves but would *license* it to other vendors who might be interested. Early response was not very positive.

There is no question that ISDN is coming. The problem is in trying to determine which features will be available at what point in time and at what locations, which puts the system designer in a very precarious position. After bringing in an innovative system from a carrier, it is possible that within some months or a year or two the particular system or service may be obsolete because of upgrades or changes made by the local carriers. Changes can come from natural system upgrades, or a desire to be compatible with other services or carriers, or to get into the long-distance environment. At this time it seems that it is probably better to solve the problems that you have with technology that already exists. By the

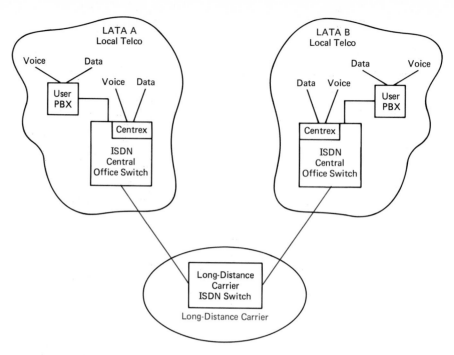

**FIGURE 16-15**
InterLATA ISDN Connections

time the proposed new services become available, your situation and problems may be very different from what they were even a short time ago, and it is always better to *let others be the pioneers* in debugging new systems. Philosophically, it seems that the two biggest promoters of ISDN today are the carriers who are beginning to offer the services and the organizational planners who see the long-range benefits but will not have to live with the day-to-day problems that occur with brand new, untried systems that are continually upgraded. Remember the axiom in the communications business: "You can always tell the pioneers by the arrows in their backs." There are usually enough pioneers out there to make most of the mistakes. If you want to save yourself a lot of grief you are probably better off waiting for a more proven and stabilized system before you go to ISDN. This comment is being made while the situation is still in a great amount of flux, but with the projections for availability of services being in the early 1990s, there is still plenty of time to learn from others' experiences. Possibly the fourth edition of this text will be able to paint a rosier picture within the next couple of years.

## QUESTIONS

1. What is the function of a DSU? A CSU?
2. Define the digital speed hierarchy for T-type transmission rates from T-1 through T-4.

3. Describe the function and operation of a digital cross-connect system.

4. What is DDS? Where is it used?

5. Derive the T-1 transmission rate starting from an analog voice signal.

6. Describe the framing process utilized in the superframe format.

7. What is meant by bit robbing (stealing)?

8. Describe the utilization of the framing bit in Extended Superframe format.

9. Why is ZBTSI or B8ZS used in digital transmission?

10. What is the overall concept for the use of ISDN?

11. Describe the characteristics of the R, S, T and U interfaces.

12. What are the differences between basic rate and primary rate interfaces?

13. Describe the functional characteristics of the ISDN hardware components TE-1, TE-2, T/A, NT-1, and NT-2.

14. What is SS #7? Where is it used?

15. What is the single most significant problem facing ISDN users in the United States today?

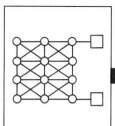

# 17

# Packet Switching

## A
## CONCEPT AND DESCRIPTION

In the late 1960s, after development of a networking concept to operate under disaster conditions, a report by the General Accounting Office (GAO) of the federal government indicated that many federal data processing facilities were grossly overutilized, while others were not used to their full capacity. To distribute the loading more evenly, the concept of a common user network was initiated. Information from sites that lacked adequate capacity could be sent to sites that had excess capacity, processed at those other sites, and the results returned to the originating location. For more effective use of the communication facilities the idea of *Packet Transmission* was introduced. Basically, Packet Transmission means that the message is divided into specific length blocks or *packets*, which are sent out individually over the network through multiple locations and then reassembled at the final location prior to being delivered to the user at the receiving end. Because there are multiple paths over which the different packets can be transmitted, they can arrive out of sequence. Therefore, each packet has appended to it the necessary control information to identify which part of which message it belongs to. The validity checking is performed at each location that the packet enters even if the packet is to be subsequently retransmitted to another point in the network. When delivered to the final packet node destination, all the

384

packets are reassembled and then transmitted to the end user in a format that is compatible with the user's equipment. Capability is also provided at the final packet node to provide an end-to-end acknowledgment back to the originating packet node saying that the entire message has reached the end node. Because of the multiple routing path capabilities, a packet network can be looked at as an adaptively routed network in which individual line failures will not cause the loss of a message.

Once the ARPANET, as it was called, was operational, it was only a matter of time before commercial organizations followed suit. One of the first companies in the United States to implement a packet network was TELENET (now GTE-TELENET), which was followed shortly thereafter by a company called TYMNET (now McDonnell-Douglas TYMNET). Together these companies now provide between 50–55 percent of all packet transmissions in the United States. The primary benefit of packet services is the capability for transmission of large volumes of data at fixed costs regardless of the distance between end points. The charge is based on the quantity of packets transmitted, not the time or distance involved. The only additional costs to a user are the connection charges at each end. Typically, a user dials in or has a leased line to the packet operator in the local environment at each end, which is paid for on a local intrastate basis. Even though GTE-TELENET charges on a packet basis and McDonnell-Douglas TYMNET charges on a character basis, the basic concept of charging by volume is the same for both. Depending on the type of traffic you have and the destinations, one service might be less expensive than the other, but other considerations must also be evaluated that will be described later.

Although packet switching originated in the United States, the packet technique was first used extensively in Europe. In fact, most of Western Europe is already tied together with one or more packet networks that work interactively with each other. The packet network vendors in the United States do not communicate with each other.

In the last few years there has been a major change in the packet environment in the United States, with many of the vendors merging. The largest, primarily because it merged with UNINET in 1986, is GTE-TELENET, which serviced more than 700 different locations and handled somewhere between 23 and 28 percent of the packet traffic by the end of 1987. McDonnell-Douglas TYMNET also served over 700 locations and handled somewhere between 23 and 28 percent of the total packet traffic. Another vendor providing packet service is Automatic Data Processing Corporation (ADP), which offers *Autonet*, used primarily for moving information between user sites and ADP offices for use of the various ADP services. Other vendors such as Compuserve, IBM (Information Network), Source, and others also provide packet switching services but have very specific and small portions of the overall markets and usually provide services for particular customer environments.

The telephone companies could be big potential players in the packet game. There is a serious problem, however, in that each of the local operating companies can develop its own interfaces which may or may not be the same as the interface developed for the long-distance carrier. Also, for calls between two different states, three organizations will be involved in the billing process, and there has been no agreement to date on how to set up the billing. In addition, common addressing and routing mechanisms must be established for all of the organizations involved so that the user data can be delivered on time and with a minimal amount of administrative overhead. Developing those mechanisms has been the biggest drawback to the telephone companies providing packet services. It should be noted, however, that Bellcore (the organization set up to provide common interfaces for the Bell operating companies) is in the process of trying to develop just such a set of interfaces. Until that is done the service providers described above will provide the majority of packet services in the United States.

In Canada there are also two services that provide the majority of packet switching capability. First is *Datapac*, which is a service provided by Telecom Canada, a consortium of Canadian telephone companies. Datapac ties together nearly all medium and large cities in Canada and connects to the U.S. packet networks. The second service, called *Infoswitch*, is a packet switching service provided by CNCP Telecommunications, a joint venture of the two large Canadian railroads, Canadian National and Canadian Pacific. Infoswitch competes directly with Telecom Canada for data communications business in packet switching.

When discussing packet network operations, it is necessary to understand the difference between the operations of the various kinds of circuits. Figure 17–1 shows a comparison of the connections of the various kinds of networks.

Figure 17–1(a) is the circuit switched configuration, shown for the connections that exist during a call. Callers A, B, and C are trying to call X, Y, and Z. A, B, and C initiate a call through an independent local switch, which routes their connection through at least one other switch to the local environments where X, Y, and Z reside. There are three separate end-to-end circuits that exist only during the time the call is in progress, but the only time the circuit is in actual use is when one of the entities at either end is physically transmitting. If neither end is transmitting, such as during pauses, then the circuit is not in use. Charges for this kind of service are based on time of use and distance.

Figure 17–1(b) describes the configuration of the connection with a leased line. In this case, A is communicating directly with Z, B with Y, and C with X. Even though the connections go through various carrier provided switches, the effect is to have a physical connection between the two communicating devices. The circuit is always there and physically available for either end to use at any time. No other user can access any segment of leased lines because they are dedicated to the connection between two specified locations. Costs for this kind of network are based on distance and fixed on a monthly basis. Leased-line circuits can be *conditioned* to improve their ability to carry data with fewer errors.

Finally, Fig. 17–1(c) is a packet switched network. In this instance there is a connection between each of the end users and a local *node*. The nodes within the packet network are connected to each other through a variety of different connections, and it is possible to transmit a message in which the segments (packets) take different paths (to be described later in this chapter) through the network. The connection between the end user and the node is utilized only when

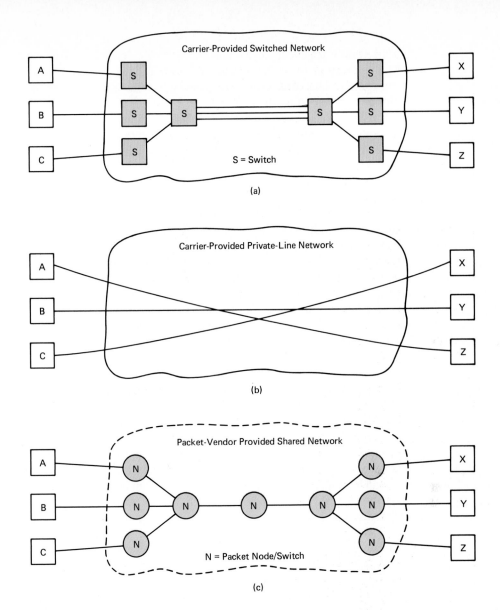

**FIGURE 17-1**

Network Comparisons. (a) Circuit Switched (circuit dedicated during call); (b) Leased Line (circuit dedicated at all times); (c) Packet Switched (circuit used only when required).

the user is communicating with that particular node (either direction), and for local calls only. The node-to-node connections in the packet network are physically there all the time but are only utilized when there is actual information to be transferred. This way, the various end users can *share* the physical connections between the nodes. At the far end there is a connection between the final node and the end user at that end. Just like the opposite end of the network, it is utilized only when the device and the node are communicating with each other. The connection from the user to the node can be either a dial or a leased-line connection. The connection between the various packet nodes are leased lines, but they are leased by the packet vendor and not the end user. With the different end users sharing the circuits, the cost is not based on time or distance but on the volume of data transmitted (either packets or characters).

Although the internal mechanism may vary greatly among the different packet providers, the operation and interface look almost identical to the end user. By referring to Fig. 17-2 you can see the basic structure of the packet network and how it is used.

The packet network is set up with a *series of nodes* (store and forward switching locations) in all of the areas where the vendor wants to provide the service. The nodes communicate with each other via an interface that is unique to each of the vendors, although they all use a variation of X.25 (to be described later). Even though Fig. 17-2 shows a symmetrical network with nodes tying to other nodes in a variety of configurations, nodes actually may have only one or two routes that they can take to get to another node. The vendor decides on the structure based on volume and location of where the service is to be provided. You must always check to see where the connections go from your particular vendor.

The nodes are connected with standard analog or digital telephone lines. The transmission rate of the user-to-network circuits can go up to 56 KBPS, although there is discussion about raising this up to 1.544 MBPS (T-1) for high-volume nodal connections.

Each node contains the necessary hardware and software to route packets to and from all adjacent nodes depending on the overhead information contained in each packet (routing, accounting, segmentation information, and so on).

The user interfaces to the network through a *PAD* (Packet Assembler/Disassembler). PADs exist in a variety of forms that provide the necessary conversion from the unique user communications environment to the standardized environment used throughout the packet network. The user interface can therefore be any of a wide variety of protocols and speeds (to be described later). The service provided is only the movement of data, so the packet vendors are *not regulated*. They are sometimes called *Value-Added Network* operators, or VANs.

The VAN designation means that the packet vendor provides some service in addition to moving the information between two points. The additional service consists of validating the information between the two end nodes and providing the necessary conversions to enter and leave the network. This *added value* to the transmission cannot be provided by the local telephone companies yet because it is considered an *enhanced* service. Also, as described earlier, because interfaces between carriers may be different, packet switching across LATA boundaries may take a while to become available.

The primary mechanism for moving information through a packet network can also be seen from Fig. 17-2. In the lower right corner, a terminal or PC generates information in one of a variety of interfaces and moves that informa-

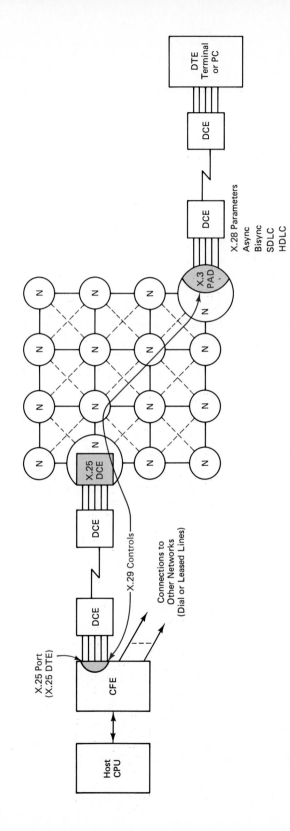

**FIGURE 17–2**
Basic Packet Network Configuration

tion into the local node through a PAD. The node puts the information in packet form with a (typical) maximum of 128 characters per packet and sends the packets through the network. The packets may take different routes but eventually get to the node in the upper left corner, where they are converted through another PAD interface for high-speed transmission to a host CPU. There can be high-speed to high-speed, low-speed to low-speed, or as was shown, low-speed to high-speed interfaces at either end of the network. The packet network can provide broadcast-type addressing, multiple addresses, and a wide variety of other delivery capabilities. What will be described in the next few sections is the mechanism whereby the information is moved through the network.

## B
## INTERFACES

A wide variety of interfaces are specified for the packet networks. The most extensively used specifications have been developed by the CCITT and are utilized in almost all packet networks throughout the world. The specifications applicable to packet networks are the X series of specs, which are known as the specifications for the Public Data Network (PDN). Chapter 5 describes the majority of specs that should be considered, but the most significant ones will be described here:

*X.1.* International Classes of services for users of public data networks.

*X.2.* International services and facilities for users of public data networks.

*X.3.* Packet assembler/disassembler facilities for a low-speed asynchronous interface facility in a public data network.

*X.21.* The interface between Data Terminal Equipment (DTE) and Data Circuit Terminating Equipment (DCTE) for synchronous operation on public data networks.

*X.21bis.* The interface between DTE and synchronous V-Series modems.

*X.25.* The interface between Data Terminal Equipment and Data Circuit Terminating Equipment for terminals operating in the packet mode on public data networks.

*X.28.* Procedures used to control the data flow between a low-speed start/stop mode DTE accessing an X.3 in a public data network.

*X.29.* Procedures necessary for the exchange of control information and user data between a PAD facility and a packet mode DTE or another PAD. Used to control a remote X.3 asynchronous PAD from a host-end X.25 DTE.

*X.75.* Terminal and transmit call-control procedures and data-transfer method on circuits between different packet switched data networks.

*X.92.* Reference connections for packets with data transmissions. Specifies the connections for the DTE to the network.

*X.96.* Call-progress signals in a public data network. Signals that describe whether the connections are or are not made.

*X.121.* International numbering plan for addressing devices in multiple different networks.

Of these interfaces, the ones that you will probably be involved with the most are the low-speed, asynchronous interfaces like X.3, X.28 and X.29, and the high-speed, synchronous interface, X.25. Since most individuals deal with a terminal or a PC, the interfaces affecting those devices are the most widely known. Of them, the X.3 low-speed, asynchronous PAD parameters affect the interface most of all. The current parameters which are factors either controlled or specified by X.3 will be described here in detail.

1. PAD recall. Escape from data mode to command mode in order to send PAD commands.
2. Echo. Defines whether PAD should provide echo for terminal characters.
3. Data forward. What characters will trigger the PAD to send partial packets (carriage return, and the like).
4. Idle timer. The time delay between characters as a signal to forward the date (this is a PAD *timeout*).
5. The PAD control for a terminal utilizing Xon/Xoff protocols.
6. Allows terminal to receive PAD messages.
7. The PAD operation when getting a *break signal* from the terminal.
8. Controls the discard of data at the PAD pending output to a terminal.
9. Provides insertion of PAD characters after carriage return is sent to the terminal.
10. Provides *folding* of data sent to a terminal when the line length is exceeded.
11. The speed of the terminal—110 BPS to 64 KBPS.
12. Provides terminal control for data transferred by PAD under Xon/Xoff.
13. Controls PAD insertion of line feed (L/F) after a carriage return (C/R) is sent to the terminal.
14. Controls PAD insertion of padding characters after L/F sent to terminal.
15. Controls whether editing by PAD is available during data-transfer mode (editing capabilities are parameters 16–18).
16. Character used to signal character delete.
17. Character used to signal line delete.
18. Character used to signal line display.
19. Controls the format of the editing PAD service signals.
20. Identifies characters not to be echoed when echo is on.
21. Parity operation.
22. Identifies the number of lines to be displayed at one time.

By looking at the parameters controlled or specified within X.3 you can see that it defines the necessary parameters for connecting asynchronous devices to the PAD. In conjunction with X.28, X.3 supports the establishment of the path, the initialization of the service, the exchange of data, and the exchange of control information.

X.28 is the next important interface specification, and it describes how the terminal users modify the X.3 parameters for the particular terminal in use. In other words, X.28 defines the procedures necessary to control the data flow between the user terminal and the PAD. After initial connection from the user's DTE, the PAD establishes the connection and provides X.28-specific services. The user's terminal (DTE) evokes the X.28 commands to the X.3 PAD, which in turn requests the necessary connection to the remote DTE. X.28, therefore, is the specific set of parameters that the user DTE is implementing. The X.28 specification provides the necessary DTE-to-PAD commands that provide for the call setup and clearing, the use of a preset X.3 PAD, resetting X.3 PAD parameters, status requests, and resets and interrupts.

X.29 is the final specification in this integrated group, and it provides the necessary directions for the PAD and a remote DTE (probably an X.25-type DTE) to exchange control information at any time. The X.29 control messages are the following:

*Set.* Changes an X.3 value.

*Read.* Reads an X.3 value.

*Set and Read.* Changes an X.3 PAD value and requires the PAD to confirm.

*Parameter Indication.* Returned in response to the preceding three commands.

*Invitation to Clear.* Allows an X.25 call clearance by the remote DTE. The X.3 PAD then clears to the local terminal.

*Indication of BREAK.* The PAD indicates the terminal has transmitted a BREAK signal.

*Error.* Response to an invalid PAD message.

These relationships can also be seen by referring to Fig. 17–2. The X.3 PAD at the local node in the lower right corner interfaces with a terminal that incorporates the modifications to the X.3 PAD parameters through X.28. In the upper left corner is the X.25 interface (to be described next), which provides the DTE control for interfacing to the X.3 PAD at the other end of the network.

The next specification may have more written about it than any other specification in the history of data communications, X.25. The term X.25 is used in a variety of forms by different people. It describes a routing methodology, a physical interface, and a mechanism for linking locations. All of these are possible at once because X.25 involves three different levels of interface.

The first level of interface is the *physical level*, which provides for a full-duplex point-to-point circuit utilizing either X.21 or X.21bis for an interface. In Europe X.21 consists of X.26 (equivalent to EIA423) and X.27 (equivalent to EIA422). In the United States X.21bis is utilized where X.26 and X.27 are used, as well as where V.28 (equivalent to EIA232) and V.35 are acceptable choices.

At the second level, the *link level*, X.25 includes procedures to set up and maintain a link between user equipment and the network. With respect to the seven-layer OSI protocol, this equates to the datalink or protocol level and consists primarily of HDLC.

The third level of X.25 interface is the *network level*, where the necessary formatting and control for the exchange of packets between user equipment and the network are established. When utilized internally within a network, this level moves packets between nodes in the network.

Because of the enormous amount of data available on the mechanics of how X.25 operates at all of its levels with all of its interfaces, it would not be practical to include all of the information here. It is the intent of this text to provide a description of the operational capabilities of the various subjects. If you need more detailed information on the structure of X.25 transmissions, refer to a text that provides the level of detail you need.

Besides the low-speed asynchronous operation utilizing X.3, X.28, and X.29, and the high-speed synchronous interface utilizing X.25, there are PADs that support asynchronous TTY, 3270BSC (bisync), 3270/3780 contention mode BSC, HASP, SDLC, HDLC, and others as the market grows. You do not have to have the specific packet switching interface specifications in your equipment to communicate to a packet network. You can use one of the very common protocols (typically IBM oriented) because there are PADs available to convert your information to the network protocols. Some of the other protocols that are supported in PADs are *Uniscope* from Univac (Unisys), *Poll/Select* from Burroughs (now Unisys also), and *VIP* from Honeywell. There is one other that is rather unique called the SDLC *pipe*. The SDLC pipe is called a *value-added* interface. It provides all necessary conversions by emulating the SNA datalink control layer (DLC layer). The way it operates is shown in Fig. 17–3. The SDLC pipe is used to connect 3274 cluster controllers utilizing SDLC into an X.25 environment. The terminal PAD intercepts the SDLC frames, strips off their header and tail, and inserts the remaining information into an X.25 packet. The host PAD puts the SDLC frame back together so that it looks like SDLC to the host.

The value-added capability comes from the fact that multiple hosts can be accessed at multiple locations, and, as an alternative protocol, bisync can be used instead of SDLC. The necessary polling takes place between the terminal PAD and the cluster controller, where the terminal PAD emulates the host. The terminal PAD then emulates the SNA functions required by the host for the SNA environment, but the information is transmitted through the packet switched network.

Before going on to descriptions of other areas of packet switching, there are some additional items of interest dealing with PADs of which you should be

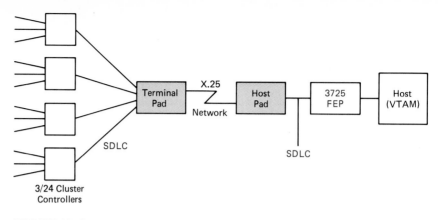

**FIGURE 17–3**
SDLC Pipe

aware. One is that it is the user device side of a PAD that distinguishes the PADs from each other. That is the side where the number of protocols, ports, security, and management capabilities are described. PADs usually run in the range of $200–$600 per port, so if you want to get the maximum capability out of a PAD you should be able to configure them either locally or remotely. Configuration refers to setting up the speed, priority, fault conditions, user mnemonics, and any other operating characteristics.

Almost all PADs support 128 character packets (by specification, packets can be 16, 32, 64, 128, 256, 512, or 1024 octets long). During the mid-1980s, an asynchronous PAD had a throughput of approximately 10 packets per second (10240 BPS) while synchronous PADs could handle up to 64 KBPS. It is reported that PADs operating at T-1 rates (1.544 MBPS) are under development.

Asynchronous PADs are typically utilized by a single user at a time for low speed operation at 300, 1200, and 2400 BPS. Newer capabilities allow asynchronous operation at either 4800 or 9600 BPS, but for the most part the higher speeds are utilized for synchronous transmission. X.25 synchronous PADs are utilized at the higher speeds and are most efficient when the network accommodates multiple users who are interleaved at high speed. Typically, the X.25 PAD can multiplex between four and 128 devices over one or two separate X.25 network links.

For interfacing into this high-speed environment, both TELENET and TYMNET have available X.25 dial-in capability. Dial-in X.25 is very useful for environments where there are clusters of terminals or PCs that do not need continuous access to a host or other clusters. Dial-in X.25 is also good for a multiuser micro, which would be in the PC/AT category, and might operate as a gateway to LANs, in which mode the packet network looks like a virtual circuit to the host for each individual user.

# OPERATION

Many buzzwords describe the procedures and operations used in packet networking. One of the common ones in use today is *connection versus connectionless* service. On a very simple level, connectionless service means that the sending station has no knowledge of the status of the receiving station (it may be available or not), while a connection-oriented transmission means that the receiving station must acknowledge receipt of information before the transmitting station can terminate the connection.

Poll/response protocols and other centralized control protocols are usually connection-oriented. Transmissions like electronic mail are connectionless and the accountability for receipt of messages is done by some higher layer of the protocol structure.

You should generally choose the methodology that suits your own application best. Public networks tend to be connection-oriented and private networks tend to be connectionless. The private networks are typically utilized for their *path* connections only, so the higher-level protocol layers will take care of all acknowledgments. The public networks need to make sure that entire messages (all the packets of a message) are available before delivery to the remote location, which necessitates end-to-end acknowledgment.

So you may get an idea of the differences between the two, some of their characteristics are listed here.

| CONNECTION-ORIENTED | | CONNECTIONLESS |
|---|---|---|
| Connection establishment | like a telephone call | Single self-contained information unit, sometimes called a Datagram (CCITT officially dropped the name Datagram in 1984, but some people still use it) |
| Information transfer | | |
| Connection release | | Point-to-point subconnections |
| End-to-end network connection | | |
| Deterministic network | | Probabilistic network |
| Typical applications: | | Typical applications: |
|   access to servers | |   broadcast |
|   file transfer | |   data collection |
|   long-term terminal attachment | |   electronic mail |
|   secure transmissions | |   inquiry/response |

Related to connection and connectionless services, but totally independent, there are connections called *virtual circuits*, of which there are two types. The first kind is a *permanent virtual circuit*, which looks like a dedicated line in operation. A specific logical path is allocated permanently so that no call set-up time is required for transmission and the path is always available for use. A *switched virtual circuit* looks like a dial connection in operation in that a specific path is established for each call and a call set-up procedure is required, meaning there will be a time delay prior to being able to initiate traffic.

## Service Providers

Many vendors provide packet services throughout the world. There are vendors in each of the major countries in Europe who can provide packet services not only within their countries, but who can interface to other countries and, eventually, the world.

In North America Datapac and Infoswitch are the two major vendors in Canada described previously, and in the United States, the two major vendors of public packet switching services are GTE-TELENET and McDonnell-Douglas TYMNET, also described previously.

Each of the local telephone companies as well as AT&T has a packet switching service, but until the end of 1987, because of the differences in interfaces, none of them could talk to each other. Interface incompatibility will be the biggest deterrent to packet services being provided by the carriers. However, a committee of Bell operating companies working together to come up with a common packet interface for all the carriers was founded in March 1986. It is called the Packet Services Compatibility Advisory Board (PSCAB) and consists of the seven Bell operating companies, Bellcore (Bell Communications Research), Cincinnati Bell, and Southern New England Telephone Company (SNET). Even though they have made some headway, standardized interfacing among the carriers is not expected until around 1990, but by the end of 1987 Southern Bell Telephone Company and TELENET had already announced an interface connecting their two networks. The mechanism allowed Southern Bell to interface within a LATA to TELENET nodes for interlata service. Right now, this is only good for operation within the Southern Bell service area, but it could be expanded to other areas if like interfaces are developed.

The primary idea behind a packet switching network is to provide a means whereby multiple users can share communications resources without being required to operate, maintain, or pay for them on a continuous basis. Payment is based on utilization. The user pays by volume, not time and distance (the way telephone calls are paid for). The goal is to provide a wide variety of connection and transmission capabilities with at least the following characteristics.

Access by dial or leased-line connection

Transmission speeds of 110 BPS through 56 KBPS (1.544 MBPS in development)

Asynchronous and synchronous interfaces

Charge for use based on volume, not time and distance

Connection to other networks, including international

Provision of detailed billing information

Utilization of analog or digital transmission capabilities, or both

Local connection in a wide geographic environment

Access through standardized interfaces or a variety of common vendor-provided interfaces, or both

The configuration for the connection of nodes within the network (store and forward switching locations) was shown in Fig. 17–1. Access to the various networks would be through the node that was closest to the end user. Even though the vendors provide similar interface environments to all end users, their internal operation and characteristics may be very different; therefore, only one vendor is typically used at any one time. Telenet and TYMNET provide the majority of the packet services in the United States, but there are other vendors available also. Typically, however, they provide substantially fewer interfaces at fewer locations.

Regardless of which vendor you use, there are certain factors that you must determine prior to contracting for service. For example, you need to know whether the vendor has a *node close to the locations* where you want to communicate. This is very important for organizations that have far-flung facilities. The host site may be in a large city where nodes are available, but remote facilities may not be near a node, which necessitates a long-distance dial connection or an expensive leased line to the closest node. The vendors' nodes are not all in the same cities, so it is quite possible that you may need two vendors for your connections and may have to use two separate interfaces.

The second thing to determine is what *protocols are available* in the nodes that you must communicate to and from. There are the low-speed and high-speed standard PADs, such as X.3 and X.25, but you may want to communicate in one of the proprietary vendor protocols and they may not be available at the nodes at the locations you are interested in.

Next you need to consider the *speed of transmission* that you will require. Although all nodes can support up to 1200 BPS and most can support up to 2400 BPS today, if you have higher speed requirements or synchronous interfaces, they may not be available at the node you are interested in. Another consideration is the type of traffic you will have. Although it is not very significant, it could have a bearing on your overall costs. TELENET charges by the packet with only one end user in a packet, while TYMNET charges on a per-character basis with multiple users possibly contained within the same packet. Studies have shown a wide variety of costs depending on location, volume, and length of transmissions, so you must get a current proposal from the vendors based on anticipated statistics to get an idea of what the cost will be if you utilize one vendor or the other.

You may also hear of the different kinds of *routing techniques*, centralized or distributed, with their advantages and disadvantages. It appears that both types operate equally well, so you do not have to be concerned with the mechanics of routing, but because so many people ask what the differences are, they will be described here.

First, there is the distributed methodology of routing, in which each node decides which path to take to the next node. The nodes constantly move status information among themselves so that each has a picture of the network and can therefore select the best path for the packet to take to its ultimate destination. This is sometimes called *Dynamic Adaptive Routing* and TELENET follows this mode of operation.

When a route is set up ahead of time the method is called *centralized*. A specific path is set up between the specific locations involved based on the defined network parameters. An alternate path will be established only when there is a problem. TYMNET follows this form of routing. When a user enters a message into the network, the nodes along a predetermined path are selected and the appropriate resources are reserved for that particular user's *session*. Traffic is transmitted in sequence one packet at a time, and they all arrive in the order that they were transmitted. The initial path is set up by a *needle* packet, and at the end of a session a *zapper* packet releases the path that the needle packet set up. In the Dynamic Adaptive Routing mode of operation each packet can take a different path and the packets can actually arrive out of sequence. In both instances, however, if a packet does not make it to the destination end, both systems will go back to the originating node and get the missing packet or packets. A typical example of the differences between distributed and centralized routing is shown in Fig. 17–4. Figure 17–4(a) shows centralized routing, where each packet of a message from an end user takes the same path through the network until the end destination, at which time the message is delivered in its entirety. Figure 17–4(b) shows distributed routing, where each packet may be routed independently through the network, possibly arrive out of sequence, but eventually get delivered as an entire message to the user at the remote site. The communication in the opposite direction conforms to the same set of rules.

One of the things you must be very careful about in choosing a vendor is the multiplicity of connections from the node that you have. The diagrams in this text show nodes that have multiple connections to other nodes, but there are many instances when a node may only have a single connection to another node. Failure of the connecting node or the transmission path to that node means failure of communication. Alternate paths may not be available and you may have to go to a dial-up mode over a long-distance connection to get back into the network.

## User-Site PADS

For the most part, low-speed asynchronous transmissions in a packet network environment involve the PAD being in the packet node. A relatively simplistic interface is then provided by the terminal or PC in accordance with X.28 parameters. If, however, you would like to communicate via high-speed synchronous transmissions, and you would like to become a node in the packet network yourself for transmitting and receiving messages, you can incorporate the X.25 PAD into your own facility. By installing a packet mode DTE into your facility that will communicate with a packet mode DCE in the packet vendor's node, you can implement the X.25 capability between the two devices.

By incorporating the X.25 interface on your own site you actually become a node in the network, but you do not pass information through like a vendor node. You are a transmit or receive node with a specific address for your traffic only. Again using TELENET and TYMNET as examples, Fig. 17–5 shows the sequence that you would normally use to become X.25 compatible. You would start off at Fig. 17–5(a), where you are communicating to a packet node utilizing one of your standard protocols such as Bisync or SDLC. When you decide to go to X.25 compatibility there is a sequence that you can use for minimum disruption to your network.

Figure 17–5(b) shows a typical first step. You would go to the vendor and request the installation of a PAD on your site. The typical TELENET PAD is a TP-3000, and the TYMNET PAD is called the TYMNET Engine. You utilize the same standard protocol that you had before, except now you go into the PAD on your site, the conversion is made on your site, and transmission is via an X.25 form to the packet node. If you get a TP-3000 you can only communicate with a TELENET node, and if you get a TYMNET Engine you can only communicate with a TYMNET node. The reason for this limitation is that when you get a PAD from a particular vendor the vendor provides a conversion so that the network interface is compatible only with what that vendor is doing internally in their own network. Another reason is that you cannot use the PAD to talk to another vendor. By using the standard protocols you used in the past there is minimum disruption to your operation. All you have to do is bring in the PAD on your site and get the communication link running, a relatively simple way of seeing whether being an X.25 node is to your advantage.

Figure 17–5(c) shows a more comprehensive interface for communicating with both TELENET and TYMNET (or others). You still use your standard protocol to talk to an X.25 PAD, but in this case it is a *generic* PAD. Generic PADs are available from a variety of vendors who have *certified software*, which means the packet vendor has certified that the software in that vendor's PAD is compatible with their network. If you need to communicate with two or more vendors (or if you want to spend less money to communicate with a single vendor) then this would be a way for you to go. Based on the address of your transmission the PAD can determine which packet network to communicate with. A related version is a PAD that may be installed in a PBX to communicate with a particular vendor, again based on address. The X.25 interfaces available in PBXs are not yet at the same capability level as the standalone PADs, but they are being developed. Generic PADs offer the most flexibility if you must communicate with two or more packet networks and you want minimal disruption of your system.

Ultimately you may want to go to Fig. 17–5(d), where you get the X.25 port directly in your Communications Front End (CFE). There are various vendors, including IBM, that provide an X.25 interface in the price range of $9000–$12,000 per port. Remember, you must make sure the vendor's software is certified by the packet vendor you expect to communicate with. Putting the X.25 port directly into your CFE provides the most efficient connection, but may be the hardest to implement. If there are troubles it will take time to debug, while your

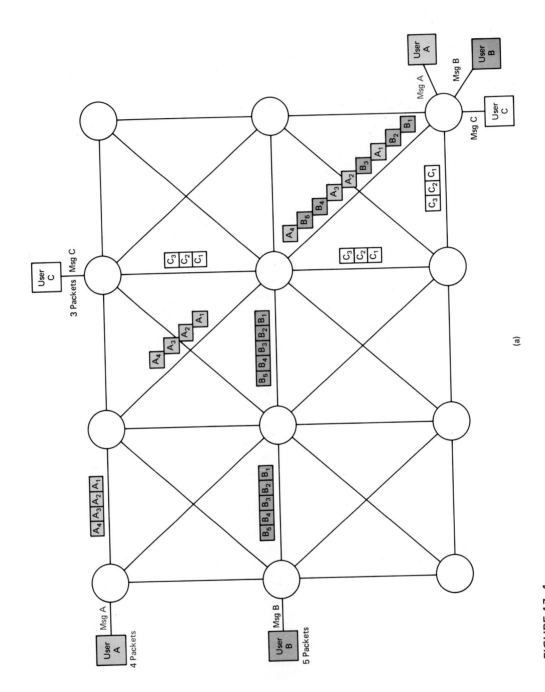

**FIGURE 17-4**
(a) Routing; (b) Telenet Routing.

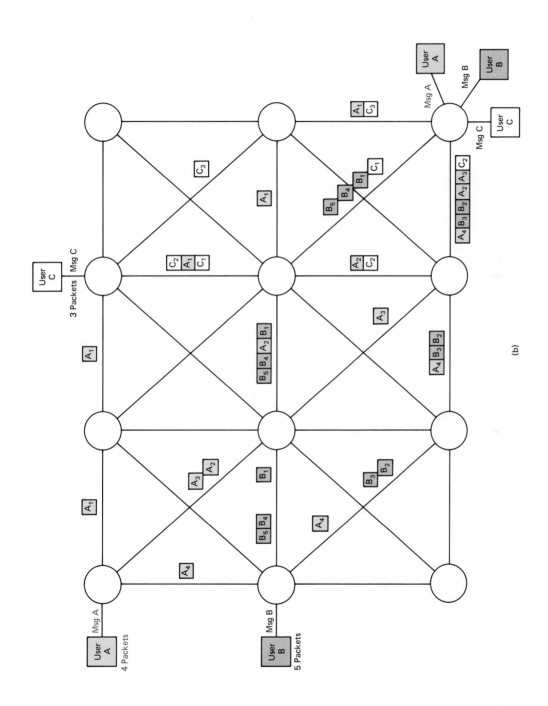

(b)

401

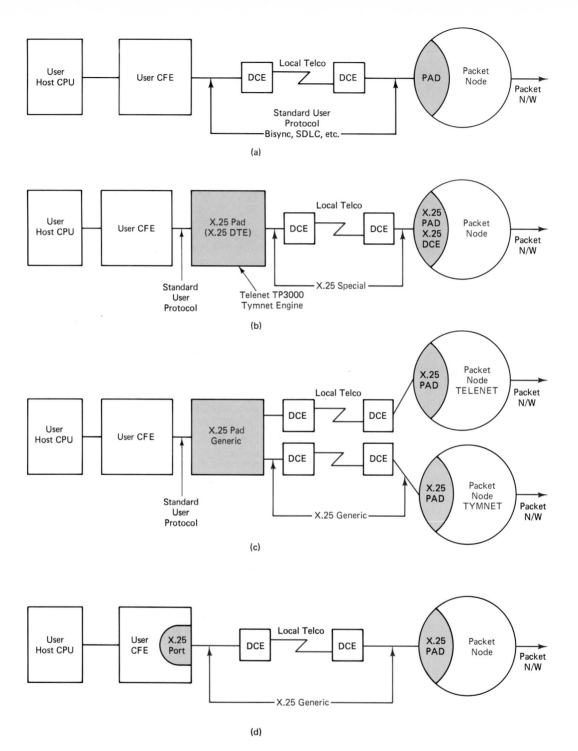

**FIGURE 17-5**
User Site X.25 PAD

network still needs to communicate. This method involves the most radical change, but in the long run it may be more efficient and less expensive for you to use once it gets up and running.

There are many reasons why you may want to implement an X.25 interface on your own site. One of the biggest is the saving of ports on the CFE. With ports costing up to $500 each, many of them can be combined to communicate through a single X.25 port, thereby potentially saving money based on the amount of ports that can be eliminated. If you have many low-speed ports that can be combined into a single high-speed X.25 port, this may be a desirable option for you.

Another reason is that an X.25 port can support up to 1024 terminals simultaneously based on logical addressing. As long as the volume of transmissions is such that the port will not be overloaded with simultaneous data, 1024 separate devices can be supported here (but typically they do not exceed 512). Eventually, with the growth of different PADs in the packet network, it may also be desirable to utilize an X.25 port, with conversions to other protocols performed for you by the packet vendor in the remote environments. Finally, using an onsite X.25 PAD is a relatively simple way to go from an asynchronous environment to a synchronous environment without incorporating new protocols. Speed may not be a big reason initially to go X.25, but as data volumes grow it will become more important.

While on the subject of X.25 PADs, you should also be aware of other products being announced by vendors for incorporation into their packet networks. TYMNET, for example, announced in 1987 a Desktop Packet Switch that they call a NANO Engine. The NANO Engine acts as a PAD for both terminals and hosts. It supports X.25, SNA/SDLC, 3270 Bisync, and asynchronous protocols. It can operate up to 64 KBPS and is self monitoring in that it supplies status information through a separate diagnostic port. TELENET is developing end-to-end voice and data switches that can be provided through multiplexers on in-house PADs. There was no date announced for availability, but this is the kind of equipment that is being developed. Other evolving services are support for dial out at 2400 BPS and higher to unattended devices and support for both X.PC and MNP.

A natural adjunct to these services will be a combined packet and circuit switch that will integrate both types of switching in a single box. Eventually this will evolve into a switch that can handle both packet and ISDN services. The device may look like a T-1 multiplexer with an ISDN interface that can tie into a packet switching network. Network management might be a problem here because there is currently no unified plan on how to provide management across networks. There are also signaling incompatibilities between the two concerning call setup and controls. Some form of gateway product will probably provide that interface. Ultimately you will probably see board-level PADs that can be incorporated right into a PC with the PC acting as a combined terminal and PAD. Here, too, the PAD must be certified for operation with a particular vendor's network.

In all of these devices and services there will be descriptions of throughput.

If you think throughput is going to be a problem for you then you must find out how the vendor is calculating it because there are many ways to do so. In addition, you need to know what the delay through a PAD or a switch is because it may affect the particular protocol you are operating with, such as Bisync. Some delays are up to 100 milliseconds through a switch, which can have an impact on timeouts for your protocols.

Finally, there will be *hybrid* switches developed for implementation on interconnected networks such as packet and SNA. A hybrid switch will be able to send both packets and SNA messages on the same physical circuit and will sort between them without a protocol conversion. Hybrid switches may also be used for switching on the B or D channel of ISDN (see Chapter 16) so that information on the B and D channel can either go to public packet network or be routed via circuit switched lines. AT&T has announced that they anticipate putting a hybrid capability into their No. 5 ESS to enable Centrex, PBX, and tandem switches on public and private networks to carry packets on public-switched telephone lines. They will then be able to use a single switch instead of multiple switches with multiplexing. Bellcore is talking about utilizing channels of between 2 and 150 MBPS where there will be a circuit switched channel for high resolution TV and packet service for all other forms of transmission (voice, data, facsimile). The problem Bellcore anticipates is integrating the multiple rates into a single common rate for uniform transmission.

Ultimately, there will be voice packet switching. The problems of voice packet switching are different from data packet switching because there is much less tolerance for packet delay in voice than there is for data. AT&T already owns some patents in this area and has described a wideband packet service for voice, data, image, and full motion video. Their system is expected to move millions of packets per second, and eventually tens of millions of packets per second, compared to today's switches that run in the range of thousands of packets per second. Some of the capability will be provided by parallel switching capabilities, speech compression down to 12.8 KBPS, and the sensing of silent periods to eliminate excess packet transmission. Switches and equipment to support this mode of operation are expected to become available in the mid-1990s.

In anticipation of the superpacket switch for central offices in the 1990s, AT&T has already demonstrated a packet telephone system that can support several hundred voice conversations. The goal is to get more than 10,000 separate voice conversations on a single broadband Metropolitan Area cable.

Initial announcements from AT&T say that their central office of the future will use both fast and wideband packet switching. They expect to have variable length packets with voice and data transmitted on the same circuit but not mixed within the same packet (voice will typically constitute a 512-bit packet). Routing will be handled by hardware logic, with the route established at the time of connection (see fast-packet switching in the next section). Every packet will follow the same path to get across up to seven switching nodes with a 55 millisecond delay maximum. To keep delay problems from affecting the voice, a predetermined amount of delay will be added to the total transmission so that when it is converted back to voice at the receive end, the signal will be *smoothed out*.

It is possible that the T-1 framing format between these new switches will allow more conversations in a single T-1 channel, with the control for each provided in the 24th channel (out of band). The ultimate goal is to have the equivalent of 100 T-1 links between switches, each with at least 100 separate conversations, resulting in a 10,000-line central office. One of the ways this will be done is to eliminate the *packets of silence*, described in Chapter 14 under speech compression. If ADPCM is used instead of PCM, and the silent periods are taken into account, it is anticipated that only 40 percent of the original 64-KBPS bandwidth will be required. Some of this technology may be in its early stages in Datakit and ISN (described in Chapter 15), which today is used for data only, may be utilized for voice packet switching in the future.

As a final topic within the subject of packet switching, a new term being used is *Fast-Packet Switching* (FPS). The concept of FPS is to utilize a packet format for internodal trunks instead of setting up a circuit between them. The FPS packets are transmitted and routed through each of the fast-packet nodes without depacketizing until the destination node is reached. The route is set up prior to the transmission of the first packet.

In the same way that operation for TYMNET was described, a predetermined route is established prior to transmission of the fast packets comprising a message (this could be a voice transmission). A single packet is transmitted through the network via the desired path, and at the same time a series of alternate paths is stored in a processor. If there is a problem during the transmission, one of the alternate paths can be utilized to transmit the remainder of the message. Once the initiating packet has reached the destination node, a return packet is sent using the same path to validate that the path is now available. Thus, minimal routing time through the switches can be accomplished, and transmissions that are less tolerant of delays can be accommodated.

Fast-packet technology is available today using the standard D-4 framing format for digital transmission, which consists of a standard 193-bit packet size that also allows for a throughput of 8000 packets per second through a T-1 facility.

Because of the critical nature of the throughput, the upper limit of one way delay will not exceed 160 milliseconds. On an individual node basis delays of less than 10 milliseconds have been reported, with a total end-to-end delay of less than 55 milliseconds.

Data to be transmitted using FPS technology must be handled differently from voice. Data can tolerate longer delays on an end-to-end basis, but it cannot tolerate any form of corruption (errors). Voice packets can be eliminated if they happen to take too long in reaching their destination, but data cannot. Data can incorporate end-to-end validation but voice does not need it. When utilized together, voice packets have a higher priority than data packets in FPS.

Considering all of the technology in progress, there will definitely be some significant evolutionary announcements in the next few years. Along with the desire of most users to have *interconnected* networks with full network management, much care must be used in incorporating these technologies when connecting multiple networks.

As a final point, there is the question of when and where to use packet switching. The most common impetus involves the connection of a single central-site processor to a multitude of remote locations where sporadic connection is required and the costs for a dial-up line would be too high. Or, a multitude of locations may be connected to another widely distributed group of locations under the same cost restrictions. These two cases constitute the most prevalent scenarios. However, packet use may simply make economic sense on a specific point-to-point basis where your dial-up costs are beginning to become significant.

Figure 17–6 describes the trade-off criteria among a dial connection, packet switching, and a leased line on a point-to-point circuit. There is no cost for the dial network if you don't use it, but the cost goes up very quickly when you do, depending on the time and distance of the call. Therefore the slope of dial-line costs is very steep. Next, the packet switching network has certain up-front fixed costs for interfacing to the packet network, but since charges are by volume, not time and distance, the slope of the cost line is much less than for a dial connection. Finally, a leased line costs the same whether it is lightly or heavily used. Therefore, it is a flat line. If your usage is below the point where the packet and dial lines cross, you are better off staying with a dial connection. Between that and the intersection of packet and leased line usage, you are better off with packet services. At or beyond the intersection of packet and leased line usage, you should definitely put in a leased line. At that point the cost is justified, and a leased line is yours to utilize in an unlimited manner, and at any speed you can reliably transmit on that line.

**FIGURE 17–6**
Cost Comparison of Services Point to Point

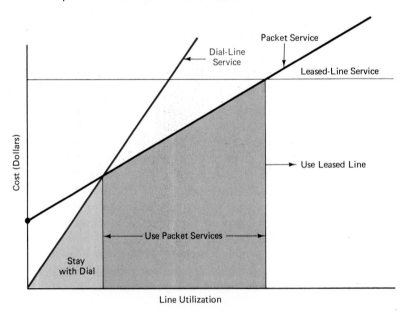

A natural question now is: Where am I going to get all this information? Much of it should already be available from your telephone bill regarding the dial costs. The leased-line cost is available from any long-distance carrier, and the packet costs can be estimated by contacting any one of the primary vendors and describing how much data you anticipate sending, the volume, and when your typical high traffic periods are. The numbers may not be exact, but you will be in a good position to know whether you are in the ballpark for any one of the three services. You can then make your selection accordingly. Obviously there are other considerations involved, but if you have a particular point-to-point situation that must be evaluated, Fig. 17–6 shows a way to perform that comparison.

## QUESTIONS

1. Briefly describe the overall concept of packet switching.
2. Describe the three primary modes of circuit configuration used to connect end-user devices.
3. What is the function of a PAD?
4. What are the three primary specifications used for asynchronous transmission in a packet network?
5. What is the primary specification used for synchronous transmission in a packet network?
6. What is the difference between a connection-oriented and a connectionless transmission?
7. How does a user access a packet network?
8. What do you need to consider when deciding whether to use packet switching?
9. What do you need to consider when deciding on which packet vendor to use for vendor-provided network facilities?
10. What is the operational difference between a dynamic routing system and a fixed routing system?
11. What is the typical implementation sequence for a user to incorporate an X.25 PAD on user-owned facilities?
12. What will be the primary use for fast-packet switching?

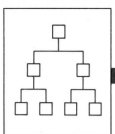

# 18

# Network Architectures

## A
## BACKGROUND

One of the biggest areas of network evolution over the last 15 years has been the movement toward standardized networking and internetworking. From the proprietary schemes of individual vendors in the 1970s to the internetworking standards of the 1980s, we are in the process of heading toward a so-called *global data network* in the 1990s. The ultimate goal is to allow any device on any network to communicate with any other device on any other network regardless of where the individual devices are, the networks are, or most important, who the vendors are. Some vendors have been reluctant to move toward total interconnectivity because they fear the loss of potential proprietary product sales. But to maintain proprietary equipment sales, it must be possible for the equipment to communicate with devices and networks provided by other vendors in different geographic and network environments. This chapter will describe both the international and proprietary network interfaces that have evolved since the early 1970s.

# OPEN SYSTEMS INTERCONNECT (OSI)

The Open Systems Interconnect (OSI) is a specification describing seven layers of interface that was developed by the International Standards Organization (ISO). The specification is sometimes called the OSI or ISO *model*. OSI was developed because of the need to interconnect different vendors' products and services utilized at either the same or different locations. The aim of the OSI model is to provide a standardized set of parameters which, if followed by the different vendors, would provide a methodology for communicating at all levels in the user's environment. OSI is known as a *layered protocol*, where each layer has a specific set of functions to perform. Each layer should have a standardized interface to the layers both above it and below it and should be able to communicate directly with the equivalent layer of another device.

A simplified version of the OSI reference model is shown in Fig. 18–1. The functions of each one of these layers are as follows:

**LAYER ONE** Layer One is called the *physical* layer and includes those functions required to activate, maintain, and deactivate the physical connections. It is responsible for getting the bits of information to and from the physical medium. Layer One defines both the functional and procedural characteristics of the interface to the physical circuit. Included in this layer are the electrical specifications, the cabling and wiring characteristics, and a functional description of the data and control flow across the interface to the medium.

**FIGURE 18–1**
OSI Reference Model

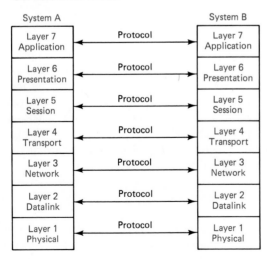

**LAYER TWO**     Layer Two is called the *datalink* layer and incorporates the mechanism for synchronizing the transmission of information over the physical link. It includes error control and is independent of the information the bits represent. In OSI Layer Two is called *High Level Data Link Control* (HDLC). On a practical level, it is the mechanism whereby information is transmitted between two adjacent locations, or two adjacent nodes within a larger network. HDLC is roughly equivalent to what the vendors typically call a protocol that moves data between devices. HDLC moves the information within a predetermined set of parameters. At this level there are options allowing multilink communications (splitting a single communication across multiple physical channels). Level Two controls connection-oriented, connectionless, and single-frame transmissions. Connection-oriented service means that a connection must be established between the two end systems before the initiation of communications. The connection can be a physical one (actual wire) or a virtual one (predetermined routes through which packets will be moved from end to end, possibly on different circuits). This is similar to making a telephone call in which the circuit is established by dialing and then a conversation can take place between the two parties connected. The path can be different each time you dial.

A connectionless service involves transmission of data in a packet form with each packet traveling independently. The path may be established on an end-to-end basis with nodes in between on a predetermined basis, or each node can determine the next path to take when a packet enters that node. This is similar to mailing a letter that will be moved to its destination regardless of any other letters sent to the same location and regardless of which route is taken.

In single-frame transmission only a single frame is sent at one time.

Datalink layer protocols may have the ability to break up data into separate frames or packets that are transmitted in order one at a time. Individual frames may require acknowledgment after receipt. If an acknowledgment is not received the packet will be retransmitted. The datalink layer thereby provides packet flow control, which in turn allows the system to change speeds at either end.

**LAYER THREE**     Layer Three is called the *network* layer. It provides the necessary switching and routing functions required to establish, maintain, and then terminate any connections between transmitting and receiving locations. Layer Three is known as the X.25 layer and includes the disassembly, reassembly, and error correction for packets transmitted in a packet switched network. This is the layer that determines how the routing will be performed in moving a packet or a message from end to end through a network consisting of many nodes. At this level there can be many different types of networks, and each family of protocols developed for use within this layer will have a unique identifier so that it can be identified and changed if necessary during the transmission of a message.

**LAYER FOUR**     Layer Four, the *transport* layer, provides for an end-to-end control of the information interchange between two devices. It incorporates flow control, error recovery, and end-to-end acknowledgment. Layer Four incorporates such functions as multiplexing independent message strings over a single connection and segmenting data into appropriately sized units for handling by the network layer. It provides a level of isolation designed to keep the user independent of the physical and operational functions of the network. An analogy applicable to this layer is the case of sending a certified or registered letter through the postal system. Moving the letter from node to node (Layer Two) is handled by the sign-off of the letter at each physical location that it reaches, and the ultimate receiver at the final location signs the return card and sends it back through the network. When the return card is received by the original transmitter, you have an end-to-end acknowledgment. Layer Four protocols typically validate that data is not modified, duplicated, or lost in transmission. It also provides end-to-end error checking.

**LAYER FIVE**    Layer Five is the *session* layer, which provides the necessary interface to support a dialog between two separate locations and provides two forms of that dialog. The first is a two-way alternating (half-duplex) mode, and the second, a two-way simultaneous (full-duplex) mode. Layer Five incorporates the establishment of a communication session, which is equivalent to logging on to a particular application. Each of the transmissions to and from that application is part of that session. The session will be terminated when the user wants to communicate with a different application, so the user must log off the existing application and log on to the new one.

**LAYER SIX**    Layer Six, the *presentation* layer, insures that information is delivered in a form that the receiving system can understand and use, in other words, that the syntax or physical representation of the data is compatible. Layer Six is not concerned with the meaning of information, only that it is presented in a form that is recognizable to the application layer. An example of the need for this layer would be two terminals communicating with each other with one using ASCII code and the other using EBCDIC. The presentation layer provides the negotiation and determination as to which end does the translation of the code, while maintaining the meaning of the information. Included in this layer are the processes of screen formatting, encryption, compression, and all other forms of bit manipulation that involve display on the receiving device.

**LAYER SEVEN**    Layer Seven, the *application* layer, is involved in the support of the actual end-user application. At this level the meaning of the information is important, and the function is to support all applications as well as to manipulate information (not bits). Layer Seven's function is to provide for transfer of files, graphic information, document processing, and any other function that is required for the unique user environment. Included at this level is the capability for distributed processing.

When two compatible systems communicate with each other, it is the two application layers that actually move the information back and forth. If a communication link is involved, the information starts at Layer Seven in one device and moves down through all the layers, including the physical layer, where the bits of information are transferred to the medium. Either a local connection is provided or a long-distance carrier environment is traversed. The information is inserted back into the first layer of the receiving device and then works its way up through Layer Seven.

One of the larger issues today concerning network protocols is the variety of specifications that are applicable to each layer. It is a very controversial subject, because most users and many of the vendors who build *clone-type equipment* would like to see universal interfaces. Others feel that the availability of different specifications in each of the layers leads to a *proprietary* set of equipment, even though they favor the overall OSI specification.

For example, the ideal device is capable of communicating with any other device through each of the seven layers, but a variety of specifications can be used in each layer. Foremost of the different standards is right at the physical level. One of three completely incompatible interfaces, the IEEE 802.3/.4/.5 specifications can be used. 802.3 is an Ethernet equivalent using collision detection, 802.4 is token passing, and 802.5 is token ring, which is IBM's favorite mode of transmission. They are radically different hardware and software interfaces for the physical level, although they do not correspond exactly to the first level of ISO. You can utilize any one of these specifications (the actual ISO spec is 8802/3, 8802/4, and 8802.5) and be ISO compatible, but you still may not be able to communicate with other devices. Interfaces such as RS232 or CCITT X.21 may also be used.

For economic reasons it does not make sense to incorporate all three interfaces into a single device, so your equipment will have one of the three primary types of interface. You will probably use the interface that is most applicable to your particular application. You will be OSI compatible, but may still not be able to talk to another device that is also OSI compatible if it has a different standard interface.

At the second level, with HDLC, different parameters can be selected by different end users. For example, the transmission can be specified as to different maximum packet lengths. If you choose a longer length than other users, they will be able to transmit to you but you cannot transmit to them.

There are opportunities for incompatibility all the way up through each layer, and there are areas in Layers Five and Six that are not even completely defined yet. As a user, you can select the specific parameters you want for your application, but your choices may be different from those of another user with the same application. An example of selecting different parameters in the same layers will be described in Section E, on MAP/TOP. As an end user you may want to see a single set of standards being used, but in all likelihood a *series* of standards will be used in the future.

To get an idea of some of the different specifications that are applicable at each level, refer to Fig. 18–2.

The primary functions for the network layer, Layer Three, include network connections, data transfer, reset, and connection/release functions in conform-

Level

| Level | | |
|---|---|---|
| 7 | Electronic Mail<br>File Transfers<br>Virtual Terminals<br>CAD/CAM | Process Control<br>Robotics<br>Graphics<br>Document Exchange |
| 6 | ASCII          EBCDIC<br>Data for Specific Applications — FAX/Graphics/etc.<br>ISO 8824 | Binary Stream<br><br>ISO 8825 |
| 5 | ISO 8326 | ISO 8327 |
| 4 | ISO 8072          ISO 8073<br>ISO INTERNET 8473 | |
| 3 | ISO 8348          ISO 8473          X.25 | |
| 2 | IEEE 802.2 (LLC)          HDLC<br>ISO 8802 | |
| 1 | IEEE 802.3/.4/.5          CCITT X.21<br>RS232          RS449          ISO 8802/3/4/5 | |

**FIGURE 18–2**
*Layer Specifications and Descriptions*

ance with the X.25 standard and ISO standards 8348 or 8473. At this level there can be many different types of networks and therefore each family of protocols developed for use within this layer must have a unique identifier so it can be changed if necessary during the transmission of the message.

At the transport layer, Layer Four, ISO 8073 specifies the multiple classes of protocols for *connection-oriented* communications, while ISO 8072 specifies the type of service that must be provided at this level. Typically, a Layer-Four protocol validates that data is not modified, duplicated, or lost in transmission. It can include end-to-end error detection or pass on the validation that may be provided in the network layer.

At the fifth layer, ISO 8326 specifies the type of service, while ISO 8327 specifies the protocol. There is still a lot of work being performed at this level, but it will definitely contain two separate subsets of service: (1) the *session kernel* for establishing and releasing a session, and (2) *token management*, which is a request for use of resources that is added to the kernel.

Within the sixth layer, ISO 8824 provides the rules for defining and recording the meaning of individual messages. In conjunction with ISO 8824, ISO 8825 defines basic encoding rules that are necessary to convert notations into actual messages for subsequent transfer.

The seventh, or application layer contains the functions for transfer of files, accessing information, transferring jobs, manipulating data, message handling, virtual capabilities, and other applications. The application layer is normally oriented toward a particular type of business, such as banking, automation, and electronic mail, where typical uses might include graphics, facsimile, robotics, document exchange, CAD/CAM, and virtual terminals.

Without getting into the mechanics of bit manipulation, the seventh layer typically works as follows. A message is generated at the user's application and inserted at the seventh layer. The application layer adds a header identifying the appropriate parameters and sends the message down to the sixth layer, which puts its own header on. The process continues, with each layer adding its own information to the length of the message until it reaches Layer Two, where the message is put into packet form within an X.25 transmission frame. The physical level transmits the bits. At the receiving end each piece of the header is stripped off as the information works its way back up the ladder. Finally, the user's application at the receiving end can look at the message in a form that can be utilized by the user at that location.

Many people have found it hard to conceptualize this transmission layering with each layer providing its own unique function. An analogy is used for clarification, showing the generation, transmission, and reception of a letter between two locations where the language is different, such as the United States and Japan. A diagram is shown in Fig. 18–3.

Let us assume that a Japanese factory manager has read about a new product being manufactured in the United States and would like to obtain manufacturing rights. The need for information translates into the application process. The product manager consults an engineer, who becomes the *application layer*. The engineer prepares the appropriate questions to be asked about the product in a letter, primarily concerning the technical aspects.

**FIGURE 18–3**
OSI Example

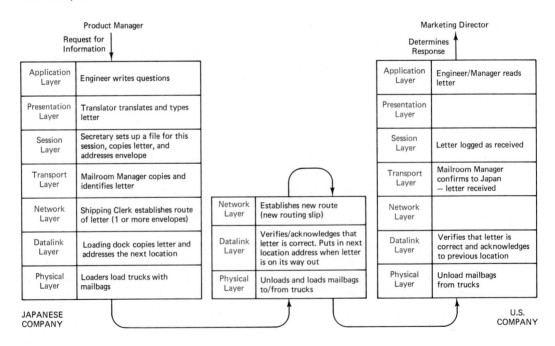

The engineer writes the questions in Japanese and gives them to a translator who prepares the actual letter so that it not only utilizes the correct format but also provides the specific questions in English. This is the primary function of the *presentation layer*, to make sure that information is in a form that the recipient can understand and use.

After typing the letter, the translator gives it to a secretary, who represents the *session layer*. The secretary sets up the file dealing with the particular product, copies the letter for the file, and addresses the envelope to the location in the United States where the request must be sent.

The secretary then takes the letter to the mailroom manager, who represents the *transport layer*. The job of the mailroom manager is to guarantee receipt of the letter in the United States. He does this by first making a copy of the letter. This level of validation is an *end-to-end* mechanism and is equivalent to the transmission of a certified or registered letter in the United States with a return receipt requested. The return receipt is the green postcard which you, as the transmitter, attach to the letter. Regardless of the route that the letter takes to the recipient, the recipient signs the card and it comes back to you, even if by a different route.

The mailroom manager then sends the letter to the shipping clerk, who is the *network layer*. The shipping clerk has to make sure the letter is an appropriate size. For example, if drawings or attachments must be sent, different *envelopes* may have to be used. For example purposes, let us say the shipping clerk must make up five separate envelopes. The shipping clerk addresses and transmits one envelope at a time with the address of the next location to receive that letter. If the letter has to go from Tokyo to St. Louis, for example, the shipping clerk must determine the route from Tokyo to that point. The letter could go through Honolulu, Los Angeles, San Francisco, or directly to St. Louis. In addition, each of the five envelopes can take a different path.

The shipping clerk sends each letter with an individual city address to the loading dock, the *datalink layer*, where the loaders copy each one and put on the physical address of the next specific location identified by the shipping clerk. The loaders then put the letters on a truck or other vehicle (the medium) and ship them out. The vehicle is the *physical layer*.

A single relay point is shown in the middle of Fig. 18–3, representing one of the interim cities. At the physical layer, the loaders bring in the mailbag with the specific letter and verify that the letter is correct and was not damaged in transmission (has no bit errors).

The letter is then sent up to the relay point shipping clerk, who establishes the route for the next leg of the trip. The loaders then put the specific address on and ship it out again.

There can be any number of relay points in the process, with each letter potentially taking a different path until they all get to the U.S. company in St. Louis. At the company location the loaders unload each mailbag from the truck. The loaders verify that each letter is correct and acknowledge back to the last relay point that sent the letter.

The letter is then sent to the shipping clerk, who only has to pass the letter on to the mailroom manager because there is no additional routing to be performed. The network layer block is therefore empty on the U.S. side of Fig. 18–3. The mailroom manager then assembles the five letters, validates that all of the individual letters that make up the total package have been received, and sends an acknowledgment back to the mailroom manager in Japan indicating that the entire letter has been received in the United States. The mailroom manager hands the letter to the secretary in the U.S. company, who logs the letter as received and sets up a file (the session layer).

There is no function to be performed at the presentation layer because translation was already done in Japan. Therefore the presentation layer block is empty. The secretary can now give the entire letter to the applications engineer (Layer Seven), who reads the letter, interprets it, and decides which questions can be answered and how. The engineer goes to the marketing director of the U.S. company to determine what kind of response needs to be generated, and the process is then reversed to Japan.

Each letter transmitted back and forth between the two companies becomes part of the *session* (file) that was set up. Whether the two companies decide to work together or not, the session continues until they either drop the project or go into the next phase of working together, which could potentially be a different session.

If you go back through the process, you will see that each of the individuals involved (each layer) adds additional information to the letter itself to promote the process of communications. Each of the seven layers of the OSI protocol performs its specific function so that all of them can work together connecting the two diverse locations.

Reams and reams of descriptions and explanations have been written on the OSI model, especially as it applies to packet switching, so they will not be discussed in more detail here. There are also other protocols based on the OSI model, and some of them will be described here.

## C
## SYSTEMS NETWORK ARCHITECTURE (SNA)

Systems Network Architecture (SNA) was first introduced in the early 1970s. By 1987 over 25,000 SNA networks were in use around the world and over the years SNA has generated thousands of articles, descriptions, and interpretations. Although there is general agreement as to what SNA is, there are always variations in the interpretation of what it does and how it does it. This text will attempt to describe the overall concepts, major components, and functional operation of SNA, as well as many of the software packages that interface with it. It should be noted at the outset that SNA is a continually evolving environment and there will always be changes and new products or interfaces being added to it. Therefore, whatever is described here should be verified prior to utilizing the information in any evaluation you are performing.

SNA has been described as a set of formalized architectural specifications or architectural philosophy with a set of design specifications for all future IBM communication products such that all those products can be interconnected.

SNA is actually a layered set of protocols, like OSI. It provides a series of specifications in which rules of operation, logical procedures of interaction and interfacing, and formats for movement of information are defined. In other words, SNA is like a *transport* service for a host of different applications.

Some people describe SNA as a five-layer protocol structure or architecture with the physical control (equivalent to ISO Level One) and the application level (equivalent to ISO Level Seven) outside SNA, but interacting with it. Others describe all seven layers as being part of SNA. This text will treat all seven layers as if they were part of SNA, because whether they interact as a part of or as an adjunct to SNA, they are part of the overall process.

Before getting into the details of the SNA structure it would be beneficial to see how SNA relates to OSI. Figure 18–4 shows the seven OSI layers in relation to two different IBM hierarchies. The middle column contains IBM's products that are compatible with the seven OSI layers. IBM's SNA layers are on the right.

**FIGURE 18–4**
SNA Compared to OSI

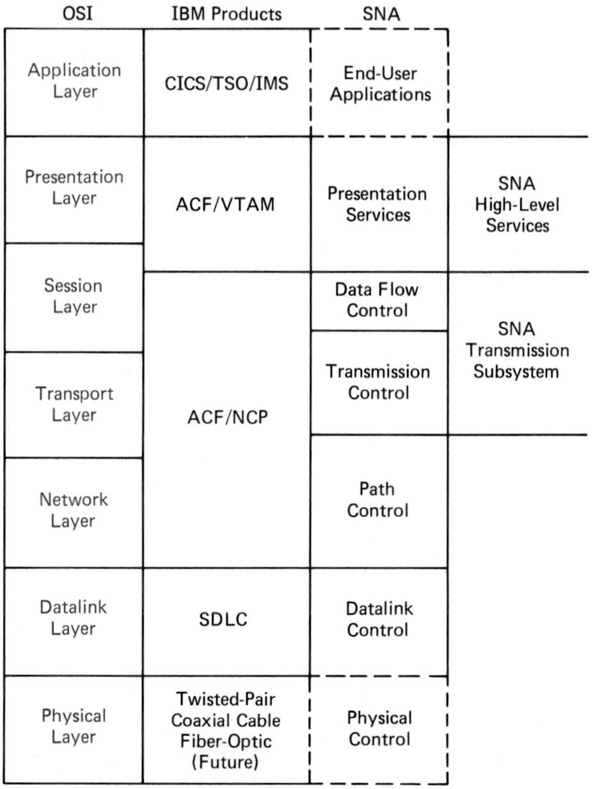

| OSI | IBM Products | SNA | |
|---|---|---|---|
| Application Layer | CICS/TSO/IMS | End-User Applications | |
| Presentation Layer | ACF/VTAM | Presentation Services | SNA High-Level Services |
| Session Layer | ACF/NCP | Data Flow Control | SNA Transmission Subsystem |
| Transport Layer | | Transmission Control | |
| Network Layer | | Path Control | |
| Datalink Layer | SDLC | Datalink Control | |
| Physical Layer | Twisted-Pair Coaxial Cable Fiber-Optic (Future) | Physical Control | |

The OSI application layer is described by SNA as the end-user application layer and is comparable to IBM's applications such as CICS (Customer Information Control System), TSO (Time Share Option), and IMS (Integrated Management System).

Except for the application layer there is no direct comparison between what SNA provides and what OSI provides. The SNA high-level services, which consist of presentation, function management, and session control, offer somewhat more capability than exists in the OSI presentation layer. The equivalent IBM product is ACF/VTAM (Advanced Communication Function/Virtual Telecommunications Access Method).

The OSI session layer covers some of the SNA presentation services and the entire data flow control portion of SNA. The session layer also includes a portion of the SNA transmission control subsystem, which in turn overlaps a portion of the OSI transport layer. Data flow and transmission control are described as the transmission subsystem in SNA.

The OSI transport layer and network layer and the major portion of the session layer all equate to IBM's ACF/NCP (Advanced Communication Function/Network Control Program), which incorporates the SNA transmission subsystem and path control.

OSI's datalink layer is HDLC, while the SNA datalink control is SDLC. SDLC is a clone of HDLC, with specific options selected for the way IBM will move bits on a communications link.

The OSI physical layer corresponds to the SNA physical control, which consists of primarily coaxial cable for IBM, but may also consist of twisted pair.

As can be seen there are seven layers in both OSI and SNA, but their implementations are very different, especially between Layers Three through Six.

A major difference between OSI and SNA is that OSI specifies that the software in a particular product must have corresponding software in the device it is communicating with. If error detection and recovery is in one device, it must also be in the second device. Also, the fifth and sixth layers of OSI still have many functions that are not yet fully defined, although the seventh layer requires Layers Five and Six to operate. Vendors are forced to assume certain characteristics of Layers Five and Six, which IBM has done. The result is that the interactions of different vendors' network architectures are all potentially different, because the vendors may make different assumptions about parameters within those layers. Another area that affects not only OSI and SNA, but also probably all other network architectures, is throughput. Recent studies have shown that OSI Layer Four (the transport layer) has a maximum throughput capability of somewhere between 600 KBPS and approximately 1.8 MBPS, which means that if a user eventually requires a higher throughput, such as T-1 and T-3 networking, there may have to be a substantial change in those architectures. The needed changes may be far off in the future, but with high-speed transmissions becoming available all the time, they may be required much sooner than you would like.

Let us now take a look at the structure and some of the components of SNA. The architectural rules specify what the SNA end users can be. The end users are either application programs, I/O devices, or terminal operators, which are not always considered part of the architecture but utilize SNA for interconnecting with other devices and sharing resources. There is a specifically defined relationship and interface between SNA and the various network components. The network components are called *logical* components and are required to interconnect and share resources between the various end users of the system. The architectural rules also specify the operating sequence for controlling the configuration and operation of a network.

The SNA architecture defines three entities as Network Addressable Units (NAU). NAUs are the components through which users communicate with each other. They are

Logical Units (LU)

Physical Units (PU)

System Services Control Points (SSCP)

All of the NAUs reside within an end point known as an SNA node. The SNA nodes are connected by the communication links that perform various SNA functions. The NAU is a logical location with a unique name and address. Figure 18–5 shows the relationship of these units.

The LU is responsible for allocating resources to the end user, such as memory, CPU cycles, records, sessions, and I/O devices like keyboards and displays. PUs are software-based devices that actually move information. The various types will be described later.

SNA operates by setting up sessions between two NAUs known as logical

**FIGURE 18–5**
*SNA/NAU Relationships*

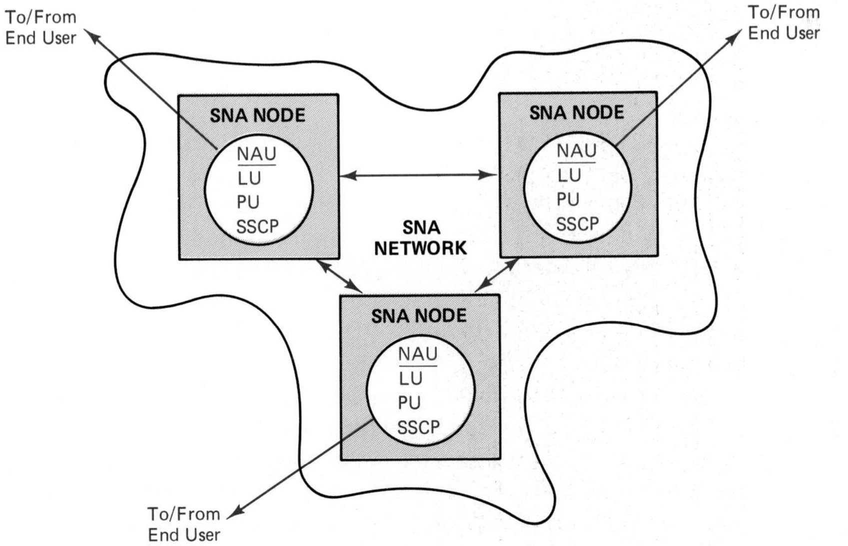

connections. Sessions that directly connect end-user application programs are known as LU–LU sessions. All other sessions, which are between SSCPs and other SSCPs, LUs, or PUs, are known as *control sessions.*

The control sessions, also known as non-LU sessions, involve a hierarchical host resident application program communicating with a *dumb* I/O device such as a terminal or a printer. These sessions are known as Types 1, 2, 3, 4, and 7.

The newer LU–LU sessions that directly connect end-user programs or devices are known as LU Type 6.0, 6.1, and 6.2. LU 6.2 is a general purpose program-to-program session (described in more detail later).

There are various types of PUs, described as follows:

*PU Type 1.* PU Type 1 was utilized prior to SNA and is also called a Terminal Node (TN). It supports non-SNA type protocols at the datalink level and consists of Async and 3270 Bisync. SDLC can also be included here. Type 1 devices consist of 3271 and 3272 terminals.

*PU Type 2.0.* Type 2.0 is a Cluster Controller Node (CLC) and consists of the 3174, 3274, and 3276 controllers. It supports the PU Control Point (PUCP) software and supports a single link connection to the next level of the SNA hierarchy.

*PU Type 2.1.* Type 2.1 is known as a Network Node (NN) or a Peripheral Node (PN). It is sometimes also called an Advanced CLC node. Type 2.1 devices consist of System 36/38, 5520, 8100, System 1, and IBM PCs. They support the Peripheral Node Control Point (PNCP) software, which is a major SSCP subset allowing PU 2.1 nodes to control SNA sessions directly.

*PU Type 4.* A Type 4 device is a Communications Controller (COMC) and consists of the 3705, 3725, 3726, 3720, 3721, and 2725, all of which support NCP (Network Control Program) software.

*PU Type 5.* Type 5 is a host node, such as the System 370, 3030, 3080, 3090, 4300, and 9370, which supports SSCP software. The PU Type 4 and PU Type 5 are also called subarea nodes because they support subarea addressing and can recognize the different network environments.

The SSCP is the host resident NAU responsible for network management; it is considered a subset of VTAM. It provides the control of a *domain*, which is defined as an SSCP with all its interacting PUs, LUs, communication links, and station addresses. The host node is the only node that would contain all three NAU types. A diagram of all PU/LU relationships is shown in Fig. 18–6.

The various physical units are shown in Fig. 18–6, such as the PU-1 which is a pre-SNA type device, and a PU-2, which is a cluster controller. No PU-3 is defined in SNA to date. The PU-4 is the communication front end, and a PU-5 is the host. The various LUs are LU Type 1, which is an application program communicating with a non3270-type printer; LU Type 2, which is an application program communicating with a 3270-type terminal display; LU Type 3, which is an application program communicating with a 3270-type printer; an LU Type 4, which includes the various office product-type programs; and the LU 6, which is

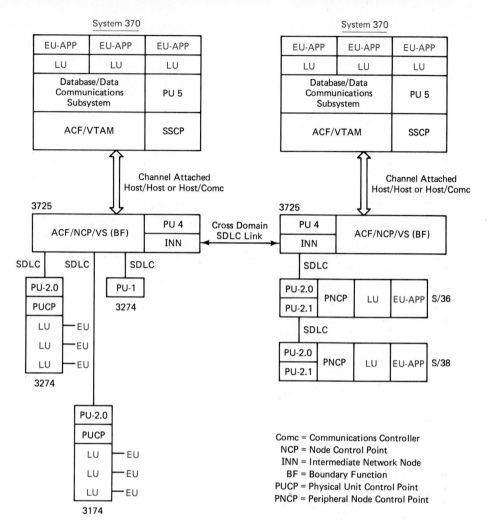

**FIGURE 18–6**
PU/LU Relationships

an application-to-application program residing in any device that is defined as a host. The LUs are micro or mainframe application programs, or both, bound to a particular character or data stream. On a functional basis, the LU Type 1 transmissions involve a character stream that is typically used for data processing, while an LU Type 2 is a 3270-oriented data stream, as is the LU Type 3.

An LU is a port through which the various users access SNA-type services. The LU software is implemented within SNA layers 3, 4, and 5. Since the various LU types utilize different SNA protocols, they are not compatible with each other. Most significant of the current LU packages is LU 6.2, which is involved with *peer-to-peer* relationships. The idea is to allow individual devices to communicate directly with each other without going through a higher level device. The compatible interfaces are included in such packages as CICS, S/36, S/38, Display Writer, Scan Master, and 5520.

Probably the best way to begin to understand the complexities of SNA is to see how the various software packages utilizing SNA services are organized. The PU manages the physical resources of the node where there is only one PU per node. The PU is a combination of hardware and software. The LU is the interface between the user and the network, and there can be more than one LU within a PU. The LU can also be a combination of hardware and software. The various programs are integrated under the architectural baseline called APPC (Advanced Program-to-Program Communication). APPC controls the point-to-point servicing of information flow between network locations and incorporates a variety of other programs. APPC/LU 6.2 allows applications and programs to communicate directly with each other once a physical connection is made. Any type of data stream, synchronous or asynchronous, can be accommodated and the communication is at the logical level so that no network tasks are required to set up or validate the transmission. Within APPC either end can initiate a conversation, which is very new for IBM. In the past, SNA permitted a hierarchical master-slave relationship in which only the higher level device could initiate the communication.

The primary advantage of APPC is the ability to provide distributed processing within a network that includes many hosts, minicomputers, and PCs. Because of its peer-to-peer relationship, APPC is not good for hierarchical applications such as inquiry response to and from a centralized database. Its code is very complex and cannot be used with other SNA applications, so all APPC software must be newly created for each network application.

Because of the requirement for new software generation those users who are going to APPC are typically developing new applications under LU 6.2 or are going to new systems designed around LU 6.2. Very few users are converting their existing software packages to LU 6.2 because of the expense involved. With the amount of time and effort involved in developing the original application software, end users are reluctant to go about changing that software with another large developmental program, so primarily only new systems and applications are being developed within APPC. APPC will continue to evolve and will eventually either coexist with the SNA hierarchical mode or replace it.

Some of the programs in SNA perform particular kinds of functions. The major ones are as follows.

## SNADS (SNA Distribution System)

SNADS is a set of programs running within LU 6.2 that provides end users with a capability for store and forward distribution of information. IBM calls SNADS an asynchronous communication (this is not a strict communications transmission definition) because the transmitter and receiver do not have to be available at the same time (more like a connectionless or noninteractive service). Here asynchronous means not directly connected, either physically or logically. The users of SNADS are addressable locations that can originate or receive transmissions, defined as originating and/or destination nodes. The transmissions are called *distributions* and the hardware associated with SNADS is called a *Distribution Service Unit* (DSU).

SNADS operates within DISOSS (to be described later) under the CICS/VS operating system, which itself is on an MVS type host. Typical SNADS units are system 36/38, 5520, Series 1, or 8100s. The originating or destination users of SNADS can be PCs, display writers, or scan masters.

To communicate within the SNADS environment a *session* must first be established. Although IBM calls the communication asynchronous, the actual transmission between SNADS nodes must be synchronous (SDLC). Communication under SNADS involves the non-real time delivery of documents and/or files, which means that the various nodes in the network can store information indefinitely until the receiver decides to access it, very much like electronic mail.

## DIA (Document Interchange Architecture)

Document Interchange Architecture is application level software that describes how documents and files can be interchanged between different systems. It describes the protocols and data structures that allow functions like electronic mail, document storage/retrieval/distribution, library-type searches, file transfer, and library services such as document filing and retrieval.

DIA consist of four separate services, as follows.

*DDS (Document Distribution Services).* DDS distributes documents and messages to one or more distributed recipients.

*DLS (Document Library Services).* DLS allows distributed users to search for, retrieve, file, and/or delete files or documents within a DIA document library.

*FTS (File Transfer Service).* FTS is software that supports the movement of information within DLS.

*APS (Application Processing Services).* APS provides the necessary document processing services within *sessions*.

The various users reside at nodes called Office System Nodes (OSN) or Source Recipient Nodes (SRN). The users at SRNs are devices like PCs, scan masters, and display writers. An SRN communicates through OSN to a CICS/VS MVS host, System 36/38, 5520, Series 1, or 8100. This is done within a DISOSS environment.

The difference between DIA and SNADS is that SNADS provides the *remote* document distribution between adjacent SNADS DSUs, which include DIA OSN, while DIA supports *local* document distribution services between SRN and OSNs.

## DCA (Document Control Architecture)

Document Control Architecture software incorporates a data stream that standardizes the contents of documents transmitted through a network. There are three forms of DCA:

*RFT (Revisable Form Text).* RFT supports the generation of revisable documents designed to be edited, such as text and format information.

*FFT (Final Form Text).* FFT software describes a document that is destined for final display on a printer. No modification of the information is allowed.

*MFT (Mixed Form Text).* With MFT multiple information types can be included within the same data stream, such as text with facsimile and text with graphics.

The products that support DCA (as well as DIA) are the PC, 5520, System 36/38, and DISOSS 370.

## DDM (Distributed Data Management)

Distributed Data Management is software very much like SNADS and DIA, but it can operate independently of APPC. It provides the necessary data connectivity for distributed, record-oriented files and therefore it involves a distributed data management type of architecture. However, IBM does not call it a distributed Data Base Management System (DBMS). DDM supports the file creation, deletion, renaming, loading, unloading, locking, and unlocking characteristics for multiple file entities. The files must be handled in their entirety, while a true DBMS would provide the movement of segments of files across different systems. Therefore, DDM really is not a distributed DBMS.

## LEN (Low Entry Networking)

Low Entry Networking is described as an architectural extension of a PU Type 2.1 node. It allows small networks previously regarded as peripheral nodes to function as full network nodes so that programmers do not have to configure networks or connections and may add nodes without a new host SYSGEN (System Generation).

To an ACF/NCP node, the LEN nodes appear as a PU Type 2.0 CLC running as a PUCP, but the LEN nodes themselves recognize each other as peer type 2.1 nodes running PNCP. You do not need either a mainframe or a communications front end to set up a LEN node.

The LEN consists of two different levels:

*Network nodes,* which have directories of the peripheral nodes connected to them.

*Peripheral nodes,* defined as the devices that are communicating. The network nodes send messages between themselves on behalf of the peripheral nodes that are connected to them.

The first implementation within LEN is APPN (Advanced Program-to-Program Networking). APPN supports intermediate nodal routing functions similar to those that pass through a PU Type 4 node (3725). APPN initially supported this kind of function between System 36/38 environments. APPN provides the end-to-end sessions between non-adjacent nodes, and provides a significant change from the classical SNA hierarchy, which always included centralized tables that had to be updated manually. An example of an APPN environment is shown in Fig. 18–7.

In APPN, applications can communicate transparently with applications on other machines on a peer-to-peer basis. If a file to be accessed is not local, then a directory at a central location can be accessed and the location of the physical file obtained and accessed regardless of where it resides in the network.

To operate, APPN is loaded into each machine (the System/36 here) with a definition of all of the physical network components. The parameters of the links between all the locations are stored and a set of routing tables is created so that access is possible between any two devices.

**FIGURE 18–7**
APPN

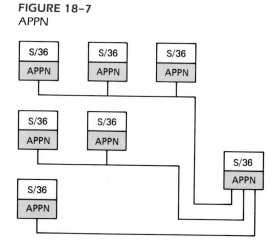

Files can be moved from one location to another for access or account tracking purposes, and any software changes regarding either the links or devices must be transmitted to all locations. It is even possible to go to the focal point System/36 to get to a file in another System/36 not directly connected. In turn, the central machine can access any one of the remotes for coordinated files and reporting purposes.

A common application for the APPN environment is an organization with many remote offices that have a lot of local processing to do on individual accounts. If an account moves from location to location, the entire file can be moved to the processor at the new location, while the centralized processor accesses and integrates management reporting information from all subsidiary locations. Since many organizations have this type of application, it is anticipated that APPN will grow very quickly.

## DISOSS

DISOSS is an application program that normally resides in a host processor. It provides for the storage, retrieval, and distribution of documents created by various IBM products that are compatible with a PC. DISOSS is sometimes called the mainframe backbone, because it moves documents between mainframes. As a departmental processor, DISOSS is incorporated into the System 36/38, the 5520 Administrative System, and the 8100 Distributed Office Support System. The DISOSS-to-DISOSS connections are provided through SNADS for the non-real time delivery of documents; in other words, documents do not have to be delivered in real time and can be stored within SNADS for an indefinite period of time. On a single user workstation, DISOSS is supported on the PC, 6580 Displaywriter, and 8815 Scanmaster. With regard to moving documents in a network, the DCA software can be described as a letter being generated, while DIA is the envelope, and DISOSS is the service that moves the envelope from one location to another. All of these coexist within SNA.

## APPC/PC (Advanced Program-to-Program Communication/PC)

Advanced Program-to-Program Communication/PC is software designed for PCs within SNA for utilizing application programs in a distributed transaction processing environment. APPC supports LU6.2 and PU2.1 peer-to-peer communication and includes the necessary lower-level network management functions, the conversation and session-level security requirements, and other necessary software to support PC use within SNA.

If the PC has APPC, then SNA is supported down to the PC level. The PC then becomes the *lowest peer* in the network, but because of all the software involved, the PC must have a much larger RAM memory capability.

Utilizing APPC/PC, the token-ring LAN is able to access host processors regardless of their location. All of the necessary interfaces will be in place to allow communication between low-level devices as well as to higher level intermediate minicomputers and, ultimately, the host processors.

## Netview-Netview/PC

Netview-Netview/PC is the IBM network management software announced in 1986. It provides for the consolidation of various SNA host resident programs that previously performed network management functions under SNA. Because of the extensive level of detail involved with Netview and Netview/PC, it will be described in more detail in Chapter 22.

To show the architectural relationships of the various SNA products, Fig. 18-8 identifies where they reside. There are obviously many more relationships, but this will give you an idea of the systems in which all the programs are generally used.

Finally, Fig. 18-9 provides an overview of where all of the various hardware components fit in with the product numbers that may be more familiar. A similar diagram of the software incorporating SNA products would be much too extensive for inclusion here, but you can probably provide your own relationships by reviewing the SNA architectural diagrams and the network configuration diagrams. Keep in mind that these products and services are constantly changing. New features are being added and relationships to other networks, especially OSI, are growing all the time. A disadvantage of putting together a text like this is that the subject changes so dynamically, but what is included should give you a good basis for evaluating what you need for your own purposes.

FIGURE 18-8
SNA Relationships

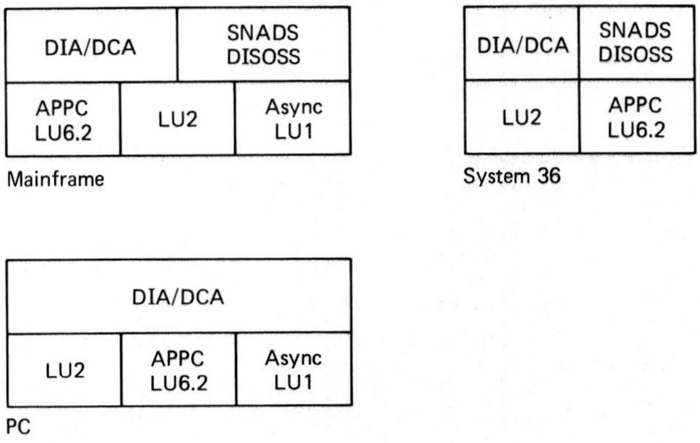

| DIA/DCA | | SNADS DISOSS |
|---------|------|--------------|
| APPC LU6.2 | LU2 | Async LU1 |

Mainframe

| DIA/DCA | SNADS DISOSS |
|---------|--------------|
| LU2 | APPC LU6.2 |

System 36

| DIA/DCA | | |
|------|-----------|----------|
| LU2 | APPC LU6.2 | Async LU1 |

PC

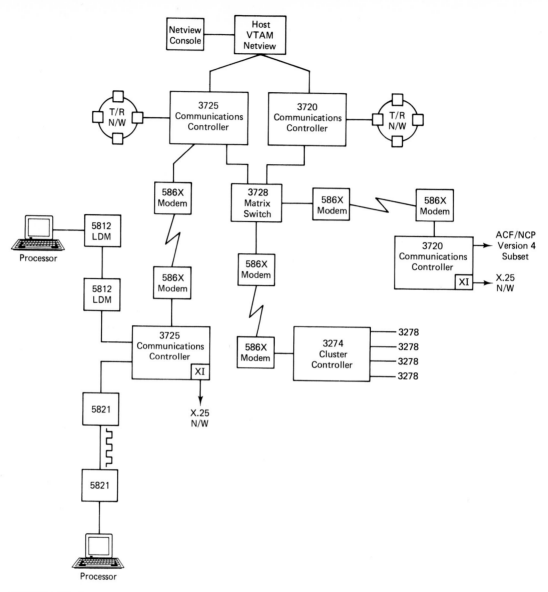

**FIGURE 18-9**
IBM Network Configurations

## D

# OTHER NETWORK ARCHITECTURES

IBM is not the only vendor that has an alternative plan for a networking architecture. Most of the other vendors have equivalents to OSI, but, just like IBM, they are all unique. Even though many of the vendors have committed to integrating

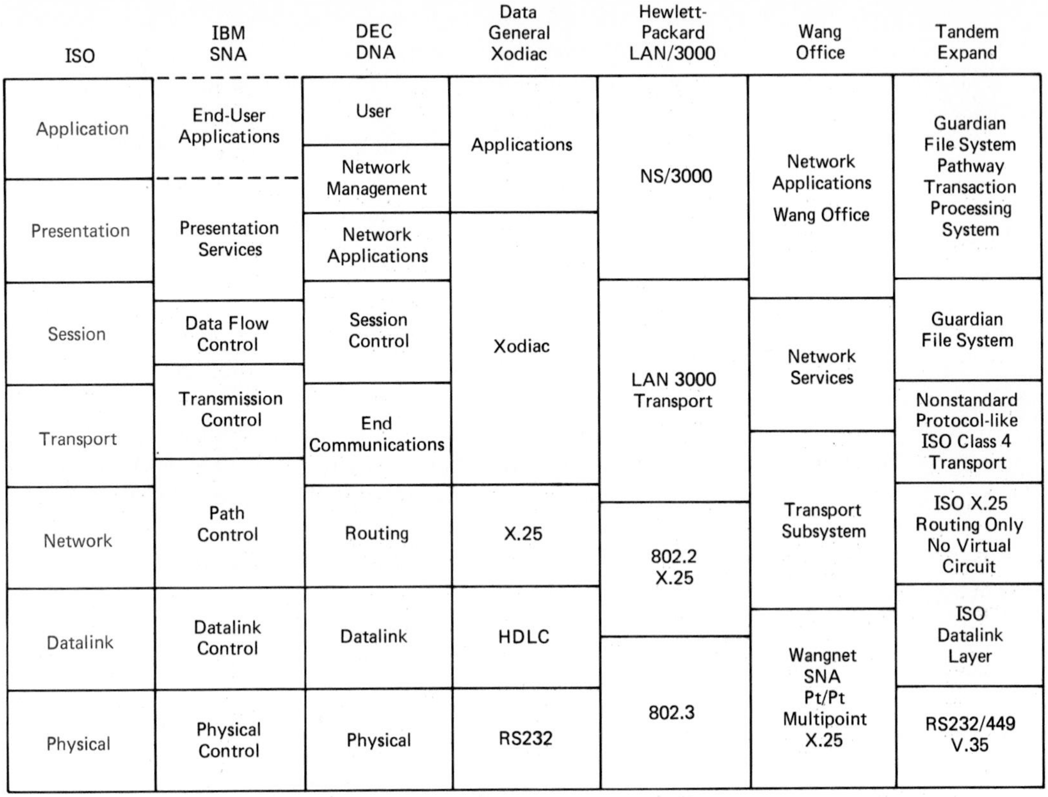

| ISO | IBM SNA | DEC DNA | Data General Xodiac | Hewlett-Packard LAN/3000 | Wang Office | Tandem Expand |
|---|---|---|---|---|---|---|
| Application | End-User Applications | User | Applications | NS/3000 | Network Applications / Wang Office | Guardian File System Pathway Transaction Processing System |
| | | Network Management | | | | |
| Presentation | Presentation Services | Network Applications | Xodiac | LAN 3000 Transport | Network Services | |
| Session | Data Flow Control | Session Control | | | | Guardian File System |
| Transport | Transmission Control | End Communications | | | | Nonstandard Protocol-like ISO Class 4 Transport |
| Network | Path Control | Routing | X.25 | 802.2 X.25 | Transport Subsystem | ISO X.25 Routing Only No Virtual Circuit |
| Datalink | Datalink Control | Datalink | HDLC | 802.3 | Wangnet SNA Pt/Pt Multipoint X.25 | ISO Datalink Layer |
| Physical | Physical Control | Physical | RS232 | | | RS232/449 V.35 |

**FIGURE 18–10**
Other Network Architectures

OSI into their product line, they are currently utilizing proprietary architectures. The evolution of the product vendor lines is expected to occur over the next 10 years, but much may happen in the interim, especially with SNA expansion, that may change present-day thinking. To give you an idea of what other architectures look like, Fig. 18–10 shows network architectures of IBM, DEC, Data General, Hewlett-Packard, Wang, and Tandem. Because of the expansion and continuous change of the networks, only an overview and some of the current products will be provided here. SNA has already been described, so we will first take a look at Digital Equipment Corporation (DEC), which has its own architecture called DEC Network Architecture (DNA). DEC is one of the strongest supporters of OSI and is steadily moving toward conformance, but at the same time, they are selecting specific options within OSI to build proprietary products. DEC's products are application-oriented and doing very well in the marketplace. As shown, DEC utilizes eight different layers of which the top three—user applications, network management, and network applications—are comparable to the top two layers of OSI. The DNA functions at these levels are the terminal access and file-transfer capabilities. Session control and end communications involve what DNA calls task-to-task communications. The routing level, comparable to the OSI network level, is described as the adaptive routing function within DNA. The data-link and physical levels are very much comparable to OSI and include point-to-point connections, X.25, and Ethernet. DEC has also made substantial progress in interfacing with SNA through *gateway* products in which the gateways look like PU Type 2s. The existing SNA gateway is a PDP11-type device with network management capability that connects DECnet to an SNA front-end controller like a 3725 so the DECnet will look like an LU6.2 device to SNA. DEC's products will continually undergo change as DEC moves closer to OSI.

Current indications are that DNA Phase V, destined for the 1990s, will have very specific layer relationships that correspond to OSI, and that OSI will be treated as a subset of DNA so that the user can use either one and take advantage of the features of both. A probable description of those relationships is shown in Fig. 18–11.

UNISYS has also announced their architectural structure for the 1990s. UNISYS is going to keep a separate Sperry architecture, which they call the Sperry Distributed Communications Architecture (DCA), as well as the Burroughs Network Architecture (BNA). These architectures are illustrated in Fig. 18–12. As shown, the structure for both equipment architectures is very much

**FIGURE 18–11**
DNA for the 1990s

| OSI | DNA Phase IV | DNA Phase V 1990s | |
|---|---|---|---|
| Applications | User Applications Network Management | Network Applications Office Systems Electronic Mail File Transfer | FTAM OSI CCITT V.400 |
| Presentation | Network Applications | Network Management DECnet Services Others | OSI Presentation |
| Session | DECnet Session | DECnet Session | OSI Session |
| Transport | DECnet Transport | Common Transport I/F | |
| | | DECnet Transport | OSI Transport |
| Network | DECnet Routines | ISO Connection Oriented Services Over X.25 ISO Connectionless Service ISO Routing Protocol | |
| Link | DDCMP HDLC | DDCMP X.25 802.3 Ethernet HDLC | |
| Physical | Ethernet | | |

**UNISYS Architecture and OSI Evolution**

| OSI Layers | Sperry Distributed Communications Architecture (DCA) | | Burroughs Network Architecture (BNA) | |
|---|---|---|---|---|
| | 1988 | Future | 1988 | Future |
| Application | Proprietary Applications | Proprietary Applications and New OSI Services FTAM/X.400/Directories Others | Proprietary Applications | Proprietary Applications and New OSI Services FTAM/X.400/Directories Others |
| Presentation | Application Dependent | Application Dependent | Application Dependent | Application Dependent |
| Session | Interprocess Communications | OSI Connection-Oriented | Burroughs Session Transport Protocols | Burroughs Transport Protocol OSI Connection-Oriented Transport Protocol 0, 2, 4 |
| Transport | Data Transport Protocol | Data Transport Protocol / Transport Protocol 0, 2, 4 | Burroughs Session Transport Protocols | Burroughs Transport Protocol OSI Connection-Oriented Transport Protocol 0, 2, 4 |
| Network | Telecom Network Access Protocol \| X.25 | Telecon Network Access Protocol \| X.25 \| Internet Protocol | Burroughs Integrated Adaptive Routing System (BIAS) | BIAS Internet Protocol |
| Datalink | Univac Datalink Control \| X.21 | Univac Datalink Control \| X.21 \| 802.2 | Burroughs Datalink Control \| X.25 X.21 Others \| CSMA/CD 802.3 | Burroughs Datalink Control \| X.25 X.21 Others \| CSMA/CD 802.3 |
| Physical | RS232 RS449 \| Others | RS232 RS449 \| Others \| 802.3 | | |

**FIGURE 18–12**
UNISYS Architectures

oriented toward the OSI model right now, but many of the processes are unique to UNISYS. The structures will stay basically the same in the future but the levels will continue to be developed toward OSI. Therefore both Sperry and Burroughs can advertise that they are moving toward OSI while maintaining their proprietary functions. IBM has done the same thing, and we will see later that most of the other vendors will also.

Back in Fig. 18–10 we have *Xodiac* from Data General. Xodiac is an architecture in which the bottom three layers conform to OSI, but Layers Four, Five, and a part of Six are grouped together and applications include the remainder of Layer Six and all of Layer Seven. There is also a commitment by Data General to move toward OSI, with future plans shown in Fig. 18–13 along with some Xodiac products. As can be seen, Xodiac is quite a bit different from OSI today but will be moving toward OSI in the future. More details should be available in the next few years.

Hewlett-Packard and their LAN/3000 network are also moving toward OSI, but it appears that they will be doing so with very specific software that does not conform exactly to OSI layers. In addition to their 802.2 and 802.3 layers for communicating on a LAN, Hewlett-Packard also has an X.25 interface. Their equipment looks like an 8100 device to SNA and can link up with a 3725 controller and emulate a PU Type 2 and either an LU Type 2 or an LU Type 3. HP is not only moving toward OSI, but also maintaining a tie-in with SNA where many of their products are utilized for specific remote applications and then tie into host processors.

Wang is another major player in the OSI and SNA compatibility game with

**FIGURE 18–13**
Xodiac of the Future from Data General

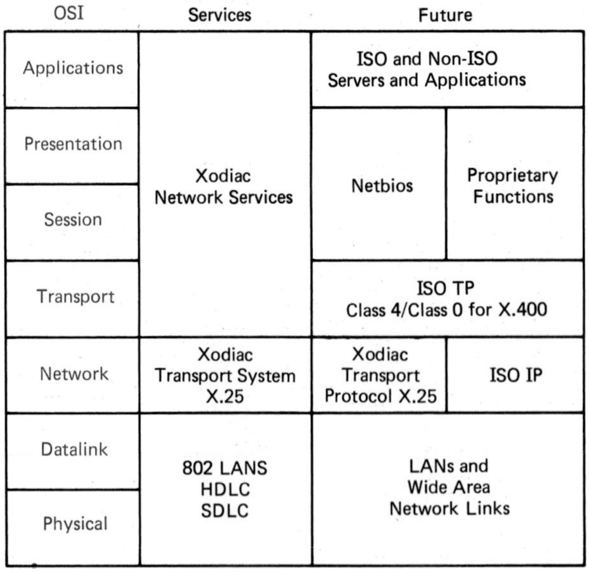

| OSI | Services | Future | | |
|-----|----------|--------|---|---|
| Applications | Xodiac Network Services | ISO and Non-ISO Servers and Applications | | |
| Presentation | | Netbios | Proprietary Functions | |
| Session | | | | |
| Transport | | ISO TP Class 4/Class 0 for X.400 | | |
| Network | Xodiac Transport System X.25 | Xodiac Transport Protocol X.25 | ISO IP | |
| Datalink | 802 LANS HDLC SDLC | LANs and Wide Area Network Links | | |
| Physical | | | | |

what is called the *Wang Office*. At the network applications level, Wang Office is the interface between the user and the Wang Network and includes the network administrative functions. Network services provide for the interchange of information among Wang users and include Information Distributed Services (IDS) and VS terminal emulation, which allow them to run as a CICS application in an SNA environment. The transport subsystem provides an interface to other networks that are comparable to the bottom level including Wangnet, SNA, point-to-point, multipoint, and X.25 connections. Direct correlation with OSI is not apparent, and it would seem that the Wang intent in integrating into the OSI world is to provide gateway functions.

Even further away from OSI is the Tandem architecture, called *Expand*. Expand is designed around an intersystem networking architecture that is both proprietary and closed, but because Tandem controls both ends of the communications links in their typical application environments, cross compatibility is not a problem. Tandem provides something unique with their fault tolerant and modular expansion capabilities. This is one of the primary reasons why users go to Tandem equipment. Expand supports networking standards that move transactions to and from other networks through gateways that support both SNA and X.25 from ISO. The SNA connectivity is what Tandem calls SNAX (SNA Access Services Software). SNAX allows SNA devices to be configured on Tandem systems so that applications running in SNA can communicate with applications running on Expand. It is not anticipated that there will be very many changes in Expand because of the unique niche that Tandem has in the data processing world.

Finally, although detailed information is not yet available, AT&T has announced their intention to move toward OSI. They have indicated that their products such as the 3B-type computer will provide for interconnection, but it is not known exactly how. It may very well be a combination of proprietary interfaces and gateway products.

Although all of the vendors have different network architectures and most of them have indicated that they will move toward OSI, many people feel that the vendors will stay with their unique architectures to allow for continuous promotion of proprietary products in specific application environments. The connectivity to OSI and other networks will come from gateways that each of the vendors will build so their proprietary equipment can communicate with other networks, which sounds like a good business decision. The vendors then can stay in business selling the kinds of products they make best, while at the same time promoting interaction with other networks. *Clone vendors* will not be able to come up with comparable equipment to be sold at lower cost without doing at least some of their own development.

It is the author's opinion that in the world of the future there will be many different network architectures with gateways to each other so that specific applications can be optimized and the user can take advantage of specific features for specific applications. The idea of a single terminal providing all capabilities will be much too expensive, especially if some of the capabilities will only be used for a small portion of the total time.

# SYSTEMS APPLICATION ARCHITECTURE

Systems Application Architecture (SAA) was developed by IBM to provide distributed program development and database access across their own existing incompatible environments. The objective is to provide connectivity among devices like the PS/2, System/3X, and large hosts. The initial focus was on the OS/2 operating system, which was designed for the PS/2. Next, guidelines will be applied to DCA, DIA, SNADS, SNA network management, LEN, token ring, and any other interface that applies. The standards will apply primarily to local and departmental systems where peer-to-peer communications based on APPC for token-ring clusters and PC networks will be used. SAA's goal is to create an environment in which a single software package will be capable of running on PCs, System/3X, and mainframes.

SAA consists of four major components as follows:

*Common User Access* defines a consistent user interface across the various SAA product lines, including screen layouts, menus, selection techniques, keyboard layouts, and displays. It is expected to look like the OS/2 end-user interface.

*Common Programming Interface* will include a set of programs that include high-level languages and their necessary support services. The primary languages are ANSI, COBOL 1985, ANSI FORTRAN, FORTRAN 77, and ANSI-C based on the X3J11 proposal. The procedural languages will be REXX and VM/SP System Interpreter, and the application generator will be the Cross System Product (CSP) set. CSP is known as EZ RUN on the IBM PC. Other significant languages will be the SQL Database language, QMF Query Interface, ISPF Dialog Interface (called EZ-VU on the IBM PC), and the GDDM Presentation/Graphics Interface.

*Common Applications* are the application programs that will run on OS/2, System/3X, Silverlake when it becomes available, and Compatible 370 mainframe systems that will run under MVS/XA and/or VM/SP. Also included in this group will be the 3080, 3090, 4381, and 9370 product lines. As new SAA compatible products become available they will also support these application programs.

*Common Communications Support* will support peer-to-peer SNA networking along with connections to X.25, Token Ring, Netview, and other communication services to be announced.

IBM is committed to implementing a consistent interface across all of their network products. Their goal is to make the service available in some form on all of the connected systems. There must also be a standardized method of addressing and formatting the data and SAA organizes those guidelines.

SAA is based on the LU 6.2 protocol as defined under ACS/VTAM 3.2, which became available in 1989. IBM has announced their intention to provide full compliance and incorporation of every element of SAA in all future products. They have also stated that other interfaces, especially CICS and IMS, which are operating independently now, will also be considered for upgrading into the SAA environment.

SAA will also support the full communications evolution, where it will be included in VTAM. System/3X will have SAA built into its operating system. The PC without OS/2 may have an extension added to its operating system to include SAA. Higher-level programming services will be added on top of communication services so that the programmer will be able to call in the VTAM operating system and PC extensions. Regarding LU 6.2, SAA will operate at a higher level for consistency across equipment while LU 6.2 will operate at a lower level that might be different for each system. SAA will provide the capability for LU 6.2 devices to communicate across different networks. PCs will have to be designed to operate much faster and have more memory to incorporate the features required to support SAA.

Figure 18–14 is provided to give you an idea of the relationship of SAA to both SNA and OSI. The figure is a functional comparison, not a direct layer-by-layer comparison. Because of the newness of SAA, it is quite possible that these relationships may change over time, so if you intend to integrate SAA into your organizational philosophy, you should make sure that you have all the current information required.

# F
## MAP/TOP

Directly related to OSI model implementation, and a subject of continuing debate, is the Manufacturing Automation Protocol and the Technical and Office Protocol (MAP/TOP). MAP is a very specific implementation of OSI that was developed by General Motors in the early 1980s in an effort to automate their factory floor. A common form of communications and interfacing was needed to tie together computers, terminals, robots, and management functions. The various products they were using were all built by different vendors. So that all of the vendor products could communicate on the factory floor, GM decided to encourage a particular use of OSI that evolved into MAP. Because of the early state of the OSI protocols at the time, GM decided to select very specific options. The specific parameters selected by GM cover a wide variety of alternatives that are beyond the scope of this text, so only an overview diagram is provided in Fig. 18–15.

While the evolution of MAP was continuing, in 1985 the Boeing Corporation decided that a similar type of environment would be applicable to their Timeshare network. They developed the Technical and Office Protocol (TOP), which performs the same functions as MAP, except TOP is oriented toward the movement of documents and files, while MAP primarily concerns the control of

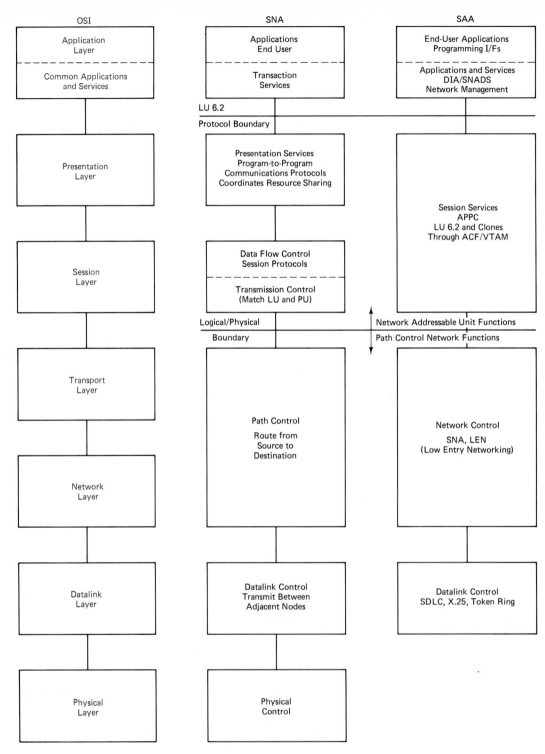

**FIGURE 18–14**
SAA Relationship to SNA and OSI

| Layer | TOP Protocols | MAP Protocols |
|-------|---------------|---------------|
| 7 | ISO FTAM* 8571<br>File Transfer<br>Limited File Management | ISO FTAM 8571<br>File Transfer Protocol<br>Manufacturing Msg. Format Std. (MMFS)<br>Common App. Service Elements (CASE)<br>ISO 8649 |
| 6 | Null — Using ASCII and Binary Data Only | |
| 5 | ISO 8327 — Session Kernel; Full Duplex | |
| 4 | ISO 8073 — Transport Class 4 | |
| 3 | ISO INTERNET 8473 — Connectionless<br>X.25 Subnetwork Dependent Convergence<br>Protocol (SNDCP) | |
| 2 | ISO 8802/2 — Logical Link Control (LLC)<br>IEEE 802.2 Type 1 Class 1 | |
| 1 | ISO CSMA/CD 8802/3<br>IEEE 802.3 | ISO Token Passing Bus 8802/4<br>IEEE 802.4 |

*File Transfer Access Method

**FIGURE 18–15**
MAP/TOP Model

robotic devices. As shown in Fig. 18–15, layers two through six are the same for both protocols but the first and seventh layers are very different. The difference at the seventh level is because of the different applications; TOP's are for text and documentation, while MAP's relate to the control of machines. At the first level, MAP utilizes IEEE 802.4 token passing, which is necessary to guarantee a maximum access time for any one device (especially the control computer). TOP uses IEEE 802.3, which is collision detection methodology, such as Ethernet. MAP is described as a *deterministic* process that *guarantees* a maximum access time, while TOP is described as *probabilistic*. Probabilistic means no time guarantee for access can be provided because of the Ethernet form of operation, in which collisions can occur when two or more devices try to transmit at the same time (you must try again).

The difference between protocols creates a very interesting situation. Both protocols are OSI compatible, yet they cannot communicate with each other because their methods of medium access at the first level are different, a perfect example of why proprietary products will continue to proliferate. Besides requiring unique interfaces, unique applications require different protocols at the seventh level, and the users of those protocols have chosen to optimize the use of particular applications. It is interesting that MAP and TOP are described by OSI proponents as perfect examples of why OSI will work. If there is any confusion here, it is because many people assume that compatibility means that devices will communicate across all applications and media, so that a single universal terminal can be used. But MAP and TOP are examples of the benefits of having proprietary systems that may within their own networks provide compatibility upward and downward within the seven-layer OSI structure. It is not really necessary to communicate across those boundaries, so it makes sense to keep them separate.

On an operational level MAP operates in a broadband token-passing environment with messages occupying only two channels of the LAN (broadband operation is described in Chapter 15). Other channels within the MAP environment can be used for other applications such as data transfer, security, video, and others. MAP utilizes a *bus* arrangement on 75-Ohm coaxial cable. It can run at either 5 or 10 million bits per second and can incorporate up to 1000 different stations. Ethernet is used in TOP, with a bus of shielded coaxial cable at 50-Ohms impedance. Ethernet operates at 10 megabits per second with a total capacity of 1024 stations. Ethernet is a baseband system in which only one user can communicate at a time. Both systems incorporate the necessary network management capabilities to configure the system and the necessary fault isolation to find and fix network problems.

MAP specializes in the interfaces for controlling robotic-type devices, while TOP utilizes the same interfaces for the control and distribution of text. TOP specifies a network for distributed information processing in a multivendor environment and addresses the necessary technical and business office functions like electronic mail, document processing, and interchange of graphics. Documents can be generated on one system, edited on a second, and printed on a third with integrated text and graphics, a difficult process to achieve with standalone programs.

TOP specifies a selected set of options within each OSI layer to provide the specific function for document interchange. It specifies remote file transfer, which is the reading or writing of a file on another system; electronic mail in either ASCII or other TOP-defined formats; graphic exchange; document exchange; and virtual terminal operation.

Version 3.0 of TOP provides for the X.400 series specification of electronic mail. Electronic mail is different from file transfer because the users cannot access each other's files with electronic mail, as they can with file transfer capabilities.

MAP and TOP were expected to grow very quickly because of their ability to communicate across networks, but many of the MAP vendors are reducing their projections because the market has not grown as fast as they anticipated. As with many other new products and services, it will take time for MAP and TOP to be accepted, and that acceptance will be based on the economics of the particular service or application required by the end-user organization. Opting for environments like MAP, TOP, or any other OSI environment will not be done solely because of the desire for compatibility, but because there is both an operational and economic benefit to be derived from their use.

# TRANSMISSION CONTROL PROTOCOL/INTERFACE PROTOCOL (TCP/IP)

The Transmission Control Protocol/Interface Protocol (TCP/IP) was developed within in the Department of Defense to promote interconnection of DOD networks in the early 1970s (it became a military standard in 1978). Movement within the OSI framework was not occurring fast enough so the DOD decreed that only computer systems compatible with TCP/IP would be able to connect to the Defense Data Network (DDN). This specific development came from the Defense Advanced Research and Projects Agency (DARPA).

In 1988 Congress mandated that within two years a switch to GOSIP (Government Open Systems Interconnect Profile) must be made. GOSIP was developed by the U.S. Government Users Committee and is comparable to MAP and TOP. The changeover mandates federal usage of interoperable protocols at all seven layers of the OSI model and is definitely an evolutionary step upward from TCP/IP. TCP/IP was always viewed as an interim method of connecting networks together, with OSI being the ultimate goal. GOSIP will accomplish that goal.

Even though the change is supposed to take place by 1990, not all networks will immediately go to GOSIP. TCP/IP will continue to be supported on existing networks for many years because of the high cost of upgrading, and, in addition, there is a loophole in the directive. If an organization can show some pressing need due to specifications, security, cost, or other reason, it may still use TCP/IP. Also, because there is such a heavy and growing commercial use of TCP/IP with a wide variety of products and vendors to support them, the switch to GOSIP will be tough to implement in the time frame mandated. As of the middle of 1988 GOSIP already supported the seventh-layer FTAM file structure as well as the X.400 electronic mail terminal. However, many governmental locations are still incorporating TCP/IP, so it may very well last a lot longer than was originally intended. In 1987 there were over 2000 major nodes in the network, such as the National Science Foundation, which has a super computer at the head of a large pyramid with raw data being brought in, processed, and returned to terminals. CAD/CAM environments are heavy users of TCP/IP to connect to each other as well as to other systems.

In performing its functions, TCP/IP is closely related to OSI but different. The original packet switching network from which TCP/IP evolved was called ARPANET, a layered set of protocols that supported application-oriented functions as well as application-to-application communications. The original design consisted of connecting two host processors with a communications protocol that was called Network Controlled Program (NCP). NCP allowed one message at a time to be in process with no end-to-end validation (only node-to-node). TCP was designed to replace NCP. The part of NCP that was responsible for the movement of packets between networks (internetworking), was called IP, and the resulting combination is called TCP/IP. ARPANET was converted to TCP/IP over a period of time.

A wide variety of applications was developed to sit on top of TCP/IP for individual users, including graphics, remote diagnostic and maintenance, packetized speech, and, most often, data. The various components of TCP/IP are as follows:

*TCP.* TCP establishes sessions between user processes on different networks. It is a reliable method of communications because there is end-to-end error recovery. A user's application program interface (API) interfaces with TCP to initiate either an outgoing or an incoming session.

*IP.* IP allows the interconnection of multiple networks and uses global source and destination addressing schemes so that no two networks have the same addresses anywhere within their destination definitions.

*UDP (User Datagram Protocol).* UDP is a method of sending and receiving internetwork packets without end-to-end error checking or session management. It is a one-way mechanism for sending information.

*ICMP (Internet Control Message Protocol).* ICMP is part of the network management process in which status messages are generated by internetwork gateways that describe a malfunction or error condition, such as unavailability, and are sent back to a control location.

*Telnet.* Telnet is an application-level protocol that makes a remote terminal look like a local terminal to the host processor with which it is communicating.

*FTP (File Transfer Protocol).* FTP provides for the transfer of data files consisting of one or more segments through the multiple networks connected in the system.

*SMTP (Simple Mail Transfer Protocol).* As the name implies, SMTP is an electronic mail transfer between users.

A diagram of the relationship of the various protocols is shown in Fig. 18–16.

The form used by TCP/IP for sending information is an Ethernet packet. The relationship of the various levels of recognition is shown in Fig. 18–17. If a user is generating data that is moved to another network, the first thing added to the data is a TCP header. When it is determined that the information must be moved to another network, the IP header is added. Finally the address header is added, which is the unique address on the remote network. The entire packet is sent out in Ethernet form so that the TCP/IP device can receive the message from the originator and route it to the appropriate receiving network. A local header is the header for the network that the packet exists in at any given time, such as X.25, ARPA, or Ethernet. The IP header supports the internetworking packet routing, which also indicates the type of higher level protocol being used. Finally, the TCP supports communication between the application's processes and/or programs in the host communicating devices.

TCP/IP is used extensively for interconnecting LANs with current development taking place in connecting LANs at different locations. Many vendors are

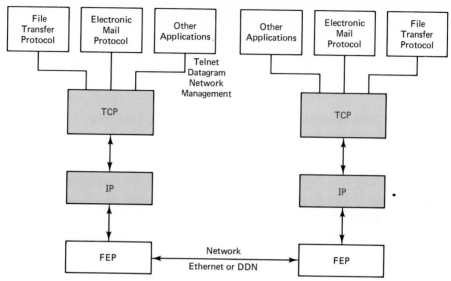

FEP = Front End Processor

**FIGURE 18-16**
TCP/IP Interconnection

**FIGURE 18-17**
TCP/IP Data Format

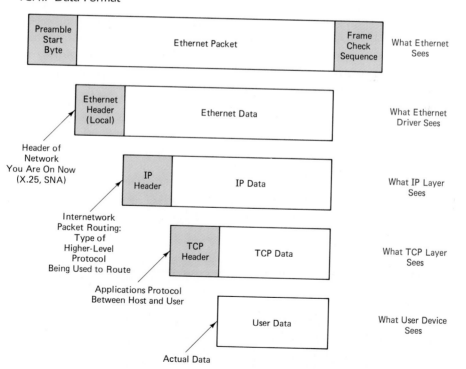

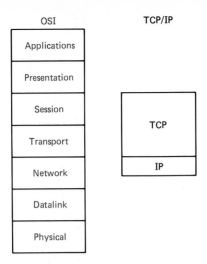

**FIGURE 18–18**
*TCP/OSI Relationships*

still providing products for TCP/IP interfaces even though it is considered an interim substitute for OSI. If you intend to use TCP/IP you should be aware that many of the devices do not have network management capabilities and may have limited file access or sharing capability. In addition, an important factor to consider is that initial implementations do not have any user-level security authentication. TCP/IP is used primarily for moving files through different networks without consideration for who is doing the transmitting or who is doing the receiving. Security and authentication processes are being developed so that more sensitive applications can be incorporated.

Finally, there is a relationship between TCP/IP and OSI. TCP incorporates many of the functions of the fourth and fifth layers of OSI and IP incorporates a portion of the third, or networking level (shown in Fig. 18–18). It is expected that the future development of TCP/IP will involve more internetwork compatibility such as packet size and addressing schemes, but the major use of TCP/IP will probably remain in the governmental DDN environment. It is also possible that nongovernment network users will take advantage of TCP/IP until more or better OSI interfaces become available.

## H
## THE FUTURE

With OSI coming into its final phases of definition, there is already an effort underway to take on the next generation of interface standards. While OSI is oriented toward communications, especially point-to-point, the next level of development will be in what is being called Open Distributed Processing Architecture (ODPA or ODP). ODP will be developed for multiprocessor environments in which a single task is divided among many processors that may exist on different networks. ODP is anticipated to be the primary area of interface specification work throughout the 1990s.

Meanwhile, in Europe, the European Computer Manufacturer's Association (ECMA) has developed a structure equivalent to OSI to be used for security of data transmissions. The structure is described as a *security framework* made up of building blocks called *security features* that operate within an environment called the *security domain*.

The ECMA structure provides an architecture for the application-specific design of security features in a network. Tentative descriptions of the various building blocks are as follows:

*Authentication* defines the uses of a password for user IDs.

*Association management* is the specific link between the user and the application. If the user does not use the appropriate code set, encryption, or compression, access to information can be denied.

*Security state* is a network status report of who is physically on the network at any time. The report can be kept as a log for future analysis.

*Access authorization* is the set of rules governing decisions on who can access and who has control of access to the network.

*Security attributes* describe the security classifications of the various users and resources such as files.

*Interdomain* describes the process whereby two domains with different security policies can interact with each other.

*Security audit* refers to any collection of events occurring in the network to be analyzed either immediately or later.

*Security recovery* is an automated method for dealing with suspected breaches of security. The methods are implemented according to predetermined rules.

*Cryptographic support* involves the distribution of security management data, such as the movement of information regarding the classifications of users or files.

*Subject sponsor* facilities handle the necessary set-up procedure when more than one application or service is to be used by any particular user. It incorporates the necessary restrictions predetermined by the user when two or more applications are utilized simultaneously.

Since this is a brand-new set of definitions that has not been adopted by any of the formal standards organizations, there will be many changes before it is formally adopted, if it is ever adopted for network security issues. The ECMA's framework does not involve the incorporation of cryptographic equipment, which is a separate and independent process dealing with individual links. The security framework is intended to enable you to set up a structure for handling sensitive files and information in your network.

# QUESTIONS

1. What is the overall concept of the OSI model?
2. Describe the functional characteristics of the seven layers of the OSI model.
3. Develop your own analogy for Fig. 18–3 and describe the functions of each of the layers.
4. What is SNA? Is it comparable to OSI?
5. What is the difference between a PU and LU in SNA?
6. Do other vendors have their own network architectures? How do they compare with OSI and SNA?
7. What is the device that will allow you to communicate between two different network architectures?
8. What is meant by SAA?
9. How can two devices that are OSI compatible not be compatible with each other?
10. Where would you most often use TCP/IP?

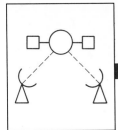

# 19

# Satellites, Video, Radio, Facsimile, and Microwave

In the mid-1980s we saw a great change in the use of facilities for data communications. Satellites had been in use for many years, and although their use did not grow as fast as anticipated, there were some very economical satellite applications. At the same time we saw the growth of cellular radio, which was used almost exclusively for voice at first, but then began to be used for data. Video techniques were also tied in extensively, including the Teletext and Videotex applications as well as video conferencing and video telephones. Finally, we saw the growth of facsimile, which is the movement of documents or pictures by transmission of the image of the document, not the characters or the binary representation of them. This chapter will describe the various products and services that became available during the 1980s, some of their operational descriptions, and some projections for future use.

## A

## SATELLITES

Satellites are divided into two major functional groups. Standard satellite communication takes place directly between user sites, or connections can be made to a third party, who then communicates via the satellite. The second group, which seems to be growing (especially in remote environments), is called VSAT.

445

VSAT is the utilization of smaller antennas at widely distributed or changing geographic locations where traffic volumes are not great. There is a centralized control for transmission and all of the remotes share a single satellite transponder. VSAT costs much less than a full band of satellite transmission capacity and is being implemented more and more where terrestrial facilities become too expensive. Both groups of satellites will be described here.

## Standard Satellites

The prevalent form of satellite utilization involves a direct link between user facilities with a satellite in between, or connection to a third party over a satellite link. The satellite acts like a *microwave in the sky*. Instead of going through a direct terrestrial link, the communication path goes through a satellite.

Satellite transmission has the advantage of costing the same regardless of the distance between transmitter and receiver, and regardless of the number of receivers (everybody receives at the same time). The bandwidth of available channels is very high (1.544 MBPS is very common and higher rates are available). Disadvantages include the propagation delay (the time it takes to go from the transmitter to the receiver and back to the transmitter), which is a minimum of 500 ms due to distance; lack of security because of the broadcast nature of satellite transmissions; and, depending on the frequencies used, varying amounts of environmental degradations due to moisture in the air.

Satellites used for standard application are called *geosynchronous* satellites. Geosynchronous satellites always maintain the same relative position over the face of the earth. In other words, as the earth turns the satellite moves with it. The satellites orbit at approximately 22,300 miles above the earth's surface, which is the optimum distance for orbiting dynamics.

Various organizations were originally involved in launching and operating satellites, but during the mid-1980s there was a major change in owners and operators. The volumes of data traffic had not met expected growth projections, so a lot of satellite capacity went unused. By the end of 1987, only about 70 percent of the satellite capacity was being used in the western hemisphere. Some of the companies who stayed in or bought into the business were AT&T and GTE, both original operators; MCI, who ended up in the satellite business by taking over Satellite Business Systems and then buying RCA Globecom; Contel ASC, who bought American Satellite Corporation; and Hughes Network Systems, who bought out Western Union, which was an original operator that had serious financial problems in the beginning of 1988. Many organizations are involved with satellites outside the United States, but this description will focus on U.S. owners and operators (Canadian satellite services are described in Chapter 3).

A schematic representation of a potential satellite system configuration is shown in Fig. 19–1 which shows two different configurations for satellite communications. User A communicates via its own antennas directly to the satellite and User B connects through carrier loops to a third-party vendor, who provides the satellite communications. The differences are primarily in the volume of traffic

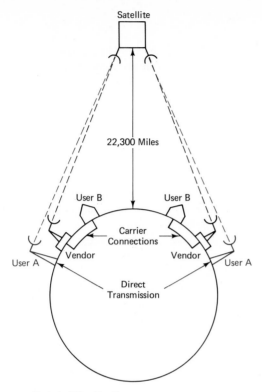

Satellite

22,300 Miles

User B                    User B

Carrier
Connections

Vendor          Vendor

User A                              User A

Direct
Transmission

Technical Considerations

Total volume of data to be transmitted
Peak system loading
Block size for optimum throughput
Propagation delays
Type of protocol to be used
Speed of transmission link
Costs of dedicated link vs. costs of vendor service
Compatibility of user system to vendor offerings
Ease of expansion to multiple locations

**FIGURE 19–1**
Satellite Considerations

to be sent. User A's high volume makes it economically feasible to utilize a dedicated circuit even with the combined costs of ground stations and leased satellite link. User B, on the other hand, does not have a sufficient volume of traffic to warrant a dedicated satellite path and therefore uses ground connections (or a digital termination system) to get to a satellite vendor, who will then multiplex or concentrate the low-volume traffic. When their traffic is combined, it is economically feasible for the low-volume users to use satellite circuits.

The satellite acts as a relay on a direct path to move information from one ground location to another. Communication to and from the satellite is in the microwave range at a minimum speed of 56,000 BPS, although it may go up to 1.544 MBPS or more.

Once a user is large enough to afford a dedicated satellite link, there is only one serious disadvantage to the utilization of that link: the propagation delay inherent in moving information from the ground to the satellite and back again. With a height of 22,300 miles, it takes approximately $\frac{1}{8}$ second for an electromagnetic transmission to reach the satellite and another $\frac{1}{8}$ second to come back to earth. The processing time between the ground stations and the satellite adds approximately another 50 ms to a one-way link, giving approximately a 300-ms time delay from transmission to reception. For applications where a response is required, at least another 300 ms is required for the response to get back to the transmitter, which results in an absolute minimum time of 600 ms round trip. Satellite users actually experience somewhere between 1- and 2-second response times for acknowledgments to individual transmissions.

For typical 56,000-BPS transmissions, there must be adequate buffering at both the transmit and receive ends to accommodate not only a single round-trip delay time, but for the total amount of retransmissions allowed. If the allowable amount of retransmissions of an error block is 3, for example, and there is a single satellite link, the user will need storage for a minimum of 168,000 bits for each link. The problem is compounded when you consider multiple satellite hops, such as might occur on international communications. If end-to-end communications are required, the propagation delay must be factored in and a decision made as to whether to transmit end to end or to use store-and-forward techniques every time the message comes back to the ground. One possible alternative to the end-to-end link is connection to a packet switching network, where the virtual circuit will take over and handle all the error detection and correction for the user. (The packet network may use satellites, too, so response times must still be considered.) The primary concern here is the satellite link for a dedicated in-house system where a single user must accommodate the propagation delays inherent in transmission.

Another alternative is the use of a satellite delay compensation unit (SDCU) on the ground at each end of the satellite link. At the local end it operates as a far-end emulator to the host site, which communicates with the SDCU as if it were the remote location. At the far end, another SDCU emulates the host to the remote site. The user equipment, therefore, does not have to worry about buffering, which is accommodated in the SDCU. What must be considered is the sequence of acknowledgments for messages that may come from a local SDCU, but which never reach the far end. Again, there are alternatives to accommodate this situation, and satellite service vendors are coming up with new ways to relieve the end user of the problem of propagation delay.

Still, for interactive processing there are delays that cannot be eliminated, because the user needs the response to the previous transmission before retransmitting. The *time-out* values in the protocol must be made longer so they will not be exceeded when a satellite path is incorporated into the network. The protocol involved must also be considered. SDLC, for example, has an option that allows only seven blocks for transmission before the transmitter will automatically cease transmitting. On faster satellite links, such as 1.544 MBPS (T-1 carrier), there will be more than seven average-sized blocks in the pipe before the first transmission ever gets to the far end. Transmission shutdown would then make SDLC operate as if it were a half-duplex protocol and reduce much of the efficiency for which it was designed. One way to improve this is to have more blocks in the path, which is possible but involves modification to the protocol. Other vendors allow more blocks prior to cessation of transmission, such as Burroughs with 127 and DEC with 255 blocks. HDLC, of which SDLC is a subset, also allows the implementation of a mechanism called *extended format* that provides for up to 7 bits for message identification (127 blocks). It is not enough to obtain a link on a satellite because of the volume you have; you must also consider the impact on the timing and software at both ends.

Satellites that are usable over North America are restricted to orbits between 67° and 143° west longitude. In those positions the satellites have a direct line-of-site path to both the east and west coasts of the United States, which is required because microwave transmission is used and the transmitting and receiving antennas must *see* each other. Table 19–1 shows most of the satellite positions assigned to date. The orbital position is shown in the first column, the name of the system is in the second, and the third column shows the microwave frequency bandwidth in gigahertz at which the satellite operates.

If they use different frequency bands, it is possible for two satellites to be in the same position because the antennas for one will not be receptive to signals for the other. The two primary bands in use today are the 4/6- and 12/14-GHz bands. In the future, however, it is anticipated that satellites will utilize the band between 20 and 30 GHz. The 4/6-GHz band is called the C band, the 12/14-GHz band is known as the Ku band, and the 20/30-GHz band is known as the Ka band. Because the bands are getting crowded, the FCC has authorized moving the satellites in the C band from 4° and 3° apart down to 2° apart, which will open additional slots for new satellites if required in the future. There must be specific spacing between satellites because the *up links* all transmit at the same frequencies. The ground antenna must aim its beam within a very narrow band to hit only the satellite it is aiming for. If the beam dispersion is too wide there will be an overlap on another satellite, which will interfere with its reception. Designing and building antennas for narrower dispersion beams requires more money, so there was much objection to the 2° spacing; but it appears that in the future all satellites will move to 2° apart because there is sufficient time for the vendors to develop the equipment and the technology is already available.

Another method for increasing the available satellite bandwidth is with the use of special antennas that transmit in *orthogonal planes* (planes that are 90° to each other like an X), which allow the same frequencies to be used at the same satellite twice. These transmissions are said to be *linearly polarized*. In addition, at the satellite there will be antennas that will provide *beam shaping,* which will provide a higher power output to specific geographic areas like large cities. Eventually there will be *spot beam* antennas, which will require even less power, yet be able to transmit to specific sites utilizing smaller antennas.

The difference between the C band and the Ku band is that their frequencies

**TABLE 19–1**
Satellite Positions

| POSITION (DEGREES) | SYSTEM | FREQUENCY (GHz) |
|---|---|---|
| 143° | Satcom V | 6/4 |
| 141 | Unassigned | — |
| 139 | Satcom 1-R | 6/4 |
| 137 | Unassigned | — |
| 134 | Galaxy 1 | 6/4 |
| 132 | Rainbow 1 | 14/12 |
| 131 | Satcom 3-R | 6/4 |
| 130 | ABCI 2 | 14/12 |
| 128 | American Satellite 1 | 6/4 and 14/12 |
| 125 | Comstar 4 | 6/4 |
| 124 | SBS 5 | 14/12 |
| 122 | Spacenet 1 | 6/4 and 14/12 |
| 120 | USSSI 2 | 14/12 |
| 119.5 | Westar V | 6/4 |
| 117.5 | Canada | 14/12 |
| 116.5 | Mexico | 6/4 and 14/12 |
| 113.5 | Mexico | 6/4 and 14/12 |
| 112.5 | Canada | 14/12 |
| 111.5 | Canada | 6/4 |
| 110 | Canada | 14/12 |
| 108 | Canada | 6/4 |
| 107.5 | Canada | 14/12 |
| 105 | Gstar 2 | 14/12 |
| 104.5 | Canada | 6/4 |
| 103 | Gstar 1 | 14/12 |
| 101 | Unassigned | — |
| 99 | SBS 1 | 14/12 |
| 98.5 | Westar IV | 6/4 |
| 97 | SBS 2 | 14/12 |
| 96 | Telstar 1 | 6/4 |
| 95 | Comstar D1/D2 | 6/4 |
| 94 | SBS 3 | 14/12 |
| 93.5 | Galaxy 3 | 6/4 |
| 91 | Westar III | 6/4 |
| 89 | SBS 4 | 14/12 |
| 88.5 | Telstar 2 | 6/4 |
| 87 | RCA K1 | 14/12 |
| 86 | Westar VI | 6/4 |
| 85 | USSSI 1 | 14/12 |
| 83.5 | Satcom IV | 6/4 |
| 83 | ABCI 1 | 14/12 |
| 81 | American Satellite 2 | 6/4 and 14/12 |
| 79 | Rainbow 2 | 14/12 |
| 78.5 | Westar II | 6/4 |
| 77 | RCA K2 | 14/12 |
| 76 | Telstar 3 | 6/4 |
| 75 | Unassigned | — |
| 74 | Galaxy 2 | 6/4 |
| 73 | Unassigned | — |
| 72 | Satcom 2-R | 6/4 |
| 71 | Unassigned | — |
| 69 | Spacenet 2 | 6/4 and 14/12 |
| 67 | Satcom VI/RCA K3 | 6/4 and 14/12 |

450

require different operational considerations. The C-band signals are weaker than the Ku-band's and so require larger antennas. The C-band signals are less susceptible to atmospheric noise, but they cannot be used near large cities because some terrestrial microwave transmissions are in the C-band range. Satellite transmissions in the same area would cause interference. Therefore, the ground stations for C-band satellite transmissions are in rural areas, with communications to and from cities on high-speed analog or digital links.

The Ku signal is a stronger signal and therefore uses smaller antennas. It is capable of delivering *spot beams* that are concentrations of transmissions to small geographic areas. Because of the Ku signal's higher frequency range, it is more sensitive to atmospheric conditions. The Ka band (20–30 GHz) has potential for the future, but its transmission would be the most sensitive to atmospheric conditions, again because of its frequency range. For a comparison of the bands' technical parameters, refer to Table 19–2.

Another satellite use being proposed is the direct user device to satellite transmission with no switching, involving spot-beam satellites that will use the extremely low frequencies. The original proposal suggests 1.618 and 1.653 GHz as the frequency for these devices, which will be utilized for mobile communications such as from a car, truck, bus, boat, or out of doors. The spot beam will use a data rate of approximately 300 BPS on a continuous basis, and 16 KBPS in a *burst* mode. Voice can also be transmitted by spot beam if it is compressed, probably at 4800 BPS (obviously not toll quality). One of the anticipated uses for spot-beam transmission is vehicle or object location because the antenna can be extremely small, as small as nine inches in diameter. Power needs will fluctuate depending on the data rate. The path is unique in that it will be initiated from the device, go directly to the satellite, down to a hub location, back to the satellite, and then to the final device. In other words, there are two satellite hops with the inherent propagation delays. Still, for its intended application, spot beam may turn out to be a popular service.

Two primary methods of modulation techniques are used for satellite transmission. Satellites do not perform any signal regeneration, only amplification, which makes the received signal bigger but does not regenerate it. If a transmission becomes deteriorated on the uplink side, it can only get worse on the down-

**TABLE 19–2**
Satellite Comparison Parameters

| PARAMETER | C BAND | Ku BAND | Ka BAND |
|---|---|---|---|
| Wavelength | 7.5 cm | 2.5 cm | mm range |
| Minimum beam width | 2°–3° | 1° | < 1° |
| Transponders | 24 | 10–12 | ≈ 20 |
| Earth antenna size | 12 ft | 6 ft | 9–12 in |
| Slots available | Almost full | Some used | Not used yet |
| Frequencies used | 4–6 GHz | 12–14 GHz | 20–30 GHz |
| Transmission effects | Minimal | Moderate | Severe |
| Cost | Least | Midrange | Highest |

link side, so care must be taken in selecting the particular frequency bands to be used and the type of modulation.

One type of modulation is *Frequency Division Multiple Access* (FDMA). With FDMA the transponder is divided into 45-KHz channels with either analog or digital modulation. It is not as efficient as TDMA, and there is some power loss due to signal separation, but it is very simple and less expensive. FDMA is usable for channels where the user does not require high transmission rates.

The second form of modulation is called *Time Division Multiple Access* (TDMA). In TDMA every receiver has a predetermined frame to receive and only looks at that frame. Transmission is also on a predetermined time basis, which means that it must be very accurately synchronized. The cost is higher than FDMA and timing is an extremely critical factor. TDMA utilizes a full satellite transponder (there are usually up to 24 transponders per satellite) and requires the full output of that transponder.

One advantage in using a satellite instead of a terrestrial microwave circuit is the reduction in the amount of transmission errors. Whereas a cross-country terrestrial link may require up to 60 segments of circuits, the satellite uses one primary segment plus possibly a couple of others at each end. The probability of transmission degradation is reduced, because once the microwave signal rises above the atmosphere (approximately eight miles), there is nothing to degrade the signal.

That does not mean there are no other problems. There are two things that affect satellite transmission. The first is a solar eclipse, which in this case refers to when the earth gets between the sun and the satellite, interfering with operation of the satellite's solar panels. The time of the year during which this occurs is for 23 days on either side of March 21 and September 21. The absolute worst times are on March 21 and September 21. There is a strong likelihood of transmission difficulty for a 72-minute period on each of those days, with possible serious degradations.

The second form of solar problem is called *sun transit;* a "satellite eclipse" in which the satellite comes between the sun and the ground station antenna. When the sun is lined up behind the satellite, thermal noise can drown out a weak satellite signal. Sun transit also occurs twice a year (the time frame depends on the orbital position), and there are five consecutive days during which there can be up to 10 minutes each day when problems may occur. It is quite possible to get by with voice, but data would have serious problems. Some satellite vendors offer the user an alternative path during the problem times, but not all of them do this. If you think sun transit will be a problem for your environment, you must make your own alternate plans.

When discussing the various satellites, one parameter that needs to be defined is the amount of transponders that are carried, because each transponder provides an independent link capability and quantifies total satellite capacity. The C-band satellites usually carry 24 transponders, while the Ku-band satellites usually carry 10 to 12. It is anticipated that the Ka-band satellites will have approximately 20 transponders when the first is launched in 1992.

When comparing satellite vendors, be sure to evaluate the proposed maintenance of the circuit. That is: Will the vendor provide just the satellite link or take end-to-end responsibility for the entire link? When there is a problem in the total link, and the satellite vendor is responsible for only the satellite portion, there is the potential for each carrier to say the other is at fault, leaving you, the end user, with the problem (not them). AT&T is one company that will take end-to-end responsibility. They also have a *one-call* maintenance service called Service-Plus, in which they agree to take all maintenance calls, isolate the problem, either fix it or refer it to the vendor who is at fault and then oversee final correction of the problem, even if they are not the vendor on any portion of the link. The force of competition may make others do the same. Because many factors can cause degradation in a network, eliminating one significant potential source of delay in problem identification may be well worth the additional expense (look at it as an insurance policy).

## Very Small Aperture Terminals (VSAT)

Toward the latter part of the 1980s there was a glut of unused satellite capacity, primarily because of the growth of fiber links throughout the United States. At the same time, however, one service that used satellites started to grow very fast—the *Very Small Aperture Terminal* (VSAT) system. A VSAT system uses the same satellites that the standard satellite systems use, but the VSAT system uses a much smaller antenna, between 1.2 and 1.8 meters (4′ and 6′). VSAT systems use either receive-only (R/O) or transmit/receive stations at all of the sites to be connected. A diagram of a VSAT system is shown in Fig. 19–2. Each remote has a direct path to the satellite, as does the host CPU. The diagram shows a terrestrial link between the host and the master station ground antenna, which is what the situation would be if you used a third-party vendor for your satellite paths. Alternatively, you could have the master site antenna at your own location if you wanted to implement a VSAT network of your own. The central site is called a *hub,* or *master earth station.* Communication takes place in a *star* configuration. The hub transmits to all remotes simultaneously (there is a separate address for each remote) and the remotes have a variety of ways to communicate back to the hub.

When utilizing the C-band satellites, the uplink is typically in the range of 5.925–6.425 GHz, and the downlink is 3.7–4.2 GHz. The Ku-band uplink is typically 14–14.5 GHz, and the downlink is 11.7–12.2 GHz. The C band requires a bigger antenna diameter (4.5 meters) because of wavelength. In addition, if the C band is used near large cities, it may overlap terrestrial microwave. The Ku band is applicable to more locations because of its lack of frequency overlap, but it is more environmentally sensitive. Ku band can also utilize higher transmit power levels, and so it permits higher data rates. Ku-band transmissions are *asymmetric,* which means that the outbound transmission from the hub can be high power, with a capacity of 512 KBPS or more, while the inbound transmissions from the remotes may have lower power, capable of transmitting only up to 128 KBPS (and typically much lower).

Transmitting from the remotes to the host site is done in a variety of ways.

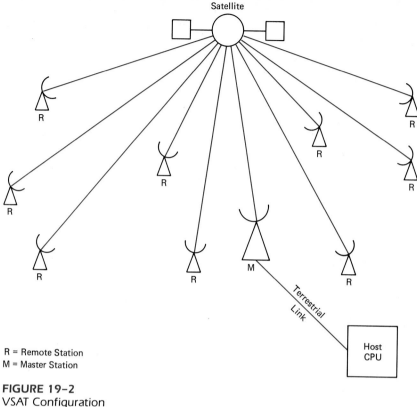

Satellite

R = Remote Station
M = Master Station

**FIGURE 19–2**
VSAT Configuration

First is *TDMA* (Time Division Multiple Access), which involves a high burst of information transmission into a preassigned time slot. TDMA requires extreme sensitivity with respect to timing relationships of all the remotes. The more remotes you have, the more critical the timing becomes.

*Random Aloha* is very much like Ethernet CSMA/CD. The remote transmits when it is ready, and if there is no acknowledgment, it tries again after a preset random delay. A collision level of 10 percent is unacceptable for normal operation, and the whole system becomes unstable with about 18-percent collisions. When collisions reach the unacceptable rate, the random delays change dynamically so that there is a higher probability of transmissions getting through the next time.

The third method for transmission is called *Slotted Aloha*. Slotted aloha involves a full transmission within a predetermined time boundary, or slot. It is a good method for short, uniform message lengths and for link loading up to approximately 20 percent. Slotted aloha becomes unstable at about 36-percent usage, because there will be too many collisions that require retransmission because of overlapping transmission times (even with fairly accurate timing synchronization).

A fourth method is called *Reservation Access.* Reservation access is a good method for low-volume users with variable-length messages that may include very long messages. The remote sends a request to the hub by way of a dedicated subchannel. The hub assigns particular time slots for the required traffic, giving the remote a dedicated time frame for transmitting its particular amount of information.

A final transmission method is called the *Stream Method,* which incorporates a dedicated stream of time slots allocated to a particular remote, whether the remote needs it or not. The stream method is good for applications that require a steady flow of data or voice.

For flexibility, if you require a variety of applications, you can use a combination of all of the transmission methods at predetermined times.

As for ground equipment, you need an antenna and a *feed,* which is a method for providing Radio Frequency (RF) power to the antenna. Along with the feed there are the necessary transmit-and-receive radio electronics and the digital electronics for moving the bits to and from the antenna. The cost for these remote transmitting stations is coming down significantly because of higher volume use, but a small antenna still costs up to $10,000. The hub, on the other hand, may cost up to $1 million, which means that you need a fairly large network to justify its installation. If the cost is not justifiable, you could contract with a third party to provide all of the hub communications and you communicate to and from the hub antenna by way of a terrestrial link.

Hubs are usually redundant, but the remote VSATs are not. An advantage of a VSAT network is that it can be configured and reconfigured very quickly because there are no physical circuits to set up or take down. Antennas can be mounted on a pole or on a free-standing mount because they are small and portable. In addition, a VSAT network can be configured for transmitting full motion, color video, which is very good for those applications requiring broadcast messages.

Most VSAT networks come with full monitoring and control systems (of course you have to buy them) that can detect degradations or failures and perform dynamic reconfigurations when available.

The primary application for VSATs seems to be to replace networks that require multidrop or broadcast type communications. One system installed in 1987 consisted of a motel reservation system in which the corporate office communicated directly with remote locations through a VSAT network provided by a third party. The users installed their own antennas at their geographically dispersed locations. When reservations traffic was necessary the remotes would transmit to the hub, from which a high-speed terrestrial digital link was established to the reservation system in another city. The reservation could then be confirmed by transmitting back to the hub, which in turn transmitted to the remote confirming the request. The savings for the user organization was estimated to be in the range of tens of thousands of dollars a month compared to the terrestrial links that they previously used, because most of their properties were in remote locations. A third-party vendor was selected to provide the hub services because the user felt they did not have the personnel or the expertise to set up a system on their own from scratch. Their plan is to fine-tune the network while using the third party, and then, if the economics are right, put in their own hub and run their own network—a very sensible way to go because they can get experience without the high up-front expenditures of setting up a hub location.

It is apparent that when deciding how to incorporate a VSAT service, one of the primary decisions to make is whether to own and operate your own network or to lease the service from a *shared-hub* vendor. Some of the larger shared-hub vendors are Contel ASC, which provides a service called Equastar; Hughes Network Systems, which provides a service called Integrated Satellite Business Network (ISBN); and AT&T. Each of these vendors made a heavy commitment to the VSAT business between 1986 and 1988. They are all large companies that can provide the kinds of service you would like to have from a shared-hub vendor.

You probably have a small network if you decide to use a shared hub, in which case the vendor will provide the entire package. On the other hand, if you own and operate your own network, you will put in your own system including all of the antennas, radio transmission equipment, and support facilities, which is very expensive and should only be done by large users. For example, Holiday Inn is in the process of putting in their own reservation system using a VSAT network to over 2000 locations, to be supported out of their own hub in Memphis, Tennessee.

If you are going to use a network with a shared hub (probably the most common for users getting into the VSAT environment), you must consider having an alternative to what is called the *backhaul* connection for reliability purposes if it goes down. The backhaul connection is the circuit that connects your data processing center to the vendor's hub and typically consists of leased land lines. You need to identify how much of the shared hub you will need, how many remote VSAT units you will need, and what your capacity requirements will be during both average and peak utilization.

When you compare the cost trade-offs between sharing a hub and owning your own, these are the things that must be considered:

Investment in hub facilities

Staffing

Network operations center

Experience of shared hub vendor versus user personnel

Startup costs

Startup problems

Locations for satellite coverage

Antenna sizes depending on location

Anticipated link performance parameters (bit error rates)

Methodology for transmission (speed and size of transmission)

Since VSAT is a currently evolving technology (and an even smaller antenna system called USAT has been announced), it is strongly recommended that, regardless of the size of your system, you *start off* with a shared-hub network so that you and your organization can become familiar with VSAT network operation along with its advantages and disadvantages. Only after you have had experience with how the network works should you consider installing one of your own. By that time you'll have a better idea of what to expect, especially in terms of the problems and the costs.

An alternative to VSATs in local environments is the use of FM radio transmission. Radio modems are used in the UHF and VHF transmission bands utilizing frequency modulation. FM radio systems typically are good for up to approximately 30 miles and can operate up to 9600 BPS, but because of noise, channel sharing, and other degradations, FM broadcast is usually operated at 300 BPS.

The protocol typically used for this kind of transmission is known as *Radio Carrier Sensed Multiple Access* (RCSMA), which is very much like Ethernet. When you transmit and a collision occurs, you will retransmit after a random delay because there will be no acknowledgment. Utilization of RCSMA is not high, but for a localized environment it is an alternative to VSAT (remember that VSAT is good for both local and extremely diverse geographic environments).

The FCC has already allocated channels for RCSMA in the 900-MHz range, and users get unlimited use of an assigned channel. Asynchronous devices talk to each other through an interface that looks very much like an X.3 packet-switching pad, where each device has X.28 parameters for compatibility. Any asynchronous device can talk to any other through the standardized interface. For synchronous transmission (at the higher data rates), bisync is typically used in a poll/call mode, which is a master-slave relationship. In the poll/call mode there will be no collision because the only time a particular remote will transmit is when it is polled or called by the master site. Synchronization time is typically 25 ms or less, so it will not be a factor in communicating.

So, in relatively limited geographic environments, such as buildings in an industrial park, FM transmission is a good choice for moving information between locations. If, however, you are dispersed geographically, then VSAT becomes an alternative method of communication, as opposed to relying only on a carrier line or facility.

# B
## VIDEO

### Video Conferencing

Data communications networks (not commercial broadcasters) have supported video communications for many years. One of the first forms implemented was the transmission of pictures that AT&T called *Picturephone,* which was available in the 1960s, but was not feasible to implement at the time because of the cost and bandwidth requirements. In the early 1980s the costs began to come down, and there was a big pitch to set up video conferencing capabilities, which many organizations did. For this operation, the cost of the actual communications links is insignificant compared to the setup of the facilities at either end. Video conferencing therefore suffered early on from the high cost of studio equipment, and the pictures were of poor quality and distorted because vendors tried to compress the amount of bandwidth required for transmission. Operational personnel manning the cameras in the beginning were not professional, so the users at the receive end got images that were nothing like they expected (home video quality was expected). Also, strict time limitations on transmission link rental caused a lot of anxiety and pressure, which discouraged other potential users.

Two entire transponders on a satellite or two separate video capacity transmission links are required for two-way video conferencing. Time during peak hours is expensive and necessitates setting up specific time frames for video conference meetings. Although there are organizations who have studios available for rent, very little is said about their profitability, and independent evaluators feel that few are profitable. There is no question that time and travel dollars can be saved if a good video conference can be set up, but it may still not be economical to supply the service.

The economics of video conferencing and video phone service may improve with the recent availability of video at 56 KBPS (digitized) using compression techniques that retain a fairly high-quality image (but not broadcast grade). The device that performs the compression is known as a video *codec*. The picture is good enough for two-way telephone conversations, but additional development is needed to further improve its quality. For use with video phones (telephones with TV cameras and screens) a video codec in 1988 cost in the range of $35,000–75,000 but was expected to get down to $10,000 by 1990. The cost of a communication link at 56 KBPS runs in the range of $2500 per month for a private link, depending on distance, in addition to approximately 80¢ per minute for a link over 500 miles.

The following description illustrates the complexity of video compression techniques. The TV screen can be divided into 512 horizontal and 480 vertical elements called *pixels* (picture elements, for a total of 245,760 per frame). Eight bits per pixel with 256 shades of grey results in full motion video at 30 frames/sec requiring 59 MBPS (512 × 480 × 8 × 30). Color usually requires up to 90 MBPS, which can be reduced to 45 MBPS if you go to 15 frames per second. Even at 15 frames per second, to reduce transmission down to 56 KBPS there must be an 800:1 compression ratio, which results in a large degradation in picture quality. As you can see, compression is not a simple matter.

Voice is usually sent separately from the video transmission because if it were to be sent as part of the video it would require another 4–8 KBPS of bandwidth, degrading the picture even more. More exotic video capability comes from the high-resolution cameras and monitors that have 520 × 910 pixels per frame (instead of the 512 × 480). This kind of resolution, however, will require higher data rates, not lower ones.

There will probably be many more developments in video conferencing, but it must still be determined whether there is really a market for this service at prices of $10,000 or more per end. Related somewhat to this was a new video telephone product which became available in 1987. It was the size of a notebook and had a three-inch diagonal screen with a black-and-white video camera. *Snapshots* are transmitted in 1.5–5.5 sec, depending on the image size. The picture interrupts the voice, and the screen is split between the live image of the caller and a photo of the remote location (you can see yourself moving, but the individual at the other end looks like a continuously updated snapshot). The device reduces the quantity of pixels and brightness, which reduces the bit transmission requirements, and the camera is able to focus within a range of 24–52 in. Costs were not firmly established during its demo time, so it will be interesting to see whether the device is a viable product and where the video market is heading in general. There seems to be no doubt, however, that until the price comes down to a more affordable level, video conferencing will not be widely implemented.

## Videotex/Teletext

In the early 1980s two competing forms of information transmission using video began to evolve called Videotex and Teletext. Both originated in Britain but are very different in operation. *Teletext* is a one-way only broadcast operation, like a TV set, where the information to be transmitted utilizes an unoccupied portion of the standard TV signal. Between each of the 30 frames of a standard video transmission there is a period of time called the *Vertical Blanking Interval* (VBI). Information, which can be several hundred individually numbered pages, can be repeatedly transmitted every minute or two during the VBIs. A special decoder (either standalone or built into the receiver) selects the page number for display on a spare TV channel. In the United States, either Channel 3 or Channel 4 is not used in any given geographic area. Whichever of the two is not being used can be used for display of the Teletext transmission. The first Teletext pilot was in operation in 1972 and used 24 rows of 40 characters each with a 5 × 7 dot matrix for the characters.

    *Videotex* had its pilot installation in 1976 (called Prestel). It required a 1200-BPS modem for transmission from the database to the receiver and utilized a 75-BPS reverse channel for requests. Transmissions took place on a standard telephone line.

    A French system called Teletel could access either Videotex or Teletext, and an early Canadian Videotex system was called Telidon. The first AT&T version was compatible with Telidon, and because of the way the interfaces were designed the U.S. and Canadian systems could access the comparable European systems, but the reverse was not true. As time moved on, the various systems seemed to prosper in Europe but fail in the United States. France, however, is presently in the process of converting the entire country to a Videotex operation. The government is providing terminals to users with directory services available via Videotex so that printed directories are not necessary. This will save a lot of money in printing and distributing directories, although it is still not clear whether the system is truly economically viable. An attempt to make it more so would be to include the various *Yellow Page* services on Videotex, but that is not likely to work in the United States because one of the most profitable ventures for all telephone companies is the generation of Yellow Pages. Therefore, unless the phone companies themselves provide the Videotex service and charge advertisers for it, the probability of their giving up the printed Yellow Page services is very remote.

In the United States some fairly large organizations tried Videotex but gave it up, including Knight-Ridder, Times-Mirror, CBS, Centel Corporation, and others. Even with all the past negative experience, it seems that somebody is always willing to try this kind of service. A series of three new tests were announced in 1987, to be implemented between 1988 and 1992.

The first new system is *Prodigy,* from Trintex (in mid-1988 the name was officially designated as Prodigy), to be supported by IBM and Sears. Trintex provides news, weather, sports, electronic mail, movie reviews, and brokerage services. Future services would include banking and shop-at-home services. The starting cost is in the range of $9–12 per month after a sign-up fee of approximately $30, which compares with the approximate $35 per month charged by the previous systems. The low cost is based on getting advertising revenue for the system. Prodigy can only be accessed by a computer with a modem running at least at 1200 BPS, and preferably at 2400 BPS. The need for higher speed is because of the graphics displays. One of the serious problems facing systems like these in the past was the slow *refresh* of the screen, which took about 10–15 sec. The Trintex software is faster because of a multiple-frame transmission sequence based on an assumption of what the user *probably* wants next. If a different screen is requested, the normal extended time delay will be encountered. Initial projections are that Trintex will be profitable by the mid-1990s, and it will be interesting to see whether the service is accepted by the marketplace.

A second system, called *Telaction,* from JC Penney is planned primarily as a shopping service. The initial system is to be set up in the Chicago area using touch-tone telephones for ordering from screens. The user selects an assigned channel on cable TV and then dials a number on a touch-tone phone (no physical connection is required between the TV and the phone). Once the number is dialed, the user can call up various screens for purchasing items. More numbers are then dialed to select the items. One initial drawback is that users will be grouped in nodes of 15 subscribers each, all viewing the same screen. Each must wait until the previous node user stops using the node before accessing the system. Many other systems attempted to develop shop-at-home services, but with newer services utilizing their own cable TV and UHF channels and 800 dial-in WATS lines (which cost the user nothing) in many of the metropolitan areas of the country, the demand for additional shop-at-home services does not seem as great as it used to be. However, if Penney's is successful they will expand to other areas of the country.

The third form of Videotex under development is *Alex* from Bell Canada. Alex provides a gateway to all kinds of information services that can be accessed by a PC, similar to the access to database services provided in the United States. Bell Canada expects the terminals to lease for less than $15 Canadian per month, and is considering the possibility of using telephone directories (like France) as a future service.

At present there are high hopes for all of these Videotex services and others that are still on the drawing board. With more consumers buying PCs that can be used as home terminals, the potential for at-home services is growing. However, it still remains to be seen whether the services are worth the operating charges. Most services are just information providers at present, so there will probably have to be other types of services that will be offered in conjunction with database services to make them more economically attractive. Maybe by the time the next edition of this text comes out, there will be more positive news to present for this business.

One last item: A related term used in the video environment is *Viewdata,* a generic term for any information retrieval service. Viewdata refers to any menu listing the selections of databases available to an end user. Some confusion exists because Viewdata is also the name of a specific Videotex service provided by a British company. There is also confusion between Videotex and Teletext. The CCITT distinguishes between the two by specifically identifying Videotex as a two-way communication and Teletext as one way only. Recently there was talk of a new Telex service to be called Teletex (notice that there is no letter *t* at the end). Teletex is to be an upgraded version of the existing five-level Baudot Telex system, which is the largest communication system in the world. If the upgrade is successful there will be additional confusion in terms. Teletex is only a message switching and delivery system, while Teletext is a one-way information provision service. If these terms are used in conversation, make sure you are aware of the specific service being discussed.

# C

# CELLULAR RADIO

Cellular radio is a system designed to replace the older *mobile radio,* which only had 12 separate channels for an entire geographic area. The areas had a 35–50 mile radius and used specially assigned frequencies. The equipment would select an unused channel, and the user would dial an operator and specify the number to be called. In cellular radio, as shown in Fig. 19–3, a series of cells each covers 1–8 square miles and together resembles a *honeycomb.* Each cellular radio market is assigned two blocks of 333 channels each in the 825–90 MHz band. All of the cells are controlled by a Network Switching Office (NSO), which connects to each of the cell transmitter/receivers through telephone land lines. The NSO then provides the connection to the regular carrier network. Adjacent cells use different channels, so there is no interference from calls in neighboring cells. Frequency modulation is used for the voice transmission, with a spacing of 3 KHz between channels. Two different frequencies are used for FDX operations.

Each cellular radio mobile phone has a 10-digit identification number, which is converted into a 34-bit binary code known as the *Mobile I/D Number* (MIN). All calls are dialed directly. Each cell has at least one channel delegated for the set up and control of calls that is separate from the voice channel.

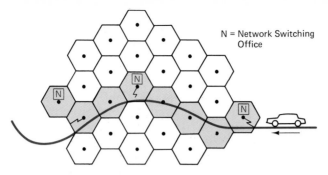

**FIGURE 19–3**
Cellular Radio Configuration

To initiate a call, the mobile phone tunes in to the strongest set-up channel it hears (typically the closest base station). The set-up channel is always transmitting so that it can be heard by all devices in the area. When no specific devices are being called, filler transmissions are provided to make sure that all devices in the area can determine which is the closest base station.

When a call is made *to* a cellular phone, the cell base-transmitters send out the unique binary code identifying the called device. When the call is recognized, the phone tries to seize the *set-up* channel in the cell that it is currently in, but may have to wait for other respondents to complete their processes. The called phone then sends its MIN, which is relayed to the NSO over a 2400-BPS link. The NSO keeps track of all the channels in use and assigns an unused channel for each call. The assignment is sent to the mobile phone over a *forward* set-up channel. The mobile device tunes to the assigned channel and acknowledges to the cell base-station by sending back a 6-KHz tone, which is in turn relayed to the NSO. The serial number of the mobile transceiver is converted to the 32-bit binary sequence and is also transmitted automatically, which facilitates billing and reduces theft (the serial number is a built-in function in each mobile phone).

*Hand off* among cells is accomplished by the NSO in a given area. When a mobile device leaves one cell and enters another, the old NSO informs the new NSO of the transference so that a new channel can be set up. A 200-ms burst on the voice channel is transmitted, which tells the mobile device what new voice channel is being assigned in the new cell. A burst sequence on the reverse set-up channel is transmitted and the conversation continues. The talkers on the circuit usually are not aware of the bursts because voice is not audibly affected, but the transfer can have a very serious effect on data.

Of course, you will probably not be entering information into a machine while you are driving, but devices are being developed to be capable of transmitting in an unattended mode while a vehicle is moving. Some private systems already have this capability, but whether it will be practical in the public environment remains to be seen. Mobile radio is growing at a very fast rate, but is currently used almost exclusively for voice communications. Its future may be

**TABLE 19–3**
Top 30 Cellular Radio Markets

| | | | |
|---|---|---|---|
| 1. | New York–Nassau–Suffolk–Newark–Jersey City–Paterson–Clifton–Passaic | 14. | Baltimore |
| 2. | Los Angeles–Long Beach–Anaheim–Santa Ana–Garden Grove–Riverside–San Bernardino–Ontario | 15. | Minneapolis–St. Paul |
| | | 16. | Cleveland |
| 3. | Chicago | 17. | Atlanta |
| 4. | Philadelphia | 18. | San Diego |
| 5. | Detroit–Ann Arbor | 19. | Denver–Boulder |
| 6. | Boston–Lowell–Brockton–Lawrence–Haverhill | 20. | Seattle–Everett |
| | | 21. | Milwaukee |
| 7. | San Francisco–Oakland | 22. | Tampa–St. Petersburg |
| 8. | Washington, D.C. | 23. | Cincinnati |
| 9. | Dallas–Fort Worth | 24. | Kansas City |
| 10. | Houston | 25. | Buffalo |
| 11. | St. Louis | 26. | Phoenix |
| 12. | Miami–Fort Lauderdale–Hollywood | 27. | San Jose |
| 13. | Pittsburgh | 28. | Indianapolis |
| | | 29. | New Orleans |
| | | 30. | Portland (Oregon) |

affected by the convenience of the handheld device used for direct satellite communications (described in Section A of this chapter). Even though the demand for data support on the cellular network may not be great, direct satellite transmission is attractive because it involves no switching. Table 19–3 shows the 30 largest cellular markets in operation today.

# D
# FACSIMILE

Although facsimile has been around for many years, in late 1986 a tremendous growth began in the facsimile market. Vendors came out with new equipment that provided document transmission in less than 10 seconds, which was described as a *revolution* in communications. It may not have been quite a revolution, but there is no question that facsimile has made a very big dent in the information transmission market. The idea behind facsimile transmission is the transmission of a picture or document in which the image on the paper is converted to binary form. The result is called an electronic *bit map*.

A typical page is broken up into areas of 200 dots/in. resolution, from both a left-to-right and top-to-bottom scan, totaling 3.7 million dots on an 8.5 × 11 in. page. The high speed of transmission is due to an algorithm that provides compression of the bits to be sent. On an average document with alphanumeric text, the copy is typically 85 percent white and 15 percent black. If the black areas are specified by boundaries only, even more compression is possible. If successive rows of bits are similar, they can be further compressed by describing only the differences instead of the specific values (known as two-dimensional coding in facsimile). By combining the various forms of compression along with some of the higher data-transmission rates, documents can be transmitted in fewer than 10 seconds.

To provide a standardized methodology for the development and production of facsimile equipment, the CCITT has established four groups of facsimile standards. They are

|  | SIGNAL | COMPRESSION | SPEED |
|---|---|---|---|
| Group 1 | Analog | None | 6 minutes |
| Group 2 | Analog | Limited | 3 minutes |
| Group 3 | Digital | Complex | <1 minute |
| Group 4 | Digital | Complex | <10 seconds |

Within the Group 4 category there are three classes of operation:

| BITS/INCH | CLASS I | CLASS II | CLASS III |
|---|---|---|---|
| Mandatory resolution | 200 | 300 | 400 |
| Optional resolution | 300/400 | 200/240/400 | 200/240/300 |

As can be seen there is a wide variety of equipment available and, with mass production, the prices are coming down all the time. Some organizations transmit information quickly via facsimile and then use *scanning* equipment to convert the images for storage and display. With software conversion the image can be converted to ASCII code for alphanumeric storage after transmission in less than the time it would take to convert the text to binary, and then transmit. Facsimile can use standard telephone lines, so only voice-grade facilities need to be paid for. As users opt for ISDN and 56-KBPS transmission, the ability to move entire documents, including the graphics used in desktop publishing applications, will become indispensable. Facsimile should not be overlooked as a mechanism for moving high volumes of data, especially for long-term data or image storage.

## E
## MICROWAVE

Microwave transmission is related to satellite and radio transmission. Entire texts have been written about the technical and operational characteristics of microwave, so only the use of microwave by the end user (as opposed to the carriers, who have their own microwave requirements) will be discussed here. Excluding direct satellite transmission, end-user microwave implementation is typically in a local environment for short distances in what is called *bypass*. Bypass is available in two forms. *Service bypass* is a special connection to the local telephone company's central office, possibly with fiber cables bypassing copper local loops. A more common kind of bypass is *facility bypass,* which is a direct connection to a long-distance carrier. Long-distance carriers cannot put cables in the street, but can connect to end users via microwave. End users can also set up their own short-distance microwave for communicating between facilities up to approximately 15 miles apart. Voice, data, video, and almost any other kind of transmission in a point-to-point connection can be made.

Even though the entire range of 2–23 GHz is utilized for microwave, the lower bands are very congested, so in the early 1980s two specific bands were allocated for this kind of transmission, the 18-GHz and 23-GHz bands. The 18-GHz range provides a greater path length, more information-carrying capability, and better performance in poorer atmospheric environments, but it is more expensive. There is a relatively short installation time for these bands, but an FCC license is required for their use, which can take six to nine months to obtain. As part of obtaining the license you must perform *path engineering,* which determines whether there are overlapping frequency areas or interfering circuits. The user must also identify expected radiation levels and incorporate many other parameters before the FCC will determine whether to issue a license. Cost is another factor. A low-capacity circuit with a single link may cost about $10,000. A T-1 or higher capacity usually starts at $50,000 and goes up from there. You should also be aware that although a particular system works well in one location, it may not necessarily work as well in another because of environmental or physical path conditions. Finally, because of potential physical link degradations, you should also determine whether to incorporate alternate or back-up facilities (or at least have a plan) so you can still operate when the link is degraded.

Some organizations have installed entire networks with multiple microwave links, but they are usually provided by a third party (especially by the carriers themselves), so they will not be discussed here. If you think you can justify your own microwave network, it is strongly recommended that you go to one of the carriers or third-party microwave vendors. They have the technical expertise, but even more important, they know the process, and are familiar with the FCC, all necessary for installing your system in an optimum fashion.

## QUESTIONS

1. Describe the operational differences between the two primary forms of commercial satellite communications.
2. What does geosynchronous mean? Why is it important for communications users?
3. What are some of the problems associated with satellite communications? What is the most significant one? Why?
4. What do C band and Ku band mean?
5. What are the two primary modulation techniques used with satellites, and where are they used?
6. Why must communication satellites be placed in specific orbital positions?
7. Describe the operation of a typical application using a VSAT system.

8. Describe the technique used to transmit video at 56 KBPS.

9. What is the primary difference between Videotex and Teletext? Is it significant from an application point of view?

10. Describe the operation of a cellular radio system between two cities. Include the initiation and termination processes.

11. What is the difference between facsimile and data transmission?

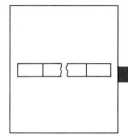

# 20

# Communication System Transactions, Applications, and Formats

## BACKGROUND

Any communications system, whether it is based on a single processing site or multiple processing sites, such as for a distributed processing application, will have to process a wide variety of applications. The handling of applications may be different in the central processor mode from the distributed processing modes, where specific functions may be handled in specific CPUs. A set of definitions has been developed that is applicable to both methods of implementation. These definitions are not necessarily accepted industry standards, since there are none, so the reader must use them as a baseline for describing, discussing, and analyzing the method whereby each transaction is handled.

## B

## INQUIRY/RESPONSE (I/R)

Of all the different transactions used in a network, the one used most often in communications systems is the inquiry/response (I/R). Inquiries from both local and remote locations are placed to the databases at one or more central processing sites, and responses are returned to the inquirers. An I/R is defined as the entry of a request from a terminal for information from a database, regardless of where that database resides in the system, and the return of the requested information to the operator in a real-time mode. Real time in this case means that an operator is waiting for the system to respond; the longer the system-response time, the longer the operator has to wait. As will be seen in Chapter 23, response time is a critical design criterion.

## C
## RECORD UPDATE (R/U)

A *record update* is defined as the modification or deletion of an existing record in the *system* database. Record update should not be confused with *file update,* which refers to any change made in the database. R/U has a very specific meaning because of the methods whereby different changes to the database must be handled. R/U can be done by an operator in a real-time situation, or it can be done in a non-real-time mode with inputs that may have been "batched" previously. Batching will be described in Section I of this chapter. The advantage of R/U being done in real time is that it is available to all users of the system immediately after the update. When the update is not done in real time, it is not available to users until it gets to the database, after its initial entry into the system. The initial entry usually occurs at a terminal where the data is collected. Data collection will be described in Section E of this chapter.

## D
## DATA ENTRY (DE)

Data entry (DE) is the creation of a new record in the *system* database in real time. Because the process whereby the database management system creates a new entry in the database is different from the process it goes through to access an already existing file, the data-entry function has been given a separate transaction definition. The newer database management systems are being designed to be physically resident in a single CPU dedicated to a single database. The new CPUs are called *back-door* or *back-end* machines and are now becoming available for both IBM and non-IBM systems. The creation of a new record in the database will take longer than a straight access, and even though it is not a significant period of time, it is being defined as a separate transaction because the internal process is different.

# DATA COLLECTION (DC)

Data collection (DC) is the collection of information in a local or remote environment for *subsequent* update into the *system* database. The information is put into a machine-readable form so that, when the appropriate time and facilities are available, the collected information can be applied to the database in either the record update or data entry mode. The function of data collection implies that the information is not available to users of the system at the time it is collected and will be only after being applied to the database. For those systems where the information collected can be accessed locally, the local user may perform inquiries against that information; but from an overall system point of view, no other user will be able to access it, and therefore this particular transaction must have a unique definition.

The fact that data collection is implemented in a local environment implies that the local environment has a storage medium to collect the information. Information can also be transmitted incrementally or in a batch mode to a central site, where two more alternatives exist. If, at the time of transmission, the information is applied to the database and is available to all users, it becomes the combined function of record update and data entry. If, however, the information is collected again at the central site for subsequent update, it is still considered data collection. The data collection procedure itself may involve the transmission of the information from a terminal to the central site directly for off-line storage purposes, in which case we have storage only at the central site instead of at each of the remote sites, still considered data collection because the information is not available to the system users. Until the information becomes available to the system users it cannot be considered a part of the database accessing system and must be handled separately. Central-site collection of information for subsequent database updating is sometimes called *spooling*.

# MESSAGE SWITCHING

Message switching defines what is required when a message must be transmitted between three or more processing sites, which can be terminals, CPUs, or both. Message switching requires three or more locations because no routing is involved when there are only two locations. Routing is only required when a decision must be made at a particular site as to where the message must be sent. Even where a single central site has multiple terminals connected to it, if a terminal on one line has to communicate with a terminal on another line, the message must go through the central site, where a determination as to the output location must be made. If the message is routed intact, which means its contents are not manipulated in any way, message switching has occurred. All the queuing, buffer management, and routing table functions of the communications software must be included when message switching is required. Most systems do not perform message switching because of these handling overheads; but if it is done, it is usually performed by a separate front-end processor (see Chapter 12).

## G
## PROCESS CONTROL (PC)

A process control transaction is one where a physical process is monitored automatically. Information regarding that process is transmitted to another location, where controls are generated *automatically* regarding the physical environment. Responses may be sent to a third location. Typical applications of process control are an electrical-power grid system, an oil refinery, and a chemical plant. Process control is completely automatic, needing no human intervention. Only where limits exceed the capability of the control units will human action be required.

## H
## COMMAND AND CONTROL (CC)

The command and control environment is very much like the process control environment, except that in C/C there may be manual and automated monitoring of a physical process and the control is always initiated by a human. Even though the controls at the physical locations may be implemented by machines, the initiation is still done by the human. The latest buzz word describing this process is $C^3$ (Communications, Command and Control).

## I
## BATCH

A *remote batch* is defined as the collection and transmission of all the information needed to perform a particular standalone job to another location for processing. After processing at the second location, the response is collected and returned to the transmitter all at one time if required. A *local batch* is sometimes described as the processing of a particular function at one site and transmitting the results to a second site. Either term is acceptable if it is assumed that the information and results are transmitted together as one sequence for either processing or use by the other site. A batch can consist of a particular application to be processed as a complete standalone job, or it may be a group of data collection functions that will be processed separately once they reach the application site. Batch processing is almost always performed in a non-real-time mode.

# J

## DIAGNOSTICS

All the previous transactions involve the day-to-day operation of a typical communication system. They are the functions that must be performed for the user to conduct business. An important function that is usually overlooked is validation that the system is operating properly so that any malfunction can be corrected quickly. To accommodate this kind of application, the user must consider the implementation of a series of diagnostic capabilities (over and above the communication facilities) that will continually test the system operation to determine if malfunctions are occurring or if a failure has occurred. Many times degradations or failures occur, but are not recognized right away because the particular process involved is not used all the time. If a diagnostic capability exists the failure or malfunction can be recognized almost immediately, and corrective action can be taken long before the process has to be used again. Because vendors do not normally provide validation in minicomputers and terminals (some mainframe vendors do), it is important for the user to consider implementing diagnostics as a separate application when designing the system. The diagnostics should include the communications software and all the individual hardware elements that make up the system. Tests can be performed either in a standalone environment or in conjunction with other elements of the system. Because of the already existing capabilities, however, the communications system can be considered a separate item and treated independently. (See Chapter 22 for the latest diagnostic capabilities.)

# K

## DISTRIBUTED APPLICATIONS

When discussing distributed applications there is a tendency to confuse the application with the network. The fact that applications are performed in different locations or under different sets of conditions really has no effect on the physical network itself, which consists of either dedicated or dial-up circuits operating on either half-duplex or full-duplex facilities. To reduce some of the confusion, three definitions will be given relative to distributed processing applications. Keep in mind that they are actually specialized system configurations that are implemented with half- and full-duplex circuits and other types of standard communications facilities.

The first definition is of *hierarchical distributed processing,* in which there are multiple levels of processing capability, starting at the terminal level and going to some nodal level. Anything that cannot be done at either the terminal or one of the nodes is then done at some high-order central site. There may be multiple levels of nodes in a hierarchical network, but those connections are either point-to-point or multipoint circuits usually configured in full duplex. Hierarchical distributed processing is shown in Fig. 20–1 and was representative of IBM's distributed network environment, System Network Architecture (SNA) when it was first announced.

The second type of distributed processing is *remote distributed processing,* which is shown in Fig. 20–2 and consists in this particular case of three independent processing sites, each with the same level of network controls and capability. In the hierarchical process, what cannot be done at one terminal goes upward through the network until it finally reaches a location where the particular processing can be performed. In remote distributed processing, each site has specific functions to perform at a certain control level, and therefore what cannot be processed at one site is moved to the next site to see if it can be processed there. If not, it goes to the geographic location where it can be processed. In remote distributed processing, it is also possible for the same applications to be performed at different sites (load sharing), because it is possible that the databases to be used with the application might be different.

The third type of distributed processing is *functional distributed processing*

**FIGURE 20–1**
Hierarchical Distributed Processing

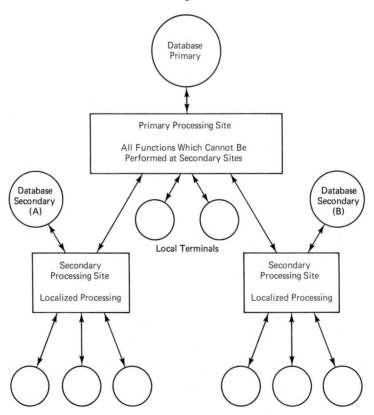

COMMUNICATION SYSTEM TRANSACTIONS, APPLICATIONS, AND FORMATS

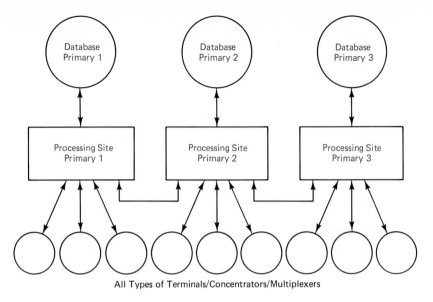

All Types of Terminals/Concentrators/Multiplexers

**FIGURE 20–2**
Remote Distributed Processing

and involves the separation of processing functions into separate CPUs. The three functions that are logically separated are transaction processing, application processing, and database processing. A diagram of this configuration is shown in Fig. 20–3 and, as shown, it consists of three separate processors. Minicomputer vendors initiated this kind of configuration, but today many standalone processor vendors are developing software packages to fit into this framework. The transaction-processor software already exists in many environments and functionally is configured very much like the front end in Fig. 20–3. The purpose of the transaction processor is to handle all the networking functions and interfaces and to interface with the processors connected to it on a separate communications path. Also in Fig. 20–3, a separate path connects the transaction processor with both the applications processor and the database processor on a bus, which may be a LAN. The transaction processor is sometimes called a *front-end processor.*

The *back-end processor* is the database management processor, which has all the system databases tied to it (there may be more than one database processor). The primary function of the processor is to read, write, or modify data in the database. It does not handle any application software. This concept is a radical departure from previous database management systems, which integrated parts of the applications software into the database manager for supposed efficiency purposes. With the reduced cost of memory and processing equipment today, it is becoming more feasible to duplicate the hardware interfaces making the software simpler.

Even though there are many large-scale database management systems in

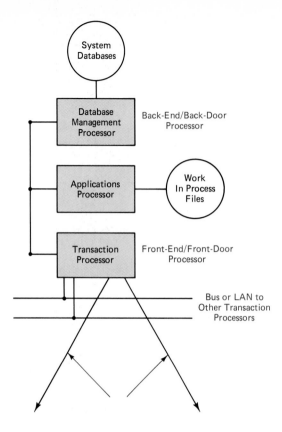

**FIGURE 20–3**
Functional Distributed Processing

operation, the standalone database manager is making headway for the following reasons:

1. There is faster database access because the machine is specifically designed to be a high-performance database access device and does not have to live within the host operating system.
2. It can off load the host because it takes the overhead software out of the host, leaving the host to do more of its *number crunching*.
3. It can be a network database server because it can provide shared databases for different users in a network. If an individual machine cannot handle the size database required, then additional back-end database management processors can be tied to the same bus until the total database can be accommodated. The transaction processor will have the appropriate address tables to direct traffic to the specific database processor that contains the file being requested.
4. Back-end database machines can accommodate a shared database across

many hosts. The hosts can also be from different vendors and have different characteristics because the entire interface is a common one. Each host machine only needs to have the interface format and message characteristics to access the database management processor.

5. The overall cost will probably be less because the cost for doing database accesses in a machine designed strictly for that purpose will be less than the cost from the host, where database accesses would use up resources that could be utilized for additional applications processing.

6. Because of its special-purpose design, a standalone database management processor can be optimized for use in a *relational* database. Any required changes will not affect any other process or processor (especially not applications).

7. This type of machine will provide a universal database interface because the microprocessors at its interface can convert the operating parameters of any host CPU its operating parameters of this machine.

All in all, it would appear that the time has come for the implementation of a standalone database management machine, and if you look at most PC LANs today (see Chapter 15) you will see individual PCs functioning as database servers (called file servers).

The third processor in Fig. 20–3 is an applications processor, which is defined as the machine that performs all data processing that is not directly involved with the network (the transaction processor) or database management (which is the responsibility of the database management processor). All previously defined applications are included here, as well as any of the interface functions not directly related to the processing in the other machines. Any reports that have to be written, statistics that have to be generated, interfacing between applications, and the like, are considered unique applications. The applications processor may also have peripheral storage devices connected to it so that it can avail itself of temporary storage (work files) needed for specific processing as defined within the application requirement. As networks have been evolving, however, the concept of one LAN for transaction processors and a separate LAN for applications and database machines has given way to a single LAN connecting all the devices.

This *functional distributed processing* configuration can be included in either of the hierarchical or remote distributed processing locations by replacing the primary processing sites with this configuration. There is nothing to preclude the use of these configurations at lower levels in the hierarchical mode; but, for a start, it would only be done at the primary sites.

Most companies start off with a single central site and add to it, starting with terminals and adding CPUs at remote locations. At any given time there will probably be a combination of remote and hierarchical configurations. A diagram of this configuration is shown in Fig. 20–4. As shown, there is remote distributed processing along with the primary sites, and each primary site has associated with it a hierarchical type of network. It might be possible in some of these networks for the secondary processing sites to have communications paths to

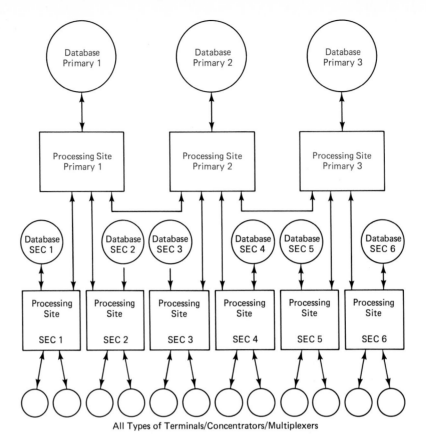

**FIGURE 20–4**
Combined Remote/Hierarchical Processing

other secondary sites, but this may not always be true. This diagram is a fairly accurate picture of what IBM's SNA offers.

# L

## FORMATS

By far, one of the most critical functions to be implemented in a data communications system is the format of the message to be transmitted. The format tells the logical processing equipment at either end of the communication line what to do with the message and how to do it. Part of the format may also involve the sequence of operations (handshaking) that must be completed to permit modem synchronization and network routing. Data formats can only be recognized after the communications equipment has completed its handshaking and are therefore related most to the system-level design; but because the code type, length, and transmission validation technique are also involved, the format must be considered an integral part of any data communication system.

There are three fundamental segments of a data transmission format: the *header,* the *text portion,* and the *trace* or *tail segment.* Since all applications may be implemented differently, a generalized format is shown in Fig. 20–5. Not all the functions that will be described are necessary for all applications, while other applications may require additional functions. Included here is a basic format that contains the majority of the key functions that must be considered when

**FIGURE 20–5**
Generalized Message Format

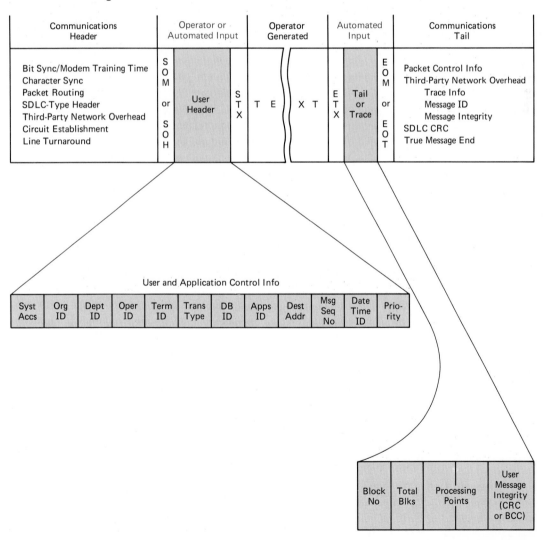

designing the format; the user can select those that are applicable to the situation and add those that are required beyond what is described here.

Another factor to consider relative to formats is that in a network, especially a hierarchical network, the lower-level communication links may have complete formats defined for them, while the links at the upper levels or between central processing sites may add additional information fields to create a *superformat*. Superformats allow the movement of entire blocks of information from low-order processing locations, so that when the information reaches its intermediate or ultimate destination, all the original information is available for processing. Superformat information is used for multiple link routing (interprocessor) and error-detection capabilities.

In describing the components that make up the message format, we refer to Fig. 20–5 and see at the left two portions of a sample message header. The first portion is the communications header, which verifies that the communication link exists both electrically and logically and provides the capability for synchronization in synchronous transmission (handshaking). It also provides the capability for the communications hardware at the receive end to establish bit and character synchronization when necessary. In a high-level communication link, where messages have been routed from a lower-order processing location, there may also be a communications routing segment in the communications header, which determines the necessary routing between the higher-order links.

Once the communications header has been identified, a user header is initiated by a character identified as a *start of message* (SOM). In ASCII, it is known as the SOH (start of header) character. The user header is terminated by an STX (start of text) character. It is up to the user to determine the information to be contained within the header. The items of information within the user header can be bits, bytes, words, combinations, or any other sequence that the user finds convenient and feasible to implement. The information can be either operator generated or automatically generated by software, firmware, or both. Each potential segment of the header will be described next as to function and probability of use.

**SYSTEM ACCESS** The system access segment can be considered a password through which the potential accessor of the system must provide identification as an authorized user. Depending on the type of equipment involved, system-level access can be detected and validated at the remote terminal, the nodes, the central site processors, and even at the database manager. This access-type identification will permit at least a first-level identification as to whether a particular user is authorized to utilize the system. For applications where dial-up connections are made, this password is just about mandatory. Even if dedicated lines are primarily used, if dial-up is used for backup capability, system access identification should still be required because the user must not allow data to be compromised by an unauthorized user.

**ORGANIZATION ID/DEPARTMENT ID** Organization ID and department ID identify the specific organization within the user environment that is trying to access the system facility. Neither of them, one, or both may be required, or further levels of definition within the organization might be required to gain access. Organization/department ID provides control of who within the spectrum of authorized users will be allowed to access the different types of databases available within the system. Where all users are not allowed to access all databases (manufacturing operations is not allowed to access financial information or personnel files, for example), this level of identification allows the database management system to determine which users are authorized to access not only specific databases, but even records within a single database. In the future, however, it may also be desirable to have a sublevel organization ID that will permit certain users to access specific applications, while other users will be excluded.

**OPERATOR ID**   In all systems today that are part of a network, and where many terminals can be used by different personnel, it is becoming increasingly critical to identify the operators using a terminal. Identification is necessary not only for security and accessing purposes, especially where database access is limited to specific operators within specific organizations; it is also necessary to identify users who are using the system in an unauthorized manner or making an inordinate amount of accesses, which may indicate a training problem. Since all tracking and auditing relies ultimately on identifying the individual who accesses the system, operator ID is one of the most important functions to be included in the header of a message. The ID information may be entered in each message by the operator or, after a log-on procedure, it can be inserted automatically by terminal software or firmware.

**TERMINAL ID**   The first four segments of the header described thus far may or may not be entered by an operator. It is quite possible for an unauthorized user to obtain a valid operator's number and try to access the system illegitimately. By installing a terminal ID at each terminal location in hardware or firmware, an additional level of security can be implemented by forcing operators to use only previously authorized terminals for their respective accesses. Thus, if an unauthorized user has a valid operator's number, the unauthorized user must also get to a terminal that is authorized to accept inputs with that operator ID. The system manager may then limit accessibility at all remote levels, and by changing both the operator IDs and the terminal IDs in a predetermined manner, any compromise of the system will only last until the next change occurs. Terminal ID can also be used to prevent users who are authorized to use the system from accessing specific databases. For example, if payroll information should not be available to terminals used on the production floor, specific limitations can be imposed within the database manager so that only specifically identified payroll access terminals can access the payroll files. Terminal ID is a powerful level of system security because it is non-operator dependent.

In the newer distributed processing networks, for the processing CPUs to determine what is supposed to be done with a message, the type of transaction it contains must be defined (see the definitions earlier in this chapter). Since specific types of transactions are handled differently by the various CPUs, it is necessary to identify the specific type of transaction quickly so that is can be routed to the appropriate CPU for processing. It is possible that the transaction may not have to be specified, but if management and applications functions are processed in different CPUs, the transaction definition is extremely important for efficient handling of messages.

*DATABASE ID/APPLICATIONS ID*   Since the newer systems are using smaller computers and PCs, not only are the databases being segmented but the applications are being performed in separate CPUs. Where different databases reside with different CPUs and different applications are performed by different computers, it is necessary to identify both the database and the application of a particular message so that the proper inter- and intrasite routing functions can be performed. The IDs can be used with the transaction definitions to identify the final destination address in those networks where it is desired to have the terminal operator transparent to where its data are physically resident. Even though it takes more software to implement this implied addressing, it relieves the operator of having to determine where the appropriate application or database physically resides.

*DESTINATION ADDRESS*   If the system design is such that implied addressing is not incorporated or if the requirement for terminal-to-terminal communications exists, it is necessary to include a destination address segment in the header. Even when implied addressing is involved, there may be situations when an operator must communicate with some administrative or control location, and it may therefore be necessary to have both the implied addressing and destination address capability included in the same format.

*MESSAGE SEQUENCE NUMBER*   Some form of message sequence number identification must be incorporated into a communication system so that the users of the system, both manual and automated, will have a means of identifying whether duplicate transmissions are being received and whether messages are missing. In all networks where multiple paths for messages exist, it is quite possible for a message to take one path to get to its ultimate destination and for the acknowledgment to take a different path. It is also possible for a message to be received in error, while the negative acknowledgment for that message is lost or held up on the way back to the transmitter. For example, if there is no way for the database manager to determine whether a particular update has already been received, it is possible to apply the same update to a record twice or to lose an update completely. Imagine this happening in a typical banking situation in the following manner. A customer goes into one of the bank branches and wants to cash a check. The teller inquires against the database to determine whether there is enough money in the account to cash the check. Once the amount is validated, the teller cashes the check for the customer, and the customer leaves the bank. The teller goes back into the system with an update that debits the account for the amount of the check. The update can be made to the database, but the acknowledgment coming back to the terminal can be held up in a queue, lost, or garbled, so that the terminal operator never gets an acknowledgment. If, after the appropriate time out, the operator retransmits the message, the file will be updated again, thus debiting two checks to the same file instead of one. Now, the acknowledgment for the first update comes back, and it appears to the operator that the second transmission has just been acknowledged.

In the meantime, another transaction, such as a deposit, takes place with a different customer. A file update transaction is transmitted into the system, which, for typical reasons in a communications network, does not get to the file for update immediately, but the acknowledgment from the second transmission of the previous debit transaction now comes back and appears to the operator to be an acknowledgment for the deposit update. As far as the operator is concerned, everything is all right within the file, but we actually have two erroneous records.

One means of overcoming this situation is to identify each transaction with the terminal ID and message sequence number, so that the database manager will be in a position to compare the new update on a particular record with the previous update. If they are the same, the second one is acknowledged without changing the file. There is, of course, a probability of error here, too, in that in between the first and second update received by the database manager an update from another source can come into that record (a deposit or check at a different branch or a previously written check cleared through the system). The database manager now looking at the sequence numbers that appear to be different will process both if only the single previous transaction is stored.

A brute-force solution to this situation would be to have the previous two transactions stored, but the same type of sequence could occur again (where a third input is processed between the two that are stored), so some limit has to be placed by the user on how many of the previous transactions will be stored. It must be recognized that all storage of previous transactions adds a significant amount of overhead to the system in processing time, and especially in information storage on the peripherals. An alternative approach might be to require an operator to reinquire into the database any time an acknowledgment is not received for a transmission, to validate whether an update has already reached the file. This is not foolproof either, in that the original update can be held up in a queue while the new inquiry, taking a different path, can go into the database and look at the data in its original unchanged state. The operator will then initiate a new update, while the first update, having overcome its delay in the queue, updates the file. Shortly thereafter, the second update comes in and updates the file again. The risk factors involved in implementing these methods must be evaluated by the user to determine which method, or combination of methods, must be incorporated to provide the least amount of exposure in the customer environment. Without some form of message sequence number identification, however, this becomes an almost impossible task. For that reason, it is quite possible that additional levels of message ID must be incorporated within the header of a message so that the database manager can determine whether or not to apply an update to a file.

The foregoing description is not meant to imply that banks suffer from this problem in day-to-day operation, as their software is probably the most extensive in prohibiting problems like these from occurring. It was used as a generic example to describe out-of-sequence conditions that could occur on less sophisticated systems such as inventory management or other sequence-sensitive applications.

**DATE/TIME ID**   One level of message ID that can be used to validate the applicability of a particular update is the date/time ID, which can also be put in the header portion of a message. The database manager can then be designed so that date/time comparisons must be made, in sequence, before an update to the file can be made. A new date/time stamp must be put on each message when it is transmitted, so some kind of real-time clock must be installed at all the terminal locations. This is not a totally clean method either. Multiple terminals at different locations may try to access the same record for updating and, because of propagation delays or queues, arrive out of sequence. For this particular case, the terminal ID can be used with the sequence number and the date/time stamp to determine whether a particular update should be made. Here, again, the user must determine how much identification is required within the message to provide the least tolerable amount of exposure to erroneous file handling.

**PRIORITY**   For the communications network with multiple paths and multiple transmission lines, terminals or lines being down are a day-to-day possibility. When these conditions occur, queues of messages destined for those terminals or lines build up. Over time the queues can become very long. When the failed unit becomes operational again, the messages must be sent out one at a time, on a first in/first out basis, unless some form of priority scheme has been established for permitting urgent messages to be transmitted first. Without some form of priority scheme, it is quite possible for urgently required information to wait its turn behind lower-priority information (which may also take a long time to transmit) and not arrive at the destination in time to be of any use. For example, the response to an inquiry with a waiting operator should take precedence over a batch-type transmission that will go to a printing device at a remote site. For some applications this may not be a problem because the system is *transaction driven,* which means that only terminal operators are accessing the system and they are all waiting for responses. If the responses do not come, the operators have procedures either to reinquire or to use alternative methods of obtaining the information. In the future, however, for those applications where information is transmitted from terminals for batch processing and requires long printouts, it may be possible for priority to be mandatory.

A typical example of a priority problem can be seen in the airline environment, where the passenger manifest is transmitted to the boarding station so that the airline service agents can identify passengers with valid reservations. If a manifest is held up due to a long transmission where no priority scheme has been implemented until after the flight has left, it is of no use to the service agent. The problem can be overcome with a priority scheme that allows passenger manifests to precede other predefined low-priority transmissions. A single bit will allow two levels of priority, and 2 bits will allow four levels of priority. Priority handling software is one of the items that makes communications software more complex. If it is not necessary in the beginning, the user should evaluate long-term needs in detail to determine whether the priority capability should be implemented anyway at the beginning of the design, when it is easiest to do so.

The preceding items do not necessarily all have to be implemented, and there may be others that should be implemented. The user can at least evaluate the criteria that must be incorporated, and this list can be used as a checklist for incorporation of the required functions. Another point to remember is that the sequence of these individual segments is not necessarily critical and can be changed according to user requirements. Also, one or more segments, if applicable, can be put in the trace portion of the message. By the same token, one or more segments in the trace can be put in the header if it is so desired. The reason for putting information in specific sequences in the header or the trace portion of the message is that the decoding of each segment can be done in firmware instead of software; and if the segments always occur in the same location relative to the control characters (SOH, STX, ETX, EOM), the firmware can be used to detect the same locations every time for the same quantity of characters, which reduces the amount of software that must be used to perform those functions. This in turn allows the applicable software required to be accommodated in less main memory of the CPU.

**TEXT**   The text portion of the message format is the information that the operator has generated for transmission to the location where it is to be processed (or from the CPU back to the operator as a response). It may contain a fixed or variable amount of characters. Almost all systems today use variable-length text portions with a maximum limitation, which is usually based on communication interface buffer size. Also, the text portion itself may contain multiple blocks of information that can be processed separately by the applications CPUs. Within the ASCII code there is an ETB (end of text block) character that can be used to segregate the message blocks. As long as all the blocks pertain to the same function described by the header and the trace, they can be accommodated within the same text portion. If, however, there are different applications, updates, or inquiries, they must be transmitted using different message sequence numbers, because they may be applicable to different databases or locations. The text portion of a message is terminated by the insertion of an ETX (end of text) character which, at the same time, defines the start of the tail or trace portion of the message format.

The trace portion of the message, like the header, consists of two parts. The first part deals with the integrity of the block, as well as its routing through the system, which helps in the analysis of problems when message blocks do not get delivered. The second portion deals with the integrity of the message from the user's protocol standpoint. For the most part, messages that use formats like those described here are synchronous transmissions. Therefore, the use of an error-detection scheme such as CRC will be fairly common, although a block check character (BCC) is also used on some systems. The specific function of each of these items is described next.

**BLOCK NUMBER/TOTAL BLOCKS**  For those cases where messages must be broken up into smaller blocks for buffer or transmission-length purposes, some block number identification must be provided so that the ultimate receiver can put all the blocks back together to reassemble the original message and know for certain that all the blocks have been received. By identifying the block number and the total blocks in a particular message, the receive equipment can perform that function. It is also possible for block number and total blocks to be contained in the header portion instead of in the tail portion.

**PROCESSING POINTS**  Because many routing functions in a network depend on the quality and loading of the network at the time of transmission, it is possible for a message to take a different path each time it goes between two network end points. In addition, the message can go through many different processing points where the routing software at each point must determine the next location to which the message must be sent. It is also possible for the message to be transmitted, and due to some hardware or software problem, keep going between two or more CPUs in a *round robin* effect so that it never gets to its desired destination. There has to be some limited number of locations to which a message can be transmitted before it must be considered *lost*. Once this number has been reached, the message has to be sent to an administrative location where an operator can determine what is to be done with it. A segment of the trace portion of the message must be added at each processing location to store the location ID to show where the message has been. This will also be of great use for tracking lost messages to determine what kind of problems may have been encountered. The user portion of the trace information is then terminated by an EOM (end of message) character, which is sometimes called EOT (end of transmission).

**USER MESSAGE INTEGRITY**  Since almost all protocols in use today, especially those used with synchronous transmissions, have a method for detecting errors in the transmission, the user message integrity block is normally included in all transmissions that use the format described here. For example, SDLC has CRC built into it, while bisync has either CRC or block check characters (BCC) built into it. Bisync would not have a format exactly like the one described here, but SDLC definitely would.

Where a user is transmitting information through the packet switching environment, the user's block has its own error detection scheme, which is what is shown here, and there will also be a separate error-detection method in the communications tail. If the network components that are moving the message do not have their own error-detection scheme, the error-detection scheme that is built into the protocol must determine if errors are encountered in the block received.

Once the user portion of the tail or trace has been completed, there may also be a communications tail or trace, which is oriented toward the communication link control. The tail may consist of a message error detection function such as CRC, a communications routing trace for network use only, a transmission ID for link-to-link transmission of the message, and a message end, which tells the communication equipment that the transmission is truly over. The communications trace is transparent to the user except for when transmission errors are detected, requiring extra transmissions which in turn appear to cause the propagation time to increase. The user is unaware of the reason for the propagation delay. Therefore the communications tail can be considered transparent from a processing point of view but not from a user point of view.

To summarize the pieces that make up a particular format, there are the user-oriented functions of header, text, and trace, and a system-oriented header and trace, which is usually user transparent. For the typical network, the user header, text, and trace can be identified as the user-generated portions of a message or response, while the communications header and tail can be associated with a communication overhead, such as SDLC or packet, which is used to move the information between the specific individual sites.

Now that you have the information to develop your own system message formats, you also need to know that for all practical purposes, the vendors have done almost all of it for you in their network architectures and software for standardized protocols. Also, since real-time message switching is becoming obsolete because of electronic mail, the necessity for developing your own message format is almost nonexistent today. As such, the next edition of this text will probably delete this whole section.

## QUESTIONS

1. Describe the following types of transactions: inquiry/response, record/update, data/entry, data/collection.
2. What is meant by a hierarchical distributed system?
3. What are typical applications for a remote distributed processing configuration?
4. What are the five primary segments of a typical message format?

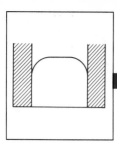

# 21

# Transmission Bandwidths and Impairments

## A
## BACKGROUND

The bandwidth of a communications channel is one of the parameters that determine the maximum data rate that can be supported by that channel. There are two limits involved here. First, according to Nyquist, the signalling rate (baud) cannot exceed twice the bandwidth. Therefore, on a voice-grade line, 6000 baud (3300–300 Hz) × 2 is the maximum signal change rate. Secondly, according to Shannon, in the absence of noise you must have at least one half of a cycle to detect the specific amplitude, frequency, or phase of a signal (used in modulation).

Given these limitations and the practicalities of what actually exists in the real world, the majority of modems today operate with their carrier frequency in the middle of the voice band at 1800 Hz. At this frequency normal line degradations have their least effect. As such, referring to Shannon as the limiting case here, there are a maximum of 3600 half cycles available. Naturally, we cannot attain this theoretical rate, so the optimum trade-off between speed and cost with today's technology is 2400 baud (signal changing every three quarters of a cycle). With only 1 bit of information per signal change, this would seem to indicate a maximum data rate of 1800 BPS. The reason we can get much higher data rates on the voice-grade line is because of multibit modulation, described in Chapter 10.

It is within these parameters that the detailed parameters of the voice-grade line will be discussed.

# B
## CHANNEL BANDWIDTH AND FREQUENCIES

To provide an idea of the total frequency spectrum, Fig. 21–1 describes various frequency ranges all the way from the low-end audible range to the cosmic-ray range, where wavelengths are described in fractions of a micrometer, which is 1/1,000,000 of a meter. The audible bandwidth spectrum is shown in the upper half of Fig. 21–2, where human hearing, human speech, and the telephone channel are superimposed on a logarithmic scale. The lower diagram shows the specific band pass of the telephone line, which describes all voice-grade line channels and consists of a total of 4.2-kHz bandwidth, of which 0 to 300 Hz is reserved for non-voice use (low-speed teletype traffic) and the high end of 3.3 to 4.2 kHz is used for telephone company signaling and test purposes (not for establishing circuits, which is done by *touch tones,* two-tone combinations within the voice spectrum). The band of 300 to 3300 Hz remains open for transmission of voice and/or data; it carries all information in the voice-grade telephone network. It is up to the user as to whether voice, data, or both are to be transmitted, and it is up to the various equipment vendors who design systems to interface with these specific bandwidth capabilities.

# C
## TRANSMISSION IMPAIRMENTS

Assuming the user has at least some voice-grade lines, this section contains descriptions of the principal impairments to data transmission and some of the steps taken to overcome them. There is a unique set of impairments inherent in both analog and digital transmission techniques, but the specific items discussed here are only the voice-band parameters that most affect data communications on voice-grade lines.

To understand better what each term means and how it affects the line, one must recognize and understand the key parameters relevant to the impairments and the techniques used to analyze them. One of the first definitions that must be made is the decibel (dB). The *decibel* is defined as the ratio of output signal power to input signal power. The formula is as follows:

$$\text{Power Gain in dB} = 10 \log_{10} \frac{\text{output power}}{\text{input power}}$$

| Band Designation | From | | To | |
|---|---|---|---|---|
| | Frequency | Wavelength | Frequency | Wavelength |
| Audible | 20 Hz | – | 20 kHz | – |
|   Bass Viol | 40 Hz | – | 200 Hz | – |
|   Trombone | 70 Hz | – | 500 Hz | – |
|   Human Voice | 100 Hz | – | 1100 Hz | – |
|   Trumpet | 200 Hz | – | 900 Hz | – |
|   Violin | 200 Hz | – | 3 kHz | – |
|   Flute | 260 Hz | – | 2.1 kHz | – |
|   Piccolo | 500 Hz | – | 4.2 kHz | – |
| Radio (CCIR) | 3 kHz | 100 km | 3000 GHz | 0.1 mm |
|   Very Low Frequency VLF | 3 kHz | 100 km | 30 kHz | 10 km |
|   Low Frequency LF | 30 kHz | 10 km | 300 kHz | 1 km |
|   Medium Frequency MF | 300 kHz | 1 km | 3 MHz | 100 m |
|   High Frequency HF | 3 MHz | 100 m | 30 MHz | 10 m |
|   Very High Frequency VHF | 30 MHz | 10 m | 300 MHz | 1 m |
|   Ultra High Frequency UHF | 300 MHz | 1 m | 3 GHz | 10 cm |
|   Super High Frequency SHF | 3 GHz | 10 cm | 30 GHz | 1 cm |
|   Extremely High Frequency EHF | 300 GHz | 0.1 cm | 3000 GHz | 0.1 mm |
| Infrared | 1000 GHz | 300 $\mu$m | $10^5$ GHz | 3 $\mu$m |
| Visible | – | 1 $\mu$m | – | 0.3 $\mu$m |
|   Red | – | 1 $\mu$m | – | 0.69 $\mu$m |
|   Orange | – | 0.69 $\mu$m | – | 0.62 $\mu$m |
|   Yellow | – | 0.62 $\mu$m | – | 0.57 $\mu$m |
|   Green | – | 0.57 $\mu$m | – | 0.52 $\mu$m |
|   Blue | – | 0.52 $\mu$m | – | 0.47 $\mu$m |
|   Violet | – | 0.47 $\mu$m | – | 0.3 $\mu$m |
| Ultraviolet | – | 0.3 $\mu$m | – | $10^{-5}$ $\mu$m |
| X-Rays | – | $10^{-3}$ $\mu$m | – | $10^{-7}$ $\mu$m |
|   Soft | – | $10^{-3}$ $\mu$m | – | $10^{-5}$ $\mu$m |
|   Hard | – | $10^{-5}$ $\mu$m | – | $10^{-7}$ $\mu$m |
| Gamma Rays | – | $10^{-6}$ $\mu$m | – | $10^{-7}$ $\mu$m |
| Cosmic Rays | – | $10^{-7}$ $\mu$m | – | $< 10^{-7}$ $\mu$m |

k = Kilo = 1000  
M = Mega = 1,000,000  
G = Giga = 1,000,000,000  

c = centimeter = 1/100  
m = millimeter = 1/1000  
$\mu$m = micrometer = 1/1,000,000 (micron)  

**FIGURE 21–1**
Frequency Spectrum

    Logarithms are used because a signal level in dB can be easily added and subtracted and because the human ear responds naturally to signal levels in an approximately logarithmic manner. If the output power is less than the input power, the logarithmic result is negative (logs of fractions are negative values) and the line is said to have a loss of that many dB. For reference purposes, the individual output and input signal power is related to a specific level called a dBm, where zero dBm (Log 1 = 0) equals 1 milliwatt (mW) at 600-ohms impedance. For most circuits the reference frequency used is 1004 Hz. Any measure-

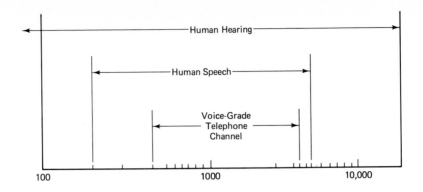

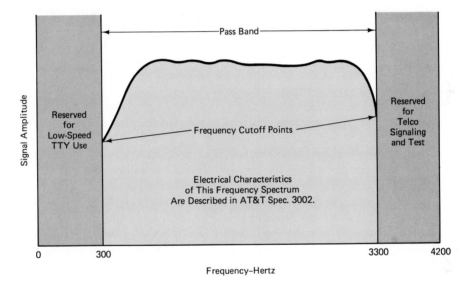

**FIGURE 21–2**
Telephone Channel Frequency Spectrum

ments made relative to the reference frequency are expressed in decibels relative to 1 mW (dBm), where

$$\text{Power Level in dBm} = 10 \log_{10} \frac{\text{signal power mW}}{1 \text{ mW}}$$

Therefore zero dBm equals 1 mW and absolute power levels may be expressed as so many dBm. Other test signals can be used at 1004 Hz, but they would be at different levels.

Many people have asked why the test tone is set at the odd number of 1004 Hz. Originally the tone was 1000 Hz, but when the long-distance network started moving toward the digital environment with 8000 samples per second of the voice signal, sampling of the 1000 Hz caused a synchronization problem in the T-1 frames (the 193 framing bit in each frame was the same as a digitization of the 1000 Hz signal). A *false framing* condition resulted, which confused the channel banks that were moving the T-1 signals, causing out-of-sync conditions. To eliminate the false syncing problem, the test tone was reset at 1004 Hz.

To reference measurements back to the original test-tone level, another unit of measurement is used, the signal decibel level relative to 1 mW (dBm) with respect to test-tone level (dBm 0), defined as

$$\text{dBm } 0 = \text{signal level (dBm)} + \text{test-tone level (dBm)}$$

Data is normally transmitted at a level that is 13 dB below the test-tone level. Therefore the data level is $-13$ dBm 0. For example, if the 1 mW test tone is received at $-5$ dBm, the modem would be set to transmit at $-8$ dBm.

Data transmission-line measurements for much of the impairment testing are made with the 1004-Hz tone, which is also called a *holding* or *test tone.* The testing is performed at the normal transmit level and does not necessarily describe the dB loss at other frequencies.

According to communication line theory, noise is the primary limiting factor for data transmission. The noise itself does not cause a significant amount of errors in low-speed transmission up to 2400 BPS, but for transmission rates above that the combined effects of other impairments make the actual noise encountered a significant contributing factor. Other names for the noise, which is an audible hiss on a telephone line, are message circuit noise, background noise, Gaussian noise, amplifier noise, white noise, and hiss. The noise is measured in decibels, also above some reference, which is assumed to be $-90$ dBm, the level that represents the lowest noise level that is encountered in a voice-grade line. Therefore, the reference noise level defined at 0 dBrn is $-90$ dBm.

Another type of noise is called *transient noise.* Names typically used for transient noise are impulse noise, fortuitous noise, burst noise, and clicks. Transient noise usually occurs at random, unpredictable times. Steps cannot be taken to eliminate random noise, while predictable impairments may be compensated for in some way through *conditioning,* which will be described later in this chapter.

Sources of noise in the data communications channel are crosstalk on adjacent channels, switching, power fluctuations, component failures, impedance mismatches, atmospheric conditions, interface mismatches, analog to digital conversion, and inherent design of the equipment being used. The primary effect of noise on data being transmitted is signal distortion, which modifies or destroys the original bit value.

To analyze the noise relative to its impact on the telephone, a filter based on the response of the telephone, called a *C-message filter,* is used as a band limiting device with a level meter that gives a representative noise measurement. C-message filters simulate the telephone response. Even though the filter is used primarily for voice, it is also used for data transmission purposes. The C-message filter measures in units called *decibels above reference noise, C-message weighted* (dBrnc).

Since noise on a telephone line is also signal dependent, an increase in signal level will cause a corresponding increase in noise. To simulate and then measure these conditions, the 1004-Hz test tone at the data level is transmitted on the line. At the receiving end a *notch filter* removes and measures the test tone. Testing in this mode is defined as *C-notched noise measurement*. A circuit configuration for the various filters on the line is shown in Fig. 21–3.

Aside from noise effects, the primary impairment on a telephone line is the loss of energy at each frequency, which may vary. Because the frequency band we are interested in extends from 300 to 3300 Hz, the amplitude loss at each frequency is referenced to the loss at 1 kHz. The curve referred to as the amplitude response or attenuation distortion of a transmission channel is shown in Fig. 21–4 for a standard voice-grade line.

The second primary source of distortion is caused by different frequencies moving down the telephone line at different rates. Thus even though all the frequencies are transmitted at the same time, they will be received at slightly different times, known as *envelope delay, group delay,* or *frequency delay,* which may be expressed in either microseconds or milliseconds of delay. The absolute delay cannot be determined because the length of the path varies. Actually, only the relative difference between the frequencies is important anyway. The differences at the receive end are known as *envelope delay distortion at a given frequency* and can be measured as the difference in microseconds when compared with the delay experienced by a reference tone at 1800 Hz. (The 1-kHz tone is not used in this case.) Actual methods used to measure envelope delay distortion are very sophisticated due to the complexity of making accurate frequency determinations; for descriptive purposes the relationships are shown in Fig. 21–4.

The next level of distortion is caused by power line harmonics, especially in telephone carrier multiplexed systems, which create a forward and backward movement of the zero crossings of the individual frequency known as *jitter.* The jitter represents phase changes and is measured by looking at the zero crossing point of a particular test tone (1004 Hz). Noise, because it also affects the zero crossings, can heavily influence the measure of jitter; therefore, to make accurate measurements, the holding tone should be at the data level. In addition, the notched noise measurements should be made in conjunction with the phase jitter

**FIGURE 21–3**
Noise Measurement

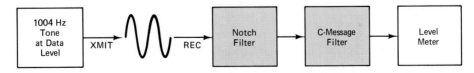

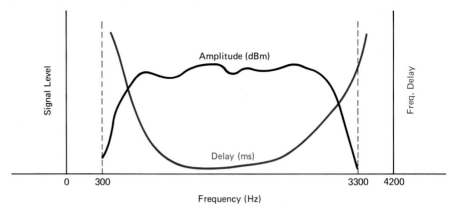

**FIGURE 21–4**
Amplitude and Delay Response

measurements to help determine what is actually being experienced—true phase jitter caused by equipment or the effects of a high noise level.

For low-speed data transmissions, phase jitter is rarely noticeable over the effects of amplitude response distortion, envelope delay distortion, and transient errors. Since the telephone channel may be made up of many active components, such as diodes, transistors, and LSI circuitry, and passive components, such as coils, capacitors, and resistors, there is another mode of distortion called *nonlinear distortion,* which is caused by the specific nonlinear characteristics of the components themselves. The components and companders on the telephone circuit will distort a data signal, because they cause the generation of unwanted harmonics that add to the information signal in a detrimental manner. Figure 21–5 shows clipping, one of the effects of nonlinear distortion. Although the figure exaggerates the effect, many harmonics cause this type of distortion.

Nonlinear distortion is measured on specific test equipment. Two sets of very closely paired frequencies are used. Their harmonics and cross harmonics are measured to determine the total amount of nonlinear distortion, which is called either *intermodulation distortion* or *harmonic distortion.*

Line conditioning and equalization (described in Section E of this chapter) correct many of the effects of amplitude distortion, envelope delay distortion, and nonlinear distortion, but there are limits as to how much of those impairments can be compensated for on any given facility.

A separate kind of transmission error, the transient type, is also known as a *line hit* and is the primary source of errors in low-speed transmissions. Line hits cause errors because they totally destroy or significantly modify the bits being transmitted. Transient distortions are divided into three general categories:

> **Drop out.** A sudden large reduction in signal level that lasts more than several milliseconds.

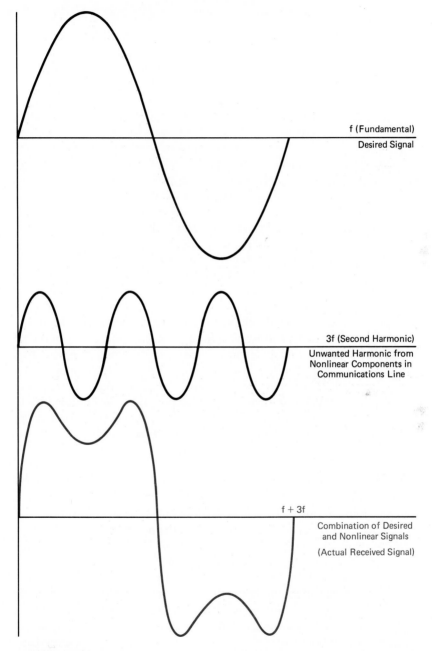

f (Fundamental)

Desired Signal

3f (Second Harmonic)

Unwanted Harmonic from
Nonlinear Components in
Communications Line

f + 3f

Combination of Desired
and Nonlinear Signals

(Actual Received Signal)

**FIGURE 21–5**
Clipping Effects

493

*Phase hit.* A sudden uncontrolled change in phase of the receive signal.

*Gain hit.* A sudden spike of noise of very short duration, which sounds like a click on the telephone line.

Names for the different types of distortion are not used in exactly the same way by all vendors and users and, in some cases, different names are given. However, the user should always pinpoint the specific type of distortion to be measured and relate it to the terms described in this section to establish accurate measurement methods and readings.

One other type of distortion warrants discussion here, and that is *echo*. Echo was described in Chapter 10 but bears repeating here in the context of line degradations. Echo is caused by different network elements, two of which are the telephone handset and a device called a *hybrid*. A hybrid is a converting coil that converts a two-wire local loop to a four-wire circuit for long-distance transmission in the Class 5 telephone office. Another hybrid at the other end of the line converts the four-wire connection back to two wires for the two-wire termination at the other end. Hybrid coils and handsets may have a different *characteristic impedance* from the telephone lines, which in practical terms means that not all the energy transmitted in one direction will be absorbed by the receive end, and that some of it will actually be reflected back toward the transmitter. Energy reflection, which can be recognized by the transmitter, is what is known as echo and exists primarily on dial-up lines. A practical example of impedance matching occurs on standard TV antenna connections. The flat twin lead wire and the coaxial wire must be connected to different points in the back of the TV because they are of different impedances. To eliminate echos from circuits, the telephone company has installed either *echo suppressors* or echo cancelers (described in Chapter 10), which cause a unidirectional transmission. Failures of echo suppressors on dial-up circuits allow the echo to come back with enough energy to distort the transmitted signal or prevent it from dropping out fast enough to avoid the loss of the initial bits each time the direction of the transmission changes (which results in another form of clipping).

When a call is made to transmit data in today's telephone environment, the *called* unit issues a *tone* that indicates that it is ready to receive data. This tone is in the range of 2235 Hz, which is the frequency the telephone company uses to disable echo suppressors. Internationally, V.21 echo suppression is 2100 Hz. Since modems are designed to work in the presence of some echo signals (remember, while transmitting, an echo does not bother the modulator), the echo suppressor may be disabled without detriment to the data traffic.

As a corollary to echoes, it is possible to insert too much power from the transmit end onto the communication line, and this condition causes what is known as *singing*. Singing is normally controlled by decreasing the power output of the transmitting modem, but if it is caused by the carrier it can be compensated for by inserting extra losses in the line. In either event, the modem output signal must be within the specifications of the voice-grade line specification.

# D

## ERROR RATES AND THEIR MEASUREMENT

The most often used measure of the quality or the degree of impairment of a communications channel used for data transmission is the *error rate test*. The error rate is established by using test equipment that generates specific sets of bits and/or blocks of data and then compares the receive information with what was transmitted. The difference between the receive bits and the transmitted bits is known as the *bit error rate* (BER). The sequences of bits transmitted are known as *patterns* and can range from the gross test of all 1s (all mark) and alternate mark–space patterns to extremely complex patterns that will not repeat themselves for many millions of bits. Common pattern lengths, however, are usually in the range of 63, 511 and 2047 bits, with the worst-case pattern being the 2047-bit sequence as established by the CCITT. Because a larger pattern can encompass many more combinations of bits, it is more likely to isolate an otherwise elusive channel problem.

The BER alone is not the best measure for determining the effective information throughput of the transmission line, because interference, errors, and noise of a level significant enough to cause errors usually come in a burst. The burst may cause multiple bits within a particular block to be in error, but if the same amount of bits in error were distributed among all the bits transmitted, there would be a much higher block error rate. Therefore the user must also take into account the specific block length being measured or perform block error testing to get a more accurate indication of what the actual line performance will be.

In general, testing is done with a pattern length that most closely matches the block size that is expected to be transmitted. Once the block error rates are within the user's established limits, bit error rate testing can be used to fine-tune the line.

The *block error rate* (BLER) is most closely related to the definition of *effective information throughput*. If the BLER is specified as 1 percent, then for every 100 blocks of information at the test length there will be 1 in error, for which a single block will have to be retransmitted. The BLER is significant for all modes of transmission, but especially for protocols that use the *go back N* technique (described in Chapter 9). The *go back N* technique requires the transmission of any block that is received in error, in addition to all blocks that were transmitted *after* the block in error.

Another term used when describing the various error rates is called the *error-free second* (EFS). The EFS is very similar to the BLER except that it describes the probability of success for getting a 1-second-long block through correctly, as opposed to the probability of failure, which is described by the BLER. Even though errors do not occur for an entire second, a gross level probability of determining how much data can be throughput can be calculated, because the second can be related directly to the amount of bits being transmitted. For example, with a 2400-BPS transmission, a typical 1-s block would contain 2400 bits or 300 characters. If the block size is in the range of 300 characters, then a direct correlation can be made as to the probability of success for individual blocks. Since most communication lines have error rates specified for a typical line, it is relatively simple for the user to determine what a particular line, at a particular transmission rate, is expected to experience relative to errors and retransmissions.

In reviewing all these error-rate parameters, we can see that the block size is a critical factor in the effective data throughput. On an intuitive level we can visualize extremely short blocks getting through with a very high degree of probability, but the effective throughput is limited by the fact that the network overhead must be accommodated for each transmission. Thus, as the block length gets longer, the effective throughput will also become greater. An increase in length is only good up to a certain level, because as the block gets longer it will eventually get to a length that just about guarantees that an error will occur. There is an optimum block-size definition for each individual line at a particular transmission speed with a particular error rate.

Based on an analysis provided by the telephone company for typical voice-grade lines without conditioning, optimum block sizes range from about 100 plus characters at 9600 BPS up to approximately 520 characters for transmissions at 1200 BPS. Thus, for most applications on voice-grade lines, block sizes should be limited to a maximum of between 500 and 600 characters where practical. The minimum block size should be 100 characters if the user would like the most effective throughput rate for a given line. Each application and each line must be considered separately, because error rates can vary greatly from line to line.

One other factor to consider in this environment is that the increase in transmission speed does not result in a proportionate increase in effective throughput. For example, a transmission rate at 2400 BPS will not produce twice the throughput as at 1200 BPS, although it closely approximates that. At 4800 BPS there is an effective increase in throughput of about 1.6 to 1.7 over the throughput at 2400 BPS.

At 9600 BPS, however, the effective throughput, even using the optimum block sizes for both 9600 and 4800, may only increase the throughput by 1.2 to 1.3 of the throughput at 4800 BPS. These numbers relate to a typical voice-grade line where long distances are involved (500 miles or more) and are not indicative of connections with direct computer-to-computer transmission on high-quality or conditioned lines. Also, any particular location may have lines that are better or worse than a typical voice-grade line and therefore have better or worse experience than the average. What the user can expect in a specific environment can only be identified with any degree of confidence by specific operation and tests utilizing the equipment and facilities that are to be installed.

Thus the user, prior to initial design, should recognize that 9600 BPS is not always the most effective means of high data rate transfers, and it is quite possible for a 4800- or 7200-BPS transmission rate to actually have a better effective information throughput.

Another factor to consider is that 9600 BPS is almost never used on a multi-drop line today, not only because of the errors, but because of the polling/calling, networking overhead, and, especially, synchronization sequences (described in Chapter 8), which effectively lower the throughput on the multidrop line to something equal to or less than what would be expected on a 4800-BPS line. It is quite possible that with improved hardware and line parameters, the throughput can be improved, but at this time 9600 BPS should not be considered for a multidrop environment.

Finally, with the newer modems transmitting at 14,400, 16,800, and 19,200 BPS, the exponential increase of error rates with transmission speeds is a critical factor in the selection of modem speeds for user networks.

## E
## LINE CONDITIONING AND EQUALIZATION

The carrier usually provides most of the potential improvements that can be made to the voice-grade communication line, because the carrier has control over most of the facilities. For dial-up circuits, which change from call to call, conditioning lines for data transmission is not practical for the carrier because the transmissions take a different path on each call. Therefore, most modem manufacturers provide *automatic equalization modems,* which correct for some circuit-induced signal distortions on both dial-up and multidrop circuits. Equalization is normally required only for transmission speeds of 2400 BPS and up.

Even with carrier line conditioning (equalization), there is a choice as to the amount and the type of conditioning that is provided. C-type conditioning has been provided by AT&T for many years and comes in five different levels, of which only three (C1, C2, and C4) are available to leased line users of the DDD network. Conditioning now also comes in what is known as D type, which provides for additional improvement on the line for two areas that were not covered with C-type conditioning. Because of the new long-distance carrier environment existing since divestiture, the user should always check in advance as to whether a carrier provides equalization. If not and it is required later, an alternative carrier may be required, which involves a whole new process of ordering, installing, and testing. If you think you will need equalization, use a carrier that provides it now, and remember that only leased lines can be conditioned by the carrier.

It is not really hard to understand the difference between the two types of conditioning and when and where they will help a transmission line's performance. The various kinds of line impairments were covered earlier; of them, 11 are described in AT&T Spec. 3002. Eight can be controlled by the carrier so that they are maintained within the limits described in FCC tariff number 260, and four can be controlled to additional optional limits. All are shown in Table 21–1. Attenuation distortion and envelope delay distortion are controlled through C-type conditioning, while signal-to-noise ratio and harmonic distortion are controlled through D-type conditioning. Each type of conditioning within both C- and D-type levels is tariffed separately. They can be obtained either independently or together on any leased line.

**TABLE 21–1**
Conditioning Areas and Costs

| LINE IMPAIRMENT | BASIC AT&T INTERNAL CONTROL | AREAS OF C-CONDITION CONTROL | AREAS OF D-CONDITION CONTROL |
|---|---|---|---|
| Attenuation distortion | × | × | Same as basic |
| Envelope delay distortion | × | × | |
| Signal-to-noise radio | × | Same as basic | × |
| Harmonic distortion | × | | × |
| Impulse noise | × | Same | |
| Frequency shift | × | as | |
| Phase jitter | × | basic | |
| Echo | × | 3002 | |
| Phase hits | | | |
| Gain hits | Not controlled | | |
| Drop outs | | | |

**TYPES OF AVAILABLE CONDITIONING**

| | |
|---|---|
| C1 Point to point | D1 Point to point |
| C1 Multipoint | D2 Multipoint (3 remotes) |
| C2 Point to point | D5 Multipoint (20 remotes) |
| C2 Multipoint | |
| C4 Point to point | |
| C4 Multipoint (3 remotes) | |

The second major group of impairment parameters in Table 21–1 includes impulse noise, frequency shift, phase jitter, and echo. Because the telephone company knows what is intended to be transmitted over those lines, it tends to maintain them within certain internally set limits even though they are not obligated to do so. The three remaining kinds of impairments—phase hits, gain hits, and drop outs—are not controlled at present because they are transient electrical occurrences (see Section C) and therefore cannot be compensated for as permanent conditions.

C-type conditioning is the term given to the capability provided by the telephone company to make voice-grade lines meet more restrictive specifications for attenuation distortion and envelope delay distortion.

C-type conditioning, which is available in five varieties, C1 through C5, applies to voice-grade lines. C1, C2, and C4 apply to voice-grade private lines between user sites, while C3 is similar to C2 and applies to lines that are part of some large dedicated network, such as the military AUTOVON and CCSA (Common Control Switching Arrangements). Point-to-point international links can be conditioned to C5, which is also similar to C2.

In Fig. 21–6, Sections II, III, and IV, the heavy lines refer to the attenuation distortion and envelope delay limits for C1, C2, and C4 conditioning. The thinner lines represent a typical line characteristic that meets those limits. The greater

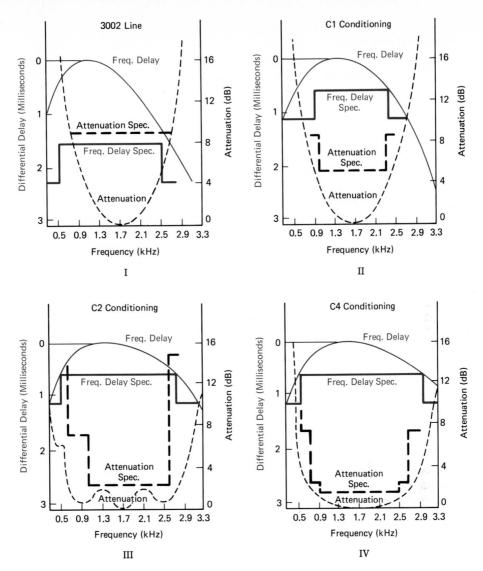

**FIGURE 21–6**
Conditioning Levels and Limits

the degree of C-type conditioning, the more the attenuation distortion and delay distortion are reduced at both ends of the frequency band.

C1, C2, and C4 conditioning can be provided for any point-to-point 3002 line, and C1 and C2 conditioning can also be provided on any multipoint 3002 line without restriction as to number of points. C4 conditioning, however, is not provided on multipoint lines with more than one central and three remote points. Charges are made on the basis of a one-time installation charge and a monthly rate for each point on the line, whether point-to-point or multipoint circuits are conditioned. More than 50 percent of the conditioning provided by the carriers is C2.

D-type conditioning is an option that was developed primarily for 9600 BPS operation and higher on a 3002 line. The standard 3002 specification requires a signal-to-noise ratio of not less than 24 dB, a second harmonic distortion of not more than $-25$ dB, and a third harmonic distortion of not more than $-30$ dB. For D-type conditioning, we have a signal-to-noise ratio specification of 28 dB, a signal-to-second harmonic distortion ratio of 35 dB, and a signal-to-third harmonic distortion of 40 dB.

The harmonic, or nonlinear, distortion occurs because attenuation varies with signal amplitude, and a sine wave sent through such a channel will be flattened at the peaks (clipping). The same distortion would result from adding harmonics of low amplitude to the signal in the first place. Therefore, harmonic distortion is measured in terms of the amount of second and third harmonic content that would cause the same amount of flattening. Noise and nonlinear distortion are critical to data transmission because they interfere with the accurate reproduction of the transmitted wave forms at the receiver. In contrast with the problems caused by delay distortion, their effect cannot be reversed. No amount of hardware sophistication in the receiving modem can recreate the original signal shape once it has been changed by harmonic distortion. The only protection against harmonic distortion is to make the signal less susceptible to it, by maximizing the differences between the unique wave shapes that have to be distinguished by the demodulator. D-type conditioning provides just such an improvement by specifying a lower allowable harmonic content.

D1 conditioning is offered for point-to-point circuits, and D2 is offered for two- or three-point circuits. Charges are also based on a one-time installation charge, plus a monthly rate for each point on the line. A new level of D-type conditioning called D5 was introduced in 1983; it provides for up to 20 points in a multidrop circuit as long as the total circuit distance is less than 4000 miles. D-type conditioning is not necessarily available at all locations throughout the country and therefore must be implemented on a location-by-location basis.

Early in 1988 AT&T announced D6, a new level of conditioning designed to improve the operation of analog modems at 19.2 KBPS. D6 will complement C and other D conditioning levels, although the specific degradations to be improved and D6's specifications are not yet available. When D6 does become available, the parameters will be provided to modem vendors, allowing them to incorporate compatible interfaces into their equipment to keep 19.2-KBPS analog transmissions competitive with some of the digital transmissions up to that speed. Given the new level of conditioning, it might then be possible for modem vendors to consider designing modems that can operate at even higher data rates, perhaps at the next logical level of transmission speed, 21.6 KBPS.

At this point it is natural to ask, "What is the maximum throughput that can be obtained on a voice-grade line?" For the answer we refer to Claude Shannon, who derived a formula that provides an answer. Shannon determined that the factors that limit signal transmission on a communication line are the available bandwidth, the available signal power, and the noise encountered on the circuit. The formula he derived is:

$$C = W \log_2(1 + \frac{S}{N})$$

where
$C$ = the theoretical limit of data transmission in BPS
$W$ = the available bandwidth in Hertz
$S/N$ = the ratio of signal power to noise power

For the established parameters of a 3002 voice-grade circuit, which is the type of circuit provided by the carriers, $C$ is approximately 25 KBPS. $C$ is the theoretical maximum throughput that is possible on a voice-grade line, although under real-life considerations it will probably never be attained. Vendors may approach this magic number with modems that cost more and more to incorporate the features necessary to get the higher data rate, but at some point you will probably be better off considering a digital circuit. As ISDN (described in Chapter 16) comes closer to being a reality, the need for higher-speed analog transmissions will probably decrease.

## QUESTIONS

1. What is the primary factor that limits the ability to transmit data on a communications line? What are four other names for this impairment?
2. What are five sources of line degradation?
3. What are the two primary effects on the received communications signal that have the most impact on the transmission of data?
4. What are three types of measurements that can be used to identify the amount of errors encountered in a particular time frame?
5. What is the relative effect of block size on total information throughput?
6. What line degradations are compensated for with C-type conditioning?
7. What line degradations are compensated for with D-type conditioning?

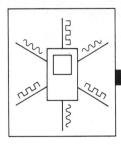

# 22

## Network Management
## and Control

A

### BACKGROUND

Based on past experience it would appear that the primary design goal has been to develop a communications network that provides the necessary paths for the user to move data most efficiently. More recently, however, it has become increasingly apparent that it is even more critical to consider the operation and maintenance of the network once it has been installed.

If the user considers the *life cycle cost* of a complete system, which includes a network, he will find that, excluding carrier costs, the two most significant costs involved are for the operation and maintenance of the network. The network is the most error-prone of the system components, there are usually multiple vendors involved, and there are too few qualified personnel available to support all the networks implemented today.

Since maintenance is such a significant part of the success of a network, this chapter is longer than the others. Entire texts deal with the subject in depth, so this chapter provides only an overview of the common carrier environments and typical types of test equipment and procedures. Relatively simple examples are used so the reader should keep in mind that the actual testing and isolation of problems involve the use of specialized test equipment used by experienced and specially trained network maintenance personnel.

When discussing the complex subject of network management, there are many different ways of attacking the problems. Different people will have different methods of solution although the desired end result is the same: *Get it working again*. The concept and methods described in this text were derived from personal experience in conjunction with the experiences of many others who are involved in network management. Therefore, although there may be alternative methods, what is presented here can be used as a basis for developing an in-house plan for managing your network.

There are three primary ways to provide service restoration after degradation: redundancy, rerouting, and reconfiguration. *Redundancy* refers to duplicate hardware and network facility segments that are available at all times so that if the primary path degrades or fails a secondary path can continue network operation.

*Rerouting* is the transmission of information along alternative paths so that the end-to-end transmission initially required can still be obtained. One of the simplest ways of rerouting is *dial backup;* if a leased line fails, you can dial the end location and transmit the information over the dial backup circuit. Of course, there are speed and protocol considerations to take into account, especially in environments where 9600 BPS or higher transmissions are used. Rerouting is discussed in more detail later in this chapter.

*Reconfiguration* is the manual or automatic reconfiguration of equipment and/or lines to achieve the original end-to-end connections. In general, reconfiguration may involve reorganizing priorities to give a failed application higher priority than another application on a different circuit, terminal, or CPU. Reconfiguration may be the most costly in time because it requires knowledgeable personnel who are familiar with the network operation and the appropriate switching equipment.

The preceding three modes of operation are short-term solutions meant to keep information moving. A better solution is to correct the degraded or failed circuit and/or equipment so that normal operation is restored. The following parameters are desirable for an efficient network management system:

1. Management should be integral to the network itself.
2. Multiple network management access points must be supported.
3. There must be a centralized network information and statistics database with an understandable presentation of information for operators to use when required.
4. Network control messages must have priority over data messages so that network status can be maintained in its optimum form.
5. Security must be built in to limit access, because unauthorized access may be able to shut down all transmission.

6. Network management functions must be transparent to the different types of transmission media. Regardless of whether you use cable, fiber-optic, microwave, or other medium, the network management functions must be capable of providing test information and results without being affected by that media.

7. Changes and rerouting must be simple to make and flexible so that degraded operation can be restored to normal with minimal operator decision making and/or *tinkering* with the network.

8. There must be a database of all network resources, components, facilities, and users so that it is possible to determine what the impacts will be for any action taken by the network operations personnel at any time.

Many organizations have not put the appropriate emphasis on getting their network operational again after degradation or failure because they consider the network control center (NCC) to be a *cost center,* not a profit center. But in the long run the NCC can actually provide a substantial amount of savings. To accomplish this, there must be an appropriate number of personnel who have the responsibility and *authority* to correct problems encountered in network operation. It is a paradox that many individuals who are assigned the responsibility for network management and who must make decisions regarding the correction of network problems, sometimes in the middle of the night or on weekends, do not have the authority to make those decisions. The result is that problems cannot be fixed during off hours but only during the day when the majority of the organization must try to function with a malfunctioning network. *Responsibility without authority is meaningless.*

The network manager must know what is happening, be able to determine the cause of problems and correct them, and plan for network growth. Here, too, the network manager must have input to the decision-making apparatus in an organization to make sure that problem correction and eventual expansion are coordinated throughout the entire organization. The quick vendor response times that were once available for reconfiguring and adding new capabilities are being stretched out more and more, and even new leased lines may require more than three months for installation and operation.

The sequence of operations required for efficient network management control consists of the following:

1. *Monitor the Physical Status.* Includes the hardware, transmission facilities, personnel, and interfaces.

2. *Monitor the Performance.* Includes network utilization, traffic volume, response time, line and interface availability, and capacity.

3. *Network Control.* Correct identified problems.

4. *Network Management.* Combines monitoring and control for management of network operations, growth of the system based on use, improvement of existing services, correcting and reconfiguring in conformance with user changes, and identifying required performance parameters.

Given these conceptual requirements we can further discuss the methods of identifying, isolating, and correcting network problems.

Network testing is changing significantly because of the growth of digital network capability. Testing in the voice network has always been considered as much of an *art* as it is a science because of the variable nature of the different impairments encountered. On the other hand, the digital network has been designed with more diagnostic capability, making it much easier to identify and isolate problems, but the testing is done in the carrier environment, not in the user environment. This text, therefore, deals primarily with the analog network, although digital testing parameters will be described also.

Testing is required because of network degradations. Most users have reported a decline in the quality of voice circuits since divestiture. The combination of procedural changes, cutbacks, multivendor circuits, and personnel turnover makes it much harder now to obtain centralized testing capability. End-to-end circuit testing cannot be done by an individual telephone company, although some long-distance carriers provide end-to-end maintenance for a fee (if your circuit is totally contained within a single LATA the local telco can provide end-to-end testing). Local testing has suffered also because multiple vendors provide separate test equipment for voice and data, which are of equal importance to the using organization. Vendor support cannot necessarily provide all the answers. They may know their own equipment very well, but they may not know other vendors' equipment or be familiar with the network.

There are three basic approaches to network testing, each with its own advantages and disadvantages.

A. *Rely on Vendors.* If you rely on a vendor for testing, you probably have a single vendor's products in your network and are therefore *locked in* to that vendor. Fewer vendors today are capable of providing this complete capability. With the recent announcement of network management architectures from IBM (Netview), and AT&T (UNMA—Universal Network Management Architecture), there is a movement toward integrating test equipment into the network, but these will be a while coming. Other vendors will probably incorporate the new standards in their equipment so they can typically talk to Netview, UNMA, or any others. But the more architectures there are for network management, the more diversity there will be in equipment, and we may end up with more sets of standards that are not compatible with each other. If the two major interfaces from IBM and AT&T take hold and become dominant, then it is possible that equipment can be built to interface with both, and the user will be better off, but experience tells us that this probably will not happen.

B. *Utilize an Organization Dedicated to Network Problem Solving (Third Party).* At one time third-party problem solving was considered a viable alternative, but today the expertise required is so vast and covers such a wide variety of products and services that it is not really feasible to provide the service, although some companies do. The organizations in the best position to provide network problem solving are the carriers themselves, especially the long-distance carriers, because a big portion of the network is within their own domain. Of course, Vendor X is not likely to give you the same level of service for Vendor Y circuits as for their own. The carrier providing the majority of your circuits is the best for handling your end-to-end network management, which will include noncarrier equipment at either end. However, not only is this a difficult position for the carrier to be objective in, but it is also usually not very cost effective.

C. *In-House Network Management.* In-house network control is by far the most flexible in design and operation. Users typically understand their problems and situations better than any carrier or vendor could, therefore they are in a much better position to isolate problems. Network problems are not always the result of network conditions; they may actually be operational problems or human problems in utilizing the network. It is therefore to your advantage to have an in-house network operations and control center so that you can not only isolate a problem, but also determine the best way to fix it by considering all of the factors involved. A disadvantage of in-house network control is that it requires more resources such as knowledgeable people, equipment, space, power, management, and all of the other support overheads. As you convert to a digital network you will again be at the mercy of the vendor, because the carriers are the only ones in a position to test and debug the circuit portion of your network.

Many network controllers hesitate to rely on the vendors to debug their digital circuit problems, a carryover from their experiences with analog, when there was a lot of controversy as to where problems originated and how best to fix them. Sometimes carriers were reluctant to admit that a problem existed or that they were responsible for the problem. Network controllers are also concerned that if the carrier does all the circuit testing, the controller's job may become obsolete. This is a *job security* situation.

All in all, it seems that most users are setting up their own network control centers today to make sure they have complete control over their networks. As the digital world evolves, test equipment will be developed to pinpoint problems as being inside or outside the network, so that carriers can be told with more certainty that a problem is truly in their environment and the user can fix noncircuit network related problems. If any test equipment is to be purchased, the user should make sure that it provides problem-isolation capabilities.

## C
## ACCESS INTERFACE DEVICES

To be effective as a network operational tool, test equipment must be attached to the line that is to be tested in some manner, if it is not permanently built into the line circuitry. Table 22–1 is a list of the major access and interface equipment used to provide line attachment.

**TABLE 22–1**
Access and Interface Devices

A. Jacks
  1. Analog
    a. Monitor
    b. Patch
  2. Digital
    a. Monitor
    b. Patch
B. Switches
C. Relays
  1. Manually operated
  2. Automatic

One of the most effective line access units is the jack and plug. Analog jacks are usually placed in the analog line circuit to provide both a parallel and a serial access to the line, as shown in Fig. 22–1. Parallel access is used for the monitoring function by attaching the test equipment via a plug to the line circuit to be monitored without interrupting the circuit path from the line to the equipment (modem in this example). Attaching the monitor equipment should be done by first connecting the monitor to the plug cord and then inserting the plug into the monitor jack. The monitor equipment must have a high electrical impedance to the circuit so that it will not appreciably affect the line's operation.

Serial or series-access jacks are connected so that the circuit (line) passes through the jack, allowing the circuit to be interrupted and carried through the plug and cord to a different line interface unit (modem in the example). Such an arrangement allows a known operational modem to replace a modem that is thought to be malfunctioning by *patching* the good modem into the circuit. The patching operation disconnects the potentially bad modem. Electrical contact is made between the upper normal jack contacts for the line circuit and continues through the plug and cord to the spare modem. A corresponding set of digital connectors, sometimes called digital jacks, on the other side of the two modems allows the spare modem to be connected to the user's interface (DTE) through the middle normal jack contacts. As contact is made between the line and cord plug, the regular or normal modem is isolated from the circuit on the analog side and similarly isolated from the DTE on the digital side by the digital plug insertion. Since the digital interface to a modem is usually the 25-wire RS232C standard, digital jacks must be 25-circuit units, rather than the 2-circuit units used for analog jacks. The jack and plug combinations drawn in Fig. 22–1 would be arranged in line, equipment, and monitor connections similar to those of the 2-wire analog jacks at the top. The names *tip* and *ring* used for the analog circuits come from the tip and ring contacts on the plug.

The jack shown at the top of Fig. 22–1 is an analog jack for connecting to the tip and ring pair of the local loop. Other jack arrangements were discussed in Chapter 5. One that was not included in that chapter is the *RJ71C*. This jack provides 12 data over voice modem connections.

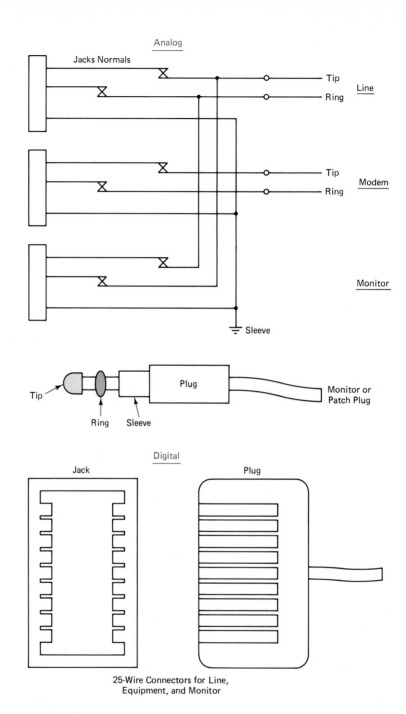

**FIGURE 22-1**
Access Jacks

Related to all the jacks is other interface equipment used by the carrier in the end-user environment. For example, the 829 Data Station Termination Unit, commonly called an 829 test set, is activated manually or by a 2713-Hz tone and is designed to provide diagnostic capability to the carrier by looping back the local loop to the carrier office. The 829 comes in three versions:

*829A* No amplifier included

*829B* Amplifier included

*829C* Amplifier and equalization circuitry included

The carrier may require you to have an 829 test set on any voice line you obtain, and you must pay for it. The ability to provide testing from the central office is a distinct benefit, and therefore the use of 829s is recommended, especially where local loops are erratic.

Another device provided by the carrier that is commonly used is the Terminator Block, which is known as a 42A. A 42A terminates a carrier-provided circuit (typically a single local loop). Since 42A blocks may exist within a facility, there may be a question as to where carrier responsibility ends and user responsibility begins. In today's deregulated environment, that responsibility is usually at the main/intermediate distribution frame, used in your building for business purposes, or the *protector block,* used in your home. Any 42A terminators therefore are probably your responsibility.

Two other terms used extensively in the analog environment are described here, because you may run into them when discussing networks with the carriers. The first one is *Common Channel Interoffice Signaling* (CCIS), a switching method that was the precursor of the ISDN 23B + D transmission, which used the D channel for signaling purposes. In CCIS the necessary signaling for call setup, supervisory commands, addressing, take down, and management is sent on a path separate from the voice. CCIS can only be done from special processor equipped telephone offices, and although its use is growing within AT&T, it will be superseded by digital signaling in the 24th channel once Signaling System #7 is implemented (refer to ISDN in Chapter 16 for further description).

The other term you may run into is *Common Controlled Switching Arrangement* (CCSA), which refers to the use of a four-wire switch (as opposed to a two-wire switch). CCSAs were first installed around 1960 and are in fairly common use today for four-wire circuits. They should have no impact on your operation as they are provided by the carrier and do not affect your normal operations.

# D
## TEST EQUIPMENT CONFIGURATIONS

Before getting into a more detailed identification of test equipment and testing parameters, it is appropriate to identify the major levels of network test capability. There is an implied cost differential among the levels in initial implementation, but as you go higher in the four levels described, you will find that less human intervention is needed and therefore ongoing costs are reduced. For most installations, the additional cost for the more sophisticated equipment is paid back in relatively short periods of time (as little as 24 months) through reductions in personnel and network downtime. Since every user environment is different, the parameters of your particular environment must be evaluated to determine what is best for you. Although it may require fewer personnel to operate the more advanced equipment, they will have to be more knowledgeable (and therefore more costly) to be able to use the information effectively.

The four levels of test configuration are manual, semiautomatic, computerized access, and computer-controlled test and access.

***LEVEL 1: MANUAL***  Level 1 involves having manual jacks on each line with the test equipment being primarily a data line monitor (to be described later) and possibly a bit error rate tester (BERT). Fig. 22–2 shows the manual configuration.

At this level testing must be done manually with the network operator *patching* the necessary test equipment into the patches of the network control center (NCC). A spare modem or DSU (both are DCE) must be available for patching out the existing line DCE to eliminate the original DCE as a problem cause. Manual configurations like these can identify approximately 80 percent of network problems. The fact that they are all manual increases the probability of human error, and the larger a network becomes, the more that is involved in carrying out the test procedures.

***LEVEL 2: SEMIAUTOMATIC***  Level 2 is shown in Fig. 22–3 and involves the installation of electromechanical relay contacts in place of manual jacks. Activation of the jack configuration is through a controller that has either a keypad or thumbwheel-type switches. The operator sets the appropriate switches to patch the spare DCE in or out or patch test equipment onto the line to monitor either the digital side or the analog side.

**FIGURE 22–2**
Manual: Level 1 Test Configuration

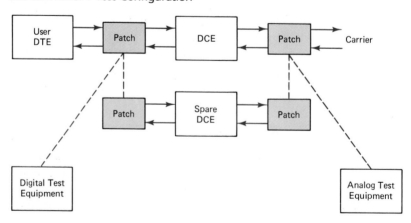

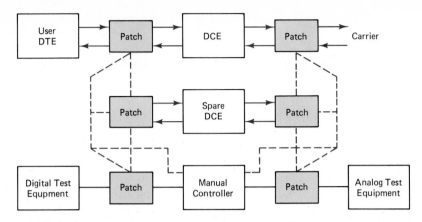

**FIGURE 22–3**
Semiautomatic: Level 2 Test Configuration

***LEVEL 3: COMPUTERIZED ACCESS*** Level 3 devices have been installed since the late 1970s; in them the electromechanical controller is replaced by an intelligent computer. The operator controls all tests through a CRT keyboard. A self-contained database is usually available that allows the operator to determine what the configurations were prior to degradation. After all tests are run, there is automatic restoration to the original configuration, if required. A diagram of level 3 access is shown in Fig. 22–4.

***LEVEL 4: COMPUTER-CONTROLLED TEST AND ACCESS*** Level 4 involves the total automation of the test function. A computer controls the access and the test

**FIGURE 22–4**
Computerized Access: Level 3 Test Configuration

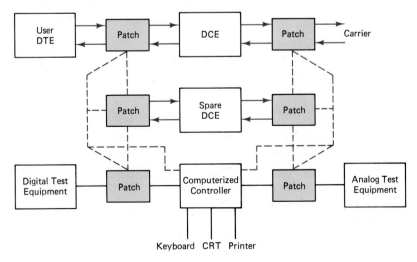

equipment itself so that testing can be performed in an unattended mode, such as during the evening, for monitoring and level checking purposes. With predetermined levels of acceptable operating parameters, these tests can also be run all the time, and only under conditions that exceed specific predetermined parameters is additional testing and/or operator involvement required. More and more test equipment is being designed to operate in this fashion because it takes less operator expertise to actually perform the test. However, knowledgeable personnel are still required to interpret the results and determine what the corrective action should be. Fig. 22–5 shows level 4 operation.

A gross approximation of the kind of configuration to use when you have a specific network is made as follows. If you have up to 50 circuits and they are predominantly point-to-point, the level 1 configuration is probably adequate. With multipoint, or up to 100 circuits, or both, a level 2 configuration would be more appropriate. If you have a distributed environment with point-to-point, multipoint, or more than one specific network, or up to 150 circuits, the level 3 test configuration is probably the best choice. If you have a combination of the preceding networks or 200 circuits or more, it would probably be best to have a level 4 test configuration. The equipment is provided by both standalone vendors and vendors who provide modems. Typical vendors are Atlantic Research, Codex, Avant Garde, General DataComm, Halcyon, Hewlett-Packard, NEC (digital network), Northern Telecom, Paradyne, Racal Milgo, and Tektronix. Costs for equipment from these vendors vary over a very wide range, from a few thousand dollars all the way up to $500,000 for a level 4 configuration that can monitor

FIGURE 22–5
Computer-Controlled Test and Access: Level 4 Test Configuration

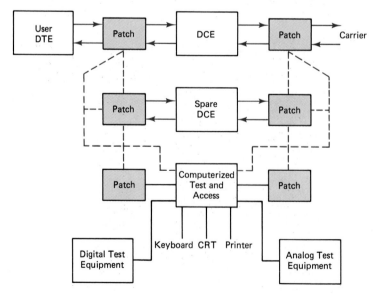

and control over 1000 lines with over 65,000 terminals. The equipment you purchase should not only accommodate the existing environment but be flexible enough to adapt to any changes you will have over at least the next two to three years. DCE equipment with automated test features should be considered at the same time.

Reference has been made in this section to the Network Control Center (NCC). The Network Control Center is probably the single most critical point in all of network operations. All lines coming in and out of the centralized facility go through the NCC for monitoring and diagnostics. NCCs are typically manned 24 hours a day, seven days a week when the network is operational (although some may not be manned to this level if the network is not operational during particular times of the day). The NCC houses all of the necessary diagnostic and test equipment (described later in this chapter) and is the place where network users can obtain help. A typical NCC is divided into three major segments. They are the help desk, operations, and tech support.

A. *Help Desk.* The help desk is the most important part of the NCC from the network user's point of view, because it is a focal point for user-friendly, nontechnical help. Over the years it has become obvious that many *perceived* network problems were not truly network problems, but procedural problems in which the users either did not conform or did not know the correct procedures. Procedure verification and help with particular applications are provided by the help desk. The help desk helps to track problems by keeping a log of each problem along with its corresponding solution. As a particular problem recurs, it can be solved more quickly by referring to the *solution log*. The help desk also starts the problem determination process after all procedures have been verified, so it usually has access to the appropriate problem-solving group. The people at the help desk must be knowledgeable regarding procedures, applications, and network anomalies, and intuitive about how problems may manifest themselves so that solutions can be readily obtained. It is important to maintain coordination among shifts of help-desk personnel so that problems extending beyond a shift can be tended to easily by the next shift's personnel.

B. *Operations.* Operations involves the actual network problem isolation and maintenance, which must take place at both planned and unplanned times. Operations involves the activation and deactivation of network elements such as circuits, modems, and other components and maintains all interfaces with the carriers to isolate and fix network problems, especially where non-network operations are concerned.

C. *Tech Support.* Tech support is the technical support given for non-network problems, such as software problem determination, and involves application support, programming, procedures, organizational interfacing, and integration of all user network resources. Tech support involves solving problems related to general network use, rather than specific network component failures. The tech support people must be knowledgeable as to the operation of the entire organization, not just specific applications, procedures, or circuits.

# E

## TEST STANDARDS

Before discussing specific equipment, a word on standardization is in order. The most prevalent interface is the IEEE-488 bus, an internationally accepted method of connecting test instrumentation with a controlling computer, regardless of manufacturer or speed. IEEE-488 defines the interface for the required functional, electrical, and mechanical parameters. All devices that meet IEEE-488's specification operate in accordance with the defined parameters on a defined mechanical plug-and-cable interface with electrical signals of appropriate levels. All devices must do one or more of the following:

*Listen.* Receive addressed data

*Talk.* Transmit addressed data

*Control.* Specify transmit and/or receive functions for information transfer

The major parameters of the IEEE-488 interface are as follows:

15 devices maximum on a single bus

Maximum transmission distance, 20 m (63 ft)

Eight data lines plus eight information and communication management lines

The message transfer in bit parallel, byte serial, asynchronous, with a three-wire handshake

A transfer rate of 1 MBPS (8-bit bytes transmitted serially) for a limited distance and 500 KBPS over the full 20-m path

Up to 31 transmitters and 31 receivers connected to the bus, but only 1 transmitter and 14 receivers operating at any one time (totaling the 15-device maximum)

The vendors who make automated test equipment are not necessarily the same vendors who make automated switching matrices. Test devices may operate on multiple networks through automatic or manual line switching matrices; therefore the actual configuration for utilizing test equipment can cover an entire network.

A factor for the user to consider is whether the system can transmit at lower data rates while test equipment is determining the network problem, which can only be done when the entire line or a portion of it does not have to be taken out of service for standalone testing.

Another standard used for testing is the CCITT V.54 specification, which describes standardization for loopbacks, described later in this chapter.

# F

## ANALOG SIGNAL PARAMETERS

Two separate signal-quality parameters must be measured: the analog and digital signals (on the line and also the user side of the modem). This section describes the analog parameters; Section G discusses the digital parameters.

Even though analog systems have been around a lot longer than digital, less is typically known about how to troubleshoot analog signals and fewer people know how to diagnose the problems encountered with them. Analog functions can be unstable, producing both acceptable and nonacceptable signal ranges within short periods of time. Also, analog signals are modified by noise or line degradation. The demodulator at the receive end may think it sees the signal originally generated when it actually sees a degraded (modified) signal, and so it puts out different digital bits from what were originally generated by the DTE at the transmit end. With the multiplicity of vendors of carrier services and test equipment, today's user must be knowledgeable about what can possibly happen on a carrier line, how to use the necessary test equipment, and how to analyze the results.

A detailed analysis of each signal to be measured is not warranted here, but a description of the functions to be measured will be given.

In analog networks there are two types of degradation parameters: *transient* and *steady-state*. Transient degradations occur intermittently and are rarely predictable, so they are usually defined by a specific quantity of occurrences over a given period of 5, 15, or 60 minutes or more. Transient degradations include the following:

1. *Impulse Noise.* Large, short-lived changes in circuit noise waveform, other than background noise, which usually result from electrical transients like switches and relays changing state.
2. *Gain Hits and Phase Hits.* Short-lived also, but when they are over the signal may either return to the value it had before the hit or stay at the new or in-between value. Phase hits of at least 3-ms duration are called impulse hits. Also, gain hits that exceed 4 dB and that change over a 200-ms period, rather than the specified 20-ms period, are called 2-dB gain hits.
3. *Drop Outs.* Negative gain hits that last for at least 10 ms and are of a magnitude of 12 dB or more (signal value is less than one-sixteenth of what it should be). Drop outs are the least common of transient degradations but cause the most errors.

*Steady-state degradations* include the following:

1. *Attenuation.* Also called *amplitude degradation.* Attenuation is an inherent characteristic associated with the voice-grade telephone network. When a signal is inserted on the line at the transmit end with the same amplitude across the entire 300- to 3300-Hz bandwidth, the received signal magnitude will be greatest toward the middle of the band and then slope off toward the edges of the band. Attenuation is reduced by C-type conditioning (described in Chapter 21), and, although it is not critical for voice applications, it is extremely critical for high-speed data applications.

2. *Envelope Delay.* Sometimes called frequency delay. Envelope delay is the same functional type of degradation as attenuation, but here the different frequencies arrive at the remote end at different times. Frequencies around 1200 Hz are received first, with frequencies above and below 1200 Hz coming in later. Frequencies in the 2900-Hz range may come in more than 2 ms later. Envelope delay may also be compensated for by C-type conditioning.

3. *Nonlinear Intermodulation Distortion.* The result of compressing and clipping of signals by carrier network components. New signal components are generated that distort the original signal, with the first result being bit errors. Also called harmonic distortion, nonlinear intermodulation distortion can be compensated for by D-type conditioning.

4. *Background Noise.* A result of the many environmental parameters affecting transmission over longer distances. Background noise is typified by the *hissing* that you may hear on a long-distance call. Background noise is also called white noise, Gaussian noise, amplifier noise, ambient noise, and hiss.

5. *Frequency Shift.* An occurrence primarily in the long-distance carrier environment where signals are modulated onto microwave carriers and then demodulated back into the local environment. Sometimes the frequencies that go into the carrier environment come back slightly different, resulting in a change of modem carrier signals.

6. *Phase Jitter.* Also known as just plain jitter. Phase jitter occurs because of power line harmonics in the carrier environment. Jitter causes a slight shifting of the position of the rise and fall times of the output digital bits to the user.

7. *Echo.* The degradation parameter that occurs when some of the original signal is reflected back to the transmitter because of mismatched *impedances* that exist naturally on the circuit. Echoes will get all the way back to the transmitter if there is a malfunction in the 4-wire echo-suppression circuitry of the carrier. Echoes will normally occur in dial-up situations, because in order to provide full-duplex data flow on a 2-wire half-duplex circuit, the echo-eliminating circuitry is disabled by the dial-up modem using a tone (described in Chapter 10).

Background noise refers to noise that is present without a signal on the line. Since user-generated signals cause additional noise to be generated, when looking for steady-state degradation parameters you must also look for *notched* noise, the noise present *with* a signal (usually the AT&T 1004-Hz standard test signal). A test signal is introduced on the line, which causes the signal-induced noise to also come on the line; then the test signal is filtered out by the measuring devices, which use a *notch filter,* and the noise induced by the signal remains so it can be measured.

In discussions of degradation parameters you may also hear the following terms:

Measuring noise impairments in the absence of a signal:
Background noise
Crosstalk (signals from another path)
Impulse noise
Signal-frequency interference
Frequency-division multiplexing signal-induced impairments:
Amplitude hits
Amplitude jitter
Drop outs
Erratic carrier
Frequency translation (change of frequency)
Phase hits
Phase jitters
Pulse code modulation signal-induced impairments:
Aliasing products
Compandor-missed tracking
Quantizing distortion
Timing bias
Timing jitters
Signal-induced distortion:
Second harmonic
Third harmonic

The terms may sound like a different language to you, but they are all important for network controllers, who analyze and identify degradation parameters so they can point to the appropriate carrier vendor for problem resolution. The easy solution would be to have the carrier take on the responsibility for identifying and fixing problems, which may cost more initially but be cheaper in the long run because you would need less equipment and your personnel would not have to be familiar with the excruciating details of analog line degradation. Even with a knowledgeable individual you may not always isolate a problem, because the impairments can change fairly quickly, and what appears to be a problem at one time may not be the problem a few minutes later (the appropriate test equipment can make a big difference).

The analog parameters discussed here are measured in two ways: out-of-band testing and in-band testing. *Out-of-band* testing involves testing with a portion of the 300- to 3300-Hz bandwidth (300 to 600 Hz) while data is being transmitted in the remainder of the band (the primary band). The quality of the test is not as good as that of a full-band test, although a bad line will usually show up. The data rate in the primary band has to be reduced because some of the available bandwidth is used for the test band.

*In-band testing* is done with the line in a test mode, so data cannot move and the line is out service. With the appropriate equipment, in-band testing can be done between message transmissions, although there is a delay before information transmission can occur because the user must disconnect the test equipment and initiate synchronization for transmission of the data. A better time to do in-band testing would be when the traffic is either very low or nonexistent.

Although it is not a true test, *sealing current* is sometimes used in the analog environment to break down the film that can build up on mechanical switches. A constant direct current (dc) of several microamperes is put on the circuit to break down the film, permitting a good, solid electrical connection. Sealing current does not affect data and is sometimes required to keep the signal *gain* constant. It is almost always applied by the local carrier.

## G

## DIGITAL SIGNAL PARAMETERS

As stated before, the carriers provide the majority of testing for digital circuits. Since many of the errors that occur in digital circuits are corrected by the carriers or transmitted through the network with the corresponding logic errors in them (see DS-1 signaling in Chapter 16), some of those parameters may be tested for in the end-user environment.

In the digital network certain performance parameters are identified by AT&T, such as 99.4 error-free seconds out of every 100 for DDS (Dataphone Digital Service), which translates into 218.4 seconds (3 minutes and 38.4 seconds) per day during which time an error *may* occur. Availability of DDS circuits is 99.96 percent over a year's time, which equals an outage maximum of 3.5 hours. Within that outage, no single event will exceed two hours.

T-1 performance is rated at 95 percent error-free seconds over a 24-hour period, which equates to 3 minutes per hour or 72 minutes per day. Although this seems very high, considering the transmission rate available at T-1 (1.544 MBPS) the actual information throughput is substantial. Availability for T-1 over a 12-month period is 99.7 percent, which means an average outage of 26.28 hours over the year with no single outage maximum specified. (This criteria is identified in AT&T publication 41451.)

There is a variety of causes for errors, and the tests for them are as follows:

**A.** *Bipolar Violations.* Testing can determine whether two or more consecutive pulses for a bipolar signal are in the same direction. As described in Chapter

16, there are certain conditions under which bipolar violations are generated by the carrier but removed when transmitted to the next location, even if that location is at a user site. Therefore, bipolar violations should not occur unless there is an error.

**B.** *Low-Level Signal.* Pulse levels are established in the specifications for digital transmission. If those levels are not maintained, the pulse may be lost. Low-level signal testing determines whether the pulse parameters are in spec or not. Testing is also done for the total loss of signal, which may be due to low signal level or absence of signal completely.

**C.** *Frame Synchronization.* In the testing for appropriate *framing* of a transmission, there is either the superframe (SF) or extended superframe (ESF) format, which involves different uses of the 193rd bit in DS-1 signaling. Many degradations such as multiple clock references can cause loss of frame synchronization; testing for it can determine whether additional diagnostics can be performed to determine what problems may have caused *frame slippage* or *loss of synchronization*.

**D.** *Pulse Density.* Related to bipolar violations is the case where too many zeros occur in sequence. As described in Chapter 16, the B8ZS method is used to insert extra 1 bits (by bipolar violations) into a bit stream where there are more than 15 consecutive 0 bits (or an 8-bit byte that has no 1 bits in it). If signals are received with excessive sequences of 0 bits, synchronization or timing problems can occur between switches.

**E.** *CRC (Cyclic Redundancy Check).* The CRC is only performed for ESF transmissions and can determine whether bits have been changed during a transmission between two adjacent switches. Unless both ends of the connection have ESF, CRC cannot be utilized. This CRC is done only in a link-by-link basis in the network and does not involve the CRC that the user may have as part of the transmission protocol. CRC in the network is designed to isolate specific connections that have problems, while CRC in the protocol is designed at the logical level to determine whether the messages have errors. The two are very different.

Since testing and diagnosis of degradations and failures are one of the most important functions in any communication link, it is of significant value to the customer to determine what is available either from the carrier or from other equipment vendors. For the DDS-II services, it is possible with a special DSU and carrier equipment to determine whether errors are occurring in your links. If ESF is used with the B8ZS form of ones density coding, it is possible to diagnose degraded line conditions. To do so, however, the local carrier equipment must be capable of supporting those functions. AT&T can support those functions in their network, but if the local carriers cannot, the user will not have access to those capabilities unless there is a direct connection to AT&T.

The DSU/CSU has the capability for providing loopback to the local telephone companies' CO. Testing can then be performed from the AT&T ABATS (Automatic Bit Access Test System). The test locations work in conjunction with the local telephone company equipment and can check the entire network. The line loopback provides for end-to-end CSU testing. The DSU to CSU connection can also be tested, but those tests are *in band,* and the lines must be taken out of service to perform them. The tests can again be performed by AT&T personnel at the ABATS sites. The carrier is able to perform all the testing, rather than requiring the user to acquire the necessary equipment and personnel to perform the tests.

In conjunction with the ABATS testing capability, there is also a service called Customer Test Service (CTS). End users can access CTS through an asynchronous terminal by dialing the CTS computer in Chicago, which provides the necessary loopbacks in both directions to test your DSU/CSU at both ends of your lines. At present this is available only on interstate circuits, but they can be either point-to-point or multipoint. If you need regularly scheduled diagnostic services for preventive maintenance, you can schedule test time in advance with AT&T. Both the ABATS and the CTS service capabilities will probably be expanded by the time this text gets into print, so it is advised that you determine what the latest capabilities are.

As a final note, you should also be aware that there are other vendors who provide test equipment for diagnostic testing, although they may use a *subchannel.* Depending on the vendor, *robbed bits* may be used to convey test information, which may affect the user's throughput. If the ABATS and CTS services become widely used, it is quite probable that individual vendor equipment may obtain only a very small portion of the total test market.

## H
## DIGITAL INFORMATION PARAMETERS

On the digital side of the DCE it is much easier to define what you are looking for and interpret what you see, because the information is in binary form (bits). Digital testing equipment usually combines qualitative and quantitative values in determining line performance. The measurements and parameters are frequently listed under different categories, so the descriptions given here should not be taken as the only way to identify them.

Line quality:
   Character analysis
   Message analysis
   Protocol analysis
Network access control:
   Configuring
   Emulator evaluation
   Modem/multiplexer evaluation
   Protocol converter evaluation
   Switching

Status and performance:
    Application
    CPU
    Network
    Terminal
    Traffic error rates
    Traffic type
    Traffic volume
Service levels:
    Applications analysis
    Availability
    Capacity analysis
    Growth planning
    Scheduling
    Simulation
    Statistical evaluations and comparisons
    Utilization

Statistics should be gathered on a line basis, group basis, and at network level. Included within these parameters are response time, total system loading, and utilization of all equipment. A directory of network elements should be provided so that the network manager can understand and recognize what flexibility exists for problem resolution and growth.

## I

## TEST EQUIPMENT

Numerous test products are available, and many vendors provide test equipment. Some vendors have more capability than others, and some provide specific test equipment for specific problems. Because of the wide variety of product availability, the descriptions provided here for test equipment are generic; they describe the major functions to be performed rather than the specific vendor products or product lines.

The easiest set of equipment to specify is the analog test equipment. Made up of many components, each making individual measurements, the equipment may be called a *transmission-impairment measurement system* (TIMS). The TIMS will perform one or more of the following measurements:

Signal-level
Signal-to-noise ratio
Harmonic distortion

Envelope delay

Noise level (usually C-message weighted)

Noise in the presence of 1004-Hz signal (notched noise)

Attenuation vs. frequency

A new class of test set, the ITIMS (In-Service TIMS) performs nearly all these measurements by observing a high-speed data signal, already on the line, without taking the line out of service. It is expensive, but saves time and reduces service interruptions.

Digital information test equipment includes the following:

*Bit Error Rate Tester (BERT).* A BERT performs bit matching of data patterns. A transmitted bit stream is *looped back* through various parts of the network and compared to the received bit stream to see if all the transmitted bits came back the same way as they were sent out.

*Character Error Rate Tester (CERT).* A CERT does the same thing as a BERT, but in a character mode.

*Block Error Rate Tester (BLERT).* A BLERT does the same thing as a BERT and CERT, but in the block or message mode. BLERTs provide a very effective means of testing message transmissions because they can emulate real-world transmission parameters. The user needs to know how many messages are in error, not just the bit error rate.

For example, given 1000 messages with 100 bit errors, the actual effect on the network could be the retransmission of 100 messages (if there were 1 bit error in each of 100 messages), or 10 percent of the messages. On the other hand, if all 100 errors occurred in just one message due to a burst of noise (most common), there is only one message to retransmit (0.1 percent). For this reason, even if you have a BERT, you should have some way of determining how many messages were in error, or, as the telephone company now does, you should have a parameter telling you how many error-free seconds (EFS) there are so that you know how many messages would be received and how many would have to be retransmitted per unit time. It is the total amount of retransmissions that you are interested in, not just the amount of bit errors.

BERTs, CERTs, and BLERTs, all being digital devices, go on the DTE side of the modem.

The tests described for BERTs, CERTs, and BLERTs are nonprotocol-oriented tests (BLERTs, however, could block messages like a protocol). There are other test devices that generate multiblock transmissions and emulate both terminals and system-level equipment in the specific protocol you use. If you cannot find out what a problem is by using the BERT, CERT, or BLERT, you may need an emulator to give you additional information with respect to the timing and protocol actually occurring on your transmission line. Emulation devices are almost always geared to a specific product and are provided by several vendors.

For simplistic testing, especially in a field environment, a device known as a *breakout box* (also called an EIA interface test set) is put in series with the digital path between the DTE and the DCE. The breakout box allows jumper connections to be made in or between any signal on the RS232 interface, and it allows the external insertion of signals on particular lines. Monitoring can also be done using this device because each line is individually accessible on the breakout box. Since they are very simple devices with simple indicators, breakout boxes are available for less than $50 today. If you would like to connect to signal-generating equipment, that capability can be included at a higher price.

Another device, the *loop-back adapter,* provides digital-type loop backs in the same location that a breakout box would be installed. It loops back pins 2 and 3 for data, pins 4 and 5 for request to send and clear to send, and pins 6, 8, and 20 for control purposes. A loop back tests segments of a circuit so that isolation of line problems may be accomplished from the central site.

As stated in Section E, CCITT Specification V.54 identifies the full-circuit loop-back configurations, which are shown in Fig. 22–6. Figure 22–6(a) shows

**FIGURE 22–6**
Loopback Configurations

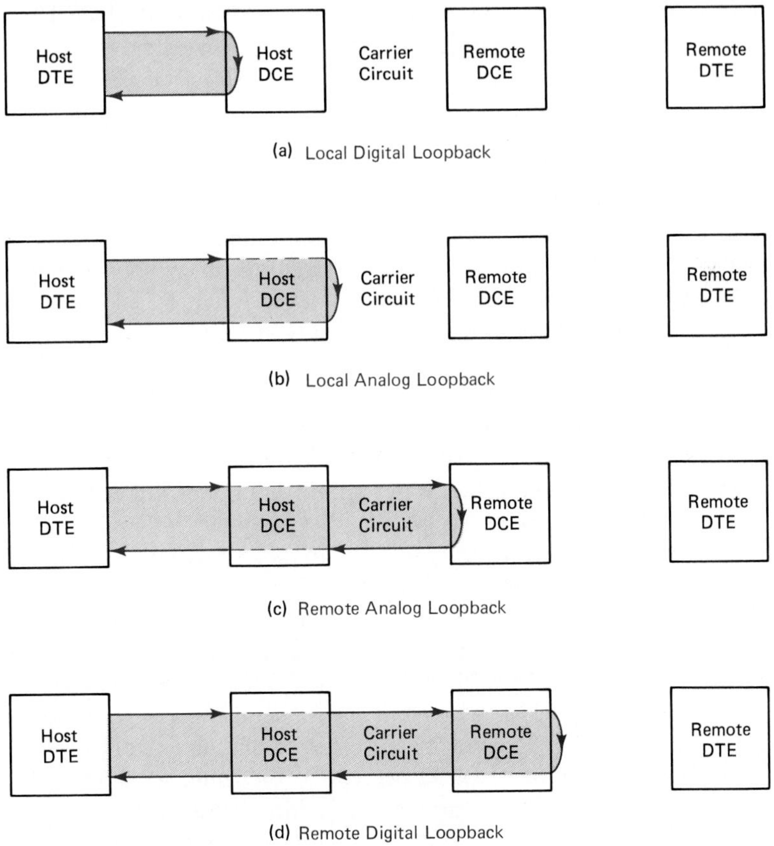

(a) Local Digital Loopback

(b) Local Analog Loopback

(c) Remote Analog Loopback

(d) Remote Digital Loopback

the local digital loop back, which can be accomplished by a switch setting in the host-end modem. The local digital loop back connects the incoming and the outgoing lines, so the host DTE will get the signal it generates sent back to it. If test equipment is integrated into the circuit between the host DTE and DCE, all the local digital loop-back tests can be performed using the test set. In this configuration the signals coming out of and going back into the host DTE can be examined. You are more likely to use the host itself if the software in the host is capable of generating and receiving its own signals. The local digital loop back tests the logical operation of the DTE as well as the connection between the DTE and the DCE.

Figure 22–6(b) shows a local analog loop back, which can perform the same tests as the local digital loop back, except the signal goes through the host DCE, which in turn tests the operation of the local DCE. Although the host DCE plays itself back to back, because of the relationships of the data and timing coming in from the remote it may be on the borderline and therefore not truly operational when connected in a full end-to-end circuit.

Figure 22–6(c) shows the remote analog loop back that tests not only the host DCE, but the circuit from end to end. The remote DCE not only must loop back the signal, but must also amplify it, because there is a loss in the transmission going from the host to the remote site. The remote DCE must generate a signal at the same output level as it would if it were fully operational.

Figure 22–6(d) shows the remote digital loop back, which tests the remote DCE to determine whether it is operating. The timing relationships of the signals coming from the remote should be the same as under normal conditions; this may also help test the host DCE, although if this particular configuration does not work, it does not necessarily mean that the remote DCE is at fault. A timing relationship or a potential circuit degradation may put the host DCE over the edge of its marginal operation. If the circuit problem shows up in this configuration, the host DCE should be first patched out with a known operational host DCE to determine whether the original host DCE or the remote DCE is causing the problem.

Note that none of these connections tests the remote DTE. It is a sad but true fact that the majority of terminal vendors do not provide diagnostic capability for testing their devices in a remote environment. Because the need for problem resolution is increasing, it is possible that many will do so, but the additional cost, with its resultant competitive disadvantage, will make the vendors think twice before they incorporate features to make it easier to diagnose a circuit problem that they feel is not of their doing.

Many DCEs are capable of performing the local and remote loop-back connections under some form of automated control, either from the host DCE or from computerized test equipment. If the same vendor is used to provide the automated test configuration and the modems, an integrated test facility results that should be very reliable in identifying potential network problems. It has been estimated that better than 90 percent of the time, with the full test capability, a particular network component or facility included within the four loop-back conditions can be identified in less than 10 minutes. If you think of the time and effort needed to do this manually, you will see why this kind of equipment can pay for itself within a relatively short period of time. If different vendors are used to provide the test equipment and the DCE equipment, the configuration is called a *wraparound*. Although there's bound to be some finger pointing, if all the equipment is IEEE-488 bus compatible, there should be few problems in integrating the devices.

The range of prices is wide, as shown next in a list of equipment that analyze and troubleshoot a network.

Breakout boxes: $50–300

Intelligent breakout boxes: $1200–1500

BERTs, CERTs, BLERTs: $500–3500

Response-time analyzers: $1500–5000

Data line monitors:

Monitor and collect data only: $2000–6000

Interact and generate data (and display control characters): $3000–12,000

Terminal emulation: $12,000–30,000

Analog testers: $200–13,000

Digital test sets: $5000–15,000

All the equipment should come with some form of training manual to teach the user how to use it, and especially how to interpret the results. In addition, the user must have some inherent knowledge of the troubles that might occur and how to interpret test results to correct the indicated problems. Experience is therefore very important; it always pays to hire someone who has had some experience so that you will not have to spend extra time and expense training. However, once the individual is trained in your system, he or she becomes a prime target for hiring by another organization at a significant increase in salary. For this reason, network knowledgeable personnel should be given competitive pay scales and attractive work environments. Pressure is an inherent part of the network management environment, and if management will support the resolution of problems, it will be a lot easier for the *troops* to operate and to stay in that environment.

At the time of this writing much of the digital signal test equipment was still handled by the carriers, but it is anticipated that the following kinds of equipment will be available so that the end user can perform the same types of tests.

*DS1 Test Set.* A device that will be able to measure all of the parameters relative to DS1 signaling, such as bipolar violations, synchronization determination, pulse density, and low signal levels. The DS1 test set will have a CRC incorporated into it if used for testing on a circuit with ESF.

*CSU/DSU Emulator.* A standalone device that will emulate the user connection in a digital interface environment. It does not necessarily have to be a separate piece of test equipment, but may be a spare CSU/DSU. It will provide all the necessary interface levels, loopback capabilities, and diagnostic procedures that can be used with the carrier equipment to test the local loop in a digital circuit or an end-to-end digital circuit.

## J
## TEST SEQUENCES FOR PROBLEM ISOLATION

As stated earlier in this chapter, two basic types of tests, digital information testing and analog or digital signal testing, are performed to isolate problems that occur on a communications line. Digital information testing refers to the test of information in its digital information form; analog or digital signal testing refers to tests performed on the communications line itself. Many tests utilize the loop back, which for purposes of this section means the return of information to the source at any one of a number of locations in the network (the digital side of DCE at transmit end, the circuit side of DCE at transmit end, the circuit side of DCE at receive end, or the digital side of DCE at receive end).

The most prevalent test mode by far is the digital information test, which can be performed by a large range of equipment, from the so-called *free* equipment on the communications devices themselves to sophisticated self-contained units. Since most tests performed by these devices are in the loop-back mode in analog systems, they will be described first.

When a problem has occurred and the communications line is suspected, the very first test should be a *modem self-test*. Depending on the particular unit, the test may consist of one or more pushbuttons for which the end result is the same: generating an internal test pattern. The test pattern resembles as closely as possible the normal digital input (which has been disconnected) and travels through more than 90 percent of the internal circuitry, a simulated telephone line, and then returns to its originating circuitry. The return pattern is compared with the transmitted pattern, and the user is advised of differences by an indicator lamp. It is remotely possible that an error could be caused by the self-test circuitry itself, so if errors occur here a spare modem should be substituted and the same testing repeated. If the substitute modem seems fine, the original modem may have had a problem. Testing with the line should continue if an additional problem exists.

Modem self-tests, even when performed at both ends, do not necessarily guarantee that a modem is operational. First, the test patterns do not go through the complete set of circuits that are required for interfacing with the communications line, and second, the bit pattern generated may not be the specific pattern that is causing the communication line problem. In addition, an even more common problem, often hard to find, is an out-of-tolerance timing condition.

The next test to perform is a *remote self-test,* in which one modem generates a test pattern and transmits the information down the actual line through the modem at the other end, where it is digitally looped back and returned to the communications line for comparison at the transmit end.

Two alternatives exist with the remote self-test. First, without the benefit of line-test equipment, if both modems have passed the local self-test, passing the remote self-test indicates that a problem is probably external to the modem or line, possibly in the software, terminal, or front end; if the remote self-test fails, the modem vendor or the carrier should be contacted.

If external test equipment is available, the same test should be repeated with externally generated patterns that are more complex. If the results are the same as the self-test results, the same conclusions can be drawn with a high probability of accuracy, but the external test equipment should be able to provide a more accurate representation of where the fault really lies.

If, however, the local loop fails with the test equipment, a modem failure is extremely probable. If the remote digital loop results agree with the results of the remote self-test, no conclusion may be drawn.

At this point the carrier should be called and the specifics of the problem described. The carrier will check the line problems that are the most common and easiest to test. If testing results in no trouble being found (NTF), ask the carrier which checks were made, and then try to use the line again. In many instances, the carrier has indicated that they have been unable to find a problem after testing the line, yet the line has been found to be good after the test sequences have been completed.

If the communications line is still not operational, the carrier should be called again and specifically requested to perform a noise check and a frequency run (FREQ), if those tests were not performed before. The FREQ consists of testing the attenuation at various frequencies throughout the telephone bandwidth. If this doesn't work, the modem vendor should be called, and, assuming the user does not have any specific internal test capability, the modem vendor and the carrier must work together to try to isolate the problem. The present deregulated environment consisting of multiple carriers is one of the strongest arguments for having internal operating procedures to facilitate interaction between the modem vendor and carrier maintenance personnel.

With the appropriate equipment, end-to-end testing can also be performed (one way each way). The same type of test can be performed utilizing the test equipment on an end-to-end basis without a loop back. The information goes through the modems and the logic hardware at each end, so the probability of detecting errors is better than on a loop back because the actual signal path is involved. A remote analog loop back should not be performed unless the signal goes through an amplifier at the remote end, because without the amplifier the user ends up with a communication line that appears to be twice as long as what it was designed to operate over. (The remote modem normally outputs a signal level that is the same as the signal level at the transmit end, but if an analog-*only* loop back is performed, the level being looped back at the receive modem will be the receive signal level ($-16 \pm 4$ dB) of the remote end, instead of $0 \pm 4$ dB, its normal transmit signal level.)

Another test is performed through polling and calling sequences, which can be used to determine the operational sequences of the individual modems, especially critical in a dial-up situation where all the modem-terminal equipment interfaces must have specifically defined relationships with each other.

One other level of digital test capability is available, with automated test equipment on the digital side at each end. Specific signals as well as data blocks can be sent from one test equipment to the other so that comparisons can be made at each end of a line without a loop back. The entire live system is utilized for the test. It is also possible for the communications software to be tested automatically if the test equipment allows for external input of information (very expensive, however, if remote sites are to have separate test equipment).

The second significant area of testing is analog testing, the hardest to describe. The analog world is much different from the digital world, in which people discuss *discrete* elements instead of the varying elements that normally occur in the analog network. As with digital testing, analog tests can be performed in a loop-back or end-to-end mode, although the loop backs must be on the analog side of the modem at each end of the circuit. With very few exceptions, analog testing performed in a loop-back mode is nearly 100 percent valid. With some of the newer network test equipment and built-in modem test capabilities, some environments have line problem isolation definition rates of better than 90 percent within time frames of ten minutes or less. As stated previously, the equipment costs a lot but usually pays for itself quickly.

If the problem still cannot be isolated, then in all likelihood carrier and possibly modem vendor personnel probably will be required at both ends of the line for coordinated troubleshooting. The coordinated tests take quite a bit of time, and the line could be unavailable for extended periods (hours or days). Even after a problem is identified, correcting it in the carrier environment may still take hours or days.

The first test performed on the line in an analog mode is called *continuity,* which shows whether the connection is broken somewhere, one of the easiest problems to isolate. If continuity is not the problem, the next test that should be performed is *level testing,* the measurement of power levels at various points in the circuit. The measurements can be made in many ways, but with a telephone line it is most convenient to use a decibel (dB) measuring device, as described in Chapter 21.

In the telephone company environment a typical communications path has a receive level that is 16 dB less than the transmit level. The 3002 specification identifies the normal transmit and receive levels, with $\pm$ 4 dB deviation allowed. If the measurement is anything other than what was expected, the circuit is identified as *long* if the difference is more than 16 dB or *hot* if the signal is stronger than expected (less than 16 dB different). Level testing gives a very good indication of the loss of signal strength on the line.

A second analog test regards *frequency response;* it is a measurement of the line response for all frequencies between 300 and 3300 Hz. The allowable amount of deviation from the norm for each of the frequencies is identified in the 3002 specification.

Another analog measurement is *noise measurement.* The only noise we are really interested in is that which exists between 300 and 3300 Hz, because those are the frequencies at which we will be transmitting our data. To do this measurement, a C-message filter, described in Chapter 21, is used to simulate the line characteristics. Although a C-message filter allows some of the noise in from outside the band and reduces some of the in-band noise, it is sufficient for giving a fairly accurate indication as to whether noise is a problem. The noise measurement should be made with the end of the circuit properly terminated, because if it is not, additional noise or other kinds of problems such as echoes can be injected back into the circuit.

A generalized noise measurement using the C-message filter is not always adequate to identify the total impact of noise, because some of the noise is only generated in the presence of a signal. Therefore, some type of signal must be generated and transmitted, and then the signal must be eliminated and the noise measured that is a result of that signal. The test signal is known as the test tone, and its frequency is 1004 Hz. This test tone is erased, or *notched* out, by a notch filter that eliminates the 1004-Hz signal but leaves the signal-generated noise component. Although the noise at 1004 Hz is also eliminated, the effect of its elimination is barely noticeable.

Another analog test that may be performed measures *envelope delay.* Envelope delay rarely changes significantly without a corresponding change in other parameters that are routinely measured, so envelope delay is only suspected with a new or changed circuit. Another unique type of noise is *nonrandom noise,* which is a single-frequency interference. It is practically impossible for the single-frequency noise to be out of tolerance if the total noise is within tolerance, and therefore the C-notched filter noise measurement would find this problem before it would be tested for independently.

A third type of analog measurement is *frequency shift,* in which a particular frequency is shifted up or down by the time it gets to the receive end. A 5-Hz change up or down is allowable, and most carrier testing finds frequency-shift problems very quickly.

A fourth type of analog problem is *phase jitter,* which is actually a frequency shift that occurs frequently and continuously. Jitter is not normally a common problem and is hard to recognize because of the relationship between the phase jitter and the noise that is created by the testing equipment. Noise will always affect a phase-jitter meter, and vice versa. Since the measurements are hard to differentiate, it is usually recommended that they be performed by the carrier.

The testing described thus far is for impairments that are fairly constant and does not apply to the hit type of noise, which is random and has values that can change instantaneously. Hits, unless they are on a continuous basis, normally result in random errors detected in data transmissions.

The tests described here are generic and have been used for many years to test analog circuits. If you would like to follow the formalized AT&T methodology for testing, there are certain standards you can use. Bell System Publication (BSP) 41008 (dated July 1974) describes transmission standards for voice-grade telephone lines. The techniques used to measure transmission characteristics are described in Bell System Publication 41009 (dated May 1975), which recommends a series of tests that are still applicable. Some of the tests are briefly described here.

The basic tests performed on the line to determine its operational capability utilize the 1004-Hz test tone at the transmit end and measure the following parameters on the receive end:

Amplitude Jitter
C-Message Noise
C-Notch Noise
Dropouts
Frequency Translation (Change of frequency)
Gain Hits
Idle Channel Noise
Phase Hits
Phase Jitter
Signal Loss in dB
Signal/Noise Ratio

Other tests are recommended that utilize *tone responders* in telephone locations or user facilities, primarily for loop-back testing (in this case a *tone* is used for line testing). The tones activate the 829 test set and a unit called the Remote Isolation Device (RID) to initiate Bell Code Tests 100–107.

The 100–107 tests are conducted by calling the responder and transmitting a predetermined series of test tones in particular timing sequences. The most common series is the Code 100, which is the simplest of the signal loss and noise tests. Code 105 tests are the most useful from a circuit point of view because they measure two-way analog loss plus many degradations such as signal/noise ratio, phase jitter, nonlinear distortion, and peak/average signal ratio. The Code 107 test is the most exotic of the code tests in that it is utilized to isolate transient problems and conditions.

Users can set up their own tone generators to access the various central office responders so that tones can be generated and looped back to isolate problems in the local loop or central office. The carriers frown on this because they do not like anyone changing the configuration of their equipment without their knowledge.

Carriers can utilize the 829 test set and the RID to provide loop-back testing to the telephone company test center. The 829 is at the end of a four-wire leased line, where it accepts the 1004-Hz tone and loops it back to the Central Office. The receipt of the signal is what is looked for, NOT the level (in other words this is not a level test, only a continuity test). The RID does the same test for a two-wire circuit (not widely used).

The tests that give the most information are tests for the following parameters:

*Loss.* The power loss of a signal from the transmit end to the receive end.

*Noise.* The background signal energy on a line or channel that has no signal on it.

*C-Notched Noise.* The noise on a voice-grade line with the 1004-Hz test tone applied. The 1004 Hz is filtered, or *notched,* out when the measurement is made so that the noise generated by the test tone can be measured. C-notched noise is sometimes called *signal-induced* noise.

*C-Message Noise.* The noise on a particular line measured in relation to a particular frequency.

*Envelope Delay Distortion.* The measurement of the various times it takes for different frequencies to get to the end of the line when generated simultaneously. This is a relative measurement, not an absolute one.

*Phase Jitter.* A measurement of the signal instability with respect to phase.

*Amplitude Jitter.* A measure of signal instability with respect to amplitude of the signal.

*Intermodulation Distortion.* A measure of the harmonics on the line. A harmonic is a multiple of the frequency or frequencies that exist on the line.

*Peak to Average Ratio (P/A Ratio).* A measurement of the peak values of a particular signal compared to the average values of that signal for determining distortion of the overall signal on a particular path.

*Impulse Noise.* A particular band of received signal noise that exceeds the Route Mean Square (RMS) noise in that particular band by 12 dB or more.

*Hits.* Sudden and rapid changes in the gain or phase of a received signal.

*Drop Outs.* Sudden losses of signal.

With all the various tests that can be run in the analog network, you must remember that they are not always conclusive. For example, if you run loop-back tests the only thing you know with certainty is whether there is loss of continuity on the path. It takes knowledgeable personnel with a good idea of what the circuit is physically made up of to run the appropriate tests to determine what is causing the particular line problem.

One final area of problem determination must be pointed out here: power problems. With more devices relying on *house power* to operate, it is necessary to consider what your power sources are and what you would need to do in the event of power failure. Many people do not consider the short-term problem of degraded power availability.

Examples of power-line problems are noise, brownouts, blackouts, surges, faults, sags, and spikes. Each can have a serious effect on your communications equipment (and any other equipment) and therefore must be considered in the design of the network environment. There are many ways to provide alternate power including Uninterruptible Power Supplies and batteries, but these usually can be used for only a relatively short time. If you are susceptible to longer-term outages, you must consider alternative backup such as a diesel generator or some other form of power generation that is external to the commercial source.

Going one step further, if you need dual power sources, you should make sure that the wiring leaves your building from two separate locations and does not have any common path to the source of the power.

Other equipment used for monitoring, measuring, and improving power sources are

>*Power Line Monitors.* Monitor the incoming power levels.
>
>*Filters.* Provide *smoothing out* of input power to eliminate surges or spikes.
>
>*Surge Suppressors.* Reduce surges caused by transient factors; very important for computers and PCs.
>
>*Isolation Transformer.* Reduces the effect of sudden changes in input power to the equipment.
>
>*Constant Voltage Transformer.* Provides a constant level of source power, regardless of the incoming power, over a very wide range.
>
>*Regulator.* Keeps input power within a predetermined range.

Your network does no good for you when it is down, so if you are dependent on commercial power to keep it up, you must make the same kind of backup decisions for power that you do for circuits.

## K
## BACKUP AND ALTERNATIVE PROCEDURES

In all network management and control procedures, the concepts of backup and alternative procedures are mandatory. They can cover numerous possibilities, and the extent of implementation is normally limited only by the amount of available financial resources. Basic backup procedures will be described here, rather than specific types of equipment.

First, the concept of backup should be identified. What does the user really need? Is immediate backup required, or is some time available before service must be restored? What is the maximum length of time that the system and/or particular components of the system can be unavailable to users? These are some of the major parameters that must be evaluated when determining how much alternative capability is required.

If the entire system must be immediately available, the user would need a completely duplexed set of hardware and software capability at all levels, from the peripheral storage devices at the central sites all the way out to the display devices at the remotes, which is usually impractical. The majority of cases have single pieces of equipment in the remote network, while the central site normally has the duplexed capability. Since we are concentrating on the communications network in this text, only functions that relate to it will be described here.

At the central site, the best hardware backup to have is the ability to switch the communication lines from one communications computer to another in the event one fails. A second level of protection is to have alternative termination equipment that can be automatically switched in, and a third is to have alternative modulation equipment that can be replaced in a circuit in the event of a failure at the central site. The latter type of switching (the modem) is normally done manually or automatically through a tech-control panel after a problem has been identified (it could be done automatically through a console or keyboard as described in Section D of this chapter). If an individual circuit fails and is not backed up with a spare, it will have to be fixed in order to restore service to the remote location.

Because of the usual lack of full backup capability in a network (due primarily to cost), the user may consider alternative communication paths to be used in the event of a failure. The primary capability is the use of dial-up facilities for leased-line failure. It is recommended that the dial-up capability originate at the central site since central site hardware can be shared across the entire network. In addition, if there are problems in the host site hardware or software, you do not want the remote sites calling in because the central site may not be capable of communicating anyway. With dial-up facilities the user can contact the remote sites in a prioritized sequence that would be the most efficient from a processing or application point of view at the central site.

With the growth of personal and business computers, modems should have full-duplex transmission capability on two-wire circuits for use on the backup line, because almost all protocols on those machines require simultaneous two-way communication.

As a last resort, if it appears that circuit failure will last for an extended time and alternative communication paths are not available, the user can consider using any of the express mail or regular mail services to move information from one remote site to another remote site, or to the central site for entry at a later time. Actual use depends on the particular application and time available before information must be included in the system.

When a dial-up sequence is used after a leased line has broken down, the dial-up modem must operate differently and is therefore usually a different modem. Because of the expense of putting two modems at every remote site, the user probably has dial-up modems only at the sites that require the quickest reconnection. Some of the newer modems can operate on either a dial *or* a leased line by switch positions and, although they are more expensive than regular modems, they are less costly than two separate modems. If the modem fails, however, the site will be out of service.

Because maintenance personnel are not available at all sites, and remote site personnel rarely have the necessary technical capability, most backup and alternative procedure must be performed at or from the central site.

Backup planning must include some thought given to *disaster* planning. In other words, what happens if your central facility goes down because of flood, earthquake, or fire? What would you do if the entire network was going to be down for a period of time? Disaster planning could be the subject of an entire text all by itself, but you must consider alternatives in the event that you lose your primary facility. Will you be down for hours, days, weeks, or even months? What would be the resources required to bring you back up to minimal operating capability? Could anyone else provide the resources? Where could you get those resources? When would they be available?

You must perform a *risk analysis* to determine what your liabilities would be in the event of a major outage, and what the costs would be to get back to an operational condition (even to a lesser mode of capability). Some organizations perform a risk analysis and decide that, although they will keep their facility as protected as possible, if it is destroyed for any reason they will *go out of business*. The costs for a backup facility apparently may not be worth the expense, so that some would much rather provide predetermined levels of fire suppression, flood suppression, and other ways to keep their primary facility operating. Even then, provisions for alternative power and communications backup are still needed as described before.

To sum up the backup capabilities, you need communications backup, power backup, and disaster planning to keep your network up and running.

## L
## VENDOR-PROVIDED NETWORK MANAGEMENT FACILITIES

Although there has always been a need for coordinated network testing, it was not until the breakup of the Bell System that the necessity for single source network troubleshooting became a high priority. Before divestiture in 1984, network problems were typically resolved by the carriers with the user providing additional support from network control centers, which provided interfacing devices to get to the network. With the growth of a multivendor environment, different products in the user and carrier environment make coherent testing mandatory. In addition, with standardized networks evolving like OSI and SNA, it will be necessary not only to get your network up and running, but also to find out what the problems were when the network degraded or malfunctioned. A wide variety of products from individual vendors has surfaced that are purported to be the *single-source solution*. The "solution" involves the use of the same vendors' equipment in all parts of the network and is therefore not always practical. In 1986, however, a major product from IBM called Netview and Netview/PC was announced, the first of the truly integrated management systems that included all of the pieces of the network. Netview was not the first system to perform management functions, but the first to perform them in a particular network environment, which in this case was SNA. Many other vendors, especially those providing network products such as modems, followed with their own architectures. Codex, General Data Comm, Paradyne, and others announced products to support network management capabilities. In 1987, AT&T announced their Unified Network Management Architecture (UNMA). UNMA was the AT&T answer to integrated network management and control. Shortly after that announcement, many of the other vendors announced interface compatibility to UNMA, and at the same time, still others indicated compatibility with Netview and Netview/PC.

Because of the diversity of products and the probability that only the two major architectures from IBM and AT&T have a chance of really becoming de facto standards, only they will be described. However, the information given here is only preliminary. There is no doubt that features will be added on a continuing basis, and that vendors will continue to come out with new support for these architectures. If you are in the market for a network management system, you should make sure you have the latest information from all of the vendors before making a decision, since this is one of the fastest changing areas in data communications.

## Netview and Netview/PC

Netview's purpose is to provide full network management capabilities in the IBM SNA environment. Netview/PC has the additional capacity to provide interfaces for diagnosing and testing the products which, for the first time, do not have to be IBM or IBM-compatible products. The philosophy behind Netview is to provide network management for

Bypass and Recovery
Diagnosis
Problem Detection and Correction
Problem Determination
Resolution of Problems

In addition, network performance parameters are to be collected so that they can be provided to the end user, including:

Accounting
Availability
Component Delay Monitoring
Response Time
System Utilization

Included within these capabilities are configuration and change management and control, along with status information on the different network resources. Netview was designed to replace (and therefore includes) most of the functions of the following software packages that were previously available:

NCCF: Network Communications Control Facility
NLDM: Network Logical Data Manager
NMPF: Network Management Productivity Facility
NPDA: Network Problem Determination Application

Netview operates under the VTAM, Virtual Telecommunications Access Method, and MVS (the mainframe operating system). Netview/PC provides a series of extensions and simplifications for Netview to operate on the IBM PC, including interfacing to voice communications, the IBM token-ring network, and, most importantly, interfaces to other manufacturer products. IBM has designed Netview as an *open communication architecture* that other vendors can support through an interface called the Application Program Interface (API). IBM can test the vendors' equipment in either SNA or other devices when they tie into SNA.

A diagram of Netview and Netview/PC is shown in Fig. 22–7. If you have a 370 host, Netview provides help facilities, customization facilities, and a control facility that includes the ability to monitor the hardware, sessions, and status.

Operating through VTAM, Netview/PC provides a wide variety of additional capabilities. It provides interfaces and control for IBM devices, monitoring and control of non-IBM devices, the token ring, the interface to the Rolm CBX, and even the ability to communicate with remote Netview/PC devices. Netview/PC runs on an IBM XT or AT.

One of the big features of Netview is that it can monitor both peer-to-peer and hierarchical sessions so that all of the performance parameters can be identified for those kinds of applications. When information is collected in a Netview/PC system, a file transfer between the Netview/PC and the host uses an LU 6.2 protocol to move that information. Reporting, billing, and other processing can be moved to the host using the LU 6.2.

Netview and Netview/PC can also remotely determine modem problems. Initially only IBM modems were compatible, but when other vendors saw the popularity of Netview, they began to incorporate Netview/PC-compatible interfaces.

The three following terms are used frequently concerning Netview:

*Focal Point.* A central host system that provides the generalized network management services.

*Entry Point.* The point at which a user's terminal enters the IBM communications system. These devices are SNA-addressable products such as System 3X, 3X74 Cluster Controllers, and 37XX Communication Controller Products.

*Service Points.* Products that provide ancillary network management service to products having no direct SNA network management support. They

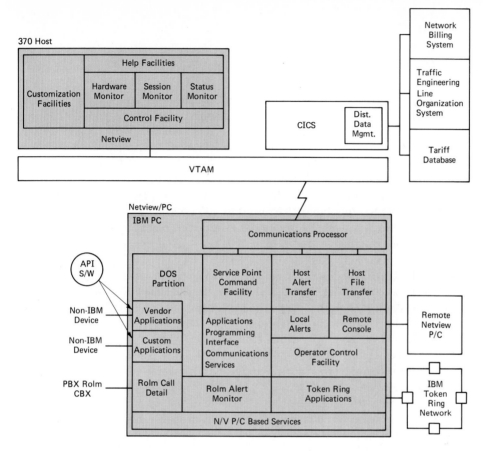

**FIGURE 22–7**
Netview and Netview PC

perform the necessary conversion between SNA management messages and the messages used by non-IBM or non-SNA devices.

## Universal Network Management Architecture (UNMA)

In 1987 AT&T announced the Unified Network Management Architecture (UNMA), the network management methodology to be used for all future AT&T products. Its stated goal is to provide the following functions:

Accounting
Configuration Management custom features
Fault Isolation
Integrated Control

Operations Support
Performance Monitoring
Planning
Security

UNMA is to be designed into AT&T Dataphone II and System 75 and 85 PBXs and integrated into new products announced at the same time. The first new product is the Accumaster Consolidated Work Station, which communicates with a Dataphone II system controller, a Dataphone II 839A dial backup, various modems, multiplexers, T-1 multiplexers, and the Starkeeper Management System for Datakit. The other product is the Accumaster Trouble Tracker, which stores and routes alarm conditions to the appropriate control locations. The Trouble Tracker is able to communicate with up to 400 separate System 75, 85, and dimension PBXs. Many other vendors of network equipment announced that they would produce interfaces compatible with UNMA as soon as more of its parameters were known.

As part of the UNMA architecture, AT&T has made their Network Management Protocol (NMP) available which conforms to the OSI model. NMP specifies a common transport through the applications layers of OSI. Because most network architectures from the various vendors are also going to move toward OSI (although not necessarily to full conformance), UNMA may provide a methodology for collecting operational statistics efficiently for any architecture that does conform to OSI. The specific application messages to be used with NMP were to be released late in 1988.

Although many critics say that UNMA does not go far enough, because of AT&T's position in the industry, UNMA will probably become one of the de facto standards in the network management world.

One last point should be mentioned here, and that is OSI. As of 1987 there was no set of standards or criteria for OSI network management, and projections were that those standards would not be available until the early 1990s. If there is one reason why OSI itself will not progress as fast as it might have, it is that there is nothing available to provide monitoring and control of the OSI network. As has been stated many times throughout this text, just to get your network up and running is not the primary force behind data communications, but *keeping* the network up and running. Any network will suffer if it does not have the ability to identify, diagnose, and solve network problems when they arise. An even more critical problem is that of connectivity to other networks. If you have a group of LANs, SNA networks, or packet networks, or use any other network in your organization, you must be able to identify a problem no matter where it arises. Those vendors whose products allow intranetwork troubleshooting followed by internetwork troubleshooting will have an advantage over the vendors that do not. If it takes OSI several years to come up with a method of network management, too many other networks may already be implemented that could preclude or at least slow down the incorporation of OSI standards. Only time will tell what the user's preference will be on this controversial subject.

No discussion of network management would be complete without including the voice telephone system. Although an entire book could be written on the subject, a brief description will be given here.

Most users today do not understand what their voice costs truly are. A manual reconciliation between the bill and the actual equipment on the user's premises is required each month. For example, some organizations request further definition of what is contained in their bill and then receive a bill for a different dollar amount covering different equipment. There are errors in equipment, lines, foreign-exchange circuits, and other facilities. Sometimes equipment is listed that had either been cancelled months before or not yet delivered. There are obvious communication problems among the organizations within the carrier who sends the bill.

A total inventory is required of all the telephone equipment and services in your organization, possibly a huge task, but you must know what you have before you can decide what you will need in the future. It is not uncommon to discover circuits, equipment, or facilities that are really not needed, while others may be overloaded. Overloading is often due to a lack of knowledge of what is available. The user may even be able to reconfigure existing lines and services to provide better response times within available facilities.

There are also big misconceptions about WATS service. WATS is not free. The more you use it, the more it costs. Many personal and other nonrelated business calls are made using WATS lines because employees think that WATS is free. Without measuring the actual utilization of the various carrier services, there is no way to tell what the required business utilization is versus what it should be.

Another abuse of the in-house phone system is the use of special exchanges for horoscopes, time, weather, dial-a-joke, dial-a-prayer, or the local porno number. If you do not measure the use of these special numbers, you cannot prevent or limit their use.

With the newer PBX equipment available today, many kinds of restrictions can be placed on individual phone extensions so that business calls can be accomplished while most unauthorized, nonbusiness calls can be restricted. If certain employees should be able to make personal calls, that can be implemented also. For example, calls can be restricted based on area codes (which have a 0 or a 1 as a second digit), by exchange, or even by specific numbers. Included is the ability to route calls by the least-cost method, which starts on existing leased lines and then goes to tie lines, foreign-exchange lines, WATS lines, and finally dial lines.

The way to limit nonbusiness calls is first to obtain station message detail recording (SMDR), which can tell you who made the call, where it was made, time and length of call, the day, the account billed, and the cost. Without some form of SMDR, there is no way to control these costs. Once you have the necessary information, you can make intelligent decisions regarding cost allocation, cost control, sales management, chargebacks, network analysis, third-party telephone purchase and/or resale, and many others.

In summary, if you do not know what you are doing now, you cannot make an intelligent decision regarding where to go with changes and growth.

Consider a study made by RCA/Cylix in 1983 of 150 companies of all sizes nationwide with respect to how their communications costs were allocated. The percentages were as follows:

Leased lines and modems: 79 percent

Staffing: salaries and benefits: 9 percent

Corporate overhead: personnel not directly related to the network; space, utilities, and so on: 7 percent

Other equipment: test and backup capabilities: 3 percent

Switching computers in large in-house networks: 2 percent

The percentages lead to many possible conclusions, the primary one being that if there were some way to reduce the amount of lines and modems there would be substantial cost savings. If you compare equipment costs to the 3 percent spent on test and backup equipment—the equipment that tells you how well the network is running and where to optimize—you can see the disproportionate expense. A little more spent on optimization (which includes the SMDR equipment) may provide a substantial reduction in the cost of lines and modems (which also includes the dial services). The potential impact is grossly out of proportion to the amount of money spent initially. Many years of experience have shown that you cannot overestimate the value of diagnostic and control equipment, but most management does not pay enough attention to them.

A more recent study, performed in 1987 by a different organization, indicated that staffing costs had increased significantly with respect to the total cost of the network, and the percentage increase was almost exactly matched by the reduction in cost of leased lines and modems. On further examination it was determined that much of the staffing cost was for the end users of the equipment, not the network personnel. Information was not available on the breakdown of end user and operating personnel so there was no way to compare the two studies directly. But since the rest of the costs did not seem to change significantly, you can assume that the overwhelming cost of network operation involves the components such as the lines, equipment, and services provided on the lines. It is important to look at your network every 12–18 months to make sure that it is running in an optimum form, because if you want to save money, the first place to look is within the network components.

## QUESTIONS

1. What is the primary purpose of a network management system?
2. Describe the three primary ways to restore service after a failure.

3. Describe the major functions that should be incorporated into a network management system and give examples.

4. Describe the major functions involved with managing a network and give an example of each.

5. What are three organizational ways to implement a network management plan? Which is best for you?

6. What are the functions of plugs and jacks and terminator blocks?

7. Describe the operation of a typical jack (patch) panel.

8. What is the most common host-site-oriented network test configuration in use today? Why?

9. What are the functions of the three major segments of a Network Control Center?

10. Describe three typical examples each of transient and steady-state analog line degradations.

11. What is the difference between in-band and out-of-band testing?

12. What is the function of sealing current?

13. Describe five types of test that are used in the evaluation of digital circuits.

14. Describe the purpose and typical operations of a TIMS.

15. What are the functions of a BERT, CERT, and BLERT?

16. What is the purpose of a loopback? What result does each of the four primary loopback configurations provide?

17. From a conceptual point of view what process is incorporated for isolation of network problems?

18. Describe the three major methods for providing network/system backup.

19. Describe the functions of Netview and Netview/PC.

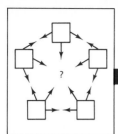

# 23

# Design Considerations

Chapters 1 through 22 have described the basic elements and functions that comprise a data communications network. Also brought out were some of the considerations involved when planning such a network. This chapter will bring those items together and provide the reader with an idea of the system tradeoffs that must be considered when designing a complete system.

## A
## CENTRALIZATION VERSUS DECENTRALIZATION

A major consideration in all system design is to determine the primary mode of processing data. Will it be done at a centralized site, at multiple centralized sites, at remote sites, or in some mixture of remote and centralized processing?

Even though it is not solely a technical consideration, it appears that in today's environment, the primary decision as to whether to incorporate a centralized or decentralized type of data processing has become a political decision. Many of today's managers and decision makers grew up in the environment of the "big machine," where IBM had an extensive impact on users' decision-making processes. The IBM philosophy was that control was mandatory in all system operations, and since it was much easier to control the operation at a single site, a single mainframe processor at one location would be the best choice.

Today's environment is somewhat different, however, in that control techniques do not have to be maintained at only one site. Functions such as down-line loading, up-line loading, and automated monitoring and logging techniques allow control to be resident at single or multiple central sites, while distributed processing can still take place in the network. Once management recognizes that they do not have to give up control when they go into a distributed form of processing, the decision to go decentralized is much easier.

If the political environment can be eliminated when the decision is made to go centralized or decentralized, the decision becomes a standard one of cost versus benefits. The benefits must be looked at from the point of view that they have both advantages and disadvantages, and they also have cost impacts over and above the purchase or lease of computing equipment. Typical of these hidden costs is the need for more capable personnel at the remote sites when decentralized processing is implemented. Additional capabilities add to the basic cost for the operation of the entire system. The second most obvious area of additional cost is for maintenance. No single organization can afford to have maintenance personnel for all equipment at all sites, so the right vendor must be called at the right time to fix any problem. It takes a more qualified person to determine the cause of the problem so that the correct vendor can be summoned. To help the personnel perform this function, automated and semiautomated test equipment can be employed (described in Chapter 22), but it also adds to the cost of system operation.

When trying to make the decision as to whether a system should be decentralized or not, the user must objectively evaluate the type of business the company is engaged in and whether that type of business lends itself to a distributed environment. For example, is the company geographically distributed in multiple locations? Are different applications performed at different sites? Do the reporting requirements mandate centralized distribution with short time turnarounds, or is time available for coordinating the reports and submitting them less often? How are orders handled? How are the files utilized? Can multiple copies of a database be utilized within the system with decision-making capability based on the access of only those separate files? These are only some of the decision factors that must be considered on an overall company basis as to how the system will be used. Other decisions are more pertinent to the day-to-day operation of the network, and they are somewhat more technical in nature.

Technical/operational decisions usually have response time as the primary requirement. If the system operation is primarily terminal/operator oriented, the operator will most often wait for a system to respond to an inquiry. The longer the operator has to wait, the greater the wasted time will be and the greater the overall cost of the system. Response time of the system/network is therefore critical and in most cases is designed to be within six seconds maximum, with two seconds or less the desired response time. If the system is batch-oriented, and data are collected remotely and processed at one or more central sites, the response time may not be as critical; but depending on the length of the transmissions between the two locations, first for the generation of information and then for the return of the results, the network response-time design parameters are still critical because of the costs involved in the network for transmission time. Right along with the response time, the total volume of traffic must be estimated so that the appropriate network components and facilities can be designed to accommodate those loads. The next section discusses design requirements in more detail.

Other basic questions must be answered relative to what the system will be required to accomplish with respect to the user's applications. Of the transactions described in Chapter 20, which ones must be incorporated into the system operation for each different application for each location? Have the various dispersed operations of the company done their processing independently in the past with different code sets, equipment, programming languages, and procedures? What is the total system cost for doing business in the present environment? If the present system was expanded to accommodate the new requirements, what would the same mode of operation cost for the expanded configuration? These questions must be answered in their total system environment, which includes hardware/software, people, network facilities, and maintenance costs. It is mandatory that this be done because it is no longer feasible to compare just the hardware/software costs. The operation and maintenance costs of a distributed network can be substantially greater than for a system that was central-site oriented in the first place. Cost factors of ten to one in operations are not uncommon, so it is necessary to take a look at the total system operation, which includes all the factors that make up the total cost to the company.

Another very important factor to consider is the increase or expansion of services that can be offered to the users or customers of the system. Expanding a given system may cost much less than distributing the capabilities over multiple locations, but the improved response time may considerably improve user environment. Where external customers are involved, it may mean either obtaining or maintaining a competitive position. The additional costs involved are therefore allocated over improved or additional services as opposed to maintenance of existing services, which makes the evaluation more subjective because you end up comparing apples and oranges.

Costs for the decentralized approach must be generated independently for each potential mode of implementation. If some applications are to be performed at the central site while others are at the remote sites, consideration should be given to altering the mix if a significant cost savings can be attained (as long as operational requirements are still met). Along with the location of applications processing, the method of system control must also be considered because the controls can add a significant amount of overhead in both hardware and software to the basic cost of the system. A substantial amount of human decision is involved here, because the overhead traffic will be greatly increased, and the managers who are to perform the control at the central sites must assimilate significantly increased amounts of data from multiple sites. The load can be partially allayed by generating software to perform those assimilations, but that also adds to the central site overhead and the total system cost. If some mode of control can be delegated to the remote processing sites and reporting takes place on a weekly, monthly, or quarterly basis, then a more reasonable approach can be incorporated that will optimize the use of the system for applications versus the necessity for controls.

As can be seen, the decision as to whether a system should be centralized or decentralized has many subjective areas, so all facets should be looked at on an individual objective basis for impact on the overall system. A small increase in cost of initial hardware, for example, could result in a significant savings in operating costs, which mean a lower overall cost to the organization. A good example of this tradeoff is the use of PCs at the remote sites, which decreases central site costs and potentially reduces network costs (offset somewhat by additional terminal, operator, and maintenance costs).

# B
# DESIGN REQUIREMENTS

Once the decision has been made to implement a network, whether centralized or decentralized, certain basic criteria must be established so that an optimal network can be implemented to meet the basic system requirements. The design requirements for the network, which must be established as a base, are listed here. Note that the functions are not necessarily in a priority sequence for any particular application. The user must determine which of the design criteria have the higher priority for the system to be implemented. The functions are communications oriented, as well as total-system oriented, so that the impact of one on the other can be determined.

1. What are the geographic points to be connected?
2. What is the data traffic volume on each line (connection between two points)? Include the traffic that is anticipated to come in from individual terminal locations on a multidevice controller. Volume should be estimated by application.
3. What are the peak traffic volume requirements on each line (also collected by application)?
4. What is the response time required to the user, average and maximum?
5. What level of data modification should be considered (such as error detection, data compression, forward error correction)?
6. What level of security is required on the individual network segments (encryption)? What about internal privacy?
7. What is the anticipated growth by the time the system is physically implemented?
8. What is the growth projection for the next five years on a yearly incremental basis?
9. Of the existing applications, how many will have to be changed and how many eliminated?

10. How many new applications must be supported?

11. What are the preliminary budgetary limitations?

Once these primary design requirements have been established (there are others that will probably be application oriented), the various alternatives in designing a network can be investigated. The alternatives involve such things as multidrop lines, multiplexing techniques, types of protocol, transmission formats, use of microprocessors with firmware, utilization of specialized common carriers, use of alternative phone company services, and use of third-party vendor equipment. In evaluating the different implementation methods, the impact on all areas must be considered, and cost is not the only parameter. Additional people, higher-paid personnel, network alternatives, user impacts, and capability for meeting operational objectives must all be evaluated when performing the trade-off analysis.

It is extremely important that the user generate the information for the design requirements internally. Outside help would only charge you money for collecting information that your own people must generate anyway. If technical expertise is needed when evaluating the collected information, that is the time to get outside help. Pay only for the capability you don't have in house. Besides, what would you do if you wanted to change or upgrade later and the outsider was no longer available?

## C
## RESPONSE TIMES

*Response time* is the total time it takes for a transaction to be processed from the moment an operator hits the "enter key" on the terminal until the response starts to display on either the CRT or the printer at the operator's location. Response time can be isolated and defined independently, although in part it consists of the processing times of the different sites that process the transaction as well as the transmission paths over which the transaction must travel.

The calculation and use of the term *response time* seems to be misunderstood by most people. When someone says there is a two-second response time for a system, many people expect all responses to be within the two-second time frame. Nothing could be further from the truth. Response time is an *average* time, and only for a certain percentage of the total amount of transactions. The actual formula for response time is:

Response Time = $x$ seconds for $y$ percent of the time

The formula indicates that the response time occurs for a particular percentage of the total transactions. For example, you may have a two-second response time 95.5 percent of the time, a four-second response time 98.6 percent of the time, or ten seconds 99.9 percent of the time. Everyone tends to describe a system as having a typical specific response time, but response times are used most often regarding average or above average usage times. It is quite possible for the response time to slow down during peak usage times, and of course that is when everyone would like to see the shortest response time. Users of the system should be aware that during peak times the response time gets longer. It is not a defect in the system, but part of the design.

If you truly need a short response time, even during peak usage, the cost of your network will go up significantly because you will need faster transmissions, and possibly separate circuits instead of multidrop. Decisions like these need input from all parties involved, not just the technical types who try to optimize network operation. If you have outside customers who judge you every time you respond to them on the phone, you may have to expend the extra time, effort, and money to give the shorter response time so that they will feel you are being responsive to their needs.

A good example of this kind of application is the stock brokerage business. If you want to buy or sell a stock very quickly because of news you just heard, you definitely want the absolute shortest response time, whether it is from your own terminal, telephone conversation with your broker, or the broker's own terminal executing your transaction. The brokers must be responsive and quick to keep your business. Other businesses may also have critical time limitations, which may or may not be as stringent. You must decide, along with all of the operational personnel, what response time you can accommodate while meeting end users' and customers' expectations.

If it is necessary to include the total preparation time of a request plus the utilization of the results after the inquiry has been processed, the time interval should be called *transaction time,* which is the time it takes from the initiation of one transaction until the initiation of the next transaction, regardless of the processes that must be undertaken in between, including nonproductive *dead time.*

Since response times on multidrop lines may also be affected by the amount of drops on the line, the speed of transmission, and the processing at the appropriate application site (which includes recognition and database access), it is necessary to identify as many of the other factors as possible that can impact response time. They are

**TERMINAL BUFFERING** If the terminal has a buffer of adequate size to take a complete transmission, it will require only one transmission for an inquiry against a database and a response to that inquiry. If multiple transmissions must be sent because of limited buffer size or because the operator is transmitting directly on line, the response time is lengthened by the amount of time it takes for each transmission to be sent and acknowledged.

**LINE SPEED** The transmission line speed can have a significant effect on response time in two different areas, terminal-to-node transmission time, and node-to-node transmission time. For example, if the terminal-to-node transmission time is at the rate of 300 BPS, we have a transmission rate of 30 characters per second asynchronous, so a 150-character message would take 5 seconds to transmit. If the transmission rate is 2400 BPS synchronous, it would only take $\frac{1}{2}$ second for the same transmission. If the system design requirement is such that a maximum 2-second response time is required, it is obvious that at least a 2400-BPS transmission rate is required between the terminal and the first node.

The other area in which line speed is significant is between the nodes and central sites. On these particular segments, it is usual to see a minimum of 9600 BPS and not uncommon to see 56 KBPS or up to 1.5 MBPS transmission rates. The higher rates between nodes or between nodes and central sites are required because they are, in effect, concentrator points. They must move much more data and therefore need a greater line capacity, which is accomplished by speeding up the transmission rate. Remember from Chapter 22 that the effective throughput at higher speeds must be considered (doubling speed does not necessarily double throughput).

The effect on response time must be measured by examining every leg over which a message must move and determining the minimum, average, and peak load time transmission rates to realize the overall impact. It is also necessary to look at the alternative paths that must be taken by either the initial inquiry or the response to determine what potential impacts they have if queuing or line problems cause rerouting. Depending on the application, it might be necessary to specifically limit the paths over which long transmissions must be sent, such as batch entries or long reports to be printed out at the terminal.

**QUANTITY OF PATHS**   As seen previously, the quantity of possible paths that may be taken between the terminal and the ultimate destination, and by the return of the response, is critical to response time. The system designer must make intelligent selections with respect to the routing for each application to determine whether it is operationally feasible or desirable to send long transmissions over the same paths as shorter transmissions. Remember that the longer the transmission takes on individual legs, the longer the overall response time will be.

**QUEUING AT TRANSMISSION NODES**   Almost all transmission nodes are store-and-forward types of devices, meaning that an entire message must be brought in and validated before it can be transmitted to the next destination. Because there are many lines and sometimes multiple terminals on the same lines, the possibility of malfunctioning or inoperative equipment or of queues building up at a particular node must be analyzed. The longer these queues build up, the longer it will take for a particular transmission to get to and leave that node for the next location, which may have a very significant impact on the response time.

**QUEUING AT ACCESS SITES**   Along with the queuing at a transmission node, queuing at an access site can be encountered. When it comes to the determination of the capacity of a particular central site, one of the biggest areas of uncertainty is the quantity of database accesses that can be accommodated per unit of time. Many users will put multiple disk drives on the same controller because it is less expensive, but this configuration forces a queuing situation to develop for files that are connected to controllers that can access one disk at a time (some controllers can read to one and write to another). Instead of a new or different CPU to perform database accesses, all that may be needed to improve throughput at the database accessing site is to add more peripheral controllers in parallel and reconfigure the database so that more accesses are available per unit of time. If database accesses must be queued because of the volume of accessing required, the response-time values increase, and the recovery problems that can occur as the result of a failure at the central site are also increased significantly.

**POINT-TO-POINT VERSUS MULTIPOINT LINES** We saw in Chapter 6 that only one terminal on a line can be transmitting or receiving at a time (except for broadcast addressing, where there is still only one transmitter, but two or more receivers may get the message simultaneously). Therefore, in the case of a multidrop line, if one terminal is busy, another cannot transmit at the same time. Even with the use of full/full-duplex protocols, only one terminal can transmit while a different terminal receives. If two terminals have to transmit at the same time, one must wait its turn while the other finishes its transmission or reception. Terminal queuing is an important factor to consider. It is possible that the multiplexing techniques described in Chapter 11 can be used to give each location the capability of point-to-point connections even though single high-speed long-distance lines are still used; so the response-time analysis must also consider the response-time requirements at each location, the length of messages to be transmitted, and the possible queuing that would occur during low traffic times, average traffic times, and peak traffic periods.

**LENGTH OF TRANSMISSION** It is obvious that the length of transmission must be considered in the response time, because even with different transmission rates the total amount of information must still be moved. As the messages get longer over a fixed capacity transmission line (regardless of the speed), the response time must increase. Transmissions should not necessarily be shortened, since that may not be operationally feasible, but the applications should be investigated to make sure that the transmissions are the most efficient for that application. Excess data transmission should be avoided at all locations because the excess data will have to be transmitted not only from the terminal to the first node, but also on every path it must take to get to the final destination.

One of the most flagrant abuses of this factor is the transmission of entire screens of data when only the variable portions must be sent. Fixed-screen formats are typical examples. It means more programming in the beginning with its additional expense; but it is only a one-time cost, whereas higher-speed lines and equipment are a continuing monthly expense or, at best, a higher one-time communications equipment purchase cost. All potential software effort that would reduce overall communication line time requirements should at least be considered.

**DIAL-UP CIRCUITS VERSUS POINT TO POINT** If a system utilizes dial-up circuits, the dial-up time, connection time, and answer of the circuit time (handshaking) must all be included in the response time. These cases are point to point, where the terminal usually dials the site to be accessed directly (the central site could also dial out to remotes but there would still only be a single path). The time it takes to establish the dial-up connection must be included in the response time for at least the response to the first transmission. Once a circuit has been established, subsequent transmissions (during the time the circuit is there) will only require consideration of the other factors described for leased-line circuits.

***PROPAGATION DELAYS***   Here propagation refers to the propagation of electrical signal, not the data transmission rate, and it is only significant when you have very long transmission distances to cover. The most common of these is for a satellite, where absolute minimum round-trip times are on the order of 600 ms. In practical situations today a satellite response time with a single satellite hop is on the order of one to two seconds. A propagation delay is time over and above the data transmission rate, because regardless of what the data transmission rate is, it still takes the same amount of time for the signal to reach a satellite, be retransmitted to the receiving station where an access is made, and then return via the same path. For applications where two or three satellite hops are to be accommodated, the system designer must not only look at the propagation delay with its impact on response time, but at the impact on the error-handling procedures that may occur on any leg of the total transmission path. The satellite problem is not an easy one to solve and was discussed further in Chapter 19.

***PRIORITY HANDLING***   For systems with two or more priority levels, the sequence and time frames for the different priorities must be established so that a projected queuing sequence can be set up and the user can be made aware of the probability of queues being delayed due to higher-priority messages. Priority analysis must be made for transmissions *from* terminals as well as *to* terminals and must also be reviewed for node-to-node transmission and node-to-central site transmission. Remember, priorities may not only be on a message basis, but also on line or terminal address, which gets even more complex when you consider multidrop circuits along with the unique message priorities.

***AVERAGE VERSUS PEAK LOADS***   Although we have discussed some related impacts on the preceding items, average and peak loading must also be considered as a separate entity. The reason for this separate consideration is the impact on the design of the system relative to the implementation of point-to-point circuits, multidrop circuits, and multiplexing requirements. Many operational situations have maximum response time needs even during the peak load situations. The user should be aware, however, that to design a system for peak load handling may be extremely expensive because of the excess unused capacity available during the time that peak load handling is not required. To alleviate this situation, if possible, it might be more advisable to schedule the work load so that the peaks of the peak load times are not as high relative to the average load as they might otherwise be. Functions that do not have to be done at certain times should be moved to off-peak times, which is usually opposed by data processing departments because of the added work load, but the overall savings to the organization could be substantial.

**QUALITY OF TRANSMISSION MEDIA**   Transmission media quality is very often ignored. Most users assume that transmission facilities are the same regardless of the locations connected because the telephone company must meet the same basic set of requirements at all locations, but this is definitely not true. The basic criteria for data transmission can be met with different kinds of facilities that have their own inherent error rates as well as different facilities (usually newer versus older). Even at one location, the quality of the lines can vary significantly, which means that one of them may exhibit a much higher volume of errors than another. Each location and its connection to the local telephone company serving office must be evaluated separately because the local loops usually have the most problems. For locations where the error rate is higher, the system designer must include those factors in the response time calculation. Each time a message is transmitted, if there is an error, it must be retransmitted unless a forward error correcting code is used, but then, too, the length of the message will have a substantial impact on the response time if it must be retransmitted.

**TYPE OF APPLICATION**   Some response time calculations are affected by the particular application that must be processed. In some cases information has to be obtained from different locations and assembled prior to a response. Other applications require a certain amount of physical data processing on the information being obtained. For those types of functions, the time for calculation, assembly, and so on, must be included in the anticipated response time.

**SPEED OF OUTPUT DEVICE**   Output device speed is only pertinent when a printing device with a limited printing speed is used. If the information to be used starts at the beginning of the print cycle, in most cases, except for Teletypes, the response time will not change. But there are other applications in which the information to be used is in the middle or at the end of the response message. If the response is printed out on a printer that has a limited print speed (characters per second versus lines per minute), the total response time consideration must include the total of the time for initial input plus the print time it takes to get to the area of the response that the operator has requested.

The preceding factors have the most significant impact on response time, but the user and designer must always be aware that individual applications and operations can have additonal factors that may affect the response time. Any additional time required by the operator, transmission facilities, or data processing facilities between the time the enter key is depressed and the usable information begins to display at the operator's location increases the reponse time and must therefore be factored into the response time considerations.

The factors described here are oriented toward a network using carrier facilities. With the tremendous growth of the PC and its integration into LANs, there is another whole series of response time characteristics that must be considered just for LANs. A PC on a LAN communicating through a gateway to a remote location through the carrier network is subject to most of the previously described factors. However, if the PC is part of a LAN that contains all of the necessary processing sites, databases, printers, and servers, then response time must be determined for that particular network alone, with the specific limitations imposed by the network components. Usually the response time on a LAN is dependent almost exclusively on the ability of the *server* devices to respond to users. Another area that is becoming important is the access and utilization of files that must be assembled from multiple servers in a network, which may take more time than originally anticipated because of file size and the limited transmission size allowed on the LAN. These problems must be solved on an application-by-application basis, not on a LAN-by-LAN basis. Multiple users on the same LAN may have different requirements for processing their applications.

As one last point here, one of the primary limiting factors in LAN use is the *print server,* if the printer is not fast enough to keep up with all of the network users who share it. Faster printers (like laser printers) may partially solve the problem, but you should also consider what would happen if the printer failed. Some users provide extensive buffering at the printer location to absorb the peak loads, but careful calculations must be made first so that optimum use is obtained from the printer without spending too much for the extra buffering and software to handle it.

## D
## CAPACITY/THROUGHPUT

Many factors affect the capacity and throughput of a data communications system. The most obvious is the transmission rate of information on the communication lines between the central and remote sites. Transmission rate has a further limitation in those configurations where terminals are multidropped on the line because only one remote location on the multidrop line can transmit at one time. Therefore, it is not really just the capability or capacity of a terminal controller but the quantity of terminal controllers on any one line and the volume of traffic that they will generate.

Another area, which is not as obvious as the first, is the capability of the central site hardware to handle multiple incoming and outgoing communication lines. Regardless of the speed of the lines and the capabilities of the terminals on those lines, if the central site hardware cannot handle the lines simultaneously, the capacity of that particular system is seriously degraded. Factors such as communications software design, availability of peripheral storage and buffer areas in main memory, and types of protocol all have differing effects on the potential capacity of the system, regardless of the size of the front end communications handling CPUs. Since there is an extremely wide variety of hardware and software capabilities for different machines, and good comparative methods are not available, this section will deal with the capacity and throughput of the primary limitation of transmission capability, which is the potential capacity of a communication line itself.

Describing a communications line in terms of its transmission speed is actually a method of specifying the absolute maximum instantaneous data rate. That speed, however, is not attainable on a continuous basis because of overhead transmission requirements (polls and calls) and errors that cause retransmission of the same information. The parameter of real importance is how many usable characters of information can be transmitted per second.

The term usually used to describe the effective rate of information transfer is *transmission rate of information bits* (TRIB), which is a measure of the effective quantity of true information transmitted over a communication line per unit time. The TRIB depends on the various components that make up the communication line. The efficient use of those components is also important because different modes of utilization have a different impact on the TRIB, such as the type of protocol and the error detection and correction techniques.

To calculate the throughput of a particular communication line we will consider a point-to-point case in which a transmission line is terminated with a modem at either end and a data processing device on the digital side of the modem. A specific formula has been derived by various network designers to take into account the significant parameters affecting the information-carrying capacity of a communication line. The formula is

$$TRIB = \frac{B(L - C)(1 - P)}{L/R + T}$$

Where TRIB = net quantity of information bits (true rate of information bits) that are effectively transmitted per unit time (in this case, seconds)
   $B$ = number of information bits per character
   $L$ = total block length in characters
   $C$ = average number of noninformation characters per block (overhead characters like the SDLC frame characters)
   $P$ = probability of an error occurring in a particular block
   $R$ = modem transmission speed in characters per second
   $T$ = time interval between blocks of the transmission in seconds

This equation has been derived by a number of sources and is applicable to both full- and half-duplex operations for one-way transmissions. For a system that has yet to be designed, this particular equation can be used to calculate an optimum-sized block length. The equation shows that TRIB increases as the block length increases until a specific point is reached, at which time the TRIB will begin to decrease as the block length increases. The point at which the TRIB is the maximum is the optimum block size. For determining the effective throughput on an already existing system, all one has to do is plug in the different parameters in the equation to determine the effective data throughput on that particular communication line.

For a half-duplex protocol, where each block transmitted is separated by the time it takes for an acknowledge to be received, the $T$ parameter will decrease the effective data throughput significantly. The bisync protocol is a half-duplex protocol and can be measured in this mode. For a full-duplex protocol such as SDLC, the $T$ parameter disappears as long as continuous transmission is taking place. If, over a period of time, occasions arise where the seven-block maximum transmission takes place from one end to the other before an acknowledgment has been received, then some factor for $T$ must be included in the equation (on some form of average basis depending on observed characteristics). The only function that is of a random nature in this equation is $P$, which is the probability of error. Also, since errors on a communications line occur in bursts, the fact that there are multiple bit errors does not mean that multiple blocks will have to be transmitted. Typically, however, using a block length of approximately 400 characters, $P$ for a typical communication line can be assumed to be, for calculation purposes, 0.01 (one message out of a hundred will probably be in error) but it should also be recognized that $P$ could vary over a very wide range, which has a substantial impact on the TRIB. For a full-duplex case, we have a calculation with the following assumptions:

$B$ = 7 information bits per character (ASCII code)
$L$ = 400 characters
$C$ = 10 overhead characters per block
$P$ = 0.01
$R$ = 300 characters per second (CPS) (2400 BPS synchronous)
$T$ = 0 (this is a full-duplex link where continuous transmissions are occurring in one direction)

Performing the calculation we get the following equation:

$$\text{TRIB} = \frac{7(400 - 10)\,(1 - 0.01)}{400/300 + 0} = 2027 \text{ BPS}$$

As can be seen, the effective throughput at 2400 BPS, even with continuous transmission, is 2027 BPS.

One additional factor must be considered here, and that is the case specifically for SDLC. Because SDLC does not retransmit only the error block, but the error block and all subsequent blocks that have been retransmitted, a slightly different formula must be used for SDLC. The SDLC formula will take into account the fact that multiple blocks may be retransmitted when an error occurs because of the *go back-N technique*. The formula to be used is as follows:

$$\text{TRIB}_{\text{SDLC}} = \frac{B(L - C)\,(1 - NP)}{L/R + T}$$

As can be seen, the formula differs only by the addition of $N$, which stands for the average number of blocks that must be retransmitted. For typical point-to-point circuits where continuous communication is involved, $N$ has been observed to be on the order of magnitude of 2. Using this factor, we can now calculate the effective SDLC throughput using the same parameters as in the previous example:

$$ \text{TRIB}_{\text{SDLC}} = \frac{7[400 - 10]\ [1 - (2)\ (.01)]}{400/300 + 0} = 2007 \text{ BPS} $$

In this case we have an effective throughput of 2007 BPS. Also, for these particular parameters, as $N$ increases, the effective throughput will go down by approximately 20 BPS for each additional block of information that must be retransmitted. Since $N$ can be a maximum of 7, the effective throughput can be reduced by more than 100 BPS as long as continuous transmission is maintained. If such a case arises where seven blocks are transmitted and an additional wait time is required before the acknowledgment is received, the entire equation must be recalculated to further include the $T$ factor (continuous retransmission of multiple blocks is extremely rare and should therefore not be given much weight during analysis).

The SDLC calculations shown here are for point-to-point continuous transmissions. In the case of the multidrop lines, the probability is substantially increased for more blocks to be retransmitted when an error occurs, because the central site may be transmitting to one remote terminal while receiving from another remote terminal, meaning continuous two-way transmission between the same two points is not taking place, which complicates the calculation. Multidrop lines must really be analyzed as to observed characteristics, rather than with a quantitative calculation where the parameters can be more easily identified and specified. The other factors that must be considered are polling and calling, which are required to determine whether individual remote sites have messages to transmit or whether they are in a condition to receive messages. The particular timing sequence, and the timing used to answer the polls and calls when there is no information to be transmitted, are a function of software and add to the time between message blocks. It is necessary to use measured characteristics for determining what the poll/call cycle times are to calculate the impact on line capacity.

When the anticipated loading on a line is relatively light and then begins to increase, the calculated capacity can be used to determine when a new line will be needed. Note, however, that the parameter $P$ increases as the transmission rate increases, and if observed characteristics so indicate, it might be advisable to reduce the transmission rate to something like 4800 BPS, because a lower error rate may actually increase the TRIB, depending on the quality of the communication lines. In many installations the effective throughput has been demonstrated to be better at 4800 BPS than at 9600 BPS because of the difference in error rates encountered. If a modem vendor, for example, insists its device will truly come close to doubling a throughput with a doubling of transmission speed, ask the vendor to sponsor a test in your specific environment to prove the capability assertion.

Another factor, which may possibly completely override the line capacity calculation, is the fact that the traffic load may be so low that transmission rate capacity is a negligible parameter. Low traffic flow usually permits multidrop operation, which increases response time, but really does not affect the actual transmission time of bits between the central site and the remote once transmission starts. Because of the overhead functions that must occur on each line for line control and error detection and correction, it is really the processing capacity at the central site communications line interface that contributes to the reduced transmission capability on an overall line basis instead of just an individual BPS basis on an individual group of lines. The transmission speed for the existing lines can actually increase and yet have relatively minor impact on the computer capacity; but if a new line is added, even at a lower transmission rate, its impact may be very significant.

## E
## NETWORK MODELING

Over the years many vendors have tried to develop software to design a network after being given the operational parameters. To date, none of them have been shown to work very well. There are two basic kinds of design models: the analytical model and the simulation model. The *analytical model,* which uses a mathematical formula to approximate responses, is relatively fast and good for implementation on PCs. The *simulation model,* which mimics the actions of the network hardware and software, is a more precise method than the analytical model, but it takes a large amount of CPU processing cycles and typically must be done on a mainframe.

Modeling packages are available into which you can incorporate an already existing network and then calculate the effects of various potential changes in parameters. The model is actually a replica of the existing network in mathematical form. Typically, these packages run in the neighborhood of $100,000 each for a mainframe-based product and $50,000–100,000 per year for a time-shared product. That cost is just for the use of the program, to which you must add the necessary time to enter network traffic parameters, which could be a major investment.

These packages can give you a performance analysis of your network and can optimize the topology utilizing the various forms of network connection, such as multidrop, multiplex, concentration, or packet. If you also want a cost analysis, you must incorporate the current tariff data for all of the vendors you are using. Since this data changes on a continuous basis, you are again looking at another significant investment of time and effort to keep that database updated.

Two of the organizations that have packages like these are IBM and AT&T. The IBM program (called SNAP/SHOT) simulates the performance of IBM systems only. Others are available, but before you use them you need to know what the ongoing expense of operating that program will be. You would be better off taking a look at your network once every 12 to 18 months with *SNAP/SHOT* to see if there are any significant areas that need to be changed. It is not a bad idea to examine your network at least that often anyway, because with fast changing applications and products your operations 12 to 18 months from now may be quite different from what they are today. Not only might you take better advantage of existing facilities, but you may be in a position to incorporate new products and services that could further optimize your network expense. As described in Chapter 22, if 80 percent of your network expenditure is in the facilities, would that not be the best place to look when you need to optimize network costs?

## QUESTIONS

1. What is the primary trade-off when evaluating centralized versus decentralized processing? What are some of the secondary parameters?
2. Describe five significant criteria that must be included when establishing a set of communication system design requirements.
3. Define response time. Describe six factors that affect response time.
4. What are some of the factors that affect the capacity and throughput of a communications system?
5. Compare the capabilities of the two primary kinds of network design models.

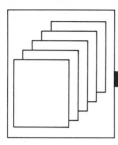

# 24

# System Implementation and Support

## BACKGROUND

When implementing a data communications system, certain functions, although they may appear to be peripheral in nature, have a very strong bearing on the successful operation of the system. They involve documentation, standards, procedures, personnel, and vendor interfacing. Without the appropriate documentation for personnel to refer to, a communications system is destined to be down for much longer periods of time than necessary. The establishment of standards for both procurement and operational interfaces is mandatory for orderly growth or expansion of the system. At the same time, a definitive and detailed set of procedures is necessary for maintaining and operating the equipment. The appropriate personnel must be hired and trained so that they are aware of the operational considerations, not only for the communications system but also for the user's applications. Last but not least are the vendor-support interface requirements, which must be established and maintained early in the implementation sequence. Many problems can only be resolved with the vendor's help, and if an appropriate path is not established early, the system will be down for longer periods than necessary.

# B

## DOCUMENTATION

The primary area where system implementors fail in their responsibility is in the generation and maintenance of appropriate documentation. No design can take place unless the requirements are specified and all the design personnel know what they are, which can only be done by documenting the requirements and making the documentation available to designers. During the design phase all changes, additions, and deletions must be integrated into the documentation as they occur, or different designers will be designing to different requirements. As new requirements and specifications are established, they too must be documented so that there is a continuous record of what is happening in the development of the system, and all designers must be made aware of those changes. It is an outright fallacy, as proven by the experience of almost all designers, to believe that changes to existing documentation can be assembled externally to the document and upgraded later. As a practical fact, this almost never gets done, and during the interim different people have different versions of what is supposed to be the same document.

In many cases it is advisable to establish a separate internal organization that has the sole responsibility for maintenance and upkeep of system documentation. No document can be considered correct unless that document matches what is in the central source or library. Individuals assigned the responsibility of keeping the documentation updated must make sure that the changes are continually fed into the central library, because the central library will then provide copies of that documentation to other users. The "central library" can be just a bookcase, but some centralized location must be established as the master document location.

A significant problem that usually arises with documentation is the actual implementation of changes. There can only be one person or one specific group authorized to change the documentation. Whatever review cycles are used, there must be a signoff to changes to the basic documentation. Even though changes may appear to be desirable, they must be incorporated through the appropriate change-control organization so that an accurate record of how many changes and what they are can be maintained. As a general rule, it is usually grossly inefficient to add or change requirements during the design phase unless there is an outright error in the original design. The implementation and integration of the changes means that the original design will be delayed and, in most cases, that the acceptance criteria will be changing at the same time. The best procedure to use is to keep potential changes in a separate "to be implemented" list, and only after the basic system is operational should the changes be implemented. A side advantage is that the changes can usually be combined so that the total amount of effort involved in installing them is less than it would have been if they had been done one at a time. Many of them may affect the same areas of hardware and software design.

At the top of the list of required basic documentation must be the *functional specifications*. The functional specifications, defined from a user-level point of view, is what the system is supposed to be doing when it is operational. A separate subset of specifications is needed for the communications network, applications processing, database, and software for both on-line and off-line functions.

The next level of specification is the *hardware design specification,* which defines the design criteria for each piece of hardware that will go into the system—devices such as the CPU, controllers, modems, tech control, test equipment, communications media, power sources, peripherals, recovery hardware, and cabling. Each specification must be defined so that it meets the overall functional specifications. Also, each must be validated so that it is compatible with the other hardware items being specified.

The third level of system documentation is the *system design specification* for both hardware and software. These specifications establish the detailed design specifications for implementing the functions defined under functional specifications, and include such items as the I/O system, restart/recovery, formats, forms control, protocols, statistics gathering, editing requirements, routing, file management, system start/load, the transaction processing subsystem, the database management subsystem, the file management organization, the details of the applications, and the support software. Also included within the system design specifications are the hardware/software interfaces, such as the controllers, communication line interfaces, peripheral interfaces, and network connectivity requirements.

The next level of documentation involves *facilities specifications,* which include such functions as power distribution, cable ducting, environmental controls, floor loading, fire and smoke detection, security access, storage, libraries, and the repair and maintenance criteria. The specific layouts must also include appropriate locations for personnel to provide the necessary operation and maintenance functions for the system.

Included also within the documentation requirements are the *system operational and maintenance specifications,* which describe the requirements for operating the system and the levels of operational capability that must be maintained. Such functions as MTBF (Mean Time Between Failure), MTTR (Mean Time to Repair), and UTR (Up Time Ratio) are some of the parameters that can be specified here.

Any other document that specifies the requirements for a particular application or activity must be defined in a specification for that function. Without a clear, concise, and comprehensive set of specifications the actual system design activity may be completed with errors or the absence of required functions. It is up to the system designer to determine that all of the basic requirements called out in the functional specifications are truly included in both the hardware and system design specification.

# C

# PROCEDURES

Along with the specification documentation, there is another set of documents that is every bit as important, the procedures required to physically implement the applications once the system has been designed and is operational. Primary among these are the *operating procedures,* which describe in extreme detail the step-by-step sequences of operations that must be performed by the operators to accomplish each specific application inherent in the system. Operational procedures are designed to describe the way the system should run if it is running correctly. If there are errors or malfunctions in the system, another set of procedures must be implemented: the *error procedures.*

Error procedures are the steps that must be taken if the system does not operate in accordance with the operational procedures. They must be exercised first so that alternative operations can be implemented to accomplish the application if backup facilities are available. Error-handling procedures are different from the error-detection and diagnostic procedures that are used to isolate and correct problems.

A complete set of diagnostic procedures is necessary for each area of the system, as well as for the system as a whole. Once the system procedures for diagnosing a problem have isolated the problem in a specific subsystem, the subsystem procedure can be used to further isolate the specific problem. In the case of a communications network, where the actual facilities being tested may not be in a local environment, it is necessary to have a comprehensive set of test equipment and substitution facilities that will allow for the replacement of potentially defective components (such as modems) with spare units so that quicker isolation of the problem can be done.

Another set of procedures that is every bit as important as the operational and maintenance procedures are the *change control procedures.* Without a specific sequence for the change control process, it is possible to have different versions of the same document existing at the same time, and there will be cases of personnel being unaware of the changes because they did not know that somebody else was making them. Part of the requirement for all procedures, therefore, is to make sure that changes are incorporated immediately when issued and identified as to the level and date of the change incorporation.

Although they involve a procedure and a specification, the preventive maintenance (PM) requirements and procedures must be adhered to, not only to ensure that the system components remain within the appropriate warranties, but to prevent failures that result during normal system operations. Typical PM procedures are applicable to peripherals with mechanical components, but they also apply to data processing equipment, especially in the communications area where there can be degradation of components or facilities over a period of time.

## D
## STANDARDS

To design a system with minimal interfacing problems among the various subsystems such as communications, applications, and database, a set of standards must be established that provide definition of what is supposed to take place when those functions interface with each other. Interface standards include not only the physical interfacing, but also the electrical signal interfacing and the functional interfaces.

There must typically be common hardware standards, such as for the processors, disks, magnetic tapes, modems, and terminal interfaces, all of which allow the necessary traffic to move from one device to another as well as from one physical location to another. In the software area, another set of standards must be established for such functions as file structures, I/O access methods, directory structures, audit control software, security, privacy, recovery, diagnostics, program languages, forms, edits, and software module interfaces.

With respect to network standards, there must be standard code sets, formats, protocols, queuing, and physical electrical level interfaces such as RS232C, which allow the user to interface with external communications equipment. Many specific network standards have been defined throughout this text for interfaces dealing with such functions as modems/terminals, user interface/packet network, and specific message protocols.

## E
## PERSONNEL

Another area of critical implementation sensitivity is the need for sufficient trained personnel to operate and maintain the system. Independent of system users, there are two functions that the operational personnel must perform, operations and maintenance. During the times of normal system operation, there may be relatively little activity for the personnel to perform, other than to make sure the appropriate operational capabilities exist when a particular application must be accomplished.

When the system begins to degrade or actually malfunction the capability of the operational personnel is most critical. They must be able to isolate, define, and then correct any problems that are degrading the performance of the system. In most organizations, very few people pay much attention to system operation when all is going well, but when the system is malfunctioning all eyes and pressure are on the applicable maintenance personnel to correct the problem as soon as possible, especially in systems where on-line, real-time applications are taking place. For all of the time the system is either degraded or nonoperational, operators are nonproductive, and business is probably being lost.

The best way to ensure that the system is maintained in an operational state is to hire and train experienced personnel. The basic background must include familiarity with the function to be performed, and then the using organization can add the necessary local or in-house training to adapt the capabilities and background of the individual to the requirements of the organization. The key, however, is the availability of adequate and comprehensive material and competent instructors. It is extremely difficult for new personnel, even though they may be experienced in the appropriate discipline, to adapt to a new system without training, and to understand not only the specific system components for which they will be responsible, but how those components relate to the overall organizational use and application.

The actual education can start either on an in-house basis or externally with classes. Many vendors offer classes to using organizations on either a low- or minimum-cost basis that train operations personnel in the use of individual pieces of hardware. It is up to the using organization, however, to provide the training as to how those hardware and software elements are used to accomplish the actual system applications.

For those personnel to whom the basic disciplines are known adequately, the best training is OJT (on the job training). OJT can be augmented by classroom exercises that incorporate the use of equipment in the environment in which it is actually being used.

In addition, overview course material can be presented either on an in-house or external basis, even for experienced personnel, so that their own particular job functions can be viewed in the context of the overall system operation. Individuals may obtain this type of education as a group or on a self-study basis as long as there is adequate material and instructional personnel to answer any questions that may arise. Many of the procedures and techniques used by experienced personnel have only been discovered because they have performed the same job at other locations or for a period of time at the present location. It would be extremely desirable to document procedures as they evolve so that future personnel can have the benefit of the experience of those people who have already developed system expertise.

As it pertains specifically to the communications environment, the real-world situation is such that very few people are available who have the appropriate background and knowledge to maintain a large network. As such, they are very hard to find and keep after they have obtained even more experience. It is therefore necessary to provide the appropriate incentives, both monetary and professional, to retain personnel in whom a significant investment in time and effort has been made.

One other major function must be discussed with regard to personnel requirements: organization. The organization as it refers to a communications network must be set up to function 24 hours a day, seven days a week, since most network environments are operational 24 hours a day. Even though the utilization may not be high during certain times, the potential for failure is the same at all times. There must be appropriate shift coverage not only for the standard five-day week but also for the weekends, even if it is on a limited basis, because dedicated communication facilities can degrade or fail at any time. The use of automated monitoring and test equipment may reduce the amount of personnel required for maintenance. In most cases, where systems have 16 lines or more, automated test equipment, even though there may be a high initial cost, will probably pay for itself within a year or two due to reduced personnel and the reduced cost involved in isolating and correcting problems over a period of time.

The organization responsible for system operation and maintenance must have a clear-cut path of authority for correcting problems within its own environment and a very specific path for correcting problems in which other organizations are involved. At the same time, there must also be a good working relationship with the system users and designers, because many problems can arise that are operational and not due to the failure or malfunction of any specific piece of hardware or software. Appropriate chains of command must be established so that they are clear and known to all operating personnel. It is also necessary to identify the contact personnel in other using organizations so that if specific line managers are not available the necessary coordination for correction of interdisciplinary problems can continue. Naturally, specific procedures must be written and adhered to for correction of those problems that affect other organizations, especially where there is the possibility for either degradation or absence of service for a period of time.

## F
## VENDOR INTERFACING

Last but not least in the system implementation and support area is the interface requirement for dealing with vendors. Vendors include hardware, software, network, and system suppliers who provide either a product or a service to the using organization. It is mandatory to establish the appropriate communication links between the various vendors and using organizations, and, depending on the specific implementation, it may also be necessary to establish communication links between some of the vendors directly. It is very common for the user to experience problems for which a vendor does not want to take responsibility, whether for technical or financial reasons. It is therefore necessary to have a very good in-house understanding of vendors' products or services so that a strong case can be made for identifying a particular vendor as the cause of the problem. It is also very common for a particular problem to be the fault of more than one vendor, and in some instances the user may be a part of the problem. Again, it is mandatory to have a good understanding of the overall system so that the appropriate vendors can be identified to fix such problems.

If there are problems in which multiple vendors are potentially involved, a procedure must be established whereby all the involved vendors can be brought together to try to solve the problem. It does no good to have one vendor at a time try to solve the problem, because it will take no responsibility for the other vendor's product or service; therefore, a problem may still exist even though one vendor has done all it can do for its own product. The user must also have a qualified representative to make any necessary interface decisions, because during the time the vendors are discussing the problem, the user is the one who has the degraded or nonexistent operational capability.

As an additional level of management control, the necessary communication paths to the various levels of vendor management organizations must also be established, because maintenance personnel often do not have the authority to make changes involving either time or money. Many times problems must be solved by the addition of new facilities, extra modification to existing facilities, new software, or additional time utilization, which the vendor site personnel do not have the authority to order. If critical problems arise involving significant user impact, it is necessary to have immediate access to the appropriate vendor management levels so that at least interim authorization can permit resumption of operation. It should also be recognized that all applicable documentation generated by the vendor due to changes that arise as a result of the maintenance activity must be made available to both the vendor's site personnel and the user personnel so that in the future the same problem can be corrected more quickly.

On the subject of vendors, you have to keep an open mind. Many promises are made with good intentions, but many times the commitments cannot be met. Through all of these situations, a variety of vendor claims and comments has been developed. So with a little humor we can end the text on an upbeat note with a list of some of those vendors' claims.

"It looks different, but it's an exact replacement."
"You'll never need a spare."
"The end user will never see the difference."
"The software will be upward-compatible with all new releases."
"It is a very simple upgrade."
"It is not the cost that is important."
"The documentation is complete."
"The system is very user friendly."
"Anyone can understand and follow the manuals."
"The documentation will follow shortly."
"It can be easily modified in the field after delivery."
"Didn't you know there was a modification charge?"
"The estimates are very conservative."
"We are testing the fix now."
"The software was fully checked out at the factory."
"We are just a phone call away."
"All we have to do is put a few more people on it."

"It is the other vendor's fault, not ours."

"It can't happen in our system."

"Your order is next in the queue."

"Your order will be shipped first thing tomorrow morning."

"Your version is not supported anymore."

"The warranty does not cover your situation."

"You should have told us sooner."

"The software has *hooks* for all the additional features you will need."

"It is an interface problem, not our hardware."

"Your delivery will be delayed because our vendors are late."

"Management is working on the problem."

"It is our people who make the difference."

"The discount is only good until the close of business today."

"Your system is an off-the-shelf configuration."

"This is the best package for the money in town."

"Trust us, we know exactly what you need."

"The year-old equipment you have has no trade-in value."

"If you sign the order now there is a better chance of getting the changes."

"You are our most important customer."

## QUESTIONS

1. Describe at least four levels of documentation required to support a communications system. What is the biggest problem facing the maintenance of these documents?

2. Describe four types of procedures required to effectively implement a communications system.

3. Describe four types of standards involved in communications networks.

4. Describe three methods for providing training to communications personnel.

5. Describe a method that can reduce vendor interfacing problems to a minimum.

6. Can you add five more common "vendor claims"?

# Organization Addresses

**American National Standards Institute**
1430 Broadway
New York, New York 10010
(212) 354-3471
(ISO standards are also available from ANSI)

**AT&T Technologies Commercial Sales**
P.O. Box 19901
Indianapolis, IN 46219
(800) 432-6600
AT&T Publications

**Canadian Standards Association (CSA)**
178 Rexdale Blvd.
Toronto, Ontario M9W 1R3
(416) 744-4044
(ANSI and ISO standards are available from the CSA)

**CCITT**
General Secretariat
International Telecommunications Union
Place des Nations
1211 Geneva 20, Switzerland

**Electrical and Electronic Manufacturing Association**
One Yonge Street
Suite 1600

Toronto, Ontario M5E 1R1
(416) 862-7152

**Electronic Industries Association** (EIA Standards)
2001 Eye Street N.W.
Washington, D.C. 20006
(202) 457-4966

**European Computer Manufacturers Association** (ECMA Standards)
114, Rue de Rhone
CH-1204 Geneva, Switzerland
Tele: 41 22 35-36-34

**Institute of Electrical and Electronic Engineers** (IEEE)
345 East 47th Street
New York, New York 10017
(212) 705-7900

**International Organization for Standardization** (ISO)
Central Secretariat
1, Rue de Varembe
1204 Geneva, Switzerland
(ISO standards may be purchased from CSA or ANSI)

# APPENDIX B

## Data Communications Reference Texts

Black, Uyless D. *Data Communications and Distributed Networks,* 2nd ed. Reston, Va.: Reston Publishers, 1987.

Folts, Harold C., ed. *McGraw-Hill's Compilation of Data Communications Standards,* 2nd rev. ed. New York: McGraw-Hill Book Company, 1983.

Kruglinski, David. The Osbourne-McGraw-Hill *Guide to IBM PC Communications.* New York: Osbourne/McGraw-Hill Book Company.

Martin, James. *Computer Networks and Distributed Processing: Software, Techniques, and Architecture.* Englewood Cliffs, N.J.: Prentice Hall, 1981.

Martin, James. *Introduction to Teleprocessing.* Englewood Cliffs, N.J.: Prentice Hall, 1972.

McNamara, John E. *Technical Aspects of Data Communication,* 2nd ed. Digital Press—Digital Equipment Corporation, 1982.

Seyer, Martin D. *RS-232 Made Easy: Connecting Computers, Printers, Terminals, and Modems.* Englewood Cliffs, N.J.: Prentice Hall, 1984.

Stallings, William. *Local Networks: An Introduction.* New York: Macmillan Publishing Co., Inc., 1987.

# Glossary

A

**Access method**  A software/hardware method of transferring data between host-resident application programs and remote devices. This term is usually used to describe communications software residing in a mainframe computer.

**ACD, automatic call distributor**  A switching system that automatically distributes incoming calls in the sequences they are received to a centralized group of receivers without human interface. If no receivers are available, the calls will be held until one becomes free.

**ACK or acknowledge**  A character or sequence of characters sent by a receiver to notify a sender that the last message was received correctly. ACK is also sent by a remote device as a "go-ahead" response to a selection sequence.

**Acoustic coupler**  A type of modem that permits use of a telephone handset as a connection to the public telephone network for data transmission by means of sound transducers.

**Adaptive differential pulse code modulation**  One of the methods of pulse code modulation utilized in digitizing an analog signal (32 KBPS is typical).

**Adaptive equalization**  A modem feature allowing it to automatically compensate for distortions on the line.

**Adaptive predictive coding**  A methodology used in compressing digitized voice signals.

**ADCCP, Advanced Data Communications Control Protocol**  A communications protocol endorsed by the American National Standards Institute.

**ADPCM**  *See* Adaptive differential pulse code modulation.

**Algorithm**   A prescribed set of well-defined rules or processes for arriving at a solution to a problem. A mathematical process.

**Alphanumeric**   Made up of letters (alphabetic) and numbers (numeric).

**Alternative route**   A secondary communications path used to reach a destination if the primary path is unavailable.

**AM, amplitude modulation**   Transmission of information on a communications line by varying the voltage level or amplitude.

**Ambient noise**   Signal interference that is present on a communications line at all times (background noise).

**Amplifier**   A device that increases the power or amplitude of a signal.

**Amplitude variation (ripple)**   Unwanted variation of signal voltage at different frequencies on a communications line.

**Analog signal**   A signal that changes in a nondiscrete manner (smooth transitioning to different levels).

**Answer back**   A transmission from a receiving data processing device in response to a request from a transmitting data processing device that it is ready to accept or has received data.

**APC**   *See* Adaptive predictive coding.

**Application program**   The computer program that performs a data processing rather than a control function.

**ARPANET**   A network installed in the 1970s that became the forerunner of packet switched networks.

**ARQ, automatic retransmission request**   A generic description of a protocol mechanism that involves retransmission of message blocks received in error. There are several types of ARQ operation.

**ASCII, American Standard Code for Information Interchange**   A data communications code set.

**ASR**   Automatic send-receive. Typically pertains to teleprinter equipment.

**Asynchronous**   A data transmission which does not require a separate clock signal for the reception of data. In code sets, character codes containing start and stop bits.

**Asynchronous transmission** (start–stop transmission)   Provides transmission of one character at a time with a start bit and one or more stop bits appended on each one. Any amount of time can elapse before the next character can be sent.

**Attenuation**   Loss of communication signal energy.

**Audio frequencies**   Frequencies that can be heard by the average human ear, usually between 15 and 20,000 Hz.

**Automatic dialer**   A device that will automatically dial telephone numbers on the network. Operation of the dialer may be manual or automatic.

**AWG, American Wire Gauge**   Wire size standard used in communications line media descriptions.


## B

**Backup**   The hardware and software resources available to recover from a degradation or failure of one or more system components.

**Backward channel** (also called reverse channel)  A channel used for sending data in the opposite direction of the primary (forward) channel. The backward channel is usually used for sending data at low speeds for either control purposes or keyboard data.

**Balanced circuit**  A circuit terminated by a network whose impedance balances the impedance of the line so that the return losses are negligible.

**Bandwidth**  The information carrying capability of a communications channel or line.

**Baseband**  The frequency band occupied by individual information bearing signals before they are combined with a carrier in the modulation process. In LANs, one transmitting device at a time on the circuit.

**Base group**  Twelve communications paths capable of carrying the human voice on a telephone set. A unit of frequency-division multiplexing systems bandwidth allocation.

**Baud**  Data communication rate unit taken from the name Baudot. Defined as the number of signal level changes per second regardless of the information content of those signals.

**Baudot**  A five-level code set named for the early French telegrapher who invented it. International Telegraph Alphabet (ITA) Number 2 is the formal name.

**BCC, block check character**  A single character that follows a sequence (block) of characters used for error-checking purposes. For example, LRC appended to the end of a block is often called "the BCC."

**Beam**  Another name for microwave radio systems that use ultra- and superhigh frequencies (UHF, SHF) to carry communications, where the signal is a narrow beam rather than a broadcast signal.

**BER**  The bit error rate encountered on a transmission line per unit time.

**BERT, bit error rate testing**  Testing a data line with a pattern of bits that are compared before and after the transmission to detect errors.

**Bias**  Communications signal distortion with respect to bit timing.

**Bit**  Binary digit contraction. The smallest unit of data communications information, used to develop code representations of characters.

**Bit-oriented protocol**  Refers to those data communications protocols that move bits across a data link without regard to the meaning of those bits. Nearly all bit-oriented protocols follow the international HDLC recommendations

**Bit rate** (*See* BPS)  The rate at which bits (binary digits) are transmitted over a communications path. Normally expressed in bits per second (BPS). The bit rate is not to be confused with the data signaling rate (baud), which measures the rate of signal changes being transmitted.

**Bit stream**  Refers to a continuous series of bits being transmitted on a transmission line.

**Blank**  A condition of "no information" in a data recording medium or storage location, which can be represented by all spaces or all zeros, depending on the medium.

**BLAST**  *See* Blocked asynchronous/synchronous transmission.

**BLER**  The block error rate encountered on a transmission line per unit time.

**BLERT, block error rate testing**  Testing a data line with groups of information arranged into transmission blocks for error checking.

**Block**  Some set of contiguous bits, bytes, or both that make up a definable quantity of information.

**Block check character**  A single character appended to the end of a data block for error-checking purposes. The BCC is usually LRC but could also be checksum results.

**Blocked Asynchronous/Synchronous Transmission**  A proprietary software package for sending asynchronous and synchronous information, used primarily by personal computer interfaces.

**Blocking**  A condition in a switching system or PBX in which no paths or circuits are available to complete a call and no dial tone is returned to the calling party. In this situation there is no alternative but to hang up and try the call again. Also referred to as denial or busy condition.

**Block multiplexer channel**  A computer peripheral multiplexer channel that interleaves blocks of data. *See also* Byte multiplexer channel. Contrast with selector channel.

**BPS, bits per second**  The basic unit of data communications rate measurement. Usually refers to rate of information bits transmitted.

**Break**  A signal used to "break in" when the opposite party or unit is sending. A feature of dial, point-to-point teletypewriter systems operating in half duplex.

**Breakout box**  A test device utilized for monitoring and inserting signals at the RS232 interface.

**Bridge**  Equipment and techniques used to connect circuits and equipment to each other, ensuring minimum transmission impairment. Bridging is normally required on multipoint data channels where the drop for the local loop is separated from the circuit that continues on to the next drop.

**Broadband**  Refers to transmission facilities whose bandwidth (range of frequencies they will handle) is greater than that available on voice-grade facilities; sometimes called wideband. Also used to describe a particular kind of local area network configuration where multiple different users can share the same cable facility in different channels.

**Broadcast**  The ability to send messages or communicate with many or all points on a circuit simultaneously.

**BSC, bisynchronous**  An IBM-developed data link control procedure using synchronous transmission.

**BTAM, Basic Telecommunications Access Method**  An IBM communications software product for interfacing between applications software and the communications network.

**Buffer**  A storage area for data.

**Burst**  A series of events occurring as a group.

**Burst error**  A series of consecutive errors in data transmission. Refers to the phenomenon on communication lines where errors are highly prone to occurring in groups or clusters.

**Bus**  A single connective link between multiple processing sites (co-located only) where any of the processing sites can transmit to any other, but only one way at a time.

**Byte**  Some set of contiguous bits that make up a discrete item of information. Bytes are 8 bits long.

**Byte multiplexer channel**  Multiplexer channel that interleaves bytes of data from different sources. Contrasts with selector channel.

## C

**Call forwarding**  Calls to one station can be automatically switched to another specified station.

**Call setup time**  The overall length of time required to establish a switched call between pieces of data terminal equipment.

**Camp-on**  A feature of a switching station or device that notifies a calling station that a called station is busy and allows the calling station to wait and be automatically connected when the line is free.

**Carrier**  An analog signal at some frequency modified by information (changes to frequency or amplitude or phase or combinations of amplitude and phase) to represent that data in a communication system.

**Carrier system**  A method of obtaining or deriving several channels from one communication path by combining them at the originating end, transmitting a wideband or high-speed signal, and then separating the original information at the receiving end.

**CATV**  Cable television.

**CBX**  Computerized branch exchange (switchboard).

**CCITT, Consultive Committee for International Telephone and Telegraph**  An international standards group.

**CCSA, common control switching arrangements**  A methodology of provision for dedicated network switching controls.

**Central office** (also called end office or wire line office)  A telephone company office where switching of subscriber lines takes place.

**Centrex**  A type of private branch exchange service where the equipment is physically located in the local telephone exchange.

**CERT, character error rate testing**  Testing a data line with test characters to determine error performance.

**Chain**  A series of processing locations that information must pass through each location on a store-and-forward basis in order to get to a final location.

**Channel**  A data communication path.

**Channel bank**  Communication equipment performing multiplexing. Typically used for multiplexing voice-grade channels.

**Character**  A language unit composed of bits.

**Character parity**  A technique of adding an overhead bit to a character code to provide error-checking capability.

**Character synchronization**  The process through which a receiving device can determine which bits, sent over a data link, should be grouped together into characters.

**Checksum**  A BCC or BCS that is computed using simple binary addition.

**Circuit**  The electrical path that provides communication between two or more locations.

**Circuit switching**  A method of communication in which an electrical connection between calling and called stations is established on demand for exclusive use of the caller until the connection is released.

**Clocking**  Time synchronizing of communication information.

**Cluster**  A group of user terminals co-located and connected to a single controller through which each terminal is afforded the opportunity to access a single communication line.

**Cluster controller**  An intelligent device, usually located at a remote site, that allows several "dumb" terminals or similar devices to connect to a single modem on a data link.

**Coaxial cable**  Cable with a shield against noise around a signal-carrying conductor.

**CODEC, Coder/Decoder**  A device for digitizing a voice signal or converting the digitized signal back to voice. Performs the opposite function of a modem.

**Communication line controller**  A hardware unit that performs line control functions with the modem.

**Compandor**  A device used on some telephone channels to improve transmission performance. The equipment compresses the outgoing speech volume range and expands the incoming speech volume range on a long-distance telephone circuit.

**Concentrator**  An electronic device that interfaces in a store and forward mode with multiple communication lines at a message level and then retransmits those messages via one or more high-speed communications lines to a processing site.

**Conditioning**  A technique of modifying electrical circuit parameters on a communication line to improve the capability of that line to support higher data transmission rates. (*See* Equalization.)

**Contention**  User competition for use of the same communications facilities; a method of line control in which terminals request or bid to transmit. If the channel is not free, the terminals must wait until it is.

**Control character**  A character that is normally nonprintable and used for control purposes rather than for the exchange of information.

**Controlled carrier**  A feature of a modem that allows the modem carrier signal to be turned on or off under command of the DTE. A controlled carrier is necessary at remote locations on multipoint lines.

**CPS, characters per second**  A data rate unit.

**CPU, central processing unit**  The computer control logic used to execute the programs.

**CRC, cyclic redundancy check**  An error-checking control technique utilizing a specifically binary prime devisor that results in a unique remainder.

**CSMA/CD, carrier sensed multiple access/collision detection**  A method of transmitting information in the local area network environment (LAN) where only one transmitter may be on the line at any one time. If two devices transmit simultaneously, the signals "collide" and both must cease transmission. Each will try again at a later time determined by a different internal delay.

**CSU, channel service unit.**  A digital interface device for connecting the end user equipment to the local digital telephone loop.

**CTS, clear to send**  A control line between a modem and a controller used to operate over a communication line.

**Current loop**  An interface in which the absence or presence of current flow (as opposed to voltage levels) is used to provide signaling between devices.

**Cursor**  A lit area on an electronic display screen used to indicate the next character location to be accessed.

## D

**DAA, data access arrangement**  A telephone-switching system protective device used to attach nonregistered equipment to the carrier network.

**Data compression**  The technique that provides for the transmission of fewer data bits without the loss of information. The receiving location expands the received data bits into the original bit sequence.

**Dataphone**  The generic name given to the modems offered by AT&T.

**Dataphone II**  The generic name given to the diagnostic modems (also known as networking modems) offered by AT&T.

**Data set (modem)**  An electronic terminating unit for analog lines used for data signal modulation and demodulation.

**dBm**  Power level measurement unit in the telephone industry. 0 dBm is 1 mW at 1004 Hz terminated by 600-Ω impedance.

**DCE, data communication equipment**  The equipment installed at the user's premises that provides all the functions required to establish, maintain, and terminate a connection; the signal conversion and coding between the data terminal equipment; and the common carrier's line (for example, data set, modem).

**DDCMP, digital data communications message protocol**  A DEC data communications line protocol.

**DDD, direct distance dial**  The North American Telephone dial system. Also called PSTN, Public Switched Telephone Network.

**DDS, Dataphone Digital Service**  A Bell System digital data link offering. Speeds of 2400, 4800, 9600, 19,200, and 56,000 BPS are offered. DDS offers error rates that are about ten times better than analog (voice-grade line) services.

**Decibel (dB)**  Power level measurement unit.

**Dedicated line**  A communication line that is not dialed. Also called a leased line or private line.

**Delay**  A period of time that elapses between the end of one event and the start of another.

**Delay distortion**  A distortion that occurs on communication lines due to the different propagation speeds of signals at different frequencies. Some frequencies travel more slowly than others in a given transmission medium and therefore arrive at the destination at slightly different times. Delay distortion is measured in microseconds of delay relative to the delay at 1200 Hz. Delay distortion does not affect voice, but it can have a serious effect on data transmissions.

**Demodulator**  A functional section of a modem that converts the received analog line signals back to digital form.

**DES, data encryption standard.**  A standard issued by the National Bureau of Standards that describes a technique for encryption.

**Dial line**  A communication line that is dialed.

**DID, direct inward dial**  A method for an outside call to be routed through a switchboard direct to the extension dialed.

**Digital**  A two-discrete-state signal.

**Distortion**  The unwanted modification or change of signals from their true form by some characteristic of the communication line or equipment being used for transmission (such as delay distortion, amplitude distortion).

**DOV, data over voice**  Used in PBX environments on voice telephone lines to send modulated data using carrier frequencies well above the voice band.

**DPCM, differential pulse code modulation**  A method of digitizing an analog signal.

**DQM, data quality monitor**  A device used to measure data bias distortion.

**Drop**  Refers to the place on a multipoint line where a tap is installed so that a station can be connected.

**Drop outs**  On a communication line, the signal can temporarily disappear, causing loss of data. Drop outs are often caused by environmental influences such as lightning.

**DSU, data service unit**  A device used in digital transmission for interconnecting a DTE to a CSU. It converts compatible DTE signals to bipolar pulses.

**DTE, data termination equipment**  Equipment comprising the data source, the data sink, or both, that provides for the communication control function (protocol). Data termination equipment is actually any piece of equipment at which a communication path logically begins or ends.

**DTMF, dual tone multifrequency**   A method of providing tones for dial purposes. The AT&T trademarked term is Touch Tone.

**DTS, digital termination system**   A method of bypassing local loop service that may use either microwave or fiber-optic cable.

**DUV, data under voice**   On microwave links, the low-frequency bands are used for data. The higher-frequency bands are used for voice. Hence, data is "under" voice.

## E

**Echo distortion**   A telephone line impairment caused by electrical reflections at distant points where line impedances are dissimilar.

**Echoplex**   An error-detection method in which characters sent by a terminal to a host are sent back to the terminal and displayed.

**Echo suppressor**   A device installed in long-distance telephone lines for eliminating echo back to the speaker. Echo suppressors can cause difficulties with simultaneous two-way communications unless they are disabled by the modems.

**EFS, error free second.**   A standard established by AT&T for identifying the amount of errors on a transmission line per unit time.

**EIA, Electronic Industries Association**   An organization of electronic manufacturers in the United States that establishes standards.

**Emulation**   The act of imitating or performing as if a device or program were something else.

**Encryption**   The technique of modifying a known bit stream on a transmission line so that it appears to be a random sequence of bits to an unauthorized observer.

**End office**   The first telephone office that a data line is connected to over the local loop or access line. The end switching office for a dialed connection.

**Envelope delay**   An analog line impairment where a variation of signal delay with frequency occurs across the data channel bandwidth (*see* Delay distortion).

**EP, emulation program**   An IBM program that allows their communications front-end equipment to utilize the BTAM access method.

**EPABX, electronic private automatic branch exchange**   Another name for a switchboard. May or may not be digital.

**Equalization**   A technique used to compensate for distortions present on a communication channel.

**ER, error rate**   The number of errors per unit of information in the test to establish the error rate.

**ESS**   *See* Electronic switching system.

## F

**Facility**   A transmission path between two or more locations without terminating or signaling equipment. The addition of terminating equipment would produce either a channel, a central office line, or a trunk. Various types of signaling would also be used depending on the application.

**FCS, frame check sequence**   The name of the error checking information appended near the end of the frame in bit-oriented protocols. Equivalent to the BCS in character-oriented protocols.

**FDM, frequency-division multiplexing**   A multiplexing technique with which a data line bandwidth is divided into different frequency subchannels used to share a data line between several user terminals.

**FDX, full duplex**   The capability of transmission in both directions at one time. Also, a four-wire circuit.

**FEC, forward error correcting**   A coding technique used to correct errors in transmission at the receiver by use of redundancy included in the transmission block.

**FEX**   *See* Foreign exchange service.

**Fiber-optics**   Glass fibers that carry visible light containing information in cables.

**Filter**   Electronic circuitry that blocks some components of a signal while allowing other components to pass through uniformly. For example, a high-pass filter blocks all frequencies in a signal that are below a specified frequency called the "cut off."

**Firmware**   A set of software instructions set permanently or semipermanently into a read-only memory.

**Fixed equalization**   A simple equalization technique for modems by which the amount of compensation is preset internally or externally to the modem.

**Flag**   A bit field or character of data used to set apart the data on either side of the flag. A delimiter.

**Flow control**   A procedure by which a sending station can be "throttled" so that it does not send more data into the data link or network than can be handled by the link or network.

**FM, frequency modulation**   A method of transmitting digital information on an analog line by changing the carrier frequency between two different values.

**Foreign exchange service, FEX**   A service that connects a customer's telephone to a remote exchange, providing the equivalent of local telephone service to and from the distant exchange.

**Format**   A structure of a message or data such that specific controls or data can be identified by their position during processing.

**Forward error correction**   The technique that provides for the transmittal of additional information with the original bit stream so that if an error is detected the correct information can be recreated at the receive end without a retransmission.

**Four-wire circuit**   A circuit that consists of two twisted pair cables. A four-wire circuit provides two separate circuits between stations.

**Frame**   Bit-oriented protocols refer to data blocks as frames. Also, in T-1 transmissions, 8 bits from each of 24 channels plus 1 frame bit for a total of 193 bits.

**Frequency**   The number of cycles of an alternating current signal per unit time.

**Frequency shift keying, FSK**   A form of frequency modulation in which the carrier frequency is made to vary or change in frequency at the instant there is a change in the state of the signal being transmitted (the carrier frequency on the line during a one or marking condition would be shifted to another predetermined frequency during a zero or spacing condition).

**Frequency stacking**   Another name for FDM, which indicates how the multiplexing is performed.

**Front end**   An auxiliary computer system that performs network control operations, freeing the host computer system to do data processing.

**FSK**  *See* Frequency shift keying.

**Full duplex**  A four-wire circuit, or a protocol that provides for transmission in both directions at the same time between the same two points.

**Full-duplex modem**  Provides a channel for sending data in each direction. Full-duplex modems are required for two stations to send data to each other at the same time.

## G

**Gain**  The degree to which the amplitude of a signal is increased. The amount of amplification realized when a signal passes through an amplifier or repeater. Normally measured in decibels.

**Gaussian noise**  A noise whose amplitude is characterized by the Gaussian distribution, a well known statistical distribution (white noise, ambient noise, hiss).

**General poll**  In IBM BSC protocol, a general poll is used for abbreviated addressing on lines where cluster controllers are used. The cluster controller responds to a general poll and indicates whether any of its connected devices has data to send.

**Geosynchronous**  A communication satellite orbit at the correct distance from earth and at the correct speed to appear fixed in space as the earth rotates.

**Gigahertz (GHz)**  An analog frequency unit equal to 1 billion Hz.

**Go-back-N**  A form of continuous ARQ in which all blocks or frames following a block received in error are discarded and need to be resent.

**Group address**  Used to address two or more stations in a predesignated group.

**Guardband**  The unused frequency band between two channels that provides separation of the channels to prevent mutual interference.

## H

**Half duplex**  A communication line consisting of two wires or a protocol capable of transmitting only one direction at a time.

**Handshaking**  Line termination interplay to establish a data communication path.

**Harmonic**  Frequencies that are multiples of some fundamental frequency.

**Harmonic distortion**  A data communications line impairment caused by erroneous frequency generations along the line.

**HDLC, high-level data link control**  An ISO standard data communications line protocol.

**Hertz**  Internationally recognized unit of measure for electrical frequency. The number of cycles per second. Abbreviated Hz.

**House cables**  Conductors within a building used to connect communications equipment to termination blocks.

**Hybrid**  An inductive device that converts a two-wire circuit into a four-wire circuit or a four-wire circuit into a two-wire circuit.

**Hz**  *See* Hertz.

## I

**IDF, intermediate distribution frame**  An equipment unit used to connect communications equipment to the carrier local loop.

**Impedance**   The total opposition offered by a component or circuit to the flow of an alternating or varying current; a combination of resistance, capacitance, and inductance.

**Impulse noise**   A type of interference on communication lines characterized by high amplitude and short duration. This type of interference may be caused by lightning, electrical sparking action, or by the make–break action of switching devices.

**Insertion loss**   Signal power loss due to connecting communication equipment units with dissimilar impedance values.

**Integrity of data**   The status of information after being processed by software or transmitted over a communication link.

**Interference**   Refers to unwanted occurrences on communications channels that are a result of natural or man-made noises and signals, not properly a part of the signals being transmitted.

**Interleaving**   The process of alternately sending characters, blocks, or messages in a system.

**Intermodulation distortion**   An analog line impairment where two frequencies create an erroneous frequency, which in turn distorts the original data signal representation.

**ISDN, integrated service digital network**   An acronym for the *digital pipe* where any one of a number of services can be transmitted on a common network.

**ISO**   International Standards Organization.

**Isochronous**   The term given to the movement of start–stop data (asynchronous transmission) over a synchronous data link with each intervening time interval being an integral number of character times.


## J

**Jitter**   Type of analog communication line distortion caused by the variation of a signal from its reference timing positions, which can cause data transmission errors, particularly at high speeds.

**Jumbo group**   The FDM carrier system multiplexing level containing 3600 voice frequency (VF) or telephone channels (six master groups).


## K

**KBPS, kilobits per second**   A data rate equal to 1000 BPS.


## L

**LAN**   Local area network.

**Leased line, private line, dedicated line**   A communications line, usually a four-wire circuit, for voice, data, or both leased from a communications carrier on a monthly basis.

**LDM, limited distance modem**   A "short-haul" modem that can only operate properly over relatively short distances (up to about 20 miles). LDMs must operate over metallic wire circuits that are *nonloaded*.

**Line driver**   An inexpensive amplifying device that allows two or more devices to communicate over inexpensive twisted-pair cable up to 2000 feet and up to 19,200 BPS.

**Loaded wire**   Refers to local loops that have loading coils installed.

**Loading coils**   Inductive devices that improve the quality of voice transmissions (distorts data signals and must therefore be compensated for by standard modems).

**Local loop**   The access line from either a user terminal or a computer port to the first telephone office along the line path (also called station loop, end loop, or subscriber loop).

**Logging**   The act of recording something for future reference, such as error events or transactions.

**Loopback**   Directing signals back toward the source at some point along a communications path.

**Loop current**   A teletypewriter-to-line interface and operating technique that involves switching an electrical current on and off to represent data bits.

**LPC, linear predictive coding**   A method of compressing digitized voice information.

**LRC**   Longitudinal redundancy checking.

**LSI, large-scale integration**   A classification of electronic device comprising many logic elements in one very small package (integrated circuit) to be used for data handling, storage, and processing.

**LTA, line turnaround**   On a two-wire circuit, the amount of time it takes for one end to stop transmitting and then begin receiving from the other end.

## M

**Mark**   Interface standards define a mark to be the condition of the data line when sending a logic one.

**MBPS, mega bps**   A data rate equal to $10^6$ or 1 million BPS.

**MDF, main distribution frame**   An equipment unit used to connect communications equipment to lines with connecting blocks.

**Megahertz, MHz**   A unit of analog frequency equal to 1 million Hz.

**Message switching**   Routing messages among three or more locations by store-and-forward techniques in a computer.

**Metallic circuits**   Refers to circuits that use metal wire (copper) from end to end. Implies that no loading coils or any other devices are interposed between the ends of the circuit. Metallic circuits have electrical (dc) continuity from end to end.

**Microcode**   A set of software instructions that executes a macro instruction.

**Microwave**   A radio carrier system using frequencies whose wavelengths are very short.

**Milliampere, mA**   Electric current measurement unit equal to 0.001 Ampere.

**Milliwatt, mW**   A power unit of measurement equal to 0.001 watt.

**MIL-STD 188**   A military standard interface equivalent to RS232 between a DCE and a DTE.

**Modem** (data set)   An acronym taken from functions the unit performs by modulating and demodulating the digital information from a terminal or computer port into an analog carrier signal to be sent over an analog line.

**Modem eliminator**   A device that allows two DTE devices to be connected without using modems.

**Modem sharing unit**   A device that allows several terminals or other devices to share a single modem.

**Modulator**   The sending function of a modem.

**MTA, modem turnaround**   *See* LTA.

**MTBF, mean time between failure**   The average time between failures of a particular device based on statistical or anticipated experience.

**MTTR, mean time to repair**  The average time it takes to repair a device once it has failed.

**Multiplexer**  A device that accepts many data lines and combines them into a single high-speed, composite data stream.

**Multipoint line**  Also called a multidrop line. A communications line having several subsidiary controllers that share time on the line under control of a central site.

**Multistation controller**  A terminal controller having more than one terminal device connected to it for subsequent access to the communication line.

## N

**Narrowband**  Refers to a LAN configuration in which only one user can transmit at any one time (sometimes called baseband).

**NCTE, network channel terminating equipment**  The equipment at a user's facility that is used to terminate a digital circuit.

**Noise**  A communications line impairment that is inherent in the line design or induced by transient bursts of energy.

**Null modem**  *See* Modem eliminator.

## O

**Octet**  A group of eight bits that usually, though not necessarily, represents a byte, or word, and so on.

## P

**Packet switching**  The transfer of data by means of addressed packets whereby a channel is only occupied for the duration of transmission of the packet. The channel is then available for the transfer of other packets.

**PAD, packet assembler/disassembler**  Equipment providing packet assembly and disassembly facilities.

**Parity error**  An error that occurs in a particular entity of data in which an extra or redundant bit is sent with the data. Detects only odd numbers of bit errors. Even numbers of bit errors are not detected.

**Pass-band filters**  Filters used in modem design to allow only the frequencies within the communication channel to pass, while rejecting all frequencies outside the pass band.

**Patching jacks**  Series-access devices used to patch around faulty equipment using spare units.

**PBX**  Private branch exchange; a telephone switchboard.

**PCM, pulse code modulation**  A generic method of converting an analog signal to a digital form.

**Phase hits**  A sudden electrical disturbance on a communication line which causes the phase of the carrier signal to change, causing bit errors on the data link.

**Phase jitter**  An analog line impairment caused by power and communication equipment along the line, shifting the signal phase relationship back and forth.

**PM, phase modulation**  A method of combining digital information onto a line-carrying signal by variation of the phase relationship of the signal. May also indicate preventive maintenance in the form of service functions provided during periods of normal operation to reduce the probability of failure later on.

**Point to point**   A communications line connected directly from one point to another, as opposed to multipoint lines.

**Polling**   A control message sent from a master site to a slave site as an invitation for the slave site to transmit data to the master site.

**Privacy**   The techniques used for limiting or preventing access to specific system information from otherwise authorized system users.

**Propagation delay**   The time necessary for a signal to travel from one point on the circuit to another.

**Protocol**   A formal set of conventions governing the format and control of inputs and outputs between two communicating processes. Includes handshaking and line discipline.

**PSK, phase shift keying**   A method of analog modulation utilizing differences in phase only as representing data bits (*see* PM).

**PTT, Postal Telephone & Telegraph**   A government organization in foreign countries responsible for telephone and telegraph services.

**Pulse modulation**   The modification of the characteristics of a series of digital pulses in one of several ways to represent an analog signal. Typical methods involve modifying the amplitude (PAM), width or duration (PDM), or position (PPM). The most common pulse modulation technique in telephone work is pulse code modulation (PCM). In PCM, the analog signals are sampled at regular intervals and a series of binary bits representing the amplitude of each pulse is transmitted, representing the amplitude of the information signal at that time. The standard sampling in today's environment is 8000 times per second with 8 binary bits representing each sample pulse giving a required transmission rate of 64,000 BPS.

## Q

**QAM, quadrature amplitude modulation**   A method of modulation in which two carriers in quadrature are used for modulation. One carrier is used for modulating the $X$ axis and the other carrier is used for modulating the $Y$ axis.

**QTAM, queued telecommunications access method**   An IBM communications software product for accessing data lines through a communications controller.

**Quadrature distortion**   Analog signal distortion frequently found in phase modulation modems.

**Queuing**   The process of sequentially storing messages for subsequent delivery.

## R

**Recovery**   The necessary actions required to bring a system to a predefined level of operation after a degradation or failure.

**Regenerative repeaters**   A device interposed between the ends of a data link or between nodes of a network to regenerate distorted signals. Used in digital transmission.

**Response time**   The time measured from the depression of the enter key at a terminal to the display of the first character of the response at that terminal site.

**Reverse channel**   An optional feature provided on some modems that provides simultaneous communication from the receiver to the transmitter on a two-wire channel. It may be used for circuit assurance, circuit breaking, and facilitating certain forms of error control and network diagnostics. Also called backward channel.

**RTS, request to send**   An RS232 control signal that requests a data transmission on a communication line.

## S

**SDCU, satellite delay compensation unit**   A device utilized for providing compensation for the time delays involved in a satellite transmission. Usually provided by the satellite communications vendor.

**SDLC, synchronous data link control**   An IBM data communications message protocol. A subset of HDLC.

**Sealing current**   A current utilized by the local telephone company to provide better contact of switches in their office. The current is used to burn away impurities that develop over time on metal switch contacts.

**Selector channel**   A channel designed to operate with only one I/O device at a time. Once the I/O device is selected, a complete record is transferred one byte at a time. Contrast with block multiplexer channel.

**Short-haul modems, SHM**   *See* Limited distance modem.

**Slicing level**   A voltage or current level of a digital signal that determines whether a one or zero bit will be recognized.

**Slot**   A unit of time in a TDM frame in which a subchannel bit or character is carried to the other end of the circuit and extracted by the receiving TDM unit.

**S/N, signal-to-noise ratio**   The relative power levels of a communication signal and noise on a data line, expressed in decibels.

**SNA**   *See* Systems Network Architecture.

**Space-division multiplexing**   Refers to using a separate circuit or channel for each device. Essentially this means no multiplexing at all. If, for example, a new terminal needs to be added to a system, a separate wire is run to accommodate it.

**Start bit**   In asynchronous transmission, the start bit is appended to the beginning of a character so that the bit sync and character sync can occur at the receiver. The start bit is always a "0" or "space" condition.

**Start-stop**   Also known as asynchronous transmission. A transmission technique in which each character is preceded by a start bit and followed by a stop bit.

**Stop-and-wait ARQ**   A form of ARQ in which the sender sends one block of data and stops sending until an acknowledgment for that block is received from the receiver. An example is bisync.

**Stop bit**   In asynchronous transmission, the stop bit is appended to the end of each character. The stop bit is always a "1" or "mark" condition. It sets the receiving hardware to a condition where it looks for the start bit of a new character. May be 1 or 2 bits.

**Store and forward**   A data communication technique that accepts messages or transactions, stores them until they are completely in the memory system, and then forwards them to the next location as addressed in the message or transaction header.

**Streaming**   A condition of a remote modem when it is sending a carrier signal on a multidrop communication line and will not turn off.

**String coding**   A technique for combining multiple sequential occurrences of the same character or bits.

**Subscriber loop**   *See* Local loop.

**Switched service**   A common carrier communications service that requires that call establishment take place before a data link can be established. For example, DDD is a switched service.

**Sync (syn)**   A bit or character used to synchronize a time frame in a TDM. Also a synchronizing sequence used by synchronous modems to perform bit synchronization and by the line controller for character synchronization.

**Synchronous modem**   A DCE that utilizes a clocking signal to perform bit synchronization with the incoming data.

**Synchronous transmission**   Messages sent in blocks where all characters or bits are sent contiguously. No start or stop bits are appended to characters. Each block begins with a sync sequence and a start of message sequence so that character framing can occur at the receiver and ends with an end of message sequence to prepare the receiver to look for a new message.

**Systems Network Architecture (SNA)**   The name of IBM's networking strategy to integrate their computer systems.

## T

**Tariff**   The rates, rules, and regulations concerning specific equipment and services provided by a communications carrier.

**TCAM, telecommunications access method**   An IBM communications software product for interfacing communications lines with applications software.

**T-Carrier**   The AT&T name for their digital carrier system used for carrying data or digitized voice signals.

**TDM**   *See* Time-division multiplexing.

**TDMA, time division multiple access**   A method utilized primarily in satellite transmission in which various users share their time on the same satellite link (portions of separate users are multiplexed onto the same link through a satellite).

**Telemetry**   Collection and transmission of data obtained from remote locations by sensing conditions in a real-time environment.

**Telex**   A teletypewriter service that allows subscribers to send messages to other subscribers on an international level over the public telephone network.

**Terrestrial circuits**   Nonsatellite channels.

**Text**   That part of a message or transaction between the control information of the header and the control information of the trace section or tail that constitutes the information to be processed or delivered to the addressed location.

**Thermal noise**   A type of electromagnetic noise produced in conductors or in electronic circuitry that is proportional to temperature. *See also* Gaussian noise.

**Time-division multiplexing, TDM**   A technique for combining several information channels into one facility or transmission path in which each channel is allotted a specific position in the signal stream based on time. At the receiving end, the signals are separated to reconstruct the individual input channels.

**Time-out**   A protocol procedure that requires a device to make some response to a command or message block within a certain period of time. If the response does not occur within that period of time, a time-out condition occurs, which is considered an error condition.

**Time sharing**   A processing technique by which multiple users at their own remote terminals have the ability to share common computer resources at the same time.

**TIMS, transmission impairment measurement system**   A generic name for a system that can diagnose and isolate network problems.

**Trailer or trace block**   Control information transmitted after the body or text of a message or transaction used for tracing error events, timing the communications through the network, and recovering misplaced blocks or transactions after system failures.

**Transparency**   A transmission mode achieved when both the sending and receiving devices do not react to the content of the data they are sending.

**Trunk**   A multiple line circuit that connects two switching or distribution stations or centers. Also a circuit from a PBX to a Class 5 telephone office.

**Turnaround time**   The time required for a modem to reverse direction of transmission on a two-wire circuit.

**TWX**   Teletypewriter Exchange Service. Uses 8-bit ASCII characters whereas Telex uses 5-bit characters.

## U

**UTR, up time ratio**   The average amount of time that a device is operational compared to the total time being measured.

## V

**Validity checking**   The techniques used to check the accuracy of data after transmission on data lines.

**VF, voice frequency or voice-grade line**   A 4.2-kHz bandwidth telephone channel designed to carry the human voice from one telephone set to another. The usable portion of the band is 300 Hz to 3300 Hz.

**VHF, very high frequency**   A radio carrier frequency band used in radio transmissions.

**VRC, vertical redundancy checking**   A method of character parity checking.

## W

**WATS, Wide Area Telephone Service**   A flat rate or measured bulk rate long-distance telephone service provided on an incoming or outgoing basis. By use of an access line, WATS permits a customer to make telephone calls to any dialable telephone number in a specific zone for an hourly rate. INWATS permits reception of calls from specific zones over an access line in like manner but the *called* party is charged with the call. The United States has been divided into five zones of increasingly greater coverage depending on the location of the customer.

**White noise**   *See* Gaussian noise; Thermal noise.

**Wideband**   In LAN systems, the ability for multiple users to communicate simultaneously in different channels. Same as broadband.

**Word**   One or more contiguous bytes, which may also be used to identify a class of computer.

# Index

## M

McDonnell Douglas, 31, 385
Maintenance service, 453
Make/break signal, 194, 195
Manchester code, differential, 347
MAP, 435–38
Mark, 15, 85
Mark parity, 265
Mark/space signal, 194, 195
Masking information, 281
MCI, 28, 446
  development of, 42
  and software defined networks, 47
  and WATS, 36
Medium access control, 319
Meridian, 302
Message-framed data, 139
Message sequence number, 480–82
Message switching, 469–70
Microwave, 33, 68–71, 344, 464–65
MIL-STD 188, 85–93
Mixed form text, 424
MNP, 176, 177, 178–79, 280
Mode, 160, 253
Modem, 10, 17, 85, 115, 140, 167, 190, 198,
    204, 526
  autobaud, 219–20
  autodial, 227–31
  automatic equalization, 497
  Codex, 203
  comparison chart of, 209
  considerations in choosing, 211–18
  dial-up, 280
  equalizers in, 220–21
  fast-train, 215
  frequency agile, 328
  KBPS, 203
  medium-distance, 193
  multidrop, 216
  null, 221–24
  reverse-channel, 205, 206
  RF, 304
  short-haul limited-distance, 192
  split-channel, 205, 206, 207
  split-stream, 143, 215
  streaming, 141, 215
  TCM-type, 202
  212A, 205
  two-wire full-duplex, 205
  Y, 174
  Z, 174
Modem eliminator, 221–24
Modem emulator, 221–24
Modem pooling, 306
Modem self-test, 526
Modem simulator, 221–24
Modem synchronization time, 141, 145
Modem training time, 141, 145
Modem Turnaround (MTA), 167, 208
Modes, 66

Modulation, 61, 190
  adaptive differential pulse code, 300
  amplitude, 197, 198
  analog modes of, 196–98
  continuously variable slope delta, 301
  frequency, 196
  frequency division multiple access, 452
  multibit, 124, 198–211
  phase, 197–98, 199, 200
  pulse amplitude, 291, 298
  pulse code, 291, 297, 300
  pulse duration, 298
  quadrature amplitude, 200
  techniques of, 451
  time divison multiple access, 452
  trellis coded, 202
Modulator, 190
Monitor bit, 334
Morse, Samuel, 3, 12, 125, 277
Morse code, 125, 126, 277
Multibit modulation, 124, 198–211
Multidrop limitation, 143
Multidrop line, 151, 555
Multidrop line environment, 264
Multidrop synchronous operation, 143
Multilink communications, 410
Multiplexer, 236, 243–48, 356
Multiplexing, 4
  byte, 241
  code division, 217
  frequency division, 44, 238, 239–40
  intelligent, 243–48
  networking, 356
  statistical, 243–48, 253
  time-division, 238, 240–42, 291
  T–1, 248–51, 356
Multipoint/multidrop circuit, 119–20
Multistation access unit, 318, 332–33
Multistation circuit, 119–20

## N

Narrowband, 316, 321, 331
National Academy of Sciences, 42
Negative bias, 144
Negotiation, 280
Netview, 427, 535–37
Network
  architectures of, 427–33
  broadband, 321
  bus, 317
  circuit switched, 387
  definition of, 117
  global data, 408
  in-house, 318
  mesh, 318
  metropolitan area, 320
  packet switched, 182, 386–90, 448
  ring, 318
  RS232, 345
  software defined, 47–49